W9-BTB-634

www.wadsworth.com

www.wadsworth.com is the World Wide Web site
for Thomson Wadsworth and is your direct source
to dozens of online resources.

At *www.wadsworth.com* you can find out about
supplements, demonstration software, and student
resources. You can also send email to many of our
authors and preview new publications and exciting
new technologies.

www.wadsworth.com
Changing the way the world learns®

From the Wadsworth Series in Mass Communication and Journalism

General Mass Communication

Anokwa/Lin/Salwen, *International Communication: Issues and Controversies*
Biagi, *Media/Impact: An Introduction to Mass Media,* Seventh Edition
Bucy, *Living in the Information Age: A New Media Reader,* Second Edition
Craft/Leigh/Godfrey, *Electronic Media*
Day, *Ethics in Media Communications: Cases and Controversies,* Fourth Edition
Dennis/Merrill, *Media Debates: Great Issues for the Digital Age,* Third Edition
Fellow, *American Media History*
Gillmor/Barron/Simon, *Mass Communication Law: Cases and Comment,* Sixth Edition
Gillmor/Barron/Simon/Terry, *Fundamentals of Mass Communication Law*
Hilmes, *Connections: A Broadcast History Reader*
Hilmes, *Only Connect: A Cultural History of Broadcasting in the United States*
Jamieson/Campbell, *The Interplay of Influence: News, Advertising, Politics, and the Mass Media,* Fifth Edition
Kamalipour, *Global Communication*
Lester, *Visual Communication: Images with Messages,* Third Edition
Overbeck, *Major Principles of Media Law,* 2005 Edition
Straubhaar/LaRose, *Media Now: Understanding Media, Culture, and Technology,* Fourth Edition
Zelezny, *Communications Law: Liberties, Restraints, and the Modern Media,* Fourth Edition
Zelezny, *Cases in Communications Law,* Fourth Edition

Journalism

Bowles/Borden, *Creative Editing,* Fourth Edition
Chance/McKeen, *Literary Journalism: A Reader*
Craig, *Online Journalism*
Fischer, *Sports Journalism at Its Best: Pulitzer Prize—Winning Articles, Cartoons, and Photographs*
Fisher, *The Craft of Corporate Journalism*
Gaines, *Investigative Reporting for Print and Broadcast,* Second Edition
Hilliard, *Writing for Television, Radio, and New Media,* Eighth Edition
Kessler/McDonald, *When Words Collide: A Media Writer's Guide to Grammar and Style,* Sixth Edition
Laakaniemi, *Newswriting in Transition*
Miller, *Power Journalism: Computer-Assisted Reporting*
Poulter/Tidwell, *News Scene: Interactive Writing Exercises*
Rich, *Writing and Reporting News: A Coaching Method,* Media Enhanced Fourth Edition
Rich, *Writing and Reporting News: A Coaching Method, Student Exercise Workbook,* Media Enhanced Fourth Edition
Stephens, *Broadcast News,* Fourth Edition
Wilber/Miller, *Modern Media Writing*

Photojournalism and Photography

Parrish, *Photojournalism: An Introduction*

Public Relations and Advertising

Diggs-Brown/Glou, *The PR Styleguide: Formats for Public Relations Practice*
Hendrix, *Public Relations Cases,* Sixth Edition
Jewler/Drewniany, *Creative Strategy in Advertising,* Eighth Edition
Newsom/Haynes, *Public Relations Writing: Form and Style,* Seventh Edition
Newsom/Turk/Kruckeberg, *This Is PR: The Realities of Public Relations,* Eighth Edition
Sivulka, *Soap, Sex, and Cigarettes: A Cultural History of American Advertising*
Woods, *Advertising and Marketing to the New Majority: A Case Study Approach*

Research and Theory

Baxter/Babbie, *The Basics of Communication Research*
Baran/Davis, *Mass Communication Theory: Foundations, Ferment, and Future,* Third Edition
Littlejohn, *Theories of Human Communication,* Seventh Edition
Merrigan/Huston, *Communication Research Methods*
Rubin/Rubin/Piele, *Communication Research: Strategies and Sources,* Sixth Edition
Sparks, *Media Effects Research: A Basic Overview*
Wimmer/Dominick, *Mass Media Research: An Introduction,* Seventh Edition

LIVING

in the

INFORMATION AGE

A New Media Reader

Second Edition

Erik P. Bucy
Indiana University

WADSWORTH

THOMSON LEARNING

Australia • Canada • Mexico • Singapore • Spain
United Kingdom • United States

WADSWORTH

THOMSON LEARNING

Publisher: Holly J. Allen
Assistant Editor: Shona Burke
Editorial Assistant: Laryssa Polika
Technology Project Manager: Jeanette Wiseman
Marketing Manager: Kimberly Russell
Marketing Assistant: Andrew Keay
Advertising Project Manager: Shemika Britt
Signing Representative: Lori Grebe
Project Manager, Editorial Production: Megan E. Hansen

Art Director: Maria Epes
Print/Media Buyer: Doreen Suruki
Permissions Editor: Stephanie Lee
Production Service: Gretchen Otto, G&S Book Services
Copy Editor: Laurie Baker
Cover Designer: Annabelle Ison
Cover Image: Courtesy of Getty Images
Compositor: G&S Book Services
Printer: Webcom

COPYRIGHT © 2005 Wadsworth, a division of Thomson Learning, Inc. Thomson Learning™ is a trademark used herein under license.

ALL RIGHTS RESERVED. No part of this work covered by the copyright hereon may be reproduced or used in any form or by any means—graphic, electronic, or mechanical, including but not limited to photocopying, recording, taping, Web distribution, information networks, or information storage and retrieval systems—without the written permission of the publisher.

Printed in Canada

1 2 3 4 5 6 7 08 07 06 05 04

For more information about our products, contact us at:
    Thomson Learning Academic Resource Center
    1-800-423-0563

For permission to use material from this text or product, submit a request online at http://www.thomsonrights.com.

Any additional questions about permissions can be submitted by email to thomsonrights @thomson.com.

Library of Congress Control Number: 2004105369
ISBN 0-534-63340-4

Thomson Wadsworth
10 Davis Drive
Belmont, CA 94002-3098
USA

Asia
Thomson Learning
5 Shenton Way #01-01
UIC Building
Singapore 068808

Australia/New Zealand
Thomson Learning
102 Dodds Street
Southbank, Victoria 3006
Australia

Canada
Nelson
1120 Birchmount Road
Toronto, Ontario M1K 5G4
Canada

Europe/Middle East/Africa
Thomson Learning
High Holborn House
50/51 Bedford Row
London WC1R 4LR
United Kingdom

Latin America
Thomson Learning
Seneca, 53
Colonia Polanco
11560 Mexico D.F.
Mexico

Spain/Portugal
Paraninfo
Calle Magallanes, 25
28015 Madrid, Spain

Brief Contents

PREFACE   xi

I   THE NEW INFORMATION AND ENTERTAINMENT ECOLOGY   1
     1   The Communications Revolution   3
     2   New Media Theory   33

II   CONVERGENCE AND CONCENTRATION IN THE MEDIA INDUSTRIES   65
     3   Convergence, Content, and Interactivity   67
     4   Media Concentration   92

III NEW TECHNOLOGIES, THE SELF, AND SOCIAL LIFE   115
     5   At the Interface: New Intimacies, New Cultures   117
     6   Media Saturation and the Increasing Velocity of Everyday Life   139

IV   SOCIAL IMPACTS OF INFORMATION AND COMMUNICATIONS
     TECHNOLOGIES   163
     7   Networked Computing: Promises and Paradoxes   165
     8   Questioning Information Technology   188

V   NEW TECHNOLOGIES AND THE PUBLIC SPHERE   219
     9   Electronic Democracy   221
     10   The Digital Divide   255

VI   POLICING THE ELECTRONIC WORLD: ISSUES AND ETHICS   283
     11   Copyright and Regulation   285
     12   Privacy and Surveillance   308

INDEX   333

Detailed Contents

PREFACE   xi

I   THE NEW INFORMATION AND ENTERTAINMENT ECOLOGY   1

    1   The Communications Revolution   3
        1-1   The Roots of Revolution   3
              Frances Cairncross

              The Trendspotter's Guide to New Communications   7
              Frances Cairncross

        1-2   Technological and Economic Origins of the Information Society   11
              James R. Beniger

        1-3   Renaissance Now! Media Ecology and the New Global Narrative   21
              Douglas Rushkoff

    2   New Media Theory   33
        2-1   Principles of Mediamorphosis   33
              Roger Fidler

        2-2   A New World (Small Pieces Loosely Joined)   42
              David Weinberger

        2-3   Remediation   50
              Jay David Bolter and Richard Grusin

        2-4   Uses of the Mass Media   59
              Werner J. Severin and James W. Tankard Jr.

II CONVERGENCE AND CONCENTRATION IN THE MEDIA INDUSTRIES   65

    3   Convergence, Content, and Interactivity   67
        3-1   Convergence and Its Consequences   67
              John Pavlik and Shawn McIntosh

        3-2   The Civil War Inside Sony   73
              Frank Rose

        3-3   The Fast-Forward, On-Demand, Network-Smashing Future of Television   80
              Frank Rose

              TiVo's Turning Point: It Redefined Television. Now Comes Competition.   84
              Josh McHugh

        3-4   Digital Cinema, Take 2   86
              Michael A. Hiltzik

    4   Media Concentration   92
        4-1   The New Global Media   92
              Robert W. McChesney

	4-2	Global Media *Benjamin Compaine*	97
	4-3	The Threat to the Net *Pat Aufderheide*	102
	4-4	Big World: How Clear Channel Programs America *Jeff Sharlet*	106

III   NEW TECHNOLOGIES, THE SELF, AND SOCIAL LIFE   115

5	**At the Interface: New Intimacies, New Cultures**		**117**
	5-1	A Nation of Voyeurs *Neil Swidey*	117
	5-2	Toy Soldiers *Mark Frauenfelder*	125
	5-3	Weblogs: A History and Perspective *Rebecca Blood*	129
	5-4	Love.com *Anna Mulrine*	133
6	**Media Saturation and the Increasing Velocity of Everyday Life**		**139**
	6-1	Supersaturation, or The Media Torrent and Disposable Feeling *Todd Gitlin*	139
	6-2	Prest-o! Change-o! *James Gleick*	146
	6-3	Spam Wars *Evan I. Schwartz*	151
	6-4	The First Law of Data Smog *David Shenk*	157

IV   SOCIAL IMPACTS OF INFORMATION AND COMMUNICATIONS TECHNOLOGIES   163

7	**Networked Computing: Promises and Paradoxes**		**165**
	7-1	The World Wide Web Unleashed *John December*	165
	7-2	The Productivity Puzzle *Thomas K. Landauer*	172
	7-3	Computer Age Gains Respect of Economists *Steve Lohr*	177
	7-4	The Computer Delusion *Todd Oppenheimer*	181
8	**Questioning Information Technology**		**188**
	8-1	Further Explorations into the Culture of Computing *Clifford Stoll*	188
	8-2	Plan 9 from Cyberspace: The Implications of the Internet for Personality and Social Psychology *Katelyn Y. A. McKenna and John A. Bargh*	193
	8-3	Absolute PowerPoint: Can a Software Package Edit Our Thoughts? *Ian Parker*	205
	8-4	The Myth of Order: The Real Lesson of Y2K *Ellen Ullman*	212

V   NEW TECHNOLOGIES AND THE PUBLIC SPHERE   219

    9   Electronic Democracy   221

        9-1   Media Participation: A Legitimizing Mechanism of Mass Democracy   221
                Erik P. Bucy and Kimberly S. Gregson

        9-2   Smart Mobs: The Power of the Mobile Many   231
                Howard Rheingold

        9-3   Universal Access to E-mail   239
                Robert H. Anderson, Tora K. Bikson, Sally Ann Law, and Bridger M. Mitchell

        9-4   Fragmentation and Cybercascades   245
                Cass R. Sunstein

    10   The Digital Divide   255

        10-1   Rethinking the Digital Divide   255
                Jennifer S. Light

        10-2   Routes to Media Access   264
                John E. Newhagen and Erik P. Bucy

        10-3   The Rise of the Overclass: How the New Elite Scrambled Up the Merit Ladder—
                and Wants to Stay There Any Way It Can   272
                Jerry Adler

        10-4   Tech Savvy: Educating Girls in the New Computer Age   277
                Sherry Turkle, Patricia Diaz Dennis, et al.

VI   POLICING THE ELECTRONIC WORLD: ISSUES AND ETHICS   283

    11   Copyright and Regulation   285

        11-1   Who Will Own Your Next Good Idea?   285
                Charles C. Mann

        11-2   The Next Economy of Ideas   291
                John Perry Barlow

        11-3   Free   296
                Lawrence Lessig

        11-4   The Race to Kill Kazaa   303
                Todd Woody

    12   Privacy and Surveillance   308

        12-1   Remembrance of Data Passed: A Study of Disk Sanitization Practices   308
                Simson L. Garfinkel and Abhi Shelat

        12-2   In Defense of the Delete Key   318
                James M. Rosenbaum

        12-3   Privacy and the New Technology: What They Do Know Can Hurt You   322
                Simson L. Garfinkel

        12-4   The Challenge of an Open Society   327
                David Brin

INDEX   333

Preface

A lot has happened since the dust settled from the dot.com bust of 2000, in whose wake the first edition of this reader went to press. Venture capital has become leery of investing in Silicon Valley start-ups with more logo appeal than business sense; the convergence model that drove the AOL Time Warner merger has proven itself, once again, not quite ready for prime time (and AOL Time Warner has reverted to just Time Warner); and, the hastily enacted Patriot Act, written and passed by Congress in the immediate aftermath of the September 11 terrorist attacks, has reaffirmed the intrusive potential of new technologies—especially when given legislative cover in the context of a national security threat. These and related events have changed the popular outlook on new technologies away from the rosy scenarios of utopian prognosticators to a more sober consideration of the actual value of digital/networked communications. From an entrepreneurial standpoint, the climate for investing in digital technologies has become more cautious, whereas, from a civil liberties perspective, the information environment is being viewed as a space of increased monitoring and surveillance.

At the same time, networked media have become normalized as a routine part of daily life. Digital technologies continue to have a profound influence on the media industries, affecting the production and distribution of content as well as the ways in which audiences approach and make use of media products. Two developments are still having far-reaching social, economic, and professional implications —the transition from analog to digital systems and the rapid expansion in the reach, capabilities, and user-friendliness of the Internet through the World Wide Web. In conjunction with cyber-related developments, interactive devices such as TiVo and PlayStation are transforming the way audiences approach and utilize media technologies, causing consumers to be seen as active *users* of communication technologies rather than passive *receivers* of content. Amidst this change, content providers must continually retool their operations to remain viable in a media environment characterized by heightened competition, program experimentation, and audience restiveness.

Just as the media industries are not immune from Moore's law—the tendency for computer processing power to double every 18 months to 2 years—so citizens of the information society cannot escape the forces unleashed by technological advancement. Consumers are reaping the rewards of revolution, but access to new technology remains uneven, and research is beginning to reveal usage gaps between sophisticated users and those who lack the skills and motivations necessary for full media access. Digital media clearly do not benefit everyone equally, as studies of the digital divide repeatedly reveal. For the student of new information and communication technologies, however, the dynamism of this theory/practice interface affords ample opportunity for intellectual exploration and engagement.

PURPOSE AND ORIENTATION

While staying true to the original purpose of this reader—to illuminate the social, psychological, and professional impact of technological trends in the evolving information and entertainment ecology—the second edition of *Living in the Information Age* represents a substantial revision of the first edition. My goal with the second edition was to reprint a slightly smaller number of readings than the first edition (47 compared to 64) that were more substantial in length (though not any less readable) and that could, to the extent possible, "stand the test of time." Given the short shelf life of the more industry-oriented readings in the first edition, I significantly refashioned the second part of the book, which had been focused on industry concerns, and condensed the overall number of chapters from 16 to 12. The result is a more focused set of readings that explore the issues in somewhat greater depth. Altogether, over half the readings in this revised edition are new.

The articles comprising this revised edition have thus been selected not only on the basis of their conceptual import and industry relevance but also for their in-depth treatment of topics. Reflecting the dynamism of developments at the interface, the scholarly and popular literature is growing in sophistication and scope. Included here is a representative cross section of that literature, which elucidates important Information Age issues (e.g., spam wars, PowerPoint woes, and the costs of information exposure) while exploring the broader, enduring role of communication technology in society. Developments addressed in this reader range from online dating and mobile swarming to media saturation and videogame culture. More broadly, readings examine

- How multitasking and the accelerated pace of everyday life can be viewed as byproducts of both computer efficiency and seemingly harmless devices such as the remote control
- How the Internet can be profitably thought of as a *communication* medium that enables different levels of social and professional interaction
- How interactivity made possible by networked computing also increases opportunities for surveillance and incursions on personal privacy

To assist learners in a classroom setting, each reading is again prefaced by a brief introduction and three questions for critical thinking and discussion. The questions are offered to encourage in-depth consideration of the issues raised in the readings and spark spirited discussion of the material. Following each article are suggestions for performing relevant follow-up searches using the InfoTrac® College Edition full-text article database.

ORGANIZATION

Living in the Information Age is divided into six major thematic parts that trace the development, survey the literature, and assess the impact of new technologies on the media landscape, examining both conceptual and practical aspects of life in an information society. *Living in the Information Age* thus provides students (and other readers) with a broad understanding of new communication technologies while encouraging original thinking about media, both old and new, in relation to theory.

Living in the Information Age is intended to enhance college-level courses addressing media and technology, social informatics, cyberculture studies, new communications technologies, or mass communication and society, with an emphasis on the changing media environment. Dozens of courses are beginning to emerge in this area—indeed, new media offerings are cataloged by the Resource Center for

Cyberculture Studies (http://www.com.washington.edu/rccs)—but despite growing student and scholarly interest in new media, there still are few satisfactory texts. *Living in the Information Age* is designed to help bridge this gap.

Part I of *Living in the Information Age* consists of articles dealing with the evolution of the information society and summarizes a set of theories relevant to understanding the new media. New to this part are readings about the control revolution, media ecology, remediation, and coordination issues between the real and virtual worlds. Part II examines how the media industries are being transformed through digital convergence and corporate concentration; all of the readings about convergence are new to this edition, while the chapter on media concentration features new entries about global media trends and consolidation in the radio industry, focusing on the growth and influence of Clear Channel Communications.

Part III highlights issues "at the interface" of new media and society, exploring new technologies, the self, and social life as well as media saturation, the consequences of e-mail spam, and the increasing velocity of everyday life. New readings are included about the practice of "Googling" prospective dates and job applicants, blogging, the videogame threat to old media, and the media torrent, or never-ending flow of images and sounds that characterize contemporary life. Part IV addresses social and economic impacts of networked computing and presents a set of readings questioning information technology, including new articles addressing the implications of intensive Internet use and the limitations of PowerPoint as a communication platform. Part V delves into issues surrounding electronic democracy and uneven access to the Internet, commonly referred to as the "digital divide." New readings take up questions about media participation, mobile computing, and the fragmentation of common concerns that occurs online. Finally, Part VI raises concerns about copyright violations, privacy, and surveillance—legal and ethical dilemmas that are perhaps unique to our Information Age—with new readings about file sharing, information exposure, and free expression in cyberspace.

ACKNOWLEDGMENTS

Several people, notably Burcu Bakioglu, Alexander M. Campbell Halavais, Eszter Hargittai, and Thom Gillespie provided some valuable article suggestions for the revised edition, as did members of the Media Ecology Association (www.media-ecology.org) and Association of Internet Researchers (www.aoir.org) listservs. Amanda Berry assisted with important aspects of the project with her trademark resolve and characteristic pizzazz, while April Easter lent a helping hand with the permissions process.

David Silver, who founded the Resource Center for Cyberculture Studies, deserves a round of applause for facilitating a considered discussion of the first edition of this reader to take place on the RCCS Web site in the form of two book reviews and an author's response (see http://www.com.washington.edu/rccs/booklist.asp). I would also like to extend my gratitude to those authors who recognized the educational value of this project and permitted their work to be reprinted in this collection either at a nominal fee or free of charge. Sharing knowledge and freely circulating ideas is the essence of the educational enterprise and provides students and professors alike with the intellectual raw materials necessary to arrive at new insights.

The editorial team in Wadsworth's communication division was instrumental in making this revision happen. I particularly appreciate the enthusiasm and support of Wadsworth's communication publisher and mass communications editor, Holly Allen, who recognized the value of a second edition and championed its development. Kimberly Russell, Shona Burke, Laryssa Polika, and other members of the Wadsworth marketing and editorial team who travel around the country and help promote the catalog also deserve special praise. Finally, Gretchen Otto and the helpful professionals at G&S Book Services once again brilliantly managed the production aspects of this project.

For their thoughtful suggestions and guidance in the preparation of this revised edition, the following reviewers warrant generous recognition: Benjamin J. Bates, University of Tennessee; Alexander M. Campbell Halavais, State University of New York at Buffalo; R. Lance Holbert, University of Missouri at Columbia; and Sean Zdenek, University of Texas at San Antonio.

Finally, the following individuals initially helped make this project a reality by reviewing the first edition of this reader: David Atkin, Cleveland State University; Ronald C. Bishop, Drexel University; Robert H. Bohle, University of North Florida; Phillip G. Clampitt, University of Wisconsin at Green Bay; Paul D'Angelo, College of New Jersey; Joseph Dominick, University of Georgia; Junhao Hong, State University of New York at Buffalo; Dorothy Kidd, University of San Francisco; Rebecca Ann Lind, University of Illinois at Chicago; Linda Lumsden, Western Kentucky University; Maclyn McClary, Humboldt State University; Stephen McDowell, Florida State University; John E. Newhagen, University of Maryland at College Park; Maurice Odine, Tennessee State University; Paula Otto, Virginia Commonwealth University; Arthur A. Raney, Florida State University; Brad L. Rawlins, James Madison University; David Silver, University of Washington; and Danney Ursery, St. Edward's University.

Erik P. Bucy, Ph.D.
Indiana University, Bloomington
ebucy@indiana.edu

PART I

≈

The New Information and Entertainment Ecology

Part I establishes a foundation for examining the development and consequences of the new information and entertainment ecology. The use of the word *ecology* to describe the information landscape evokes the environmental nature of today's communications media; in many ways, media serve as a primary source of sensory stimulation, knowledge gain, and need satisfaction. Information technologies and entertainment media literally saturate modern life to the point where it has become difficult to imagine life *without* them. The readings in Chapter 1 explain the origins and development of the information revolution, highlighting the developments that made our current mediated existence possible. The convergence of digital technology and enhanced telecommunications systems since the early 1980s has resulted in the explosive growth of new media in recent years, yet, as the reading on the technological and economic origins of the information society by James Beniger explains, the trends that set this process in motion were long in the making. The readings in Chapter 2 present several theoretical approaches relevant to studying new media, including *mediamorphosis,* which describes the process of media evolution as well as how new technologies diffuse or spread throughout society, and *remediation,* which is the repurposing or refashioning of old media with new. Additionally, readings on two audience-centered theories of media use are presented. The first, on *uses and gratifications,* addresses the needs that media fulfill and the sources of need satisfaction that media compete with, and the second, on the *new world* of cyberspace, describes how the Web is changing our understanding of social interaction, knowledge, and morality.

1

The Communications Revolution

Reading 1-1

The Roots of Revolution

Frances Cairncross

→ utopian narrative
→ linear & (maturation): history

EDITOR'S NOTE

In this excerpt from the Death of Distance: How the Communications Revolution Will Change Our Lives, *Frances Cairncross discusses the major changes that have occurred to the three communications technologies most important to the Information Age—the telephone, television, and networked computer—since 1980. She also offers 30 predictions of how the "death of distance"—her phrase for the ability to reach anyone in the world at any moment through electronic media—will shape the future in* The Trendspotter's Guide to New Communications.

CONSIDER

1. What important advances in communications technology have occurred since 1980?

2. In your opinion, do the transformations that have taken place in communications technologies deserve to be called "revolutionary"?

3. Which predictions do you agree with in *The Trendspotter's Guide to New Communications*? Which do you disagree with, and why?

It is easy to forget how recently the communications revolution began. All three of today's fast-changing communications technologies have existed for more than half a century: the telephone was invented in 1876; the first television transmission was in 1926; and the electronic computer was invented in the mid-1940s.[1] For much of that time, change has been slow, but, in each case, a revolution has taken place since the late 1980s. In order to approach the future, we need first to ask why the really big changes have been so recent and so far-reaching.

THE TELEPHONE

Since the 1980s, the oldest of the three technologies has undergone two big transformations—an astonishing increase in the carrying capacity of much of the long-distance network and the development of mobility. They result, in the first case, from the use of glass fibers to carry digital signals, and, in the second, from the steep fall in the cost of computing power.

For much of its existence, the telephone network has had the least capacity for its most useful service: long-distance communication. A cross-Atlantic telephone service existed early on: indeed, by the 1930s, J. Paul Getty could run his California oil empire by telephone from European hotels, in which he chose to live because their switchboard operators could make the connections he needed.[2] But even in 1956, when the first transatlantic telephone cable went on-line, it had capacity for only eighty-nine simultaneous conversations between all of Europe and all of North America.[3] Walter Wriston, former chairman of Citibank, recalls the way it felt to be an international banker in the 1950s and 1960s: "It could take a day or more to get a circuit. Once a connection was made, people in the branch would stay on the phone reading books and newspapers all day just to keep the line open until it was needed."[4]

Since the late 1980s, capacity on the main long-distance routes has grown so fast that, by the start of 1996, there was an immense and increasing glut, with only 30 to 35 percent of capacity in use.[5] The main

reason for this breathtaking transformation was the development of fiber-optic cables, made of glass so pure that a sheet seventy miles thick would be as clear as a windowpane. The first transatlantic fiber-optic cable, with capacity to carry nearly forty thousand conversations, went on-line only in 1988. The cables that will be laid at the turn of the century will carry more than three million conversations on a few strands of fiber, each the width of a human hair.

Meanwhile, new cables are being laid; new satellites, which carry telephone traffic on less popular routes, are due to be launched; and a range of low-orbiting satellites may eventually carry international traffic between mobile telephones. In addition, new techniques are starting to allow many more calls to travel on the same fiber. It is as though an already rapidly expanding fleet of trucks could suddenly pack several times as many products into the same amount of space as before.

This massive growth in capacity is increasingly reflected in tariffs. MCI's generous Mother's Day gesture [of free long-distance calls in 1995 and 1996] cost the firm plenty, but would have been impossible without the growth in capacity on the American network, where the traffic on that day is probably the heaviest of any day, anywhere in the world. Already, international and long-distance call rates have been falling, changing our mental map of the world. But the cost of carrying an extra telephone call across the Atlantic and on many other long-distance routes has fallen much further and now approaches zero. This fall in rates is the drive behind the death of distance.

By the middle of 1997, the threat of a glut had receded. The reason was the enormous increase in demand created by the Internet, which carries messages of many sorts at prices that ignore distance. When distance carries no price penalty, people communicate more, and in new ways. In the future, the lavish plans to build more capacity and ingenious technologies to compress signals will continue to push prices down, until it costs no more to telephone from New York to London than to the house next door.

While capacity has been increasing, the telephone has become mobile. Cellular communication, which dates back to the period immediately following World War II, became commercially viable only in the early 1980s, when the collapse in the cost of computing made it possible to provide the necessary processing power at a low enough cost.

Now, the mobile telephone may arguably be the most successful new way of communicating that the

From *The Death of Distance: How the Communications Revolution Will Change Our Lives* by Frances Cairncross (Boston, MA: Harvard Business School Press, 1997), pp. xi–xvi, 4–12. Copyright © 1997 by Frances Cairncross. Reprinted by permission of Harvard Business School Press.

world has ever seen—already, more than one telephone subscription in seven is to a mobile service. Mobile telephony's share will continue to rise: in 1996, it accounted for 47 percent of all new telephone subscriptions.[6] For conversations, people will come to use mobile telephones almost exclusively.

They will be able to communicate from every corner of the globe: in the course of 1996, two stranded climbers on Mount Everest used mobile telephones to call their wives. One wife, two thousand miles away in Hong Kong, was able to arrange her husband's rescue; the other, sadly, could merely say a last farewell.[7]

The mobile telephone also allows better use of the most underused chunk of time in many people's lives: traveling time. People will use their commuting time more fully, but other benefits may be even greater: passengers can be checked in for flights during the bus ride to the airport, for example, and maintenance staff can schedule visits more efficiently, knowing exactly when equipment in transit will arrive. The mobile telephone thus raises productivity by using previously idle time.

THE TELEVISION

At the end of the Second World War, a mere eight thousand homes worldwide had a television set. By 1996, that number had risen to more than 840 million—two-thirds of the world's households.[8] The basic technology of television sets has not changed over those fifty years, but the transmission of programs has been revolutionized by the development of communications satellites. Now another revolution—in channel capacity—has begun.

In fall 1963, people around the world witnessed for the first time an important but distant political event as it was taking place. The 1962 launch of Telstar, the first private communications satellite, had made possible the live global transmission of the funeral of President John F. Kennedy.[9] The psychological impact was huge: this unprecedented new link among countries would change perceptions of the world, creating the sense that the world's peoples belonged to a global, not merely local or national, community.

The 1988 launch by PanAmSat of the first privately owned commercial international (as opposed to domestic) satellite constituted another milestone, cutting the cost of transmitting live television material around the world. As recently as the 1970s, more than half of all television news was at least a day old. Today, almost

all news is broadcast on the day it occurs.[10] Big events—the fall of the Berlin Wall, the Gulf War, the O. J. Simpson trial verdict—go out to billions of viewers as they happen.

Until recently, most television viewers around the world have had access to perhaps half a dozen television channels at most—and often to only two or three. The main reason is purely physical: analog television signals are greedy users of spectrum. Only in the United States and a handful of other countries, and mainly only since the 1980s, have cable-television networks—less constrained by the limits of spectrum—brought people real viewing choice.

Now choice is expanding with breathtaking speed. Toward the end of the 1980s, communications satellites began to broadcast directly to a small dish attached to people's homes, thus inexpensively distributing multichannel television. Suddenly, more viewers had more choice than ever before.

In the mid-1990s came another revolutionary change: broadcasters began to transmit television in digital, not analog, form, allowing the signal to be compressed and, consequently, far more channels to be transmitted, whether from satellite, through cable, or even over the air. Like the long-distance parts of the telephone network, a service that had been constrained by capacity shortage for most of its existence has suddenly begun to build more capacity than it knows what to do with.

The result will be a revolution in the nature of television. For those who want it (most of us), the old passive medium will remain, a relaxing way to pass the evening after a day spent at work. But television—the business of transmitting moving pictures—will develop many more functions, including new roles in business. The finances of television will also change, and in a way that many viewers will resent. The scarcest thing in television is not transmission capacity, but desirable programs, especially live programming. In the future, these will rarely be available at no cost to viewers. Increasingly, viewers will pay directly for what they most want to watch.

THE NETWORKED COMPUTER

The newest of the three building blocks of the communications revolution, the electronic computer, has evolved fastest. In 1943 Thomas Watson, founder of IBM, thought that the world market had room for about five computers.[11] As recently as 1967, a state-of-the-art IBM, costing $167,500, could hold a mere thirteen pages of text.[12]

Two key changes have altered this picture: First, computing power has grown dramatically. As a result, the computer can be miniaturized and has become a consumer durable, with computing power embedded in everything from automobiles to children's toys. The main processor on Apollo 13 contained less computing power than does a modern Nintendo games machine.[13] Second, computers are increasingly connected to each other. The Internet, essentially a means of connecting the world's computers, makes apparent the spectacular power of such networked computers.

The increase in computing power has followed a principle known as "Moore's Law," after Gordon Moore, co-founder of Intel, now the world's leading maker of computer chips, the brains of the modern computer. In 1965, Moore forecast that computing power would double every eighteen months to two years. So it has done for three decades, as engineers have found ways to squeeze ever more integrated circuits of transistors onto chips—small wafers of silicon. A 486 chip, standard in a computer bought around 1994, could perform up to fifty-four million numerical calculations per second. A Pentium chip, the standard three years later, could perform up to two hundred million calculations per second. And Moore's law continues to apply. By 2006, according to Intel forecasts, chips will be one thousand times as powerful and will cost one-tenth as much as they did in 1996.[14]

As the power of the chip has multiplied, the price of computing power has fallen, computer size has decreased, and computer capacity has risen. This has had implications for many aspects of communications: the development of mobile telephones, for example, and of the "set-top boxes" that decode encrypted television signals. A landmark occurred in 1977, when Steven Jobs and Stephen Wozniak, two young computer enthusiasts, launched the Apple II, opening the way for the computer to become a household good. Today, 40 percent of homes in the United States contain a computer.

Meanwhile, responding to the limitations of computers in the 1960s, when they were large, expensive and scarce, the American Defense Department's Advanced Research Projects Agency (ARPA) backed an experiment to connect computers across the country as a way to exchange messages and share their processing power. This effort yielded a nationwide network that initially linked only university computers. Because different computers in those early days had different operating standards, a common standard or protocol became a fundamental requirement of the network. In response, Transmission Control Protocol/Internet Protocol (TCP/IP) was developed and, since the early 1980s, has provided the format for packaging all data sent over the Internet.

TCP/IP is the essence of the Internet. It provides an electronic Esperanto: a common language and a set of rules through which computers all over the world can talk to one another, regardless of whether they are PCs or Apple Macs, whether they are vast university mainframes or domestic laptops. Through the Internet, any number of computer networks can connect with one another and behave as a single network.

Although the use of the Internet grew rapidly in the 1980s and early 1990s, doubling every year, its transformation into a popular success dates only from about 1993 to 1994. At that point, the World Wide Web made it possible to accommodate on-line graphics, sound, and moving pictures, rather than just text, making the Internet more versatile and more interesting to look at. This was thanks to Marc Andreessen, a young programmer, and his colleagues at the University of Illinois. They developed the most successful graphical Web browser, which allowed navigation fairly easily from one screenful (or "page") of information to another, even if that second page was held on a different computer in another part of the world, simply by using a hand-held "mouse" control to point and click on a shaded word on the screen.

These transformations have had three main consequences. First, they vastly increase the world's computing power. Even if Moore's law stopped grinding inexorably along, the Internet has the potential to allow immense multiplication of computing power simply by linking many different computers. Second, the Internet has emerged almost by accident, as the first working model of the "global information superhighway" that politicians and big communications companies talked so much about in the early 1990s.[15] It has become not only a new global means of communicating but also a new global source of information on a gigantic scale. Third, the Internet has given birth to a vigorous new industry dedicated to developing ways to use it and services to sell across it. Only in 1994 did the number of commercial computers connected to the Internet overtake the number of academic computers. Now, tens of thousands of companies, many of them small start-ups, are racing to find profitable uses for this new technology. Never in history have so many entre-preneurs attempted, in so short a space of time, to develop uses for an innovation.

The Internet is thus a global laboratory, allowing individuals as well as the marketing departments of multinationals and academics in top universities to pioneer uses for communications technology. Already it carries telephone and video conferences as well as live television and radio broadcasts. All sorts of communications experiments, carried out on the Internet, will feed through into the other media, changing and developing them. The Internet thus functions as both a prototype and a testing ground for the future of communications. Watching its evolution, we can catch a glimpse of what lies ahead.

Reading 1-1 (continued)

The Trendspotter's Guide to New Communications
Frances Cairncross

How will the death of distance shape the future? Here are some of the most important developments to watch.

1. *The Death of Distance.* Distance will no longer determine the cost of communicating electronically. Companies will organize certain types of work in three shifts according to the world's three main time zones: the Americas, East Asia/Australia, and Europe/Africa ? *[handwritten: /Africa ?]* *[handwritten circled: B]*

2. *The Fate of Location.* No longer will location be key to most business decisions. Companies will locate any screen-based activity anywhere on earth, wherever they can find the best bargain of skills and productivity. Developing countries will increasingly perform on-line services—monitoring security screens, running help-lines and call centers, writing software, and so forth—and sell them to the rich industrial countries that generally produce such services domestically.

3. *The Irrelevance of Size.* Small companies will offer services that, in the past, only giants had the scale and scope to provide. Individuals with valuable ideas, initiative, and strong business plans will attract global venture capital and convert their ideas into viable businesses. Small countries will also be more viable. That will be good news for secession movements everywhere. *[handwritten: + terrorism!]* *[handwritten circled symbol]*

4. *Improved Connections.* Most people on earth will eventually have access to networks that are all switched, interactive, and broadband: "switched," *[circled: switched,]* like the telephone, and used to contact many other subscribers; "interactive" *[circled: interactive]* in that, unlike broadcast TV, all ends of the network can communicate; and "broadband," *[circled: broadband,]* with the capacity to receive TV-quality motion pictures. While the Internet will continue to exist in its present form, it will also be integrated into other services, such as the telephone and television.

5. *More Customized Content.* Improved networks will also allow individuals to order "content for one"; that is, individual consumers will receive (or send) exactly what they want to receive (or send), when and where they want it.

6. *A Deluge of Information.* Because people's capacity to absorb new information will not increase, they will need filters to sift, process, and edit it. Companies will have greater need of boosters—new techniques—to brand and push their information ahead of the competition's.

7. *Increased Value of Brand.* What's hot—whether a product, a personality, a sporting event, or the latest financial data—will attract greater rewards. The costs of producing or promoting these commodities will not change, but the potential market will increase greatly. That will create a category of global super-rich, many of them musicians, actors, artists, athletes, and investors. For the successful few and their intermediaries, entertaining will be the most lucrative individual activity on earth.

8. *Increased Value in Niches.* The power of the computer to search, identify, and classify people according to similar needs and tastes will create sustainable markets for many niche products. Niche players will increase, as will consumers' demand for customized goods and services.

[handwritten: ngl. "long tail" economy]

9. *Communities of Practice.* The horizontal bonds among people performing the same job or speaking the same language in different parts of the world will strengthen. Common interests, experiences, and pursuits rather than proximity will bind these communities together.

10. *Near-Frictionless Markets.* Many more companies and customers will have access to accurate price information. That will curtail excessive profits, enhance competition, and help to curb inflation, resulting in "profitless prosperity": it will be easier to find buyers, but hard to make fat margins.

11. *Increased Mobility.* Every form of communication will be available for mobile or remote use. While fixed connections such as cable will offer greater capacity and speed, wireless will be not just to send a signal over a large region, but to carry it fixed point to users in a relatively small radius. Satellite transmission will allow people to use a single mobile telephone anywhere, and the distinctions between fixed and mobile receiving equipment (a telephone or a personal computer) will blur.

12. *More Global Reach, More Local Provision.* While small companies find it easier to reach markets around the world, big companies will more readily offer high-quality local services, such as putting customers in one part of the world directly in touch with expertise in other places, and monitoring more precisely the quality of local provision.

13. *The Loose-Knit Corporation.* Culture and communications networks, rather than rigid management structures, will hold companies together. Many companies will become networks of independent specialists; more employees will therefore work in smaller units or alone. Loyalty, trust, and open communications will reshape the nature of customer and supplier contracts: suppliers will draw directly on information held in databases by their customers, working as closely and seamlessly as an in-house supplier now does. Technologies such as electronic mail and computerized billing will reduce the costs of dealing with consumers and suppliers at arm's length.

14. *More Minnows, More Giants.* On one hand, the cost of starting new businesses will decline, and companies will more easily buy in services so that more small companies will spring up. On the other, communication amplifies the strength of brands and the power of networks. In industries where networks matter, concentration may increase, but often in form of loose global associations under a banner of brands or quality guarantees.

15. *Manufacturers as Service Providers.* Feeding information on a particular buyer's tastes straight back to the manufacturer will be easier and so manufacturers will design more products specially for an individual's requirements. Some manufacturers will even retain lasting links with their products: car companies, for instance, will continue electronically to track, monitor, and learn about their vehicles throughout the product life cycle. New opportunities to provide services for customers will emerge, and some manufacturers may accept more responsibility for disposing of their products at the end of the cycle.

16. *The Inversion of Home and Office.* As more people work from home or from small, purpose-built offices, the line between work and home life will blur. The office will become a place for the social aspects of work such as celebrating, networking, lunching, and gossiping. Home design will also change, and the domestic office will become a regular part of the house.

17. *The Proliferation of Ideas.* New ideas and information will travel faster to the remotest corners of the world. Third world countries will have access to knowledge that the industrial world has long enjoyed. Communities of practice and long-distance education programs will help people to find mentors and acquire new skills.

18. *A New Trust.* Since it will be easier to check whether people and companies deliver what they have promised, many services will become more reliable and people will be more likely to trust each other to keep their word. However, those who fail to deliver will quickly lose that trust, which will become more difficult to regain.

19. *People as the Ultimate Scarce Resource.* The key challenge for companies will be to hire and retain good people, extracting value from them, rather than allowing them to keep all the value they create for themselves. A company will constantly need to convince its best employees that working for it enhances each individual's value.

20. *The Shift from Government Policing to Self-Policing.* Governments will find national legislation and censorship inadequate for regulating the global flow of information. As content sweeps across national borders, it will be harder to enforce laws banning child pornography, libel, and other criminal or subversive material and those protecting copyright and other intellectual property. But greater electronic access to information will give people better means to protect themselves. The result will be more individual responsibility and less government intervention.

21. *Loss of Privacy.* As in the village of past centuries, protecting privacy will be difficult. Governments and companies will easily monitor people's movements. Machines will recognize physical attributes like a voice or fingerprint. People will thus come to embody their identity. Civil libertarians will worry, but others will accept the loss as a fair exchange for the reduction of crime, including fraud and illegal immigration. In the electronic village, there will be little true privacy—and little unsolved crime.

22. *Redistribution of Wages.* Low-wage competition will reduce the earning power of many people in rich countries employed in routine screen-based tasks, but the premium for certain skills will grow. People with skills that are in demand will earn broadly similar amounts wherever they live in the world. So income differences within countries will grow; and income differences between countries will narrow.

23. *Less Need for Immigration and Emigration.* Poor countries with good communications technology will be able to retain their skilled workers, who will be less likely to emigrate to countries with higher costs of living if they can earn rich-world wages and pay poor-world prices for everyday necessities right at home. Thus inexpensive communications may reduce some of the pressure to emigrate.

24. *A Market for Citizens.* The greater freedom to locate anywhere and earn a living will hinder taxation. Savers will be able to compare global investment rates and easily shift money abroad. High-income earners and profitable companies will be able to move away from hefty government-imposed taxes. Countries will compete to bid down tax rates and to attract businesses, savers, and wealthy residents.

25. *Rebirth of Cities.* As individuals spend less time in the office and more time working from home or traveling, cities will transform from concentrations of office employment to centers of entertainment and culture; that is, cities will become places where people go to stay in hotels, visit museums and galleries, dine in restaurants, participate in civic events, and attend live performances of all kinds. In contrast, some poor countries will stem the flight from the countryside to cities by using low-cost communications to provide rural dwellers with better medical services, jobs, education, and entertainment.

26. *The Rise of English.* The global role of English as a second language will strengthen as it becomes the common standard for telecommunicating in business and commerce. Many more countries, especially in the developing world, will therefore adopt English as a subsidiary language. It will be as important to learn English as to use software that is compatible with the near-universal MS-DOS.

27. *Communities of Culture.* At the same time, electronic communications will reinforce less widespread languages and cultures, not replace them with Anglo-Saxon and Hollywood. The declining cost of creating and distributing many entertainment products and the corresponding increase in production capacity will also reinforce local cultures and help scattered peoples and families to preserve their cultural heritage.

28. *Improved Writing and Reading Skills.* Electronic mail will induce young people to express themselves effectively in writing and to admire clear and lively written prose. Dull or muddled communicators will fall by the information wayside.

29. *Rebalance of Political Power.* Since people will communicate their views on government more directly, rulers and representatives will become more sensitive (and, perhaps, more responsive) to lobbying and public-opinion polls, especially in established democracies. People who live under dictatorial regimes will make contact more easily with the rest of the world.

30. *Global Peace.* As countries become even more economically interdependent and as global trade

and foreign investment grow, people will communicate more freely and learn more about the ideas and aspirations of human beings in other parts of the globe. The effect will be to increase understanding, foster tolerance, and ultimately promote worldwide peace.

NOTES

1. Melvin Harris, *ITN Book of Firsts*. London: Michael O'Mara Books, 1994, pp. 108, 124, 162.

2. John Pearson, *Painfully Rich: J. Paul Getty and His Heirs*. London: Macmillan, 1995, p. 68.

3. A cable from the mainland United States to Hawaii that went on-line the following year had only 91 such "voice paths." See Gregory C. Staple (Ed.), *TeleGeography 1995: Global Telecommunications Traffic Statistics and Commentary*. Washington, DC: TeleGeography, 1995, p. 84.

4. Walter B. Wriston, *The Twilight of Sovereignty: How the Information Revolution Is Transforming Our World*. New York: Scribner's, 1992, p. 36.

5. Gregory C. Staple (Ed.). *TeleGeography 1996–97: Global Telecommunications Traffic Statistics and Commentary*. Washington, DC: TeleGeography, 1996, p. xv.

6. International Telecommunication Union. *International Telecommunication Union Database*, Geneva, May 1997.

7. "Trapped on Everest? I'm on My Mobile?" by Stephen Goodwin, *London Independent*, April 27, 1996, p. 3.

8. International Telecommunication Union. *World Telecommunication Development Report 1996/97*, Geneva, 1997.

9. *Defining Moments*. London: A. T. Kearney, 1996, p. 46.

10. Robert H. Frank and Philip J. Cook, *The Winner-Take-All Society: How More and More Americans Compete for Ever Fewer and Bigger Prizes, Encouraging Economic Waste, Income Inequality, and an Impoverished Cultural Life*. New York: The Free Press, 1995.

11. Quoted in "Tomorrow Never Knows," by Victor Navasky. *New York Times Magazine*, September 29, 1996, p. 216.

12. *Defining Moments*.

13. Christopher Anderson, personal communication, February 1997.

14. "Computer Power and Data Storage Capacity," *Screen Digest*, December 1996, p. 287.

15. "The Accidental Superhighway: A Survey of the Internet," by Christopher Anderson. *The Economist*, July 1, 1995, p. S3.

RELATED LINKS

- International Telecommunication Union (http://www.itu.int/home/index.html)
- TeleGeography, Inc. (http://www.telegeography.com)
- Frances Cairncross: On Technology (http://www.ispa.org/ideas/cairncross.html)
- Anthony Pennings' History of IT (http://www.academic.marist.edu/pennings/ithistory.htm)

FOR FURTHER RESEARCH

To find out more about the topics discussed in this reading, use InfoTrac College Edition. Type in keywords and subject terms such as "communications revolution," "fiber-optic networks," and "networked computing." You can access InfoTrac from the Wadsworth/Thomson Communication Café homepage: http://communication.wadsworth.com.

Reading 1-2

Technological and Economic Origins of the Information Society

technological → determinist

James R. Beniger

EDITOR'S NOTE

The origins of today's information-based society have their roots in a remarkable series of developments that transformed industrialized countries in the last decades of the nineteenth century. As James Beniger astutely chronicles in this excerpt from The Control Revolution *(Harvard, 1986), the accelerated processing demands precipitated by industrialization (i.e., a dramatic speedup in the pace of manufacturing and transportation) led to a crisis of control that was resolved only by the development of key information technologies from roughly 1870 to 1910. Before this time, he notes, control of society and the economy had depended on personal relationships and face-to-face interactions. Since the industrial era, however, control has been accomplished by means of bureaucratic organization, transportation and telecommunications networks, and mass media. Attendant with this change has been a shift from agricultural and manufacturing jobs to service and information-oriented work.*

CONSIDER

1. Why does Beniger consider the period from 1870 to 1910 so influential and decisive for society as we know it today?

2. In what sense can bureaucracy, a form of human organization, be considered a *control* technology, as Beniger uses the term?

3. When did the shift from an agricultural-based economy begin to shift to a manufacturing foundation—and when did manufacturing give way to the rise of the service and information industries?

To say that the advanced industrial world is rapidly becoming an Information Society may already be a cliché. In the United States, Canada, Western Europe, and Japan, the bulk of the labor force now works primarily at informational tasks such as systems analysis and computer programming, while wealth comes increasingly from informational goods such as microprocessors and from informational services such as data processing. For the economies of at least a half-dozen countries, the processing of information has begun to overshadow the processing of matter and energy.

Reprinted by permission of the publisher from *The Control Revolution: Technological and Economic Origins of the Information Society* by James R. Beniger (Cambridge, MA: Harvard University Press, 1986), pp. v–viii, 1–26. Copyright © 1986 by the President and Fellows of Harvard College.

But why? Among the multitude of things that human beings value, why should it be information, embracing both goods and services, that has come to dominate the world's largest and most advanced economies? Despite scores of books and articles proclaiming the advent of the Information Society, no one seems to have even raised—much less answered—this important question.

Even if we could explain the growing importance of information and its processing in modern economies, I realized, we would immediately confront a second question: Why now? Because information plays an important role in all human societies, we would also have to explain why it has only *recently* emerged as a distinct and critical commodity. Material culture has also been crucial throughout human history, after all, and yet capital did not displace land as the major economic base until the Industrial Revolution. To what comparable technological and economic "revolution" might we attribute the emergence of the Information Society?

My answer, as the title of this book indicates, is what I call the Control Revolution, a complex of rapid changes in the technological and economic arrangements by which information is collected, stored, processed, and communicated, and through which formal or programmed decisions might effect societal control. From its origins in the last decades of the nineteenth century, the Control Revolution has continued unabated, and recently it has been accelerated by the development of microprocessing technologies. In terms of the magnitude and pervasiveness of its impact upon society, intellectual and cultural no less than material, the Control Revolution already appears to be as important as the Industrial Revolution.

But history alone cannot explain why it is information that increasingly plays the crucial role in economy and society. The answer must be sought in the nature of *all* living systems—ultimately in the relationship between information and control. Life itself implies control, after all, in individual cells and organisms no less than in national economies or any other purposive system.

Identifying the crisis of control and the resulting Control Revolution has helped me to answer another question that has nagged me since my days as an American history major, namely, why the period 1870–1910 is so interesting to modern students and seems so decisive for society as we know it today.

The Information Society, I have concluded, is not so much the result of any recent social change as of increases begun more than a century ago in the speed of material processing. Microprocessor and computer technologies, contrary to currently fashionable opinion, are not new forces only recently unleashed upon an unprepared society, but merely the latest installment in the continuing development of the Control Revolution. This explains why so many of the computer's major contributions were anticipated along with the first signs of a control crisis in the mid-nineteenth century.

THE CONTROL REVOLUTION

Few turn-of-the-century observers understood even isolated aspects of the societal transformation—what I shall call the "Control Revolution"—then gathering momentum in the United States, England, France, and Germany. Notable among those who did was Max Weber (1864–1920), the German sociologist and political economist who directed social analysis to the most important control technology of his age: bureaucracy. Although bureaucracy had developed several times independently in ancient civilizations, Weber was the first to see it as the critical new machinery—new, at least, in its generality and pervasiveness—for control of the societal forces unleashed by the Industrial Revolution.

For a half-century after Weber's initial analysis bureaucracy continued to reign as the single most important technology of the Control Revolution. After World War II, however, generalized control began to shift slowly to computer technology. If social change has seemed to accelerate in recent years (as argued, for example, by Toffler [1971]), this has been due in large part to a spate of new information-processing, communication, and control technologies like the computer, most notably the microprocessors that have proliferated since the early 1970s. Such technologies are more properly seen, however, not as causes but as consequences of societal change, as natural extensions of the Control Revolution already in progress for more than a century.

Revolution, a term borrowed from astronomy, first appeared in political discourse in seventeenth-century England, where it described the restoration of a previous form of government. Not until the French Revolution did the word acquire its currently popular and opposite meaning, that of abrupt and often violent change. As used here in Control Revolution, the term is intended to have both of these opposite connotations.

Beginning most noticeably in the United States in the late nineteenth century, the Control Revolution was certainly a dramatic if not abrupt discontinuity in technological advance. Indeed, even the word *revolution* seems barely adequate to describe the development, within the span of a single lifetime, of virtually all of the basic communication technologies still in use a century later: photography and telegraphy (1830s), rotary power printing (1840s), the typewriter (1860s), transatlantic cable (1866), telephone (1876), motion pictures (1894), wireless telegraphy (1895), magnetic tape recording (1899), radio (1906), and television (1923).

Along with these rapid changes in mass media and telecommunications technologies, the Control Revolution also represented the beginning of a restoration —although with increasing centralization—of the economic and political control that was lost at more local levels of society during the Industrial Revolution. Before this time, control of government and markets had depended on personal relationships and face-to-face interactions; now control came to be reestablished by means of bureaucratic organization, the new infrastructures of transportation and telecommunications, and system-wide communication via the new mass media. The new societal transformations—rapid innovation in information and control technology, to regain control of functions once contained at much lower and more diffuse levels of society—constituted a true revolution in societal control. Here the word *control* represents its most general definition, purposive influence toward a predetermined goal.

Inseparable from the concept of control are the twin activities of information processing and reciprocal communication, complementary factors in any form of control. Information processing is essential to all purposive activity, which is by definition goal directed and must therefore involve the continual comparison of current states to goals, a basic problem of information processing.

Simultaneously with the comparison of inputs to goals, two-way interaction between controller and controlled must also occur, not only to communicate influence from the former to the latter, but also to communicate back the results of this action (hence the term *feedback* for this reciprocal flow of information back to a controller). So central is communication to the process of control that the two have become the joint subject of the modern science of cybernetics, defined by one of its founders as "the entire field of control and communication theory, whether in the machine or in the animal" (Wiener 1948, p. 11). Similarly, the pioneers of mathematical communication theory have defined the object of their study as purposive control in the broadest sense: communication, according to Shannon and Weaver (1949, pp. 3–5), includes "all of the procedures by which one mind may affect another"; they note that "communication either affects conduct or is without any discernible and probable effect at all."

Because both the activities of information processing and communication are inseparable components of the control function, a society's ability to maintain control—at all levels from interpersonal to international relations—will be directly proportional to the development of its information technologies. Here the term *technology* is intended not in the narrow sense of practical or applied science but in the more general

sense of any intentional extension of a natural process, that is, of the processing of matter, energy, and information that characterizes all living systems. Respiration is a wholly natural life function, for example, and is therefore not a technology; the human ability to breathe under water, by contrast, implies some technological extension.

Technology may therefore be considered as roughly equivalent to that which can be done, excluding only those capabilities that occur naturally in living systems. This distinction is usually, although not always, clear. One ambiguous case is language, which may have developed at least in part through purposive innovation but which now appears to be a mostly innate capability of the human brain. The brain itself represents another ambiguous case: it probably developed in interaction with purposive tool use and may therefore be included among human technologies.

Because technology defines the limits on what a society *can* do, technological innovation might be expected to be a major impetus to social change in the Control Revolution no less than in the earlier societal transformations accorded the status of revolutions. The Neolithic Revolution, for example, which brought the first permanent settlements, owed its origin to the refinement of stone tools and the domestication of plants and animals. The Commercial Revolution, following exploration of Africa, Asia, and the New World, resulted directly from technical improvements in seafaring and navigational equipment. The Industrial Revolution, which eventually brought the nineteenth-century crisis of control, began a century earlier with greatly increased use of coal and steam power and a spate of new machinery for the manufacture of cotton textiles.

Because control is necessary for such processing, and information, as we have seen, is essential to control, both information processing and communication, insofar as they distinguish living systems from the inorganic universe, might be said to define life itself—except for a few recent artifacts of our own species.

Each new technological innovation extends the processes that sustain life, thereby increasing the need for control and hence for improved control technology. This explains why technology appears autonomously to beget technology in general (Winner 1977), and why, as argued here, innovations in matter and energy processing create the need for further innovation in information-processing and communication technologies. Because technological innovation is increasingly a collective, cumulative effort, one whose results must be taught and diffused, it also generates an increased need for technologies of information storage and retrieval—as well as for their elaboration in systems of technical education and communication—quite independently of the particular need for control.

As in the earlier revolutions in matter and energy technologies, the nineteenth-century revolution in information technology was predicated on, if not directly caused by, social changes associated with earlier innovations.

CRISIS OF CONTROL

The later Industrial Revolution constituted, in effect, a consolidation of earlier technological revolutions and the resulting transformations of society. Especially during the late nineteenth and early twentieth centuries, industrialization extended to progressively earlier technological revolutions: manufacturing, energy production, transportation, agriculture—the last a transformation of what had once been seen as the extreme opposite of industrial production.

Increasingly confounding the need for integration of the structural division of labor [attendant with the Industrial Revolution] were corresponding increases in commodity flows through the system—flows driven by steam-powered factory production and mass distribution via national rail networks. Never before had the processing of material flows threatened to exceed, in both volume and speed, the capacity of technology to contain them. For centuries most goods had moved with the speed of draft animals down roadway and canal, weather permitting. This infrastructure, controlled by small organizations of only a few hierarchical levels, supported even national economies. Suddenly —owing to the harnessing of steam power—goods could be moved at the full speed of industrial production, night and day and under virtually any conditions, not only from town to town but across entire continents and around the world.

To do this, however, required an increasingly complex system of manufacturers and distributors, central and branch offices, transportation lines and terminals, containers and cars. Even the logistics of nineteenth-century armies, then the most difficult problem in processing and control, came to be dwarfed in complexity by the material economy just emerging.

RATIONALIZATION AND BUREAUCRACY

Foremost among all the technological solutions to the crisis of control—in that it served to control most other technologies—was the rapid growth of formal bureaucracy first analyzed by Max Weber at the turn of the century. Bureaucratic organization was not new to Weber's time; bureaucracies had arisen in the first nation-states with centralized administrations, most significantly in Mesopotamia and ancient Egypt, and had reached a high level of sophistication in the preindustrial empires of Rome, China, and Byzantium. Indeed, bureaucratic organization tends to appear wherever a collective activity needs to be coordinated by several people toward explicit and impersonal goals, that is, to be *controlled*. Bureaucracy has served as the generalized means to control any large social system in most institutional areas and in most cultures since the emergence of such systems by about 3000 B.C.

Because of the venerable history and pervasiveness of bureaucracy, historians have tended to overlook its role in the late nineteenth century as a major new control technology. Nevertheless, bureaucratic administration did not begin to achieve anything approximating its modern form until the late Industrial Revolution. As late as the 1830s, for example, the Bank of the United States, then the nation's largest and most complex institution with twenty-two branch offices and profits fifty times those of the largest mercantile house, was managed by just three people: Nicholas Biddle and two assistants (Redlich 1951, pp. 113–124). In 1831 President Andrew Jackson and 665 other civilians ran all three branches of the federal government in Washington, an increase of sixty-three employees over the previous ten years. The Post Office Department, for example, had been administered for thirty years as the personal domain of two brothers, Albert and Phineas Bradley (Pred 1973, chap. 3). Fifty years later, in the aftermath of rapid industrialization, Washington's bureaucracy included some thirteen thousand civilian employees, more than double the total—already swelled by the American Civil War—only ten years earlier (U.S. Bureau of the Census 1975, p. 1103).

Further evidence that bureaucracy developed in response to the Industrial Revolution is the timing of concern about bureaucratization as a pressing social problem. The word *bureaucracy* did not even appear in English until the early nineteenth century, yet within a generation it became a major topic of political and philosophical discussion. As early as 1837, for example, John Stuart Mill wrote of a "vast network of administrative tyranny . . . that system of *bureaucracy,* which leaves no free agent in all France, except the man at Paris who pulls the wires" (Burchfield 1972, p. 391); a decade later Mill warned more generally of the "inexpediency of concentrating in a dominant bureaucracy . . . all power of organized action . . . in the community" (1848, p. 529). Thomas Carlyle, in his *Latter-Day Pamphlet* published two years later, complained of "the Continental nuisance called 'Bureaucracy'" (1850, p. 121). The word *bureaucratic* had also appeared by the 1830s, followed by *bureaucrat* in the 1840s and *bureaucratize* by the 1890s.

That bureaucracy is in essence a control technology was first established by Weber, most notably in his *Economy and Society* (1922). Weber included among the defining characteristics of bureaucracy several important aspects of any control system: impersonal orientation of structure to the information that it processes, usually identified as "cases," with a predetermined formal set of rules governing all decisions and responses. Any tendency to humanize this bureaucratic machinery, Weber argued, would be minimized through clear-cut division of labor and definition of responsibilities, hierarchical authority, and specialized decision and communication functions. The stability and permanence of bureaucracy, he noted, are assured through regular promotion of career employees based on objective criteria like seniority.

Weber identified another related control technology, what he called *rationalization*. Although the term has a variety of meanings, both in Weber's writings and in the elaborations of his work by others, most definitions are subsumed by one essential idea: control can be increased not only by increasing the capability to process information but also by decreasing the amount of information to be processed. The former approach to control was realized in Weber's day through bureaucratization and today increasingly through computerization; the latter approach was then realized through rationalization, what computer scientists now call *preprocessing*.

Perhaps most pervasive of all rationalization is the increasing tendency of modern society to regulate interpersonal relationships in terms of a formal set of impersonal and objective criteria. The early technocrat Claude Henri Comte de Saint-Simon (1760–1825), who lived through only the first stages of industrialization, saw such rationalization as a move "from the government of men to the administration of things" (Taylor 1975, p. 3). The reason why people can be governed more readily *qua* things is that the amount of information about them that needs to be processed is thereby greatly reduced and hence the degree of control—for any constant capacity to process information—is greatly enhanced. By means of rationalization, therefore, it is possible to maintain large-scale, complex social systems that would be overwhelmed by a rising tide of information they could not process were it necessary to govern by the particularistic considerations of family and kin that characterize preindustrial societies.

In short, rationalization might be defined as the destruction or ignoring of information in order to facilitate its processing. One example from within bureaucracy is the development of standardized paper forms. This might at first seem a contradiction, in that the proliferation of paperwork is usually associated with a growth in information to be processed, not with its reduction. Imagine how much more processing would be required, however, if each new case were recorded in an unstructured way, including every nuance and in full detail, rather than by checking boxes, filling blanks, or in some other way reducing the burdens of the bureaucratic system to only the limited range of formal, objective, and impersonal information required by standardized forms.

Equally important to the rationalization of industrial society, at the most macro level, were the division of North America into five standardized time zones in 1883 and the establishment the following year of the Greenwich meridian and International Date Line, which organized world time into twenty-four zones. What was formerly a problem of information overload and hence control for railroads and other organizations that sustained the social system at its most macro level was solved by simply ignoring much of the information, namely that solar time is different at each node of a transportation or communication system. A more convincing demonstration of the power of rationalization or preprocessing as a control technology would be difficult to imagine.

So commonplace has such preprocessing become that today we dismiss the alternative—that each node in a system might keep a slightly different time—as hopelessly cumbersome and primitive. With the continued proliferation of distributed computing, ironically enough, it might soon become feasible to return to a system based on local solar time, thereby shifting control from preprocessing back to processing—where it resided for centuries of human history until steam power pushed transportation beyond the pace of the sun across the sky.

NEW CONTROL TECHNOLOGY

The rapid development of rationalization and bureaucracy in the middle and late nineteenth century led to a succession of dramatic new information-processing and communication technologies. These innovations served to contain the control crisis of industrial society in what can be treated as three distinct areas of economic activity: production, distribution, and consumption of goods and services.

Control of production was facilitated by the continuing organization and preprocessing of industrial operations. Machinery itself came increasingly to be controlled by two new information-processing technologies: closed-loop feedback devices like James Watt's steam governor (1788) and preprogrammed open-loop controllers like those of the Jacquard loom (1801). By 1890 Herman Hollerith had extended Jacquard's punch cards to tabulation of U.S. census data. This information-processing technology survives to this day—if just barely—owing largely to the corporation to which Hollerith's innovation gave life, International Business Machines (IBM). Further rationalization and control of production advanced through an accumulation of other industrial innovations: interchangeable parts (after 1800), integration of production within factories (1820s and 1830s), the development of modern accounting techniques (1850s and 1860s), professional managers (1860s and 1870s), continuous-process production (late 1870s and early 1880s), the "scientific management" of Frederick Winslow Taylor (1911), Henry Ford's modern assembly line (after 1913), and statistical quality control (1920s), among many others.

The resulting flood of mass-produced goods demanded comparable innovation in control of a second area of the economy: distribution. Growing infrastructures of transportation, including rail networks, steamship lines, and urban traction systems, depended for control on a corresponding infrastructure of information processing and telecommunications. Within fifteen years after the opening of the pioneering Baltimore and Ohio Railroad in 1830, for example, Samuel

F. B. Morse—with a congressional appropriation of $30,000—had linked Baltimore to Washington, D.C., by means of a telegraph. Eight years later, in 1852, thirteen thousand miles of railroad and twenty-three thousand miles of telegraph line were in operation (Thompson 1947; U.S. Bureau of the Census 1975, p. 731), and the two infrastructures continued to co-evolve in a web of distribution and control that progressively bound the entire continent. In the words of business historian Alfred Chandler, "the railroad permitted a rapid increase in the speed and decrease in the cost of long-distance, written communication, while the invention of the telegraph created an even greater transformation by making possible almost instantaneous communication at great distances. The railroad and the telegraph marched across the continent in unison. . . . The telegraph companies used the railroad for their rights-of-way, and the railroad used the services of the telegraph to coordinate the flow of trains and traffic" (1977, p. 195).

This coevolution of the railroad and telegraph systems fostered the development of another communication infrastructure for control of mass distribution and consumption: the postal system. Aided by the introduction in 1847 of the first federal postage stamp, itself an important innovation in control of the national system of distribution, the total distance mail moved more than doubled in the dozen years between Morse's first telegraph and 1857, when it reached 75 million miles—almost a third covered by rail (Chandler 1977, p. 195). Commercialization of the telephone in the 1880s, and especially the development of long-distance lines in the 1890s, added a third component to the national infrastructure of telecommunications.

Controlled by means of this infrastructure, an organizational system rapidly emerged for the distribution of mass production to national and world markets. Important innovations in the rationalization and control of this system included the commodity dealer and standardized grading of commodities (1850s), the department store, chain store, and wholesale jobber (1860s), monitoring of movements of inventory or "stock turn" (by 1870), the mail-order house (1870s), machine packaging (1890s), franchising (by 1911 the standard means of distributing automobiles), and the supermarket and mail-order chain (1920s).

Mass production and distribution cannot be completely controlled, however, without control of a third area of the economy: demand and consumption. Such control requires a means to communicate information *advertising*

~~about~~ goods and services to national audiences in order to stimulate or reinforce demand for these products; at the same time, it requires a means to gather information on the preferences and behavior of this audience —reciprocal feedback to the controller from the controlled (although the consumer might justifiably see these relationships as reversed).

The mechanism for communicating information to a national audience of consumers developed with the first truly mass medium: power-driven, multiple-rotary printing and mass mailing by rail. At the outset of the Industrial Revolution, most printing was still done on wooden hand presses—using flat plates tightened by means of screws—that differed little from the one Gutenberg had used three centuries earlier. Steam power was first successfully applied to printing in Germany in 1810; by 1827 it was possible to print up to 2,500 pages in an hour. In 1893 the *New York World* printed 96,000 eight-page copies every hour—a 300-fold increase in speed in just seventy years.

The postal system, in addition to effecting and controlling distribution, also served, through bulk mailings of mass-produced publications, as a new medium of mass communication. By 1887 Montgomery Ward mailed throughout the continent a 540-page catalog listing more than 24,000 items. Circulation of the Sears and Roebuck catalog increased from 318,000 in 1897 (the first year for which figures are available) to more than 1 million in 1904, 2 million in 1905, 3 million in 1907, and 7 million by the late 1920s. In 1927 alone, Sears mailed 10 million circular letters, 15 million general catalogs (spring and fall editions), 23 million sales catalogs, plus other special catalogs—a total mailing of 75 million (Boorstin 1973, p. 128) or approximately one piece for every adult in the United States.

Throughout the late nineteenth and early twentieth centuries, uncounted entrepreneurs and inventors struggled to extend the technologies of communication to mass audiences. Alexander Graham Bell, who patented the telephone in 1876, originally thought that his invention might be used as a broadcast medium to pipe public speeches, music, and news into private homes. Such systems were indeed begun in several countries—the one in Budapest had six thousand subscribers by the turn of the century and continued to operate through World War I (Briggs 1977). More extensive application of telephony to mass communication was undoubtedly stifled by the rapid development of broadcast media beginning with Guglielmo Marconi's demonstration of long-wave telegraphy in

1895. Transatlantic wireless communication followed in 1901, public radio broadcasting in 1906, and commercial radio by 1920; even television broadcasting, a medium not popular until after World War II, had begun by 1923.

Many other communication technologies that we do not today associate with advertising were tried out early in the Control Revolution as means to influence the consumption of mass audiences. Popular books like the novels of Charles Dickens contained special advertising sections. Mass telephone systems in Britain and Hungary carried advertisements interspersed among music and news. The phonograph, patented by Thomas Edison in 1877 and greatly improved by the 1890s in Hans Berliner's "gramophone," became another means by which a sponsor's message could be distributed to households: "Nobody would refuse," the United States Gramaphone Company claimed, "to listen to a fine song or concert piece or an oration—even if it is interrupted by a modest remark, 'Tartar's Baking Powder is Best'" (Abbot and Rider, 1957, p. 387). With the development by Edison of the "motion picture" after 1891, advertising had a new medium, first in the kinetoscope (1893) and cinematograph (1895), which sponsors located in busy public places, and then in the 1900s in films projected in "movie houses." Although advertisers were initially wary of broadcasting because audiences could not be easily identified, by 1930 sponsors were spending $60 million annually on radio in the United States alone (Boorstin 1973, p. 392).

These mass media were not sufficient to effect true control, however, without a means of feedback from potential consumers to advertisers, thereby restoring to the emerging national and world markets what Durkheim had seen as an essential relationship of the earlier segmental markets: communication from consumer to producer to assure that the latter "can easily reckon the extent of the needs to be satisfied" (1893, p. 369). Simultaneously with the development of mass communication by the turn of the century came what might be called *mass feedback* technologies: market research (the idea first appeared as "commercial research" in 1911), including questionnaire surveys of magazine readership, the Audit Bureau of Circulation (1914), house-to-house interviewing (1916), attitudinal and opinion surveys (a U.S. bibliography lists nearly three thousand by 1928), a Census of Distribution (1929), large-scale statistical sampling theory (1930), indices of retail sales (1933), A. C. Nielsen's audimeter monitoring of broadcast audiences (1935), and statistical-sample surveys like the Gallup Poll (1936), to mention just a few of the many new technologies for monitoring consumer behavior.

Although most of the new information technologies originated in the private sector, where they were used to control production, distribution, and consumption of goods and services, their potential for controlling systems at the national and world level was not overlooked by government. Since at least the Roman Empire, where an extensive road system proved equally suited for moving either commerce or troops, communications infrastructures have served to control both economy and polity. As corporate bureaucracy came to control increasingly wider markets by the turn of this century, its power was increasingly checked by a parallel growth in state bureaucracy.

In the modern state the latest technologies of mass communication, persuasion, and market research are also used to stimulate and control demand for governmental services. The U.S. government, for example, currently spends about $150 million a year on advertising, which places it among the top thirty advertisers in the country; were the approximately 70 percent of its ads that are presented free as a public service also included, it would rank second—just behind Proctor and Gamble (Porat 1977, p. 137). Increasing business and governmental use of control technologies and their recent proliferation in forms like data services and home computers for use by consumers have become dominant features of the Control Revolution.

THE INFORMATION SOCIETY

One major result of the Control Revolution had been the emergence of the so called Information Society. The concept dates from the late 1950s and the pioneering work of an economist, Fritz Machlup, who first measured that sector of the U.S. economy associated with what he called "the production and distribution of knowledge" (Machlup, 1962). Under this classification Machlup grouped thirty industries into control in the 1870s and especially the 1880s; the information sector has grown steadily but only modestly over the past two centuries.

Temporal correlation alone, of course, does not prove causation. With the exception of the two discontinuities, however, growth in the information sector has tended to be most rapid in periods of economic upturn, most notably in the postwar booms of the 1920s and 1950s, as can be seen in Table 1-1. Significantly, the two periods of discontinuity were punctuated by economic depressions, the first by the Panic of 1837, the second by financial crisis in Europe and the Panic of 1873. In other words, the technological origins of both the control crisis and the consolidation of control occurred in periods when the information sector would not have been expected on other economic grounds to have expanded rapidly if at all. There is therefore no reason to reject the hypothesis that the Information Society developed as a result of the crisis of control created by railroads and other steam-powered transportation in the 1840s.

A wholly new stage in the development of the Information Society has arisen, since the early 1970s, from the continuing proliferation of microprocessing technology. Most important in social implications has been the progressive convergence of all information technologies—mass media, telecommunications, and computing—in a single infrastructure of control at the most macro level. A 1978 report commissioned by the President of France—an instant best-seller in that country and abroad—likened the growing interconnection of information processing, communication, and control technologies throughout the world to an alteration in "the entire nervous system of social organization" (Nora and Minc 1978, p. 3). The same report introduced the neologism *telematics* for this most recent stage of the Information Society, although similar words had been suggested earlier—for example, *compunications* (for "computing + communications") by Anthony Oettinger and his colleagues at Harvard's Program on Information Resources Policy (Oettinger 1971; Berman and Oettinger 1975; Oettinger, Berman, and Read 1977).

Crucial to telematics, compunications, or whatever word comes to be used for this convergence of information-processing and communications technologies is increasing digitalization: coding into discontinuous values—usually two-valued or binary—of what even a few years ago would have been an analog signal varying continuously in time, whether a telephone conversation, a radio broadcast, or a television picture. Because most modern computers process digital information, the progressive digitalization of mass media and telecommunications content begins to blur earlier distinctions between the communication of information and its processing (as implied by the term

Table 1-1. U.S. Experienced Civilian Labor Force by Four Sectors, 1800–1980

Year	SECTORS (PERCENT OF TOTAL)				Total Labor Force (in millions)
	Agricultural	Industrial	Service	Information	
1800	87.2	1.4	11.3	0.2	1.5
1810	81.0	6.5	12.2	0.3	2.2
1820	73.0	16.0	10.7	0.4	3.0
1830	69.7	17.6	12.2	0.4	3.7
1840	58.8	24.4	12.7	4.1	5.2
1850	49.5	33.8	12.5	4.2	7.4
1860	4.06	37.0	16.6	5.8	8.3
1870	47.0	32.0	16.2	4.8	12.5
1880	43.7	25.2	24.6	6.5	17.4
1890	37.2	28.1	22.3	12.4	22.8
1900	35.3	26.8	25.1	12.8	29.2
1910	31.1	36.3	17.7	14.9	39.8
1920	32.5	32.0	17.8	17.7	45.3
1930	20.4	35.3	19.8	24.5	61.1
1940	15.4	37.2	22.5	24.9	53.6
1950	11.9	38.3	19.0	30.8	57.8
1960	6.0	34.8	17.2	42.0	67.8
1970	3.1	28.6	21.9	46.4	80.1
1980	2.1	22.5	28.8	46.6	95.8

SOURCE: Data for 1800–1850 are estimated from Lebergott (1964) with missing data interpolated from Fabricant (1949); data for 1860–1970 are taken directly from Porat (1977); data for 1980 are based on U.S. Bureau of Labor Statistics projections (Bell, 1979, p. 185).

compunications), as well as between people and machines. Digitalization makes communication from persons to machines, between machines, and even from machines to persons as easy as it is between persons. Also blurred are the distinctions among information types: numbers, words, pictures, and sounds, and eventually tastes, odors, and possibly even sensations, all might one day be stored, processed, and communicated in the same digital form.

In this way digitalization promises to transform currently diverse forms of information into a generalized medium for processing and by the social system, much as, centuries ago, the institution of common currencies and exchange rates began to transform local markets into a single world economy. Indeed, digitalized electronic systems have already begun to replace money itself in many informational functions, only the

most recent stage in a growing systemness of world society dating back at least to the Commercial Revolution of the fifteenth century.

REFERENCES

Abbot, Waldo, and Richard L. Rider (1957). *Handbook of Broadcasting: The Fundamentals of Radio and Television,* 4th ed. New York: McGraw-Hill.

Bell, Daniel (1979). The Social Framework of the Information Society. In Michael L. Dertouzos and Joel Moses (Eds.), *The Computer Age: A Twenty-Year View* (pp. 163–211). Cambridge, MA: MIT Press.

Berman, Paul. J., and Anthony G. Oettinger (1975). *The Medium and the Telephone: The Politics of Information Resources,* Working Paper 75-8 (December 15). Cambridge,

MA: Harvard University Program on Information Technologies and Public Policy.

Boorstin, Daniel J. (1973). *The Americans: The Democratic Experience*. New York: Random House.

Briggs, Asa (1977). The Pleasure Telephone: A Chapter in the Prehistory of the Media. In Ithiel de Sola Pool (Ed.), *The Social Impact of the Telephone* (pp. 40–65). Cambridge, MA: MIT Press.

Burchfield, R. W. (Ed.) (1972). *A Supplement to the Oxford English Dictionary, vol. 1*. Oxford: Oxford University Press.

Carlyle, Thomas (1850/1898). *Latter-Day Pamphlets*. New York: Charles Scribner's Sons.

Chandler, Alfred D., Jr. (1977). *The Visible Hand: The Managerial Revolution in American Business*. Cambridge, MA: Belknap Press.

Durkheim, Emile (1893/1933). *The Division of Labor in Society*, trans. George Simpson. New York: The Free Press.

Fabricant, Solomon (1949). The Changing Industrial Distribution of Gainful Workers: Some Comments on the American Decennial Statistics for 1820-1940. *Studies in Income and Wealth,* vol. 11. New York: National Bureau of Economic Research.

Lebergott, Stanley (1964). *Manpower in Economic Growth: The American Record since 1800*. New York: McGraw-Hill.

Machlup, Fritz (1962). *The Production and Distribution of Knowledge in the United States*. Princeton, NJ: Princeton University Press.

Mill, John Stuart (1848). *Principles of Political Economy, with Some of Their Applications to Social Philosophy, 2 vols*. Boston: Little, Brown.

Nora, Simon, and Alain Minc (1978/1980). *The Computerization of Society: A Report to the President of France*. Cambridge, MA: MIT Press.

Oettinger, Anthony G. (1971). Compunications in the National Decision-Making Process. In Martin Greenberger (Ed.), *Computers, Communications, and the Public Interest* (pp. 73–114). Baltimore: Johns Hopkins University Press.

Oettinger, Anthony G., Paul J. Berman, and William H. Read (1977). *High and Low Politics: Information Resources for the 80's*. Cambridge, MA: Ballinger.

Porat, Marc Uri (1977). *The Information Economy: Definition and Measurement*. Washington, DC: Office of Telecommunications, U.S. Department of Commerce.

Pred, Allan R. (1973). *Urban Growth and the Circulation of Information: The United States System of Cities, 1790–1840*. Cambridge, MA: Harvard University Press.

Redlich, Fritz (1951). *The Molding of American Banking, Men and Ideas*. New York: Johnson Reprint Corporation.

Shannon, Claude E., and Warren Weaver (1949). *The Mathematical Theory of Communication*. Urbana: University of Illinois Press.

Taylor, Keith (Ed.) (1975). *Henri Saint-Simon (1760–1825): Selected Writings on Science, Industry, and Social Organization*. New York: Holmes and Meier.

Thompson, Robert Luther (1947). *Wiring a Continent: The History of the Telegraph Industry in the United States, 1832–1866*. Princeton, NJ: Princeton University Press.

Toffler, Alvin (1971). *Future Shock*. New York: Bantam Books.

U.S. Bureau of the Census (1975). *Historical Statistics of the United States, Colonial Times to 1970*, 2 vols. Washington, DC: U.S. Government Printing Office.

Weber, Max (1922/1968). *Economy and Society: An Outline of Interpretive Sociology, 3 vols.*, Eds. Guenther Roth and Claus Wittich. New York: Bedminster Press.

Wiener, Norbert (1948). *Cybernetics: or Control and Communication in the Animal and the Machine*. Cambridge, MA: MIT Press.

Winner, Langdon (1977). *Autonomous Technology: Technics-Out-of-Control as a Theme in Political Thought*. Cambridge, MA: MIT Press.

 ## RELATED LINKS

- Internet Modern History Sourcebook: Industrial Revolution (http://www.fordham.edu/halsall/mod/modsbook14.html)

- Smithsonian National Museum of American History (http://americanhistory.si.edu)

- BBC: Industrialisation (http://www.bbc.co.uk/history/society_culture/industrialisation/index.shtml)

- James R. Beniger (http://www-rcf.usc.edu/~beniger)

FOR FURTHER RESEARCH

To find out more about the topics discussed in this reading, use InfoTrac College Edition. Type in keywords and subject terms such as "information society," "control revolution," and "pre-processing." You can access InfoTrac College Edition from the Wadsworth/Thomson Communication Café homepage: http://communication.wadsworth.com.

Reading 1-3

Renaissance Now! Media Ecology and the New Global Narrative

Douglas Rushkoff   *Utopian/elitist?*

EDITOR'S NOTE

Since the early 1970s, scholars have pointed to the consequences of an unfolding information and communications revolution, in which the economy becomes information-based and media occupy an increasingly central role across important domains of social influence, such as politics, economics, and mass culture. In this reading, writer Douglas Rushkoff (known for his books Media Virus *and* Coercion) *puts forth a slightly different interpretation: new technologies are not creating a revolution so much as creating the conditions for a renaissance, or rebirth, of culture and ideas. As society continues to assimilate the results of the shift caused by recent technological progress, the networked lifestyle will assume increasing importance, and fixed narratives, whether religiously grand or culturally mundane, will become more open to revision and redirection. In the process, Rushkoff argues, networked citizens will become active cocreators of both cultural and political programs, determining their own destiny to a greater extent than ever before.*

CONSIDER

1. In Rushkoff's view, how do networked technologies allow users to write their own narratives, as opposed to simply accepting a story or process as unchangeable?

2. Has the original Internet community of grassroots activists and curious cybertravelers completely vanished, in Rushkoff's opinion, or has it morphed in something else?

3. What is the basis for Rushkoff's claim that "the average American home now has more information and broadcast resources than a major television network newsroom did in the 1970s"? Do you agree—why or why not?

HACKING BORDERS: REVOLUTION OR RENAISSANCE?

So often we hear people using the word *revolution* to describe the current overwhelming cultural shift fostered

From "Renaissance Now! Media Ecology and the New Global Narrative," by Douglas Rushkoff, in *EME: Explorations in Media Ecology, 1*(1) (2002), pp. 41–57. Copyright © 2002 by Hampton Press. Reprinted with permission.

by technology and new media. However overwhelming it might be, can we really describe the current transition as a revolution? For me, the word *revolution* evokes images of a violent upheaval and guillotined heads. There's certainly very little progress implied by *revolution;* it is simply someone spinning around in circles. Digital culture may be marginally revolutionary in the sense that it is characterized by what so many companies and institutions have called "thinking outside the box"—a willingness to challenge conventions and consider meta-narratives. But this notion of thinking outside the box and gaining perspective is not simply moving in a circle. We are coming to a new understanding of what had always been considered literal reality; we are seeing it instead as a picture of reality. Our new tools are also leading us to feel empowered enough to adjust the frame around that picture. Such an upscaling of perception, intention, and design is better described as *renaissance*.

Renaissance literally means "rebirth." Old ideas emerge in a new context. A renaissance is a reconfiguring of the constructed ways we experience the world in order to reconnect with it, the adaptation of our cultural lenses to conform to our changing vision. In the last Renaissance, a number of discoveries and inventions changed our most basic experience of the real. Perspective painting allowed us to create representations of reality that simulated dimensionality. The discovery that the world was round and the ability to circumnavigate it radically redefined our notion of space and our sense of agency. The development of calculus allowed us to relate planes to spheres and spheres to four-dimensional fictional objects, performing conceptual calculations never before possible. The printing press allowed the widespread distribution of ideas and data, connecting people in expanded social and political communities. By the Enlightenment, coffee imported from Morocco encouraged people to stay up late at night and talk, giving rise to a "bohemian" culture dedicated to challenging conventional models of reality through the new perspectives they had gained.

The late 20th century brought discoveries and inventions whose collective impact could be considered a renaissance of at least equal magnitude. While perspective painting allowed Renaissance artists to create two-dimensional images, the holograph now allows us to create three-dimensional representations that approximate our vision even more closely. By manipulating the laws of perspective, some Renaissance painters created deliberately skewed or "trick" representations of reality, challenging the reliability of our vision and suggesting the possibility that illusion exists in reality. The mechanics of the holograph offer a similar challenge because when a holographic plate is shattered into many pieces, the image is not fragmented. Each shard of the plate will contain a smaller image of the entire original, suggesting that fractal relationships may underlie much of our illusions as well as our reality. The underlying technology of holographs further extends our understanding of dimensionality and has been used to understand everything from society to brain anatomy.

Although Renaissance explorers discovered that the world was round, modern scientists discovered atomic energy and took us to the moon. Having already mastered the globe through exploration, we were now able to explore beyond it, to see it as an object from another position in space, and even to destroy it. Meanwhile, chaos math and systems theory opened complex conceptual possibilities in much the same way calculus had for Renaissance mathematicians.

The computer and the Internet have changed communication, publication, and the idea of community to a degree comparable to the printing press. LSD and psychedelics, like the coffee beans of the Renaissance, had people staying up late together and experimenting with the status quo.

A renaissance is a shift in perspective, the shift from living within a model to moving outside of it. Or, as video gamers might express it, from *game* to *meta-game*. Young people who spend a lot of time immersed in video game environments understand this phenomenon well. There are two ways one can learn to play a game. The first is to read the rules, practice, and use old-fashioned trial and error. The second is to find the magazines and Web sites that will share secret codes to avoid traps, win levels, and gain special advantages in the game. Are the people using these "cheat sheets" really playing the game? Certainly, but the game they are playing is the meta-game.

Likewise, there are moments when we, as society, as a culture, or even as individuals, shift from simply playing the game by the rules to playing the meta-game and changing the rules. These are renaissance moments. Renaissance moments happen when we experience a shift in perspective so that the stories, models, and languages that we have been using to understand our reality are suddenly up for grabs. But these renaissance moments are transitory, because almost as soon as our perspectives are shifted, we settle into new conventions. Alas, the possibilities opened by our new perspective close up, and we once again mistake the map for the territory. We forget that the new stories and metaphors we have developed are just representations, and we mistake them for literal history.

But before things have been locked down, ideas compete for consensus. The challenge, and the opportunity, during these moments is to make a positive impact in that struggle. For me, this means preserving the notion that the ideas that win consensus approval may be useful, but they are still arbitrary. This is the true *border hack:* to move outside the frame of the picture and show others how this is possible. I would argue that we are currently in a period of renaissance, still in the process of assimilating the results of a shift in perspective caused by remarkable technological progress. We are still aware that the shift is going on and hoping to preserve some aspect of our newfound sensitivity into the next phase of human society. It is akin to the realization we have in the heightened state of awareness caused by a mystical or psychedelic experience: At the height of a visionquest we wonder how we will be able to remember that state of awe or insight once the experience is over. We wonder how to plant a seed or landmark of some kind that will be remembered after the return to waking-state consciousness.

Likewise, those of us aware of the power of the current renaissance are attempting to preserve and extend the notion that much of reality itself is "open source"—that the "codes" by which we organize our experiences are more accessible than we generally assume. For artists, cultural producers, and, of course, activists, there is an imperative to influence what will become the new consensus and to mark it with sense of possibility that will help us maintain a sense of agency over our own collective and individual perspectives.

A lucky beneficiary of the digital renaissance, I have been encouraged to believe that our reality is, indeed, open source—or at least that much of what we have been regarding as permanent *hardware* is, indeed, only *software* and subject to change. For me, the most important insight of cyberculture is that we all have access to its codes; we are all potential reality programmers.

Media constitute the realm in which our reality is negotiated. I used to stay up nights wondering: What are media? It was a perplexing question. A zipper is a medium; open, it means one thing and closed, another. A face is a medium; we read people's appearance and expressions for information about them. Even our DNA is a medium—arguably, the best medium nature has developed, capable of sending codes through the millennia. Ultimately, only a person's most essential consciousness—one's agency, will, and intention—isn't a medium. As consciousnesses swimming in media, we create and control narratives to negotiate reality and our places within it. Through competing stories we negotiate what is going on. But by making up rules and creating tools for storytelling, we negotiate how those stories will be told: the meta-story.

Renaissances are, in part, the moments when we pull out of a particular story long enough to consider the way in which it is being told. The game and the meta-game, the stories and the meta-stories, have been regulated and controlled for centuries. As Aristotle

well understood, stories work by creating a character whom the audience likes and having that character make a series of decisions that lead to terrible danger. This brings the audience into a heightened state of tension about this poor character who has made all these wrong decisions. Then, once the audience can't take it anymore, the storyteller invents a solution. In a Greek play that solution might have been Athena coming down to save the day.

This same storytelling technique has perhaps been perfected by the advertising industry, which has exploited the mainstream mediaspace for its ability to tell very influential little stories called commercials. In 28 seconds, we identify with, say, an aggravated executive, follow him into his hellish day, up the inclined plane of tension. Because we are a captive audience, with no access to the tools of storytelling, we must take that pain-relieving pill with him at the end of the commercial to relieve our anxiety. The storyteller chooses what pill the listener has to swallow at the end of the story—whether it is a new president or an old religion.

LET THERE BE NETWORKS

I saw a bumper sticker on a minivan in Wisconsin recently that read, "In case of rapture, this car will be empty!" I suppose that little quip means my car will still be occupied. But I am less troubled by the inevitability of my damnation, according to their schema, than the delight with which those Milwaukee passengers were anticipating Armageddon. They are looking forward to the apocalypse!

This is what happens when people take the stories their religions offer a bit too literally. Sure enough, the narratives of the Bible—like those of many other religions—tell a version of the history of the human race, from God's creation of the universe through the life and death of a messiah right on to the end of everything and the tallying of the score. If you subscribe to the right story and follow the rules, all you have to do is wait for the ending and you'll be saved. Best of all, the real quandaries of human existence—questions such as "Where do we come from?" and "Where do we go when we die?"—are now a matter of preordained fate. A closed book.

But these kinds of stories were developed back before the days of interactive media. When you're part of a captive, passive audience without keyboards or even joysticks, the only way out of a story is to wait. You have to accept the storyteller's solution because it's the only one. Either that, or reject the story altogether and risk damnation.

This was the sad fate of poor infidels like me, until pretty recently. Thanks to the Internet, we now have a way out of the story: We can write our own endings.

After all, this interactive medium is, at its core, an invitation to talk back—television with a keyboard. The online world is one in which we are entitled to voice our own opinions, however much they might contradict the status quo. We are challenged to reflect on the stories we're being told, even create our own versions—our own, personal, sacred truths.

What a terrific weapon the Internet gives us against extreme fundamentalism!

And it comes just in time now that we're facing the darkest terror of true believers who blindly follow the unilateral decrees of their leaders. For fundamentalists are simply people who insist that their religion's narrative become everyone else's literal truth.

Interactive media tend to loosen up those fixed narratives by allowing users to contribute their own ideas to the story. Try giving a sermon in an AOL chat room, or a list of commandments on the Yahoo Internet Life bulletin boards. The people you're preaching to won't remain silent, at all. The clergy I know who have taken their messages online have had to reassess their roles as ministers of faith and accept new ones as partners in spiritual learning. When religion is practiced on the Internet, participants quickly realize that we're all in this together.

The Internet undermines the blind obedience of fundamentalism by offering alternative points of view, promoting pluralism, and encouraging feedback. Not that this interactivity is all that new. While the fundamentalist priests of ancient Israel sacrificed animals on the altar, those interested in hypertext were sitting around a table arguing together as they wrote the Talmud. While fundamentalist Islamists were declaring their first Holy Wars, liberals in old Baghdad were sharing wine and finding common ground with similarly inclined Christians and Jews.

Today, the Internet deconstructs the narratives that religions use to explain the world, while inviting people from every race and culture to participate in the conversation. No wonder fundamentalists are getting upset.

In this light, it's easy to see the entire personal computing revolution as a new sort of spiritual movement. Is it coincidental that these technologies were developed in California's Bay Area, the breeding ground for alternative spiritual practices? Even the first easily networkable personal computer—the Apple—was conceived by Steve Jobs on the bongwater-stained carpets of a Reed College dorm room. And Jobs, a Buddhist at the time, didn't call it an Apple for nothing. The personal computer was the forbidden fruit—a way of access to the Tree of Knowledge, and an affront to those who would sequester any information from the formerly little people. The meek would indeed inherit the earth.

The realms of computing and, even more so, networking were unfamiliar turf. They were hard to navigate and harder still to design. People were creating a universe now, and it was as challenging as a lucid dream: Anything we could imagine, we would behold. It's no wonder that many Silicon Valley firms were forced to rely on the skills of many wild young members of the counterculture, people whose own mystical excursions had brought them into intimate contact with realities as mutable and hallucinatory as any graphical user interface.

Those of us lucky enough to get online in the early years were immediately struck by how plastic, fluid, and malleable the world can be. Online communities have no real form—they are the ever-changing consensus reality of their members. One's value in an interactive conversation is not his or her ability to obey, but the capacity to hear and then express. The interactive universe does not exist without the active participation of its people—and this participation is the ongoing act of creation itself. Talk about playing God.

THE END OF THE OLD STORY

Interactivity changed our relationship to other media, too. It was hard to watch television in quite the same way, especially with a remote control in your hand. Whether we simply channel-surfed away from the surfers on *Baywatch,* or went online and posted alternatives to a CNN story, our interactive tools gave us the ability to deconstruct the stories we were being told, and to begin to construct our own.

This is actually something very rare, especially in the spiritual realm.

There are a few faiths in which congregants are invited to participate in the creation and interpretation of the underlying narrative. Certain Jewish sects spurn answers in favor of more questions and interpretation; Quakers enjoy a dogma-free, town-meeting style Sabbath. Most religious traditions, however, simply treat their believers as a "mass," who must depend on their priests or ministers for access to the "story." But just as the Internet has led patients to information about alternative medical treatments (often against doctor's orders), it has given congregants the ability to find alternative stories about who we are, who made us, and why.

More important than any one story we may have discovered or written, the experience of sifting through them all, taking them apart, and writing our own has changed our relationship to religion, perhaps forever. The Internet is anathema to narrative. If you want to understand life as a story etched in stone, you had better stay away.

Cyber culture, based on an ethic of interactivity, releases the captive audience from the spell of the story and offers them the opportunity for active participation, instead.

The television remote control represented the first in a series of liberating interactive technologies. Imagine a man sitting in his LaZBoy chair in 1958, with popcorn on his lap, watching a painful commercial. The TV programmer is dead-set on throwing this poor man into a terrible state of anxiety. If the viewer wants to get out of that imposed state of tension, he's got to move the popcorn off his lap, lift himself out of his chair, walk up to the TV, and turn the channel—which is, perhaps, 50 calories of human labor. If he sits through to the end of the commercial, however, he may use up only 10 calories of anxiety. The brain is lazy; it makes the lazy decision. It will take the 10 calories and submit to the programming. After all, the material on TV is called programming for a reason; it's designed to program us as we sit passively in our seat. But the remote control changes the equation. Imagine a 14-year-old today, watching a commercial, and feeling the first signs that he's being put into an imposed state of tension. With the .0001 calorie that it takes to press a button, he's out of tension and out of the arc of that story. Kids with a remote control watch TV in a new way, following 10 stations at once, surfing back and forth through different stories. When they experience TV like this they're not watching television at all, but watching the television, deconstructing it as television.

The second liberating interactive device was the videogame joystick. For most of you, your inaugurating videogame experience was Pong. And, perhaps amazingly, you probably still remember that first mo-

ment you played. Pong was a simple game based on ping-pong, with two white squares on either side of the screen that would move up and down along with your movements on a control knob. People remember their first time playing Pong the way they remember where they were when President Kennedy was shot. This isn't because Americans loved table tennis so much and were happy to have the convenience of practicing it on TV. It wasn't about the literal meaning of the metaphor, it was about experiencing something on the television as metaphor. It was a thrill just to move the little white square up and down on the screen, to control the pixel. We had never had control of the pixel before. The TV screen was the holy and inaccessible realm of newscasters and movie stars, a magical place where things simply appeared. But just as the remote control deconstructed television's stories, so the joystick demystified its technology—making it an accessible medium and rendering it safe.

Finally, the computer mouse and the keyboard liberated the receive-only monitor, and turned it into a portal through which we could express ourselves. The mouse and keyboard spawned a do-it-yourself (DIY) Internet culture in which people created, uploaded, and shared their own content. In a sense, people were the content; we used technology to connect with other people.

The resulting cyberpunk culture was a renaissance culture. It was a chaotic space, where new ideas could spring up from almost anywhere. It was a gift economy, where new programs were created and shared—for free. It was a community, where new members were introduced and escorted around as if they had just bought a home in a fantasy suburb. Best of all, Internet users came to understand that the mainstream media-space no longer represented their reality. From now on, Internet users would represent their own.

In those days—the 2400-baud, ASCII-text era of ten long years ago—the Internet had nothing to do with the NASDAQ index. In fact, until 1992 you had to sign an agreement promising not to conduct any business online just to get access to the Internet! Imagine that. It was a business-free zone.

How could such rules have ever been put in place? Because the Internet began as a public project. It was created to allow scientists at universities and government facilities to share research and computing resources. Everyone from the Pentagon to Al Gore saw the value of universally accessible information-sharing network, and invested all sorts of federal funds in building a backbone capable of connecting computers around the world.

What they didn't realize was that they were doing a whole lot more than connecting computers to one another. They were connecting people to one another, too. Before long, all those scientists who were supposed to be exchanging research or comparing data were also exchanging stories about their families and comparing notes on the latest *Star Trek* movies. People from around the world were playing games, socializing, and crossing cultural boundaries that had never been crossed before. Because no one was using it to discuss military technology anymore, the government abandoned the network and turned it over to the public.

The Internet's unexpected social side-effect turned out to be its incontrovertible main feature. Its other functions fall by the wayside. The Internet's ability to network human beings is its very life's blood. It fosters communication, collaboration, sharing, helpfulness, and community. Then word got out.

The nerdiest among us found out first. Then came those of us whose friends were nerds. Then their friends, and so on. Someone would simply insist he had found something you needed to know about—the way a childhood friend lets you in on a secret door leading down to the basement under the junior high school.

How many of you can remember that first time you watched him log on? How he turned the keyboard over to you and asked what you want to know, where you want to visit, or whom you want to meet? That was the magic moment when you "got it." Internet fever. There was a whole new world out there, unlimited by the constraints of time and space, appearance and prejudice, gender and power.

It's no wonder so many people compared the 1990s Internet to the psychedelic 1960s. It seemed that all we needed to do was get a person online and he or she would be changed forever. And people were. A sixty-year-old midwestern businessman I know found himself logging on every night to engage in a conversation about Jungian archetypes. It lasted for four weeks before he even realized the person with whom he was conversing was a sixteen-year-old boy from Tokyo.

It felt as though we were wiring up a global brain. Visionaries of the period, like Ted Nelson, invented words like *hypertext* and told us how the Internet could be used as a library for everything ever written. A musician named Jaron Lanier invented a bizarre interactive space he called "virtual reality," in which people would

be able to, in his words, "really see what the other means." Starry-eyed authors like me wrote optimistic books announcing the new global renaissance.

The Internet was no longer a government research project. It was alive. Out of control and delightfully chaotic. What's more, it promoted an agenda all its own.

Using a computer mouse and keyboard to access other human beings on the other side of the monitor changed our relationship to media and the power they held. The tube was no longer a place that only a corporate conglomerate could access. It was Rupert Murdoch, Dan Rather, and Heather Locklear's turf no more. The Internet was *our* space.

The Internet fostered a DIY mentality. We called it *cyberpunk*. Why watch packaged programming on TV when you can make your own online? Who needs corporate content when you can be the content? This was a whole new world we could design ourselves, on our own terms. It felt like a revolution.

That's why it fostered such a deep sense of community. New users were gently escorted around the Internet by more seasoned veterans and shown where and how to participate. An experienced user would delight in setting up a newbie's Internet connection. It was considered an honor to rush out into the night to fix a fellow user's technical problem. To be an Internet user was to be an Internet advocate.

It's also why almost everything to do with the Internet was free. Software was designed by people who wanted to make the Internet a better place. Hackers stayed up late making new programs and then distributed them free of charge to anyone who cared to use them.

All the programs we use today are actually based on this shareware and freeware. Internet Explorer and Netscape are just fat versions of a program called Mosaic, created at the University of Illinois. Streaming media technology is really just a dolled up version of CUSeeMe, a program developed at Cornell. The Internet was built for love, not profit.

And that was the problem—for business, anyway. At the time almost no one was making money on the Internet. Not that this bothered any of the Internet's actual users, but the effects of the remote control, the mouse, and the joystick had to be undone. As more and more people got online, they spent less and less time consuming television programs and commercials. Studies showed that families with Internet connections were watching 3 or 4 hours less TV a week, seeing fewer commercials, and buying fewer TV-advertised products. Furthermore, people who are having fun and feeling connected to other people are less easily coerced into purchases. Something had to be done.

viral or 'buzz' marketing

WHOSE STORY IS IT, ANYWAY?

Thus began the long march to turn the Internet into a profitable enterprise. It started with content. Dozens, then hundreds of online magazines sprang up. But because the Internet had always been free, no one wanted to pay a subscription charge for content. It just wasn't something one did online. So most of the magazines went out of business.

The others, well, they invented the next great Internet catastrophe: the banner ad. Web publishers figured they could sell a little strip on top of each web page to an advertiser, who'd use it as a billboard for commercials. But everyone hated them. They got in the way. It was like scuba diving with someone putting bumper stickers over your mask. And the better we got at ignoring banner ads, the more distractingly busy they grew and the more time-consuming they were to download. They only taught us to resent whichever advertiser was inhibiting our movement.

So advertising gave way to e-commerce. First, the mediaspace deconstructed by the remote control had to be put back together. People doing what comes naturally online, like typing messages to one another, don't generate revenue. The object of the game, for Internet business, was to get people's hands off the keyboard and onto the mouse. Less collaboration, more consumption. Companies developed concepts such as *stickiness, attention economy,* and *eyeball hours* in an effort to keep people glued to Web sites as they were once glued to TV stations. In response to panicked articles from the mainstream media about a channel-surfing culture and decreasing attention spans, attention deficit disorder diagnoses and Ritalin prescriptions rose over 100%. Children's ability to enact renaissance was curtailed through drugs.

In order to regain control of the pixel, which the joystick had liberated, professional designers remystified the computer's interface so that it was no longer two-way. Users were forced to rely on the "wizards" built into their software programs to work magic they didn't understand. Consider the increasing opacity of the interface from DOS to the Macintosh to Windows2000. Look at the colorful and confusing interfaces used on the World Wide Web compared with the text-only bulletin boards of the early Internet. And "information architecture" turned into the science of getting people to click on the "buy" button. The only way to participate on the Web is through the mouse; the only opportunity to use the keyboard is to enter one's credit card information (if it's not already on a cookie, somewhere deep on our hard drive). The increasing and deliberate opacity of new interfaces is designed to keep us out.

Finally, in order to undo the DIY culture that had grown out of the keyboard and the mouse, commerce replaced community and content replaced people as the soul of the Net. It was announced that we were in an "Information Age" rather than a "Communication Age" because information can be bought and sold as a commodity.

Anyone logging onto the Internet for the first time in the year 2000 encountered a very different Internet than the interactive playground of ten years earlier. Browsers and search engines alike were designed to keep users either buying products or consuming commercial content. Most of those helpful hackers were now vested employees of dot.com companies. And most visions of the electronic future had dollar signs before them.

In the interests of the investment community, the Internet was restyled as an online mall. A direct marketing platform. An interactive mail-order catalog! This little scheme seemed to hold more promise. So much promise, in fact, that Wall Street investors took notice. Not that many of these e-commerce businesses actually made money. But they looked like someday they could.

Besides, Wall Street cares less about actual revenues than the ability to create the perception that there might be revenues at some point in the future. That's why it's called speculation. Others might call it a pyramid scheme. Here's how it works: Someone writes a business plan for a new kind of e-commerce company. That person finds "angel investors"—very in-the-know people who give money to write a bigger business plan and hire a CEO. Then comes the "first round" and "second round," where other, slightly less in-the-know people invest a few million more. Then come the institutional investors, who underwrite the now-infamous Initial Price Offering (IPO) on NAS-DAQ. This final ground level is called "going public." At the very bottom of the pyramid, come retail investors. That's you and me. We're supposed to log into an e-trading site and invest our money. So what's all that got to do with the Internet, you ask? Exactly. The Internet was merely the sexy word, the come-hither, the bright idea at the top of the pyramid. Sure, there were and are still plenty of entrepreneurs creating vibrant, successful online businesses—look at Yahoo, Amazon, and eBay. But the Internet wasn't born to support the kind of global economic boom that venture capitalists were envisioning. And by turning the Internet's principal use from socializing toward monetizing, business went against the Internet's very functionality.

No longer able to deconstruct, demystify, or develop our own media, we succumbed to an entirely new story about the promise of new media: money. Of course, by the time the general public was buying shares online, the people at the top of the pyramid disappeared—taking away their money as the pyramid collapsed beneath them in what is called an "exit strategy." That's another way of saying carpet bag.

IT'S ALIVE

The real Internet was hiding underneath this investment charade the whole time. It was a little harder to find, perhaps, and no one in the mainstream press was writing about it anymore, but plenty of people were still sharing stories, e-mailing relatives, finding new communities, and educating themselves. The spirit of the Internet was dormant, maybe, but very much alive.

This is why those schemes were doomed to fail. The behavior control being implemented by more nefarious online merchants, the mercenary tactics of former hackers, and the commercial priorities of the Internet's investors were blatant contradictions of the Internet's true nature. Sure, the Internet could support some business guests the way that a tree can support some mushrooms at its base and a few squirrels in its branches. But businesses attacked the Internet like a set of chainsaws. Or, better, a parasitic fungus. It needed to be rejected.

The dot.com pyramid schemes eventually failed because all pyramid schemes eventually run out of money. The dot.com collapse was also aided, in part, by the Internet's own structure and function. Its organic and interactive make-up shrugs off interventionist government controls. Just a bit more effort halted the corporate attacks that followed. It's no different than when the government abandoned the Internet in the 1980s. Instead of talking about defense contracts, the scientists online began talking about science fiction stories. The Internet never does what it's supposed to do. It has a mind, and life, of its own.

Now that the dot.com pyramid has failed to establish itself as the overarching metaphor of the Digital Age, digital reality—and perhaps our social reality—is once again up for grabs. That's because we're alive, too.

The many great applications that real people and organizations have developed to make all of our lives better are taking center stage. They are compelling and surpass even some of our wildest dreams for what the Internet might someday achieve. The ideas, information, and applications now launching on Web sites around the world capitalize on the transparency, usability, and accessibility that the Internet was born to deliver.

As long as we can maintain our renaissance sensibility and our awareness of the implications of the open source reality in which we live, we have access to enormous opportunities for cultural progress. These opportunities imply profound consequences for any of us who have become conscious of how to hack the borders of reality.

People who have been exposed to the Internet and to other interactive and virtual systems understand that our world—any system—is made up of intentionally designed interfaces. Spending so much time in virtual space, we are more aware of real space, political space, and ideological space, and the way it shapes interaction. We are more sensitive to the power and the way it is exploited. Right now, as a result of our renaissance sensibility, the definitions and conventions of our reality are becoming the component parts of a new language. Nothing is only itself, because its identifying characteristics become a self-conscious manifestation of its underlying essence. An ironic distance. A self-conscious reframing of almost everything.

Renaissance awareness is a form of self-protection, really. A defense. We are trying to focus on the mediated feeling of things. We want to stay awake in renaissance awareness as long as possible before the next reality template concretizes itself and self-conscious similes become tight metaphors. We now see that this is like that, sort of like that—it is as if. But we know that eventually "it is like" and "it is as if" will collapse into "it is." The world is that. Reality's transparency and accessibility lost yet again. At the same time, however, there is great longing to let go, to trust that the world is not trying to do something to us—to engage in an experience without fear and suspicion. Artists and writers have been working on this problem for centuries. Shakespeare often wrote prologues for his plays in which a character lets the audience in on the metaphor: "oh pardon gentles all, that we would presume that the stage would represent . . ." The modesty and honesty give your audience permission to relax. They know they are not going to be manipulated. If we can communicate this sort of goodwill in ritualized contexts, we should be able to do it in the real world of communication, as well.

It is the responsibility of programmers and designers, in particular, to realize that genuine social engagement and genuine discourse are what will keep people out of the traps and trances they are now at pains to avoid. If we can create online and mediated experiences that foster this kind of interaction and discourse —experiences that facilitate people as people, rather than subjugating them to other intentions—we will prolong our sense of freedom as well as our ability to hack even more of world's imaginary borders.

RENAISSANCE NOW

To those of us who really love it, the Internet is looking and feeling more social, more alive, more participatory, and more, well, "Internety" than ever before. Not slumping or waning, slowing up or winding down. This might sound surprising, given the headlines on most newspapers' business pages these days, which have proclaimed the technology bubble officially burst. Likewise, analysts on the financial cable channels and the venture capitalists of Silicon Alley now shun any company whose name ends in .com, and have moved on to more promising new buzzwords like "wireless."

But the metrics fly in the face of conventional wisdom. Internet use is up in terms of real hours spent online and the number of people getting new accounts every day. More surprisingly, although countless dot.coms have gone under for failure to meet their investors' demands, e-commerce is actually up, as well —more than 30% up from 2001. More than 100 million Americans now buy goods and services online.

The Internet is more capable now than it ever was of supporting the vast range of individual, community, and commercial interests that hope to exploit the massive power of networking. Still, countless investors, analysts, and pundits have fallen off the Internet bandwagon.

I say good riddance. The experts jumping ship today can't see the Internet as anything other than an investment opportunity that has dried up. Sure, the Internet made a lot of people money, but its real promise has always been much greater than a few upward stock ticks. If we can look past the size of our 401K plans to the underlying strength of our fledgling networked society, all signs are a-okay. The Internet has never been in better health.

Maybe this kind of optimism requires us to look at the Internet as less of an investment opportunity than a new kind of life form. Take MIT's newly announced web curriculum. The university has promised that, over the next ten years, it will carry the notes, course outlines, and assignments for hundreds of its most popular courses in science, humanities, and the arts. Instituting a policy that would make an Internet investor shudder, MIT plans to release all of this material, to anyone in the world, for free.

Or have a look at www.blogger.com. It's not just a Web site, but a set of publishing tools that allows even a novice user to create a Web log, automatically add content to a Web site, or to organize Web links, commentary, and open discussions. In the short time Blogger has been available, it has already fostered an interconnected community of thousands of users. These are not simply people who surf the Web, but who are now empowered to create it.

Taking their cue from old-school Internet discussion groups like USENET, Web sites such as www.metafilter.com allow anyone to begin a discussion about almost anything found online. Each conversation begins with a link, then grows as far as its participants can take it. This is the real beauty of hypertext, and it's finally catching on. Although hackers have employed bulletin board interfaces on sites like www.slashdot.org since the Web's inception, more commercially minded endeavors like www.plastic.com are now using the very same model to generate open dialogues about culture and media.

Even Yahoo's biggest growth area is conversation. Yahoo Groups, a set of bulletin board discussions and mailing lists, contain thousands of the best discussions happening online—and almost all of them have been started by real people. Based on an old but still widely used style of e-mail conversation called listserv, it allows group members to read postings and add to the conversation without ever opening their browsers. Some of these special interest groups are narrowcast to a degree only possible on a global network where people interested in anything from absinthe drinking to zither tuning can find one another across great distances.

And now that international trade and open markets are no longer the Internet's chief global agenda, much more humanitarian efforts are taking shape. My friend Paul Meyer helped launch Internet Project Kosovo (IPKO) just days after NATO stopped shelling the Serbs in 1999. A single satellite dish allowed Albanian refugees to find lost members of their families and international aid agencies to allocate their resources. Today, Meyer and others are helping people in this and other war-torn and developing regions to network, publicize their plights, and even open businesses.

For those whose refugee status ended long ago, Ellis Island has teamed up with the Mormon Church to create a database containing arrival records for the 22 million immigrants who came through the New York port between 1892 and 1924. Linked databases, accessible to anyone via the Internet. Is this starting to sound familiar?

Or remember how the Internet was supposed to provide all of us with alternative sources of news and information? Although it was almost crushed under the avalanche of content during the dot.com gold rush, www.alternet.org has emerged as a vibrant source of news stories and opinions that won't appear in your evening paper anytime soon. It's the ultimate alternative news weekly, available on the Web or through e-mail, using the Internet to collect and syndicate content from a variety of sources that just couldn't get published any other way. And it's all free.

The original Internet community didn't go into some sort of remission. No, not at all. Although the mainstream news media were busy covering the latest corporate mega-mergers, the Internet's actual participants were continuing to develop and extend their favorite forums for interaction.

Although e-commerce customers were waiting for "return authorization" numbers for misordered merchandise from Pets.com, the participants of AOL's chat rooms were exchanging tips on caring for their chihuahuas. While DoubleClick was reckoning with plummeting click-through rates on their banner ads, the personal ads in Nerve.com's singles' classifieds were exploding. While the value of many E-Trade portfolios were falling into the red, people who never sold anything before in their lives were learning to make huge sums selling the old items in their basements and attics through the auctions on eBay.

Likewise, while newspaper headlines panicked investors about the failure of broadband, the massive communities built on IRC chat channels and other early live networking platforms were finding new, more advanced avenues for social and intellectual exchange. For-profit streaming media companies like Icebox may have failed, but the streaming video technologies they used have survived and flourished as social tools like IVisit and Netmeeting.

While the client lists of business-to-business service companies like Scient and Sapient have diminished, peer-to-peer networks, from Napster to Hotline, still grow in popularity and resist all efforts to quell the massive exchange of data, illegal or not.

In fact, the average American home now has more information and broadcast resources than a major television network newsroom did in the 1970s. A single Apple laptop is a sophisticated video production studio, allowing for the complex editing of home videos and independent films. Add a fast Internet connection, and a home producer can broadcast around the globe. My own Aunt Sophie, armed with a scanner and e-mail account, has inundated the family with photos of all our relatives' new babies.

Independent radio stations run through DSL and cable modems out of studio apartments around the world find loyal audiences through Shoutcast.com and other amateur media networks. And, as the word *amateur* suggests, these are radio stations borne out of the love for a particular genre of music. They allow aficionados from any node on the planet to enjoy their favorite styles—from raga to reggae—round the clock.

The early Internet was often compared to the Wild West—an anarchic realm where a lone hacker could topple any empire—and that spirit of independence is still dominating the culture and ethic of the interactive space. Any group or individual, however disenfranchised, can serve as the trigger point for an extraordinarily widespread phenomenon.

Media viruses like "all your base" and irreverent Flash or Quicktime video parodies of commercials like Budweiser's "Wassup" campaign are launched from the bedrooms of teenagers and distributed by e-mail to millions of office cubicles, eventually finding their way to the evening news.

Thousands of hackers around the world still represent a great threat to major software companies, the DVD industry, and any corporation whose interests rely on closed source computer code or encrypted files. No sooner is a new closed standard released than it is decoded by a lone hacker or, better, a team of hackers working in tandem from remote and untraceable locations. The "crack" is then published on countless mirror sites, making its dissemination inevitable and unsquashable.

Activists of all stripes have seized on the Internet for its ability to cultivate relationships across vast distances and promote new kinds of alliances between formerly unaffiliated groups. The Internet-organized demonstrations against World Trade meetings in Seattle and Quebec are the most notable examples of such networking. Protestors communicated online for months in advance of their well-attended rallies, yet they took the authorities and mainstream media reporters utterly by surprise.

No, despite the many efforts to direct its chaotic, organismic energy toward the monolithic agenda of Wall Street, the Internet can't help but empower the real people whose spirit it embodies.

And I've only mentioned a very few of the thousands of equally vital new buds blooming on the Internet today. They thrive because they promote the life of the Internet itself. They are not parasites but fruit, capable of spreading their own seeds and carrying the Internet's tendrils even further. They are the Internet.

They share the very same qualities that make the Internet so compelling and valuable: transparency, participation, openness, and collaboration. They are the ideals and communities that allowed the Internet to fend off all efforts to harness its power for a single, selfish objective. They are also what will keep the Internet resilient enough to withstand the next attack.

So do not mourn. Rejoice. While you may never be able to sell that great dot.com name or stock you bought last year, you're getting to participate in something that no civilization in the history of the planet has ever had the privilege of experiencing until now: the Internet.

FROM NARRATIVE TO EMERGENCE

Every early culture across the globe composed stories —myths—to explain what was going on here. For centuries, we have understood our world—even our sciences—as being somehow authored: that things were set in motion by someone or something. We cling to the belief that existence proceeded by design.

That's why Darwin's theory of evolution was such a threat to our narrative understanding of the world,

and why creationists resist its implications to this day. But even those of us who believe in evolution like to impose a kind of narrative sentimentality on top of it, where we imagine matter and life to be groping steadily and consciously toward complexity.

Now our computers have forced us to entertain new, even less linear models for why things happen, and for how nature has gotten so very organized. One of these models, described in Steven Johnson's book *Emergence,* explores the way everything from ant colonies to ancient cities find their order. It turns out there are no decrees from the queen ant. Ancient cities still in existence today had no official planners. Conditions can be set up, but life, organisms, communities, and order now appear to arise—emerge, in other words— from the bottom up. There is no author of the story.

And what is the chief prerequisite for emergence to occur? You guessed it: networking. Interconnectivity is what allows an "it" to become a "they." Instead of acting on its own, each atom, molecule, cell, organism, or entire community now begins to act as part of a larger complex—a networked being.

This is challenging stuff for those of us who have understood creation very differently. It's as big an insight as the theory of evolution, and it's bound to create as much of a stir. Where will the next set of Monkey Trials take place? Surely not on the Internet. Because in an interactive mediaspace, the proponents of emergence have a home-field advantage.

THE EMERGING INTERNET

Almost anyone who has been online has seen—and experienced—evidence of emergent behavior. Just watch the way communities form around authors on Amazon.com or the way opinions pile on to discussions at Slashdot.org or the way fan Web sites spring up about the latest sci-fi movie.

And consider what the Internet did to television. The current TV season is littered with so-called "reality" shows. We are so fed up with authored stories that we don't even want to watch them anymore: We'd rather see programs that are authored by their participants: real people (for the most part) in unscripted situations.

This is because we think of ourselves no longer as actors, behaving according to a script, but as co-creators, responsible for the collective development of our world. The experience of democracy, free markets, free speech, and, now, an interactive media space has made us reluctant to live by decree. Fundamentalism—the notion that our world is completely ordained, and that our job is simply to follow the rules written by God—does not jibe with our newfound experience of collective will.

This doesn't mean that God needn't exist—just that we may be more partnered with Her than we at first presumed. In any case, we must accept responsibility for the course of human events from now on, and we'd better use our interactive technologies to get the conversation going about where we want to take this little blue ball on which we're living. Narrative is not the enemy, as long as we can participate in writing it.

If nothing else, the Internet teaches us to see the value of diversity and plurality. All the opinions of all the people matter. Fundamentalism teaches that there is only one path, one story, and one author. Whether they are attacking the free market, women's rights activists, civil libertarians, or homosexuals and whether they are using purchased airwaves or hijacked airplanes, such fundamentalists are fighting a losing a battle. We will be networked.

REFERENCES

Blogger: *Push-Button Publishing for the People*. Pyra Labs. 22 Dec. 2001. Retrieved from http://www.blogger.com.

Johnson, Steven. *Emergence: The Connected Lives of Ants, Brains, Cities, and Software*. New York: Scribner, 2001.

Massachusetts Institute of Technology. "Mellon, Hewlett Foundations Grant $11M to Launch Free MIT Course Materials on Web." 18 June 2001. MIT. 22 Dec. 2001. Retrieved from http://mit.edu/newsoffice/nr/2001/ocwfund.html.

RELATED LINKS

- Douglas Rushkoff (http://www.rushkoff.com)
- Media Ecology Association (http://www.media–ecology.org)
- The Media and Communication Studies Site (http://www.aber.ac.uk/media/Functions/mcs.html)
- Slashdot: News for Nerds (http://slashdot.org)
- Plastic: Recycling the Web in Real Time (http://www.plastic.com)

FOR FURTHER RESEARCH

To find out more about the topics discussed in this reading, use InfoTrac College Edition. Type in keywords and subject terms such as "media ecology," "border hack," and "Internet culture." You can access InfoTrac College Edition from the Wadsworth / Thomson Communication Café homepage: http://communication.wadsworth.com.

2

New Media Theory

Reading 2-1

Principles of Mediamorphosis

Roger Fidler

EDITOR'S NOTE

The emergence of new media rarely precipitates the death of old media; instead, existing media forms evolve and adapt to the changing communication environment in a gradual process that is comparable in some ways to the evolution of species. In this reading, Roger Fidler introduces a unified way of thinking about media transformation and adaptation, a process he calls mediamorphosis. *Instead of studying each new media form separately, mediamorphosis regards all media as constituent elements of an interdependent system. By studying the communication system as a whole, Fidler asserts, it becomes clear that new media do not arise spontaneously and independently—they emerge gradually from the metamorphosis of old media.*

CONSIDER

1. To better understand technological change, why must we first discard most of our commonly held assumptions, particularly about the pace of change?

2. What are the dangers of *technomyopia*? How do inflated short-term hopes distort initial expectations for new media and cause us to treat future growth phases with skepticism?

3. How can the six principles of mediamorphosis be used to predict what will happen in the next stage of media evolution?

Change is not something most people look forward to or are particularly good at predicting. Even for the inventors and innovators who stimulate technological and social changes, visualizing the future presents an enigmatic problem. Yet, despite the anxieties often caused by change, humans seem to have a remarkable propensity for rapidly assimilating new ideas, products, and services once they are perceived to fit into their personal and cultural definitions of reality. While no one, it seems, is ever completely prepared for change or able to accurately predict outcomes, we can all begin to discern probable shapes of the future by learning to recognize the historic patterns and mechanisms of change. This chapter introduces several frameworks for assessing change and evaluating new media technologies.

YESTERDAY'S FUTURE, TODAY'S PAST

Much of what is now taken for granted has, in fact, only recently emerged. Just one human generation ago, at the beginning of the 1970s, electronic pocket calculators were just starting to compete with slide rules and mechanical adding machines; computers were big and impersonal; and AT&T was still a monopoly that leased nearly all private telephones in the United States. Portable communicators and voice interaction with computers only existed in the imaginary twenty-third-century universe of the original Star Trek television series.

Twenty-five years ago, electronic media were confined to broadcast radio and television. Lasers and fiber-optic networks, miniature video cameras and handheld television sets, compact disc players and music CDs, digital fax machines, cellular phones, and laptop computers were all unknown outside of a few research and development laboratories.

Information retrieval was something one only did in libraries with printed books and periodicals, or microfilm, using pencils and paper. The Internet and electronic mail (e-mail) were still confined to the rarefied and generally secret world of defense-related research.

Newspapers and magazines had just begun converting their newsrooms from mechanical typewriters to electronic text-editing systems and their composing rooms from hot-type to cold-type technologies. Few journalists then could have imagined the electronic news gathering and production technologies that are common today or foreseen desktop publishing and the explosion of news graphics made possible by personal computers.

A mere decade ago, few people could have imagined that by the mid-1990s digital fax machines, electronic mail services, and miniature cell phones would be routinely used to communicate just as easily and inexpensively with individuals in distant countries and rural communities as within large cities and office buildings. In the mid-1980s, most publishers abandoned consumer online services (then called videotex) after collectively losing several hundred million dollars and promptly declared that electronic publishing would not emerge as a viable business until well into the next century. Who then would have envisioned the frenzy of activity that now surrounds consumer online services and the World Wide Web?

THE 30-YEAR RULE

While we may never be able to foretell the outcomes of technological change with a high degree of precision, we can sharpen our focus. To do so, we must first enlarge our perspective and discard most of our commonly held assumptions, particularly about the speed of change.

Changes may seem to be occurring more rapidly in the world today, but studies of historical records have shown that this is a common misconception. Paul Saffo, a director at the Institute for the Future in Menlo Park, California, posits that the amount of time re-

From *Mediamorphosis: Understanding New Media* by Roger Fidler (Thousand Oaks, CA: Pine Forge Press, 1997), pp. 1–29. Copyright © 1997 by Roger Fidler. Reprinted by permission of Sage Publications, Inc.

quired [for new ideas to fully seep into a culture] has consistently averaged about three decades for at least the past five centuries. He calls this the 30-year rule.

As a new media forecaster, Saffo has learned from experience that our short human memories all too often confuse surprise with speed. When it comes to emerging technologies, he finds that the slowness of change is the rule rather than the exception. Most ideas take much longer to become "overnight successes" than anyone is ever prepared to admit.

The reason life feels so much more rapid today, Saffo contends, is not that individual technologies are accelerating at a faster rate or that things are happening more quickly than they have in the past. What's actually occurring is that "more technologies are coming up at the same time. It is the unexpected cross-impact of maturing technologies that creates this powerful acceleration that we all feel."[1] Cross-impacts are also the variables, he says, that make new media forecasting so difficult.

STAGES OF DEVELOPMENT

There is, however, a relatively consistent pattern of accelerated development that takes place as each new technology moves from laboratory to marketplace. Saffo has identified three typical stages within the 30-year rule. "First decade: lots of excitement, lots of puzzlement, not a lot of penetration. Second decade: lots of flux, penetration of the product into society is beginning. Third decade: 'Oh, so what?' Just a standard technology and everybody has it."[2]

Which Development Stage Are We In?

As we attempt to peer into the future of communications, it would seem, therefore, that the critical question to be asked with regard to emerging media technologies is, Which development stage are they in? But, as we will discover, the answer to such an apparently simple question is not always obvious. To know the stage, we must also have some idea of when the clock started, and how innovations are likely to be affected by other technological and social developments, which are not easily determined in the midst of change.

Example: Xerox's Alto

When the first personal computer designed specifically for nontechnical users was switched on at the Xerox Palo Alto Research Center (PARC) in the early 1970s, most of the underlying ideas and technologies had been under development for one to three decades. The scientists who created the Alto, as this early computer was called, believed they were already in the second stage and that their invention could quickly penetrate the office market, but the company's senior executives and market researchers were unconvinced.[3]

While Xerox's decision not to immediately begin marketing Alto systems is often held up as an example of corporate incompetence, it may have been based on a more accurate assessment than the pundits have acknowledged. With the benefits of hindsight, we can now see that personal computing in the 1970s was still in its first stage. Beyond a small cadre of scientists and amateur enthusiasts, few people then were ready to believe they might soon have a practical use for their own desktop computer. Additionally, many of the component and manufacturing technologies needed to make personal computers affordable to general consumers were not yet available.

Another decade would pass before a personal computer system comparable to the Alto would enter the consumer marketplace. And even in the 1980s there was uncertainty as to which stage personal computers were in. Many financial bets were made on the assumption that they were then in the third stage, only to be lost when the market for home computers faltered toward the middle of the decade. What we can see only now is that the cross-impacts of video game, electronic mail, online information, and Internet technologies coupled with faster and cheaper telecommunications and a growing home office market in the 1990s finally thrust personal computers into the third stage.

RESTATING THE RULE

The 30-year rule may not be foolproof, but it does put the development of new technologies into a more realistic perspective. We need to remember, however, that this rule is not intended to fix a precise time frame for the widespread adoption of new technologies. Saffo's essential point is that impressions of spontaneous technological advancements are generally wrong. This rule can be restated in two different ways: (1) Laboratory breakthroughs and discoveries nearly always take longer than anyone expects to become successful commercial products or services. (2) Technologies that appear to have suddenly emerged as successful new products and services have been under development for much longer than anyone admits.

THE DANGERS OF TECHNOMYOPIA

While the time required for new technologies to migrate from laboratories to store shelves may span several decades, Saffo also cautions industry leaders against complacency. History, he says, shows that once consumers perceive a new technology to be useful and affordable, widespread adoption can take place rather quickly. Yet, despite the frequent repetition of this pattern, he has found that people are still nearly always caught by surprise.

The relatively flat, slow ramp followed by a steep, rapid climb is the growth model upon which most start-up companies build their business plans. But that model can be misleading. The actual pattern for enterprises attempting to exploit new technologies rarely conforms to a smooth ascending curve. More often than not, the typical, real-life trend line resembles a roller coaster. Several moderate ups and downs generally precede the final grand ascent to market success, although there are never any assurances that there will, in the end, be a final grand ascent. This tendency to undergo several initial ups and downs may contribute to the surprise factor when a new technology finally does take off. Typically, a great deal of publicity will follow the announcement of a discovery or new invention. But when the first rush of excitement is dampened by disappointments and setbacks, we usually treat future growth phases with skepticism. Saffo calls this affliction technomyopia.

> [Technomyopia] is a strange phenomenon that causes us to overestimate the potential short-term impacts of a new technology. And when the world fails to conform to our inflated expectations, we turn around and we underestimate the long-term implications. First we over-shoot and then we under-shoot.[4]

Example: The Video Game Roller Coaster

The development of video game technology illustrates this phenomenon. Beginning in 1972 with two simple ball-and-paddle games called Odyssey and Pong, video games quickly captivated the minds, and wallets, of teenagers and young adults. A steady stream of popular video arcade games, such as Pac Man and Space Invad-ers, followed in the late 1970s. Within 10 years, Americans were spending more money on home video game systems and at video arcades than they spent on movies and music—a total of more than $11 billion. Then, even more suddenly, the market collapsed. By 1985 total sales of home video game systems had dropped from more than $3 billion at its peak to only $100 million.[5]

The crash forced nearly all U.S. video game companies into other computer businesses or bankruptcy. Most industry executives and analysts saw this as a sign that video games were merely a fad. But just as the U.S. market was collapsing, Nintendo, a Japanese toy company, introduced a new game system in Japan called Famicon. And two years later, Nintendo swept across the Pacific with the speed and power of a tsunami. Armed with a wider selection of fast-action games that incorporated sophisticated graphics, Nintendo quickly revived interest among those who had become bored with earlier systems and attracted a new generation of players as well. By 1989 Nintendo controlled 80 percent of the U.S. video game market, which had recovered to its $3 billion pre-crash level. By the beginning of the 1990s, one out of every five U.S. households owned a Nintendo set.

TECHNOLOGICAL ACCELERATORS AND BRAKES

Rogers's diffusion theory is perhaps the simplest model for visualizing the historic adoption patterns of established technologies, but it only partially explains why a new media technology will suddenly diffuse into the general consumer market and attain a dominant position. Early adopters may encourage others to try a new technology, but they alone have not been shown to provide the energy needed for rapid acceleration, or to have sufficient influence to significantly affect the introduction and diffusion of a technology.

Diffusion theory cannot adequately explain, for example, why FM radio (which was invented in the early 1930s and provided a far superior means of broadcasting than the original AM radio technology) floundered for three decades and then, in less than 10 years, managed to dethrone its rival all across North America. What was the accelerator? And what had applied the brakes for so long? These are the questions that Brian Winston, a journalism professor at the University of Wales, has attempted to answer.[6]

Winston blends a strong cultural perspective with the history of media technologies to arrive at a comprehensive explanation of how new media are born and developed. His ideas are based on the following convictions:

- Social, political, and economic forces play powerful roles in the development of new technologies.
- Inventions and innovations are not widely adopted on the merits of a technology alone.
- There must always be an opportunity as well as a motivating social, political, or economic reason for a new technology to be developed.

SUPERVENING SOCIAL NECESSITIES

In Winston's view, the accelerators that push the development of new media technologies are what he calls *supervening social necessities*. He defines these as "the interfaces between society and technology." They derive from the needs of companies, requirements of other technologies, regulatory or legal actions, and general social forces. In the case of FM radio, the supervening social necessities that emerged in the 1960s fit into all four categories.

Needs of Companies

Competition with television was cutting deeply into the profits of large established AM stations, and their future seemed in doubt. By contrast, the dramatically lower costs associated with FM broadcasting made the operation of smaller stations that targeted niche audiences quite profitable and appealing to media companies, entrepreneurs, and investors. Manufacturers were also attracted to FM because it created a new and potentially even larger market for radios.

Requirements of Other Technologies

Advances in recording and playback technologies, significant improvements in home equipment, and the growing popularity of hi-fi and stereo recordings created the need and demand for high-quality broadcasting technology, which FM readily provided. Stereo, introduced on FM in 1961, offered radio audiences yet another incentive to switch. The miniaturization of electronic components also made it possible for radio manufacturers to combine AM and FM technologies in more compact receivers, which, in turn, increased the demand for FM stations and new equipment.

Regulatory and Legal Actions

The resolution in the mid-1960s of patent infringement suits finally removed a serious legal impediment to FM's development. But even more important was the 1967 Public Broadcasting Act. This regulatory action established National Public Radio (NPR) as a production center for educational and public affairs broadcasting and reserved space on the FM dial for new public radio stations.

General Social Forces

However, FM owes a great deal of its ultimate success to rock 'n roll music and to teenagers in the late 1950s and 1960s. Because of AM's broad reach and large undifferentiated audiences, stations tended to broadcast only Top 40 popular music and avoid so-called underground recordings, such as rock, jazz, and blues. The smaller FM stations could afford to target niche audiences, which allowed them to satisfy the musical tastes of teenagers and to provide an outlet for small, independent recording studios.

The increasing popularity of FM music stations among teenagers helped drive demand for new portable and car radios with FM receiver technology. It also attracted advertisers who were trying to reach the affluent young audience, which was rapidly becoming a social and economic force to be reckoned with. By 1969, the average FM listener was about 10 years younger than the average AM listener, and more than half of all Americans listening to radio were tuned to FM stations.

THE LAW OF SUPPRESSION OF RADICAL POTENTIAL

The law of suppression of radical potential, in Winston's view, applies the brakes that slow the disruptive impact of a new technology upon the social or corporate status quo. Brakes arise from the same four broad categories identified with supervening social necessities. The [suppression] law helps us understand why FM radio took so long to succeed in the general consumer market despite its obvious technical and economic superiority over AM broadcasting.

Needs of Companies

In 1933, when Howard Armstrong demonstrated his FM prototype to David Sarnoff, president of the powerful Radio Corporation of America (RCA), AM radio was already well established and generating high profits for manufacturers and broadcasters. Sarnoff recognized that FM represented a revolutionary new radio technology that was far better than AM, but he was not eager to disrupt RCA's substantial profits from AM radio, especially in the midst of the Great Depression.

Requirements of Other Technologies

In the 1930s RCA was also investing heavily in the development of television, and many of the company's patents involved using the same portion of the radio spectrum that Armstrong was proposing for FM radio. Sarnoff saw television as RCA's next great opportunity and marshaled the company's resources to protect its position.

Regulatory and Legal Actions

When Armstrong realized that RCA would not back his invention, he decided to push its development on his own. After the Federal Communications Commission (FCC) allocated a small range of the radio spectrum for FM broadcasting, he secured licenses to build several stations and begin manufacturing FM radios. Buoyed by his early success, he confidently predicted in 1940 that the existing AM broadcast system would be largely superseded by FM within five years.

But, however farsighted he was about technology, Armstrong underestimated the interest Sarnoff and other broadcasters had in maintaining the status quo, as well as their political clout, particularly with the FCC.[7] At the insistence of RCA and the network broadcasters, the FCC began hearings in 1944 into the appropriate spectrum allocations for television and other broadcast technologies that were poised to take off as soon as the war ended. Using dubious evidence to justify its decision, the FCC in 1945 approved the recommendations of the broadcasters to move FM to a different location in the radio spectrum and give TV broadcasters the portion previously allocated to FM.

With this one ruling, the FCC rendered all of Armstrong's installed FM broadcast equipment and radios obsolete and useless. At the time, there were more than 50 FM broadcast stations and half a million FM radios in operation in the United States.

General Social Forces

The 1929 stock market crash and subsequent global depression significantly reduced consumer demand for new radio sets and caused a shakeout in the radio manufacturing business. Enthusiasm for a new radio technology that would require replacement of existing sets and broadcast equipment was understandably low.

However, even with the financial constraints posed by the Depression, Armstrong managed to attract a credible number of early adopters and investors. Unfortunately, just as FM broadcasting was poised to take off, its commercial development and expansion were abruptly halted by the United States' entry into World War II. After the war, FM technology still had a strong following, but the obsolescence caused by the FCC's change of radio spectrum allocations seriously inhibited continuing support. Moreover, by the end of the 1940s, TV was already rapidly drawing consumer and investor attention away from both AM and FM radio.

THE MEDIAMORPHIC PROCESS

While the preceding hypotheses are integral to the process I call mediamorphosis, they only provide general insights into the pacing and timing of technological developments. Before we can even begin to make reasonable judgments about emerging technologies and the future of mainstream media, we need to acquire a broad, integrated knowledge of human communications and the historic patterns of change within the overall system. This knowledge is central to our understanding of the mediamorphic process, which I have defined as: *The transformation of communication media, usually brought about by the complex interplay of perceived needs, competitive and political pressures, and social and technological innovations.*

Mediamorphosis is not so much a theory as it is a unified way of thinking about the technological evolution of communication media. Instead of studying each form separately, it encourages us to examine all forms as members of an interdependent system, and to note the similarities and relationships that exist among past, present, and emerging forms. By studying the communication system as a whole, we will see that new media do not arise spontaneously and independently—they emerge gradually from the metamorphosis of old media. And that when newer forms of communication media emerge, the older forms usually do not die—they continue to evolve and adapt.

The example of FM's delayed success and radio's transformation from a mass-audience medium to a niche-audience medium can also be used to illustrate this key principle of mediamorphosis. As TV began its grand ascent, general-audience radio went into a steep decline that led some analysts to predict the eminent death of the medium. But radio didn't die. Nor was AM entirely subsumed by FM. Instead, AM adapted and through the adoption of new technologies and marketing strategies has steadily become more competitive with FM. Since the beginning of the 1990s, AM radio has been showing strong signs of revival in the United States and elsewhere.

The rapid diffusion of TV also brought about significant transformations within the newspaper, magazine, and film industries. Each was declared a dying medium without the capacity to compete with TV's immediacy and compelling images, yet each proved to be more resilient and adaptable than expected. This also illustrates an important corollary to the metamorphosis principle: Established forms of communication media *must* change in response to the emergence of a new medium—their only other option is to die. The metamorphosis principle, as well as several other key principles of mediamorphosis, derive from three concepts—coevolution, convergence, and complexity.

COEVOLUTION

All forms of communication are, as we shall see, tightly woven into the fabric of the human communication system and cannot exist independently from one another in our culture. As each new form emerges and develops, it influences, over time and to varying degrees, the development of every other existing form. Coevolution and coexistence, rather than sequential evolution and replacement, have been the norm since the first organisms made their debut on the planet. The wealth of communication technologies we now take for granted would not have been possible if the birth of each new medium had resulted in the simultaneous death of an older medium.

Communicatory Codes

Specific forms of media, as with species, have life cycles and eventually do die out, but most of their defining traits will always remain part of the system. Just as biological characteristics are propagated from one generation to another through genetic codes, media traits are embodied and carried forward through communicatory codes that we call languages. Languages have been, without compare, the most powerful agents of change in the course of human evolution.

The development of spoken language and written language brought about two great transformations, or mediamorphoses, within the human communication system. Each of these two classes of language has been responsible for reordering and greatly expanding the human mind in ways that made modern civilization and culture possible. Countless transforming technologies affecting all aspects of human life and communication have been inspired and energized by these two agents of change.

Now a third great mediamorphosis resulting from the recent development of a new class of language is poised to once again radically influence the evolution of communication and civilization. For the past two centuries, industrial age and information age technologies have been conjointly contributing to the rapid development and spread of this language, which has only become known to most people in the past two decades. This new class of language is called digital language. It is the *lingua franca* of computers and global telecommunication networks.

CONVERGENCE

Nearly every personal computer sold today offers users the ability to play CD-ROMs that blend text and still images with audio and video clips, as well as the opportunity to conveniently dial into global networks and access vast stores of textual and audio/visual information. This is just one of the more obvious examples of the concept known as media convergence. The idea that diverse technologies and forms of media are coming together now seems almost commonplace, but not so long ago it was considered quite visionary.

In 1979, when Nicholas Negroponte began popularizing the concept in his lecture tours to raise funds for a building to house the Media Lab at the Massachusetts Institute of Technology, few people had any comprehension of convergence. Audiences were often astonished by Negroponte's revelation that "all communication technologies are suffering a joint metamorphosis, which can only be understood properly if treated as a single subject."[8] To illustrate this concept, Negroponte drew three overlapping circles labeled "broadcast and motion picture industry," "computer industry," and "print and publishing industry" (see Figure 2-1). Since then, the notion that these industries are coming together to create new forms of com-

vg. social) cultural convergence (Jenkins)

1978

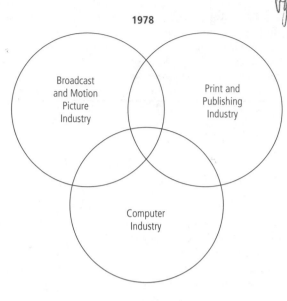

2000

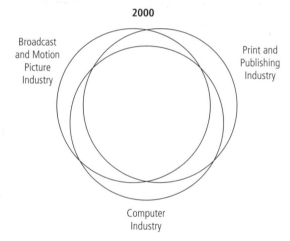

FIGURE 2-1. The MIT Media Lab's construct of convergence.

known, is generally defined as any medium in which two or more forms of communication are integrated.

Within the broadest definition of the term, most printed newspapers and magazines qualify as forms of multimedia because they convey information through a blend of written words, photography, and graphics displayed on a paper medium. However, the visions of multimedia popularized in the past two decades have tended to dismiss paper as an "old" medium. The preferred "new" medium for displaying blended content is the electronic screen. With an electronic display medium, such as a computer monitor or television screen, new multimedia systems are capable of conveying information through various blends of full-motion video, animation and sounds, as well as still images and written words.

COMPLEXITY

During periods of great change, such as we are now experiencing, everything around us may appear to be in a state of chaos and, to a large extent, it is. Chaos is an essential component of change. Without it, the universe would be a dead place and life would be impossible. Out of chaos comes the new ideas that transform and vitalize systems.

Chaos Theory

A central tenet of contemporary chaos theory is the notion that seemingly insignificant events or slight initial variations within chaotic systems, such as the weather and the economy, can trigger cascades of escalating, unpredictable occurrences that ultimately lead to consequential or catastrophic events. This aspect of the theory is often illustrated by the example of a butterfly flapping its wings in China and causing a hurricane to develop off the coast of Florida.

Chaotic systems are essentially anarchistic. That is, they exhibit nearly infinite variability with no predictable long-term patterns, which explains why precise long-range weather and national economic forecasts are all but impossible. It also explains why no one will ever be able to accurately predict which specific new media technologies and forms of communication will ultimately succeed and which will fail.

The importance of chaos to our understanding of mediamorphosis and the development of new media is actually less in the theory than in its connection to

munication has shaped much of the thinking about the future of mass media and human communications.

Multimedia Forms of Communication

Negroponte and others at MIT are credited with being among the first to recognize that this convergence of media industries and digital technologies would ultimately lead to new forms of so-called multimedia communication. Multimedia, or mixed media as it is also another related concept—complexity. In this context, *complexity* refers to the events that take place within certain apparently chaotic systems.

Chaos and order, like birth and death, are opposite extremes of all complex, or so-called *living systems*. According to physicist Mitchell Waldrop, the edge of chaos is "where new ideas and innovative genotypes are forever nibbling away at the edges of the status quo."[9]

Complex, Adaptive Systems

As scientists studied the behavior of complex systems, they discovered that the richness of the interactions that occur within living systems allows them to undergo *spontaneous self-organization* in response to changing conditions. In other words, Waldrop observes, complex systems are *adaptive,* in that "they don't just passively respond to events the way a rock might roll around in an earthquake. They actively try to turn whatever happens to their advantage."

By recognizing that the human communication system is, in fact, a complex, adaptive system, we can see that all forms of media live in a dynamic, interdependent universe. When external pressures are applied and new innovations are introduced, each form of communication is affected by an intrinsic self-organizing process that spontaneously occurs within the system. Just as species evolve for better survival in a changing environment, so do forms of communication and established media enterprises. This process is the essence of mediamorphosis. *(evolution theory) (of: I.D.?)*

PRINCIPLES OF MEDIAMORPHOSIS IN PERSPECTIVE

This discussion furnishes a number of general insights into the adoption and implementation of new media technologies that can guide our thinking about the next stage in the transformation of mainstream media and emerging computer-mediated communications. The following *six fundamental principles of mediamorphosis* flow from the preceding discussion:

1. *Coevolution and coexistence:* All forms of communication media coexist and coevolve within an expanding, complex adaptive system. As each new form emerges and develops, it influences, over time and to varying degrees, the development of every other existing form.

2. *Metamorphosis:* New media do not arise spontaneously and independently—they emerge gradually from the metamorphosis of older media. When newer forms emerge, the older forms tend to adapt and continue to evolve rather than die.

3. *Propagation:* Emerging forms of communication media propagate dominant traits from earlier forms. These traits are passed on and spread through communicatory codes called languages.

4. *Survival:* All forms of communication media, as well as media enterprises, are compelled to adapt and evolve for survival in a changing environment. Their only other option is to die.

5. *Opportunity and need:* New media are not widely adopted on the merits of a technology alone. There must always be an opportunity, as well as a motivating social, political, and/or economic reason for a new media technology to be developed.

6. *Delayed adoption:* New media technologies always take longer than expected to become commercial successes. They tend to require *at least* one human generation (20–30 years) to progress from proof of concept to widespread adoption.

By combining the principles of mediamorphosis with an understanding of the attributes that have shaped the development of communication media in the past, we can gain valuable insights into the new forms that may emerge as well as the ways in which existing forms may adapt and continue to evolve.

NOTES

1. "Paul Saffo and the 30-Year Rule," *Design World, 24* (1992): 18.

2. Ibid.

3. The story of Xerox's development of the first personal computer system is told by Douglas K. Smith and Robert C. Alexander in *Fumbling the Future: How Xerox Invented then Ignored the First Personal Computer.* New York: Morrow, 1988.

4. "Paul Saffo and the 30-Year Rule," p. 18.

5. Steven Lubar, *InfoCulture: The Smithsonian Book of Information Age Inventions.* Boston: Houghton Mifflin, 1993, p. 274.

6. Brian Winston, "How Are Media Born and Developed?" In John Downing, Ali Mohammadi, and Annabelle Sreberny-Mohammadi (Eds.), *Questioning the Media: A Critical Intro-*

duction. Thousand Oaks, CA: Sage Publications, 1995, pp. 54–74.

7. Tom Lewis, *Empire of the Air: The Men Who Made Radio.* New York: HarperCollins, 1991, pp. 300–301.

8. Quoted in Stewart Brand, *The Media Lab: Inventing the Future at MIT.* New York: Viking Penguin, 1987, p. 11.

9. M. Mitchell Waldrop, *Complexity: The Emerging Science at the Edge of Order and Chaos.* New York: Touchstone, 1992, p. 12.

RELATED LINKS

- The Poynter Institute's New Media Timeline (http://www.poynterextra.org/extra/Timeline/index.htm)

- Xerox Palo Alto Research Center (http://www.parc.com)

- The Pulse of Tablet Technology (http://www.ojr.org/ojr/technology/1017968908.php)

- Roger Fidler (http://www.ici.kent.edu/fidler.htm)

FOR FURTHER RESEARCH

To find out more about the topics discussed in this reading, use InfoTrac College Edition. Type in keywords and subject terms such as "mediamorphosis," "media evolution," and "new technology adoption." You can access InfoTrac from the Wadsworth/Thomson Communication Café homepage: http://communication.wadsworth.com.

Reading 2-2

A New World (Small Pieces Loosely Joined)
David Weinberger

EDITOR'S NOTE

To author David Weinberger, the Internet represents a new world that we are just beginning to inhabit. However, unlike the real world, cyberspace has few rules of behavior and fewer lines of authority. Although the effects of online communication are only now coming into vague relief, the new environment is allowing users to explore and seek out new aspects of themselves. In cyberspace, the very notion of self is becoming more fluid and flexible. As Netizens negotiate the social and psychological terrain of this new world, the Web is redrawing the rules of social interaction in ways that still do not make complete sense. Whatever the outcome of these negotiations, social and cultural life may never be the same. "It is a measure of the importance of the Web," Weinberger observes, "that to understand it we find ourselves rethinking bedrock notions of our culture . . . such as space, time, perfection, social interaction, knowledge, matter, and morality." For a similar perspective, consult Reading 1-3 on media ecology and the new global narrative by Douglas Rushkoff.

CONSIDER

1. Why does Weinberger conclude that, for all the overheated, exaggerated news coverage of the World Wide Web, the Web has not yet been hyped *enough*?

2. How is the problem of drawing a clear line between what's public and what's private in cyberspace part of the more general problem of understanding how to coordinate the virtual and real worlds?

3. Why is the fact that the Web is "profoundly unmanageable," in Weinberger's view, so crucial to its success as a communication and information medium?

The Web [unlike earlier software systems] breaks the traditional publishing model. The old model is about control: a team works on a document, is responsible for its content and format, and releases it to the public when it's been certified as done. Once it's published, no one can change it except the original publisher. The Web ditches that model, with all its advantages as well as its drawbacks, and says instead, "You have something to say? Say it. You want to respond to something that's been said? Say it and link to it. You think something is interesting? Link to it from your home page." By removing the central control points, the Web enabled a self-organizing, self-stimulated growth of contents and links on a scale the world has literally never before experienced.

The result is a loose federation of documents—many small pieces loosely joined. But in what has turned out to be simply the first cultural artifact and institution the Web has subtly subverted, the interior structure of documents has changed, not just the way they are connected to one another. The Web has blown documents apart. It treats tightly bound volumes like a collection of ideas—none longer than can fit on a single screen—that the reader can consult in the order she or he wants, regardless of the author's intentions. It makes links beyond the document's covers an integral part of every document. What once was literally a tightly bound entity has been ripped into pieces and thrown into the air.

What the Web has done to documents it is doing to just about every institution it touches. The Web isn't primarily about replacing atoms with bits [i.e., the physical world with electronic elements] so that we can, for example, shop online or make our supply chains more efficient. The Web isn't even simply empowering groups, such as consumers, that have traditionally had the short end of the stick. Rather, the Web is changing our understanding of what puts things together in the first place. We live in a world that works well if the pieces are stable and have predictable effects on one another. We think of complex institutions and organizations as being like well-oiled machines that work reliably and almost serenely so long as their subordinate pieces perform their designated tasks. Then we go on the Web, and the pieces are so loosely joined that frequently the links don't work. But that's okay because the Web gets its value not from the smoothness of its overall operation but from its abundance of small nuggets that point to more small nuggets. And, most important, the Web is binding not just pages but us human beings in new ways. We are the true "small pieces" of the Web, and we are loosely joining ourselves in ways that we're still inventing.

While the Web consists of many small pieces loosely joined . . . we can be individuals only because we are members of groups. Our families, our communities, and our culture make us what we are. So if a new infrastructure comes along that allows us to connect with everyone else on the planet and to invent new types of connections, this is big news indeed.

Even so, the conversation needs to take one step more. Our social connections until now have almost all been constrained by geography: the real world. These constraints feel natural to us because that's exactly what they are. They're so natural that they're usually invisible: it's inconspicuously true that we generally have to travel longer to get to places that are farther away; that to be heard at the back of the theater, you have to speak louder; that when a couple moves apart, their relationship changes; that if I give you something, I no longer have it; that our presence in the world is continuous from birth until death. Our every social act implicitly conforms itself to the geographic and material facts of the real world. But the Web is an unnatural world, one we have built for ourselves. The facts of nature drop out of the Web. And so we can see reflected in the Web just how much of our sociality is due not to the nature of the real world but to the nature of ourselves. The Web confronts us with a different sort of brute fact: we are creatures who care about ourselves and the world we share with others; we live within a context of meaning; the world is richer with meaning than we can imagine.

The Web gives us an opportunity to rethink many of our presuppositions about our nature and our

From *Small Pieces Loosely Joined: A Unified Theory of the Web* by David Weinberger (Cambridge, MA: Perseus Publishing, 2002), pp. viii–xii; 1–25. Copyright © 2002 by David Weinberger. Reprinted with permission.

world's nature. Only by so doing can we begin to discern why the Web has excited us far beyond reasonable expectation. The hype about the Web hasn't been unwarranted, only misdirected. The conversation I believe we need to have is about what the Web is showing us about ourselves. What is true to our nature and what only looked that way because it was a response to a world that was, until now, the only one we had?

A NEW WORLD

When Michael Ian Campbell used an online alias, no one was suspicious. After all, choosing a name by which you'll be known on the Web is a requirement for using America Online. Known as "Soup81" to his AOL buddies, the eighteen-year-old Campbell was considered a polite, even kind young man in the Florida town where he lived with his mother. At the end of 1999, he had finished his first semester at a community college and was working in a retail store during the day; at night, he pursued his dream by acting in plays at the Cape Coral Cultural Theater. On December 15, he and millions of others were using America Online's "instant messaging" facility to type messages back and forth to their friends old and new. Instant messaging opens a window on your computer screen in which the letters being typed by your conversant show up as they're being typed. It's like watching over the shoulder of someone typing—even the effect of the Delete key is eerily evident—although that person can be thousands of miles away. Indeed, Soup81 was chatting with sixteen-year-old Erin Walton in Colorado, someone he had never met before. He did know something about her, though: eight months earlier, a pair of teenagers had killed thirteen people at Walton's high school, Columbine, in Littleton, Colorado.

After some initial chitchat, Campbell typed a warning onto Walton's screen. Don't go to school the next day, his message said, because "I need to finish what begun [sic] and if you do [go to school] I don't want your blood on my hands."

When Walton, understandably shaken, alerted Columbine's school officials, they closed the school for two days and postponed exams. Three days later, the FBI got a court order in Denver forcing AOL to name the person behind the screen name "Soup81." The agents moved in quickly, questioning Campbell for ninety minutes and taking custody of his computer. A judge ordered Campbell to remain in the county jail without bail until his hearing a few days later.[1]

Campbell's mother blamed this aberrant behavior on the death of her son's father a month earlier. Campbell's lawyer, Ellis Rubin, made up a type of insanity —"Internet intoxication"—to excuse it. But Michael Campbell gave a different explanation. On *The Today Show* a few days later, seemingly trying to puzzle out his own behavior, he said that, as a dedicated actor, he was trying on a role. He was seeing what it would be like to be his favorite actor, John Malkovich.

"Internet intoxication" makes about as much sense as the "Twinkie defense"[2]—Dan White's supposed claim that junk food threw off his moral judgment —but at least it acknowledges that something about the Internet contributed to this event. At the very least, had Campbell met Walton in person, his "channeling" of Malkovich would probably have come off as nothing more than a celebrity impression. The Internet allowed Soup81 to assume a persona and become someone that Michael Ian Campbell wasn't. In fact, Soup81 didn't usually go around threatening people online; this seems to have been an isolated incident. Although Soup81's actions on December 15, 1999, were atypical of the tens of millions of chats that take place every day, it is not at all unusual on the Web for someone to "try on" a personality and to switch personalities from chat room to chat room: behavior that would cause your family to plot an intervention off the Web is the norm on the Web. The very basics of what it means to have a self-identity through time—an "inner" consistency, a core character from which all else springs—are in question on the Web.[3]

Michael Campbell is, of course, an exception, which is why he got onto *The Today Show* and the other 300–400 million users of the Web did not. And that's why he served four months in a Florida jail as part of a plea bargain that also forbade him from using the Internet for three years. Fortunately, Campbell's story is not typical. But even the typical, everyday world of the Web is more alien than it at first seems.

The Web has sent a jolt through our culture, zapping our economy, our ideas about sharing creative works, and possibly even institutions such as religion and government. Why? How do we explain the lightning charge of the Web? If it has fallen short of our initial hopes and fears about its transformational powers, why did it excite those hopes and fears in the first place? Why did this technology hit our culture like a bolt from Zeus?

Suppose—just suppose—that the Web is a new world that we're just beginning to inhabit. We're like the early European settlers in the United States, living

colonialism (11)

on the edge of the forest. We don't know what's there and we don't know exactly what we need to do to find out: Do we pack mountain climbing gear, desert wear, canoes, or all three? Of course, while the settlers may not have known what the geography of the New World was going to be, they at least knew that there was a geography. The Web, on the other hand, has no geography, no landscape. It has no distance. It has nothing natural in it. It has few rules of behavior and fewer lines of authority. Common sense doesn't hold there, and uncommon sense hasn't yet emerged. No wonder we're having trouble figuring out how to build businesses in this new land. We don't yet even know how to talk about a place that has no soil, no boundaries, no near, no far.

New worlds create new people. This has always been the case because how we live in our world is the same thing as who we are. Are we charitable? Self-centered? Cheerful? Ambitious? Pessimistic? Gregarious? Stoic? Forgiving? Each of these describes how we are engaged with our world but each can also be expressed as the way our world appears to us. If we're egotistical, the world appears to revolve around us. If we're gregarious, the world appears to be an invitation to be with others. If we're ambitious, the world appears to await our conquest. We can't characterize ourselves without simultaneously drawing a picture of how the world seems to us, and we can't describe our world without simultaneously describing the type of people we are. If we are entering a new world, then we are also becoming new people.

Obviously, we're not being recreated from the ground up. We don't talk in an affect-less voice, express curiosity about the ways of earthlings, and get an irresistible urge to mate once every seven years. But we are rewriting ourselves on the Web, hearing voices we're surprised to find coming from us, saying things we might not have expected. We're meeting people we would never have dreamed of encountering. More important, we're meeting new aspects of ourselves. We're finding out that we can be sappier, more caustic, less patient, more forgiving, angrier, funnier, more driven, less demanding, sexier, and more prudish—sometimes within a single ten-minute stretch online. We're falling into e-mail relationships that, stretching themselves over years, imperceptibly deepen, like furrows worn into a stone hallway by the traffic of slippers. We're falling into groups that feel sometimes like parties and sometimes like battles. We're getting to know many more people in many more associations than the physics of the real world permits, and these molecules, no

longer bound to the solid earth, have gained both the randomness and the freedom of the airborne. Even our notion of self as a continuous body moving through a continuous map of space and time is beginning to seem wrong on the Web.

If this is true, then for all the overheated, exaggerated, manic-depressive coverage of the Web, we'd have to conclude that the Web has not yet been hyped enough.

In 1995, when media coverage of the Web was at its most hysterical, psychologists at Carnegie Mellon University gave computers, software, and Internet access to ninety-three Pittsburgh families who had never been online before. While a significant portion of the globe was wearing out the thesaurus in the hunt for synonyms for "exciting" to describe the promise of the Web, and another portion with equal passion saw the Web as the final smut-filled convulsion of civilization, the Carnegie Mellon scientists calmly studied these families for two years, asking them questions about their patterns of usage, their outside interactions, and their mental states. In the fall of 1998, the results began to leak out: for a significant number of these families, "Internet use led to their having, on balance, less social engagement and poorer psychological well-being" [see Reading 8-2].[4] Not surprisingly, the study was featured on the front page of the *New York Times*.

Two years later, in the fall of 2000, another study was featured in the *New York Times*. Headlined "Who Says Surfers Are Antisocial?" and ignoring the obvious riposte that it was the *Times* who had said it just two years earlier—the article reported that a study of 2,000 people by the University of California at Los Angeles had found that Internet users increased their contact with others, made online friends, and spent just as much time with their families as before. They were also watching 28 percent less television.[5]

The studies caused controversy individually and in comparison. Were the samples fair? Why didn't the Carnegie Mellon study use a control group? Had the Internet changed in the five years between the start of the first and the end of the second study, as suggested by one of the first study's authors?[6] But more was at stake than the quality of the science. That each of these opposing stories was front-page news exposed some of the disquiet behind the public passion for the Web. At the time the media were focused on how the Web was making twenty-five-year-old software jockeys into billionaires, how upstart companies were threatening the largest "bricks and mortar" corporations, and how investors were grumbling if they didn't make ten times

3rd Language (p. 39)

their money in eighteen months. But we—the great mass of Web users—knew there was more to the story than how the money was being made and, later, lost. We knew the Web was affecting more than our bank accounts and our "shopping experience." It was changing the way we're social, for example.

The truth is that neither of these studies could really answer the question "Is the Web making us more or less social?" much less the broader question "What is the Web doing to us as social animals?" Even if we assume that both studies are paragons of the scientific method, the best they could do is answer some highly specific questions: Are Net users watching more or less television? Are we spending more or less time with our friends in the real world? These questions are only interesting, however, because they give us factual pegs on which to hang our intuitive sense that something big is happening.

We're worried, we're giddy, we're confused. If our way of being social is different on the Web, it surfaces questions that give us vertigo. For example, much of our sociality depends upon drawing the line between our private and our public lives: a friend is close if you can tell her that you're secretly quite religious, that your sex life is other than she thought, that you're not as confident as you may seem. Likewise, it's a serious transgression to ask questions more personal than we're entitled to ask; "So, how much money do you make?" and "You and your spouse doing it much?" are more likely to prevent intimacy than to foster it. Because the line between public and private is so important to us—we use words such as "embarrassment" and "humiliation" to describe what happens when the line is crossed—we generally know the rules so well that we don't have to think about them. But the Web is putting us into positions where the lines are not just blurry but have been redrawn according to a new set of rules that don't yet make sense to us. Even something as straightforward as e-mail is catching many of us unwittingly on the wrong side of the line. For example, in October 1999, Xerox fired forty people for e-mail abuse.[7] At the beginning of December 1999, the *New York Times* fired twenty-three employees at a Virginia payroll processing center for sending "inappropriate and offensive" e-mail—reportedly off-color jokes. At the same time, the navy reported that it had disciplined more than five hundred employees at a Pennsylvania supply depot for sending sexually explicit e-mail. These crackdowns on e-mail "abuse" expose a fissure. On the one side, e-mail is like mail—you type it in and send it

to someone. On the other, e-mail is like a conversation—you talk about whatever you want, you make jokes, you don't bother to re-read it before you send it, and you forget about it ten minutes later. So which is it? A formal letter or an informal conversation? Get it wrong, draw the line between public and private inaccurately, and you could end up being fired [see the readings in Chapter 12].[8]

Or worse. In May 2000, John Paul Denning found himself locked up in the Bellevue Hospital's ward for the mentally disturbed—his shoelaces confiscated as a precaution against suicide—because he'd written an e-mail to an old friend in which he said, "Maybe I should stop showing people my new gun, but I'm so proud of it. Makes me feel like a real New Yorker," as well as some references to the mayhem he could commit.[9] New York University expelled Denning when they heard about this, although eventually a board of inquiry readmitted him when he was able to show that the e-mail was simply dark humor sent to a close friend.

The problems we have finding the new lines between the public and the private are part of the more general problem of understanding how to coordinate the two worlds, one real and one virtual.

We can learn more by looking at something perfectly ordinary on the Web. For example, if we want to study the Web's effect on our sociality, we could look at "weblogs" [blogs] or online journals, for there you can see the redrawing of the line between public and private [see Reading 5-3]. In 2000, a few sites began offering tools that made it so easy to create and maintain a weblog that all you had to do was type in the content. As a result, an estimated 100,000 weblogs exist now, although the actual number is unknowable.

Let's take a random example. Someone named .Zannah (yes, the leading dot, the visual equivalent of a pierced tongue, is part of her Web identity) has a weblog titled "/usr/bin/girl" (the technoid-sounding name refers to standard Unix directories.)[10] The page's main serving consists of frequent write-ups about Web sites that .Zannah finds interesting:

> This site [www.compugarg.com] sells Computer Gargoyles, to watch over you as you surf the 'net'. . . .
>
> Taco Joe's graphics are silly at best, which led me to believe that I wouldn't like this game. However, upon giving it a chance, I found myself somewhat enthralled with the taco making, roach squashing business. . . .

Open Cola, the world's first open-source cola. I have no idea how it tastes, but I'm fairly amused at the idea of an open-source food or drink. . . .

Good information that might help a hapless browser find some useful sites. But .Zannah isn't merely conveying information. In the left-hand margin, .Zannah lifts her veil, providing lists of what matters to her, including "recently acquired items" ("blue vinyl pants, rhinestone chain, hair toys, replicant shirt, glowsticks . . .") and a list that's harder to categorize:

mixellanea randomosity:

I am 65.465% insane.

I'm 42% bitchy.

I'm an idealist.

I'm also sensitive.

My geek quotient is 63.

I'm a pink grapefruit.

I'm right between pessimism & optimism.

If you follow the links, you find that these are the results of various sarcastic quizzes around the Web. Despite—or is it because of?—the irony and sarcasm, the reader begins to get a sense of this young woman.

Then, in one corner, there's a link to a personal home page, a second place for .Zannah to expose herself to the public in highly controlled ways.[11] The weblog page is updated more frequently than her home page, but the two pages also differ in the types of disclosures they publish. It's almost as if they were the views two different friends might have of her, each site drawing the line between the public and the private differently. The home page doesn't feel quite as free; it appears to be tied more closely to her offline self—for example, she discloses her physical location—although the differences are more in tone than content. In the upper left corner of her home page, there's a picture of her. She looks as if she's in her early twenties. Head bent down, black hair falling in parentheses past her face, her eyes looking up to make direct contact. An appealing, knowing face. But, if you leave your mouse cursor over the face for more than a few seconds, up pops a caption. It reads: "[just some random chick]." So, is the photograph of .Zannah or is it truly just a random photo? Her webcam is off right now, but the last image it recorded is there. The random chick is

.Zannah all right. The caption is just some misdirection. Probably.

What's going on here? Personal revelations, but enough irony to make sure we don't trust them too much. A name that begins with punctuation, a carefully constructed set of sarcastic lists that tell us about herself, and a clue that what we're reading is a mix of self-revelation and self-invention. Is she being sociable on the Web? She is certainly playing in public with others. But how can we make sense of the evidence about whether the Web is making us less social if we're not certain what it means to be social in this new world?

.Zannah is no Michael Ian Campbell; she is not channeling John Malkovich and making idle threats to a student recently terrorized in a school shooting. She's not insane and she's not an anomaly. For all her oddness, her quirkiness, her postmodern irony, .Zannah is the norm of the Web. She is what's ordinary. The real problem we face with the Web is not understanding the anomalies but facing how deeply weird the ordinary is.

If we're to make any progress in understanding the Web's effect on us—including but certainly not limited to the question, "Is the Web making us more or less social?"—we need something more. We have a hundred ways of considering the Web, from bytes in flight to technological infrastructure to economic playing field to entertainment medium to global conversation to a wanker's paradise. But none seems adequate to the task. Our ways of thinking about the Web have tended to make the Web too small to account for the effect it's having.

If we were to investigate a "big idea" such as democracy, we would look at how its introduction in the eighteenth century affected a suite of related terms basic to our understanding of ourselves in a world of others: citizen, rights, duties, equality, justice, nation, government, authority, legitimacy, law, morality, human nature. In a parallel fashion, as we've looked at just one sample question about the Web—does it make us more or less social?—we've found ourselves brought to consider terms as basic as self, society, friendship, knowledge, morality, authority, private, and public. It is a measure of the importance of the Web that to understand it we find ourselves rethinking bedrock notions of our culture.

But democracy had such a powerful effect, overturning governments and changing the social order, only because it occurred within an oppressive culture of monarchy and aristocracy. Who you were depended on who you were born as, and clearly not everyone was born equal. Democracy was an explosive idea only because this context of inequality pressed so hard against it. The Web's power likewise comes from the pressure of the atmosphere into which it was born. Just as the opposite of democracy was aristocracy, the opposite of the virtual world of the Web is the real world. The Web explodes out with precisely the same force with which the real world pushes in.

It's easy to see what was so oppressive about aristocracy and all that went with it, but what's so oppressive about the real world? Yes, having to travel distances to get where we're going is a bother, but the Web's distancelessness isn't enough to explain the force with which the Web has hit us. After all, telephones and faxes also eliminate distance. Something more has to be going on.

A few years ago, I listened to a woman calling in to a legal expert on a radio talk show. Her basement apartment had taken in a few feet of water in a flood. She didn't have insurance and the landlord's insurance didn't cover the damage. The legal expert explained that the caller was out of luck. Floods happen. The caller was outraged. Who was going to replace her appliances and furniture, not to mention the keepsakes now ruined forever? This was an injustice! I listened with sympathy, for I had been through a flood many years ago, but I also listened with amazement. A bad thing had happened to this woman, so she expected compensation to make it all better. It was as if the world had not lived up to its side of a contract.

Her demand was unreasonable, but her premises, I believe, are widely shared in our culture. Bad things aren't part of "the deal." There isn't a problem we don't assume we will solve eventually. Cancer will soon be cured. AIDS is on the run. We'll figure out a way to mend the hole in the ozone layer and to reverse global warming. Terrorism will be rooted out. We just need to marshal the facts and manage the project. The dinosaurs could only look up in dismay as the asteroid slammed towards them, but we'll organize an international project, preferably with Bruce Willis at the helm, and we'll nuke that sucker back to the Stone Age. We are the masters of our fate. We can manage our way out of any problem.

The building of the Hoover Dam is perhaps the emblematic example of the power of traditional management. The six companies responsible for the project had to construct a city in the desert to house 5,000 workers, complete with a water and sewer system, a city hall, laundries, schools, police and fire departments, and a hospital. They had to build a 222-mile extension of the power system to bring electricity to the site. They spent seven months building a 22.7-mile railroad and a 400-car switchyard. To deliver materials, they built a cableway 1,580 feet long. Even the simplest aspects of the dam's construction often turned out to be hideously complex, requiring ingenious solutions. For example, moving pipes a mile and a half from their fabrication plant required building specially designed 16-wheeled, 38-foot-long trailers with tractors in the rear devoted simply to braking, and two-tier cars to bring the pipes to their final destination.[12] The Hoover Dam is a masterpiece of management as well as of engineering.

The Web, however, is teaching us a different lesson about management. Consider the Web as a construction project. It's the most complex network ever created. It is by many orders of magnitude the largest collection of human writings and works in history. It is far more robust than networks far smaller, yet it was created without managers. In fact, it succeeded only because its designers made the conscious decision to build a network that would require no central control [see Reading 7-1]. You don't need anyone's permission to join in, to post whatever you want, to read whatever others have posted. The Web is profoundly unmanaged, and that is crucial to its success. It takes traditional command and control structures and busts them up into many small pieces that then loosely join themselves—and that, too, is crucial to its success.

As a result, the Web is a mess, as organized as an orgy. It consists of voices proclaiming whatever they think is worth saying, trying on stances, experimenting with extremes, being wrong in public, making fun of what they hold sacred in their day jobs, linking themselves into permanent coalitions and drive-by arguments, savoring the rush you feel when you realize you don't have to be the way you've been.

Our real-world view of *space* says that it consists of homogenous measurable distances laid across arbitrary geography indifferent to human needs; the Web's geography, on the other hand, consists of links among pages, each representing a spring of human interest. Real-world *time* consists of ticking clocks and the relentless schedules they enable; on the Web, time runs as intertwining threads and stories. In the real world, *perfection* is held as an ideal we humans always disappoint; on the Web, perfection just gets in the way. In the real world, *social groups* become more impersonal as they get larger; on the Web, individuals retain their faces no matter what the size of the group—even in the "faceless mass" of the public. In the real world, we have thinned our knowledge down to a flavorless stream of verifiable facts; on the Web, knowledge is fat with stories and voice. Our "realistic" view of *matter* says that it's the stuff that exists independent of us, and as such it is essentially apart from whatever meanings we cast over it like shadows; the matter of the Web, on the other hand, consists of pages that we've built, full of intention and meaning. In the real world to be *moral* means we follow a set of principles; while on the Web, resorting to principles looks like prissiness, and authenticity, empathy, [spontaneity], and enthusiasm instead guide our interactions.

If the Web is changing bedrock concepts such as space, time, perfection, social interaction, knowledge, matter, and morality, no wonder we're so damn confused. That's as it should be. A new world is opening up, a world that we create as we explore it. .Zannah is inventing it, Michael Ian Campbell is abusing it, and every person browsing and posting is setting bytes in flight that shape this new world. Space, time, perfection, social interaction, knowledge, matter, and morality—this is the vocabulary of the Web, not the bits and the bytes, the dot-coms and not-coms, the e-this and B2That. The Web is a world we've made for one another. It can be understood only within a web of ideas that includes our culture's foundational thoughts, with human spirit lingering at every joining point.

NOTES

1. Dave Bryan, "Parent: Teen Accused of Threatening Columbine Student Was 'Bored,'" AP, December 18, 1999; http://www.newstimes.com/archive99.

2. In 1978, former San Francisco supervisor Dan White murdered Mayor George Moscone and supervisor Harvey Milk. White was found guilty of involuntary manslaughter rather than first-degree murder because the jury accepted that he was operating under "diminished capacities." According to the Urban Legends Reference Page, the Twinkie defense was never actually offered. Instead, an expert witness testified that White's abandoning of his usual health food regime was evidence of his deep depression. The witness did not claim that eating junk food caused the depression. Barbara and David Mikkelson, 1999, http://www.snopes.com/snopes.asp.

3. Sherry Turkle has written two excellent and prescient books on the nature of the self online: *The Second Self: Computers and the Human Spirit* (New York: Simon & Schuster, 1984) and *Life on the Screen: Identity in the Age of the Internet* (New York: Simon & Schuster, 1995).

4. Lawrence Biemiller, "Lonely and Unhappy in Cyberspace? A New Study Prompts Online Debate," *Chronicle of Higher Education* 45, no. 4 (1998).

5. John Schwartz, "Who Says Surfers Are Antisocial?" *New York Times,* October 26, 2000.

6. Ibid., citing Robert Kraut.

7. Maura Kelly, "Your Boss May Be Monitoring Your E-mail," *Salon* (December 8, 1999), http://www.salon.com/tech/feature/1999/12/08/email_monitoring/index.html.

8. York, "Invasion of Privacy? E-mail Monitoring Is on the Rise," *Information Week* (February 21, 2000).

9. Fred Kaplan, "Words that Haunt: Student's Dark Humor Brings a Hospitalization Order," *Boston Globe,* May 2, 2000.

10. See http://www.stormwerks.com/linked.

11. See http://www.stormwerks.com/found2.

12. William Joe Simonds, "The Boulder Canyon Project: Hoover Dam," Online: http://www.usbr.gov/history/hoover.htm.

 ### RELATED LINKS

- *Small Pieces Loosely Joined* website (http://www.smallpieces.com)
- *JOHO: Journal of the Hyperlinked Organization* (http://www.hyperorg.com)
- Evident: David Weinberger's Table of Contents (http://www.evident.com)
- stormwerks (http://www.stormwerks.com)

 ### FOR FURTHER RESEARCH

To find out more about the topics discussed in this reading, use InfoTrac College Edition. Type in keywords and subject terms such as "networked communication," "social impact of the Internet," and "HomeNet study." You can access InfoTrac College Edition from the Wadsworth/Thomson Communication Café homepage: http://communication.wadsworth.com.

Reading 2-3

Remediation

Jay David Bolter and Richard Grusin

EDITOR'S NOTE

Different forms of media are continuously influenced by and exert influence over each other. In this essay, media scholars Jay David Bolter and Richard Grusin refer to this process as the reciprocal logic of remediation—*the repurposing or refashioning of old media with new media, not just in terms of content or retelling of stories but through the incorporation of old media into new media forms. To make their case, Bolter and Grusin show how the desire for* immediacy—*the sense of "being there," through media—is pursued in digital graphics by adapting earlier strategies from linear perspective painting, as well as photography, film, and television. Similarly, through* hypermediacy—*the presentation of multiple media forms in a single communication medium—digital multimedia also borrow techniques from modernist painting and previous forms. Illuminating and challenging, this article formed the basis of a book co-written by Bolter and Grusin,* Remediation: Understanding New Media *(MIT Press, 1999), on the use and the cultural significance of the World Wide Web and other textual and visual electronic environments. It concludes with some proposals for remediation as a general theory of media production.*

CONSIDER

1. According to Bolter and Grusin, how is photography more immediate than painting, film more immediate than photography, and television more immediate than film?

2. Does this progression mean that cyberspace and other forms of virtual reality now fulfill "the promise of immediacy"?

3. How do digital multimedia applications and art forms seek to get to "the real" by both multiplying and simultaneously denying the act of mediation?

THE DOUBLE LOGIC OF *STRANGE DAYS*

"This is not like TV only better," says Lenny Nero in the futuristic film *Strange Days*. "This is life. It's a piece of somebody's life. Pure and uncut, straight from the cerebral cortex. You're there. You're doing it, seeing it, hearing it . . . feeling it." Lenny is touting a black-market device called "the wire" to a potential customer. The wire is a technological wonder that deserves Lenny's praise. It fits over the wearer's head like a skull cap, and sensors in the cap somehow make contact with the perceptual centers in the brain. In its recording mode, the wire captures the sense perceptions of the wearer; in its playback mode, the device delivers these recorded perceptions to the wearer. If we accept the popular view that the role of media is to record and transfer sense experiences from one person to another, the wire threatens to make obsolete all technologies of representation. Lenny mentions television, but we can extend his critique to books, paintings, photographs, film, and so on. The wire's appeal is that it bypasses all forms of mediation and transmits directly from one consciousness to another.

Strange Days itself is less enthusiastic about the wire than Lenny and his customers. Although the wire embodies the desire to get beyond mediation, *Strange Days* offers us a world fascinated by the power and ubiquity of media technologies. Los Angeles in the last two days

From "Remediation" by Jay David Bolter and Richard Grusin, *Configurations*, 4(3) (1996), pp. 311–358. © The Johns Hopkins University Press and Society for Literature and Science. Reprinted with permission of The Johns Hopkins University Press.

of 1999, on the eve of "2K," is saturated with cellular phones, voice- and text-based telephone answering systems, radios, and billboard-sized television screens that constitute public media spaces. And in this media-saturated world, the wire itself is the ultimate mediating technology, despite or indeed because the wire is designed to efface itself, to disappear from the user's consciousness. Two scenes, in which Lenny coaches the "actors" who will appear in a pornographic recording, make it clear that the experience the wire offers can be as mediated as a traditional film. And if the wire itself is cinematic, the whole of *Strange Days* is also conscious of its own cinematic tradition, with its obvious debts to films from *Vertigo* to *Blade Runner*. Although Lenny insists that the wire is "not TV only better," the film ends up representing the wire as "film only better."

Strange Days is a compelling film for us because it captures the ambivalent and contradictory ways in which new digital media function for our culture today. The film projects our own cultural moment a few years into the future in order to examine that moment with greater clarity. The wire is just a fanciful extrapolation of contemporary virtual reality, with its goal of unmediated visual and aural experience, and the proliferation of media in 2K L.A. is only a slight exaggeration of our current media-rich environment, in which digital technologies are proliferating faster than our cultural, legal, or educational institutions can keep up with them. In addressing our culture's contradictory imperatives for immediacy and hypermediacy, the film enacts what we understand as a double logic of "remediation." Our culture wants both to multiply its media and to erase all traces of mediation: it wants to erase its media in the very act of multiplying technologies of mediation.

We are in an unusual position to appreciate the double logic of remediation—not only because we are bombarded with images (in print, on television, in films, and now on the World Wide Web and through other digital media), but also because of the intensity with which these two logics are being pursued in all these media. "Live" point-of-view television programs show us what it is like to accompany a policeman on a dangerous raid or indeed to be a skydiver or a race car driver hurtling through space. Filmmakers routinely spend tens of millions of dollars to film "on location" or to recreate period costumes and places in order to make their viewers feel as if they were "really" there. Internet sites offer stories, images, and now video that

is up-to-the-minute, all in the name of perceptual immediacy. Yet these media enact another logic with equal enthusiasm: web sites are often riots of diverse media forms, including graphics, digitized photographs, animation, and video—all set up in pages whose graphic design principles recall the psychedelic 1960s or dada in the 1920s. Hollywood films, like *Natural Born Killers* or *Strange Days* itself, routinely mix media and styles. Televised news programs now feature multiple video streams, split-screen displays, composites of graphics and text—a welter of media that is meant to make the news more perspicuous to us.

What is remarkable is that these seemingly contradictory logics not only coexist in digital media today, but are mutually dependent. Immediacy depends upon hypermediacy. In the effort to create a seamless moving image, filmmakers combine live-action footage with computer compositing and two- and three-dimensional computer graphics. In the effort to be up to the minute and complete, television news producers assemble on the screen ribbons of text, photographs, graphics, and even audio without a video signal when necessary (as was the case during the Persian Gulf War). At the same time, even the most hypermediated productions strive for a kind of immediacy. So, for example, music videos rely on multiple media and elaborate editing to create an immediate and apparently spontaneous style. The desire for immediacy leads to a process of appropriation and critique by which digital media reshape or "remediate" one another and their analog predecessors such as film, television, and photography.

THE LOGIC OF IMMEDIACY

Virtual reality is "immersive," which means that it is a technology of mediation whose purpose is to disappear. Yet this disappearing act is made difficult by the apparatus that virtual reality requires. In *Strange Days,* users of the wire had only to put on a slender skull cap, but in today's virtual reality systems, the viewer must wear a bulky "head-mounted display," a helmet with eyepieces for each eye. In other systems known as "caves," the walls, (and sometimes the floor and ceiling) are themselves giant computer screens. Although less subtle than the wire, current virtual reality systems strive to serve the same purpose in surrounding the viewer with a computer-generated image. With the head-mounted display in particular, virtual reality is literally "in the viewer's face." The viewer is given a first-person point of view, as she gazes on a graphic world from within that world, from a station point that is always the visual center of that world. As the computer scientists themselves put it, the goal of virtual reality is to foster in the viewer a sense of presence: the viewer should forget that she is in fact wearing a computer interface and accept the graphic image that it offers as her own visual world.[1]

The desire for immediacy is apparent in the claim that digital images are more exciting, lively, and realistic than mere text on a computer screen, and that a videoconference will lead to more effective communication than a telephone call. The desire for immediacy is apparent in the increasing popularity of the digital compositing of film and in Hollywood's interest in replacing stunt men and eventually even actors with computer animations. And it is apparent in the triumph of the "graphical user interface" for personal computers. What designers often say they want is an "interfaceless" interface, in which there will be no recognizable electronic tools, no buttons, windows, scroll bars, or even icons as such. Instead the user will move through the space interacting with the objects "naturally," i.e., as she does in the physical world. In fact, virtual reality, three-dimensional graphics, and graphical interface design are all seeking to make digital technology "transparent." In this account, a transparent interface is one that erases itself, so that the user would no longer be aware of confronting a medium, but instead would stand in an immediate relationship to the contents of the medium.

The transparent interface is one more manifestation of the desire to deny the mediated character of digital technology altogether. To believe that with digital technology we have passed beyond mediation is also to assert the uniqueness of our present technological moment. However, the desire for immediacy itself has a long history that is not easily overcome. At least since the Renaissance, it has been a defining feature of Western visual (and for that matter verbal) representation, and to understand immediacy in computer graphics, it is helpful to keep in mind the ways in which painting, photography, film, and television have sought to satisfy this same desire. These earlier media sought immediacy through the interplay of the aesthetic value of transparency with techniques of linear perspective, erasure, and automaticity, all of which are again deployed in digital technology.

Computer graphics create images in linear perspective but apply to linear perspective the rigor of contemporary linear algebra and projective geometry.[2] Computer-generated projective images are mathematically perfect, at least within the limits of computational error and the resolution of the pixelated screen. Renaissance perspective was never perfect in this sense, not only because of hand methods, but also because the artists often manipulated the perspective for dramatic or allegorical effect.[3] (Of course digital graphic perspective can be distorted too, but even these distortions are generated mathematically.) Computer graphics also express color, illumination, and shading in mathematical terms,[4] although so far less successfully than perspective. So, as with perspective painting, when computer graphics lay claim to the real or the natural, they seem to be appealing to the Cartesian or Galilean proposition that mathematics is appropriate for describing nature.

Furthermore, to Cartesian geometry, computer graphics adds the algorithmic mathematics of John von Neumann and Alan Turing. Computer programs may ultimately be human products, in the sense that they embody algorithms devised by human programmers, but once the program is written and loaded, the machine can operate without human intervention. Programming, then, employs erasure or effacement. Programmers seek to remove the traces of their presence in order to give the program the greatest possible autonomy. In digital graphics, human programmers may be involved at several levels: the computer operating systems are written by one group of specialists; graphics languages (such as Open GL) are written by others; and applications are programs that exploit the resources offered by languages and operating systems. All these classes of programmers are simultaneously erased at the moment in which the computer actually generates an image by executing the instructions they have collectively written.

Immediacy can also be promoted by involving the viewer more intimately in the image. The production of computer animation seems to be automatic, but the viewing can also be interactive, although the interaction may be as simple as the capacity to change one's point of view. In painting and photography, the user's point of view was fixed. In film and television, the point of view was set in motion, but it was the director or editor who controlled the movement. Now computer animation can function like film in this respect, for it too can present a sequence of predetermined camera shots. However, the sequence can also be placed under the viewer's control, as it is in animated computer video games or virtual reality.

It is remarkable how easily a player can project herself into a computer game like *Myst* or *Doom,* despite the low resolution and limited field of view afforded by the screen. It is also a creed among interface designers that interactivity increases the realism and effectiveness of a graphical user interface. The icons become more present to the user if she can reposition them or activate them with a click of the mouse. When interactivity is combined with automaticity and the five-hundred-year-old perspective method, the result is one account of mediation that millions of viewers today find compelling.

vgl. Ananova? game trailers?

THE LOGIC OF HYPERMEDIACY

Like the desire for immediacy, the fascination with hypermediacy also has a history, both as a representational practice and as a cultural logic. In digital media, the practice of hypermediacy is most evident in the heterogeneous, windowed visual style of World Wide Web pages, the desktop interface, multimedia programs, and video games. It is a visual style, in the words of William J. Mitchell, "that privileges fragmentation, indeterminacy, and heterogeneity and that emphasizes process or performance rather than the finished art object."[5] Such interactive applications are often grouped under the rubric of "hypermedia." Hypermedia's "combination of random access with multiple media" has been described with typical hyperbole by Bob Cotten and Richard Oliver as "an entirely new kind of media experience born from the marriage of TV and computer technologies. Its raw ingredients are images, sound, text, animation and video, which can be brought together in any combination. It is a medium that offers 'random access'; it has no physical beginning, middle, or end."[6] This definition suggests that the logic of hypermediacy had to wait for the invention of the cathode ray tube and the transistor. However, we believe the same logic is at work in the frenetic graphic design of cyberculture magazines like *Wired* and [the now defunct] *Mondo 2000,* in the patchwork layout of such mainstream print publications as *USA Today,* and even in the earlier "multimediated" spaces of Dutch painting, medieval cathedrals, and illuminated manuscripts.

When in the 1960s and 1970s, Douglas Englebart, Alan Kay, and their colleagues at Xerox PARC and elsewhere invented the graphical user interface and called their resizable, scrollable rectangles "windows," they were implicitly relying on Alberti's metaphor [of a rectangular surface representing "an open window

through which the subject to be painted is seen"].[7] Their windows opened onto a world of information made visible and almost tangible to the user; their goal was to make the surface of these windows, the interface itself, transparent. However, as the windowed style has evolved, transparency and immediacy have had to compete with other values. In current interfaces, windows multiply on the screen: it is not unusual for sophisticated users to have ten or twenty overlapping or nested windows open at one time. The multiple representations inside the windows (text, graphics, video) create a heterogeneous space, as they compete for the viewer's attention. Icons, menus, and toolbars add further layers of visual and verbal meaning. This graphical user interface was to replace the command-line interface, which was itself wholly textual. By introducing graphical objects into the representation scheme, designers believed that they were making the interfaces more "natural," but they were in fact creating a more complex system in which iconic and arbitrary forms of representation interact.

Unlike a perspective painting or three-dimensional computer graphic, the windowed interface does not attempt to unify the space around any one point of view. Instead, each text window defines its own verbal, each graphic window its own visual, point of view. Windows may change scale quickly and radically, expanding to fill the screen or shrinking to the size of an icon. And unlike the painting or computer graphic, the desktop interface does not erase itself. The multiplicity of windows and the heterogeneity of their contents mean that the user is repeatedly brought back into contact with the interface. The user learns to read the interface as she would any hypertext. She oscillates between manipulating the windows and examining their contents, just as she oscillates between looking at a hypertext as a texture of links and looking through the links to the textual units as language.

With each return to the interface, the user confronts the fact that the windowed computer is both automatic and interactive at the same time. We have argued that the automatic character of photography contributes to the photograph's feeling of immediacy, but the situation is more complicated with the windowed computer. Its interface is automatic in the sense that it consists of layers of programming that are executed with each click of the mouse. The interface is interactive in the sense that these layers of programming always return control to the user, who then initiates another automated action. Although the programmer is not visible in the interface, the user as a subject is constantly present, clicking on buttons, choosing menu items, and dragging icons and windows. Both the apparent autonomy of the machine and the user's intervention can be interpreted as contributing to the transparency of the technology. On the other hand, the buttons and menus that provide user interaction can also be seen as getting in the way of the transparency of the digital image. If some software designers now characterize the two-dimensional, desktop interface as unnatural, they really mean that it is too obviously mediated. They prefer to imagine an "interfaceless" computer offering some brand of virtual reality. However, the possibilities of the windowed style have probably not been fully explored and elaborated.

One reason that this style has not been exhausted is that it functions as a cultural counterbalance to the desire for immediacy. If the logic of immediacy leads one to erase or automatize the act of representation, the logic of hypermediacy acknowledges multiple acts of representation and makes them visible. Where the logic of immediacy suggests a unified visual space, hypermediacy offers a heterogeneous space, in which representation is conceived of not as a window onto the world, but rather as "windowed" itself—with windows that open onto other representations or other media. The logic of hypermediacy calls for representations of the real that in fact multiply the signs of mediation and in this way try to reproduce the rich sensorium of human experience.

In the twentieth century, as indeed earlier, it is not only high art that wants to combine heterogeneous spaces. Graphic design for print, particularly for magazines and newspapers, is becoming increasingly hypermediated. Magazines like *Wired* or [the defunct] *Mondo 2000* owe their conception of hypermediacy less to the World Wide Web than to the tradition of graphic design that grows out of pop art and ultimately lettrisme, photomontage, and dada. The affiliations of a newspaper like *USA Today* are more contemporary. The paper has been criticized for lowering print journalism to the level of television news. However, visually *USA Today* does not draw primarily on television: its layout resembles a multimedia computer application more than it does a television broadcast. The paper attempts to emulate in print the graphical user interface. For that matter, television itself, especially news programs, also shows the influence of the graphical user interface when it divides the screen into two or more frames and places text and numbers over and around the framed video images.

In all its various forms, the logic of hypermediacy

expresses the tension between regarding a visual space as mediated and regarding it as a "real" space that lies beyond mediation. What characterizes modern art is an insistence that the viewer keep coming back to the surface, or in extreme cases an attempt to hold the viewer at the surface indefinitely. We are making an argument here that in the logic of hypermediacy the artist (or multimedia programmer or web designer) strives to make the viewer acknowledge the medium as a medium and indeed delight in that acknowledgement. She does so by multiplying spaces and media and by repeatedly redefining the visual and conceptual relationships among mediated spaces—relationships that may range from simple juxtaposition to complete absorption.

Initially, most rock music adhered to the logic of immediacy. However, as early as the 1960s and 1970s, as electric and electronic instruments and recording systems became more sophisticated, performers such as Alice Cooper, David Bowie, and Kiss began to create elaborate, consciously artificial productions. The traditional "musical" qualities of these productions, never very complicated, became progressively less important than the visual and aural spectacle. Today the stage presentations of rock musicians like U2 are often celebrations of media and of the act of mediation, while "avant-garde" artists like Laurie Anderson, the Residents, and the Emergency Broadcast Network are creating [works] that reflect and comment upon such stage presentations with their seemingly endless repetition within the medium and multiplication across media.

As Michael Joyce reminds us, replacement is the essence of hypertext, and in a sense the whole World Wide Web is an exercise in replacement.[8] When the user clicks on an underlined phrase or an iconic "anchor" on a web page, a link is activated that calls up another page. The new material usually appears in the original window and erases the previous text or graphic, although the action of clicking may instead create a separate frame within the same window or a new window laid over the first. The new page wins our attention through the erasure, tiling, or overlapping of the previous page. Beyond the World Wide Web, replacement is the operative strategy of the whole windowed style. In using the standard computer desktop, we pull down menus, click on icons, and drag scroll bars, all of which are devices for replacing the current visual space with another.

Replacement is at its most radical when the new space is of a different medium—for example, when the user clicks on an underlined phrase in a web page and a graphic appears. Hypermedia and windowed applications replace one medium with another all the time, confronting the user with the problem of multiple representation and challenging her to consider why one medium might offer a more or less appropriate representation than another. In doing so, they are performing what we would characterize as acts of "remediation."

REMEDIATION

In the early and mid–1990s, perhaps to a greater extent than at any time since the 1930s, Hollywood produced numerous filmed versions of classic novels—including works by Hawthorne, Wharton, and even Henry James. There has been a particular vogue for the novels of Jane Austen (*Sense and Sensibility, Pride and Prejudice* twice, and *Emma*). Some of the adaptations are quite free, but (except for the odd *Clueless*) the Austen films, whose popularity swept the others aside, are historically accurate in costume and setting and very faithful to the original novels. Yet the Austen films do not contain any overt reference to the novels on which they are based: they do not acknowledge that they are adaptations. Acknowledging the novel in the film would disrupt the continuity and the illusion of immediacy that Austen's readers expect, for they want to view the film in the same seamless way in which they read the novels. The content has been borrowed, but the medium has not been appropriated. This kind of borrowing, extremely common in popular culture today, is also of course very old. An example with a long pedigree would be paintings illustrating stories from the Bible or from other literary sources, where apparently only the story content is borrowed. The contemporary entertainment industry calls such borrowing "repurposing": to take a "property" from one medium and reuse it in another. With reuse comes a necessary redefinition, but there may be no conscious interplay between media. The interplay happens, if at all, only for the reader or viewer who happens to know both versions and can compare them.

Marshall McLuhan remarked that "the 'content' of any medium is always another medium. The content of writing is speech, just as the written word is the content of print, and print is the content of the telegraph." [9] As his problematic examples suggest, McLuhan was not thinking of simple repurposing, but perhaps of a more complex kind of borrowing, in which one medium is itself incorporated or repre-

sented in another medium. Dutch painters incorporated maps, globes, inscriptions, letters, and mirrors in their works. All our examples of hypermediacy are characterized by this kind of borrowing, as is also ancient and modern *ekphrasis,* the literary description of works of visual art, which W. J. T. Mitchell defines as "the verbal representation of visual representation." [10] We will argue that remediation is a defining characteristic of the new digital media. What might seem at first to be an esoteric practice is so widespread that we can identify a spectrum of different ways in which digital media remediate their predecessors, a spectrum depending upon the degree of perceived competition or rivalry between the new media and the old.

At one extreme, an older medium is highlighted and re-presented in digital form without apparent irony or critique. Examples include digitized paintings or photographs and collections of literary texts on CD-ROM. There are also numerous World Wide Web sites that offer pictures or texts for users to download. In these cases, the electronic medium is not set in opposition to painting, photography, or printing; instead, the computer is offered as a new means of gaining access to materials from these older media, as if the content of the older media can simply be poured into the new one. Since the electronic version justifies itself by granting access to the older media, it wants to be transparent. The digital medium wants to erase itself, so that the viewer stands in the same relationship to the content as she would if she were confronting the original medium. Ideally, there should be no difference between the experience of seeing a painting in person and on the computer screen, but this is of course never so. The computer always intervenes and makes its presence felt in some way, perhaps because the viewer must click on a button or slide a bar to view a whole picture or perhaps because the digital image appears with untrue colors. Transparency, however, remains the goal.

In this kind of remediation, the older media are presented in a space whose discontinuities, like those of collage and photomontage, are clearly visible. In multimedia the discontinuities are indicated by the windowframes themselves and by buttons, sliders, and other controls, which start or end the various media segments. The windowed style of the graphical user interface favors this kind of remediation: different programs, representing different media, can appear in each window—a word processing document in one, a digital photograph in another, digitized video in a third—while clickable tools activate and control the different programs and media. The standard graphical user interface remediates by acknowledging and controlling the discontinuities as the user moves between media. Finally, the new medium can remediate by trying to absorb the older medium entirely, so that the discontinuities between the two are minimized. The very act of remediation, however, ensures that the older medium cannot be entirely effaced. The new medium remains dependent upon the older one, in acknowledged or unacknowledged ways. For example, the whole genre of computer games like *Myst* or *Doom* remediate cinema, and the games are sometimes called "interactive films." The idea is that the players become characters in a cinematic narrative. They have some control over both the narrative itself and the stylistic realization of it, in the sense that they can decide where to go and what to do in an effort to dispatch villains (in *Doom*) or solve puzzles (in *Myst*). They can also decide where to look, where to direct their graphically realized points of view, so that in interactive film, the player is often both actor and director. On the World Wide Web, on the other hand, it is television rather than cinema that is remediated. There are numerous web sites that remediate the monitoring function of broadcast television. These sites present a stream of images from digital cameras [web cams] aimed at various parts of the environment: pets in cages, fish in tanks, a soft drink machine, one's office, a highway, and so on. Although these point-of-view sites monitor the world for the web, they do not in general acknowledge television as the medium that they are refashioning. In fact, television and the WWW are engaged in an unacknowledged competition in which each now seeks to remediate the other.

Like television, film is also trying to absorb and repurpose digital technology. As we have mentioned, digital compositing and other special effects are now standard features of the Hollywood films, particularly in the "action-adventure" genre. And in most cases, the goal is to make these electronic interventions transparent. The stunt or special effect should look as "natural" as possible, as if the camera were simply capturing what really happened in the light. Computer graphics processing is rapidly taking over the animated cartoon; indeed, the takeover is already complete in Disney's *Toy Story*. And here too the goal is to make the computer disappear: to make the settings, toys, and the human characters look as much as possible like live-action film. Hollywood has incorporated computer graphics at least in part in an attempt to hold off the threat that digital media might pose for the traditional, linear film.

This attempt shows that remediation operates in both directions: users of older media such as film and television can seek to appropriate and refashion digital graphics, just as digital graphics artists seek to refashion film and television.

Paradoxically, then, remediation is as important for the logic of immediacy as it is for hypermediacy.

MEDIATION AND REMEDIATION

It is easy to see that hypermedia applications are always explicit acts of remediation: they import earlier media into a digital space in order to critique and refashion them. However, digital media that strive for transparency and immediacy (such as immersive virtual reality and virtual games) are also acts of remediation. Hypermedia and transparent media are opposite manifestations of the same desire: the desire to get past the limits of representation and to achieve the real. They are not striving for the real in a metaphysical sense. Instead, the real is defined in terms of the viewer's experience: it is that which evokes an immediate (and therefore authentic) emotional response. Transparent digital applications seek to get to the real by bravely denying the fact of mediation. Digital hypermedia seek the real by multiplying mediation so as to create a feeling of fullness, a satiety of experience, which can be taken as reality. Both these moves are strategies of remediation.[11]

Technologies of immediacy try to improve upon media by erasing them, but they are compelled to define themselves by the standards of the media they are trying to erase. The wire, Lenny claims, "is not like TV only better"; in saying this, of course, he affirms the comparison that he denies. The wire does improve upon television, because it delivers "lived" experience, as television promises and yet fails to do. Similarly, interactive computer games such as *Myst* and *Doom* define their reality through the traditions of photography and film. *Doom* is regarded as authentic because it places the user in an action-adventure movie; *Myst* because of the near photorealism of its graphics and its cinematic use of sound and background music. In general, digital photorealism defines reality as perfected photography, and virtual reality defines it as first-person point-of-view cinema.

It would seem, then, that *all* mediation is remediation. We are not of course claiming this as an a priori truth, but rather arguing that at this historical moment all current media function as remediators and that remediation offers us a means of interpreting the work of earlier media as well. Our culture conceives of each medium or constellation of media as it responds to, redeploys, competes with, and reforms other media.

REMEDIATION AS REFORM

The word remediation is used today by educators as a euphemism for the task of bringing lagging students up to an expected level of performance. The word derives ultimately from the Latin *remederi*—to heal, to restore to health—and we have adopted the word to express the way in which one medium is seen by our culture as reforming or improving upon another. This belief in reform is particularly strong for those who are today repurposing earlier media into digital forms. They tell us, for example, that when broadcast television becomes interactive digital television, it will motivate and liberate the viewer as never before; that virtual reality improves upon film by placing the viewer at the center of a moveable point of view; that electronic mail is more convenient and reliable than physical mail; that hypertext brings interactivity to the novel; and that digital audio and video improve upon their analog equivalents. The assumption of reform is so strong that a new medium is now expected to justify itself by improving upon a predecessor: hence the need for computer graphics to achieve full photorealism. Yet the assumption of reform has not been limited to digital media. Photography was seen as the reform of illusionistic painting; the cinema as the reform of the theater (in the sense that early films were once called "photoplays").

It is possible to claim that a new medium makes a good thing even better, but this seldom seems to be the rhetoric of remediation and is certainly not the case for digital media. Each new medium is justified because it fills a lack or repairs a fault in its predecessor, because it fulfills the unkept promise of an older medium. (Typically, of course, users did not realize that the older medium had failed in its promise, until the new one appeared.) The rhetorical virtue of virtual reality, of videoconferencing and interactive television, and of the World Wide Web, is that each of these technologies repairs the inadequacy of the medium or media that it now supersedes. In each case that inadequacy is represented as a lack of immediacy. So photography was more immediate than painting; film than photography; television than film; and now virtual reality fulfills

the promise of immediacy and supposedly ends the progression.

Remediation can also imply reform in a social or political sense, and again this sense has emerged with particular clarity in the case of digital media. A number of American political figures have even suggested that the World Wide Web and the Internet can reform democracy by lending immediacy to the process of making decisions. When citizens are able to participate in the debate of issues and possibly even vote electronically, we may substitute direct (immediate) democracy for our representational system. Here too, as it happens, digital media promise to overcome representation. Even beyond claims for overt political reform, many cyberenthusiasts suggest that the web and computer applications are creating a digital culture that will revolutionize commerce, education, and social relationships [see Readings 1-1, 5-1, 5-4, and 7-4]. Thus, broadcast television is associated with the old order of hierarchical control, while interactive media move the locus of control to the individual. That digital media can reform and even save society reminds us of the promise that [was] made for technologies throughout much of the twentieth century: it is a peculiarly, if not exclusively, American promise. American culture seems to believe in technology in a way that European culture, for example, may not. Throughout the twentieth century, or really since the French Revolution, salvation in Europe has been defined in political terms —finding the appropriate (radical left or radical right) political formula. Even traditional Marxists, who believed in technological progress, subordinated that progress to political change. In America, however, collective (and perhaps even personal) salvation has been thought to come through technology rather than through political or even religious action. Contemporary American culture claims to have lost much of its naïve confidence in technology. But, the gesture of reform is ingrained in American culture, and this is why American culture takes so easily to strategies of remediation.

Finally, remediation is reform in the sense that media reform reality itself. As we have argued above, it is not that media merely reform the appearance of reality. Media hybrids (the affiliations of technical artifacts, rhetorical justifications, and social relationships) are as real as the objects of science. Media make reality over in the same way that all Western technologies have sought to reform reality. Thus, virtual reality reforms reality by giving us an alternative visual world and insisting on that world as the locus of presence and meaning for us.

This fascination with media explains why <u>the self today is both mediated and remediated</u>. If immediacy were possible, if the self could be left alone with the objects of mediation, then media would not need to enter into the definition of self. We could then be just subjects in the world. But even if that utopian state were ever possible, a supposition that we would in any case take great pains to deny, it is certainly not available to us in today's media-saturated environment. Media are part of our world as much as any other natural and technical objects. Whenever we engage ourselves with visual (or verbal) media, we become aware not only of the objects of representation but also of the media themselves. Instead of trying to be in the presence of the objects of representation, the subject now defines immediacy as being in the presence of media. In this remediation of the self, the fascination with media functions as the sublimation of the initial desire for immediacy, the desire to be present to oneself.

The first generations of film technicians and producers remediated both photography and the practices of stage plays. The inventors of television remediated the vacuum tube from a device for modulating radio transmissions into a device for transmitting images. In computer graphics, paint programs borrowed techniques and names from manual painting practices. The first generation of World Wide Web designers have remediated graphic design as it was practiced for printed newspapers and magazines, which have now themselves remediated the graphic design of the World Wide Web.

NOTES

1. Larry F. Hodges, Barbara O. Rothbaum, et al., "Presence as the Defining Factor in a VR Application," GVU Technical Report #94-06 (Atlanta, Ga.: Graphics Visualization and Usability Center, 1994).

2. See James D. Foley, Andries van Dam, Steven V. Feiner, John F. Hughes, *Computer Graphics: Principles and Practice* (Reading, Mass.: Addison-Wesley, 1996), pp. 229–283.

3. See James Elkins, *The Poetics of Perspective* (Ithaca, N.Y.: Cornell University Press, 1994); Kemp, *The Science of Art;* Margaret A. Hagen, *Varieties of Realism* (Cambridge: Cambridge University Press, 1986).

4. James D. Foley, Andries van Dam, Steven V. Feiner, John F. Hughes, *Computer Graphics: Principles and Practice* (Reading, Mass.: Addison-Wesley, 1996), pp. 563–604 and pp. 721–814.

5. William J. Mitchell, *The Reconfigured Eye: Visual Truth in the Post-Photographic Era* (Cambridge, Mass.: MIT Press, 1994), p. 8.

6. Bob Cotten and Richard Oliver, *Understanding Hypermedia* (London: Phaidon Press, 1992), p. 8.

7. Leon Battista Alberti, *On Painting and On Sculpture. The Latin Texts of De Pictura and De Statua,* ed. Cecil Grayson (London: Phaidon, 1972), p. 55.

8. As Joyce puts it: "Text reproduces itself; hypertext replaces itself" (private communication).

9. Marshall McLuhan, *Understanding Media: The Extensions of Man* (New York: McGraw-Hill, 1964), pp. 23–24.

10. W. J. T. Mitchell, *Picture Theory* (Chicago: University of Chicago Press, 1994), pp. 151, 152. W. J. T. Mitchell attempts to break down the dichotomy between words and images by arguing for a hybrid, the "imagetext," but his picture theory finally assimilates images to words more than the reverse.

11. The logic of remediation we describe here is similar to Derrida's account of mimesis in "Economimesis," where mimesis is defined not ontologically or objectively in terms of the resemblance of a representation to its object but rather intersubjectively in terms of the reproduction of the feeling of imitation or resemblance in the perceiving subject. "Mimesis here is not the representation of one thing by another, the relation of resemblance or identification between two beings, the reproduction of a product of nature by a product of art. It is not the relation of two products but of two productions. And of two freedoms. . . . 'True' *mimesis* is between two producing subjects and not between two produced things." Jacques Derrida, "Economimesis," *Diacritics* 11 (1981): 3-25; p. 9.

RELATED LINKS

- *Remediation* home page (http://www.lcc.gatech.edu/%7Ebolter/remediation/index.html)
- Jay David Bolter (http://www.lcc.gatech.edu/~bolter)
- The Emergency Broadcast Network (http://www.guerrillanews.com/ebn)

- Laurie Anderson (http://www.laurieanderson.com)
- *Strange Days* Web site (http://www.rottentomatoes.com/m/StrangeDays-1066711)

 FOR FURTHER RESEARCH

To find out more about the topics discussed in this reading, use InfoTrac College Edition. Type in keywords and subject terms such as "remediation," "hypermedia," and "immediacy." You can access InfoTrac College Edition from the Wadsworth/Thomson Communication Café homepage: http://communication.wadsworth.com.

Reading 2-4

Uses of the Mass Media
Werner J. Severin and James W. Tankard Jr.

EDITOR'S NOTE

Conceptions of the media audience are changing. Increasingly, media consumers are seen as active users of communication technologies rather than passive receivers of content. From a perspective of uses and gratifications, they always were. Rather than ask what media do to people, uses and gratifications research turns the question on its head and asks what people do with media. Different people, it turns out, can use the same media message for very different purposes. As this reading by Werner Severin and James Tankard illustrates, uses and gratifications is the area of communication study that most directly acknowledges the active audience.

CONSIDER

1. Conventional wisdom assumes that media audiences are generally passive. What is the evidence that members of the media audience are, in fact, quite active?

2. What specific uses and gratifications do you derive from your media use? Do different uses and gratifications vary according to different media? If so, how and why?

3. Are new communication media such as the Internet providing uses and gratifications that the old media did not, or are they just satisfying user needs in different ways?

Many of us, both in the media and out of the media, tend to think of the media "acting" upon their viewers, listeners, and readers. Subconsciously we often con-

From *Communication Theories: Origins, Methods, and Uses in the Mass Media* (5th ed.) by Werner J. Severin and James W. Tankard Jr. (New York: Longman, 2001), pp. 293–305. Copyright © 2001 by Addison Wesley Longman, Inc. Reprinted by permission of Pearson Education, Inc.

tinue to accept the model of the media as a hypodermic needle or a bullet directed to a passive target. But audiences are not always passive; one classic study, titled "The Obstinate Audience," pointed out that the audience is often quite active (Bauer, 1964). Other researchers (Bryant & Street, 1988) echo the statement: "The notion of 'the active communicator' is rapidly achieving preeminent status in the communication discipline" (p. 162). Rubin (1994) has argued that audience activity—the deliberate choice by users of media content in order to satisfy their needs—is the core concept of the *uses and gratifications approach*.

Along similar lines, one group of authors suggested that the term "audience" be replaced with the idea of an active "reader" of mass communication content (Gamson, Croteau, Hoynes, & Sasson, 1992). These authors stress that much mass media content is rich in meaning and open to multiple readings.

The uses and gratifications approach involves a shift of focus from the purposes of the communicator to the purposes of the receiver. It attempts to determine what functions mass communication is serving for audience members. In at least one respect the uses and gratifications approach to the media fits well with the Libertarian theory and John Stuart Mill's notions of human rationality. Both stress the potential of the individual for self-realization.

BEGINNINGS OF THE USES AND GRATIFICATIONS APPROACH

The uses and gratifications approach was first described in an article by Elihu Katz (1959) in which he was reacting to a claim by Bernard Berelson (1959) that the field of communication research appeared to be dead. Katz argued that the field that was dying was the study of mass communication as persuasion. He pointed out that most communication research up to that time had been aimed at investigating the question "What do media do to people?"

Katz suggested that the field might save itself by turning to the question "What do people do with the media?" He cited a few studies of this type that were already done. One of them was, curiously enough, by Berelson (1965). It was his "What 'Missing the Newspaper' Means," a 1949 study conducted by interviewing people about what they missed during a newspaper strike.

During this two-week strike of delivery workers, most readers were forced to find other sources of news, which is what they overwhelmingly said they missed the most. Many read because they felt it was the socially acceptable thing to do, and some felt that the newspaper was indispensable in finding out about world affairs. Many, however, sought escape, relaxation, entertainment, and social prestige. These people recognized that awareness of public affairs was of value in conversations. Some wanted help in their daily lives by reading material about fashion, recipes, weather forecasts, and other useful information.

Another example cited by Katz (1959) was Riley and Riley's study (1951) showing that children well integrated into groups of peers use adventure stories in the media for group games, while children not well integrated use the same communications for fantasizing and daydreaming. This example illustrates a basic aspect of the uses and gratifications approach—different people can use the same mass communication message for very different purposes. Another study (Herzog, 1944) examined the functions radio soap operas fulfilled for regular listeners. Some listeners found emotional release from their own problems. For others, listening provided escape, while a third group sought solutions to their own problems.

USES AND GRATIFICATIONS IN AN ELECTION CAMPAIGN

Blumler and McQuail (1969) used the uses and gratifications approach as the overall research strategy in a study of the 1964 general election in Britain. The central aim of their study was "to find out why people watch or avoid party broadcasts; what uses they wish to make of them; and what their preferences are between alternative ways of presenting politicians on television" (pp. 10–11). Part of their aim was to answer the challenging question posed by earlier election studies that indicated mass media election campaigns had little effect on voters: If voters are not influenced by mass media election programming, why do they follow it at all? Also, the researchers expected that classifying viewers according to their motives for viewing might disclose some previously undetected relationships between attitude change and campaign exposure and, thus, might tell us something about effects after all.

Blumler and McQuail began the task of determining people's motives for watching political broadcasts by using open-ended questions to interview a small sample. On the basis of the responses to these questions, they drew up a list of eight reasons for watching political broadcasts. This list was used in subsequent interviewing with a large sample survey. On the basis of this interviewing, the researchers determined the frequency with which each reason was cited. The three most frequently mentioned reasons reflect a desire for what Blumler and McQuail call "surveillance of the political environment." These reasons, each cited by

vgl. deliberare vs. ritualistr. use of media ; making us.
ussing media (!)

more than half the respondents, indicate that people used the political broadcasts as a source of information about political affairs. Other data from the survey indicated that one of the specific purposes of this surveillance was to find out about campaign promises and pledges. Only about a third of the respondents chose "To remind me of my party's strong points," a reason that would indicate the political broadcasts were being used for reinforcement of existing attitudes. This casts some doubt on the indication from some earlier research that people turn to the mass media primarily for reinforcement.

CLASSIFYING INDIVIDUAL NEEDS AND MEDIA USES

A few years later, in a paper that summarized work in the field to that time, Katz, Blumler, and Gurevitch (1974) pointed out that the studies are concerned with: (1) the social and psychological origins of (2) needs, which generate (3) expectations of (4) the mass media or other sources, which lead to (5) differential patterns of media exposure (or engagement in other activities), resulting in (6) need gratifications and (7) other consequences, perhaps mostly unintended ones (p. 20).

They cited two Swedish researchers who in 1968 proposed a "uses and gratifications model" that included the following elements:

1. The audience is conceived of as active, that is, an important part of mass media use is assumed to be goal directed.

2. In the mass communication process much initiative in linking need gratification and media choice lies with the audience member.

3. The media compete with other sources of need satisfaction (pp. 22–23).

The uses and gratifications literature has provided several ways of classifying audience needs and gratifications. Some have spoken of *immediate* and *deferred* gratifications (Schramm, Lyle, & Parker, 1961); others have called them *informational-educational* and *fantasist-escapist* entertainment (Weiss, 1971).

McQuail, Blumler, and Brown (1972), based on their research in England, suggested the following categories:

1. *Diversion*—escape from routine and problems; emotional release.

2. *Personal relationships*—social utility of information in conversations; substitute of the media for companionship.

3. *Personal identity* or *individual psychology*—value reinforcement or reassurance; self-understanding; reality exploration; and so on.

4. *Surveillance*—information about things which might affect one or will help one do or accomplish something.

In 1975, Mark R. Levy (1978b) examined the cross-national applicability of the McQuail, Blumler, and Brown typology with a sample of 240 adults living in Albany County, New York. He found that their four groupings or clusters of items from England were reduced to three substantially overlapping dimensions in the United States. All three clusters contained surveillance items, and the other two clusters were equally mixed. Levy speculated that the differences may be caused by several factors, including the greater availability of television news in the United States, the fact that Americans may rely on it for a greater variety of needs, and the differences [between countries] in the style and presentation of television news.

In a more complete report of the same research Levy (1978a) concluded that besides informing viewers, television news also tests their perceptions and attitudes on "fresh" events and personalities. However, the participation is at a distance with reality, "sanitized" and made safe by the celebrity newsreader. Many viewers, he says, "actively" choose between competing newscasts, "arrange their schedules to be near a television set at news time, and pay close, albeit selective, attention to the program" (p. 25).

Katz, Gurevitch, and Haas (1973) see the mass media as a means used by individuals to connect themselves with others (or disconnect). They listed 35 needs taken "from the (largely speculative) literature on the social and psychological functions of the mass media" and put them into five categories:

1. *Cognitive needs*—acquiring information, knowledge, and understanding.

2. *Affective needs*—emotional, pleasurable, or aesthetic experience.

3. *Personal integrative needs*—strengthening credibility, confidence, stability, and status.

4. *Social integrative needs*—strengthening contacts with family, friends, and so on.

5. *Tension release needs*—escape and diversion (pp. 166–167).

In a study comparing computers with other means of satisfying needs, Perse and Courtright (1993) identified eleven needs that might be satisfied by mass, interpersonal, or computer-mediated communication: to relax; to be entertained; to forget about work or other things; to have something to do with friends; to learn things about myself and others; to pass the time away (particularly when bored); to feel excited; to feel less lonely; to satisfy a habit; to let others know I care about their feelings; and, to get someone to do something for me.

NEW TECHNOLOGY AND THE ACTIVE AUDIENCE

Researchers have only begun to study the ways that cable television and other new media offering expanded user choices relate to the user's pursuit of uses and gratifications. A few studies done so far provide clues concerning the impact of new technology on how people use the mass media.

Cable television provides new and diverse opportunities for the audience to become active. With cable, the number of channels can increase from the ten or fewer available with broadcast television to over 100. Cable viewers adopt various strategies to cope with this increased number of choices. One strategy is to narrow one's regular watching to a subset of the available channels that correspond to one's interests. This subset has been called an individual's "channel repertoire" (Heeter & Greenberg, 1985). Viewers differ in their awareness of available cable options. To some extent, viewers appear to be overwhelmed by the number of programs and channels now available. One survey of users of a 35-channel cable system found viewers were able to correctly identify an average of only nine channels by their number or location on the channel selector (Heeter & Greenberg, 1985).

About half the time, cable viewers have a program in mind when they turn on the television set. The other half of the time, programs are chosen at the time of viewing. Viewers use a variety of scanning strategies to decide which programs to watch. These strategies differ in whether they are *automatic* (going from channel to channel in the order that they appear) or *controlled* (going from one selected channel to another on the basis of some desired goal); *elaborated* (involving all or most channels) or *restricted* (involving a limited number of channels); and, *exhaustive* (searching all channels before returning to the best choice) or *terminating* (stopping when the first acceptable option is located). The most active viewers of cable television tend to use controlled, elaborated, and exhaustive searching strategies. They tend to be young adults (Heeter & Greenberg, 1985).

The videocassette recorder also gives the television viewer opportunities to be a more active viewer. It offers the user greater flexibility in terms of times for viewing and it increases the choices of available content. Levy (1980) argues that using a VCR to time-shift programs is a demanding task and that viewers who take the trouble to do it must be among the most active members of the television audience.

Several studies have looked at the uses to which people put computers as communication devices. Perse and Courtright (1993) found in a 1988 survey that computers ranked lowest among 12 types of mediated and interpersonal communication for satisfying communication needs such as relaxation, entertainment, self-awareness, and excitement. The picture changed a few years later, however. Another survey (Perse & Dunn, 1995) looked particularly at the use of computers to communicate with others through information services and the Internet, or what the authors called *computer connectivity*. People using computers for electronic communication were satisfying the following needs: learning, entertainment, social interaction, escapism, passing the time, and out of habit. Use of computers hooked to networks or information services for reasons of passing time or out of habit suggests a ritualistic use, not a use aimed at the gratifications provided by specific content. The authors suggest that this ritualistic use of computers for connectivity might actually lead some users of computer networks or information services to become addicted. [For further discussion about the effects of computer use, see Reading 8-2.]

The uses and gratifications approach may be particularly useful in helping us understand how people use the World Wide Web, e-mail, and other aspects of cyberspace.

RECENT DEVELOPMENTS IN USES AND GRATIFICATIONS RESEARCH

One recent development has been a movement away from conceptualizing audiences as active or passive to treating activity as a variable (Rubin, 1994) That is, sometimes media users are selective and rational in their processing of media messages, but at other times they are using the media for relaxation or escapism. These differences in type and level of audience activity might also have consequences for media effects. For instance, cultivation effects of the type proposed by George Gerbner and his associates might be most likely to occur when audience members are viewing television for diversion or escape.

Another new direction has been to focus on media use for satisfying particular needs. For instance, one possible use of the mass media is to relieve loneliness. Canary and Spitzberg (1993) found evidence supporting this use, but the relationship depended on the extent of loneliness. They found the heaviest use of the media to relieve loneliness was in the *situationally lonely*, or those who were temporarily lonely. They found less use of the media to relieve loneliness in the *chronically lonely*, or those who have felt lonely for a period of years. The explanation seems to be that the chronically lonely attribute their loneliness to internal factors and so do not believe that communication in itself will provide relief.

Film scholars have begun to use an active audience approach to help us understand the viewing of extremely violent motion pictures. Why do people watch films such as *Reservoir Dogs, Pulp Fiction, True Romance, National Born Killers, Man Bites Dog, Henry, Portrait of a Serial Killer, Bad Lieutenant,* and *Killing Zoe*? And what kinds of active cognitive processing strategies might they use to make the violence more tolerable? Hill (1997) studied focus groups of viewers of brutal films and found that they responded with *portfolios of interpretation*—particular methods of response that they brought to the viewing experience. Factors within the portfolio included a conceptualization of fictional violence as entertaining, anticipation of upcoming violence and readiness to choose methods of self-censorship, and establishing individual thresholds for acceptable violence.

CONCLUSIONS

The uses and gratifications approach reminds us of one very important point—people use the media for many different purposes. This approach suggests that to a large extent, the user of mass communication is in control. The uses and gratifications approach can serve as a healthy antidote to the emphasis on passive audi-

ences and persuasion that has dominated much earlier research.

The uses and gratifications approach may make a significant contribution to our understanding of media effects as we move further into the digital age and media users are confronted with more and more choices. It is obvious that the media user dealing with cable television with as many as 500 channels or with a videocassette recorder that allows time-shifting, archiving, and repeated viewing of television content is a much more active audience member than the traditional media consumer of a few years ago. The uses and gratifications approach should eventually have some things to say about the users of these new media. After all, it is the single area of theory that has attempted most directly to deal with the active audience.

At the very least, the uses and gratifications approach should direct our attention to the audience of mass communication. Brenda Dervin (1980) recommended that the development of information campaigns should begin with study of the potential information user and the questions that person is attempting to answer in order to make sense of the world. The same lesson probably applies to the producers of much of the content of the mass media. Media planners in many areas should be conducting more research on their potential audiences, and the gratifications those audiences are trying to obtain.

REFERENCES

Bauer, R. A. (1964). The obstinate audience: The influence process from the point of view of social communication. *American Psychologist, 19,* 319–328.

Berelson, B. (1959). The state of communication research. *Public Opinion Quarterly, 23,* 1–6.

Berelson, B. (1965). What "missing the newspaper" means. In W. Schramm (ed.), *The Process and Effects of Mass Communication* (pp. 36–47). Urbana: University of Illinois.

Blumler, J. G., & D. McQuail (1969). *Television in Politics: Its Uses and Influence.* Chicago: University of Chicago Press.

Bryant, J., & Street, R. L., Jr. (1988). From reactivity to activity and action: An evolving concept and Weltanschauung in mass and interpersonal communication. In R. P. Hawkins, J. M. Wiemann, and S. Pingree (eds.), *Advancing Communication Science: Merging Mass and Interpersonal Processes* (pp. 162–190). Newbury Park, CA: Sage.

Canary, D. J., & Spitzberg, B. H. (1993). Loneliness and media gratifications. *Communication Research, 20,* 800–821.

Dervin, B. (1980). Communication gaps and inequities: Moving toward a reconceptualization. In B. Dervin and M. J. Voight (eds.), *Progress in Communication Sciences, Vol. 2* (pp. 73–112). Norwood, NJ: Ablex.

Gamson, W. A., Croteau, D., Hoynes, W., & Sasson, T. (1992). Media images and the social construction of reality. *Annual Review of Sociology, 18,* 373–393.

Heeter, C., & Greenberg, B. (1985). Cable and program choice. In D. Zillmann and J. Bryant (eds.), *Selective Exposure to Communication* (pp. 203–224). Hillsdale, NJ: Lawrence Erlbaum.

Herzog, H. (1944). Motivations and gratifications of daily serial listeners. In W. Schramm (ed.), *The Process and Effects of Mass Communication* (pp. 50–55). Urbana: University of Illinois Press.

Hill, A. (1997). *Shocking entertainment: Viewer response to violent movies.* Luton, Bedfordshire, England: University of Luton Press.

Katz, E. (1959). Mass communication research and the study of popular culture: An editorial note on a possible future for this journal. *Studies in Public Communication, 2,* 1–6.

Katz, E., Blumler, J. G., & Gurevitch, M. (1974). Utilization of mass communication by the individual. In J. G. Blumler and E. Katz (eds.), *The Uses of Mass Communications: Current Perspectives on Gratifications Research* (pp. 19–32). Beverly Hills, CA: Sage.

Katz, E., Gurevitch, M., & Haas, H. (1973). On the use of the mass media for important things. *American Sociological Review, 38,* 164–181.

Levy, M. R. (1978a). The audience experience with television news. *Journalism Monographs, 55.*

Levy, M. R. (1978b). Television news uses: A cross-national comparison. *Journalism Quarterly, 55,* 334–337.

Levy, M. R. (1980). Home video recorders: A user survey. *Journal of Communication, 30* (4), 23–25.

McQuail, D., Blumler, J. G., & Brown, J. R. (1972). The television audience: A revised perspective. In D. McQuail (ed.), *Sociology of Mass Communications* (pp. 135–165). Harmondsworth, UK: Penguin.

Perse, E. M., & Courtright, J. A. (1993). Normative images of communication media: Mass and interpersonal channels in the new media environment. *Human Communication Research, 19,* 485–503.

Perse, E. M., & Dunn, D. G. (1995, August). *The utility of home computers: Implications of multimedia and connectivity.* Paper presented at the annual meeting of the Association for Education in Journalism and Mass Communication, Communication Theory and Methodology Division, Washington, DC.

Riley, M. W., & Riley, J. W., Jr. (1951). A sociological approach to communications research. *Public Opinion Quarterly, 15,* 445–460.

Rubin, A. M. (1994). Media uses and effects: A uses-and-gratifications perspective. In J. Bryant and D. Zillmann (eds.), *Media Effects: Advances in Theory and Research* (417–436). Hillsdale, NJ: Lawrence Erlbaum.

Schramm, W., Lyle, J., & Parker, E. B. (1961). *Television in the Lives of Our Children.* Stanford, CA: Stanford University Press.

Weiss, W. (1971). Mass communication. *Annual Review of Psychology, 22,* 309–336.

RELATED LINKS

- Mass Media: Uses and Gratifications (http://www.cultsock.ndirect.co.uk/MUHome/cshtml/media/effects.html#uses)

- Uses and Gratifications of the Web Among College Students (http://www.ascusc.org/jcmc/vol6/issue1/ebersole.html)

- Why Do People Watch Television? (http://www.aber.ac.uk/media/Documents/short/usegrat.html)

FOR FURTHER RESEARCH

To find out more about the topics discussed in this reading, use InfoTrac College Edition. Type in keywords and subject terms such as "uses and gratifications," "the active audience," and "need satisfaction (sources of)." You can access InfoTrac from the Wadsworth/Thomson Communication Café homepage: http://communication.wadsworth.com.

PART II

≈

Convergence and Concentration in the Media Industries

Part II surveys the different ways in which media industries and technology companies are coping with digital convergence and corporate concentration. As the readings in Chapter 3 address, converging media are offering audiences more individualized choice than ever before, from interactive mechanisms for viewer and user feedback to enhanced content availability and nonlinear story-telling techniques. Rather than spelling the end of old media, digital convergence signals a new era of media cross–fertilization. Problems arise for companies like Sony, however, when the impulses of its electronics division to make content freely available across platforms clash with the interests of its music division to in-sert copyright protections and restraints on file use. With personal video recorder systems like TiVo, control over content and programming shifts from the networks to the viewer in a way that the broadcast industry has never before experienced— or allowed. For the movie industry, nonlinear editing systems are opening creative opportunities for filmmakers everywhere, while transforming the look and feel of Hollywood productions. From the background images in movies like *Cast Away* to the interaction between mythic characters in *Lord of the Rings,* digital effects are becoming more lifelike than ever and scenarios that were once possible only in fiction are now routine. The readings in Chapter 4 highlight concerns over media concentration, which have been raised by cultural critics with growing force. Fueled by a relaxation of ownership rules and the synergies made possible by convergence, the recent wave of media mergers raises questions about content diversity, the stifling of innovation, and the ability of industry to provide low-cost, high-bandwidth access to cyberspace.

3

Convergence, Content, and Interactivity

Reading 3-1

Convergence and Its Consequences
John Pavlik and Shawn McIntosh

EDITOR'S NOTE

Convergence, or the integration of computing, telecommunications, and broadcast media in a single digital environment, is in many ways revolutionizing mass media and communication. The changes involved in the transfer from an analog mass communication system to one based on digital platforms are nothing short of sweeping, as this reading from Converging Media *by John Pavlik and Shawn McIntosh lucidly explains. From interactive mechanisms for viewer and user feedback to enhanced content availability and nonlinear storytelling techniques, converging media are offering audiences more individualized choice than ever before. To take full advantage of the potential of digital media, communications professionals will have to learn new skills and be prepared to adapt to continual technological innovation and change. Terms highlighted in bold are defined in a glossary at the end of the reading.*

CONSIDER

1. Of the key differences between analog and digital media summarized in Table 3-1, which are the most important and why?
2. How, specifically, is convergence transforming the nature of mass communication, leading to a reexamination of the term "mass communication" itself?

3. In what ways do peer-to-peer file sharing sites such as Morpheus and Kazaa illustrate the power and possibilities of converging media?

The coming together of computing, telecommunications, and media in a digital environment is known as **convergence,** although scholars still do not agree on an exact and complete definition of the word. Convergence can also be used to mean the merging of Internet companies with traditional media companies, such as AOL with Time Warner. It can also be used in talking about specific types of media, such as print, audio, and video all converging into one digital media.

Even if a specific definition is still not agreed upon, convergence is transforming the very nature of mass communication, which of course has dramatic implications. These implications fall into four areas:

1. The content of communication.
2. The relationships between media organizations and their publics.
3. The structure of communication organizations.
4. How communications professionals do their work.

Convergence is leading to a complete reexamination of the term "mass" communication. This will be a major theme of this [reading], with a central premise being that although there will continue to be "mass" communication, in the sense that media companies and others will continue to produce messages for large audiences, frequently the members of those audiences may receive messages tailored to each individual, and audiences will become much more active in their engagement with mediated communication than they have been.

Fundamentally, convergence is transforming the kinds of media audiences have grown up with. In the pre-converged world of media, the process of mass communication consisted largely of a system of messages communicated through words, images, and sound. The converged media world still features these elements but brings with it new paradigms that are possible with digital, networked media.

From *Converging Media: An Introduction to Mass Communication,* pp. 19–28, by John Pavlik and Shawn McIntosh. Published by Allyn and Bacon, Boston, MA. Copyright © 2004 by Pearson Education. Reprinted with permission of the publisher.

CONVERGENCE AND COMMUNICATION CONTENT

Stories told in a digital, online medium can make connections with other types of content much more easily than in any other medium [see Readings 2-2 and 7-1]. This is done primarily through the use of **hyperlinks,** or clickable pointers to other online content. This is just as true for news content as it is for other forms of mass communication, including advertising, public relations, and entertainment. For example, advertisements in a digital, online environment permit visitors to click on interactive ads or even images of products in which they can be purchased directly online. Or, in entertainment programming, hyperlinked content allows a viewer to explore a story in a nonlinear narrative, where the outcome of a story may be unchanged, but the path one takes to get there is unpredictable.

Content is much more fluid, dynamic, rapid, and global in an online environment, which enables better representation of events and processes in real life. Moreover, it is increasingly possible to obtain communications and content on demand. In the traditional media world, news, entertainment, or marketing information was broadcast or published on a schedule solely determined by the publisher or broadcaster. Technology exists currently that would allow the audience to even choose from which camera angles they wish to watch a sporting event, for example, and switch between angles or watch their own replays during the game. This is not to say that everyone will want to—or should be a television director whenever they watch television. Sometimes passively consuming media is all a person wants. But that is not to say that simply being able to be a more active participant in the kind of content one is watching won't alter how mass communication content and media in general are perceived.

Digitization is transforming both how and when media organizations distribute their content. They are no longer distributing content solely through traditional channels and instead are delivering digital content via the Internet, satellite, and a host of other digital technologies. They are increasingly making that content available 24 hours a day, with news organizations updating the news almost continuously, and to a worldwide audience, leading to a reexamination of the tiered approach to distribution.

The production cycle and process is similarly being transformed by digital technology. In fact, the transformation may be even deeper in terms of media content production. Whether Hollywood motion pictures, television shows, news, books, magazines, newspapers, or online, the process of producing media content is rapidly becoming almost entirely digital. Movies are shot using digital cameras and edited on computers. Reporters working for television, radio, newspapers, or any other news operation capture their raw material with digital devices as well, editing their stories digitally. Even book authors typically write on a computer, with words increasingly remaining digital throughout the entire production process.

CONVERGENCE AND MEDIA ORGANIZATIONS' RELATIONSHIPS WITH THEIR AUDIENCE

The process of analog [non-digital] mass communication was largely one-way, from the source of a message to the receiver, or audience. The audience was relatively large, heterogeneous, and anonymous. Audience members had relatively few means by which to communicate either with each other on a mass scale or with the creators and publishers of mass communication content. Audiences in the age of convergence can communicate via e-mail, online forums, and other interactive media more easily and quickly with those who create and publish mass communication content. In addition, they can also create mass communication content themselves and reach far larger audiences for much lower costs than they could have with traditional media. They are generally not anonymous, although it is easy to create an online persona that bears little resemblance to one's real life.

Automation in digital media allows for mass communication organizations to keep detailed and automatically updated records on their audiences as they track their paths within their Web sites through intelligent software agents and programs known as **cookies,** which allow a Web site to recognize when a previous user comes to the Web site and gives them personalized content. This is invaluable information for media organizations to better understand an audience's media behaviors, preferences, and habits.

INCREASED MEDIA CONSUMPTION

As the media system continues to evolve toward a digital future, audience demand for media is growing. The "15th Annual Communications Industry Forecast," prepared by Veronis Suhler, showed that audiences were consuming more and more media as part of their daily lives.[1] The report indicated that the average person in the United States would spend 10.3 hours per day with various forms of information and entertainment media by the end of 2004, an increase of an hour since 1999. Notably, U.S. media consumers are shifting away from the use of traditional news and entertainment sources, including newspapers, magazines, broadcast television, and radio—media traditionally supported primarily by advertising. Audiences are shifting their media consumption toward digital media and consumer-supported media, such as cable and satellite television, books, and the Internet. Advertiser-supported media made up 69.1 percent of total media consumption in 1995 and just 60.9 percent in 1999; and the percentage is expected to fall to 54.7 percent by the end of 2004.

ACTIVE MEDIA PRODUCTION AND DISTRIBUTION

Digital media make it easier than ever for the public to create and distribute media content, whether it is an original drawing done using illustration software, an animation or video, or a song sampled and mixed from current hits by famous recording artists.

Writing and music have led the way in media consumers creating content, although in music especially remixes of previously recorded (and copyrighted) music are more common than an amateur copying passages from a number of famous books and claiming it as his or her own work. Even before it became possible to download songs and send music files over the Internet, music fans were rerecording their favorite artists onto blank audio cassettes and making "garage band" recordings. Although by today's standards it was a laborious process, individuals could create music remixes of songs from their favorite band, for example, or certain songs from a variety of favorite artists. Distributing numerous copies of these tapes was usually too expensive and labor intensive to be worthwhile, and making subsequent copies from the copies noticeably reduced the sound quality, which is not the case in the digital world.

DISTRIBUTION ALTERS THE BALANCE OF POWER

Audiences are increasingly active in their communication both with each other and with the creators of mass communication content [see Readings 1-3, 2-2, and 2-4]. This gives them much greater control over what media they consume and shifts some of the power away from media organizations providing content and toward the audience. Through **viral marketing,** the online equivalent of word-of-mouth advertising, a popular Web site's product or piece of content can potentially reach millions of online users in a very short time, all without corporate promotion or advertising. The success of **peer-to-peer** file-sharing programs such as Morpheus and Kazaa are examples of how an Internet audience shifts the balance of power away from media organizations, even though those organizations are the ones that created and provided that content in the first place.

Audiences aren't willing to wait for the evening news or the next day's paper for developments in a breaking story. "When you don't have access to radio or TV, the Internet is the best news source," said Jarvis Mak, a senior Internet analyst for NetRatings. "It can become, in a way, your immediately updated newspaper."[2]

Audiences can get their information and entertainment from literally thousands of sources around the world. Audiences aren't content to sit back and listen in silence to what the media report. They want their own voices to be heard. The Internet enables audiences around the world to participate in a global dialog about the world's events and issues and can bring individuals into direct contact with each other, though separated by thousands of miles and political and cultural boundaries. It is not clear what the net effect of this sea change in communication will be, but it is clear the foundation is being laid for a more connected and engaged global public.

FRAGMENTATION AND "THE DAILY ME"

These changes are not without some dangers, however. Actively choosing the media you want to see, hear, or read can narrow the scope of news items or entertainment that may be encountered by accident that unintentionally engage or entertain. Former MIT Media

Lab director, the late Michael Dertouzos, called the specialization of news to one's specific interests "The Daily Me." This phenomenon could fragment audiences into small groups of like-minded individuals who do not interact with other groups or with society as a whole and choose to receive only the news and information that reinforces their beliefs and values. Media fragmentation has already been a trend in analog media, and digital media can easily accelerate that trend. Cass Sunstein, law scholar and author of *Republic.com,* voices similar concerns over the social effects in a democratic society when media audiences become increasingly fragmented and stop discussing broad social and political issues [see Reading 9-4].

However, personalization and localization of news does have benefits in potentially getting the public to become more engaged in news and in helping them become better informed about current events. Making better connections between news analysis and primary source materials is one of the most important developments in online journalism. It is important because it helps to place stories in better context and can hold journalists accountable for their reporting by enabling the audience to compare a journalist's report with the actual primary source material about which he or she is reporting. This may help slow or even reverse the steady decline in credibility suffered by U.S. news organizations during the past quarter century.

Consider how MSNBC on the Web incorporated customization capability into its reporting. On its cable channel, MSNBC transmitted a report about the five most dangerous roads in America. On its Web site, not only did MSNBC provide the text of this report, but producers linked to a federal traffic database that permitted visitors to the site to enter a ZIP code and obtain traffic fatality data for that community and see which roads are the most dangerous in their town. Within 24 hours, the site had logged 68,000 visitors interested in learning about the most dangerous roads in their own communities.

Table 3-1 summarizes the qualities of mass communication in the pre-converged (analog) and post-converged (online, digital) media worlds.

CONVERGENCE AND COMMUNICATIONS ORGANIZATIONS

In the pre-converged world, centralized media organizations created and published or broadcast content on predetermined schedules. A newspaper was printed

Table 3-1. Analog versus Digital Mass Communication

	Analog Mass Communication	Digital Mass Communication
Audience	Large, heterogeneous, anonymous, private. Bounded by geographic, cultural, and political boundaries. Passively read, watch, and listen to media to gratify needs.	Fragmented, homogeneous, known, and addressable, erosion of privacy. Geographic, political, and cultural boundaries less important. Increasingly active in consumption, creation, and participation in media.
Feedback	Few mechanisms for audience feedback and generally slow.	Instant, increasingly extensive through e-mail, online discussion forums.
Functions	Surveillance, correlation, cultural transmission, entertainment, marketing/advertising, mobilization.	Surveillance, correlation, cultural transmission, entertainment, e-commerce, mobilization.
Program/content availability	Centrally controlled schedule. One-way, dominated by centralized content providers.	Decreasingly centrally controlled schedule. Increasingly on-demand from a diverse array of voices. Less dominated by centralized content providers, often times many-to-many and audience-created.
Government regulation	Extensive for electronic, audio-visual media, little for print.	Little for print, reduced for traditional electronic media but uncertain and still evolving.
Storytelling	Stories are linear and static (i.e., they are fixed in print, on film or magnetic tape) and designed for mass audiences; modalities of expression are limited to those possible in each analog medium.	Linear and nonlinear, multimedia, interactive, exploratory, customizable, and dynamic. Content creator is more like a guide to knowledge, information, entertainment, and discovery.
Distribution channels	Separate, analog, one-to-many. Usually physical products.	Increasingly convergent, digital, many-to-many. Often not physical products.

and distributed within a certain period of time; a television broadcast appeared within a given time slot. Centralized means media organizations where content production and distribution, as well as marketing and other functions, are controlled by a central unit or individual. Internet-based media can be less centralized. Many divisions may determine the design or content of individual Web pages of an overall Web site. Web-based media are certainly not exempt from the economic consolidation of all mass media, but the nature of the Web permits more flexibility and adaptability in publishing or webcasting content.

SOCIAL, POLITICAL, AND ECONOMIC PRESSURES

The digital media system is a product of more than simply technological change. Economic, cultural, and political influences also are reshaping media, just as they have ever since Gutenberg printed his first Bible in 1455.

Governments, both domestic and international, regulate most media in an attempt to shape or control them or their content. This is true whether in the ana-

log or digital worlds of media. Broadcast media have traditionally been subject to extensive government regulation, whereas U.S. print media have been relatively free of government regulation, with strong legal independence established in the First Amendment to the Constitution of the United States.

Yet, in the digital, online realm, even "print" media organizations become subject to greater government regulation, whether in the United States or internationally. As newspapers move from the analog to the digital world and their products reach an increasingly global audience transmitted via satellite, telephone, or cable lines, they are finding themselves increasingly subject to international rules, regulations, and restrictions foreign governments may place upon the Internet. Libel and obscenity laws differ widely between countries, raising the question of whose version of libel should be used when an article published on the Internet libels someone according to local laws. Likewise, should Internet communication be considered under telephone regulations, because many people access it through telephone lines, or regulated according to the cable industry, because it is also available through cable modems? These are just some examples in which digital technology and convergence have sped ahead of our current legal framework.

CONCENTRATION OF MEDIA OWNERSHIP

Although there are many public service media, most media companies throughout the world try to make a profit. Many media companies are among the most profitable private enterprises in the world, with average profit margins often in excess of 20 percent a year—double the average for other industries.

Concentration of media ownership has been a growing trend in the analog world, and the same process is taking place in the digital media world. Convergence is in some ways fuelling media concentration, by leading traditional media giants such as Time Warner to join with an online colossus such as America Online, giving way in 2001 to AOL Time Warner. Although by mid-2002, with plummeting stock prices and executive shake-ups at a number of media giants such as AOL Time Warner [now called Time Warner] and Vivendi, some media analysts were saying that they moved too rapidly toward convergence without first figuring out a good business model. However, the trend is clear: Analog and digital media are rapidly being consolidated into the hands of a few, very large, very powerful, and very rich owners, an economic structure referred to as an **oligopoly** [see the readings in Chapter 4]. These media enterprises today are increasingly likely to be part of large, global media organizations publicly owned and accountable to shareholders whose main interest is the financial bottom line.

This centralized control over the signs and symbols of mediated communication can threaten the numbers and types of different voices heard on the Web. Inclusivity, diversity, and plurality of voices, both mainstream and marginal, have felt the increasing squeeze of global corporate owners eager to turn a double-digit profit in the online digital world. The trend is especially worrisome when a company can also control the means of distribution, such as Time Warner with its control of online access through America Online, the largest Internet Service Provider (ISP) in the United States, and through their Time Warner cable system with Time Warner's large amount of media content.

CONVERGENCE AND COMMUNICATIONS PROFESSIONALS

With all the changes brought to mass communication because of convergence, it is obvious that the way communications professionals do their jobs will also change.

Just as the differences between print, video, and audio largely disappear in a digital media world, so will the divisions between print and electronic journalists, advertising and public relations professionals. Although it is likely journalists will still emphasize one or another field, print journalists will need to learn aspects of electronic journalism and electronic journalists will have to learn more about aspects of print journalism in order to fully utilize the digital media environment. Advertising and public relations professionals will have to learn how to best attract the attention of a public that encounters ever more media and in which the public is more active than in the past.

Just what constitutes a television or radio receiver, or TV or radio programming, is in a state of flux. Once it was simple. Radio programming was what a listener heard on a radio. Today, however, there are radio stations that transmit their programming via the Internet and listeners tune in via their computers. Moreover, these radio stations can include images, graphics, text, and video. For example, some Voice of America radio reporters have been trained in digital video shooting and editing and can now be "VJs," or videojournalists, webcasting their stories visually as well as through audio. With little more than a small digital video camera and a laptop computer with video editing software, journalists can now shoot, edit, and produce a professional-quality news video segment.

But in order to take advantage of digital media, new skills will have to be learned, and it will be more important than ever that the fundamental principles and ethics of each profession are not abandoned in the march toward the digital environment.

GLOSSARY

convergence   the coming together of computing, telecommunications, and media in a digital environment. Convergence and the changes it is bringing are fundamentally changing many aspects of mass media and communication.

cookie   information that a Web site puts on a user's local hard drive so that it can recognize when that computer accesses the Web site again. Cookies allow for conveniences like password recognition and personalization.

hyperlink   a word, graphic, or image that is linked through HTML code to another Web page or media element either within the same Web site or in a different Web site on the World Wide Web.

oligopoly an economic structure in which a few very large, very powerful, and very rich owners control an industry or series of related industries.

peer-to-peer (P2P) a computer communications model in which all users have equal abilities to store, send, and accept communications from other users.

viral marketing spreading news and information about media content through word-of-mouth, usually via online discussion groups, chats, and e-mails, without utilizing traditional advertising and marketing methods.

NOTES

1. Veronis Suhler Releases 15th Annual Communications Industry Forecast. Retrieved May 15, 2002, from http://www.veronissuhler.com/publications.

2. Grenier, Melinda Patterson (updated 2002, January 16). Record Number of Office Workers Use Webcasts Last Month. *The Wall Street Journal Online*. Retrieved May 15, 2002, from http://online.wsj.com/public/us.

RELATED LINKS

- Converging Media: An Introduction to Mass Communication (http://wps.ablongman.com/ab_pavlik_convgmedia_1)

- Lectures for *The News Lab* (http://www.columbia.edu/~jp35/newslab/lectures/all_lectures.html)

- News Lab: The Center for New Media (http://www.columbia.edu/~jp35/newslab)

- Poynter Online—Convergence Chaser (http://www.poynter.org/dg.lts/id.56/aid.40727/column.htm)

FOR FURTHER RESEARCH

To find out more about the topics discussed in this reading, use InfoTrac College Edition. Type in keywords and subject terms such as "media convergence," "peer-to-peer communication," and "oligopoly." You can access InfoTrac College Edition from the Wadsworth/Thomson Communication Café homepage: http://communication.wadsworth.com.

Reading 3-2

The Civil War Inside Sony

Frank Rose

EDITOR'S NOTE

Among media conglomerates, Sony is in a unique position: It is perhaps the only international media company to have a major stake in both consumer electronics and entertainment, including movies, music, television, and videogames. The company's split personality is not without its problems, however. As Frank Rose writes in this article from Wired *magazine, "Sony's electronics side needs to let customers move files around effortlessly, but its entertainment side wants to build in restraints, because it sees every customer as a potential thief," that is, a nonpaying file-sharer. The tension between cross-platform file-sharing, preferred by Sony Electronics, and strict copyright protections, preferred by Sony Music, have put the company's internal divisions at odds. Sony Music wants to entertain you. Sony Electronics wants to equip you. The problem is that when it comes to digital media, their interests are diametrically opposed. This reading explains how the company is desperately trying to resolve this predicament (and overcome its fear of piracy) before a third party like Microsoft waltzes in and sets the new standard for the next generation of audio-video operating systems.*

CONSIDER

1. Should Sony Music give in to the desire of Sony Electronics and allow free and unfettered file-sharing across different platforms—why or why not?

2. To get around this problem, should Sony sell off its entertainment divisions and be content as an electronics manufacturer?

3. Why is the "security/digital rights management/copyright arena" a critical battlefield for media and technology companies, as the CEO of Sony Corporation of America claims?

For Keiji Kimura, the problem is small enough to fit in his pocket and just heavy enough to weigh on his mind. Kimura is a senior VP at Sony headquarters in Tokyo, and the problem in question is Apple's iPod, the snappy little music player that's revolutionizing consumer electronics the way Sony's Walkman did some 20 years ago. By rights, Sony should own the portable player business. The company's first hit product, back in the '50s, was the transistor radio, the tinny-sounding invention that took rock and roll out of the house and away from the parents and allowed the whole Elvis thing to happen. A quarter-century later, the Walkman enabled the kids of the '70s to take their tapes and tune out the world. But the 21st-century Walkman doesn't bother with tapes or CDs or minidiscs; it stores hundreds of hours of music on its own hard drive. And it sports an Apple logo.

"It's a good product," Kimura says of the iPod. "It's exciting. I am positive the hard disk is a key device that will change our lifestyle."

A broad-shouldered man with a shock of thick black hair and a ready smile, Kimura is in charge of nearly every Sony device that's portable, from laptops and handhelds to Handycams and Walkmans. And he's right: When the average consumer has a hard disk not just in the PC but in the set-top box and in half a dozen other gizmos—all connected by wireless networks that zap their contents painlessly from one to another—life will be richer. In fact, this is the vision his boss, Sony

president Kunitake Ando, laid out more than a year ago as the company's core strategy.

Ando wants nothing less than for Sony to reinvent itself. But that will never happen as long as the company is frozen by its fear of piracy. Sony's digital Walkman device is a good example. Where the iPod simply lets you sync its contents with the music collection on your personal computer, Walkman users are hamstrung by laborious "check-in/check-out" procedures designed to block illicit file-sharing. And a Walkman with a hard drive? Not likely, since Sony's copy-protection mechanisms don't allow music to be transferred from one hard drive to another—not an issue with the iPod. "We do not have any plans for such a product," says Kimura, the smile fading. "But we are studying it."

Really? No plans? When the world leader in consumer electronics takes a pass on the hottest portable music player out there, you have to wonder what gives. Sony became a global giant on the basis of innovative devices manufactured by the millions on nothing more than a hunch that people would buy them. Now Apple is delivering the innovation while Sony studies the matter.

What's changed since the original Walkman debuted is that Sony became the only conglomerate to be in both consumer electronics and entertainment. As a result, it's conflicted: Sony's electronics side needs to let customers move files around effortlessly, but its entertainment side wants to build in restraints, because it sees every customer as a potential thief. The company's internal divisions reflect those in the marketplace, where entertainment executives have declared war on consumers over file-sharing. But Sony's position is unique. It can settle the fight and flourish, or do nothing and be hobbled.

From "The Civil War Inside Sony" by Frank Rose, *Wired,* February 2003, pp. 100–103, 136–137. Copyright © 2003 The Condé Nast Publications Inc. All rights reserved. Reprinted with permission.

Instead, it's tried to play both sides. As a member of the Consumer Electronics Association, Sony [Electronics] joined the chorus of support for Napster against the legal onslaught from Sony [Music] and the other music giants seeking to shut it down. As a member of the RIAA [Recording Industry Association of America], Sony [Music] railed against companies like Sony [Electronics] that manufacture CD burners. And it isn't just through trade associations that Sony is acting out its schizophrenia. Sony [Music] shipped a Celine Dion CD with a copy-protection mechanism that kept it from being played on Sony PCs. Sony [Music] even joined the music industry's suit against Launch Media, an Internet radio service that was part-owned by—you guessed it—Sony. Two other labels have since resolved their differences with Launch, but Sony Music continues the fight, even though Sony Electronics has been one of Launch's biggest advertisers and Launch is now part of Yahoo!, with which Sony has formed a major online partnership. It's as if hardware and entertainment have lashed two legs together and set off on a three-legged race, stumbling headlong into the future.

This is not how it's supposed to work.

Outside Sony's surprisingly modest Tokyo headquarters, traffic is backed up as usual on the gently curving street people call Sony Avenue. Here, in the tree-shaded neighborhood of Gotenyama Heights, the company's home since 1947, its presence looms so large the whole area is known as Sony Village. Gracious houses with blue-tile roofs are folded into the hills alongside humble storefronts and Sony's utilitarian white tile-and-stucco office buildings. This is an outfit with 168,000 employees and annual sales of $57 billion. As president, Kunitake Ando hopes to transform Sony into a company that doesn't just sell entertainment as well as hardware but delivers it in digital form to products that are part of in-home networks. "If we can combine the strength of hardware and the strength of entertainment, we could build a unique business model," Ando says excitedly, his wide grin and even wider glasses making him seem more like an overeager kid than the second in command to CEO Nobuyuki Idei. It's a bold strategy built on a big if.

As an electronics company, Sony makes some of the coolest gadgets on the planet, even without an iPod. In its last fiscal year, it sold a staggering 56 million of them: 19 million Walkmans, 6 million stereos, 10 million television sets, 5 million video players, 4 million PCs, 4 million computer screens, 5 million camcorders, 3 million digital cameras—some $36 bil-

lion worth in all. Year after year, it beats out the likes of Ford and Coca-Cola to top the Harris Poll of brands Americans consider the best. "Wow-type products—that's Sony," Ando exclaims, waving his arms as he sits perched on the edge of his chair in a mammoth conference room. "I call it the power of hardware."

The problem of hardware is more like it, because for all this, Sony lost money on the stuff. Japan's consumer electronics giants are being squeezed by upstarts in China, Taiwan, and Korea, where manufacturing costs are far cheaper. Without entertainment, which provided 30 percent of the company's revenue and nearly all its profits, Sony would be as bad off as Matsushita, NEC, and Toshiba, its traditional Japanese rivals. "The big dinosaurs are struggling to survive," Ando admits. "And Sony is one of them, of course."

On the entertainment side, Sony is one of seven global media conglomerates that dominate the industry. The weakest link is its New York–based music arm, where sales are dropping despite hits from Jennifer Lopez, Shakira, Bruce Springsteen, and the Dixie Chicks. (A separate Japanese label is doing slightly better.) Sony Pictures is Hollywood's hottest studio, producing blockbusters like *Spider-Man* and *Men in Black II* along with some of America's top soap operas, popular sitcoms in Germany, and hit movies in China. And Sony's PlayStation unit, located in Tokyo, is the undisputed king of videogames, leading the industry in sales of game consoles and software despite a determined onslaught from Microsoft.

The theory behind Ando's "ubiquitous value network," as his strategy has awkwardly been dubbed, is that the whole company will get a lift by enabling content to move freely through its hardware. Gadgets increase in value to consumers as they're linked to other gadgets; digital delivery of entertainment creates the tantalizing possibility of luring those same consumers into a direct sales relationship. But the different entertainment units have a hard time talking with one another, much less with the sprawling electronics operations in Tokyo, San Diego, New Jersey, and Berlin. "Sony is not one company, it's about 50 companies, and there's nothing other than the CEO's office to bring them together," says Frank Sanda, CEO of Japan Communications, which provides mobile phone services to Japanese corporations. "I'm a student of Sony—I like and admire it. But it's a bunch of vertical poles that don't even hit one another in the breeze because they're too far apart."

Ando knows that things are awry. "Our intent is to

provide rich content and services to users without any frustration, without any stress," he says. "Initially, because of our content group, we tried to protect the rights of labels and artists too much, so this made it very difficult for consumers to use the machine. Now we know that for the industry to grow, we have to find an optimum balance point. We have to consider ease of use for consumers but at the same time protect content holders' rights. We think it's almost an advantage for Sony that we have both—we can understand the content side and we have hardware, so we can start thinking about this way ahead."

But the entertainment and electronics industries were at odds long before Sony tried to marry the two. Sony and the Dutch electronics firm Philips pioneered digital music two decades ago with the development of the CD, only to have music-industry execs attack it as an incitement to piracy and a threat to vinyl. Meanwhile, Universal and Disney were suing Sony over its new Betamax videocassette recorder, which they claimed promoted illegal copying as well. The overheated rhetoric was a dress rehearsal for today's music piracy debate: The president of Universal called Sony's top U.S. executive a highwayman on national television, while Jack Valenti, Hollywood's lobbyist in Washington, compared the VCR to the Boston strangler.

In the end, of course, these technologies created a bonanza for show business. CDs triggered years of double-digit sales increases as people rushed out to replace their records; home video now accounts for 40 percent of Hollywood's worldwide film revenue, more than double its box office take. But while Sony scored big with its CD players, it lost out on the VCR when Betamax was eclipsed by VHS. So in the late '80s, with the minidisc in development and cofounder Akio Morita convinced that Betamax would have won if he'd controlled a film library, the company spent billions to buy CBS Records and Columbia Pictures.

Later, when profligacy and mismanagement resulted in a $3 billion write-off, Sony's enthusiasm for the American media business faded: Reached on the golf course in January 2000 with the shocking news that AOL and Time Warner would merge, Idei told Sony's North American chief it was "a regional problem." As things turned out, it was.

Now, with the AOL Time Warner deal an acknowledged fiasco [indeed, the company is now just called Time Warner], Sony is on the front lines of digital convergence. The job of making a business out of entertainment and hardware combined falls to Sony's

chief strategist, Yuki Nozoe. Having spent several years at the company's Hollywood studio, Nozoe is one of the few in the inner circle who know both sides of the business. Sony has more than 100 online offerings up or in development in various spots on the globe—sites for videogames, video-on-demand, soap operas, even insurance. (Sony is one of Japan's biggest insurers.) Most are designed for broadband, which means they might just about be ready by the time the world switches over from dialup.

What works now is music, so chief among the prototypes for Sony's vision of the future are sites like bitmusic in Japan and pressplay, a joint venture with Universal Music in the U.S. But pressplay has delivered a hapless performance to date. Subscribers face a complicated set of limits on what they can do with the music they buy, and until recently they weren't able to get anything at all from Warner, EMI, or BMG, which have a competing joint venture called MusicNet with even tougher restrictions.

So pressplay subscribers haven't even topped the 50,000 mark, while Kazaa, the leading file-sharing service, has 60 million users.

Nozoe appears unfazed. He considers everything an experiment, and he isn't counting on any one service to succeed on its own. Sitting in his nondescript office overlooking the flat, harborside district of Shinagawa, where gleaming new Sony towers rise above rail yards and worker quarters, he points to a small vase of flowers on the windowsill and says, "A single service may not attract many customers. But when it becomes a bouquet . . . "

Moments later, a woman's voice emerges from his office walls. It's 3 pm, break time at Sony factories throughout Japan, and the voice implores us to stand up, stretch, relax. It's been saying this for decades, ever since Akio Morita decreed it. Set to ethereal Japanese music, the message exudes an eerie calm, but it's a ghost from the industrial past, a reminder of how far Sony still has to go.

Idei has been focused on making Sony able to compete in an age of digitally networked products almost from the moment he was named president in 1995. "He had a vision that AV and IT would merge someday," says Ando, who was a Sony insurance executive before Idei put him in charge of a project to break into the personal computer market. "We knew that everything must be connected." The product that resulted, an entertainment-oriented PC that was named Vaio, for video-audio integrated operation, was a big success in Japan, and eventually it made inroads in the U.S. After Idei was named CEO in 1999, he made Ando president and put veterans of the Vaio team, like Keiji Kimura, in charge of key divisions. The message was clear: IT rules.

Now Sony offers PCs with a variety of standard networking options—USB, Bluetooth, 802.11b (known in the U.S. as Wi-Fi) and its heftier cousin 802.11a, which has the bandwidth to handle high-quality video—as well as portable gadgets, like Handycams and the NetMD Walkman, that connect to them. Yet many products don't link well. Take the NetMD Walkman: Not only does it rely on a painfully slow USB 1.0 connection to transfer music to and from a PC, but it's bound by the rules set by Sony's copy-protection software, OpenMG. Introduced in 1999, OpenMG is responsible for the cumbersome check-in/check-out process and for other, even more annoying restrictions, like no copying of MP3 files without a time-consuming conversion to Sony's proprietary Atrac3 format.

Other products don't connect at all, among them Sony's new high-end car audio system, which combines a standard CD player with an in-dash hard drive. A hit in Japan and just introduced in the U.S., it lets you rip CDs to your car stereo and leave the originals at home—a big deal to anybody who's ever tried to dig under the seat for a lost disc while driving. Strangely, though, you can't connect it to a Walkman or to anything else. Kimura, the man in charge of these gadgets, certainly sees Wi-Fi in Sony's car-audio future: He's excited about the idea that you could go online when you pull into a gas-station hot spot, or download a customized mix of songs from your PC before you leave the garage. But since OpenMG doesn't yet permit file transfers from one hard drive to another, that's out for now. "We have many things to resolve," Kimura acknowledges. "Protection is one side of it—of course we have to protect our copyrights. But the challenge is how to excite the user."

Twelve time zones from Tokyo, at Sony Music headquarters in the upper reaches of a postmodern skyscraper in midtown Manhattan, you'd need a nanometer to detect much urgency about developing online services that give fans what they want. "There is a desire for the industry to live in a world of digital delivery as well as packaged goods," maintains Fred Ehrlich, the label's head of new technology. "But you have a lot of forces that need to be aligned." By "a lot of forces," Ehrlich means everything: How much can the labels

charge? Should they charge by the month or by the song? Should they offer streams or burns or downloads? How long should a download last? How many devices should you be able to play it on? And so on, until you've reinvented the entire business.

Within the music industry, Sony is regarded as the technology leader, the one the other labels look to on issues like peer-to-peer [P2P] distribution—if anyone can figure out how to adapt Napster-like technology for authorized downloads, the thinking goes, it's Sony. And Ehrlich, a nonpracticing attorney whose job is to evaluate the business potential of things like P2P, is considered one of the more forward-thinking people within Sony Music. "Tommy Mottola doesn't understand any of this stuff," says an insider, referring to the label's CEO. "He wants it all to go away. Fred sees where it's headed." But Sony also has a reputation as the most aggressive label legally, as exemplified by the massive breach-of-contract suit it filed last year against the Dixie Chicks when they claimed accounting irregularities. (The dispute was settled out of court after the group countersued, alleging "systematic thievery" by the label.) Put these two impulses together and you have a company that understands the future just well enough to go after every nickel it can get.

The key issue is online services—who'll own them, what they'll offer, and how much they'll cost. The Big Five labels staked their claims early on but divided into two rival camps; only now are all five agreeing to offer their output through both. Major acts like Radiohead have flatly refused to make their music available online, though file-swapping sites are of course beyond their control. And independent providers like Listen.com have trouble getting releases while they're hot: Months after the latest Springsteen album was on pressplay, for example, Listen still hadn't gotten clearance to offer it. The site's founder, Rob Reid, downplays the idea that the delay could be deliberate. But the Justice Department has been investigating both pressplay and MusicNet, and the judge who shut down Napster agreed to look into charges of collusion, declaring that the two ventures "look bad, sound bad, and smell bad."

Users of online services are offered only "tethered" downloads, which come with limitations on how files can be copied or burned to a CD, or transferred to a portable player. It's as if Macy's used anti-shoplifting tags to set limits on how many times your pants could be put in a suitcase or where you could go in them. "The idea of crippling legal music services is so completely misplaced I have a hard time getting inside the logic of it," Reid says. Some day, Ehrlich concedes, on-line music will offer the same flexibility you get with a CD—you'll be able to keep it forever and play it anywhere.

"I just don't think it's right now," he adds.

Comments like this explain why industry execs are considered emotionally incapable of facing the future. But there are other obstacles, and pricing is one of the biggest. When the labels offer downloads or burns, they effectively set the price at $1 per song—about the cost on a CD. User surveys show that something like 50 cents would be more realistic. But the labels don't want to undercut the retail chains that sell CDs, even if that's what it takes for Web-based services to thrive. "In theory, Sony Music would like all these services to become successful," Erlich says. "But we look at the business based on the past, while the services compete against the online world, where music has been free. It's a dance for both parties to understand each other."

Yet another hot-button issue is Internet radio, which is supposed to be just like broadcast radio except you get it online. If only it were that simple. Radio stations can play any song they want, while interactive services like pressplay have to get clearance for the songs they offer. Hence Sony's suit against Yahoo! Launch, which it argues is not a radio station but an interactive service, because it lets listeners specify which artists and genres they want to hear. Then there's the question of whether online stations should have to pay royalties when U.S. broadcast stations do not. With broadcast radio controlled by two conglomerates that keep extremely limited playlists coast to coast while sucking up hundreds of millions each year in promo fees, you'd think the labels would embrace Internet radio as a cheap way to break new talent. But they want to collect royalties, even if it means sending Net stations under.

"If you're looking for logic in this situation—hey, it's the music business," says Launch founder Dave Goldberg. "There's not a lot of logic in what they do." But to Ehrlich, the logic is in not letting another company play music gratis when it could be paying. Precedents matter: If broadcast radio hadn't been exempted from royalty payments decades ago, for reasons hardly anyone can remember, the music industry could be collecting an extra $2 billion or so a year. "It's hard to change the old world," Ehrlich declares.

"But that doesn't mean you can't change the new world."

Sony's transformation into a combined electronics and entertainment powerhouse [is foreshadowed by some of its new products]. There's CoCoon, a personal audio-video recorder that has a hard drive and can be programmed from a mobile phone. There's Room-Link, a networking hub that lets you stream video from a Vaio to a Sony Wega TV (both are already available in Japan). More important, perhaps, Sony is developing a new version of OpenMG that's supposed to make it easier to transfer files from one device to another.

The new OpenMG is one of the fruits of a program Ando and Idei started more than a year ago to get everybody at Sony working in harmony. Known internally as Symphony, the effort began with a content and technology committee that meets a few times a year—October in New York, May in Tokyo; Nozoe and Ehrlich and a couple dozen other top execs, Japanese and American, together in a room trying to hash out the company's issues. "With the arrival of digital everything, you can't get away from each other," says Howard Stringer, CEO of Sony Corp. of America, which includes the music label and film studio. "We all have to invent the business plan for the future. And even though we have sides of Sony that will disagree, finding a consensus is Sony's style."

The grunt work on the copy-protection issue is done by a subcommittee that includes Takayuki Sasaki, who heads the division in charge of OpenMG. Sasaki reports to Nozoe, who's told Sony hardware execs they can't make their decisions in a vacuum. At a meeting last May, "the content guys beat the hell out of Sasaki" because they wanted additional capabilities built into the software, says one executive. What they covet is flexibility—the ability to set the rules any way they like. "You want to be able to control the distribution of music," Ehrlich explains. "If you want to say it can go to two devices, you can do that. If you want it to time out after 30 days, you can do that."

At this point, one might reasonably conclude that Sony doesn't need a symphony, it needs some head-banging.

With OpenMG X, the version being developed, Sony will no longer set blanket rules for its own devices; it's created a digital rights management system that works on any manufacturer's hardware and allows the content owner to set the rules. Sony wants OpenMG X to be accepted across the entertainment industry—an ambition that puts it face-to-face with Microsoft. "The whole security/digital rights management/copyright arena is a critical battlefield," Stringer declares. "We're racing—*racing*—to get to a solution that has an open standard so that Microsoft doesn't waltz in and develop the audio–video operating system."

A digital rights management system isn't just a traffic cop; it's a powerful tool that gathers all kinds of information about consumers, from credit card numbers to listening habits, and dictates which devices can talk to the PC and how. Microsoft's DRM software, a key feature of its Windows Media platform, promises total flexibility for entertainment companies, and it's designed to work not just on PCs but with consumer gadgets like Sony's. "If it is the de facto standard for all digital rights management," says Stringer, "then at some point it migrates into all the networked devices, including the television set and everything else. Sony's nightmare is that the TV set becomes a monitor."

This puts Sony in a bind. Except for the Xbox, Microsoft doesn't really sell hardware. All it has to do is keep entertainment executives happy and watch them adopt its DRM platform. If Sony fails to offer every bondage option the entertainment folks can imagine for their customers, it opens the door for Microsoft to take control of its hardware. But if Sony's devices don't break out of the DRM straitjacket, it could be overtaken by manufacturers with less to lose—like Apple. To save its electronics business and make its dream of digital services a reality, Sony needs a system that doesn't punish consumers yet somehow satisfies the entertainment industry. It needs to square the circle on digital rights.

Sony thinks OpenMG X is a step in that direction. But there's no indication that other entertainment companies would rather have Sony control DRM than Microsoft—which is why Sony recently partnered with Philips to buy InterTrust, a struggling Silicon Valley outfit that holds key DRM patents. Years ago, Sony and Philips jointly developed the CD and licensed it so widely that it became an industry standard. Now they hope to do something similar with DRM

technology, so that all such systems, Sony's included, can work interchangeably. A bonus twist is that InterTrust is suing Microsoft in its own intellectual property dispute. InterTrust maintains—and Redmond [the location of Microsoft's headquarters] vigorously denies —that Microsoft illegally appropriated its DRM algorithms for the Windows Media platform. Should InterTrust win the suit, Sony and Philips could bring Microsoft into the fold as well. But Sony won't win with consumers until its two halves, electronics and entertainment, join forces to offer online services with all the freedom consumers already enjoy offline.

The stakes are huge—and yet if Sony pulls it off, the company will be unrecognizable in a few years. The networked devices and services being developed now are just an interim step. "Nobody can create a clear picture of what is a winning business model for 2010," says Idei. "The reality is transformation and constant change. We are on the sea of uncertainty, but sometimes there are small islands, and we have to navigate our company to the nearest. There are many, many Internet business trials at Sony, because we don't know if we can find a small island we want to go to, and this is the way."

Idei's ultimate goal is more distant and more radical: the dematerialization of Sony and its products. Instead of boxes stuffed with electronics, Sony will sell screens. Instead of CDs, Sony will sell sound. Ken Kutaragi, the creator of Sony's PlayStation, has made a deal with IBM and Toshiba to develop a "supercomputer on a chip" that can power network servers, pumping games with stunning 3-D graphics to Sony devices no bigger than a wristwatch. This is the future Idei envisions: invisible, interactive networks that bring sound and light to almost any nearby surface. Sony networks, Sony sound and light, Sony surfaces. If only it didn't depend on a bunch of music men who've yet to wean themselves from shiny plastic discs.

RELATED LINKS

- Sony.com (http://www.sony.com)

- Playstation.com (http://www.us.playstation.com)

- Apple iPod (http://www.apple.com/ipod)

- Apple iTunes (http://www.apple.com/itunes)

- MusicNet (http://www.musicnet.com)

- Rhapsody Digital Music Service (http://www.listen.com)

FOR FURTHER RESEARCH

To find out more about the topics discussed in this reading, use InfoTrac College Edition. Type in keywords and subject terms such as "tethered downloads," "audio-video operating system," and "interactive networks." You can access InfoTrac College Edition from the Wadsworth/Thomson Communication Café homepage: http://communication.wadsworth.com.

Reading 3-3

The Fast-Forward, On-Demand, Network-Smashing Future of Television

Frank Rose

EDITOR'S NOTE

Like the VCR in the 1980s, the digital video recorder, or DVR, is poised to take the country's living rooms by storm. In the hands of TV subscription services like TiVo and Replay, the DVR has become heralded—and feared—for its ability to let viewers skip over commercial breaks. Not surprisingly, consumers love the devices, while network executives and ad agencies scramble for ways to maintain viewer attention through "advertainment." By 2006, Forrester research predicts that 27 percent of U.S. homes will have DVRs and one-third will have video-on-demand. Either way, control over content and programming is shifting from the networks to the viewer in a way that the broadcast industry has never before experienced—or allowed. As this reading explains, the traditional broadcasting revenue model is under threat as interactive technology begins to make possible ads targeted not just by demographic or zip code but by household, based on what the people actually watch and want. The companion article describes how TiVo's fate as a company may rest in the hands of the industry it once demonized: advertising.

CONSIDER

1. What happens when DVRs give viewers control of the TV schedule, the content, and the ads?
2. How does the DVR, through services like TiVo, threaten to disrupt programming and advertising (at least as we know it)?
3. Can a service like TiVo ever really be advertiser-friendly, as the company's president claims? If so, how?

It all started with the VCR. In 1975, when Sony introduced the notion of "time shift," as cofounder Akio Morita dubbed it, television was a staid and profitable

From "The Fast-Forward, On-Demand, Network-Smashing Future of Television" by Frank Rose, *Wired,* October 2003, pp. 158–163, 176. Copyright © 2003 The Condé Nast Publications Inc. All rights reserved. Reprinted with permission.

business controlled by three national broadcast networks. *All in the Family,* the number-one show, was watched in 30 percent of American homes. Cable was something you got for better reception. The big question facing the industry was whether *Happy Days* would propel ABC to the top. (It did.)

This year's top series, *CSI,* was on in just 16 percent of households. The three broadcast networks are now six, most of them struggling to make a profit. More than 300 additional channels are available through digital cable and satellite. And time-shifting has progressed to the point that millions of viewers rely not on a VCR but on a digital video recorder, which makes it easy to find anything on those hundreds of channels and watch it anytime while fast-forwarding through the ads. The revolution that started in analog is now exploding in digital, and suddenly everything about television is up for grabs—the way we watch it and the ads that pay for it, the kinds of programs we get and the future of the networks that carry them.

The DVR, pioneered in the late '90s by TiVo, is the linchpin. It's taking hold at the same time that digital compression—which multiplies tenfold the number of signals a slice of bandwidth can carry—is enabling cable and satellite providers to pump out channels targeted to narrowly defined audiences. Throw in electronic programming guides—search functions that essentially let you Google your TV—and the implications for Hollywood are, as one exec puts it, "cataclysmic." Technology is empowering the couch potato. The fundamental premise of traditional broadcasting is its ability to control the viewer—to deliver tens of millions of eyeballs to advertisers and to direct those eyeballs from prime time all the way to late night. That control has been eroding ever since the advent of the VCR, but now it's being blasted away entirely.

As is usually the case, the revolution has not proceeded as forecast. Digital broadcasting is still stalled, and high-definition TV along with it. Although TiVo engendered panic in the industry after it appeared, it's proved a hard sell with consumers as a stand-alone device (see "TiVo's Turning Point" by Josh McHugh below). Forrester discovered last year that 70 percent of consumers didn't even know what a DVR was.

Around the same time, satellite companies started building DVRs into their set-top boxes—and sales finally started to take off. In the growing competition between cable and satellite, DVRs have become bait to lure subscribers. When cable providers started pushing video-on-demand, satellite companies—unable to deliver on-demand service—countered with DVRs. They've become so popular that cable operators like Time Warner and Comcast are now offering the systems as well. In the past year, the number of DVR-equipped households has more than doubled to 4 million. Forrester projects that in three years, 27 percent of U.S. homes will have DVRs and one-third will have video-on-demand. Either way, control shifts from the networks to the viewer.

Television is run by people who make their living telling other people what to watch and when, while cramming in more and more ads to pay for it all. Plug in a device that short-circuits the system and they're in trouble. Network execs don't get paid millions to admit their best years are behind them. But late at night, when they're sitting in their Dolby surround-sound home theaters flipping past Letterman and Leno and *Nightline* to channels 252 and 286 and beyond, or checking their TiVos to see what they missed during dinner, they know.

"This business is not broken in such a way that it's going to implode next week or next year," declares Alec Gerster, CEO of Initiative Worldwide, an agency that purchases $21 billion in ads annually on behalf of such clients as Bayer, BellSouth, and Coors. "But it is going to be increasingly difficult to do the same thing each year as if we were back in 1980. There is a freight train coming at us, and the only thing holding it back is the time it takes for consumers to bend this technology to the ways they want to use it."

"It's all about the consumer," says Jed Petrick, president of the WB network. "The question is, how does the business model find a way to maintain itself or adapt to the new consumer model?"

To some of the savvier people in advertising, the real problem isn't the DVR. The problem is the 30-second spot itself—the "30," in industry parlance. "We are dealing with a world-class disconnect between the way we're trying to communicate and the way the consumer wants us to communicate," says Gerster. All DVRs have done is force the ad business to admit the obvious—that most people will avoid commercials whenever possible. And it isn't just the spots themselves, it's their ubiquity. The networks are now squeezing 16 to 17 minutes of ads and promos into each hour of programming, up from 14 minutes a decade ago. "Technology gives you the ability to skip commercials, and clutter gives you the reason," says Andrew Green, an executive at rival buying agency OMD, which handles clients like Pepsi and McDonald's. "We are driving this thing into the ground."

So far, the networks have been able to get more and more money for fewer and fewer top-rated shows because advertisers are desperate to pile into the handful of vehicles that are left. At last spring's up-front market, where ad buyers sign up for airtime on the upcoming fall season, they dumped $9.3 billion on the six broadcast networks, well over the record $8.1 billion they'd spent the year before. But this won't go on forever. A recent Forrester survey showed that if 30 million households had DVRs—a milestone we're projected to reach in early 2007—three-quarters of the national advertisers would cut their spending on TV. And just because advertisers are buying today doesn't mean they're happy about it. "Most clients are losing faith that they're going to put the money out there and get results," says Gerster. "So how do I get my message out in a way that people will at worst tolerate it, and at best be engaged by it?"

That's the challenge. The most obvious alternative is product placement—product integration, to use the current buzzword. But ad agencies operate on commission, a percentage of the price of the ads they buy. They never bothered with product placement until their clients started pressuring them to come up with something new. Now they're faced with questions like, how do you value a Coke can that appears for 15 seconds on *Friends*? Is it worth more if Jennifer Aniston drinks from it than if it just sits on the kitchen counter? How much more?

A New York marketing entrepreneur named Frank Zazza claims to have the answer. Zazza has come up with a scheme that grades placements by 10 levels of impact, from having the product in the background to naming an entire episode after it. Mix this in with his carefully calibrated "awareness scale" plus a couple of other factors, and you get the dollar value of a placement. For $300,000 you could buy, say, 3 seconds of "verbal" (talk about the product) or 90 seconds of background. "This has the ability to completely change the dynamic of television and the way it's bought," says Peter Gardiner, chief media officer of Deutsch, one of New York's hottest ad agencies.

Zazza has his eye on an even bigger prize. He's working with a company that inserts virtual billboards into sports broadcasts to apply the same technology to product integration. Instead of having an actual Coke can on the set of *Friends,* the producers could digitally insert it before the show airs. If Pepsi offered more for the DVD version of the series, they could replace the Coke with a Pepsi. It's product integration without the product. What this means for the networks is unclear; the important thing, Zazza says, is to keep the advertisers happy: "Unilever, Procter & Gamble—they're going to be around a long time after *CSI* is kicking up daisies."

But product integration, virtual or otherwise, isn't enough. Big brands want impact—the kind you get from having your identity tied to a hit show. In the

'50s, when advertisers routinely produced their own shows, that meant programs with names like *Ford Theatre* and *Ford Star Jubilee*. Today it means Ford everywhere you look on *American Idol* and *24*.

At first, Ford tried to develop a show itself. It had been a while since anyone in Hollywood got a pitch from a carmaker, so it was news three years ago when Ford and its ad agency, J. Walter Thompson, teamed up with Lions Gate Entertainment to make a trekking-through-the-wilderness reality series. Based on a hit format from Norway, the show was titled *No Boundaries,* after the tagline for the company's SUV campaign. The WB finally aired it a year and a half later, only to drop it after six episodes. "We were very proud of *No Boundaries,*" says Rich Stoddart, a marketing manager at Ford. "But you can make the most wonderful content in the world, and without a commitment from a distribution outlet, you have an audience of one."

Since then, Ford has stuck to shows that a network has already committed to. It's had the *American Idol* contestants sing car songs: "Mustang Sally," "Fun, Fun, Fun ('til her daddy takes the T-Bird away)." It's gotten *The Tonight Show* to park a Mustang in the studio audience: "The best seats in the house," Leno quipped. And this October, for the second straight year, it's introducing the season premiere of *24,* the Fox series starring Kiefer Sutherland as a rogue CIA agent. Ford is presenting the first episode without commercial interruption, bookending it with 3-minute ads. As part of the deal, Sutherland drives an Expedition, and other models are woven into the story. "Basically, we own the show," says Rob Donnell, who heads a four-person team in JWT's Detroit office that looks for innovative ways to promote the brand on TV. It seems to work: The ad-rating service IAG reported that the pair of 3-minute commercials that introduced *24* last season, though never rebroadcast, were among the most-remembered ads of the year. No other automotive spots even placed.

Meanwhile, network execs are trying desperately to hang on to elements of the past. In August, NBC announced a scheme to sandwich minimovies between its 30-second spots in an attempt to keep viewers glued to their sets—as if there wasn't enough clutter already. But ad people are moving on. Instead of one product—the 30—Madison Avenue is developing an entire arsenal, from 3-minute "advertainment" sequences like Ford's to 5-second spots too short to skip.

The irony is that, as networks and ad agencies scramble, the ultimate advertising innovation may be brewing at TiVo: spots that lure viewers into handing over their contact info for a follow-up. The project, known as the TiVo Showcase, relies on the firm's ability to feed special programming directly to its subscribers' DVRs. This summer, for example, the company partnered with Chrysler to present video clips featuring its new Crossfire sports coupe.

DVRs may seem like an unlikely friend to advertisers, but TiVo's new president, Marty Yudkovitz, likes to talk about his company's ability to "target the viewer and take him deeper inside the message." And while TiVo makes a point of saying it doesn't collect data on individual subscribers, viewers who want to know more about the showcase product can "opt in" by requesting a CD-ROM, landing them in a database of possible customers. Ultimately, Yudkovitz argues, DVRs could let television fulfill the promise Web advertising made in the boom years: ads targeted not just by demographic, not just by zip code, but by household, based on what the people who live there watch and want. "Television has always been great at brand awareness," he says, "but that's it. Measurability, targeting, the marriage of brand awareness and direct marketing—that is the holy grail." There's only one catch: TiVo—not a network—gets the revenue from these ads.

What ads look like, how to figure their worth, who gets paid for them—"every part of the model is under threat," says OMD's Andrew Green. "Which is wonderful, really, because it makes for an exciting life."

For television executives, ads are only half the equation—the half that pays the bills, but not the only half that matters. DVRs, in tandem with the explosion of channels in digital cable and satellite, will disrupt programming as ruthlessly as they have advertising. Successful programming is why NBC can claim to have "Must See TV" on Thursday nights, and why it can charge top dollar for its ad time as well. If time slots become irrelevant, scheduling does, too.

Marty Yudkovitz argues that DVRs—make that TiVo—can help television programmers as well as advertisers. "Programmers want to know not only who's watching, but where they came from and where they're going," he says. TiVo can tell them what the patterns are. It can also program a message to appear touting, say, next week's guest star on *Will & Grace* while you're watching an earlier episode. "It's a very powerful place to be," he maintains.

But it will take more than this to make the future work, particularly for programmers at the four biggest broadcasting networks—ABC, CBS, NBC, and Fox. To people in the industry, these four are what it's all about: They get the biggest audiences, the most money, and the most buzz. Yet broadcast television is almost an anachronism—some 85 percent of U.S. households now get TV via cable or satellite—and the giant broadcast networks, with their common-denominator programming, are increasingly outdated as well. "Mass audiences, mass media—a lot of people are clinging to those old models," says Tim Hanlon, a vice president at Starcom MediaVest, a global marketing consultancy that counts TiVo among its clients. "But it's not really that way anymore."

Instead of chasing the same 18-to-49 demographic, the big broadcast networks should just admit that the time when the whole family gathered round the tube is over. Advertisers are now buying into new-style networks that deliver precisely targeted, highly desirable consumers. Take the WB, which like cable channels is known for a specific style of show: Viewers go there for relationship dramas with Gen-Y appeal and a lot of stuff about coming of age. It caters to a niche audience of 12- to 34-year-olds, especially females, and it charges advertisers a premium to reach this hard-to-get demographic. This gives the WB a brand identity the big four networks can't match.

"I watch my kids when they watch their TiVo," says Jordan Levin, the WB's programming chief, who at 35 has the soothing presence of a model suburban dad. "They have 300 channels, but they gravitate to the ones that satisfy their expectations—Nickelodeon, Disney, the Cartoon Channel, the WB. It takes a huge hit that the kids are all talking about at school to get them to try something new."

But just one show won't make them stick around. "There are going to be thousands of brands," Levin continues, "and the ones that stand for something are going to make the transition to the new playing field that digital technology is creating. The broader-based brands that don't stand for anything will go the way of *The Saturday Evening Post*."

Even the brands that stand for something will be challenged in the next phase of television. A few years from now, the 300-plus channels we have now will evolve into one: MyTV, the channel you program yourself. The increasingly sophisticated electronic programming guides that make this feasible, known as EPGs, won't be the simple onscreen listings most cable and satellite systems carry today, but interactive services with advanced search and sort functions. TiVo lets you search listings a week or two ahead and record shows when they air. Time Warner Cable is working on a system that will let you search backward in time and record shows that have already aired. (Essentially a form of video-on-demand, it works by storing programs at cable headends after they've been broadcast.) Eventually, TV listings will be marked with metatags —embedded keywords that pop up during a search, just as they do on the Web. When that happens, the amount of information your EPG picks up won't be limited to the eight or ten words most guides have now; it could include every name in the cast and a dozen other keywords as well. Want to record anything in which John Travolta had even a bit part? No problem. "Navigation is almost the crux of the future of television," says consultant Hanlon. "Not everyone has figured it out yet, but they will."

In a DVR-enabled, viewer-programmable world, with EPGs trawling the schedules to find anything you want to see, you have to wonder about the value of even a niche brand. If people end up using only the search function to assemble the programming they want to watch, the branding of networks and cable channels might not matter—and television would devolve into little more than a digitally distributed home-video business. Established brands might still have some draw, just as they do on the Internet: Google can take you anywhere on the Web, yet twice as many people head for ESPN.com as any other sports site. "But it's going to be harder and harder for any network to stand out," says Hanlon.

Right now, though, network execs have more immediate worries, like what's going to pay the overhead if the ad pie starts shrinking. "That's our biggest concern," says the WB's Levin. All that new stuff Madison Avenue is trying might work for advertisers, but there's no guarantee it will ever be the jackpot for television that 30-second spots have been. What do they do then? Try to charge subscription fees like HBO? Cut prime time from three hours to two? Put their shows on DVD and hawk them on street corners? Nobody really knows. But the freight train that used to seem such a long way off is getting closer and closer, and it won't be long before they have to decide which way to jump.

Reading 3-3 (continued)

TiVo's Turning Point: It Redefined Television. Now Comes Competition.

Josh McHugh

If TiVo CEO Mike Ramsay's life was a TV program, it would be *24*—a show he always TiVos but rarely has time to watch. Like Jack Bauer, the 53-year-old pinballs from one crisis to another as powerful enemies, shifting alliances, and relentless plot twists conspire to do him in. The specter of betrayal lurks behind every encounter. The clock is ticking. Any minute his bigger, better-financed adversaries—major cable carriers, PC and consumer electronics giants—will arrive on the scene to blow him away.

TiVo, of course, has become synonymous with DVR technology over the past five years. It established a beachhead, and although the company initially had

From "TiVo's Turning Point: It Redefined Television. Now Comes Competition" by Josh McHugh, *Wired,* October 2003, p. 162. Copyright © 2003 The Condé Nast Publications Inc. All rights reserved. Reprinted with permission.

trouble explaining its product's time-shifting capabilities to the public at large, an obsessed community of 703,000 customers sprouted, many of them proselytizing about their newfound control over TV programming and freedom from the tyranny of advertising. But the initial stage of the DVR revolution—inventing the technology and proving that there's a market for it—has ended. We're convinced: Time-shifting rules.

For TiVo, the hard part is over. Now comes the *really* hard part: competition. Making a DVR isn't rocket science: Buy a hard drive, add some graphics chips, a bit of software, and voilà! Forty-nine patents and 100 more pending make up a mere paper wall between TiVo and DVR commoditization. It took Linux programmer Isaac Richards and a handful of fellow programmers less than a year to slap together MythTV, a full-featured, open source knockoff, in their spare time. Sony, one of the original manufacturers of the

TiVo box, is now bundling its own DVR software into PCs and DVD players. Last October, Microsoft began stuffing its UltimateTV DVR technology into the Media Center platform for PCs. Then there are the cable set-top box makers, like Scientific-Atlanta and Motorola, and the promise of standard-issue DVR cable boxes—TiVo's greatest threat.

Ramsay is scrambling to compete in this new environment. First, he's sprinting to market with cheap DVRs. TiVo has always been a software play, relying on Sony and Philips to make the boxes. Last year, Ramsay hired Solectron to build TiVo-brand DVRs. The good news: TiVo picked up a new revenue stream (hardware sales went from nothing to $57 million—the majority of TiVo's $100 million in total sales) and 282,000 new subscribers. But the boxes sell at cost—$350 for the 80-Gbyte Series 2—and they put TiVo in direct competition with Sony and Philips. Best-case: cannibalization.

Then there's the cable gambit. Newly hired TiVo president Marty Yudkovitz, who was charged with new business initiatives at NBC for 20 years, is trying to convince cable operators that their customers want TiVo functionality in their cable boxes. What are his chances? TiVo recently trumped Microsoft to become DirecTV's DVR supplier. But that was a gimme: DirecTV is TiVo's fourth-largest shareholder. TiVo has by far the best DVR brand, but what's stopping Comcast from creating a new brand—say, *Comcache*—slapping it on 21 million cable boxes, and making us forget TiVo ever existed?

Ironically, TiVo's fate rests in the hands of the industry it once demonized: advertising. The company hasn't been shy about serving up users as bait to marketers, Hollywood, and networks. Last year, TiVo plunked long-form film trailers onto users' hard drives. Ramsay says 70 percent of viewers spent more than three minutes voluntarily watching previews for *Austin Powers in Goldmember.* Now TiVo is selling its subscribers' disk space to advertisers like Chrysler, 20th Century Fox, and Porsche.

TiVo is even selling data about users' viewing habits. Backend servers keep tabs on which ads people fast-forward through, which shows they record, and what scenes get viewers to rewind and watch again. This sort of information, which puts Nielsen ratings and focus groups to shame, hasn't yielded much cash yet, but Ramsay expects that to change soon. He says that before long a quarter of TiVo's revenue will come from data mining. Maybe more, when the inevitable price pressure makes the company reconsider its monthly licensing fees.

TiVo's allegiance shift may seem cold, but Ramsay's hardly apologetic in the face of his life-or-death fight. He knows that an obsessive love affair with customers can lead to critical acclaim, consumer devotion—and an Apple-esque market share. Instead, he's taking the remote away from viewers and handing it to deep-pocketed corporate interests.

Which means that the TiVo that early adopters fell in love with is dead. Can the new TiVo survive? Will Ramsay find the killer strategy? Will he just sell out? Tune in to next week's episode—or just fire up your open source DVR and watch it whenever.

RELATED LINKS

- The TiVo home page (http://www.tivo.com)
- TiVo Community Forum (http://www.tivocommunity.com/tivo-vb)
- ReplayTV (www.replaytv.com)
- DVD Recorder Connection (http://www.dvd-recorder-connection.com/index.html)

FOR FURTHER RESEARCH

To find out more about the topics discussed in this reading, use InfoTrac College Edition. Type in keywords and subject terms such as "digital video recorder," "digital compression," and "video on demand." You can access InfoTrac College Edition from the Wadsworth/Thomson Communication Café homepage: http://communication.wadsworth.com.

Reading 3-4

Digital Cinema, Take 2
Michael A. Hiltzik

EDITOR'S NOTE

Since the 1920s, Hollywood filmmakers have used special effects with—for the most part—realistic results. With the help of digital technology, the effects are becoming more lifelike than ever and scenarios that were once only possible in fiction, from the dinosaur attacks in Jurassic Park *to interaction between the mythic characters in* Lord of the Rings *to the pod races in* Star Wars, *are now commonplace on screen. The flexibility and vividness of software-generated characters and scenes seem to suggest that real actors and settings may one day become obsolete. But, for now at least, human actors have not yet lost their appeal and digital imagery still does not approach film's high visual resolution and dynamic range in terms of color and contrast. Although some pictures are shot entirely using digital cameras, most directors still favor celluloid. When it comes to postproduction enhancements and special effects, however, computers rule—film editing today is done almost exclusively through the use of video software such as Avid or Final Cut Pro. As a result, moviemakers now must expertly blend both media.*

CONSIDER

1. For Hollywood directors, what are the advantages of using traditional film cameras instead of all-digital camera technology?

2. With the growing use of software-generated characters, scenes, and settings, is anything lost from or lacking in effects-intensive films? If so, what?

3. Why is restoration of old films through the use of software like Moviepaint "the one area where digital technology is close to an unadulterated blessing"?

Hollywood being a star-making machine above all else, it was not surprising that the buzz on 2000's release of *Cast Away* was all about the weight Tom Hanks gained and then dropped to give life to his character's years of privation. The real magic behind the film wasn't revealed until much later—that the island peak over which the hero clambered was a mud pile overlooking a California parking lot, and that much of the tropical environment seen on screen, from breakers to mountaintop, had been fashioned inside a computer.

Reliving the production, George Joblove breaks into a delighted grin. "Any shot that had ocean or sky

From "Digital Cinema, Take 2" by Michael A. Hiltzik, *Technology Review*, September 2002, pp. 36–44. Copyright © 2003 Technology Review, Inc. All rights reserved. Reprinted with permission.

in it," says the senior vice president for technology at Sony Pictures Imageworks, which created the visuals, "was pretty much a special effect." The film's software-generated scenes not only featured action and compositions that would have been impractical and expensive to shoot on location, but also contained elements such as windstorms and enormous waves that are virtually impossible to create in the real world.

That a tropical island could be manufactured so seamlessly out of pixels and algorithms testifies to the ascendancy of digital technology in Hollywood, where it has all but superseded the optical and photochemical manipulations that were state of the art as recently as 10 years ago. It's no secret that 3-D digital processing is responsible for some of the grandest effects of modern blockbusters, beginning with the dinosaurs of *Jurassic Park* and leading up to the careening space runabouts of *Star Wars: Episode II—Attack of the Clones.* But what's more remarkable is how thoroughly digital technology has taken over film editing, color adjustment and other components of the so-called postproduction process —including the subtle alterations, such as the erasure of television antennas from period backgrounds and support cables from acrobatic stuntmen, that lend verisimilitude to everything from drawing-room pieces to psychological dramas.

"We call them 'invisible effects,'" says Joblove, speaking from an office that overlooks the six-hectare Sony Pictures Entertainment studio complex in Culver City, CA. "Most are things you shouldn't notice and shouldn't know about, things that shouldn't draw attention to themselves."

Indeed, without most moviegoers' noticing, digital technologies have been slowly supplanting film-based processes that have been used since the 1920s. Imageworks' vice president of marketing and communication Donald Levy estimates that the movie industry now spends roughly half a billion dollars per year on visual effects—almost all of them digital. At many postproduction houses, chemistry labs have given way to programming carrels in which computer science graduates write algorithms that will eventually simulate the wash of waves on a beach or the separation of a Saturn V rocket from its Cape Canaveral gantry—artists working in code rather than pen and ink.

And today there is scarcely a film lab in Hollywood that does not offer digital services—up to and including the restoration of archival films—to its industry clientele along with traditional developing, color timing and print services. One of the fastest-growing business lines at Technicolor, which pioneered the first two-color photochemical process in 1916, is the digital scanning of film prints in order to insert visual effects. Kodak, which sells some 80 percent of all the film stock used in U.S. movies, has hedged its bets by opening Cinesite, a Los Angeles– and London-based subsidiary that has become one of the most important and innovative purveyors of digital services—such as digital editing, special effects, and the creation of digital master copies of negatives and prints—to moviemakers.

But while large-scale digital modification of images is already rife in Hollywood, it has its limits. Clean digital files and hidden microchips haven't quite replaced reeking photochemical emulsions and temperamental celluloid stock, and the unalloyed enthusiasm many filmmakers felt for the new technology just a couple of years ago has evolved into a mature assessment of it as one tool among many, both novel and traditional. Directors and cinematographers who have worked in the new medium have generally found that its flexibility, while valuable, also comes at a steep cost.

Take Roger Deakins, an award-winning cinematographer who used digital technology to great effect in creating the distinctive look of the Joel and Ethan Coen Depression-era film *O Brother, Where Art Thou?* Deakins and the Coen brothers were determined to evoke the Dust Bowl by giving the whole film the faded look of an old-time picture postcard. This involved, among other effects, transforming the lush greens of vegetation into a sere tobacco-yellow in the film's exterior shots. While the judicious deployment of lighting and lens filters would have had the same effect, it would also have given other colors, especially skin tones, an unnatural tint. Instead, Deakins shot the entire film conventionally and had his negative digitized at Cinesite, where technicians then helped him tint out the greens without affecting the rest of the palette by adjusting the digital values of the pixels in each image —much the way audio engineers can boost the bass of a recording without changing the treble or midrange. Although the process sounds straightforward, it was much more demanding than conventional photography. Among other things, Deakins realized that he should invest his negatives with the most highly saturated colors possible, to give the technicians the maximum amount of information to work with during the color correction process. At Cinesite, he supervised the alterations like a mother hen watching over her chicks.

"I was there every day for more than 10 weeks, from testing with camera negatives until the first print was out of the lab," Deakins says. This was necessary in part because the entire project was novel, even for Cinesite. But Deakins feels that because of its very power, digital color correction demands particular watchfulness. "There's so much that can be done with the technology that if you as a DP [director of photography] aren't there, your work easily could be ruined."

In the end, he concluded that such so-called digital mastering (the conversion of a sequence or an entire film to digital form) is useful only in special circumstances—as when striving for an effect that can't be reached through conventional means. "It depends on what's right for the project, because I don't think the quality is as good as film. If you're not going outside straight RGB [red, green, and blue] timing, I don't see much point in going the digital route."

"There's a tremendous amount of hype around the word 'digital,'" agrees Steven Poster, president of the

American Society of Cinematographers. As director of photography on Sony's summer release *Stuart Little 2,* Poster also used a digital master in postproduction, since almost every frame includes the film's title character—a mouse created entirely in digital form—or one of his digital pals. "There are certain skills necessary to accomplish the shooting, making and coming out on the other end with a motion picture," Poster says. "One is cinematography. We say, if you know how to light it doesn't matter what medium you're shooting on. Likewise, if you don't know how to light it doesn't matter which medium you're shooting in." Today's filmmakers, in other words, must master not one technology but two—and then be willing to spend long hours bridging their incompatibilities.

FILM'S FIRM FOOTHOLD

The best way to grasp the degree to which digital technology has infiltrated moviemaking is to partition the life cycle of a feature into three phases: image acquisition (known in simpler days as "photography"), postproduction and exhibition.

Electronic technologies have made remarkable progress on some of these fronts—but overall, cinema hasn't changed as much as you might expect from all of this summer's buzz about digital movies. Most principal photography is still done on film, despite George Lucas's decision to shoot *Star Wars: Episode II* entirely using digital cameras. Cinematographers agree that digital hardware is getting vastly better, aided by the emergence of the so-called 24p process, which allows high-definition digital video to be shot at film's 24 frames per second, rather than the roughly 30 of conventional video (thus eliminating the need for complicated adjustments of frame rates). But even the best digital imagery still doesn't approach film's resolution and dynamic range in terms of color and contrast.

"There's still room in film to carry information beyond the capability of the eye to see it," says Brad Reinke, manager of digital restoration services at Cinesite. "Digital's not nearly there."

At the other end of the production process—your neighborhood movie theater—digital technology has barely made any headway. As of this summer only 100 or so of the country's 35,000 screens were equipped for digital movies—whether downloaded via satellite or spooled off high-density digital discs resembling DVDs. Those that were used a Texas Instruments system based

on arrays of microchips, each with about a million microscopic mirrors that pivot toward or away from the screen thousands of times per second. Digital projection is jiggle free, and unlike film projection, it doesn't degrade the print with every showing. But in part because digital projection does not create as unmistakable an improvement in the viewing experience as, say, the talkies did over silent films, theater chains are unwilling to foot the bill for the new projectors, which cost at least $100,000 per screen and might have to be upgraded every few years. Conventional film projectors, which last 20 years on average, cost $30,000.

"Digital cinema could never drive enough extra traffic through our box offices and to our concession stands to make up the difference," John Fithian, president of the National Association of Theater Owners, told a Washington, DC, technical conference last year.

Still, almost everyone in Hollywood agrees that in postproduction, digital is well on its way to becoming the state of the art. Film editing today is done almost entirely through virtual cutting and pasting on video screens, which replaces the tiresome manual method of slicing up celluloid film strips and splicing them back together with tape.

COMPLEX FX

Special effects—everything from plane crashes to acrobatic stunts to alien life forms—are now customarily computer generated, thanks to software tools like Pixar's RenderMan, or like Maya, perhaps the most widely used application for 3-D imaging. The product of Silicon Graphics subsidiary Alias|Wavefront and a direct descendant of the program that produced the dinosaurs of *Jurassic Park* in 1993, Maya is esteemed by digital-effects teams not only for its comprehensive scope and power, but for its compatibility with the special-purpose "plug-ins" (mini-programs that interact with and enhance the main software) that special-effects departments often devise to meet particular needs on feature projects. It's not unusual to hear visual-effects artists comparing the merits of, say, the ocean effects plug-in Imageworks devised to generate the breakers and swells in *Cast Away* and the one developed by Warner Brothers for *The Perfect Storm.*

Even more remarkable is the extent to which digital artists are using their tools to give life to animated characters. Every year brings improvements in the rendering of movement and organic textures like skin and hair. "We do almost all our modeling and character animation with Maya," Sony's George Joblove is explaining one afternoon as he escorts me past the darkened warrens of Imageworks' animation floor, where the finishing touches are being made on *Stuart Little 2* weeks before its scheduled release. He pulls aside a curtain to reveal a glimpse of a Maya artist working on a scene a few seconds long in which a complacent Stuart Little is suddenly snatched out of the frame by a set of talons. The scene plays over and over again as the artist refines the details.

"We have more than two dozen software engineers," Joblove continues as we tour this particular nexus of the Hollywood Hills and Silicon Valley. At any given time, he notes, some might be deployed to work on the effects for a single film, others on software that the firm will use on dozens of projects. Some of these, such as code writers and database specialists, can be found in any highly computerized organization; others, the more artistic, have expertise that can only be found in a facility like Imageworks.

I ask which is more important, artistic talent or coding skills.

"We span the whole spectrum—people who are just engineers and couldn't draw a stick figure, and others who are talented artists and never used a computer before they came here. And in the middle," says Joblove, "are a few people working on shots who have a strong and deep understanding of the science and the software and the art."

This precious breed is actually becoming more and more common in Hollywood, fueling a range of digital-movie companies from Efilm, which has developed its own laser recording technology for transferring digital images back to film, to Rhythm and Hues, where one specialty is animating unusual characters such as *Harry Potter*'s Sorting Hat—a mouthy piece of millinery that, in the judgment of the *New York Times,* had "more personality than anything else in the movie" (see Table 3-2). But it may be at Cinesite's hangar-sized facility, a few miles north of Imageworks and not far from the corner of Hollywood and Vine, that the virtues of digital postproduction are most vividly on display—along with the difficulties.

The compromises begin in Cinesite's scanning room, where technicians convert film images to streams of digital bits by playing a laser beam over the original frames. Because digital video images have an inherent "edginess," film converted to video at the standard resolution (2,048 pixels wide by 1,556 deep, known as

"2K") tends to look somewhat soft focused. That failing can be overcome by scanning at 4K—roughly 4,100 pixels across by 3,000 deep—but this generates a data file so big that a standard feature film would take 12 full days to scan. The larger digital files also impose a huge cost in storage requirements and processing time. Since the difference in image quality is almost imperceptible in a movie theater, 4K is only used for the most exacting projects, such as the conversion of *Fantasia* and *Apollo 13* for Imax presentations, where the giant screen would render even a minute loss of detail spectacularly visible.

After they leave the Cinesite scanning room, digital files continue along any of three production routes: to the insertion of visual special effects; to digital mastering, which allows color correction and conversion to DVD or video formats; or to the company's restoration service. The special-effects artists, who must carefully integrate the computer-generated objects in a frame with the real ones, get much of the glory once a film's publicity is under way. But the color timers and other professionals who oversee digital mastering probably contribute more to a film's overall look. During mastering, Cinesite's technicians use Kodak's Cineon system to adjust color values to avoid distracting video phenomena such as banding, in which slight gradations of brightness create contour lines, and clipping, in which the detail within bright images bleaches out. By adjusting the brightness of digitized images to a logarithmic curve—compressing the amount of information at the dark end of the scale and expanding it at the bright end—the system "matches the eye's perception," explains Steve Wright, Cinesite's technical director for 2-D.

RESTORED TO LIFE

But it may be Cinesite's digital restorationists who work the biggest technological miracles from day to day, making old, unviewable films look as new as they did the day they were printed. Restoration, in fact, is the one area where digital technology is close to an unadulterated blessing, for it gives technicians an unprecedented ability to remove defects caused by production mistakes or the ravages of time.

In a room rimmed with computer workstations, Corinne Pooler is painstakingly restoring a sequence from the classic 1962 film *To Kill a Mockingbird,* which Universal Studios is planning to rerelease in a pristine

Table 3-2. Digital Movie Stars (postproduction houses)

Name	Location	Specialties	Recent Film Projects
Cinesite	Los Angeles, CA	Digital mastering, visual effects, film scanning and recording, restoration	*O Brother, Where Art Thou?, Band of Brothers, Traffic, Planet of the Apes, Pleasantville*
Efilm	Hollywood, CA	High-resolution scanning from film to digital, laser recording from digital to film	*From the Earth to the Moon, Batman and Robin, Contact, Titanic*
Sony Pictures Imageworks	Culver City, CA	Scanning, color timing, modeling, character animation	*Spider-Man, Cast Away, What Lies Beneath, Stuart Little 2, Charlie's Angels*
Industrial Light and Magic	San Rafael, CA	Digital image acquisition, digital editing, visual effects	*Star Wars: Episode II—Attack of the Clones, Star Wars: Episode I—The Phantom Menace, Pearl Harbor*
LaserPacific Media	Hollywood, CA	High-definition postproduction, conversion of studio films to DVD	*Austin Powers: The Spy Who Shagged Me, Lost in Space, Wag the Dog, Magnolia*
Pixar	Emeryville, CA	RenderMan character-rendering software, feature-film animation	*Toy Story, Toy Story 2, Monsters, Inc., Pearl Harbor, The Perfect Storm*
Rhythm and Hues	Los Angeles, CA	Character animation, visual effects	*Harry Potter and the Sorcerer's Stone, Men in Black II, The Sum of All Fears, Hollow Man, Babe*

theatrical print. Because *Mockingbird*'s original negative had been damaged beyond usability, the restorers are working from two fine-grain prints unearthed in Europe and the United States and subsequently digitized by the company's scanners. Each print has its own myriad imperfections, however, which presents Pooler with the challenge of assembling one clean print from the undamaged portions of the two others.

The secret weapon is another program called Moviepaint, which Kodak specifically designed for Cinesite. On her monitor, Pooler displays a frame showing a clapboard house on the left, the branches of a spreading oak on the right, and along the frame edge the large, ugly blotch that is her quarry. Pooler carefully aligns the digital image of the previous frame over the stained image. Then she launches a function that allows her to import the pixels from the clean frame into the stained image, in effect erasing the blotch.

"It can be tedious," she says of a process that will have to be repeated, with minute variations, on thousands of scratches, stretches, dust globs and breaks. (A Cinesite program called Bitzer automates much of that process, but only manual work using Moviepaint can correct every flaw.) Pooler, nevertheless, is well aware that she holds a job that would not exist at all but for digital technology. Seven years ago, she explains, she was a housewife with a job with her local school board. As it happened, her husband, Jerry Pooler, creative di-

rector for digital restoration services at Cinesite, was beginning work on the restoration of *Sleeping Beauty*.

"I was off for the summer, and Jerry needed people to help paint out dirt hits," Corinne recalls. "He told me, 'If you can paint 150 frames a day, we'll keep you. If not, I'll have to fire you.'" Pooler had no training in art or computer science, but she did have an eye instinctively capable of distinguishing between the minuscule details on a frame that are actually part of the image and the imperfections that call for obliteration.

In this craft an innocent misjudgment can wreck hours or days of work. Pooler recalls the time her team was called upon to paint out the vestiges of stunt gear from a 3,000-frame paratrooping sequence from a big-budget adventure movie.

"Six of us divided the work. The first person saw a line of tiny black spots in the image and painted them out of the frame. The next person took a look and said, 'You erased all the parachutes!'"

MIXED MEDIA

The inadvertent erasure of real-world objects is only one of the occupational hazards awaiting moviemakers as digital technology continues to spread.

"Increasing technology always yields increasing complexity," says Daniel Rosen, Cinesite's chief technology officer. "If you're in a film theater and there's no image, your eyeballs will tell you what's wrong—a lamp burned out, or the film broke. If you're in a digital theater, what happened? Was the satellite down? Or the server? Or is there an encryption problem?"

A former TRW engineer, Rosen is Cinesite's resident technical visionary and voice of realism—equally alive to the virtues of digital technology and to its shortcomings. On the plus side, he says, is the incredible flexibility producers will gain from having digital negatives of their films, which they can feed into a multitude of formats, be they theater prints, DVDs or TV broadcasts.

On the other hand, Rosen doubts that artists or audiences will soon want to give up the unique sensory qualities of film. "If we look decades ahead, people will come to realize that digital [photography] is another way of doing things, but film will give you a different organic look," he says. "It's like oil paint and acrylic. Digital has a different texture."

And just as acrylics, watercolors and other media haven't replaced oils, digital movies may never fully replace film. More likely, the two media will coexist, with digital's practical advantages and differing qualities widening directors' and cinematographers' artistic and logistical options as the technology advances. Think of it this way: if Sony Pictures ever develops a *Cast Away 2,* and the producers discover that a digital Tom Hanks can shed 25 kilograms instantly, rather than dieting for a year, then the island may not be the only thing that's virtual.

RELATED LINKS

- Cinesite (http://www.cinesite.com)
- Efilm Digital Laboratories (http://www.efilm.com)
- Sony Pictures Imageworks (http://www.imageworks.com)
- Industrial Light and Magic (http://www.ilm.com)
- LaserPacific Media (http://www.laserpacific.com/mainmenu.html)
- Pixar (http://www.pixar.com)
- Rhythm and Hues Studios (http://www.rhythm.com)

FOR FURTHER RESEARCH

To find out more about the topics discussed in this reading, use InfoTrac College Edition. Type in keywords and subject terms such as "special effects," "digital editing," and "3-D imaging software." You can access InfoTrac College Edition from the Wadsworth/Thomson Communication Café homepage: http://communication.wadsworth.com.

4

Media Concentration

Reading 4-1

The New Global Media
Robert W. McChesney

EDITOR'S NOTE

This reading by Robert McChesney, a leading media historian, political economist, and analyst of press performance, discusses the transformation of the major American, European, and Japanese media conglomerates into a nascent global media system. As domestic markets become saturated and permit only incremental expansion, these large corporations are attempting to capitalize on growth from abroad. This often places global media at odds with local populations. McChesney's conclusion: rich media make for poor democracy.

CONSIDER

1. Why are the major media companies globalizing their operations and looking to international markets for new opportunities?

2. In what ways is the global commercial media system radical? Why, ultimately, is it politically and culturally conservative?

3. How might government subsidies and the local policies of different countries protect the culture industries abroad from American media domination?

The nineties have been a typical fin de siècle decade in at least one important respect: The realm of media is on the brink of a profound transformation. Whereas previously media systems were primarily national, in the past few years a global commercial-media market has emerged. "What you are seeing," says Christopher Dixon, media analyst for the investment firm Paine-Webber, "is the creation of a global oligopoly. It happened to the oil and automotive industries earlier this century; now it is happening to the entertainment industry."

Together, the deregulation of media ownership, the privatization of television in lucrative European and Asian markets, and new communications technologies have made it possible for media giants to establish powerful distribution and production networks within and among nations. In short order, the global media market has come to be dominated by the same eight transnational corporations, or TNCs, that rule U.S. media: General Electric, AT&T/Liberty Media, Disney, Time Warner, Sony, News Corporation, Viacom, and Seagram, plus Bertelsmann, the Germany-based conglomerate. At the same time, a number of new firms and different political and social factors enter the picture as one turns to the global system, and the struggle for domination continues among the nine giants and their closest competitors. But as in the United States, at a global level this is a highly concentrated industry; the largest media corporation in the world in terms of annual revenues, Time Warner (1998 revenues: $27 billion), is some fifty times larger in terms of annual sales than the world's fiftieth-largest media firm.

A few global corporations are horizontally integrated; that is, they control a significant slice of specific media sectors, like book publishing, which has undergone extensive consolidation in the late nineties. "We have never seen this kind of concentration before," says an attorney who specializes in publishing deals. But even more striking has been the rapid vertical integration of the global media market, with the same firms gaining ownership of content and the means to distribute it. What distinguishes the dominant firms is their ability to exploit the "synergy" among the com-

From *Rich Media, Poor Democracy: Communication Politics in Dubious Times* by Robert W. McChesney. Copyright © 1999 by Board of Trustees of the University of Illinois. As edited and published in *The Nation*, November 29, 1999. Reprinted with permission of the University of Illinois Press.

panies they own. Nearly all the major Hollywood studios are owned by one of these conglomerates, which in turn control the cable channels and TV networks that air the movies. Only two of the nine are not major content producers: AT&T and GE. But GE owns NBC, AT&T has major media content holdings through Liberty Media, and both firms are in a position to acquire assets as they become necessary.

The major media companies have moved aggressively to become global players. Even Time Warner and Disney, which still get most of their revenues in the United States, project non-U.S. sales to yield a majority of their revenues within a decade. The point is to capitalize on the potential for growth abroad—and not get outflanked by competitors—since the U.S. market is well developed and only permits incremental expansion. As Viacom CEO Sumner Redstone has put it, "Companies are focusing on those markets promising the best return, which means overseas." Frank Biondi, former chairman of Seagram's Universal Studios, asserts that "99 percent of the success of these companies long-term is going to be successful execution offshore."

Prior to the eighties and nineties, national media systems were typified by domestically owned radio, television and newspaper industries. Newspaper publishing remains a largely national phenomenon, but the face of television has changed almost beyond recognition. Neoliberal free-market policies have opened up ownership of stations as well as cable and digital satellite TV systems to private and transnational interests, producing scores of new channels operated by the media TNCs that dominate cable ownership in the United States. The channels in turn generate new revenue streams for the TNCs: The major Hollywood studios, for example, expect to generate $11 billion from global TV rights to their film libraries in 2002, up from $7 billion in 1998.

While media conglomerates press for policies to facilitate their domination of markets throughout the world, strong traditions of protection for domestic media and cultural industries persist. Nations ranging from Norway, Denmark and Spain to Mexico, South Africa and South Korea keep their small domestic film production industries alive with government subsidies. In the summer of 1998 culture ministers from twenty nations, including Brazil, Mexico, Sweden, Italy and Ivory Coast, met in Ottawa to discuss how they could "build some ground rules" to protect their cultural fare from "the Hollywood juggernaut." Their main recommendation was to keep culture out of the control of the World Trade Organization. A similar 1998 gathering, sponsored by the United Nations in Stockholm, recommended that culture be granted special exemptions in global trade deals.

Nevertheless, the trend is clearly in the direction of opening markets. Proponents of neoliberalism in every country argue that cultural trade barriers and regulations harm consumers, and that subsidies inhibit the ability of nations to develop their own competitive media firms. There are often strong commercial-media lobbies within nations that perceive they have more to gain by opening up their borders than by maintaining trade barriers. In 1998, for example, when the British government proposed a voluntary levy on film theater revenues (mostly Hollywood films) to benefit the British commercial film industry, British broadcasters, not wishing to antagonize the firms who supply their programming, lobbied against the measure until it died.

The global media market is rounded out by a second tier of four or five dozen firms that are national or regional powerhouses, or that control niche markets, like business or trade publishing. About half of these second-tier firms come from North America; most of the rest are from Western Europe and Japan. Each of these second-tier firms is a giant in its own right, often ranking among the thousand largest companies in the world and doing more than $1 billion per year in business. The roster of second-tier media firms from North America includes Dow Jones, Gannett, Knight-Ridder, Hearst, and Advance Publications, and among those from Europe are the Kirch Group, Havas, Mediaset, Hachette, Prisa, Canal Plus, Pearson, Reuters, and Reed Elsevier. The Japanese companies, aside from Sony, remain almost exclusively domestic producers.

This second tier has also crystallized rather quickly; across the globe there has been a shakeout in national and regional media markets, with small firms getting eaten by medium firms and medium firms being swallowed by big firms. Many national and regional conglomerates have been established on the backs of publishing or television empires, as in the case of Denmark's Egmont. The situation in most nations is similar to the one in the United States: Compared with ten or twenty years ago, a much smaller number of much larger firms now dominate the media. Indeed, as most nations are smaller than the United States, the tightness of the media oligopoly can be even more severe. The situation may be most stark in New Zealand, where the newspaper industry is largely the province of the

Australian-American Rupert Murdoch and the Irishman Tony O'Reilly, who also dominates New Zealand's commercial-radio broadcasting and has major stakes in magazine publishing. Murdoch controls pay television and is negotiating to purchase one or both of the two public TV networks, which the government is aiming to sell. In short, the rulers of New Zealand's media system could squeeze into a closet.

Second-tier corporations are continually seeking to reach beyond national borders. Australian media moguls, following the path blazed by Murdoch, have the mantra "Expand or die." As one puts it, "You really can't continue to grow as an Australian supplier in Australia." Mediaset, the Berlusconi-owned Italian TV power, is angling to expand into the rest of Europe and Latin America. Perhaps the most striking example of second-tier globalization is Hicks, Muse, Tate and Furst, the U.S. radio/publishing/TV/billboard/movie theater power that has been constructed almost overnight. In 1998 it spent well over $1 billion purchasing media assets in Mexico, Argentina, Brazil and Venezuela.

Thus second-tier media firms are hardly "oppositional" to the global system. This is true as well in developing countries. Mexico's Televisa, Brazil's Globo, Argentina's Clarin, and Venezuela's Cisneros Group, for example, are among the world's sixty or seventy largest media corporations. These firms tend to dominate their own national and regional media markets, which have been experiencing rapid consolidation as well. They have extensive ties and joint ventures with the largest media TNCs, as well as with Wall Street investment banks. And like second-tier media firms elsewhere, they are also establishing global operations, especially in nations that speak the same language. As a result, they tend to have distinctly pro-business political agendas and support expansion of the global media market, which puts them at odds with large segments of the population in their home countries.

Together, the sixty or seventy first- and second-tier giants control much of the world's media: book, magazine, and newspaper publishing; music recording; TV production; TV stations and cable channels; satellite TV systems; film production; and motion picture theaters. But the system is still very much in formation. New second-tier firms are emerging, especially in lucrative Asian markets, and there will probably be further upheaval among the ranks of the first-tier media giants. And corporations get no guarantee of success merely by going global. The point is that they have no choice in the matter. Some, perhaps many, will falter as they accrue too much debt or as they enter unprofitable ventures. But the chances are that we are closer to the end of the process of establishing a stable global media market than to the beginning. And as it takes shape, there is a distinct likelihood that the leading media firms in the world will find themselves in a very profitable position. That is what they are racing to secure.

The global media system is fundamentally noncompetitive in any meaningful economic sense of the term. Many of the largest media firms have some of the same major shareholders, own pieces of one another or have interlocking boards of directors. When *Variety* compiled its list of the fifty largest global media firms for 1997, it observed that "merger mania" and cross-ownership had "resulted in a complex web of inter-relationships" that will "make you dizzy." The global market strongly encourages corporations to establish equity joint ventures in which the media giants all own a part of an enterprise. This way, firms reduce competition and risk—and increase the chance of profitability. As the CEO of Sogecable, Spain's largest media firm and one of the twelve largest private media companies in Europe, expressed it to *Variety,* the strategy is "not to compete with international companies but to join them." In some respects, the global media market more closely resembles a cartel than it does the competitive marketplace found in economics textbooks.

Global conglomerates can at times have a progressive impact on culture, especially when they enter nations that had been tightly controlled by corrupt crony media systems (as in much of Latin America) or nations that had significant state censorship over media (as in parts of Asia). The global commercial-media system is radical in that it will respect no tradition or custom, on balance, if it stands in the way of profits. But ultimately it is politically conservative, because the media giants are significant beneficiaries of the current social structure around the world, and any upheaval in property or social relations—particularly to the extent that it reduces the power of business—is not in their interest.

While the "Hollywood juggernaut" and the specter of U.S. cultural imperialism remains a central concern in many countries, the notion that corporate media firms are merely purveyors of U.S. culture is ever less plausible as the media system becomes increasingly concentrated, commercialized and global-ized. The global media system is better understood as one that advances corporate and commercial interests and values and denigrates or ignores that which cannot be incorporated into its mission. There is no discernible difference in the firms' content, whether they are owned by shareholders in Japan or Belgium or have corporate headquarters in New York or Sydney. Bertelsmann CEO Thomas Middelhoff bristled when, in 1998, some said it was improper for a German firm to control 15 percent of the U.S. book-publishing market. "We're not foreign. We're international," Middelhoff said. "I'm an American with a German passport."

As the media conglomerates spread their tentacles, there is reason to believe they will encourage popular tastes to become more uniform in at least some forms of media. Based on conversations with Hollywood executives, *Variety* editor Peter Bart concluded that "the world filmgoing audience is fast becoming more homogeneous." Whereas action movies had once been the only sure-fire global fare—and comedies had been considerably more difficult to export—by the late nineties comedies like *My Best Friend's Wedding* and *The Full Monty* were doing between $160 million and $200 million in non-U.S. box-office sales.

When audiences appear to prefer locally made fare, the global media corporations, rather than flee in despair, globalize their production. This is perhaps most visible in the music industry. Music has always been the least capital-intensive of the electronic media and therefore the most open to experimentation and new ideas. U.S. recording artists generated 60 percent of their sales outside the United States in 1993; by 1998 that figure was down to 40 percent. Rather than fold their tents, however, the five media TNCs that dominate the world's recorded-music market are busy establishing local subsidiaries in places like Brazil, where "people are totally committed to local music," in the words of a writer for a trade publication. Sony has led the way in establishing distribution deals with independent music companies from around the world.

With hypercommercialism and growing corporate control comes an implicit political bias in media content. Consumerism, class inequality and individualism tend to be taken as natural and even benevolent, whereas political activity, civic values and antimarket activities are marginalized. The best journalism is pitched to the business class and suited to its needs and prejudices; with a few notable exceptions, the journalism reserved for the masses tends to be the sort of drivel provided by the media giants on their U.S. television stations. This slant is often quite subtle. Indeed, the genius of the commercial-media system is the general lack of overt censorship. As George Orwell noted in his unpublished introduction to *Animal Farm,* censorship in free societies is infinitely more sophisticated and thorough than in dictatorships, because "unpopular ideas can be silenced, and inconvenient facts kept dark, without any need for an official ban."

Lacking any necessarily conspiratorial intent and acting in their own economic self-interest, media conglomerates exist simply to make money by selling light escapist entertainment. In the words of the late Emilio Azcarraga, the billionaire head of Mexico's Televisa: "Mexico is a country of a modest, very fucked class, which will never stop being fucked. Television has the obligation to bring diversion to these people and remove them from their sad reality and difficult future."

It may seem difficult to see much hope for change. As one Swedish journalist noted in 1997, "Unfortunately, the trends are very clear, moving in the wrong direction on virtually every score, and there is a desperate lack of public discussion of the long-term implications of current developments for democracy and accountability." But there are indications that progressive political movements around the world are increasingly making media issues part of their political platforms. From Sweden, France and India to Australia, New Zealand and Canada, democratic left political parties are making structural media reform—breaking up the big companies, recharging nonprofit and noncommercial broadcasting and media—central to their agenda. They are finding out that this is a successful issue with voters.

At the same time, the fate of the global media system is intricately intertwined with that of global capitalism, and despite the self-congratulatory celebration of the free market in the U.S. media, the international system is showing signs of weakness. Asia, the so-called tiger of twenty-first-century capitalism, fell into a depression in 1997, and its recovery is still uncertain. Even if there is no global depression, discontent is brewing in those parts of the world and among those segments of the population that have been left behind in this era of economic growth. Latin America, the other vaunted champion of market reforms since the eighties, has seen what a World Bank official terms a "big increase in inequality." While the dominance of commercial media makes resistance more difficult, it is not hard to imagine widespread opposition to these trends calling into question the triumph of the neoliberal economic model and the global media system it has helped create.

RELATED LINKS

- Frontline: Media Giants (http://www.pbs.org/wgbh/pages/frontline/shows/cool/giants)
- Global Concentration: The Media Ownership Chart (http://www.mediachannel.org/ownership/chart.shtml)
- The Media Borg Wants You (http://archive.salon.com/tech/feature/2001/06/26/borg_intro/)
- Media Space: Project on Global Media and Public Space (http://www.mediaspace.org)
- Robert McChesney (http://www.robertmcchesney.com)

FOR FURTHER RESEARCH

To find out more about the topics discussed in this reading, use InfoTrac College Edition. Type in keywords and subject terms such as "media concentration," "cultural imperialism," and "globalization." You can access InfoTrac from the Wadsworth/Thomson Communication Café homepage: http://communication.wadsworth.com.

Reading 4-2

Global Media
Benjamin Compaine

EDITOR'S NOTE

Concerns over media concentration have been raised since the turn of the previous century. Recently, the issue has received renewed attention due to a sobering statistic: The number of companies that control most of what Americans read in print media, watch on television, and view at the movies has shrunk to six. By extension, it is commonly assumed that a few big companies are also taking over the world's media. However, the last few decades have seen a burst of new information sources, from cable networks to the World Wide Web, enlarging the media landscape in new ways. Still, questions abound as media influence grows for a handful of companies. In this reading, media economist Benjamin Compaine reexamines eight assumptions about global media that critics of globalization take almost as articles of faith. Upon weighing the evidence, he concludes that the world's major media conglomerates are not as big, bad, dominant, or American as critics claim. For a contrasting view of this issue, see Reading 4-1, "The New Global Media" by Robert McChesney.

CONSIDER

1. What evidence does Compaine present that suggests a few big companies are *not* taking over the world's media?

2. Critics of media concentration claim that corporate ownership is killing hard-hitting journalism. Based on this reading and your own experience, do you agree? Why or why not?

3. Most analysts of communications policy believe that stricter regulation of the mass media, particularly broadcasting, is in the public interest. Why does Compaine conclude that the opposite is true?

Big media barons are routinely accused of dominating markets, dumbing down the news to plump up the bottom line, and forcing U.S. content on world audiences. But these companies are not as big, bad, dominant, or American as critics claim. And company size is largely irrelevant to many of the problems facing today's Fourth Estate.

"A FEW BIG COMPANIES ARE TAKING OVER THE WORLD'S MEDIA"

No. Much of the debate on media structure is too black-and-white. A merger of Time Inc. with Warner

From "Global Media" by Benjamin Compaine, *Foreign Policy,* November/December 2002, pp. 20–28. Copyright © 2002 by Benjamin Compaine. Reprinted with permission of Foreign Policy; www.foreignpolicy.com.

Communications and then with America Online dominates headlines, but the incremental growth of smaller companies from the bottom does not. Breakups and divestitures do not generally receive front-page treatment, nor do the arrival and rapid growth of new players or the shrinkage of once influential players.

In the United States, today's top 50 largest media companies account for little more of total media revenue than did the companies that made up the top 50 in 1986. CBS Inc., for example, was then the largest media company in the United States. In the 1990s, it sold off its magazines, divested its book publishing, and was not even among the 10 largest U.S. media companies by the time it agreed to be acquired by Viacom, which was a second tier player in 1986. Conversely, Bertelsmann, though a major player in Germany in 1986, was barely visible in the United States. By 1997, it was the third largest player in the United States, where it owns book publisher Random House. Companies such as

Amazon.com, Books-A-Million, Comcast, and C-Net were nowhere to be found on a list of the largest media companies in 1980. Others, such as Allied Artists, Macmillan, and Playboy Enterprises, either folded or grew so slowly as to fall out of the top ranks.

Indeed, media merger activity is more like rearranging the furniture: In the past 15 years, MCA with its Universal Pictures was sold by its U.S. owners to Matsushita (Japan), who sold to Seagram's (Canada), who sold to Vivendi (France). Vivendi has already announced that it will divest some major media assets, including textbook publisher Houghton-Mifflin. Bertelsmann also has had difficulty maintaining all the parts of its global enterprise: It recently fired its top executive and is planning to shed its online bookstore. There is an ebb as well as a flow among even the largest media companies.

The notion of the rise of a handful of all-powerful transnational media giants is also vastly overstated. Some media companies own properties internationally or provide some content across borders (for example, Vivendi's Canal+ distributes movies internationally), but no large media conglomerate owns newspapers, book publishers, radio stations, cable companies, or television licenses in all the major world markets. News Corp. comes closest to being a global media enterprise in both content and distribution, but on a global scale it is still a minor presence—that is, minor as a percentage of global media revenue, global audience, and in the number of markets it covers.

Media companies have indeed grown over the past 15 years, but this growth should be understood in context. Developed economies have grown, so expanding enterprises are often simply standing still in relative terms. Or their growth looks less weighty. For example, measured by revenue, Gannett was the largest U.S. newspaper publisher in 1986, its sales accounting for 3.4 percent of all media revenue that year. In 1997, it accounted for less than 2 percent of total media revenue. Helped by major acquisitions, Gannett's revenue had actually increased by 69 percent, but the U.S. economy had grown 86 percent. The media industry itself had grown 188 percent, making a "bigger" Gannett smaller in relative terms. Similar examples abound.

"U.S. COMPANIES DOMINATE THE MEDIA"

No. Long before liberalization of ownership in television in the 1980s, critics around the world were obsessed by the reach of U.S. programming, which cultural elites often considered too mass market and too infused with American cultural values. However, in most of the world, decisions of what programming to buy traditionally lay in the hands of managers who worked for government-owned or government-controlled broadcasters. Then, as now, no nation's media companies could require a programmer to buy their offerings or force consumers to watch them. As the market becomes more competitive, with content providers such as Canal+ and the BBC marketing their products globally, it is even more important that media enterprises offer programming that people want to watch.

While Viacom, Disney, and AOL Time Warner are U.S. owned, many non-U.S.-owned companies dominate the roster of the largest media groups: News Corp. (Australia), Bertelsmann (Germany), Reed-Elsevier (Britain/Netherlands), Vivendi, and Lagardere/Hachette (France), and Sony Corp. (Japan).

The pervasiveness of a handful of media companies looks even less relevant when one looks at media ownership across countries. The United Nations' "Human Development Report 2002" examined ownership of the five largest newspaper and broadcast enterprises in 97 countries. It found that 29 percent of the world's largest newspapers are state owned and another 57 percent are family owned. Only 8 percent are owned by employees or the public. For radio stations, 72 percent are state owned and 24 percent family owned. For television stations, 60 percent are state owned, 34 percent family owned. These data suggest there is little foreign direct investment in the media sectors of most countries.

News media can tap wire services from around the globe such as Reuters, Agence France-Presse, the Associated Press, Kyodo News, Xinhua News Agency, and Itar-Tass. TV news editors can use video feeds from sources as diverse as U.S.-based CNN to the Qatar-based Al Jazeera. The variety and ownership of TV content in general has substantially increased—a reality media critics ignore. From two state-owned channels in many European countries and from three U.S. networks plus the Public Broadcasting Service, there are now dozens, often hundreds, of video options via terrestrial, cable, and satellite transmission, not to mention the offline variety of videocassettes and DVDs and the online availability of music and movies. In addition, book and magazine publishing continues to be robust worldwide. Encouraged by relatively low startup costs, new publishers are popping up constantly.

"CORPORATE OWNERSHIP IS KILLING HARD-HITTING JOURNALISM"

A bright red herring. When exactly was this golden age of hard-hitting journalism? One might call to mind brief periods: the muckrakers in the early 20th century or Watergate reporting in the 1970s. But across countries and centuries, journalism typically has not been "hard-hitting." With more news outlets and competition today, there is a greater range of journalism than was typical in the past. Further, a 2000 comparison of 186 countries by Freedom House, a nonprofit devoted to promoting democracy, suggests that press independence, including journalists' freedom from economic influence, remained high in all but two members (Mexico and Turkey) of the Organisation for Economic Co-operation and Development, where global media's markets are concentrated.

Also underlying the complaint that news has been "dumbed down" is an assumption that the media ought to be providing a big dose of policy-relevant content. Japan's dominant public broadcaster, NHEL, does so, yet is Japan a more vibrant democracy as a result? More to the point, with so many media outlets today, readers and viewers can get more and better news from more diverse perspectives, if that is what they want. Or they can avoid it altogether. The alternative is to limit the number of outlets and impose content requirements on those remaining.

The third problem with this notion of corporations killing journalism is that it assumes ownership matters. In the old days of media moguls it may have: William Randolph Hearst, William Loeb, and Robert McCormick were attracted to the media because they each had political agendas, which permeated their newspapers. Nearly a century before Italian media owner Silvio Berlusconi rose to the top of Italian politics, Hearst, whose newspapers dominated in the United States, was elected to the U.S. Congress and harbored presidential aspirations. But Hearst's dual roles did not affect U.S. politics or democracy in any lasting way. The jury is still out on the effect of Berlusconi's dual roles.

Corporate-owned newspapers may actually provide better products than those that are family owned: Research suggests that large, chain-owned newspapers devote more space to editorial material than papers owned by small firms. In many parts of South America, where regulation has restricted or prevented corporate ownership, family-run enterprises have often been closely identified with ideological biases or even with

using political influence to benefit other businesses. Brazilian media enterprise Globo, owned by the politically involved Marinho family, encompasses a TV network, radio, cable, and magazines. Yet Globo no longer opposes recent moves to liberalize Brazilian media ownership because then it could gain access to desirable foreign investment. As Latin American media shift from family-owned, partisan media to corporations, observes Latin American media scholar Silvio Waisbord, the media become less the "public avenues for the many ambitions of their owners," and their coverage of government corruption "is more likely to be informed by marketing calculations and the professional aspirations of reporters." This trade-off may not be bad.

Global media will not necessarily introduce aggressive journalism in places where press freedom has traditionally been constricted. For instance, News Corp. was criticized for dropping BBC news programming from Star TV presumably to mollify Chinese leaders in the mid-1990s. Yet satellite broadcaster Phoenix TV (in which News Corp.'s Star TV maintains a 37.6 percent stake, alongside that of the local Chinese owners) sometimes pushes the envelope in China, as when it reported on the election of Chen Shui-bian as president in Taiwan.

"GLOBAL MEDIA DROWN OUT LOCAL CONTENT"

Absolutely not. Most media—like politics—are inherently local. Global firms peddle wholly homogeneous content across markets at their peril. Thus, MTV in Brazil plays a mix of music videos and other programming determined by local producers, even though it shares a recognizable format with MTV stations elsewhere. News Corp.'s newspapers in the United Kingdom look and read differently from those in the United States. When Star TV, an Asian subsidiary of News Corp., began broadcasting satellite television into India, few tuned in to *Dallas* and *The Bold and the Beautiful* dubbed in Hindi. The network only succeeded in India once it hired an executive with experience in Indian programming to create Indian soap operas and when an Indian production house took over news and current affairs programming.

Often viewed as a negative, consolidation may have considerable social benefits. It took the deep pockets of News Corp. to create and sustain a long-awaited fourth broadcast network in the United States. And the 1990 merger in the United Kingdom of Sky Channel and

BSB created a viable television competitor from two money-losing satellite services.

"THE INTERNET HAS LEVELED THE PLAYING FIELD"

Yes. Or more accurately, it's helping to level the terrain because it is a relatively low-cost conduit for all content providers. As the old adage goes, "Freedom of the press is guaranteed only to those who own one." Make no mistake: an activist with a dial-up Internet connection and 10 megabytes of Web server space cannot easily challenge Disney for audiences. But an individual or a small group can reach the whole world and, with a little work and less money, can actually find an audience.

Worldwide, an estimated 581 million people were online by 2002, more than one third of whom lived outside North America and Europe. Yet the Internet is in its infancy. The number of users is still growing and will continue to expand to the literate population as access costs decrease.

Once online, Internet users have access to thousands of information providers. Some are the same old players—Disney with its stable of cartoon icons, Infinity with its familiar music and talk-radio broadcasting, and old government-run stations still operating in much of the world. But these coexist with newer, Internet-only options such as those found at Realguide.com, which links to 2,500 real-time audio streams from around the world, or NetRadio, which outdraws many traditional stations. These Internet-only "broadcasters" have not had to invest in government-sanctioned licenses and generally have no limits on their speech.

In countries where governments strictly control print and broadcast media, governments also can try to restrict Internet access, as China does. But some may choose not to do so: In Malaysia, the government pledged not to censor the Internet to promote its version of Silicon Valley to foreign investors. As a consequence, Malaysian cyberspace media are free of the restrictions their print and broadcast brethren face.

"PROLIFERATING MEDIA OUTLETS BALKANIZE PUBLIC OPINION"

No. The flip side of concerns that media concentration has limited available information is the concern that technology has made it possible to access so many voices that people in democratic societies can and will seek only information that supports their prejudices. A fragmented public, tuning in only to select cable channels or specific Web sites, could thus wall itself off from healthy public debate.

Recent U.S. studies show that as users gain experience with the Internet, they use it not to replace other sources of information but for more practical applications. They perform work-related tasks, make purchases and other financial transactions, write e-mail messages, and seek information that is important to their everyday lives.

Although news is low on the list of its uses, the Internet functions in much the same way as older news media: offering opportunities for both those who directly seek news sites and those who chance upon news links serendipitously. The Pew Internet and American Life Project reports that 42 percent of those who read news on the Web typically find news while they are doing other things online. This picture is not consistent with the notion that Web audiences routinely tune out information with which they disagree.

"MEDIA COVERAGE DRIVES FOREIGN POLICY"

Probably not often. Analyzing media coverage is often a chicken-and-egg dilemma: What stimulated the media to cover an event or issue? And if public policy responds to an event the news media cover, does that mean the media (or those who run the media) set the agenda?

The idea that media coverage of international crises can spark a response from politicians is termed the "CNN effect." The classic case is the coverage of starving children in Somalia in the early 1990s, which was followed by U.S. military involvement in humanitarian relief efforts. But even in the case of Somalia, some administration officials actually used the media to get the attention of other officials, and the majority of the coverage in Somalia followed rather than preceded official action.

In many places, governments are even more likely to be driving media coverage rather than the other way around, although it may suit governments to appear as if they have bowed to public opinion. The Chinese government delayed release of the crew of the U.S. EP-3 Spy plane that made an emergency landing on Hainan Island in 2001, claiming that an embittered Chinese public demanded it. Angry Web comments did precede and were then reflected in media coverage of the incident. But at the same time, the government had been fanning the flames, cultivating nationalistic sentiment through the selection and treatment of stories in the news. At other times, the Chinese government both censors Web comments and withholds information from the media when it needs to preserve its foreign policy options.

"STRICTER REGULATION OF MEDIA IS IN THE PUBLIC INTEREST"

Just the opposite. Beware when someone claims to be speaking for the "public interest." In most cases, those who invoke the term really mean "interested publics." For example, advertisers' sense of which policies on media ownership are in their interest may differ from that of regular newspaper readers or that of satellite TV subscribers.

Fostering competition has long been a central tenet of U.S. media regulation. What if preventing two newspapers from merging results in both having to trim news budgets or pages, neither having the resources to engage in investigative reporting, or worse yet, one closing shop? Media concentration may be in the public interest if it provides a publisher with greater profit margins and the wherewithal to spend some of that on editorial content, and research in fact shows this is the case.

Licensing acts as an entry barrier to new players, and antitrust laws often lag behind reality. In the market for video program distribution, for instance, ter-restrial broadcast licensees compete with cable operators and networks, who in turn compete with satellite providers. Regulation and policy limits will always be necessary, but having different regulatory frameworks for each media segment makes less sense today.

Governments that give can also take. Japanese law makes public broadcaster NHK one of the world's most autonomous public broadcasters, yet the ruling Liberal Democratic Party (LDP) strongly influences the agencies that control media licenses and that select NHK's governing board. Not coincidentally, NHK provides neutral, policy-relevant news but avoids controversial topics and investigative reporting. Where Japanese commercial television has tried to fill this gap, LDP politicians have reacted: in one case, asking an advertiser to withdraw sponsorship and in another, seeking the withdrawal of a broadcasting license.

Paradoxically, relaxing broadcast regulation may expand competition. When News Corp. put together a fourth network in the United States in 1986, the timing was not random. It followed two regulatory decisions: the Federal Communications Commission raised the limit on local licenses that a single firm could own from seven to twelve and waived a rule that kept TV networks from owning their programming. The first change allowed News Corp. to assemble a core of stations in larger markets that gave it a viable base audience, and the second sanctioned News Corp.'s purchase of 20th Century Fox, with its television production studio. Fox was thus able to launch the first successful alternative to the Big Three in 30 years. Its success also paved the way for three other large media players to initiate networks.

RELATED LINKS

- United Nations Human Development Reports (http://hdr.undp.org/reports/default.cfm)
- Global Media Monitor (http://lass.calumet.purdue.edu/cca/gmm)
- Organization for Economic Cooperation and Development (http://www.oecd.org/home)
- Benjamin M. Compaine (http://www1.primushost.com/~bcompain)

FOR FURTHER RESEARCH

To find out more about the topics discussed in this reading, use InfoTrac College Edition. Type in keywords and subject terms such as "corporate ownership," "public interest," and "global media." You can access InfoTrac College Edition from the Wadsworth/Thomson Communication Café homepage: http://communication.wadsworth.com.

Reading 4-3

The Threat to the Net

Pat Aufderheide

EDITOR'S NOTE

In this cautionary commentary about the future of broadband networks, Pat Aufderheide, a professor in the School of Communication at American University, warns that the recent wave of media mergers and acquisitions (notably AOL and Time Warner, and AT&T and TCI) may partition a large part of the Internet with a costly commercial fence, stifling innovation and hindering access. Given that the future of high-bandwidth media depends on broadband networks, Aufderheide sees the actions of the cable industry as the front line in the battle to keep access to the Internet open and free.

CONSIDER

1. In your opinion, do the mergers of AOL and Time Warner, as well as AT&T and TCI, threaten freedom of access to the Internet? Why or why not?

2. Why is the debate over broadband networks not just about the future of the Internet, but about the future of communication media in general?

3. If the cable companies succeed in becoming the dominant Internet service providers, will the innovation and creativity that has characterized the Web until now vanish?

Who owns the Internet? If you think the answer is "nobody," you're right—for now. That's why it has been such an astonishing innovation that has flourished so vibrantly at the grassroots. But this pioneering era may end badly, with an all-too-familiar finish: Big business tames a giddy and experimental phenomenon and turns it into a nice, tidy, and ever-so-profitable money-maker. And why not? That's what happened with phones, with radio, with TV. The difference this time may be that too many people have sampled an open information environment to settle for less.

The thugs of the story, who want to fence in the Internet, are the cable companies, led by communications conglomerates like AT&T. They now have something many of us want: broadband Internet service. But they plan to make us pay for it in more ways than one. And the stakes have risen dramatically since the

largest of the Internet Service Providers, America Online (AOL), announced a merger with Time Warner.

The fight is about closed access versus open access to broadband.

"Broadband" means faster transmission of more data. For Web users, that's a lot. It's the Internet squared: no waiting, no loading. With broadband, Web pages fly by like the flicked pages of a book, and Web video looks just like TV. In fact, it may be TV, and your phone, and your spreadsheet program, and your fax, and anything else that can attach to the sophisticated transmission system. That's because broadband is not simply the future of the Internet. It's the future of our communications systems.

Now, as cable companies are beginning to offer broadband, local governments are demanding open access: the ability to get on the broadband using any Internet Service Provider on the same terms as anyone else's. The cable companies are fighting for closed access: They want to force everyone who uses their broadband service to go through their preferred Internet Service Providers.

From "The Threat to the Net" by Pat Aufderheide, *The Progressive*, February 2000, pp. 17–19. Copyright © 2000 The Progressive. Reprinted with permission. www.progressive.org.

Until the announced merger, America Online had been one of the leaders in the battle for open access. But, with its merger pending, that could change. Time Warner, along with owning TV networks, movie studios, magazines, and music companies, is also the second largest cable operator. AOL executives proudly pledged their continued commitment to open access. But if the merger goes through, AOL Time Warner will have to decide whether it's still for open access or whether it will opt instead for closed access.

What AT&T does may be very important in that story. It's now the largest cable provider in the country, as well as the largest long distance phone company in the world. Back when AT&T was Ma Bell, before 1982, the phone company was an easy target for resentment. It's an easier target now. It became the largest cable company in the world last year [1999] when it bought TCI, which has had its own image problems. Before the merger, TCI was the largest cable company in the United States. Now, the two reviled giants are joined at the bottom line.

Almost two decades after government lawyers broke up the old phone monopoly and AT&T abandoned local service, the company owns a pathway to many of us again.

Cable wires reach out and touch three-quarters of U.S. homes. They also pass almost all of them, and digital cable wires could handle phone traffic. AT&T has gone on to buy other cable systems and awaits Federal Communications Commission (FCC) approval of a merger with the third largest cable company, Media-One [this approval has since been granted]. Factor in MediaOne's 25 percent interest in—you guessed it!—Time Warner, and AT&T has access to more than half of America's homes once more. AT&T may even be interested in joining forces with AOL Time Warner in some formal way down the line.

What these mergers do is threaten the freedom to access the Internet.

Today, you can choose from thousands of Internet Service Providers, and you can make that decision based on whether they offer quick hook-ups or whether they design nice chat rooms or whether they're run by your neighbor's teenager. If you want broadband service, though, cable companies will steer you to their own Internet Service Providers (AT&T's is Excite @Home).

Cable companies want to determine the speed at which any user might send information or receive it, and the Internet hardware company Cisco Systems is already selling the equipment to let them do so. AT&T, for instance, won't let you send more than ten minutes of video at a time via Excite@Home.

Since cable companies like AT&T are the first ones out of the chute with broadband, they are in a position to set terms. And they want to discourage potential competition by strangling it at birth. They have no interest in allowing anyone else to offer the equivalent of a channel over their cable lines on the same terms they offer to their own Internet Service Providers. They want people to come to cable itself for that content or to the Internet for that content, as long as it's through their system.

Content providers—be they Disney, Fox, progressive news groups, the PTA, or consumer guide services—all may lose an opportunity to reach citizens on the Net directly and to create programming that would find its own audience without paying a gatekeeper and submitting to that gatekeeper's terms.

The content providers that stand to lose the most are those without financial clout, and especially the nonprofit organizations that keep our civic culture alive. They could become second-class citizens on the Web. Their material could be transmitted at a slower speed or not at all. And if the cable companies succeed, the grassroots innovation and creativity that has characterized the Web may vanish.

Today, the Net environment is pretty chaotic, and many consumers have become accustomed to using search engines and portals and filters to find their way around. You choose the selectors; you can pick a provider that simply hauls your data around and lets you go where you want to go, or you can hook up with a more commercialized provider.

But are you ready for an Internet where you have no choice but to go through a provider that tailors your searches according to the profit-sharing deals it can cut? And are you ready to hand over to the cable company the power to determine whether to deliver your material and at what speed?

This is not some science fiction story. The battle for control over the Internet is already raging. And it is taking place on the unlikely field of local regulation, as cities and counties face off against the cable companies. Free speech and public interest advocates, along with the Internet Service Providers, joined forces to support these local officials, who confront cable companies as they apply to open or renew local franchises.

What's at stake here is not just the kinds of problems we face with cable services. That would be bad enough. On cable today, we have content problems, like having them decide for us which channels are on our systems, which news services they'll carry, and whether we can see C-SPAN II. We also have monopoly pricing problems. Cable companies give us stations we don't want and make us pay for the whole bundle. If we get only the broadband services that cable companies find it convenient and lucrative to give us, we'll certainly have these problems.

But we may have a much bigger problem: the killing of opportunity—political, social, economic—before it's even been imagined.

No one imagined the burgeoning of freedom of expression on the Net, or the skyrocketing of Net businesses, or the way that Internet communication has changed the operations of nonprofit groups, which can now instantly alert members to a zoning hearing or create an online public record of parents' complaints about school issues or post their grant applications on the Net.

The original design of the Web was responsible for its dynamism, and if the cable companies are allowed to dictate the design of broadband, the Web will take a much different shape in the future.

Why foreclose futures that stimulate competition, benefit consumers, foster innovation, boost the economy, and nurture civic life?

"The reason the Internet has been such an engine for creativity and growth is the way it was built, its architecture," Lawrence Lessig, a Harvard law professor, explained at a briefing in Washington, D.C. held by public interest advocates and underwritten by what was then America Online. Lessig's book, *Code and Other Laws of Cyberspace* (Basic Books, 1999), explains the link between this architecture and politics. Closed access services, by the way, can easily discourage unprofitable transactions. If you had wanted to see a video transmission of Lessig's presentation (which was available through nogatekeepers.com), you couldn't do it on Excite@Home.

The Internet was designed for researchers to be able to work together cheaply and easily, so it was open to any use by any user. The Net is really nothing more than the set of open and public agreements among computers about how to reach each other's code. Any computer can use the same simple software to "speak" to any other, often sending its packets of digitized data over phone lines. So long as your machine knows how to talk to all the other machines, and it has a pathway to send its data, you're part of the network. You're on

the Net. You are the Net. Users make the Net; the system evolves with the users.

When most of that data was in the form of simple text, phone lines worked perfectly to get ordinary users hooked up to the Net. Voice takes ten times as much space as data does, so there was lots of extra room.

"We've been lucky. Today's Internet ecology required no effort of design," Lessig explained. But images, especially moving images, take up gargantuan amounts of space when turned into digital code, and the great wads of data they send clog up the whole system.

So the next stage of the Net can't piggyback on existing networks. It must be built. And the way it is built will determine how it is used, and what it is used for. AT&T wants to design the system so that it controls the technology, making it closed from the start.

Broadband is not entirely the province of cable companies. In fact, local phone companies are developing what are called DSL (digital subscriber line) services—vastly speeded-up data transmission over phone lines. They are legally required to make their facilities available to anyone who wants to provide DSL service. But they are lumbering far behind in offering rapid Internet service, partly because they aren't any more eager for competition than the cable companies are, and partly because the cost of laying new wires is high.

Cable companies, which have no legal requirement to share their broadband, have told policymakers that they've paid a lot for these systems, so why should they give access away free? As Daniel Somers, the new head of AT&T's cable operations, said recently, the company didn't spend $56 billion to get into cable "to have the blood sucked out of our vein."

Portland, Oregon, has led the way for open access. But the battle with AT&T, which began in late 1998, took City Commissioner Erik Sten by surprise. He's in charge of utilities, and he went head-to-head with AT&T.

"In Portland, we had two cable companies: Paragon and TCI, and AT&T bought both of them," Sten recalls. "When they came to us for approval of their franchise license, we said that they had to offer open access, which is also called nondiscriminatory broadband service. There are about 100 Internet Service Providers in the Portland area, and we wanted them to be able to offer access to broadband on the same terms as Excite@Home. If you don't have competition with Internet Service Providers, you ultimately hand over control of the Internet to AT&T. Plus, our 100 local companies, which pay local taxes, would go out of business."

But there's more to it than that. "Access to the Internet should be as open and reasonably priced as possible," he says. "Allowing AT&T to have closed access would be just one more step in the homogenization of the information industry. It goes against the free flow of ideas, and it doesn't allow competitive pricing."

Sten attended the briefing in Washington with Professor Lessig and explained the decision to confront AT&T. "This did not look like a tough issue for us," he said. "We thought the question was, why *wouldn't* you require open access? I was astonished at AT&T's reaction. We had an amicable hearing, we saw nothing to stop us from requiring open access, we laid out the reasons, and AT&T's response was: 'We hope you have a large legal budget.'"

Sten didn't. But the city of Portland still won its first court battle. Since then, eleven other local jurisdictions have followed suit. But in Portland, rather than knuckle under and actually provide broadband service, AT&T has ordered its lawyers to appeal. And AT&T has plenty of money to spend.

To Ron Sims, the county executive who stared down AT&T in the Seattle area, the issue is uncomplicated. It's about control of content; it's about free speech; it's about choice. "No single entity should control content," he says. "We live in the heartland of high-tech development. We know high speed access is the doorway to innovation. Don't slam that door."

But how long will the door stay open? Part of the answer depends on the fate of AOL and Time Warner.

Part of the answer also lies with AT&T. It could move toward open access itself. As a result of pressure from regulators and activists, AT&T signed an agreement in principle with the large Internet Service Provider MindSpring, permitting access to AT&T's broadband service in Seattle.

The FCC has the authority to decide whether cable should provide open access, and it has a new op-

portunity to advise the Federal Trade Commission and the Justice Department about the AOL Time Warner merger.

Unfortunately, with AT&T, it has declined to decide. Instead, it has adopted a policy of "watchful waiting," in the words of FCC chairman, Bill Kennard.

"The real sad thing is that the FCC has just sat on its hands while a big company is trying to buy up something that should be publicly available," says Sten.

The problem with "watchful waiting," says Lessig, is that not mandating open access comes down to supporting closed access. And if the cable industry gets to build closed systems, it will be expensive and perhaps impossible to crack open later or to nurture the innovation that has been stifled. It's like saying you don't need to use seat belts, Lessig told the FCC, because people can always go the emergency room if they get hurt.

Under the 1996 rewrite of the nation's basic communications law, the FCC is required to streamline its regulations and phase out any that aren't conducive to competition. The FCC has argued that any regulation will stop broadband deployment. This is just what the biggest cable-telecom companies want it to say.

While the FCC treats AT&T like a tender flower of innovation, local officials are aggressively pursuing its competitors. "Innovative broadband companies are coming to Portland now, in spite of the fact that we're a pretty small market," Sten says. "That's a result of our open access decision."

Sten worries that the AOL Time Warner merger could just mean another giant with its own closed access system. "From the open access perspective, that's not any better," he says. "We should have a federal policy role here."

And the message that regulators need to hear is simple: Protect what we've got, and make sure we can build on it. Make open access the terms of doing business.

RELATED LINKS

■   Federal Communications Commission (http://www.fcc.gov)

■   Media Access Project (http://www.mediaaccess.org)

■   Lawrence Lessig (http://www.lessig.org)

■   Center for Social Media (http://centerforsocialmedia.org/aufderheide.html)

FOR FURTHER RESEARCH

To find out more about the topics discussed in this reading, use InfoTrac College Edition. Type in keywords and subject terms such as "nondiscriminatory broadband service," "Internet regulation," and "open Internet access." You can access InfoTrac from the Wadsworth/Thomson Communication Café homepage: http://communication.wadsworth.com.

Reading 4-4

Big World: How Clear Channel Programs America
Jeff Sharlet

EDITOR'S NOTE

Since the 1996 Telecommunications Act, media companies have been allowed to own as many as eight radio stations per media market and as many stations nationally as a company can acquire. Though this relaxation of the FCC radio ownership rules (which previously had been limited to two stations per market and 40 nationwide) is thought to encourage free-market competition, it has also resulted in unprecedented consolidation within the radio industry. Now the biggest radio conglomerate, Clear Channel Communications, owns some 1,225 radio stations from coast-to-coast and reaches roughly 200 million people, or 70% of the American public. This reading from Harper's *magazine chronicles the alleged control that Clear Channel exercises over local music trends, threatening artistic diversity and creativity, inflating ticket prices and advertising rates and, some would say, squelching freedom of speech—all in exchange for corporate efficiencies.*

CONSIDER

1. Does this article present convincing evidence that Clear Channel "programs America," as the title suggests? If so, in what ways does Clear Channel exercise control?

2. As a matter of communications policy, is it desirable for one company to own so many radio stations that a single broadcaster can reach 70% of the American public?

3. How does Clear Channel's ownership of billboards and concert venues and employment of local "talent buyers" shape the character of the local music scene in cities like Philadelphia?

On July 17, 2002, as a band called The Boils was preparing to play, seven men with badges, police officers and agents of Philadelphia's Department of Licenses and Inspections, walked into the basement of the First Unitarian Church at Chestnut and Van Pelt. Nobody

From "Big World: How Clear Channel Programs America" by Jeff Sharlet, *Harper's,* December 2003, Cover Story: War of the Worlds, Part One, pp. 37–45. Copyright © 2003 by Jeff Sharlet. Reprinted with permission.

knows who tipped them off, but it was clear that someone wanted the Church, as the club in the basement was called, shut down. The show's promoter, Sean Agnew, had been booking acts there for six years, but before the night when the inspectors appeared his shows had not warranted a single official complaint. A tall, lean 24-year-old with a stubbled undertaker's jaw and long, dark eyelashes, Agnew almost always wore a black mesh cap, with DORM SLUT scrawled on it graffiti-style in silver Sharpie, crammed over thick black hair.

He was known locally, and in little music magazines around the country, as "DJR500." Agnew's shows were "straight-edge," which meant that drugs and alcohol were not welcome. A local paper had recently named him a man of the year, alongside 76ers guard Allen Iverson.

The Department of Licenses and Inspections does not keep records of complaints. All the deputy commissioner could tell Agnew was that someone had gone down to City Hall, pulled the Church's permit, and discovered that the Church was not zoned to hold gatherings for entertainment purposes. No bingo, no swing dancing, and definitely no Boils. The inspectors gave Agnew a red-and-white-striped "Cease Work/Operations" sticker to affix to the Church's door and declared the concert over.

Agnew got on stage and told everyone to go home; his friends circulated through the crowd, whispering that the show was moving to West Philadelphia, to a theater called The Rotunda. Soon Agnew cut a deal to produce all his concerts there, but he was able to put on only one more show before the Department of Licenses and Inspections shut that operation down as well. Someone had gone down to City Hall, pulled the theater's permit, and discovered that it was zoned for drama only. Then inspectors visited the record shop where Agnew sold his tickets, with the news that someone had gone down to City Hall, pulled the shop's permit, and found out that it wasn't zoned for selling tickets. A few days later the inspectors were back at the shop, looking for a box under the counter in which the store kept Agnew's mail—another violation, reported by yet another concerned citizen.

Although he had no evidence, Agnew's suspicions fell on Clear Channel Communications. Clear Channel controls almost every concert venue in and around Philadelphia—from the Theater of the Living Arts on South Street to the Tweeter Center in Camden—as well as six radio stations and nearly 700 billboards. The company's local viceroy, a man named Larry Magid, once ran the city's live-music scene as a private fiefdom. Now, since Clear Channel bought him out in 2000, he manages it as a corporate franchise. Clear Channel maintains a similar chokehold on live music in almost every major city in America, as well as in most of the small ones. Agnew, who had managed to book bands that could have made far more money playing Clear Channel theaters, suspected that he was grit in the machine.

"Four or five years ago," Agnew told me one day in the record shop, where he also works as a clerk, "there were a lot more people aware of corporate power." Now, he said, money so dominated the music scene that a lot of younger kids didn't even know what "selling out" meant. When I asked him what had kept him in business, he corrected me: "I don't consider what I got into a 'business.'" Many Philadelphia music fans had rallied to his defense, he explained. After the closures, Agnew sent out word to his email list, 8,000 people who had attended at least one of his shows, and within days 1,000 of them had written to City Hall. He rented a paid mailbox. He persuaded a lawyer to represent the Church pro bono, and soon the Church had a dance-hall permit, the record shop had a ticket-selling permit, and Agnew had more events scheduled than before he was shut down.

Whoever was behind the attempt to close the Church, nearly every concertgoer I talked to blamed Clear Channel. They adored Agnew for "standing up to the evil empire," as one musician put it. Agnew, a vegetarian who lives with a cat and thousands of obsessively organized records, is now the most authentic rock and roller in the city. When he walks down the street, people nod and smile and pat him on the back. DJR500 is huge, and one day soon Clear Channel might make him an offer.

Some people complain about Clear Channel because they miss their old, independent stations, some because Clear Channel stations shrink playlists and recycle an ever smaller number of songs. Musicians say touring has become a cross-country hopscotch from one Clear Channel venue to another, each more sterile than the last; their agents and managers say that if artists don't play when and where Clear Channel says, they will suffer less airplay or none. As journalists point out, Clear Channel has made commercial radio nearly reporting-free, believing that its syndication of Rush Limbaugh to as many stations as possible fulfills its mandate to provide news and political diversity. Evangelical Christians are distressed about radio firsts pioneered by Clear Channel DJs, such as torturing and killing live animals on the air (a chicken in Denver, a pig in Florida), but this can happen only where there's a DJ: Clear Channel has put hundreds of radio veterans out of work, replacing them with canned broadcasts tailored to sound local and live. Consumer advocates argue that such robot radio is the only efficiency Clear Channel has passed along to the public. In the last several years, they point out, the cost of "free" radio—in terms of time spent enduring ads—has spiked. Concert tickets have jumped from an average of $25 to more than $40, and radio advertising rates have risen by two thirds, pricing small businesses off the airwaves.

Clear Channel says that its enemies snipe simply because it's big, and this is probably true. No one had imagined that a radio company could get so big. When Clear Channel was founded in 1972, with one station bought by a San Antonio investment banker named L. Lowry Mays, federal law forbade a company from owning more than seven FM stations and seven AMs. By the 1990s, that cap had crept up to 40 stations nationwide, no more than two per market. Then, in 1996, Congress passed the Telecommunications Act. Up to eight stations per market would be allowed, and as many overall as a company could digest. Within less than a year more than 1,000 mergers occurred; by 2000 four behemoths dominated the business. Today, Clear Channel rules.

Z-100 in New York? Clear Channel. K-BIG in L.A.? Clear Channel. KISS in Chicago? Clear Channel. KISS, POWER, the FOX, and the ZONE are all Clear Channel brands, and the dozens of radio stations nationwide that bear one of those names take their orders from San Antonio, where Clear Channel's headquarters remain, in an unassuming limestone box next to a golf course. Rush Limbaugh is Clear Channel, and so are Dr. Laura, Casey Kasem, and Glenn Beck, the rising star of rant radio who organized the "Rally for America" prowar [the second Iraq war] demonstrations.

Last June, when the FCC raised the caps on how much access to the American public any one media company could control—a move too crassly reminiscent of the days of robber barons for even the Republican-controlled House of Representatives, which voted 400-21 to roll it back—the one media company the commission hinted might actually be too big was Clear Channel. The recent debate in Congress over television ownership has focused on two numbers: 35 percent, which is the portion of American viewers to which a single TV-station owner can currently broadcast, and 45 percent, which strikes media giants as a more reasonable number. Clear Channel, meanwhile, reaches roughly 200 million people, or more than 70 percent of the American public. It owns 1,225 stations within the United States, or around 11 percent overall, and greater portions in major markets. It broadcasts from at least 200 more stations abroad, many clustered just south of the border like radio ma-

quiladoras, and it owns or controls more live-music venues than any other company. In the first six months of 2003, Clear Channel sold more tickets than the 49 next largest promoters combined; in 2001, it claimed 70 percent of the total live-music take. The billboards that ring the stadiums, line the highways, clutter the skyline? Clear Channel owns most of those too.

As a business enterprise, Clear Channel is an experiment. It is giant and potentially unstable, more reliant on muscle than on financial finesse, and to date only moderately profitable. A sort of Frankenstein's monster, it was built from the parts of once-dying industries and jolted into life by the 1996 Telecommunications Act. Supporters of the law say there was no choice; at the time, more than half the stations in the country were losing money. Opponents retort that Clear Channel is hardly a democratic solution. "I don't think there was anybody in Washington in 1996 who could have imagined that a few years later there'd be one company owning 1,200 stations," says Michael Copps, one of the two commissioners on the FCC's five-person board who opposed raising ownership caps. "We should never give anybody the ability to have that much power."

When I asked to interview Clear Channel's executives, a P.R. rep for the company told me that Clear Channel wouldn't talk to me, because it no longer needs the media: a Zen koan of consolidation. After the company learned that several underlings had talked nevertheless, radio CEO John Hogan agreed to speak with me on the phone. An amiable, 46-year-old former radio-ad salesman, he told me that "the key to radio is that it's a very personal, intimate medium." Hogan's first executive role was as the general manager of WPCH, a fully automated station in Atlanta known as "the Peach." Hogan made running the station sound like changing a diaper. "It was a 'beautiful music' station," he said. "You didn't have to make any decisions. All you did was put the tape on in the morning and you let it run for twenty-four hours and then you changed it the next day. There were no decisions to make, they were made for you. It was nice, you know, it was easy."

His idea of what radio is and can be does not seem to have changed since his days at the Peach. "People use radio 'cause it works," he told me. "If it stops working for 'em, they stop it." The "they" he was referring to were the advertisers. "For the first time ever, we can talk to advertisers about a true national radio footprint," he told me. "If you have a younger, female-skewing advertiser who wants access to that audience, we can give them stations in, you know, Boston and New York and Miami and Chicago, literally across the country. Los Angeles, San Francisco . . . We can take outdoor [ads] and radio, and *drive* people to live events and concerts and capture the excitement, the real visceral experience." The goal? "A different *kind* of advertising opportunity."

Hogan was promoted to radio CEO just over a year ago. He has tried to soften the company's image after several years of brutal acquisitions under the leadership of Randy Michaels, the former disc jockey who now manages the company's new-technologies division. Clear Channel wouldn't let me talk with Michaels, but not long after he left the radio division he gave a trade publication called Radio Ink an even blunter rationale for the company's push to dominate live music as it does radio. "People attending a concert are experiencing something with tremendous emotion," he said. "They're . . . vulnerable."

Across town from the Church, in a little club called the Khyber Pass, I went to see a show booked by Clear Channel's man in Philadelphia. The headliner was a band called The Dragons, best known for their album *Rock Like Fuck,* but the night belonged to the opening act, the Riverboat Gamblers, or, rather, to their singer, Teko. Tall, skinny, gruesomely pretty, he vibrated across the two-foot-high stage, shouting loud and hard. No one was there to see the bands; the crowd, maybe a hundred strong, was there to get drunk, or to take someone home. But everyone in the room—a cigar box painted matte black from top to bottom, beer on the floor and loose wiring dangling from the ceiling—pressed forward, chins bobbing, drunken eyes widening. Near the end of a song called "Hey, Hey, Hey," Teko jumped and landed on the two-step riser at the front of the stage. It slid away, sent him crashing onto his spine. His left hand clutched the mike, into which he continued to scream; his right hand, flailing to its beat even faster, had begun to bleed at the palm. Then he jolted off the floor, bit the mike, and launched into another song: "I get the feelin' you're gonna need a feedin'! Let's eat! Let's eat! Let's eat!"

A few minutes later, Clear Channel's man jammed himself into the edge of the crowd, grinning and rocking his head as the singer leaped from the stage and drove into the audience, swinging his bloody hand like a wrecking ball. Clear Channel's man loved it. Bryan Dilworth was a big man with small eyes and a head of thinning red hair that brought to mind Curly of the Three Stooges. He was in what he called "that mo-

ment." He grinned and rocked his head; he stopped scanning the room and actually watched the band. He elbowed me, nodding toward the Riverboat Gamblers, as if to say, "See? See?"

When the song ended, Dilworth stepped back from the crowd, returned to the bar in the next room, and ordered another Jameson's.

"Dude," he said. "*That* is what I'm fucking talking about."

Meaning the scene, the variables, "the combustibles": everything he claimed Clear Channel could never buy. That included himself. At various times, Dilworth told me he worked for Clear Channel, or didn't work for Clear Channel, or Clear Channel simply didn't matter. Sometimes he called Clear Channel "the evil empire"; sometimes he said it was the best thing that ever happened to his town. It was hard to know which Dilworth to believe: the one who took me up to the cluttered office of his private company, Curt Flood, two stories above the Khyber Pass, to play me tracks from one of his bands on a cheap boom box; or the one who took me on a tour of a Clear Channel hall and conceded that the paychecks that mattered came from Clear Channel, that he had a Clear Channel email address and a Clear Channel phone number, that he was in truth a Clear Channel "talent buyer" responsible for filling the calendars of a dozen Clear Channel venues around the city. At times Dilworth spoke of Clear Channel Philadelphia in the first person. "I am living proof," he told me more than once, "that Clear Channel Philadelphia is going to rock."

This flexibility was what made Dilworth such a valuable asset. Unlike Starbucks or Borders, Clear Channel does not build its empire from new franchises but rather goes from town to town and buys local operations. Clear Channel has Dilworths in every city with a scene, and what makes them so effective is precisely that their affiliation with the company is subject to doubt, even in their own minds. Dilworth develops "baby bands" in clubs like the Khyber on his own time and filters the most marketable of them to the more lucrative venues he books as his alter ego, a Clear Channel talent buyer. Such a double role appears to be part of the Clear Channel business plan, in which the independents—who should be an alternative to Clear Channel—instead become the company's farm team. As a result, live music is following the route taken by radio. Songs that sound the same are performed in venues that look the same and even have the same name: identically branded venues, all controlled by Clear

Channel, brick-and-mortar embodiments of KISS, the FOX, and the ZONE.

"Everything is so fucked," said Dilworth, another shot of Jameson's at his lips. "Music business my ass. Take the 'music' off and that's what it is." He drank the shot, and then he was talking about the Riverboat Gamblers again: Those dudes got it, they're going places, and Dilworth would take them there, Clear Channel all the way. That's not monopoly, said Dilworth, it's business in America. "Deregulation set this table a long time ago. I'm not taking a 'can't beat 'em then join 'em' attitude, but . . ." He trailed off, because, of course, he was.

Dilworth's contradictory relationship with Clear Channel extended even into his home life. His wife, Kristin Thomson, worked for the Future of Music Coalition, the leading activist group against consolidation. FMC's head, Jenny Toomey, had been a prominent witness against raising ownership caps during last winter's Senate hearings, at which she laid out a specific and compelling case for how Clear Channel has become a near monopoly. Thomson and Toomey had once been minor rock stars together, as the indie group Tsunami, and Dilworth thought his marriage to Thomson was a simple instance of "rocker dude meets rocker chick." He said they didn't talk about politics. Dilworth himself had given lectures for FMC on the music business. ("Fuck the art," he had advised a conference of musicians. "Put the hit first.") Thomson, for her part, felt that her husband wasn't like the rest of Clear Channel.

One night, when Dilworth and I were in his office, he showed me his first gold record, awarded for a small role he had played in the success of the band Good Charlotte. A very small role, he said; gold records get passed around freely when a record company sees a future in a relationship.

"A down payment?" I said.

"Yeah, man, it's like, a favor for a favor."

"What's the difference between that and payola?"

Dilworth guffawed and looked at me like I was the dumbest kid in school. "It's *all* payola, dude." Then his shoulders slumped and he stopped laughing.

What determines the course of music today is not a zeitgeist or a paradigm or anything that can be dismissed simply as fashion. It's not even greed. What matters now is the process. "Cross-selling." "Clustering." A confluence of car radios and concert halls, the drinks at the bar, the ticket that gets you in the door, the beat you dance to. "Anything you can do to be associated with the music, you try to do," a Clear Channel executive with forty years in radio told me. This is not entirely sinister, nor is it especially new. The music business, in its varied forms, has always depended on symbiosis. Clear Channel wants you to identify with the brand so fully that you don't recognize it as a brand at all but rather as yourself. The executive gave me an example. "Suppose you like Dave Matthews," he said. "We like Dave Matthews. We have Dave Matthews together."

To achieve this mind-meld, Clear Channel has designed itself as a self-contained, nationwide feedback loop, calibrating the tastes of its listeners and segmenting them into market-proven "formats." Today, Clear Channel operates in 13 major music formats, and although some of these formats are nearly indistinguishable, they are nevertheless finely tuned: for example, listeners can choose between "AC" (Adult Contemporary) and "Hot AC," or among "CHR" (Contemporary Hits Radio), "CHR Pop," and "CHR Rhythmic." John Hogan, the radio division's CEO, boasted that in 2003 the company would make more than 2 million phone calls to survey its listeners, a process that would produce "around 10,000 local-audience research reports." As these reports are generated, the company can respond rapidly. "If we have a CHR PD"—program director—"in, you know, Dayton, Ohio, who figures out a great way to package up a bit, or a great promotion, or comes up with something clever and innovative, we can almost *instantaneously* make it available to CHR radio stations across the country." (At the time of our interview, Clear Channel owned 89 CHRs.) Then, for a given advertiser, the company can align all its CHRs to hit one "formatic target"—a demographic. Hogan suggested teenage girls. "A great advertiser would be the Crest Whitestrips. In the past, if Crest had wanted to use radio, they would have had to call a different owner in every market. There would have been no way to link together those stations with, you know, a common theme, or a common execution."

Such harmony extends to the company's concert business as well. "There's a lot of conference calling between cities," a booking agent named Tim Borror told me, "these former independents talking to one another, letting each other know what's going on." Another independent booking agent and a Clear Channel talent buyer, neither of whom would allow themselves to be named, confirmed this practice, adding that such calls take place almost on a weekly basis. The calls can launch a band or flatten it. "At a certain point, there's only one place to go—Clear Channel—and it doesn't matter whether or not they make you a fair offer," Borror said. "And pretty soon, they don't have to make you a fair offer. And they can decide what band is playing and what band isn't."

I asked John Hogan why I should believe that Clear Channel would never use its combined dominance of radio and live events to punish an artist—or a politician—who did not cooperate with the company. "I can't imagine a scenario where it would make any business sense at all," he replied. To use the power, he said, "would be to damage it." David T. "Boche" Viecelli, another booking agent, told me: "The thing people fear—legitimately fear—is that they're going to implement the threats they've intimated with radio airplay. It's not explicit. More often it's insinuation and innuendo." Clear Channel doesn't have to actively be "the evil empire," because everyone knows that it could be. With so much of music and entertainment determined by, produced by, broadcast by, measured by, and defined by Clear Channel, the company need not exercise its control in order to wield it. Clear Channel is a system so pervasive that it relieves its participants—consumers, bands, employees, even executives—of the responsibility to object, and the ability to imagine why they would ever do so.

In Denver, Clear Channel owns half the rock stations on the dial, as well as the region's number-one station, the news/talk KOA. It owns the Fillmore, co-owns the Universal Lending Pavilion, controls the rights to the Pepsi Center, and in 2001 pried a sweetheart deal out of the city for booking shows at the legendary Red Rocks Amphitheatre, carved out of the stone of the Rocky Mountain foothills—as much of a temple as pop music can claim.

I went to Denver to meet Jesse Morreale, an independent promoter who is suing Clear Channel. Morreale is one of the biggest independents in the country, but he is also one of the last. He persuaded one of the so-called Big Four law firms in Denver to represent him, but even if they can prove that Clear Channel Radio and Clear Channel Entertainment work together to shut out other promoters and threaten artists who work with them, there's a good chance his company, Nobody in Particular Presents, will be out of business by the time the case reaches any kind of conclusion. For now, Morreale has been silenced; Clear Channel

won a protective order from the court, and although Morreale was happy to complain, he could not give me particulars.

Nor would the minor rock stars who came through town while I was there. The leather-clad lead singer of Cradle of Filth, a death-metal band from England, assured me that he would "never" say anything against Clear Channel. A punk-pop threesome called the Raveonettes at first said they hadn't heard of Clear Channel, then admitted that they had, then offered me a beer and asked if we couldn't please instead talk about rock-and-roll music. A record-company agent clinked shots with me and said, "Rock 'n roll!" but when Morreale told him I was writing about Clear Channel, he asked for my notes. "I'm going to need those," he said, trying to sound official. I would have said no, but since all I had written down was "Fred Durst," and the guy looked like he might cry, I tore the page out and gave it to him.

The next morning, I was driving around Denver listening to the radio when I heard a prerecorded spoof ad for "Butt Pirates of the Caribbean." It consisted mainly of the DJ reading, in a sneering lisp, a list of actors he considered "homo." Which is to say, it was nothing unusual. I had been listening to Clear Channel radio all over the country and had found that gay jokes ran second only to "camel jockey" or "towel head" humor. Such slurs, I began to think, were simply the comedic equivalent of the mannered rock "rebellion" in the musical rotation. Like the knee-jerk distortion of a Limp Bizkit song, the fag gags of the local morning crew are there to assure listeners that someone, somewhere, is being offended by what they are pretending to enjoy.

Back at my hotel, I called the local Clear Channel headquarters and asked for the man in charge. I was surprised to get a call back from Clear Channel's regional vice president, Lee Larsen, who invited me out to see him that very morning.

Larsen, who looked to be in his mid-fifties, was not a formal man. He put his loafers up on the coffee table between us and his arms behind his head and told me to fire away: he loved to talk about radio. Larsen wore his sandy hair in a modest pompadour, and although he had some girth on him, his tall frame and thick shoulders made him look like a linebacker. He started on the air forty years ago but made his career as a manager. On a pedestal near the center of his office sat an antique wooden radio, flanked by Broncos helmets facing inward. When I asked him what he listened to, he replied with a long and diverse list of stations—none of them Clear Channel—that marked him as a man of broad but refined tastes. Nevertheless, he was a staunch believer in Giving the People What They Want. "This whole society," he said, "is based on majority rules." There is no such thing, he said, as "lowest common denominator"; there is only democracy, and in the music world Clear Channel is its biggest purveyor. The best thing about democracy, which he likened to a pizza, is that there is so much of it. "If I take one slice of the audience, and it's the biggest slice, and it's the 'lowest common denominator' slice, whatever you want to call it, guess what? There's lots of slices for the other guy." As evidence of this bounty, he gestured over his shoulder. At first I thought he wanted me to look at the view of the Rockies behind him, but it turned out he was thinking of the franchise lined highways I'd driven to get there. "Who'd have thought there could be so many different fast-food restaurants as there are?"

There were those among us, he said, who would complain nonetheless. People "at odds with the masses." People who believe that "the mass in our country are *stupid*." People who would tell you that you "should read *Atlantic Monthly,* not *Time*." But that was all right. "You can have anything you want," he said. "You just can't have what you want everywhere." He smiled. "Some people don't like that." He leaned forward and patted the coffee table, a little gesture to let me know that he knew that I knew what he was talking about, that I was, with him, part of "the mass."

I asked him about "Butt Pirates of the Caribbean." He reared back and looked at me like I was Tipper Gore. In a gentle, rumbling tone, he asked, "What are you saying? That it should not have been on?"

"Well . . . ," I said, "switch 'Butt Pirates of the Caribbean' for something like, say, 'Jigaboos of Jamaica,' and I think you can see what I mean."

Larsen frowned. "I know clearly that you couldn't do a bit like that that's *ethnic*. I know that, okay? Maybe, in the area you're talking about, that might still be open. Society's still trying to figure out the line there. If you took that bit and put it on a classical-music radio station and played it, well the people would be outraged. It's out of context." But there was a time and place for such things. "If every radio station was doing 'Butt Pirates,' then you would be saying, 'Well, what is this?' But they are not." At the station I had heard it on, he explained, "the talent must have felt that was

within the bounds they could work within, *and* was something that the audience that was listening to *their* radio station could relate to."

I must have looked unconvinced, because Larsen seemed worried. "On the radio," he said, "the red light's on and you're talking. And you say something. Just like you do in real life. And you go"—he shaped his lips into an O and let his eyes bulge as he covered his mouth—"I. Wish. I. Hadn't. Said. That." He shrugged his shoulders, held up his palms in a "what can you do?" gesture. "But it's too late."

Regulation of radio ownership is rooted in the idea that the spectrum is a national resource, but as a reality the "public airwaves" are close to extinct. Even proponents of regulation now fight for it, perversely, in the language of business, touting ownership caps as a means to preserve the "marketplace of ideas." This phrase, or even the "free market of ideas," has become a rhetorical fixture of anticonsolidation activists, for whom it connotes a free and fair system by which ideas compete for the minds of the citizenry. Implicit in the phrase is that ideas compete in roughly the same manner as do brands of soap; that, given equal price and placement, the most effective ideas will win the day. By owning so many stations, the argument goes, Clear Channel reduces the number of songs, sounds, formats, and opinions from which American listeners can choose.

But to so frame the argument is already to have lost. Media corporations want nothing more than to create new, popular formats with which to segment their audiences on advertisers' behalf. As advocates of deregulation never tire of pointing out, the "diversity" of U.S. radio content—in terms of average number of different formats available in each market—has increased with consolidation since 1996, not decreased. In fact, nothing resembles a "free market of ideas" so much as Clear Channel itself, where infinitesimal changes in ratings are tracked, mapped, and responded to; where Boston's successful new format can appear in San Diego overnight. This is what Lee Larsen means when he speaks of giving the people what they want. Clear Channel is a supermarket of ideas, which sells scores of different products all made in the same factory.

Activists fret that Clear Channel is foisting a right-wing agenda onto its listeners. To the contrary, the company seems to advance no ideology whatsoever; nor does it seem to advance any aesthetic that could be called good, bad, ugly, or beautiful. Perhaps the most instructive example here is the controversy over what has come to be called The List: the roster of songs that, immediately after September 11, were not supposed to be played on Clear Channel stations. The List's recommendations ranged from the obvious (AC/DC's "Shot Down in Flames") to the saccharine (Billy Joel's "Only the Good Die Young") to the grotesque (Van Halen's "Jump") to the unexpectedly poetic (Phil Collins's otherwise unremarkable "In the Air Tonight"). Antiwar activists pointed out that The List "banned" Cat Stevens's "Peace Train" and John Lennon's "Imagine," but ignored the fact that The List also proscribed Judas Priest's "Some Heads Are Gonna Roll" and the Clash's "Rock the Casbah," said to have been popular with U.S. pilots on bombing runs over Iraq during the first Gulf War.

Everyone seemed to see The List as the ultimate case of censorship by a corporate head office, but in fact The List came together just as might a great promotion by John Hogan's hypothetical program director in Dayton, Ohio. On his or her own initiative (nobody knows for certain where, or with whom, The List started), a Clear Channel PD drew up a list of songs; this PD emailed The List to a PD at another station, and he or she added more songs, and so on. When, eventually, The List was leaked to the press, Clear Channel pointed out that it was the work of independent program directors who were free to play—or not to play—whatever songs they liked.

Confusing The List for ideological censorship reflects a fundamental misunderstanding of the meaning of Clear Channel. It reflects the misguided notion that the company means anything at all. All the Clear Channel talent buyers, "on-air personalities," news directors, and executives I spoke with shared a basic disregard for both the content of the product and its quality. The market would take care of those. Clear Channel's functionaries seemed to view the company as some marvelous but unfathomable machine with whose upkeep they had been charged. They knew only that it accomplished a miraculous task—satisfying the musical tastes of most of the people—and did not care to trouble themselves with how.

Bryan Dilworth swore to me he had nothing to do with Sean Agnew's show at the Church getting shut down. He said that any suggestion to the contrary was "Davy and Goliath bullshit." He claimed he walked into his boss's office and asked them if they had been involved. He told them he needed to know, because he would quit if they had. They swore innocence. I tried to confirm his story, but his bosses never returned my calls.

One Sunday I met Dilworth at his home in South Philly. His wife needed a nap, so we took his ten-month-old for a ride in his stroller. We walked through the Italian market, dead quiet at six on a Sunday evening, empty wooden stalls fronting pork shops and bakeries. We stopped to watch a group of boys on skateboards work a ramp they had set up in the street, performing for a video camera one of the kids was holding. Dilworth laughed. "The dudes who own those stores knew these kids were out here, skating on their stalls like that? They'd break their legs." This delighted him, all of it: the men who owned the stores who wouldn't give a damn for the law, the kids who took over the street who didn't give a damn for the owners. "This place is totally . . . this place," he said.

I asked him how that squared with his working for Clear Channel, which seemed dedicated to making every place the same. Dilworth didn't look at me but he smiled. His grin pushed his baby-fat cheeks up and made his eyes small.

"All of a sudden I'm supposed to be super evil?" he said. "FUCK THAT."

"No, that's not what I meant," I said.

"FUCK THAT. I just wanted to make money doing something I liked. There are different opinions about how far down the road America is businesswise, but dude, whatever, it's too far gone for anything to change."

He bumped the stroller up over a curb, and the baby began to cry. We walked without talking for a few blocks, the clackety-clack of skateboard wheels fading behind us. But closer to home, both he and the baby mellowed. Dilworth stopped smiling, and his eyes stopped squinting.

"Then," he said, "there's that feeling in your spine, and it's all right." His voice went up in pitch and grew soft, as if he were embarrassed. He was talking about rock. "When the arc is just starting to arc? And you're saying this could be Van Halen, this could be Neil Young. It's like you're bearing witness. It's not, 'Ching-ching, here we go.' It's 'I saw it. It does exist.' There's something really there. It's not just a need for chaos. It's—yeah. That's what I want." His voice deepened again, and his pace evened out. The baby had nodded off. We stopped in front of Dilworth's stoop. "Clear Channel?" he said. "That's money. I need it to buy liquor and baby clothes."

RELATED LINKS

- Clear Channel Worldwide (http://www.clearchannel.com)
- Radio's Big Bully (http://www.salon.com/ent/clear_channel)
- A Twelve-Step Program for Media Democracy (http://www.thenation.com/doc.mhtml ?i=20020805&s=larson20020723&c=1)
- Media Access Project: Media Diversity Page (http://www.mediaaccess.org/programs/ diversity/index.html)

FOR FURTHER RESEARCH

To find out more about the topics discussed in this reading, use InfoTrac College Edition. Type in keywords and subject terms such as "media consolidation," "cross selling," and "corporate efficiencies." You can access InfoTrac College Edition from the Wadsworth / Thomson Communication Café homepage: http://communication.wadsworth.com.

PART III

New Technologies, the Self, and Social Life

P art III explores issues involving new technologies, evolving conceptions of the self, and the changing nature of social life. Online, any number of activities and transactions are now becoming personalized, made possible by collaborative filtering software that compares Web users' stated preferences, purchasing history, and clickstreams (surfing patterns) with those of other users to generate custom offers. Increasingly, software is enabling users to find not just products but potential dates through online dating services like Match.com. Through search engines and other online resources, the Internet has made social life both more convenient and more exposed. Game culture has also been taken by storm, inadvertently training console warriors and influencing the content of a growing number of big-budget Hollywood movies. The readings in Chapter 5 dissect these issues at the leading edge of culture and technology, describing a range of meaningful experiences that occur at the interface. In Chapter 6, several readings take stock of the trend toward cultural acceleration and media saturation. Movies, computer games, and TV shows are moving at an ever-quickening pace, holding our attention but perhaps diminishing satisfaction. Shortened attention spans, the pressing demands of modern life, and the ready availability of personal communications devices has led to the rise of multitasking—the microprocessor-like capacity to perform several tasks simultaneously. But even the best multitaskers are having difficulty keeping up with the deluge of unwanted e-mail, or spam, which now accounts for more than half of all messages sent online, imposes huge productivity costs, and presents one of the most daunting problems for information technology officers everywhere.

5

At the Interface:
New Intimacies,
New Cultures

Reading 5-1

A Nation of Voyeurs
Neil Swidey

EDITOR'S NOTE

The Internet age has made social life both more convenient and more exposed. Gone are the days when a youthful indiscretion, heat-of-the-moment flame, or publicly recorded deed would be forgotten or remain obscure. Thanks to the vast storage capacity of the World Wide Web and precision of online search engines, notably Google, a growing part of our past is now being thrust into the present—and becoming permanent. In this reading, Neil Swidey describes how the popular Internet search engine Google, whose 10,000-plus servers field 150 million queries daily and offer search results in 36 languages worldwide, is changing what we can find out about one another—and raising questions about whether we should. From blind dates to job interviews, what it means to meet someone for the first time is changing due to the information available through networked technology. Beyond saving prospective dates and employers from embarrassment (or worse), the increasing availability of personal and public records online has some notable downsides and raises questions about the wisdom of continuous information exposure. For a related discussion of these issues, see the readings in Chapter 12.

CONSIDER

1. Have you ever Googled a friend or prospective date? If so, what was your reason and what did you find out about that person—anything you didn't already know?

2. Why is there a "profound difference" between records buried in a county filing cabinet and the one-stop precision searching available through Google?

3. Given how much of life is lived online these days, do you agree that the greater good is served by making most information accessible and permanent? Why or why not?

Michael is a clean-cut 34-year-old working in a professional job at a Boston medical school. You'd never know he did time for burglary and is a former drug addict. Well, actually, you would if you Googled him. Go to the Google.com home page and type in Michael's name (for obvious reasons, we are not including his last name here). That simple step produces more than 100 links to documents written by and about Michael. The search, Google proudly notes, takes just a 10th of a second.

Michael has never hidden from his past, and in his 20s, he even wrote for a few specialized publications about his brief stint behind bars as a 17-year-old. He was happy to share his exploits with that sliver of the population genuinely interested in the issues of incarceration. But Michael never saw Google coming— how those tiny publications would go online and into the claws of the nation's top Internet search engine, and how a bored co-worker or prospective employer would be able to get up close and personal with Michael's wild ride as a teenager.

Dazzlingly fast, vast, and precise, Google has made our lives appreciably easier. The first tool truly to make sense of the white noise that is the Internet, Google has become essential research for everyone from sales people calling on new accounts to single people taking another spin with blind-date roulette. It's reconnected long-lost biological brothers and battalion buddies. And who dials 411 anymore, when it's cheaper and faster on Google, and you don't have to explain to some headset-wearer in Terre Haute how to spell Worcester? Google saves time, saves face—it may even save lives. Instead of calling their doctor, some people type their symptoms into Google; a few have learned they were in the early stages of a heart attack.

But somewhere along the path toward changing

From "A Nation of Voyeurs: How the Internet Search Engine Google Is Changing What We Can Find Out About One Another—And Raising Questions About Whether We Should" by Neil Swidey, *The Boston Globe Magazine,* February 2, 2003, pp. 10–15. Copyright © 2003 Globe Newspaper Company. Reprinted with permission.

our daily lives, Google changed our concept of time as well. It has helped make our past—or oddly refracted shards of it—present and permanent. That's a radical notion for a medium usually defined by its ability to constantly update itself.

You don't have to have a rap sheet from deep in your past to be affected by the long arm of Google's Web crawler. Maybe it was a stupid fraternity prank or a careless posting to an Internet newsgroup in college. Perhaps you once went on a rant at a selectmen's meeting or signed a petition without stopping to read it. Or maybe you endured a bitter divorce. You may think those chapters are closed. Google begs to differ.

While most of your embarrassing baggage was already available to the public, it was effectively off-limits to everyone but the professionally intrepid or supremely nosy. Now, in states where court records have gone online, and thanks to the one-click ease of Google, you can read all the sordid details of your neighbor's divorce with no more effort than it takes to check your e-mail.

"It's the collapse of inconvenience," says Siva Vaidhyanathan, assistant professor of culture and communication at New York University. "It turns out inconvenience was a really important part of our lives, and we didn't realize it."

Google has quietly but unmistakably changed our expectations about what we can know about one another. But this search engine that fields 150 million queries a day is of no use in helping us determine how much information we *deserve* to know about one another, or how we should proceed once we know it. Should we confront friends, dates, or co-workers with the damning details we unearthed while cyber-snooping? Or should we say nothing?

Michael has felt it both ways. He first learned about the new Web order in 1999, early on in Google's life, when a woman he had just begun dating confronted him about his prison past. "Why didn't you tell me about this?" she demanded to know. The question exposed a new double standard. "When you meet someone," Michael says, "you don't say, 'I had an affair one time,' or 'I was arrested for DUI once,' or 'I cheated on my taxes in 1984.'" Since then, there have been other confrontations, but what Michael finds most disturbing are the sudden silences. "Instead of thinking, 'Was I curt last week?' or 'Did I insult this political party or that belief?' I have to think about what happened when I was 17."

When he was searching for an apartment, Michael met with no fewer than 30 potential housemates and never got so much as a callback. Once, as a finalist for a job, he was courted aggressively through three rounds of interviews and a host of phone and e-mail contacts. Then, suddenly, they stopped phoning or taking his calls. His hunch: Someone Googled him. But the worst part is, he'll never know. "If someone asks you about your past, that means they are willing to consider what you have to say about it," Michael says. "But if they don't ask, that means they've made up their minds."

Yet he finds it hard to blame Google. Asked if he uses the search engine himself, he smiles and says: "All the time."

Like every Silicon Valley story worth remembering, this one begins in a garage. Actually, it begins in the computer science department at Stanford University, but that's so much less compatible with the demands of dot-com lore. In 1995, Sergey Brin, a native of Moscow, and Larry Page, a native of Michigan, met as students in Stanford's PhD computer science program. They began tinkering with search-engine technology, focusing on how Web pages link to one another. By 1998, that work led them to found Google, with the help of nearly $1 million collected from friends, family, and a couple of Valley investors. That same year, with their new search engine online, they moved the operation out of their Stanford dorm rooms and into the garage (and three bedrooms and two baths) of a five-bedroom house their friend Susan Wojcicki had just bought in Menlo Park.

She wanted them to pay her $1,500 a month in rent and give her a piece of their new company. They were smart enough to offer her a straight $1,700, with no equity. She didn't fight too hard. Although Brin and Page were as brash and confident then as they are now, telling her, "'We're going to take over the Net,'" Wojcicki says, "I didn't take them seriously. Inktomi [the search engine powerhouse at the time] was worth like $20 billion, and these guys were renting out my garage." They were fairly good tenants, though she occasionally found herself having to bang out e-mails —"Googlers, you need to clean up!"—and was a little

freaked out when their intimate holiday gathering grew to a 400-person guest list.

In the beginning, Google—which takes its name from "googol," the mathematical term for a 1 followed by 100 zeros—was a hit mostly in techie circles. Brin and Page began building a staff; Craig Silverstein, a classmate from Stanford, was the first on board. "Google's first hire" is how he's still known around the company, even though his official title is director of technology. Wojcicki eventually began working for her tenants and is now director of product management, though most people still think of her as Sergey and Larry's former landlord.

Anyone who is anyone at Google, it seems, has a similar handle, a shorthand identifier that stresses the company's institutionalized quirkiness—from the former neurosurgeon who now operates Google's vast computer network to the former chief of staff for then-U.S. Treasury Secretary Larry Summers who now oversees one of the company's revenue streams to the former personal chef to the Grateful Dead who now dishes out organic grub in the Google cafe.

In just a couple of years, the operation has blown past its garage-band days. An infusion of $25 million from two high-powered venture capitalist firms in 1999 put it on solid footing. A contract signed the following year to provide additional search results for Yahoo! gave Google instant credibility, revenue, and exposure. The company's reputation has grown virally ever since. (Even AOL signed up Google to power its search engine last year. Yahoo Inc., while still a client, is so nervous about Google's growth that it launched a bid in December for Inktomi.)

Google now occupies three tan buildings spread across a bland office park in Mountain View, California, which is about 10 miles northwest of San Jose. The company has had to erect a heated tent and mobile kitchen to relieve the cafeteria congestion. It has more than 600 employees in 15 locations worldwide. It offers search results in 36 languages, and half its traffic comes from outside the United States.

To walk through the "Googleplex" headquarters is to step back in Silicon Valley time. While most other dot-coms have gone bust or are in full retreat, Google is living like it's 1999. All the discredited accouterments associated with the dot-com era are still on defiant display. There's the pool table (with dry-erase board hanging nearby, in case workers get inspired mid-game); the lobby featuring a baby grand piano, 1980s-style arcade games, and constellation of lava lamps; the twice-weekly staff hockey games; the on-staff masseuse; the brightly colored exercise balls that serve as extra seating for impromptu meetings; the mountain bikes and unicycles that clog the hallways (and the cramped office that the founders still share); the massive wall chart documenting the company's growth that was drawn entirely with a 64-pack of Crayolas and annotated with milestones like "Nov. 1999: Angie starts!"; and, of course, the free lunch and dinner—all-organic, all-gourmet. Brin is all of 29, his fellow founder Page is 30, and they look almost wizened next to the rest of this ultrayoung staff.

There is a palpable culture to the place that occasionally borders on the cultlike. Almost every employee I talked to, for instance, shared the conversational tic of ending sentences with an octave-climbing "right?" as if waiting for my buy-in. Many began their responses to questions with an extra slow "So-o-o," as if to say: "I'm going to make this simple for you." Employees tend to quote the founders liberally, saying things like, "As Sergey said at our holiday party, we have to think about Google's impact on the world . . ." or "As Larry and Sergey say, our goal is to organize the world's information!"

Still, there's an overall current of fun and innovation flowing through the place. And there is ample evidence of the profound impact the company is having on the rest of us. In the lobby, behind the free juice bar that doubles as a receptionist's desk, a screen displays a constant scroll of search words being typed into Google somewhere in the world at that time. As I looked up at the screen, I saw: Adult education Ontario; David Blaine; wrap around tummy tuck; Forta Patchie (honest); Oakland Fire Dept; Barbara Hershey (perhaps typed in by the actress herself, hoping to find out where her glory days went?); stinger amplifier kits; Dennis Franz salary; and a host of Asian search words I could not decipher. But Google's computers would be able to make sense of them.

Humans are hardly involved in the actual searching or sorting. That's done by more than 10,000 servers, which in Google's case are cheap PCs loaded with memory and sitting in tall racks in several high-security data storage facilities around the country. Speed and relevance have always been the hallmarks of Google's approach. All these computers help keep search times below half a second, but so, too, has the founders' refusal to accept ads with images, which would slow the process.

Google quickly distinguished itself from other search engines with its rapid responses, its refusal to let paid advertisers pervert the integrity of a search (advertisers are labeled "sponsored links" and cordoned off), and its uncanny ability to know just what you're looking for. As a measure of the founders' confidence—or cockiness—in their search algorithm, they designed an "I'm Feeling Lucky" button: Type in your search words and hit that option, and Google takes you directly to the Web site it believes you're looking for.

The Google search technology is based on something called PageRank (named after Larry Page), which determines relevance not only by counting the times a search word appears in a particular Web page but also by factoring in how many other pages are linked to that page as well as their general reputation. Google's sophisticated approach, combined with its crawler's insatiable appetite for uncovering new corners of the Web, simply works better. That has propelled its meteoric rise.

Ask people in the industry how Google was able to outdistance the competition, and they say the same thing: focus. While other Web sites tried to be all things to all people in an effort to get profitable, Google stubbornly concentrated on just building the world's best search engine. By the end of 2001, Google not only had reached its goal, but, surprisingly, it had managed to find profitability along the way. Many analysts expect Google to go public when the market's distrust of dot-coms begins to dissolve. Google embodies the original ethos of the Web—free, fast, and democratic.

But will success lead to its undoing? In the last year, Google—whose youthful founders eventually relented and brought in an adult CEO—has introduced new sites focused on news and shopping (froogle.com). In other words, it's looking a lot more like an all-things-to-everyone portal and less like simply the world's best search engine.

Amanda had been dating him for about a month. She liked his laid-back style, dug his shaved-head approach to male pattern baldness. Then, late one night, she received an e-mail from him containing a few angry words and a link to a short story she had written for an obscure online zine.

Amanda, a 26-year-old graphic artist who lived in Providence before moving west, had published the story under her real name, confident that only fiction aficionados would go to the trouble of finding the site. "Gee, thanks, Google," she says now.

She and her new beau had met online, and this particular story that he had found by Googling her revolves around a young woman who—surprise—meets a guy online. Everything goes well until he neglects to call her back a few times, and she quickly turns into an obsessive, spurned girlfriend of near-*Fatal Attraction* dimensions. "It was fiction," Amanda says, but the guy thought otherwise. She admits, "If you assumed it was me, it would make you freak out, but you should stop and ask."

Amanda decided it was pointless to argue with him. "By the time somebody's convinced you're obsessive," she says, "trying to convince him otherwise is only going to make you look more obsessive." But the more Amanda thought about it, the more steamed she got. "The hypocrisy of it all—you think I'm an obsessive person? Well, you're the one Googling me!"

So she opted for Google revenge. Amanda created an alternate digital identity for her former boyfriend —a personal Web page that would, in all likelihood, be accessed only by those people Googling him by name. On this over-the-top Web page, the guy makes a series of mock confessions that, if taken seriously, would be toxic in any future dating situation. He "admits" to being untrustworthy, jobless, sneaky, a lousy lover, and, finally, a carrier of venereal disease. Hey, Mom, let me tell you a little bit about my new boyfriend.

The cases of payback can be even worse. According to Web lore, a Midwestern college student named Libby Hoeler once sent her boyfriend a video postcard of her doing a striptease to a suggestive soundtrack of Marvin Gaye and the Divinyls. As the story goes, she eventually cheated on him; to get back at her, he shared her private peep show with the Internet masses; Libby was so embarrassed that she ended up having to drop out of school. Who knows if any of these details are true? It's not even clear that Libby Hoeler (or Hoeller) is her real name. God help her if it is, for the shadow of this performance will follow her for the rest of her life. Today, there are entire Web sites devoted to Libby, attracting disturbingly animated fans proffering marriage proposals and sharing random details about her that they gleaned from Google searches. And, naturally, there are now a host of porn sites peddling full-length footage of the dorm-room dance.

Most young single people confess to Googling their prospective dates, but there are no societal norms yet on what to do with the harvested information. If a Google search reveals that you and your blind date share an appreciation for Veruca Salt or Bavarian poetry or Leonard Nimoy's aborted attempt at a singing career, how can you bring that up gracefully, without making your snooping obvious?

Veronica Leger, a 39-year-old marketing professional from Charlestown, was sitting across the table from her blind date when the topic of clothes came up. "Oh, yeah, you're a clotheshorse," he said to her, grinning. She instantly thought back to a distant interview she had given to the *Globe* for a story about laid-off dot-commers, in which she confessed to cutting back on her shopping addiction. "Oh, you've done your homework," Leger told her date, but what she was really thinking was: "It feels kind of creepy to be Googled." Her date admitted to Googling before all first dates but said he had good reason. Once, when he delayed his search until after the date, he stumbled onto an obscure portion of an out-of-the-way Web site where the woman he had just dined with was mentioned. "That's how he learned she had been a he," Leger says.

Google has built up such a reputation for reliability that we simply assume what it produces must be what we're looking for, even though context is often absent from the search results.

Anne Savage, a 26-year-old from Brookline, once got an urgent e-mail pleading with her to provide advice on how to care for an ailing, pregnant tamarin monkey. Because she had previously Googled herself—known as "vanity Googling"—Savage knew she shared her name with a prominent veterinarian. She e-mailed back to explain and ended up starting an electronic correspondence. The tamarin ended up delivering a healthy baby.

Chris Cormier, a high-tech worker from Natick, gets e-mails all the time from people asking for bodybuilding tips. Cormier, who bears no resemblance to his impossibly chiseled, world-class bodybuilder namesake, recently got a fax inviting him to a competition in Timisoara, Romania.

Because we know Google will be able to meet whatever our informational need may be at whatever moment we need it, it has, in many ways, made us all a little lighter. "Rather than having to carry the factual baggage around in your head, you have this electronic prosthesis," says Sven Birkerts, a noted author who has written about the intersection of technology and society. "You can get it anytime, and the doors don't lock."

But as we lean so heavily on the prosthesis, will part of us atrophy? Jonathan Zittrain, co-director of Harvard Law School's Berkman Center for Internet and Society, recalls a story by the Argentine writer Jorge Luis Borges. "There's a massive library of all knowledge, but somebody messed up the card catalog, and it might as well not exist, because you have no idea where anything is," he says. "Likewise, if it's not in Google, there's an important way in which it might not exist."

Revolution is brewing inside the Boston office of the register of Suffolk Probate and Family Court, the oldest elective office in the country. A locked closet houses the wills of some of the biggest names in Boston's past—Isabella Stewart Gardner, Mary Baker Eddy, John F. Kennedy. But barely 40 feet away stands the conduit to the court's future. It looks like nothing more than a Xerox machine, but the $15,000 e-Cabinet can convert reams of court documents into searchable computer files. That means it can go a long way toward helping the register, Richard Iannella, realize his dream of creating a fully digital court.

During his six years in the post, Iannella, a kinetic former Boston city councilor who has a habit of tapping your forearm repeatedly when he's trying to make a point, has railed against the institutionalized, almost antagonistic inefficiency of the Massachusetts court system. He has worked to get his 55 employees to view each person walking through the door as a customer, or, more to the point for Iannella, a voter.

As much as he and his lieutenants have made remarkable steps toward improving efficiency, they believe the e-Cabinet offers the possibility of a giant leap. Iannella envisions a time not so far off when people can avoid coming to the courthouse altogether, instead of logging on to the court's Web site to peruse Uncle Ernie's will or file for a change in child support payments. If a judge gets a call from the cops late one Saturday night seeking an emergency restraining order, he would be able to call up the accused's complete court record from home and make a more informed decision.

Even though Iannella can only go so far without the blessing of the state's technology-tepid judicial leaders, he's determined to press ahead. So there's now a new "To Be Scanned" bin on the desk of Genevieve Donnelly, a white-haired clerk who had to fill her fountain pen with "Massachusetts standard ink" to do her recording when she joined the register's office more than 40 years ago.

But where Iannella sees efficiency, privacy advocates see danger. Robert Ellis Smith, a Providence lawyer who publishes the newsletter "Privacy Journal," worries about the benefits all these online court records will have for stalkers, identity thieves, and insidious commercial interests—especially when the online records make their way into Google's grasp. Cindy Southworth, director of technology for the National Network to End Domestic Violence, is concerned about the information-on-demand implications for women fleeing abusive relationships. "My biggest fear," she says, "is that it will take a horrific murder—because some court put something on the Web that wasn't supposed to be there—for people to begin taking this seriously."

In the absence of any standardized approach, individual courts nationwide are doing their own thing. One of the courts in the digital vanguard is in Hamilton County, Ohio, where most records are searchable through the court's Web site and, by extension, of course, through Google. I've never met Suzanne or Gregory, but by simply poking around the Hamilton County Web site, I was able to read the full appeals court judgment in their divorce, complete with their salaries and competing child support claims, down to the penny. When I then typed their full names in Google, the same document popped up instantly. Even more distressing to advocates like Southworth: The Montgomery County, Pennsylvania, court posts on its Web site the names and addresses of not just the suspects in abuse cases but the alleged victims as well.

Thankfully, many of these fears still live in the realm of the hypothetical. Pressed for concrete examples, Smith cites the horrifying 1999 case of Amy Boyer, in which a stalker paid an Internet search service for the 20-year-old New Hampshire woman's Social Security number and work address, which he used to track her down. He then shot her to death. But the Boyer case cuts both ways. After her death, her stepfather lamented that if only he had typed Amy's name into a search engine, he might have realized the danger she was in by coming across her stalker's Web site, where he had detailed his plans to kill her.

Of course, most court information has long been public. But there is a profound difference between records buried in a county filing cabinet and the one-stop precision shopping you get from Google. People now refer to the protection of the disorganized, inefficient past as "security through obscurity."

Craig Silverstein, Google's first hire, says society has tried to have it both ways for too long. "We've had this ideal of having lots of information open to the public," he says, "but in practice it hasn't been available. Now we have to decide." If Google is helping to force society's hand, he says, so be it.

So once all this information about you is out there in Googleland, is there anything you can do about it? Like so much in life, that depends on who you are. Google indexes more than 3 billion Web pages, 400 million images, and 800 million newsgroup postings (including an archive of embryonic Internet chatter it purchased from an outfit called Deja.com), but it is willing to remove certain information, under certain circumstances.

If you desperately want that picture of a bleary-eyed you in an ill-fitting toga to disappear from Google, and the search engine found the photo on a Web site you control, then all you have to do is take the picture down. (However, the image will continue to be accessible for a month or even longer to users who know to click on the "Cached" link that appears on search-results summaries.) You can also keep Google's crawler away by building code into your Web site that acts as an electronic "no trespassing" sign.

But in the more likely event that Google found the offending information on someone else's Web site, you are on your own. Google will not remove information from its index unless the Webmaster in question requests it. So say you flee an abusive relationship, move to a new state, and decide to run in a 10K road race, only to realize later that your home address got posted next to your time on the running club's Web site. If you want that information removed, you have to appeal to the good graces of the running club Webmaster, not Google.

That issue of control apparently changes, however, if you're a deep-pocketed, heavily-lawyered entity making a copyright infringement claim. Last year, lawyers for the Church of Scientology insisted that Google remove from its index links to Xenu.net, a Web site that is highly critical of the controversial church. They claimed that the site infringed on the church's copyrights and trademarks. Google promptly complied, to the horror of many Google fans who saw it as an abdication of the company's longstanding commitment to search purity. Google said it had no choice but to abide by federal copyright law, but critics pointed out that Google had in fact removed more than was required under law. In the end, Google restored some of the links and explained its reasoning to users. "Ultimately," Sergey Brin says, "where we ended up was the right conclusion, but we didn't initially handle it correctly."

Harvard Law's Zittrain says more clashes are on the way. "The cutting edge on such battles is often the Church of Scientology," he says. "They have very well honed procedures and tactics to remove information that they find objectionable." Check out a site called chillingeffects.org to see the growing list of letters from various parties demanding that Google remove information about them. What seems clear is that just as in Washington, some parties will have more power than others in the Internet democracy governing Google Nation.

I ask Brin if there is anything about him a Google search turns up that he wishes wasn't there.

"There are certainly some embarrassing photos from my younger days," he says, chuckling. "I had not the most stylish of hairdos."

How about his home address?

"I hope not," Brin says, no longer chuckling.

Would it bother him if it was there?

"Hmm, I think it would," he says.

As it turns out, his current address does not show up. Nor does the personal information for many of today's digital power brokers. Most of them were smart enough to begin years ago the process of making their personal information invisible online. So much about privacy is preventative, because once the information gets online somewhere, it spreads so fast that it's virtually impossible for it to ever be private again. (Google says its employees must follow the same procedures as the general public when requesting that information be removed.)

Brin didn't cover all of his tracks, though. Type his name into the cheery but disturbingly comprehensive Web site anybirthday.com, and up pops his birth date: August 21, 1973.

In 1996, when most Americans still didn't have e-mail addresses and most companies had yet to get their Web sites up and running, two tech guys sat in a rented office in San Francisco thinking about the earliest television work of Milton Berle, Ed Sullivan, and Dave Garroway. Actually, they were Internet guys, and they were really thinking about the future. If somebody doesn't do something, they told each other, the next generation is going to be asking the same questions of Web leaders that we ask of television's pioneers: Why didn't anyone take the time to save the early stuff?

So Brewster Kahle and Bruce Gilliat began the process of archiving the Web—literally, taking regular snapshots of as many of the Web pages as their crawler could find and putting them in a big, permanent album. That's how the Internet Archive was born, and six years later, it is still crawling away, benefiting from vastly improved technology and taking a fresh snapshot of the Web every two months. The site (archive.org) features a nifty tool called the Wayback Machine—an homage to the time-traveling duo of Mr. Peabody and Sherman of *Rocky and Bullwinkle* fame—that re-creates a Web page on various dates over the past six years. At first blush, this seems cute but superfluous. Will there ever be a time when our grandchildren will need, desperately, to get back to the actual Web site where fans of Justin Timberlake breathlessly discussed his appearance with the rest of N'Sync on the May 4, 2000, episode of *The View*?

But thinking about it in television terms, there's no question we are poorer for not being able to review the television coverage of the 1948 presidential election or most of the early episodes of the *Today* and *Tonight* shows or even the game that changed football, the 1958 overtime win of the Baltimore Colts over the New York Giants. And the Internet promises to be even more influential in shaping us in the new century than TV was in the last. "The Internet is now the information resource of first resort for millions," says Kahle. "And, increasingly, it is the resource of only resort."

So the work being done by the obscure Internet Archive and the mainstream Google in helping us order and preserve our online lives may prove vital to future generations. The irreversible course we're on will no doubt trample the privacy and security of more than a few among us.

As a nation, we need to put measures in place, before it's too late, that provide some basic protection of vital personal information, like bank account numbers and Social Security numbers and, most important, details that have personal safety implications, such as the addresses of victims. But, in the end, given how much of life is lived online nowadays, the greater good is served by making most information accessible and permanent.

In time, we will adjust. "People get used to invasions of privacy," Zittrain says. Who would have thought even a year and a half ago that we would all readily submit to taking our shoes off before boarding the shuttle to Washington? What we will likely see, though, is a privacy premium—protection far more available to people with power and money. "When pagers and high-end cellphones first came out, the only people who had them were top executives," says Sven Birkerts. "It was a mark of their prestige—they were so important that they needed to be reachable wherever they went. Then the technology trickled down. Now the mark of prestige is the person nobody can reach."

And as much as organizing all the world's informa-

tion is Google's goal, the people there insist that day is still a long way off. "Google doesn't catch everything," says Silverstein. He says the last time he Googled himself, he found a lot about his work at Google and in the computer science field, but the search produced nothing about one of his big personal-interest areas. "I am very active in the Muppets community," Silverstein says. "I maintain the FAQ list on a Muppets fan Web site."

Then again, Google gets better every day. In .17 seconds, a recent search for "Craig Silverstein" and "Muppets" produced 72 results.

PROTECTING YOUR INFORMATION ONLINE

Use "No Trespassing" Code

If you want Google to stay away from content on a Web page you control, follow the steps outlined at www.google.com/remove.html. (If you're concerned about content about yourself on someone else's site, you'll need to contact that site's Webmaster, not Google.)

Google Yourself Regularly

That's how you can find out what's out there about you and start down the path toward removing it.

Check Privacy Policies

If you're concerned about Web sites besides Google that contain information about you, check out that site's privacy section. Some offer "opt out" procedures.

Train Yourself to Say No

Decline when you're asked for your phone number or ZIP code at a store or for your Social Security number when applying for credit or insurance, advises privacy expert Robert Ellis Smith. While the request for a Social Security number is legitimate for transactions with tax consequences (getting a job, buying a house, opening a bank account), in many cases it's not necessary. Check out more tips from Smith at www.privacyjournal.net/bio.htm.

 RELATED LINKS

- Google search engine (http://www.google.com)
- Chilling Effects Clearinghouse (http://chillingeffects.org)

- Anybirthday.com (http://anybirthday.com)
- Internet Archive (http://www.archive.org)

 FOR FURTHER RESEARCH

To find out more about the topics discussed in this reading, use InfoTrac College Edition. Type in keywords and subject terms such as "Web search engine," "snoop technology," and "information exposure." You can access InfoTrac College Edition from the Wadsworth/Thomson Communication Café homepage: http://communication.wadsworth.com.

Reading 5-2

Toy Soldiers
Mark Frauenfelder

EDITOR'S NOTE

With the growing realism and sophistication of videogames, military planners have seized on the potential of even off-the-shelf programs to simulate combat situations. As this reading from eDesign *magazine points out, the relationship between games and military simulations has a long history—a relationship that has never been closer than it is today. By immersing users in difficult circumstances and challenging them with thorny problems that require split-second decision making, videogames and military simulations alike teach important skills beyond hand-eye coordination. Although battlefield commanders admit that nothing short of actual battle can completely prepare recruits for real combat, teams that train on virtual battlefield simulators perform remarkably better during war game exercises than those who don't. The generation of gamers growing up with PlayStation and the Xbox may be more prepared for military duty than we give them credit for.*

CONSIDER

1. Why are videogames and virtual simulators—forms of *virtual reality*—so ideally suited for military training when combat itself is so thoroughly *real world*?
2. Should videogame training and experience become a new measure of military readiness?
3. In what ways do military commanders share the same objectives as the entertainment industry?

In 1994, science-fiction writer Orson Scott Card wrote *Ender's Game*. Set in the future, the novel features a group of highly gifted children recruited into the armed forces to fight against a species of malevolent interstellar invaders known as "the buggers." The children,

some as young as six, are trained on combat simulators that are essentially supersophisticated videogames. (I won't spoil the ending of the book for you; I'll just say there's a reason why the games the children play are very realistic.)

Card was right about the importance of using war games to train future soldiers, but in today's world, it isn't necessary to throw the young into high-tech boot camps to make them tomorrow's generals. The videogame industry, in conjunction with the U.S. military,

From "Toy Soldiers" by Mark Frauenfelder, *eDesign: A Magazine of Interactive Design and Commerce,* October 2002, pp. 40–45. Copyright © 2002 by Mark Frauenfelder. Reprinted with permission of the author.

is preparing tots in the comfort of their own living rooms. Today's war-based videogames are often as realistic as the systems the military uses to train soldiers. In fact, the differences between videogames and military simulations are disappearing. And the reason is simple: "We want the same thing as the entertainment industry," says Dr. Michael Macedonia, chief scientist and technical director for the U.S. Army Simulation, Training, and Instrumentation Command—the place where laser tag was invented. "We want to create stories that make the training experience unforgettable."

High-level defense contractors are spinning off consumer game divisions, while traditional videogame developers are making mutant shoot-'em-ups that end up being used as Army training systems. And now simulation technologies are being integrated into real military operations. In other words, real warfare looks a lot like a simulation, where firing a cartoon missile across a candy-colored screen results in the destruction of a real building halfway across the world. War games have been turned on their head.

Games and military simulations have long been intertwined. No one knows for sure when or where chess was invented, but chesslike games have existed for thousands of years and were almost certainly created as strategy training for battle. In the 1600s, military leaders taught their lieutenants the art of war using games played on maps of real battleground sites, with pieces closely resembling actual troops and weaponry. Through the centuries, games originally developed to hone a soldier's skills found their way into the parlors of civilians looking for social diversions.

The first flight simulator, an elaborate mechanical contraption called the Link Trainer, was built in 1928 and used air pumps, valves, and bellows to simulate the experience of roaring into the wild blue yonder. In 1930, MIT scientist Vannevar Bush began working on the Differential Analyzer, a hulking, motor-driven computer programmed to simulate the trajectory of a missile. With over 2000 vacuum tubes, ISO electric motors, and 200 miles of wiring, Bush's analog computer weighed in at over 100 tons and was finally completed in 1942. The Analyzer went to work solving all manner of WWII problems until it was overtaken by the new breed of digital computers.

Videogames entered the picture in 1958, after a couple of researchers from New York's Brookhaven National Laboratory invented a game called Tennis for Two on an analog computer wired to an oscilloscope. The parameters of the game, such as wind resistance and gravity, could be adjusted, making the technology a natural choice for military ballistics simulations.

When computer games showed up in pinball arcades in the '70s, they borrowed the controls and displays developed for computerized military simulations. Almost immediately, the military began borrowing the technology back. In 1980, the U.S. Army's Training and Doctrine Command looked into videogames as low-cost tank simulators. (Realistic tank simulators, like the ones made by Lockheed Martin, cost hundreds of thousands of dollars each.) Battlezone by Atari, creators of Pong, appeared to be the perfect choice. By today's standards, Battlezone's interface was exceedingly primitive: tanks and obstacles were represented as green wire-frame objects in a barren environment. Despite its crude graphics, the game was a huge hit for two reasons: It was the first game to incorporate a true 3D landscape rendered in real time, and it delivered the thrilling experience of a tank battle for just 25 cents.

These reasons were enough to convince the Army to hire Battlezone's designers to develop a modified version that could be used as a gunnery trainer for its Bradley M2 infantry-fighting vehicle. The M2 was used to launch TOW (Tube-launched, Optically tracked, Wire-guided) missiles. At the time, the Battlezone arcade game cost $3500. Just one TOW missile cost $7000, and untrained gunners were notoriously bad at directing them: Instead of using the optical range finder on the gun, soldiers just fired missiles one after another to zero in on their target. The Army figured the games would quickly pay for themselves. For reasons that remain unclear, however, Army Battlezone was never used in training, and the few that were built ended up being enjoyed by off-duty troops in Army recreation centers instead.

In 1997, the Modeling and Simulation Office of the U.S. Marines scoured the shelves for games it could use as combat simulators. "Utilizing commercial off-the-shelf software is much more cost-effective than creating new simulations from scratch. And it is absolutely realistic enough for us," says 1st Lt. Dan Mathes, a U.S. Marines data systems engineer. The Marines purchased several copies of the violent first-person-shooter game Doom II at 550 a pop, changed the game's slobbering mutants into Naziesque soldiers, and ended up with a low-cost, networked, close-encounter combat simulator. Doom II, which used 3D graphics-rendering technology originally developed for the military, turned out to be the perfect choice for several reasons—it was first-person, real-time, and had network functionality that prepared soldiers to make team decisions.

Naturally, when the developers of Marines Doom left the service, they went to work for the gaming industry and helped make a Doom-style game called Nam, a first-person shooter that lets players run through jungles and rice paddies, obliterating depraved communist insurgents.

In 1996, the Joint Chiefs of Staff hired military software contractor OC Incorporated (OCI) to create a PC-based war simulation called Joint Force Employment. The game was designed to teach military academy students how to coordinate efforts among the four branches of the U.S. military. It became so popular that Virginia-based OCI spun off a new division to develop a civilian version of the 3D game. The result, Real War, transforms the player into an Army general with the mission of wiping out the fictional Independent Liberation Army. Just as in the original version, players can command battalions of tanks to roll across parched deserts, and order realistic-looking infantry troops to penetrate jungles and eliminate the foe.

This strange cycle of technology transferal from game to military simulation back to game has a name: "defense conversion-reinsertion." Defense contractor Lockheed Martin, which launched its own game technology company in 1995, coined this awkward term, and the company uses its knowledge of graphics cards to develop cheaper technology for the military.

"Game makers are responsible for reinvigorating the idea of making military training fun," says Dr. Dutch Guckenberger, chief scientist of SDS International in Orlando, Florida. "It used to be a dry and boring exercise." Today's military simulations are real excitement-generators, thanks to the gaming industry's emphasis on a high thrills-to-pixels ratio. One Army general told Guckenberger that he could tell the new flight simulators at a training center were good because pilots were walking out of them "sweating and smiling."

The focus on storytelling is what gives military simulations and consumer war games the power to hold users' interest. "Story is critical to learning," says Macedonia. The goal of a good military simulation, he says, is to leave a vivid impression the soldier will be able to recall and act upon, should a similar situation ever come up in actual combat. By immersing users in tricky circumstances and challenging them with thorny problems that require split-second decision-making, games and simulations both become fun. And,

according to Lt. Mathes, this approach better suits the training requirements of the new generation of soldiers. "A lot of the younger generation of Marines learn in a different way than I did," he says. "You used to be able to sit them down in front of a PowerPoint presentation, and they'd be expected to absorb information. But now they need interactivity. They need to be engaged."

Currently, the Marines are developing a new simulation called the Virtual Battlefield System (VBS), based on a suite of networked laptops and the engine behind the game Operation Flashpoint. Using the game's level editor, the Marine Corps is able to create realistic environments that teach important skills such as maneuvering, communication, and ammunition conservation. The results have been surprisingly positive. Two teams were sent into a training environment, but only one had been trained using the system. And while Lt. Mathes admits that "nothing can completely prepare you for real combat," the team that used the system prior to the training exercise did "exponentially better than the one that didn't."

Even though games and military simulations have much in common, certain elements essential to effective military training are of little use to gamers. After all, games and military simulations ultimately have different goals: Games are meant to entertain; simulations are meant to prepare soldiers for real combat. While a simulation benefits from realism, too much of it in a game will send a player to sleep. That's why Real War strips out the slow-paced, nonvisual elements, such as online quizzes and training guides, found in Joint Force Employment. And while most gamers don't want to deal with totally realistic physics, soldiers must have simulated equipment and controls that behave exactly as they would in the real world. For instance, if a tank has a tendency to tip over at a certain angle, then the simulation needs to be able to model the same center of gravity in the virtual tank. This level of verisimilitude takes a lot of fun out of a game. Players don't want to have to worry about rolling their tank while gunning their Panzer over a sand dune in pursuit of General Rommel.

In a final twist to warfare as play and vice versa, the Institute for Creative Technologies (ICT)—a partnership between the U.S. Army and the University of Southern California announced that the U.S. Army will provide the funding to develop two new consumer videogames: C-Force and CS-12. The games are real-time tactical simulations that will allow players to send foot troops into trouble spots around the world. The technologies coming out of the ICT will be used not only by the videogame and movie industries to create knuckle-chewing entertainment, but also by the military to create ultrarealistic scenarios with all the emotional impact of a wide-screen action movie.

With $45 million in funding from the Pentagon, the ICT has brought on some of the best talent in Hollywood to combine compelling story lines and scenarios, artificial human characters that act realistically, systems that simulate sight, sound, touch, and smell, and hardware that behaves like real vehicle and weapons control systems. The goal, according to ICT spokesperson Jennifer Frederick, is to create a completely immersive full-sensory VR simulation.

Thanks to the back-and-forth between gaming and military simulation developers, games have become more realistic and simulations have become more fun. What's next? Well, besides even greater realism and enhanced fun, we're going to start seeing a fusing of the two genres. As the military incorporates more computer technology into its day-to-day operations, conducting actual warfare will seem more and more like playing a videogame. The Army is adding networked war-game technology to real tanks so the tanks can be used as simulators during peacetime. This idea, called "embedded simulation," presents tank operators with a virtual world populated with virtual enemies. When the simulation is running, the tanks' guns don't fire shells. Instead, simulated explosions appear on the display screen.

The military will continue to benefit from game technology, but in light of [the September 11, 2001] terrorist-induced tragedies in the U.S., the future of consumer war games is a little fuzzy. Investment bank Wedbush Morgan Securities predicts that game sales will suffer as a result of the terrorist attacks. Some games were canceled or delayed right after 9/11. Electronic Arts pulled Red Alert 2 from shelves because the box cover showed the World Trade Center on fire. Tom Clancy's Rogue Spear Black Thorn by Ubi Soft was postponed, and Crime Patrol, a shooter game from Digital Leisure, was completely canceled. In the U.K., some chains pulled Microsoft's Flight Simulator from shelves. Microsoft removed from the game's Web site screenshots that showed the New York City skyline. Microsoft also announced that it would take the World Trade Center out of the 2002 version of Flight Simulator. And Japanese game publisher Konami considered removing certain scenes from its antiterrorism game, Metal Gear Solid.

Whether war games will rebound from 9/11 is unclear, but one thing is certain: the military will continue to borrow from gaming. "The fusion of military sims and gaming has been accelerated by the events of 9/11," says Guckenberger. "Several military programs are using both military simulations and altered videogames to provide Afghan-specific training and potential mission rehearsals. The computer fun that gamers spend so many hours on is already showing benefits when these gamers become soldiers. It's inevitable that games and military sims will become part of the soldier's future equipment."

 RELATED LINKS

- Simulation, Training, and Instrumentation Command, U.S. Army (http://stricom.army.mil)
- Modeling and Simulation Office, U.S. Department of Defense (https://www.dmso.mil/public)
- Institute for Creative Technologies (http://www.ict.usc.edu)
- IGN Entertainment, Inc. (http://www.ign.com)
- PlayStation.com (http://www.us.playstation.com)
- Xbox.com (http://www.xbox.com)

 FOR FURTHER RESEARCH

To find out more about the topics discussed in this reading, use InfoTrac College Edition. Type in keywords and subject terms such as "videogames," "military simulations," and "virtual battlefield." You can access InfoTrac College Edition from the Wadsworth/Thomson Communication Café homepage: http://communication.wadsworth.com.

Reading 5-3

Weblogs: A History and Perspective
Rebecca Blood

EDITOR'S NOTE

From a quiet beginning in the late 1990s, weblogs, or blogs, have become a mass Internet phenomenon, giving voice to over a half million people a day who go online to update their self-published e-mail journals. In this reading, Rebecca Blood, an early blogger herself, offers a history and perspective on the blogging phenomenon. She suggests that blogs do much more than provide a platform for self-obsessed narcissism. Among other things, they enable would-be writers to hone their skills (and thereby gain a certain measure of confidence); they filter the news and serve as platforms for intelligent reaction to current events; and they provide a counter voice to the ubiquitous din of media pundits. Although the content of blogs is varied and raw, some weblogs are now among the hottest places online. "Weblogs," Blood surmises, "are no panacea for the crippling effects of a media-saturated culture, but I believe they are one antidote." For more on media saturation, see Reading 6-1 by Todd Gitlin.

CONSIDER

1. In what ways do weblogs represent "an unprecedented opportunity for individual expression on a worldwide scale," as the author contends?

2. What are the key differences between filter-style weblogs and journal-style blogs, and what different functions do they perform?

3. How does blogging—the simple act of regularly writing down whatever is on your mind and posting it online—empower and provide benefits to those who blog?

In 1998 there were just a handful of sites of the type that are now identified as weblogs (so named by Jorn Barger in December 1997). Jesse James Garrett, editor of Infosift, began compiling a list of "other sites like his" as he found them in his travels around the Web. In November of that year, he sent that list to Cameron Barrett. Cameron published the list on CamWorld, and others maintaining similar sites began sending their URLs to him for inclusion on the list. Jesse's "page of only weblogs" lists the 23 known to be in existence at the beginning of 1999.

Suddenly a community sprang up. It was easy to read all of the weblogs on Cameron's list, and most interested people did. Peter Merholz announced in early 1999 that he was going to pronounce it "wee-blog"

From "Weblogs: A History and Perspective" by Rebecca Blood, *we've got blog: how weblogs are changing our culture* (Cambridge, MA: Perseus Publishing, 2002), pp. 7–16. Copyright © 2002 by Perseus Publishing. Reprinted with permission.

and inevitably this was shortened to "blog" with the weblog editor referred to as a "blogger."

At this point, the bandwagon jumping began. More and more people began publishing their own weblogs. I began mine in April of 1999. Suddenly it became difficult to read every weblog every day, or even to keep track of all the new ones that were appearing. Cameron's list grew so large that he began including only weblogs he actually followed himself. Other webloggers did the same. In early 1999, Brigitte Eaton compiled a list of every weblog she knew about and created the Eatonweb Portal. Brig evaluated all submissions by a simple criterion: that the site consist of dated entries. Webloggers debated what was and what was not a weblog, but since the Eatonweb Portal was the most complete listing of weblogs available, Brig's inclusive definition prevailed.

This rapid growth continued steadily until July 1999 when Pitas, the first free build-your-own-weblog tool launched, and suddenly there were hundreds.

In August, Pyra released Blogger, and Groksoup launched, and with the ease that these Web-based tools provided, the bandwagon-jumping turned into an explosion. Late in 1999, software developer Dave Winer introduced Edit This Page, and Jeff A. Campbell launched Velocinews. All of these services are free, and all of them are designed to enable individuals to publish their own weblogs quickly and easily.

The original weblogs were link-driven sites. Each was a mixture in unique proportions of links, commentary, and personal thoughts and essays. Weblogs could only be created by people who already knew how to make a website. A weblog editor had either taught herself to code HTML for fun, or, after working all day creating commercial websites, spent several off-work hours every day surfing the Web and posting to her site. These were Web enthusiasts.

Many current weblogs follow this original style. Their editors present links both to little-known corners of the Web and to current news articles they feel are worthy of note. Such links are nearly always accompanied by the editor's commentary. An editor with some expertise in a field might demonstrate the accuracy or inaccuracy of a highlighted article or certain facts therein; provide additional facts he feels are pertinent to the issue at hand; or simply add an opinion or differing viewpoint from the one in the piece he has linked. Typically this commentary is characterized by an irreverent, sometimes sarcastic tone. More skillful editors manage to convey all of these things in the sentence or two with which they introduce the link (making them, as Halcyon pointed out to me, pioneers in the art and craft of microcontent). Indeed, the format of the typical weblog, providing only a very short space in which to write an entry, encourages pithiness on the part of the writer; longer commentary is often given its own space as a separate essay.

These weblogs provide a valuable filtering function for their readers. The Web has been, in effect, presurfed for them. Out of the myriad web pages slung through cyberspace, weblog editors pick out the most mind-boggling, the most stupid, the most compelling.

But this type of weblog is important for another reason, I think. In Douglas Rushkoff's *Media Virus,* Greg Ruggerio of the Immediast Underground is quoted as saying, "Media is a corporate possession. . . . You cannot participate in the media. Bringing that into the foreground is the first step. The second step is to define the difference between public and audience. An audience is passive; a public is participatory. We need a definition of media that is public in its orientation."

By highlighting articles that may easily be passed over by the typical Web user too busy to do more than scan corporate news sites, by searching out articles from lesser-known sources, and by providing additional facts, alternative views, and thoughtful commentary, weblog editors participate in the dissemination and interpretation of the news that is fed to us every day. Their sarcasm and fearless commentary remind us to question the vested interests of our sources of information and the expertise of individual reporters as they file news stories about subjects they may not fully understand.

Weblog editors sometimes contextualize an article by juxtaposing it with an article on a related subject; each article, considered in the light of the other, may take on additional meaning, or even draw the reader to conclusions contrary to the implicit aim of each. It would be too much to call this type of weblog "independent media," but clearly their editors, engaged in seeking out and evaluating the "facts" that are presented to us each day, resemble the public that Ruggerio speaks of. By writing a few lines each day, weblog editors begin to redefine media as a public, participatory endeavor.

During 1999, something else happened, and I believe it has to do with the introduction of Blogger itself.

While weblogs had always included a mix of links, commentary, and personal notes, in the post-Blogger explosion increasing numbers of weblogs eschewed this focus on the Web-at-large in favor of a sort of short-form journal. These blogs, often updated several times a day, were instead a record of the blogger's thoughts: something noticed on the way to work, notes about the weekend, a quick reflection on some subject or another. Links took the reader to the site of another blogger with whom the first was having a public conversation or had met the previous evening, or to the site of a band he had seen the night before. Full-blown conversations were carried on between three or five blogs, each referencing the other in their agreement or rebuttal of the other's positions. Cults of personality sprung up as new blogs appeared, certain names appearing over and over in daily entries or listed in the obligatory sidebar of "other weblogs" (a holdover from Cam's original list). It was, and is, fascinating to see new bloggers position themselves in this community, referencing and reacting to those blogs they read most, their sidebar an affirmation of the tribe to which they wish to belong.

Why the change? Why so many? I have always suspected that some of the popularity of this form may be a simple desire to emulate the sites of head Pyra kids Ev and Meg. As the creators of Blogger, their charming, witty blogs are their company's foremost advertisement for its most popular product.

More than that, Blogger itself places no restrictions on the form of content being posted. Its Web interface, accessible from any browser, consists of an empty form box into which the blogger can type . . . anything: a passing thought, an extended essay, or a childhood recollection. With a click, Blogger will post the . . . whatever . . . on the writer's website, archive it in the proper place, and present the writer with another empty box, just waiting to be filled.

Contrast this with the Web interface of MetaFilter, a popular community weblog. Here, the writer is presented with three form boxes: the first for the URL of the referenced site, the second for the title of the entry, and the third for whatever commentary the writer would like to add. The MetaFilter interface instructs the writer to contribute a link and add commentary; Blogger makes no such demands. Blogger makes it so easy to type in a thought or reaction that many people are disinclined to hunt up a link and compose some text around it.

It is this free-form interface combined with absolute ease of use which has, in my opinion, done more to impel the shift from the filter-style weblog to journal-style blog than any other factor. And there has been a shift. Searching for a filter-style weblog by clicking through the thousands of weblogs listed at weblogs.com, the Eatonweb Portal, or Blogger Directory can be a Sisyphean task. Newcomers would appear to be most drawn to the blog—rather than filter—style of weblogging.

Certainly, both styles still exist; certainly the particular mixture of links, commentary, and personal observation unique to each individual site has always given each weblog its distinctive voice and personality; and certainly the weblog has always been an infinitely malleable format. But the influx of blogs has changed the definition of weblog from "a list of links with commentary and personal asides" to "a website that is updated frequently, with new material posted at the top of the page." I really wish there were another term to describe the filter-style weblog, one that would easily distinguish it from the blog. On the principle of truth in advertising, this would make it much easier for the adventuresome reader to find the type of weblog she most enjoys.

So, what of the weblog? Is it of interest or importance to anyone who does not produce one? Well, I think it should be.

A filter-style weblog provides many advantages to its readers. It reveals glimpses of an unimagined Web to those who have no time to surf. An intelligent human being filters through the mass of information packaged daily for our consumption and picks out the interesting, the important, the overlooked, and the unexpected. This human being may provide additional information to that which corporate media provides, expose the fallacy of an argument, perhaps reveal an inaccurate detail. Because the weblog editor can comment freely on what she finds, one week of reading will reveal to you her personal biases, making her a predictable source. This further enables us to turn a critical eye to both the information and comments she provides. Her irreverent attitude challenges the veracity of the "facts" presented each day by authorities.

Shortly after I began producing Rebecca's Pocket, I noticed two side effects I had not expected. First, I discovered my own interests. I thought I knew what I was interested in, but after linking stories for a few months, I could see that I was much more interested in science, archaeology, and issues of injustice than I had realized. More importantly, I began to value more highly my own point of view. In composing my link text every day I carefully considered my own opinions and ideas, and I began to feel that my perspective was unique and important.

This profound experience may be most purely realized in the blog-style weblog. Lacking a focus on the outside world, the blogger is compelled to share her world with whomever is reading. She may engage other bloggers in conversation about the interests they share. She may reflect on a book she is reading, or the behavior of someone on the bus. She might describe a flower that she saw growing between the cracks of a sidewalk on her way to work. Or she may simply jot notes about her life: what work is like, what she had for dinner, what she thought of a recent movie. These fragments, pieced together over months, can provide an unexpectedly intimate view of what it is to be a particular individual in a particular place at a particular time.

The blogger, by virtue of simply writing down whatever is on her mind, will be confronted with her own thoughts and opinions. Blogging every day, she will become a more confident writer. A community of 100 or 20 or 3 people may spring up around the public record of her thoughts. Being met with friendly voices, she may gain more confidence in her view of the world; she may begin to experiment with longer forms of writing, to play with haiku, or to begin a creative project—one that she would have dismissed as being inconsequential or doubted she could complete only a few months before.

As she enunciates her opinions daily, this new awareness of her inner life may develop into a trust in her own perspective. Her own reactions—to a poem, to other people, and, yes, to the media—will carry more weight with her. Accustomed to expressing her thoughts on her website, she will be able to more fully articulate her opinions to herself and others. She will become impatient with waiting to see what others think before she decides, and will begin to act in accordance with her inner voice instead. Ideally, she will become less reflexive and more reflective, and find her own opinions and ideas worthy of serious consideration.

Her readers will remember an incident from their own childhood when the blogger relates a memory. They might look more closely at the other riders on the train after the blogger describes her impressions of a fellow commuter. They will click back and forth between blogs and analyze each blogger's point of view in a multi-blog conversation, and form their own conclusions on the matter at hand. Reading the views of other ordinary people, they will readily question and evaluate what is being said. Doing this, they may begin a similar journey of self-discovery and intellectual self-reliance.

The promise of the Web was that everyone could publish, that a thousand voices could flourish, communicate, connect. The truth was that only those people who knew how to code a webpage could make their voices heard. Blogger, Pitas, and all the rest have given people with little or no knowledge of HTML the ability to publish on the Web: to pontificate, remember, dream, and argue in public, as easily as they send an instant message. We can't seriously compare the creation of the World Wide Web itself with the availability of free technology that allows anyone with a Web browser to express their unique, irreproducible vision to the rest of the world . . . can we?

There are [now] thousands of weblogs: topic-oriented weblogs, alternative viewpoints, astute examinations of the human condition as reflected by mainstream media, short-form journals, links to the weird, and free-form notebooks of ideas. Traditional weblogs perform a valuable filtering service and provide tools for more critical evaluation of the information available on the Web. Free-style blogs are nothing less than an outbreak of self-expression. Each is evidence of a staggering shift from an age of carefully controlled information provided by sanctioned authorities (and artists) to an unprecedented opportunity for individual expression on a worldwide scale. Each kind of weblog empowers individuals on many levels.

So why doesn't every bookmark list contain five weblogs? In the beginning of 1999, it really seemed that by now every bookmark list would. There was a bit of media attention and new weblogs were being created every day. It was a small, quick-growing community and it seemed to be on the edge of a wider awareness. Perhaps the tsunami of new weblogs created in the wake of Pitas and Blogger crushed the movement before it could reach critical mass; the sudden exponential growth of the community rendered it unnavigable. Weblogs, once filters of the Web, suddenly became so numerous they were as confusing as the Web itself. A few more articles appeared touting weblogs as the next big thing. But the average reader, hopefully clicking through to the Eatonweb portal, found herself faced with an alphabetical list of a thousand weblogs. Not knowing where to begin, she quickly retreated back to ABCnews.com.

I don't have an answer. In our age, the single-page website of an obscure Turk named Mahir can sweep the Web in days. But the unassailable truth is that corporate media and commercial and governmental entities own most of the real estate. Dell manages more webpages than all of the weblogs put together. Sprite's PR machine can point more man-hours to the promotion of one message—"Obey Your Thirst"—than the combined man-hours of every weblogger alive. Our strength—that each of us speaks in an individual voice of an individual vision—is, in the high-stakes world of carefully orchestrated messages designed to distract and manipulate, a liability. We are, very simply, outnumbered.

And what, really, will change if we get weblogs into every bookmark list? As we are increasingly bombarded with information from our computers, handhelds, in-store kiosks, and now our clothes, the need for reliable filters will become more pressing. As corporate interests exert tighter and tighter control over information and even art, critical evaluation is more essential than ever. As advertisements creep onto banana peels, attach themselves to paper cup sleeves, and interrupt our ATM transactions, we urgently need to cultivate forms of self-expression in order to counteract our self-defensive numbness and remember what it is to be human.

We are being pummeled by a deluge of data and unless we create time and spaces in which to reflect, we will be left with only our reactions. I strongly believe in the power of weblogs to transform both writers and readers from "audience" to "public" and from "consumer" to "creator." Weblogs are no panacea for the crippling effects of a media-saturated culture, but I believe they are one antidote.

RELATED LINKS

- Blogger.com (http://new.blogger.com)
- Eatonweb Portal (http://portal.eatonweb.com)
- MetaFilter.com (http://www.metafilter.com)
- Weblogs.com (http://www.weblogs.com)

FOR FURTHER RESEARCH

To find out more about the topics discussed in this reading, use InfoTrac College Edition. Type in keywords and subject terms such as "blogging," "metafilters," and "free-style blogs." You can access InfoTrac College Edition from the Wadsworth/Thomson Communication Café homepage: http://communication.wadsworth.com.

Reading 5-4

Love.com

Anna Mulrine

EDITOR'S NOTE

As with other areas of social life, the Internet is radically changing the dating scene. This recent cover story from U.S. News & World Report *chronicles the rise of online dating services and their appeal to the record number of American adults who are single. In a typical month, as many as half of all singles, approximately 40 million Americans, may visit an online dating site—and that's not counting the millions of teens who may also use the Web as a place to meet new friends and hook up with members of the opposite sex. According to one expert, online dating services are as important to the digital age as the automobile was in the 1920s and birth control in the 1960s; in other words, we may be witnessing a social revolution. In an age where it is now possible to meet people this way, a growing number of online users are deciding why not? For all the advantages dating sites deliver to members, there are some downsides, however: a substantial number of people using these sites—as many as 30 percent, according to one study—may already be married!*

CONSIDER

1. What factors account for the widespread popularity of online dating services, and why have they become among the most popular sites on the Web?
2. How does the matchmaking software employed by many online dating sites help members narrow the field to suitable personality types?
3. What are the potential downsides and dangers to using online dating services?

Stephenie liked what she saw the instant Craig Murphy popped up as a match on her online dating Web site. He was a good-looking 29-year-old golf pro with dark hair and darker eyes. In the year before she met Craig on Matchmaker.com, Stephenie, a 28-year-old teacher in Phoenix, had had both hits and misses courtesy of the dating service, but never a shortage of entertainment. She had groaned with her girlfriends over the dodged first date kiss—"I had to be like, 'Ah, which part of body language don't you understand?'"—and hooted over the guys who posted decades-old photos of themselves: "I mean, the picture doesn't have to be last week, but when you meet up and don't even recognize him . . ."

For his part, Craig didn't have high hopes for a Web wingman. Truth be told, he was a bit suspicious, particularly since the coworker who had persuaded him to try the service was, he says, precisely one of those unabashed frauds with the outdated photo. What's more, Craig was still stinging from a recent failed relationship.

So they were both pleasantly surprised when their initial phone conversation ranged widely and easily and spun on into the afternoon. Craig finally decided to take a leap and asked her to dinner—that night. Then came the shocker. When he gave Stephenie his address, she recalls, "My mouth just dropped." It turned out they lived in the same apartment complex, just across a courtyard from each other—and had for a year and a half. "I know I probably shouldn't tell you this," she told him. "But if you stick your head out your front door, I bet you can see me." Later, they discovered that they went to the same church, too. "How in the world did we never cross paths?" wonders Stephenie, who married Craig last year.

E-CHANGE

Craig and Stephenie are not an aberration. Across the country, a record 40 percent of American adults are single, making them one of the fastest-growing segments of U.S. households today. And in the search for love, or at least a decent date, fully half of them —40 million Americans—visited an online site last month. It is, researchers say, nothing short of a social

revolution. "We're in a period of dramatic change in our mating practices," says Barbara Dafoe Whitehead, codirector of the National Marriage Project at Rutgers University and author of *Why There Are No Good Men Left*. "I think this is as important as the automobile was in the 1920s and birth control in the 1960s."

And little wonder. Increasingly, busy singles like Craig and Stephenie are turning to the Web to help them in a way that other social institutions don't anymore. Americans are more mobile than they were a generation ago, and they're also waiting longer than ever to marry. This union of social and economic trends means that young adults are no longer relying on traditional dating venues like college to introduce them to their sweethearts. For her part, Stephenie did all of the things a woman is urged to do when looking for Mr. Right: She found a place in a sociable sort of apartment complex, complete with a swimming pool. She went to the young adult meet-and-greets at her church. She put the word out to her friends. But no luck.

Enter the Internet. Sensing a staggering demand, online matchmaking services more than quadrupled their revenue to $302 million from 2001 to 2002 [see Table 5-1]. Indeed, online personals are now the most lucrative segment of paid services on the Web, according to comScore Networks—eclipsing digital music sharing services, online investment advice, research services like LexisNexis, and gossip and entertainment sites—including what the industry calls "mainstream adult" sites like Playboy.

Awed by this sprawling online dating community—and dazzled by the speed with which they can now collect and analyze data from this community—psychologists (often employed by the sites) are delving deeper than ever before into the still-mysterious science of what makes people good companions, good spouses—in short, what makes for the lasting American romance. In the process, these social scientists are challenging some conventional wisdom about love and marriage: Do opposites really attract? What breaks up relationships, and what makes people stick together for better or worse? Which is the stronger force: the traits you find attractive in your partner, or the annoying habits that make you crazy? The truly evangelical go as far as to say that dating Web sites, located at this unique intersection of technology and psychology, could actually offer a fix for a lot of what's wrong with marriages in America.

Glenn Hutchinson and Mark Thompson are among the new Web-dating entrepreneurs, but all they

From "Love.com" by Anna Mulrine, *U.S. News & World Report,* September 29, 2003, Cover Story, pp. 52–58. Copyright © 2003 U.S. News & World Report, L.P. Reprinted with permission.

Table 5-1. Lucrative Mates

U.S. consumers spent $302 million on online services in 2002, more than any other Web category.

Category	ONLINE SPENDING (IN MILLIONS)	
	2001	2002
Games	$47	$72
Personals/dating	72	302
Business/investments	214	292
Entertainment/lifestyle	112	228
Research	58	107
Community-made directories	46	91

SOURCE: comScore Networks; *U.S. News & World Report.*

really wanted in the beginning were dates for themselves. "When we started working on this 15 years ago, Glenn and I were in grad school, not having any dates ourselves, and trying to rationalize why this is so hard," says Thompson. Since they were techie grad students (studying clinical psychology) and it was the dot-com boom of the 1990s, they did what everyone else was doing: They hatched plans for a company. They hoped weAttract.com would make money, but they also weren't opposed to the idea that it might set them up for dinner and a show, too.

When they posted an online test on their site, they really didn't expect much. As researchers, they knew how hard it is to get anyone to volunteer personal information of any kind. So they were stunned by the response. Hutchinson says: "I remember coming in after our test had been up for 18 hours. I was expecting a few dozen responses, and there were 10,000."

DATE CRUNCHERS

The two instantly realized they had the means to study millions of online subjects—an unprecedented sample in social science research. "We are able to collect data in a week with a speed faster than any academic could have dreamed about in a lifetime," says Thompson. What they stumbled upon was "this amazing natural laboratory—people having good and bad experiences, telling us what happened and why they think it happened."

Other social scientists were having the same epiphany: Not only did they have a huge study sample at

their disposal, but it was a more representative sample of the population—not the usual studies of college freshmen and sophomores. Once one goes beyond that limited group of 18-to-22-year-olds, there are some psychological surprises. For example, Duke University-trained psychologist Courtney Johnson, who works for the online site Emode, has been analyzing how people communicate, how they argue, what makes them commit. In the process of doing her studies, Johnson discovered some unexpected expectations among daters. For example, she found that men want women who are quite confident—far more confident, in fact, than women actually are on average. This counterintuitive finding would probably not have shown up in a campus questionnaire, but according to Johnson has profound implications for people trying to match their personalities.

Hutchinson and Thompson were, meanwhile, drawing on their own experiences to fine-tune their dating software. They realized, for example, that the women they ended up dating often had annoying traits, which Thompson describes as "individual quirks." "And so did we," Thompson admits. "We decided to challenge the assumption that it's our best qualities that bring us together. What really shapes relationships, we think, is what you can tolerate."

They promptly built these beliefs into their matchmaking software. "A lot of people have trouble dating due to some fundamental characteristic. But there are a lot of people who don't mind that characteristic, and others who may even find it endearing." In short, says Hutchinson: "Everyone is high maintenance. The trick is finding the precise sort of maintenance you need."

They decided to employ computer technology to find a few "simple, logical rules" that make up, well, the recipe for love. For help on the technical side, they turned to Michael Georgeff, director of the Australian Artificial Intelligence Institute. During his work on a NASA project at Stanford Research Institute, Georgeff had developed a methodology to teach Space Shuttle Discovery computers how to anticipate unexpected problems. Working with Thompson and Hutchinson, he applied the same principles to the design of dating software, employing many of the statistical methods common to social science research. "Say you score a 3 on the introvert scale, and a 6 on touchy-feely. Will you tend to like somebody who's practical?" Using Georgeff's software, Thompson and Hutchinson then developed an online quiz. Match.com, the highly popular online dating site, began using weAttract.com's software this year to give users a rough sense of what proportion of the dating population might be attracted to their particular array of personality traits.

MAKING IT LAST

Other kinds of dating software are in the works as well. Clinical psychologist Neil Clark Warren was interested in the countless relationships he had seen fall apart. "There's the mystery, the complexity—and the fact that most people get it wrong," he says. Indeed, 43 percent of married couples are not together within 15 years, and of those who do stay together, 4 in 10 say they're not happy. Warren estimates that three-quarters of marriages are in trouble the day they get started.

The reason for that dismal track record, Warren believes, is that Americans are just too easy, relying on the intangibles of "chemistry" to carry their relationships. "In this culture, if we like the person's looks, if they have an ability to chatter at a cocktail party, and a little bit of status, we're halfway to marriage," he says. "We're such suckers."

To help these suckers, Warren founded eHarmony .com, a Web site built around a 480-item questionnaire covering all sorts of personality traits and "basic subconscious wants." Singles also complete a checklist of their biggest "can't-stands": Liars and people who can't control their anger tend to top the list. Once they're matched, couples spend about eight hours online, during six to 10 dates. It's part of a structured process designed to ease things "during the awkward getting-to-know-you phase," says Warren.

The feedback from people on his site has convinced Warren of some fundamentals. People need a partner about as smart as they are. They also need someone about as curious—not necessarily someone highly curious, just well matched. Ditto with energy level: Energy or lack of it is not as important as matching up well. The matching process is rigorous enough that 14,000 benighted souls who have used his site have never scored a single match.

Warren launched eHarmony in 2000 and now gets some 10,000 new registrants a day. Alison Morrow signed up for eHarmony one year ago, and though she'd never tried an online dating site, she had met men over the Internet. Those meetings, she says, were "always big disasters." She liked the idea of eHarmony but, based on past disappointments, was skeptical. Still, she found she enjoyed reading the answers that her matches provided. "These little tidbits from all different areas of their lives. You can tell a lot even just in their grammar, their vocabulary—if they were trying to be funny, or more serious."

What's more, Morrow adds, in the past she might have been tempted to shrug off some things that "normally would be a big deal, but because you've had a few dates and feel attached, you think, 'I'm not going to let that be a big deal.'" That, she says, was a mistake. She was much more discerning with Daniel, her 100th match. By the time they had wended their way through the matching process on the site, she says: "It was like we'd been dating for three months." They were married in August.

DINNER?

Not everyone visiting a dating site is looking for a life partner, of course. In fact, fully half of Match.com's members are under 30, and they are often seeking a fun date or simple companionship. Michael Mundy fits that category. He enjoys dating, and he isn't opposed to some bar hopping, either. He goes out regularly in downtown Chicago where he lives, but even at 25 he often finds the scene exhausting: "You're there to have a good time, so you don't really want to focus on, 'OK, am I going to meet someone? Are they with someone?'"

Raised on the Net and instant messaging, Mundy says he can't imagine not signing up with an online dating site, as he did with Match.com. "We live in an age where it's possible to meet people this way," he says. "Why not?"

It's an increasingly common question. Initially, Mundy did get his share of suspicious questions. "People would ask me, 'Why is a good-looking guy like you on this site?'" he says. But Mundy, who works in advertising, is busy, without much time to date, let alone go out. "I'm also really picky." So accustomed is Mundy to E-dating that he wishes all of his potential dates had some sort of profile he could peruse first. "It's, 'OK, here's where I'm from, here's what I do, here's what I'm looking for. How about you?'"

That's what the dating services want to hear. Meredith Hanrahan, vice president of online dating at Matchmaker.com, sees these sites as *Consumer Reports* of sorts, melded with a bit of online body language. "If you want to buy a car, you get a lot of information before you even test-drive," she says. "There hasn't been a way to do that with relationships."

This presumes, of course, that people are telling the truth—a big presumption. Chris Castner of Hoboken, N.J., recalls a date he had set up through e-mail a couple of years back: "She had said she was 5-7. She was 5 feet tall. She said she was a blonde, but she was a brunet. You get the idea." And the lies can be far more egregious than hair color. One recent study found that as many as 30 percent of people using online sites may be married. And, of course, there are no profile questions that will reveal criminal behavior, including spouse abuse.

As a result, safety is a constant concern for online daters. Jill from Long Island never chatted by phone without e-mailing through an anonymous account several times first. Even then, she would make the call but block it first to be sure it didn't show up on her potential date's caller ID. She also used to tell her landlord, a cop, when she left on dates, where she was going, and the cellphone number of her new online pal. Nevertheless, she had her share of dicey experiences, like the time a guy abandoned her in a parking lot at the end of their date.

Because of these real concerns, more and more match sites are using technology and psychology tests to do some lie-detecting as well. For example, at eHarmony.com, would-be suitors answer true-or-false questions like these: "I never tell white lies." "I read all of the information that comes with any prescription I get." "I read all of the editorials in the newspaper every day." People who say yes to all such queries are immediately suspect and are asked to leave the site. So far, eHarmony has asked 16 percent of its clientele to leave based on the results of its questionnaires. Other popular sites, like Friendster.com, use circles of buddies to recommend dates of good character.

Perhaps the most interesting recent development in online dating is that it's more and more resembling old-fashioned dating. For example, there are now Match.com live events in cities throughout the country, where singles can meet up for hikes, wine tastings, and kayaking events, as well as multiday singles vacations. Ironically, these events often attract singles who just aren't comfortable with online dating.

THE SCORE

So how well does it all work? One indicator is that eHarmony has 1,500 marriages to its credit since 2000. According to Warren, the company now hears from roughly 10 couples a day who met online and are now planning a wedding. Despite plenty of mismatches—it's still real life after all—it's clear that the stigma once attached to dating services is largely gone. For his part, James Currier, CEO of Emode, envisions a time when people will be more mystified by the notion of meeting in a bar than meeting online.

But what about the romance of it all? And the serendipity? Are we losing the stories of the chance meetings, locked eyes, loss of breath? Stephenie Murphy shrugs. "We live around the corner from a video store and a little grocery shop—that would have been a cute story, reaching for the same movie or something," she says. "But this is how you meet today."

And sometimes old-fashioned good luck plays the crucial role, even on the Web. Chris Castner did eventually meet the love of his life online, even though, he emphasizes, he "never had any trouble with the ladies" in the good old bar scene either. He saw Jill from Long Island's profile and asked her out. After a hectic day at work, Jill nearly canceled her date with Chris for the evening. But she rallied, pulled a favorite blouse out of the hamper, and "sprayed Fabreze on it." She got stuck in traffic, got lost, and to top it all off was nearly hit head-on by a Mack truck. Yet they met, despite all that, and a few months later they were engaged. Today, they are married.

For her part, Stephenie Murphy feels that she got the best deal around. "I paid $100 and got a husband," she says. "Can't beat that." Especially not when that bargain comes with a bonus: a baby on the way, due in December.

 RELATED LINKS

- eHarmony.com (http://www.eharmony.com)
- Friendster.com (http://www.friendster.com)

- Match.com (http://www.match.com)
- Matchmaker.com (http://www.matchmaker.com)
- Nerve.com (http://www.nerve.com)
- Tickle.com (http://web.tickle.com)
- weAttract.com (http://www.weattract.com)

FOR FURTHER RESEARCH

To find out more about the topics discussed in this reading, use InfoTrac College Edition. Type in keywords and subject terms such as "online dating," "matchmaking services," and "online consumer spending." You can access InfoTrac College Edition from the Wadsworth/Thomson Communication Café homepage: http://communication.wadsworth.com.

6

Media Saturation
and the Increasing Velocity
of Everyday Life

Reading 6-1

Supersaturation, or The Media Torrent
and Disposable Feeling
Todd Gitlin

EDITOR'S NOTE

Media sociologist Todd Gitlin has been an astute observer of trends at the intersection of mass communication and society since the 1970s. In the decades he has been writing about the media, a growing pattern has presented itself to American society: We are now enveloped by and continuously exposed to a never ending flow of images and sounds through all manner of communication devices—televisions, cell phones, audio systems, CD and DVD players, computer screens, and digital devices of all sorts—whether we desire them or not. Statistics documenting this trend, which Gitlin refers to as unlimited media, *only begin to convey the sheer magnitude of this unprecedented exposure and 24/7 "in-touchness." Society itself seems to be well on its way to becoming as mediated and audiovisually arresting as Times Square. As Gitlin observes in this reading from* Media Unlimited, *such media saturation results from "a fusion of economic expansion and individual desire, prepared for over centuries, and nowhere more fully realized than in the United States." Welcome to the media nation.*

CONSIDER

1. What are some of the long-term consequences of a society characterized by what Gitlin refers to as *unlimited media?*

2. Carefully examine the media use statistics summarized in the early part of the reading. Which aspects of media consumption surprise you the most, and why?

3. Although the media stream that Gitlin describes is modern, it draws on "ancient springs." What are the historical origins of today's media torrent?

On my bedroom wall hangs a print of Vermeer's *The Concert,* painted around 1660. A young woman is playing a spinet. A second woman, probably her maid, holds a letter. A cavalier stands between them, his back to us. A landscape is painted on the raised lid of the spinet, and on the wall hang two paintings, a landscape and *The Procuress,* a work by Baburen, another Dutch artist, depicting a man and two women in a brothel. As in many seventeenth-century Dutch paintings, the domestic space is decorated by paintings. In wealthy Holland, many homes, and not only bourgeois ones, featured such renderings of the outer world. These pictures were pleasing, but more: they were proofs of taste and prosperity, amusements and news at once.

Vermeer froze instants, but instants that spoke of the relative constancy of the world in which his subjects lived. If he had painted the same room in the same house an hour, a day, or a month later, the letter in the maid's hand would have been different, and the woman might have been playing a different selection, but the paintings on the far wall would likely have been the same. There might have been other paintings, etchings, and prints elsewhere in the house, but they would not have changed much from month to month, year to year.

In what was then the richest country in the world, "everyone strives to embellish his house with precious pieces, especially the room toward the street," as one English visitor to Amsterdam wrote in 1640, noting that he had observed paintings in bakeries, butcher's shops, and the workshops of blacksmiths and cobblers.[1] Of course, the number of paintings, etchings, and prints in homes varied considerably. One tailor owned five paintings, for example, while at the high end, a 1665 inventory of a lavish patrician's house in Amsterdam held two maps and thirteen paintings in one grand room, twelve paintings in his widow's bedroom, and seven in the maid's room. Still, compared with today's domestic imagery, the grandest Dutch inventories of that prosperous era were tiny. Even in the better-off

households depicted by Vermeer,[2] the visual field inhabited by his figures was relatively scanty and fixed.[3]

Today, Vermeer's equivalent, if he were painting domestic scenes, or shooting a spread for *Vanity Fair,* or directing commercials or movies, would also display his figures against a background of images; and if his work appeared on-screen, there is a good chance that he would mix in a soundtrack as well. Most of the images would be portraits of individuals who have never walked in the door—not in the flesh—and yet are recognized and welcomed, though not like actual persons. They would rapidly segue into others—either because they had been edited into a video montage, or because they appear on pages meant to be leafed through. Today's Vermeer would discover that the private space of the home offers up vastly more impressions of the larger world than was possible in 1660. In seventeenth-century Delft, painters did not knock on the door day and night offering fresh images for sale. Today, though living space has been set apart from working space, as would have been the case only for the wealthier burghers of Vermeer's time, the outside world has entered the home with a vengeance—in the profusion of media.

The flow of images and sounds through the households of the rich world, and the richer parts of the poor world, seems unremarkable today. Only a visitor from an earlier century or an impoverished country could be startled by the fact that life is now played out against a shimmering multitude of images and sounds, emanating from television, videotapes, videodiscs, video games, VCRs, computer screens, digital displays of all sorts, always in flux, chosen partly at will, partly by whim, supplemented by words, numbers, symbols, phrases, fragments, all passing through screens that in a single minute can display more pictures than a prosperous seventeenth-century Dutch household contained over several lifetimes, portraying in one day more individuals than the Dutch burgher would have beheld in the course of years, and in one week more bits of what we have come to call "information" than all the books in all the households in Vermeer's Delft. And this is not yet to speak of our sonic surroundings: the music, voices, and sound effects from radios, CD players, and

From *Media Unlimited: How the Torrent of Images and Sounds Overwhelms Our Lives* by Todd Gitlin (New York: Henry Holt and Co., 2002), pp. 12–31. Copyright © 2002 by Todd Gitlin. Reprinted with permission.

turntables. Nor is it to speak of newspapers, magazines, newsletters, and books. Most of the faces we shall ever behold, we shall behold in the form of images.

Because they arrive with sound, at home, in the car, the elevator, or the waiting room, today's images are capable of attracting our attention during much of the day. We may ignore most of them most of the time, take issue with them or shrug them off (or think we are shrugging them off), but we must do the work of dispelling them—and even then, we know we can usher them into our presence whenever we like. Iconic plenitude is the contemporary condition, and it is taken for granted. To grow up in this culture is to grow into an expectation that images and sounds will be there for us on command, and that the stories they compose will be succeeded by still other stories, all bidding for our attention, all striving to make sense, all, in some sense, *ours*. Raymond Williams, the first analyst to pay attention to the fact that television is not just pictures but flow, and not just flow but drama upon drama, pointed out more than a quarter century ago, long before hundred-channel cable TV and VCRs, that

> we have never as a society acted so much or watched so many others acting. . . . [W]hat is really new . . . is that drama . . . is built into the rhythms of everyday life. In earlier periods drama was important at a festival, in a season, or as a conscious journey to a theater; from honouring Dionysus or Christ to taking in a show. What we have now is drama as habitual experience: more in a week, in many cases, than most human beings would previously have seen in a lifetime.[4]

Around the time Vermeer painted *The Concert*, Blaise Pascal, who worried about the seductive power of distraction among the French royalty, wrote that "near the persons of kings there never fail to be a great number of people who see to it that amusement follows business, and who watch all the time of their leisure to supply them with delights and games, so that there is no blank in it."[5] In this one respect, today almost everyone—even the poor—in the rich countries resembles a king, attended by the courtiers of the media offering a divine right of choice.

MEASURES OF MAGNITUDE

Statistics begin—but barely—to convey the sheer magnitude of this in-touchness, access, exposure, plenitude, glut, however we want to think of it.

In 1999, a television set was on in the average American household more than seven hours a day, a figure that has remained fairly steady since 1983. According to the measurements of the A. C. Nielsen Company, the standard used by advertisers and the television business itself, the average individual watched television about four hours a day, not counting the time when the set was on but the individual in question was not watching. When Americans were asked to keep diaries of how they spend their time, the time spent actually watching dropped to a still striking three hours a day—probably an undercount. In 1995, of those who watched, the percentage who watched "whatever's on," as opposed to any specific program, was 43 percent, up from 29 percent in 1979.[6] Though cross-national comparisons are elusive because of differences in measurement systems, the numbers in other industrialized nations seem to be comparable—France, for example, averaging three and a half hours per person.[7] One survey of forty-three nations showed the United States ranking third in viewing hours, after Japan and Mexico.[8] None of this counts time spent discussing programs, reading about their stars, or thinking about either.

Overall, wrote one major researcher in 1990, "watching TV is the dominant leisure activity of Americans, consuming 40 percent of the average person's free time as a primary activity [when people give television their undivided attention]. Television takes up more than half of our free time if you count . . . watching TV while doing something else like eating or reading . . . [or] when you have the set on but you aren't paying attention to it."[9] Sex, race, income, age, and marital status make surprisingly little difference in time spent.[10] Neither, at this writing, has the Internet diminished total media use, even if you don't count the Web as part of the media. While Internet users do watch 28 percent less television, they spend more time than nonusers playing video games and listening to the radio and recorded music—obviously a younger crowd. Long-term users (four or more years) say they go online for more than two hours a day, and boys and girls alike spend the bulk of their Internet time entertaining themselves with games, hobbies, and the like.[11] In other words, the Internet redistributes the flow of unlimited media but does not dry it up. When one considers the overlapping and additional hours of exposure to radio, magazines, newspapers, compact discs, movies (available via a range of technologies as well as in theaters), and comic books, as well as the accompanying articles, books, and chats about what's on or was on or is coming up via all these means, it is clear that the media flow into the home—not to mention outside—has swelled into a torrent of immense force and constancy, an accompaniment *to* life that has become a central experience *of* life.

The place of media in the lives of children is worth special attention—not simply because children are uniquely impressionable but because their experience shapes everyone's future; if we today take a media-soaked environment for granted, surely one reason is that we grew up in it and can no longer see how remarkable it is. Here are some findings from a national survey of media conditions among American children aged two through eighteen. The average American child lives in a household with 2.9 televisions, 1.8 VCRs, 3.1 radios, 2.6 tape players, 2.1 CD players, 1.4 video game players, and 1 computer. Ninety-nine percent of these children live in homes with one or more TVs, 97 percent with a VCR, 97 percent with a radio, 94 percent with a tape player, 90 percent with a CD player, 70 percent with a video game player, 69 percent with a computer. Eighty-eight percent live in homes with two or more TVs, 60 percent in homes with three or more. Of the 99 percent with a TV, 74 percent have cable or satellite service.[12] And so on, and on, and on.

The uniformity of this picture is no less astounding. A great deal about the lives of children depends on their race, sex, and social class, but access to major media does not. For TV, VCR, and radio ownership, rates do not vary significantly among white, black, and Hispanic children, or between girls and boys. For television and radio, rates do not vary significantly according to the income of the community.[13]

How accessible, then, is the media cavalcade at home? Of children eight to eighteen, 65 percent have a TV in their bedrooms, 86 percent a radio, 81 percent a tape player, 75 percent a CD player. Boys and girls are not significantly different in possessing this bounty, though the relative usages do vary by medium. Researchers also asked children whether the television was "on in their homes even if no one is watching 'most of the time,' 'some of the time,' 'a little of the time,' or 'never.'" Homes in which television is on "most of the time" are termed *constant television households*. By this measure, 42 percent of all American households with children are constant television households. Blacks are more likely than whites or Hispanics to experience TV in their lives: 56 percent of black children live in constant television households (and 69 percent have a

TV in their bedrooms, compared to 48 percent of whites).[14] The lower the family education and the median income of the community, the greater the chance that a household is a constant television household.

As for time, the average child spent six hours and thirty-two minutes per day exposed to media of all kinds, of which the time spent reading books and magazines—not counting schoolwork—averaged about forty-five minutes. For ages two to seven, the average for total media was four hours and seventeen minutes; for ages eight to thirteen, eight hours and eight minutes, falling to seven hours and thirty-five minutes for ages fourteen to eighteen. Here, race and social class do count. Black children are most exposed, followed by Hispanics, then whites.[15] At all age levels, the amount of exposure to all media varies inversely with class, from six hours and fifty-nine minutes a day for children in households where the median income for the zip code is under $25,000 to six hours and two minutes for children whose zip code median income is over $40,000. The discrepancy for TV exposure is especially pronounced, ranging from three hours and six minutes a day for children whose zip code incomes are under $25,000 to two hours and twenty-nine minutes for children whose zip code incomes are over $40,000.[16] Still, these differences are not vast. Given everything that divides the rich from the poor, the professional from the working class—differences in physical and mental health, infant mortality, longevity, safety, vulnerability to crime, prospects for stable employment, and so on—the class differences in media access and use are surprisingly slender. So are the differences between American and western European children, the latter averaging six hours a day total, though in Europe only two and a quarter of those hours are spent with TV.[17]

All such statistics are crude, of course. Most of them register the time that people *say* they spend. They are—thankfully—not checked by total surveillance. Moreover, the meaning of *exposure* is hard to assess, since the concept encompasses rapt attention, vague awareness, oblivious coexistence, and all possible shadings in between. As the images glide by and the voices come and go, how can we assess what goes on in people's heads? Still, the figures do convey some sense of the media saturation with which we live—and so far we have counted only what can be counted at home. These numbers don't take into account the billboards, the TVs at bars and on planes, the Muzak in restaurants and shops, the magazines in the doctor's waiting room, the digital displays at the gas pump and over the urinal, the ads, insignias, and logos whizzing by on the sides of buses and taxis, climbing the walls of buildings, making announcements from caps, bags, T-shirts, and sneakers. To vary our experience, we can pay to watch stories about individuals unfold across larger-than-life-size movie screens, or visit theme parks and troop from image to image, display to display. Whenever we like, on foot or in vehicles, we can convert ourselves into movable nodes of communication, thanks to car radios, tape, CD, and game players, cell phones, beepers, Walkmen, and the latest in "personal communication systems"—and even if we ourselves refrain, we find ourselves drawn willy-nilly into the soundscape that others broadcast around us.

Crucially, who we are is how we live our time— or *spend* it, to use the term that registers its intrinsic scarcity. What we believe, or say we believe, is less important. We vote for a way of life with our time. And increasingly, when we are not at work or asleep, we are in the media torrent. (Sometimes at work, we are also there, listening to the radio or checking out sports scores, pin-ups, or headlines on the Internet.) Steadily more inhabitants of the wealthy part of the world have the means, incentives, and opportunities to seek private electronic companionship. The more money we have to spend, the more personal space each household member gets. With personal space comes solitude, but this solitude is instantly crowded with images and soundtracks. To a degree that was unthinkable in the seventeenth century, life experience has become an experience in the presence of media.

HISTORICAL ORIGINS OF THE TORRENT

To a child growing up immersed in the culture of images, it appears the most natural thing in the world. It appears, in fact, to *be* nature. Expecting images and sounds to appear on command (or even when uncommanded and unwanted) feels as normal as expecting the sun to rise. Because it's so easy to change channels, scan for stations, surf, graze, click, go to another source of images and sounds, you assume that if you don't like what you see or hear, you can find something better (or make your own image or soundscape). No wonder each wave of technosurprises seems somehow unsurprising—the screen hanging above an airplane seat, the car that receives e-mail and plays CDs, the watch with Internet access, the digital movie camera that switches on and off at the command of a voice. Indeed, today's

inescapable hype about a brave new interconnected world has a plausible ring because a significant and growing proportion of Americans and others are already wired, or wirelessed, into numberless circuits, networks, loops of connection with images and sounds available on call.

It's easy to see how individuals grow up expecting their lives to be accompanied by image plenitude, flow, and choice. But for society as a whole, how did this blessing come to pass? Media saturation is not a gift of the gods nor of the unprovoked genius (or wickedness, or frivolity) of technological wizards. The Edisons, Marconis, Sarnoffs, De Forests, and Gateses devised and organized the media that Marshall McLuhan has called "extensions of man,"[18] but humanity came first with its hungers and competencies. Nor are our desires the unwelcome products of vast corporations, determined to stuff human time with their commodities: with products that people would be so eager to purchase, on which they would become so dependent, that they would grant their time in exchange for money to bring these commodities home. It *is* that, but it is not only that. We know that Eminem's latest CD and *The Sopranos* are human creations, but it's easy to lose sight of the fact that the media flow itself is no less human in its origins, the product of millions of people who, having been molded by a mechanical way of life, have devised a seemingly endless number of ways to relieve the strains of that way of life by mechanical means.

Unlimited media result from a fusion of economic expansion and individual desire, prepared for over centuries, and nowhere more fully realized than in the United States. The pleasures of acquisition in seventeenth-century Delft led to the pleasures of consumption in twenty-first-century New York. In both, individuals matter, and therefore so do depictions of individuals. In both, individuals clothe themselves with adornments and disguises. In both, individuals claim rights—the big difference being that once-exclusive rights have been expanded, including the right to think and feel as you like, and over time, the right to love, marry, move, work, sell, buy, vote, and otherwise act as you please. One thing that ever-growing numbers have the right to buy today is access to images at all hours and in extraordinary assortments, offering, at low cost except in time, a provisional combination of pleasure and some sense of mastery. People who were already interested in images and sounds won the time to consume them. An industrial apparatus arose to produce them cheaply and in profusion. The desire for pleasing windows on the world—and windows through which to escape the world—is nothing new, but only in modern society has it become possible for majorities to cultivate and live that desire, unwilling to accept anything less. Now, the desire for play, the desire for routine, the desire for diversion, the desire for orientation, the desire for representation, the desire to feel, the desire to flee from feeling—all these human desires in their complexity and contradiction are indulged in the vast circus maximus, our cultural jamboree of jamborees.

Although the media stream is modern, it draws on ancient springs. To feel accompanied by others not physically present is hardly unprecedented. We have a profound capacity to harbor images of actual or imaginary others who are not materially at hand—to remember or speculate about what they looked like, wonder what they are doing, imagine what they might think, anticipate what they might do, take part in unspoken dialogues with them. The fashioning of replicas extends across at least thirty thousand years of human history. Throughout this time people have lived, through images and simulations, "with" gods, saints, demons, kings and queens, heroes of fleet foot and sword, absent relations, clan members, friends, and enemies. The painting of a reindeer on the wall of a cave in the south of France, or the portrait of a dead ancestor in Egypt, or a cross on the wall, or the replica of a saint in the stained glass of a chapel, each opens a portal to an imagined world, beckoning us to cross a gap between the image *here* and what is, or was, or might be *there*.

None of that is new, nor is the manufacture and wide diffusion of popular culture. Poetry and song migrated across medieval Europe hand to hand, mouth to ear to mouth. Broadsheets circulated. From the second half of the fifteenth century on, Gutenberg's movable type made possible mass-printed Bibles and a flood of instructional as well as scurrilous literature. Even where literacy was rare, books were regularly read aloud. (In a scene at an inn from Cervantes's *Don Quixote,* published in 1605, farmworkers listen attentively to a reading of books found in a trunk.[19]) In eighteenth-century England, the uplift and piety of John Bunyan's *Pilgrim's Progress,* which went through 160 editions by 1792, was supplemented by the upstart novel, that thrilling tale of individual action, which the high-minded of the time regarded as shockingly lowbrow. From then on, reading spread, especially at home alone and silently—that is, in secret. So did the imagination of what it might be like to be, or act like, somebody else: Robinson Crusoe, Moll Flanders, Tom Jones.[20]

But even in Europe's most democratic outpost, America, the influx of reading matter into the household was retarded by the cost of books and the limits of literacy. The immense library of Thomas Jefferson was neither shared nor matched by his slaves or nearby tenant farmers. Still, sitting by his fire in the Kentucky wilderness, in the latter years of the eighteenth century, Daniel Boone read *Gulliver's Travels*—scarcely the popular image of the rough-tough wilderness man. The illiterate Rocky Mountain scout Jim Bridger could recite long passages from Shakespeare, which he learned by hiring someone to read the plays to him.[21] "There is hardly a pioneer's hut that does not contain a few odd volumes of Shakespeare," Alexis de Tocqueville found on his trip through the United States in 1831–32.[22]

In the course of the nineteenth century, long before television, stories and images entered the typical household in ever-accelerating numbers. In 1865, according to literary historian Richard Ohmann, there was probably one copy of a monthly magazine for every ten Americans; in 1905, three copies for every four Americans—an increase of more than seven-fold.[23] As for the rest of popular culture—the carnival of theater, opera, public lectures, and other live performances—its major constraint was not literacy but cost. The declining price of commercial entertainment was crucial. Sociologist Richard Butsch has calculated that in the United States of the late 1860s, about 36 million theater tickets were sold annually (about one ticket per capita, but in a population 75 percent of which was rural, and where, as Butsch writes, "the five largest markets, New York City, Boston, Philadelphia, Chicago, and San Francisco, accounted for more than half the total national box office receipts").[24] Compare this with the 4 billion tickets sold per year at the peak of moviegoing in the late 1940s (about twenty-seven tickets per person, roughly one purchase every two weeks). Compare that, in turn, with the nightly TV audience at any given moment of 102.5 million people age two and up, or almost 40 percent of the U.S. population, in the year 2001.[25]

Cost-cutting goes a long way to explain this transformation. But more time and lower cost are not sufficient to explain why people today spend roughly half their waking hours around and among these manufactured presences. A hunger has become part of us. Just as we gravitate toward food even when we're full or mealtimes are still far off, we're drawn toward the screen or the speaker not only when it is right over there in the living room and we have time on our hands but when we are with children, mates, coworkers, friends, lovers, and strangers, or the screen is in an- other room. The culture of unlimited media takes up a place in our imagination. Its language and gestures become ours, even when smuggled into our own con- versation within quotation marks ("Hel*lo*?" "Dyn-o- mite!" "Just do it!"). A bizarre event reminds us of the uncanny 1950s series *The Twilight Zone,* whereupon the *dee-dee-dee*-dah theme will pop into the mind. We choose among our cultural furnishings but unless en- sconced in a cave deep in some remote canyon, we do not choose whether to choose any more than a young man growing up in a hunter-gatherer culture chooses to hunt, or a woman to gather. These are the ways of our tribe.

NOTES

1. Peter Mundy, quoted by Geert Mak, *Amsterdam,* trans. Philipp Blom (Cambridge, MA: Harvard University Press, 2000), p. 109.

2. Dutch inventories: Simon Schama, *The Embarrassment of Riches: An Interpretation of Dutch Culture in the Golden Age* (New York: Knopf, 1987), pp. 313–19. Schama notes that research in the relevant archives is "still in its early days" (p. 315).

3. Many bourgeois Dutch houses also featured a camera lucida, a mounted magnifying lens trained on objects in the vicinity. Because the lens was movable, motion could be simulated— distant objects being brought nearer and sent farther away. But because the apparatus was mounted in a fixed location, the range of objects in motion was limited to those actually visible from the window. (Svetlana Alpers, personal commu- nication, October 8, 1999.)

4. Raymond Williams: "Drama in a Dramatised Society," in Alan O'Connor, ed., *Raymond Williams on Television* (Toronto: Between the Lines, 1989 [1974]), pp. 3–5. Flow comes up in Williams's *Television: Technology and Cultural Form* (New York: Schocken, 1975), pp. 86 ff.

5. *Blaise Pascal: Pensées,* trans. W. F. Trotter (www.eserver.org/ philosophy/pascal-pensees.txt), sec. 2, par. 142.

6. Robert D. Putnam, *Bowling Alone: The Collapse and Revival of American Community* (New York: Simon and Schuster, 2000), p. 222, citing John P. Robinson and Geoffrey God- bey, *Time for Life; The Surprising Ways Americans Use Their Time,* 2nd ed. (University Park: Pennsylvania State Univer- sity Press, 1999), pp. 136–53, 340–1.

7. This April 2001 figure for individuals fifteen and older comes from Mediamat Mediametrie (www.mediametrie.fr).

8. Putnam, *Bowling Alone,* p. 480, citing Eurodata TV (*One Television Year in the World: Audience Report,* April 1999).

9. John P. Robinson, "I Love My TV," *American Demographics,* September 1990, p. 24.

10. Robert Kubey and Mihaly Csikszentmihalyi, *Television and the Quality of Life: How Viewing Shapes Everyday Experi- ence* (Hillsdale, NJ: Lawrence Erlbaum Associates, 1990), pp. 71–73.

11. UCLA Center for Communication Policy, *The UCLA In- ternet Report: Surveying the Digital Future,* November 2000, pp. 10, 14, 17, 18 (www.ccp.ucla.edu).

12. Donald F. Roberts, *Kids and Media @ the New Millennium* (Menlo Park, Calif.: Henry J. Kaiser Family Foundation, 1999), p. 9, table 1. There were 3,155 children in the sam- ple, including oversamples of black and Hispanic children, to ensure that results in these minority populations would also be statistically significant. As best as a reader can dis- cern, this was a reliable study, with a margin of error of no more than plus-or-minus five percentage points. Since the results for younger children, ages two to seven, come from parents' reports, they may well be conservative, since par- ents may be uninformed of the extent of their children's viewing or may be underplaying it in order not to feel ashamed before interviewers.

13. Ibid., p. 11, tables 3-A, 3-B, 3-C.

14. Ibid., pp. 13–15, tables 4, 5-A, 5-B, 6. In general, fewer western European or Israeli children than Americans have TVs in their bedrooms, but 70 percent in Great Britain do. Next highest in Europe is 64 percent in Denmark. The lows are 31 percent in Holland and 24 percent in Switzer- land. Leen d'Haenens, "Old and New Media: Access and Ownership in the Home," in Sonia Livingstone and Moira Bovill, Eds., *Children and Their Changing Media Environment: A European Comparative Study* (London: Lawrence Erlbaum Associates, 2001), p. 57.

15. Roberts, *Kids and Media,* pp. 21-23, tables 8-C, 8-D.

16. Adair Turner, "Not the e-conomy," *Prospect* (London), April 2001 (www.prospect-magazine.co.uk/highlights/ essay_turner_april01).

17. Johannes W. J. Beentjes et al., "Children's Use of Differ- ent Media: For How Long and Why," in Livingstone and Bovill, Eds., *Children and Their Changing Media Environment,* p. 96.

18. Marshall McLuhan, *Understanding Media: The Extensions of Man* (New York: McGraw-Hill, 1964).

19. *Don Quixote,* pt. I, chap. 23. On reading aloud in the Span- ish Golden Age, see Roger Chartier, "Reading Matter and 'Popular' Reading: From the Renaissance to the Seven- teenth Century," in Guglielmo Cavallo and Roger Chartier, Eds., *A History of Reading in the West,* trans., Lydia G. Cochrane (Amherst: University of Massachusetts Press, 1999), pp. 269–78.

20. Ian Watt, *The Rise of the Novel* (Berkeley: University of Cal- ifornia Press, 1957), p. 50.

21. Lawrence W. Levine, *Highbrow/Lowbrow* (New York: Oxford University Press, 1988), p. 18.

22. Alexis de Tocqueville, *Democracy in America,* Ed. Phillips Bradley (New York: Vintage, 1960), vol. 2, p. 58.

23. Richard Ohmann, *Selling Culture: Magazines, Markets, and Class at the Turn of the Century* (London: Verso, 1996), p. 29.

24. Richard Butsch, *The Making of American Audiences: From Stage to Television, 1750–1990* (Cambridge: Cambridge University Press, 2000), pp. 295, 297.

25. Brian Lowry, "Turn Off the Set? Not If Media Can Help It," *Los Angeles Times,* April 18, 2001.

RELATED LINKS

■   *Media Unlimited* (http://www.fsbassociates.com/holt/mediaunlimited.htm)

■   Signals of Saturation (http://www.theatlantic.com/unbound/fallows/jf2002-04-03)

■   Media O.D. (http://www.salon.com/books/int/2002/04/15/gitlin/index.html?x)

■   Adbusters: Culture Jammers Headquarters (http://www.adbusters.org/home)

■   Todd Gitlin (http://www.jrn.columbia.edu/faculty/gitlin.asp)

FOR FURTHER RESEARCH

To find out more about the topics discussed in this reading, use InfoTrac College Edition. Type in keywords and subject terms such as "media saturation," "constant television households," and "personal communications systems." You can access InfoTrac College Edition from the Wadsworth/Thomson Communication Café homepage: http://communication.wadsworth.com.

Reading 6-2

Prest-o! Change-o!
James Gleick

EDITOR'S NOTE

The remote control exemplifies the principle of unintended consequences, the tendency of new media and communication technologies to have social impacts that weren't anticipated. In this reading, writer James Gleick traces the acceleration of media, especially television and film, to the influence of the remote control and music television. Ironically, our anti-boredom devices and ever-quickening production values often diminish program satisfaction, encouraging channel grazing and further reducing already shortened attention spans.

CONSIDER

1.   What was the original problem that the remote control was meant to solve? Has it solved this problem or made things worse?

2.   Is the accumulation of speed, and in particular the acceleration of media, a one-way street in cultural evolution, as Gleick claims?

3. What did NBC's 2000 unit, and all the other TV networks, do to prevent the dropoff in audience that would occur at the end of a typical show?

_____

We have acquired various hand-held anti-boredom devices: chiefly, the "remote." Television watchers jump from channel to channel, and filmmakers copy that by jumping from scene to scene. The more we jump, the more we get—if not more quality, then at least more variety. Saul Bellow, naming our mental condition "an unbearable state of distraction," decided the remote control was a principal villain.

> Pointless but intense excitement holds us, a stimulant powerful but short-lived. Remote control switches permit us to jump back and forth, mix up beginnings, middles, and ends. Nothing happens in any sort of order. . . . Distraction catches us all in the end and makes mental mincemeat of us.[1]

When the first remote controls appeared in the 1950s, as luxury add-ons for television sets, they seemed like innocent devices that would save viewers occasional trips from the bed or sofa to the television set. They were pitched at the lazy or infirm. "Prest-o! Change-o! Remote control tuning with 'Lazy Bones' station selector," said a Zenith advertisement. "Amazing!" The inventors and marketers thought the primary purpose of their device would be to turn the set *off* as the user drifted toward sleep. Secondary uses, they thought, could include silencing commercials and, sure, changing channels, presumably once or twice an evening, when programs ended. (*Consumer Reports,* comparing the first models, sniffed that the magazine "did not test, though it recommends judicious use of, a simple built-in control device present on every television and radio set known as the 'off-switch.'"[2]) Marketers tried not-so-subtle appeals to masculine gun and control fetishism—users could "zap" with the "Flash-Gun" and "Space Commander." No one imagined the real power waiting in the remote control. The advertising and commentary of the fifties shows that it was not seen as a time-saving device in any sense. Nor did anyone think

in terms of amplifying the television experience with dozens or thousands of channel changes per evening. Most households could get just three to five channels; how could they imagine the remote-meisters waiting a generation up the road, using their wands to create on-the-go montages, nightly sound-and-light shows?

Now every television programmer works in the shadow of the awareness that the audience is armed. The remote control serves as an instant polling device, continually measuring dissatisfaction or flagging attention, if not for Nielsen's benefit then for your own. Possession of the device means that you have a choice to make every second. *Is this dull? Am I bored yet?*

The remote control is a classic case of technology that exacerbates the problem it is meant to solve. As the historian of technology Edward Tenner puts it: "The ease of switching channels by remote control has promoted a more rapid and disorienting set of images to hold the viewer, which in turn is leading to less satisfaction with programs as a whole, which of course promotes more rapid channel-surfing." If only the programmers could tie your hands . . . for your own good! Still, isn't possession of the remote a form of power? It does serve you, as a weapon against bad programming, even if the audience does not always use it wisely. Robert Levine, a social psychologist, cites studies that find "grazers" changing channels twenty-two times a minute. "They approach the airwaves as a vast smorgasbord, all of which must be sampled, no matter how meager the helpings," Levine writes.[3] He contrasts these frenetically greedy Westerners—Americans, mostly—with Indonesians "whose main entertainment consists of watching the same few plays and dances, month after month, year after year," and with Nepalese Sherpas who eat the same meals of potatoes and tea through their entire lives. The Indonesians and Sherpas are perfectly satisfied, Levine says.

Are they really? Will they spurn that remote control when it is offered? Or is the accumulation of speed, along with the accumulation of variety, along with the accumulation of wealth, a one-way street in human cultural evolution?

Broadcasters have to worry about this, and they believe it means they must be more efficient than ever in their use of time. Just as the technology of remote

From *Faster: The Acceleration of Just About Everything* by James Gleick. Copyright © 1999 by James Gleick. Reprinted by permission of Pantheon Books, a division of Random House, Inc.

control has made it possible for you to run from boredom without leaving the couch, the Nielsen technologies have made it possible for television programmers to detect the first glimmerings of ennui, apathy, and listlessness almost before you yourself become aware of them. A minute is an ocean. At NBC, John Miller, executive vice president of advertising and promotion and event programming, explains just how fine-grained the decision-making has become. "Every station looks at every second of air time and uses it to the best of their ability," he says. "We're all bound by the laws of physics. There are only 24 hours in a day and 60 minutes in an hour and 60 seconds in a minute. Everybody looks at their time with a microscope to get the best utilization they can. It is the only real estate we have." One piece of news turned up by NBC's research dismayed the programmers: as a typical show reached its end and the credits began to roll, one viewer in four, with a remote control presumably in hand, would give in to the urge to press the Channel Up or Channel Down button. A full 25 percent of the audience would start flipping around. That was clearly intolerable. A 25-percent drop in market share in return for gratifying the egos of the cast and crew? The NBC 2000 unit addressed this problem by creating what is known as the squeeze-and-tease: the credits are compressed into one-third of the screen (carefully tested for borderline readability) while the remaining two-thirds is used for "promotainment." You might see stars bantering about and around the peacock.

If you actually take in the screenwriter's name on the right *and* chuckle at the wisecrack on the left, you are multitasking. Anyway, every network has quickly adopted the same technique, because it is just enough, it seems, to hold your attention for the critical ten or thirty seconds that would otherwise loom before you like an eternity.

The network's time obsession has changed the basic structure of standard shows like the thirty-minute (twenty-three-minute, really) situation comedy. Network programmers feel they can no longer afford the batch of commercials that used to separate the end of one show from the beginning of the next. So those commercials have moved inside the shows, creating little islands of program at the beginning and the end, cut off by several minutes from the main body. Clever writers use these for stand-alone opening jokes and codas. "It's jokes and story right from the git go— jump in and go," says Skip Collector, editor of *Seinfeld*. "That kind of relates to our lifestyle and our pace,

everybody's rushing and going and that's what we're going to do." *Seinfeld* was one show that used the split-screen closing credit time for a final joke, rather than give it up for promotainment. It also dispensed with the traditional half-minute or so of opening titles: Mary Tyler Moore throwing her hat in the air week after week, or Cosby's family dancing around. More and more sitcoms just start with running story and flash a three- to five-second art card with the name of the show.

At least the major networks still program their airtime around the quaint assumption that viewers will arrive on the hour and half-hour and stay more or less in place. Many cable-television channels have abandoned that idea. Like parents giving up on mealtime and leaving an assortment of snacks in the refrigerator, they design their programming for a perpetually restless clientele. E! Entertainment, for example, passes the minutes with a pastiche of clips, interviews, promotional tapes, and similar fare, all designed to be glittering enough to hold the attention of channel surfers whenever they happen to drop in. One of its features is Talk Soup, a compilation of brief moments from other networks' talk shows, as if talk shows weren't already in soundbite territory. We're reaching the level of distillation of an abridgement of a sampler of a *Reader's Digest*. Every meal a tasting menu. Sometimes the miniaturization is the joke. Nickelodeon's TV Land channel squeezed in Sixty-Second Sitcoms, complete with opening and closing credits, a tiny commercial, and time for, on average, two gags.

All these channels fill the gaps that used to be dead air by playing instances of a new miniature art form: "promos," "opens," "bumpers," and "channel IDs." NBC alone commissions eight thousand different promos a year. They range from ten seconds to the "long form" two minutes, and they represent an astounding deployment of technical sophistication, products of a marriage between computers and the visual arts. In the early 1980s independent designers with new computer-graphics systems, a Paintbox and a Harry, could suddenly produce complex animated effects in an hour that had previously taken a full day. With the ability to compose effects frame by frame, to create multiple layers, images dissolving into new images, designers know that the viewer cannot always keep up. But they can't always help themselves. If the technology lets them add layers, they tend to add layers. Some of the power of these bits of video lies purely and simply in their speed—the length of time between cuts steadily decreasing, to the point that we routinely absorb sequences of shots lasting eight frames, a third of a second, or less. For someone creating a ten-second channel ID that will be seen over and over again, an effect that cannot be parsed on first sight by a typical couch-bound viewer is not necessarily a bad thing. Designers sometimes don't know or care whether the viewers will actually see a four-frame image. It's an impression. Maybe they'll see more on the next viewing. A flashed image can be like a subtle allusion in a long poem, resonating just below the threshold of comprehension.

MTV ZOOMS BY

People who revile the evolution of a fast-paced and discontinuous cutting style—and, for that matter, people who like it—have a convenient three-letter shorthand for the principal villain: MTV. The most influential media consultant of modern times, Tony Schwartz, offers this doctrine of perception:

> The ear receives fleeting momentary vibrations, translates these bits of information into electronic nerve impulses, and sends them to the brain. The brain "hears" by registering the current vibration, recalling the previous vibrations, and expecting future ones. We never hear the continuum of sound we label as word, sentence, or paragraph. The continuum never exists at any single moment in time.[4]

Schwartz put his theories to work in some of the most famous political spots of the last generation, from the watershed 1964 anti-Goldwater commercial—a girl counting daisy petals juxtaposed with a nuclear explosion—to the fast-cut Read My Lips commercial that damaged George Bush in 1992. Schwartz sits now amid a treasure-house of aging tapes and memorabilia on the first floor of his Manhattan townhouse. He was one of the inventors of the supercompressed video montage—a two- or three-minute bit of film combining hundreds of nearly subliminal images of, say, the year in review. When the Cable News Network was new, its founder, Ted Turner, wanted shorter commercials to match the brisk pace of his two-minute newscasts. The thirty-second commercial, a bold innovation that had swept dizzyingly across the networks in 1971, somehow no longer seemed quite so swift. Turner hired Schwartz, who took a set of thirty-second spots and cut

them down to eight seconds, seven seconds, five seconds. Now Schwartz looks at his watch and says, "I could do a . . . let me see . . ."—apparently he is playing something back in his head—"three-second commercial that would outsell any of them." He feeds a cassette into one of a rack of videotape players and, sure enough, three-second commercials: one or two quick images plus catchphrase. "Got a headache? Come to Bufferin." "You can see why Cascade's the better buy. Try Cascade." "As long as you've been taking pictures, you've trusted them to one film."

War and Peace it wasn't. But now even Schwartz is complaining about his up-to-date colleagues: "They see the stuff that's on MTV and they imitate that."

At MTV, the creative decision-makers offer no apologies. A company fact sheet asserts, as a kind of slogan, "MTV zooms by in a blur while putting things in focus at the same time." Music Television began broadcasting in the summer of 1981, with the Buggles singing, appropriately enough, Video Killed the Radio Star, followed by the Who, the Pretenders, Rod Stewart, and others in hybrid blends of music, images of musicians performing, and other rapidly intermixed images, real or surreal, related to the music or not, but always *cut* to the music. The basic MTV unit was a three-minute movie created around a song. You might have been forgiven for thinking it was meant as a sort of wallpaper, something to put on in the background when you didn't want to watch television. Wasn't it really a descendant of television's Yule Log, burning away eternally at Christmas before a fixed camera while carols played on the audio track? Certainly the music video was premised on short attention spans. It is a three-minute format within which no single shot is likely to last more than a second or two. MTV soon became one of the United States' foremost cultural exports, playing to 270 million households, including those reached by satellites over Southeast Asia, Mexico, and South America. Besides music videos—which evolved into a fantastically crisp and artful genre—the network has sent out its own talk shows, dance shows, pick-a-date game shows, and, most intriguingly, animated cartoons, like the famous, dim-witted, super-ironic Beavis and Butthead.

The not-so-hidden premise of Beavis and Butthead is that even music videos are slow-paced and boring, so you need an overlay of comic commentary. In their own way, though, Beavis and Butthead are painfully slow—MTV going conventional and letting story, rather than music, dictate the pace. The MTV animation style is deliberately static; it makes the typical Disney feature look like a madcap action film. The dialogue staggers along as if through mud, and the comedy relies heavily on reaction shots (so standardized that the animators call them by name: Wide-Eyed 1, Wide-Eyed 2, This Sucks).

"We love pauses—pauses are like, hey!" says Yvette Kaplan, supervising director, as a bit of tape makes its way through the editing room, a segment involving an impotency clinic. "Oh, yeah," Butthead is saying in the sequence now running over and over again through the editor's screen. "Huh-huh. Me, too. Huh-huh. Maybe that place can help us score."

Of all the visual arts, animation takes the tightest control of every fraction of every second. On carefully diagrammed sheets, each consonant and vowel of each word is assigned to its precise one twenty-fourth of a second frame. The characters' mouth movements have been reduced to an essential grammar of just seven or eight basic positions, enough to cover all English speech. This particular joke strikes the team in the editing room as . . . slow. There seems to be a lag in the line. "The pacing is everything," Kaplan says. "When it's flowing, it's just safer—you don't have time to drift away and miss the humor." They delete the "me, too" and nudge the pace forward a bit more by overlapping the final fraction of a second of the sound track with the visual track for the next scene. Alternatively, they might have jumped to the next scene's dialogue before cutting away visually, or they might have started the music for the next scene early—clever pacing techniques that viewers have learned to interpret automatically and unconsciously.

"The audience has gotten more sophisticated and you can take certain leaps without people scratching their heads," says Abby Terkuhle, president of MTV animation. And of course, we're starting young. "It's intuitive," he says. "Our children are often not thinking about A, B, C. It's like, okay, I'm there, let's go! It's a certain nonlinear experience, perhaps."

NOTES

1. Saul Bellow, "An Unbearable State of Distraction." Public address to the John F. Kennedy School of Government, Harvard University, November 9, 1989. [Available: http://mirror.shnet.edu.cn/harvard/www.ksg.harvard.edu/ksgpress/ksg_news/transcripts/bellow.htm]

2. *Consumer Reports*, November 1955, p. 53.

3. Robert Levine, *A Geography of Time: The Temporal Misadventures of a Social Psychologist*. New York: Basic Books, 1997, p. 45.

4. Tony Schwartz, *The Responsive Chord*. Garden City, NY: Anchor Press/Doubleday, 1974, p. 12.

RELATED LINKS

- *Faster* Web Site (http://www.fasterbook.com)
- James Gleick's Web Site (http://www.around.com)
- Remote Control Device (http://www.museum.tv/archives/etv/R/htmlR/remotecontro/remotecontro.htm)
- Zapping (http://www.museum.tv/ETV/Z/htmlZ/zapping/zapping.htm)

FOR FURTHER RESEARCH

To find out more about the topics discussed in this reading, use InfoTrac College Edition. Type in keywords and subject terms such as "NBC 2000 unit," "squeeze and tease," and "media acceleration." You can access InfoTrac from the Wadsworth/Thomson Communication Café homepage: http://communication.wadsworth.com.

Reading 6-3

Spam Wars
Evan I. Schwartz

EDITOR'S NOTE

E-mail offers tremendous advantages for communication and enhances social life and business practices in myriad ways. But junk e-mail, or spam, now accounts for more than half of all messages sent online and imposes huge productivity costs on industry and government. More than 13 billion unwanted e-mail messages swamp the Internet each day worldwide, and spam, which already represents a majority of all e-mail sent, could soon constitute 90 percent of all message traffic. New software defenses are helping to stem the tide, but the spammers are a wily and willful bunch, and the proliferation of junk e-mail is threatening to overwhelm the Internet. According to a Federal Trade Commission study, someone with a brand new e-mail address who enters an online chat room for the first time could get hit with spam as quickly as 9 minutes later. Responding to a spam message to complain only makes the problem worse because it verifies the user's address, which invites yet more unwanted messages. Software companies are rushing to build defenses—but will the new technologies ever be able to cripple the attackers and return e-mail to its innocent roots? This reading from Technology Review *explains the vexing issues surrounding the effort to eradicate (or at least control) e-mail spam.*

CONSIDER

1. Why is stemming the rising tide of junk e-mail on the Internet one of the most daunting computer science problems to come along in years?

2. What three principal tactics are information technology specialists using in the fight to control spam?

3. Why can't the war on e-mail spam be effectively fought—and won—with technology alone?

Operating 20 computers in an abandoned schoolhouse in Rockford, IL, Jay Nelson worked with relatives to set up more than a dozen shell companies, renting equipment and Web hosting services using aliases such as "Art Fudge." Nelson and his associates then "hacked into AOL e-mail accounts," states one legal motion filed by AOL, and overwhelmed members with links to pornographic Web sites such as pamsplayhouse.com.

In 1999, AOL won a court injunction barring Nelson from such activities and fining him $1.9 million; nonetheless, he and his colleagues subsequently sent another billion e-mail messages—triggering 25 percent of AOL's spam-related customer complaints over the next two years.

From "Spam Wars" by Evan I. Schwartz, *Technology Review,* July/August 2003, pp. 32–39. Copyright © 2003 Technology Review, Inc. All rights reserved. Reprinted with permission.

Alan Ralsky, by contrast, seems almost respectable. While trying to overcome a past littered with fraud convictions, a court-ordered fine, personal bankruptcy, and a brief jail stint, Ralsky in 1997 heard about a new Internet opportunity. Repudiating pornography to his wife, Ralsky rented mailing lists and set up servers in his basement, according to media interviews he gave last year. Pitching mortgages, vacations, and online pharmacies and casinos on behalf of others, he boasted of thousands of dollars per week in sales commissions. After moving into a $740,000 house in a Detroit suburb, Ralsky set up another basement operation that was soon spewing tens of thousands of messages per hour, relayed through servers in Dallas and in Canada, China, Russia, and India. In 2001, Verizon Internet Services sued Ralsky, charging him with unauthorized use of its network.

Nelson and Ralsky are just two of the many faces

behind spam. But according to Jon Praed, an attorney with the Internet Law Group, an Arlington, VA, firm hired by the plaintiffs in both of these cases, big-time spammers have a common profile. "They have not been successful in anything else," he says. "They are hackers gone bad, or they are crooks gone geek." They also sit at the center of far-flung conspiracies to conceal their actions. (Neither Nelson nor Ralsky returned phone calls from *Technology Review*.)

The spam crisis is hardly a secret. But few could have imagined it would get this bad this fast. More than 13 billion unwanted e-mail messages swamp the Internet per day, worldwide. This tsunami of time-wasting junk will be a $10 billion drag on worker productivity this year in the United States alone, according to San Francisco-based Ferris Research. In a perverse analogy to Moore's Law of microchip processing power, the number of daily spam messages is doubling roughly every 18 months, according to the Radicati Group, a Palo Alto, CA, market research firm specializing in electronic messaging. Having risen from 8 percent of all e-mail in 2000 to more than 40 percent by the end of 2002, spam has now reached a majority, according to studies from several anti-spam software companies. Conceivably, spam could soon represent 90 percent of all e-mail, says David Heckerman, who heads the Machine Learning and Applied Statistics group at Microsoft Research, which is working on anti-spam technologies. If that happens, he says, "a lot of people will just stop using e-mail."

"Spammers are gaining control of the Internet," says Barry Shein, president of Brookline, MA-based The World, which started in 1989 as the first commercial provider of dial-up Internet service. Shein has been spending an increasing number of nights and weekends—the witching hours for spammers—trying to block barrages of spam that appear so suddenly that they threaten to overwhelm his service. He's constantly adding new spammers to a "blacklist" used to block all e-mail from rogue Internet addresses, but that's a Band-Aid. "They change their network identities every couple of hours," and then sometimes launch "revenge attacks," Shein says. And spammers are ever alert to fresh prey: according to a study conducted by the Federal Trade Commission, someone who uses a brand new e-mail address in an online chat room could get hit with spam as quickly as nine minutes later.

The problem could easily grow beyond anyone's control. "Our concern is not so much for the porn and the herbal Viagra as it is for the legitimate businesses,"

says John Mozena, cofounder of the Coalition Against Unsolicited Commercial E-mail (CAUCE), an advocacy group. "There are 24 million small businesses in the U.S. If just 1 percent got your e-mail address and sent you one message per year, you'd have 657 additional messages in your in-box every day. That is our nuclear-winter scenario."

To avert such a catastrophe, electronic warriors are fighting the scourge of spam using three principal tactics. The first involves the rapid adoption of spam-blocking-and-filtering software by consumers, corporate networks, and Internet service providers. Anti-spam software is expected to grow into a $2.4 billion industry by 2007, up from about $650 million now, according to a Radicati Group forecast. But that alone won't win the war. The second, newer approach involves instituting more drastic changes in the way e-mail and the Internet work, perhaps imposing new costs to send messages or developing the ability to trace e-mail messages like phone calls.

The third tactic is a legal one, involving not only better law enforcement and prosecution of spammers but even a ban on all unsolicited commercial e-mail. To beat back the persistent, rising tide of spam, it's probably necessary to engage on all three fronts at once. "We move based on what we anticipate from the enemy, and then the enemy reacts," says Microsoft's Heckerman. "We're already up five levels of prediction." Everyone expects further escalation—while hoping that e-mail as we know it won't be destroyed in the process.

As one of the most daunting computer science problems to come along in years, the spam jam has triggered the Internet's version of a Manhattan Project. Hundreds of software whizzes are forming teams and companies in search of the ultimate way to halt mass proliferation. At the first-of-its-kind Spam Conference at MIT in January, the overcapacity crowd of almost 600 was speckled with PhDs writing scientific journal entries, young programmers wearing beards and backpacks, and P.R. pros touting the latest anti-spam services and software. The scene struck some participants as rather pathetic. "There are some very bright people here," The World's Shein told the conferees, "and what are you spending your time doing? Blocking penis enlargement ads."

Despite deep divisions among this assemblage on who has the best tools for eradicating spam, there's broad consensus on one point: if there's one thing worse than a piece of junk e-mail, it's the prospect that a spam filter will stop a legitimate message from reaching its recipient. That's why there are two important numbers one needs to know about the spam filters now in use or under development: the filtration percentage (the proportion of junk mail blocked) and the false-positive rate (the proportion of normal mail blocked). A 95 percent filtration rate is considered good, according to Paul Judge, head of the Anti Spam Research Group, started in February as a new branch of the Internet Research Task Force, a professional society. Many filters claim even higher filtration rates, he says, but those tend to run the risk of the unacceptable false-positive rates of .1 percent or higher—meaning that one in 1,000 normal messages would be lost.

Spam fighters are relentlessly adding new weapons to their arsenal. San Francisco-based Brightmail maintains one of the most widely used filters, which has been installed on corporate e-mail servers as well as the user networks of EarthLink, Verizon, Comcast, and Microsoft's Hotmail. The filter processes about 10 percent of the world's e-mail flow, says Enrique Salem, the company's CEO. Brightmail has set up more than one million randomly generated "decoy" e-mail addresses, such as Dxodt19@anydomain.com. Since no human is attached to these accounts, no one can possibly claim that their owners ever authorized a marketer to communicate with them. Within days, weeks, or sometimes months, these phony addresses will begin receiving spam.

How can an e-mail address that's neither listed nor used start receiving spam? The answer is the "dictionary attack." So-called spambots not only harvest e-mail addresses posted on Web sites but connect to the major Internet service providers and systematically send standard address verification requests to guessed addresses, beginning with "aaa, aab, aac," or by trying "DrDebra25a, DrDebra25b, DrDebra25c." Such programs are often included with spam kits sold by organized syndicates. Whenever these programs fail to receive a "user unknown" type of message in reply, they add that address to a list of valid addresses, to be sold to other spammers. . . .

An Internet service provider can sometimes detect such a breach and throw the attacker off the system, but the attacker will attempt to connect seconds or minutes later, from a seemingly different Internet location. According to the Spamhaus Project, a U.K.-based volunteer organization funded by a British Web hosting company, earlier this year both Hotmail and MSN were buffeted by such an attack at the rate of three to four tries per second, round the clock, for at least five months straight. (Microsoft, which runs both of the targeted services, says it has identified the alleged perpetrators and is pursuing legal action in U.S. district court in San Jose, CA.)

Brightmail's decoy method is aimed at minimizing the damage of such attacks. When the in-box of Dxodt19@hotmail.com receives a message, Brightmail's software compresses that message into a unique 512-bit "signature," which is added to the database of known spam. The database is updated constantly, and a new version of it is transmitted several times per hour to Brightmail's more than 600 corporate customers. Any message that comes reasonably close to matching a known spam signature is automatically flagged as unsolicited. Eventually these pieces of presumed junk are deleted en masse. "It's like a sting operation," Salem says.

Brightmail excels in its extremely low false-positive rate. It will block only about one in a million legitimate messages, for a rate of .0001 percent. The big shortcoming of this kind of filtering is that it doesn't do a terribly good job of actually blocking junk. A new piece of spam, or even a significant twist on an old spam, will probably make it through. Indeed, Brightmail's Salem claims only a 92 percent filtration rate—and large customers such as Microsoft and EarthLink peg the actual rate at more like 70 percent. That's why Brightmail is only used as a rough filter—and why it doesn't come close to tackling the overall problem.

SMARTER SHIELDS

Seeking a more perfect form of relief, tens of thousands of users have downloaded open-source filters (most popularly, Spam Assassin) or purchased commercialized versions such as McAfee's SpamKiller. A collection of statistically valid rules created by humans, these "heuristic" filters stand guard at the user's in-box and scan every incoming message for tip-off terms such as "Viagra," "V1AGRA," or even "V★I★A★G★R★A," plus improbable return addresses, strange symbols, embedded graphics, and fraudulent routing information, indicating the message is of dubious origins. After applying hundreds of rules, the filter scores each message, discarding those whose scores exceed a threshold value. Spam Assassin and SpamKiller typically exhibit filtration rates higher than 95 percent and false-positive rates of about .1 percent, according to Matt Sergeant of MessageLabs, a maker of Spam Assassin improvements.

This relatively high false-positive rate, however, is troubling to some users. After all, much legitimate e-mail has some of the same traits as spam. Sergeant concedes that newsletters that were requested by users will occasionally be discarded. That flaw has led to novel solutions such as collaborative filters, in which users vote as to which messages should be deemed spam.

SpamNet, from San Francisco-based Cloudmark, is one example of a program that deploys democracy in this way. An add-on to Microsoft's Outlook e-mail program, SpamNet starts filtering spam automatically upon installation. If enough trusted users designate a message as spam, that message ends up in the spam folders of Cloudmark's entire base of 420,000 users. "When a new person joins, they get the benefit of the community," says Vipul Ved Prakash, Cloudmark's founder and chief scientist. False positives are rarer under this approach, and users also have the option of clicking "unblock" on any messages in their spam folders. But there are drawbacks: SpamNet demands a higher level of user vigilance, and it requires that Cloudmark's remote servers examine all incoming e-mail before passing it on.

To fend off spam that penetrates other defenses, computer scientists have turned to the 18th-century probability theory of English mathematician Thomas Bayes. Published in 1763, two years after his death, Bayes's "Essay towards Solving a Problem in the Doctrine of Chances" provides a blueprint for determining the likelihood of future events. Since one person's spam can be another person's invitation to a pleasurable afternoon, Bayesian spam filters learn over time what each individual considers unwanted e-mail. When a user deletes several unopened messages about mortgage refinancing, for instance, a Bayesian filter learns to discard e-mail with that kind of terminology. If you typically do read such messages, however, the filter will take note of that and consider it normal e-mail.

Because Bayesian filters can be trained, their effectiveness improves over time, typically attaining filtration rates of 99.8 percent, along with a false-positive rate of a mere .05 percent. "If everyone's filter has different probabilities of different messages getting through, it makes it harder for the spammers," says Paul Graham, an independent Cambridge, MA, programmer. Last August, a link to Graham's article "A Plan for Spam" on slashdot.org jump-started a rush to Bayesian filtering. These kinds of filters, Graham says, will break

the business model of the spammer. It costs about $200, he continues, to send one million messages—an endeavor that typically yields about 100 responses. If those 100 people spend an average of $2 each, the spammer breaks even. The goal, Graham says, is to drive response rates down to around one in a million so that "it would no longer be economical for a spammer to consider such a business proposition."

Microsoft Research has taken this probabilistic approach even further. Standard, so-called naïve Bayesian filters treat each word or feature in an e-mail independently, but Microsoft claims its new filter, which is offered as an option in MSN 8 software, learns probabilities for words, phrases, and other distinguishing characteristics that commonly appear together. It might flag messages containing the phrase "make money from home" and "click here" that are sent from servers based in Hong Kong and that have random characters in the subject line. Microsoft's Heckerman claims that, by correlating patterns, his filter exhibits an even lower rate of false positives.

The monkey wrench is that spam is not an inanimate adversary, but rather a tool of wily and willful humans. In fact, the very effectiveness of spam filters may actually be making the problem worse. If half of a batch of spam gets thrown into the digital garbage can, the spammer will tend to respond by sending twice as much spam the next time. "As you put more filters in place, spammers become more determined, and the spam will increase," says the Anti Spam Research Group's Judge, who is the chief technology officer at CipherTrust, an Alpharetta, GA-based provider of e-mail security systems.

To balance the higher volume, Judge says, spammers simply find ways to lower their costs, such as enlisting servers based in China or India, where labor is cheap. What's more, as spammers mount a counterattack against Bayesian methods, spam is tending to look more and more like non-spam. For example, a message that says, "Hi Jim, have you seen the party pictures—take a look!" may not raise red flags, because it doesn't contain any obvious spam terms. When spam begins to look exactly like messages from friends and colleagues, filters may fail.

That's why anti-spam researchers are cooking up more-systematic treatments. Referring to spam as a "plague," Mark Petrovic, vice president of R&D at Internet service provider EarthLink, notes that today's e-mail system was designed 20 years ago for small numbers of people who already knew one another. "The possibility of sending body part enlargement ads was unheard of," he says. Stemming the tide of spam, he says, will "require a cooperative solution to augment the basic way e-mail works."

The most widespread of these measures is a blacklist of the sort used by Shein and other Internet service providers. Also maintained by startups such as SpamCop and NetBlocks, and by nonprofits such as CAUCE and Spamhaus, blacklists are collections of Internet Protocol addresses, domain names, and server farms that have been implicated in spewing spam; any mail originating from these tainted places will be blocked. But blacklists are imprecise: they often fail to keep pace with spammers, who constantly falsify their network locations, while sometimes blocking legitimate users. Indeed, blacklists sometimes halt e-mail from entire countries with high spam rates. E-mail originating in China and South Korea, in particular, has periodically been blocked from much of the Internet.

The inverse of the blacklist is the white list—a preauthorized address book maintained by users. An option in AOL 8.0, for instance, causes any message from senders not on the high-priority list to be discarded. This method also tends to trash e-mail you might want, though, and requires a high degree of maintenance; every time you make a new contact, you have to add a name to the white list. Aside from these drawbacks for their users, blacklists and white lists also are "wreaking havoc" on legitimate mass e-mailers, says Paul Soltoff, CEO of SendTec, a direct-marketing firm. After all, many companies send out electronic newsletters and other promotional materials. These aren't as obnoxious as the come-ons that most of us consider spam, and yet they are just as vulnerable to being blocked through the widespread use of blacklists and white lists.

Another drastic anti-spam measure strikes at the heart of the Internet's culture: imposing new costs on sending e-mail. "Paying to send e-mail may be anathema to almost everybody," says Robert Hettinga of Internet Bearer Underwriting, a startup in Boston. "But eventually, bits of money will be attached to e-mail messages." Just as paper mail requires postage, e-mail would require e-stamps. A charge of one-tenth of a cent per e-mail, for instance, would hardly be noticeable to ordinary users but would levy a $1,000 tax on someone sending a million messages at once. Any piece of e-mail sent without an e-stamp would be automatically blocked. Others favor imposing a cost not in dollars but in the sender's computer time. Your PC would

have to solve a quick mathematical problem for each message it transmits, barely affecting senders of normal quantities of e-mail but crippling a spammer's microprocessor. Such a "computational cost" approach is being developed at Microsoft Research and in an open-source effort called Camram.

The World's Shein proposes an Internet market trade association, which would be an "e-mail clearinghouse," run by a group of e-mail providers. Such an organization would sell legitimate bulk mailers special license codes in return for royalties based on the size of the mailings they are sending. Spammers who buck the system would be tracked down and sued by clearinghouse lawyers using funds set aside from the royalty pool. "The goal is to monetize the processing of bulk e-mail," Shein says. He derives the idea from the long-established model by which radio stations and performers pay royalties to songwriters based on the formulas of another clearinghouse: the American Society of Composers, Authors, and Publishers. Elements of such a plan are already being adopted by the big three of e-mail providers—Microsoft, Yahoo!, and AOL—who announced in April that they are banding together to develop a way of creating a white list for legitimate marketers. The group has yet to announce whether participating marketers will pay to maintain a new infrastructure, but Shein guesses that things are heading that way.

For such a plan to work, future e-mail will have to be traceable. The telephone system has survived, in part, because there have always been ways to track phone calls back to their sources and find those who abuse the network. "Filtering e-mail without being able to establish identity is essentially futile," says EarthLink's Petrovic. He cites the problem of spam masquerading as real e-mail. "If my wife says, 'I'd like to spend some time with you this evening,' I will react differently than if a stranger says the same thing. I need to know who is talking to me before I can evaluate the meaning of the message." Indeed, Petrovic adds, the anonymity of e-mail is central to the spam phenomenon. If we cannot determine who is sending messages, all other spam-blocking measures will ultimately fail.

Establishing such traceability would require fundamental changes to the basic protocol that governs all e-mail transmission. Called the Simple Mail Transport Protocol, or SMTP, it is the 20-year-old language that virtually all e-mail software speaks in order to move messages around the Internet. If all network providers switch to an "authenticated SMTP," as EarthLink's

Petrovic calls it, only an e-mail with a verified return address and from a valid domain name would be able to get to its desired recipient.

THE LEGAL FRONT

Technology alone will never win the war. Ninety percent of spam is sent by fewer than 200 people, according to Mozena of CAUCE, the anti-spam coalition. That represents an astounding degree of concentration, but virtually everyone who fights spam for a living agrees it is roughly correct. The implication is clear: spam is a crime-fighting problem akin to the prosecution of the small number of malicious hackers who crack into networks. "These are human beings generating these messages," Mozena says. "It's not as if the Internet is broken. You can't address social problems solely with technical means." He believes that the spam plague is a criminal-justice dilemma that can be eradicated only with the active participation of legislatures and courts.

New laws, though, have yet to make much of a dent. Last year, the European Parliament passed a directive suggesting that member countries require marketers to ask permission from users before sending pitches through e-mail. So far, Austria, Denmark, Finland, Germany, Greece, Italy, and Norway have enacted such "opt-in" anti-spam legislation. But since so much spam is sent from the United States through Asia-based servers, these laws have had little effect. In 2000, the U.S. House of Representatives voted 427 to 1 to pass an anti-spam bill. But instead of including a strict opt-in provision, the bill required consumers to request the removal of their addresses from each marketer's e-mail list. After privacy advocates denounced this "opt-out" bill as useless, it died without reaching the Senate. At least two spam bills are now alive in Congress, but there is still no consensus among lawmakers on whether the government can effectively outlaw spam—or even that it should.

In April, the Federal Trade Commission held a conference to help decide how best to approach this crisis. Brian Huseman, an FTC staff attorney, says the commission has prosecuted spammers who have sold bogus wares, failed to live up to their claims, impersonated legitimate organizations, or engaged in other deceptive practices. But since the agency is mainly charged with prosecuting fraud cases, it is powerless against spam that sells legitimate products. "There is no federal law that prohibits [legitimate] unsolicited commercial e-mail," Huseman says.

Until such a law is passed, lawyers will continue to rely on precedents from similar cases, says Jon Praed of the Internet Law Group. He believes that indiscriminate mass e-mailing is "already illegal in all 50 states" based on centuries-old Common Law that prohibits unauthorized use of someone else's property—in this case, computer networks.

Armed with this argument, AOL pursued porn spammer Jay Nelson, both before and after he and his cohorts violated the 1999 court order. Since spam cases can be prosecuted anywhere damage occurs, AOL chose its hometown district court in Alexandria, VA. In October 2002, the judge held the coconspirators in contempt and awarded AOL $6.9 million in damages and fees on top of the original $1.9 million finding, according to court documents. That figure was topped in May when EarthLink won a $16.4 million judgment against Howard Carmack, a Buffalo, NY, spammer; a week later, he was arrested on charges of identity theft. Praed says spammers cannot skirt the payments by filing bankruptcy, and that the plaintiff can "hound" the guilty parties until the money is collected, preventing them from buying houses and cars. "We need to make the spammers realize they made a mistake and to discourage others from doing it," he says.

Detroit-based spammer Alan Ralsky, however, remains active. Instead of spending more time and money bringing Ralsky to court, Verizon last October decided to settle its case against the man that some call "the spam king." In return for Ralsky's paying an undisclosed sum and promising to avoid Verizon's network, the lawsuit was dropped—leaving Ralsky firmly in business.

Furious anti-spam activists posted Ralsky's home and e-mail addresses online, and soon he was deluged with piles of printed catalogues and junk mail. Yet he appears undeterred and continues to add to his list of 250 million e-mail addresses. According to his own statements, he is finding new ways to obscure his identity, laundering his Internet location data through servers in Romania and obscure parts of China. Spamhaus and CAUCE consider the 57-year-old Ralsky one of the top five spammers worldwide. "I'll never quit," he told the *Detroit Free Press*. "I like what I do. This is the greatest business in the world."

The war on spam won't be won until guys like him are somehow forced to change their minds.

RELATED LINKS

- Anti Spam Research Group (http://asrg.sp.am)
- Coalition Against Unsolicited Commercial E-mail (http://www.cauce.org)
- Spamhaus Project (http://www.spamhaus.org)
- Machine Learning and Applied Statistics Group, Microsoft Research (http://research.microsoft.com/research/mlas)
- Brightmail (http://www.brightmail.com)
- Spam Assassin (http://au2.spamassassin.org/index.html)
- McAfee SpamKiller (http://us.mcafee.com/root/catalog.asp?catid=aa)
- Cloudmark SpamNet (http://www.cloudmark.com)

FOR FURTHER RESEARCH

To find out more about the topics discussed in this reading, use InfoTrac College Edition. Type in keywords and subject terms such as "e-mail spam," "spam-blocking software," and "Bayesian filtering." You can access InfoTrac College Edition from the Wadsworth/Thomson Communication Café homepage: http://communication.wadsworth.com.

Reading 6-4

The First Law of Data Smog
David Shenk

EDITOR'S NOTE

In this reading from Data Smog, *author David Shenk suggests that the character of information, and the way we think about it, has fundamentally changed since the development of computer technology. As we have accrued more and more data and information, they have become a commodity—as well as a pollutant. Until the mid-20th century, more information was generally seen as a good thing; now we produce information much faster than we are able to process it. With information and data production at an all-time high, Shenk argues that* information overload *has surfaced as a contentious social, political, and even emotional problem.*

CONSIDER

1. What are some of the personal, societal, and professional implications of the first law of data smog?

2. Why has information production not only increased, but also accelerated, in the period following World War II?

3. What are some possible ways of counteracting the incessant barrage of information that is characteristic of a message-dense society?

Information, once rare and cherished like caviar, is now plentiful and taken for granted like potatoes.

Still, the concept of *too much information* seems odd and vaguely inhuman. This is because, in evolutionary-historical terms, this weed in our information landscape has just sprouted—it is only about 50 years old.

Up until then, more information was almost always a good thing. For nearly 100,000 years leading up to this century, information technology has been an unambiguous virtue as a means of sustaining and developing culture. Information and communications have made us steadily healthier, wealthier, more tolerant. Because of information, we understand more about how to overcome the basic challenges of life. Food is more abundant. Our physical structures are sturdier, more reliable. Our societies are more stable, as we have learned how to make political systems function. Our citizens are freer, thanks to a wide dissemination of information that has empowered the individual. Dangerous superstitions and false notions have been washed away: Communicating quickly with people helps to overcome our fear of them and diminishes the likelihood of conflict.

Then, around the time of the first atomic bomb, something strange happened. We began to produce information much faster than we could process it.

This had never happened before. For 100,000 years the three fundamental stages of the communications process—production, distribution, and processing—had been more or less in synch with one another. By and large, over our long history, people have been able to examine and consider information about as quickly as it could be created and circulated. This equipoise lasted through an astonishing range of communications media—the drum, smoke signal, cave painting, horse, town crier, carrier pigeon, newspaper, photograph, telegraph, telephone, radio, and film.

But in the mid-twentieth century this graceful synchrony was abruptly knocked off track with the introduction of computers, microwave transmissions, television, and satellites.[1] These hyper-production and hyper-distribution mechanisms surged ahead of human processing ability, leaving us with a permanent pro-

cessing deficit, what Finnish sociologist Jaako Lehtonen calls an "information discrepancy."[2]

In this way, in a very short span of natural history, we have vaulted from a state of information scarcity to one of information surplus—from drought to flood in the geological blink of an eye. In 1850, 4 percent of American workers handled information for a living[3]; now *most* do, and information processing (as opposed to material goods) now accounts for more than half of the U.S. gross domestic product.[4] Data has become more plentiful, more speedy (computer processing speed has doubled every two years for the last thirty years),[5] and more dense (from 1965 to 1995, the average network television advertisement shrunk from 53.1 seconds to 25.4 seconds and the average TV news "soundbite" shrunk from 42.3 seconds to 8.3 seconds; meanwhile, over the same period, the number of ads per network TV minute increased from 1.1 to 2.4).[6]

Information has also become a lot cheaper—to produce, to manipulate, to disseminate. All of this has made us information-rich, empowering Americans with the blessings of applied knowledge. It has also, though, unleased the potential of information-gluttony.

Just as fat has replaced starvation as this nation's number one dietary concern, information overload has replaced information scarcity as an important new emotional, social, and political problem. "The real issue for future technology," says Columbia's Eli Noam, "does not appear to be production of information, and certainly not transmission. Almost anybody can *add* information. The difficult question is how to *reduce* it."[7]

Action photographers often use a machine called a "motor drive" that attaches to 35mm cameras. The motor drive allows a photographer to shoot many separate exposures in any given second just by keeping his or her finger on a button. *Click-click-click-click-click* . . .

What an elegant metaphor for our age: With virtually no effort and for relatively little cost, we can capture as much information as we want. The capturing requires very little planning or forethought, and in fact is built right into the design of our machines. With a thumb and index finger, we effortlessly Copy and Paste sentences, paragraphs, books. After writing e-mail, we "carbon copy" it to one or one hundred others. The same goes for the photocopy machine, onto which we simply enter whatever number of copies we desire. Would you like those collated and stapled? It's no bother.

From "The First Law of Data Smog," in *Data Smog: Surviving the Information Glut* by David Shenk (San Francisco: Harper-SanFrancisco, 1997). Copyright © 1997 by David Shenk. Reprinted by permission of HarperCollins Publishers, Inc.

Only as an afterthought do we confront the consequences of such a low transaction cost. "E-mail is an open duct into your central nervous system," says Michael Dertouzos, director of MIT's Laboratory for Computer Science, exaggerating playfully to make a serious point. "It occupies the brain and reduces productivity."[8]

With information production not only increasing, but *accelerating,* there is no sign that processing will ever catch up. We have quite suddenly mutated into a radically different culture, a civilization that trades in and survives on stylized communication. We no longer hunt or gather; few of us farm or assemble. Instead, we negotiate, we network, we interface. And as we enjoy the many fruits of this burgeoning information civilization, we also have to learn to compensate for the new and permanent side effects of what sociologists, in an academic understatement, call a "message dense" society.

Audio buffs have long been familiar with the phrase *signal-to-noise ratio.* It is engineering parlance for measuring the quality of a sound system by comparing the amount of desired audio signal to the amount of unwanted noise leaking through. In the information age, signal-to-noise has also become a useful way to think about social health and stability. How much of the information in our midst is useful, and how much of it gets in the way? What is our signal-to-noise ratio?

We know that the ratio has diminished of late, and that the character of information has changed: As we have accrued more and more of it, information has emerged not only as a currency, but also as a pollutant.

- In 1971 the average American was targeted by at least 560 daily advertising messages. Twenty years later, that number had risen sixfold, to 3,000 messages per day.[9]

- In the office, an average of 60 percent of each person's time is now spent processing documents.[10]

- Paper consumption per capita in the United States tripled from 1940 to 1980 (from 200 to 600 pounds), and tripled again from 1980 to 1990 (to 1,800 pounds).[11]

- In the 1980s, third-class mail (used to send publications) grew thirteen times faster than population growth.[12]

- Two-thirds of business managers surveyed report tension with colleagues, loss of job satisfaction

and strained personal relationships as a result of information overload.[13]

- More than 1,000 telemarketing companies employ 4 million Americans, and generate $650 billion in annual sales.[14]

Let us call this unexpected, unwelcome part of our atmosphere "data smog," an expression for the noxious muck and druck of the information age. Data smog gets in the way; it crowds out quiet moments, and obstructs much-needed contemplation. It spoils conversation, literature, and even entertainment. It thwarts skepticism, rendering us less sophisticated as consumers and citizens. It stresses us out.

Data smog is not just the pile of unsolicited catalogs and spam arriving daily in our home and electronic mailboxes. It is also information that we pay handsomely for, that we *crave*—the seductive, mesmerizing quick-cut television ads and the twenty-four-hour up-to-the-minute news flashes. It is the faxes we request as well as the ones we don't; it is the misdialed numbers and drippy sales calls we get during dinnertime; but it is also the Web sites we eagerly visit before and after dinner, the pile of magazines we pore through every month, and the dozens of channels we flip through whenever we get a free moment.

The blank spaces and silent moments in life are fast disappearing. Mostly because we have asked for it, media is everywhere. Televisions, telephones, radios, message beepers, and an assortment of other modern communication and navigational aids are now as ubiquitous as roads and tennis shoes—anywhere humans can go, all forms of media now follow: onto trains, planes, automobiles, into hotel bathrooms, along jogging paths and mountain trails, on bikes and boats . . .

Information and entertainment now conform to our every orientation: Giant television screens adorn stadiums and surround theatrical stages; more ordinary-size TVs hang from ceilings in bars and airport lounges; mini-TVs are installed in front of individual seats in new airliners. Cellular telephone conversation creates a new ambiance for sidewalks and hallways. Beepers and laptop computers follow us home and come with us on vacation.

Meanwhile, the flavor of the information has also changed. It's no longer a matter of mono versus stereo or black and white versus color. TV and computer screens have been transformed into a hypnotic visual sizzle that MTV aptly calls "eye candy." With hypermedia, "dense TV," and split-screens providing a multiplicity of images at once, straining our attention has become one of our most popular forms of entertainment.

We've heard a lot lately about the moral decay evident in our entertainment packaging. But it isn't so much the content of the messages that should worry us as much their ubiquity, and it is critical to realize that information doesn't have to be unwanted and unattractive to be harmful.

Take advertising (please). Though the bulk of today's commercial messages are aesthetically appealing and can each be considered relatively harmless, in aggregate they have crept into every nook and cranny of our lives—onto our jackets, ties, hats, shirts, and wristbands; onto bikes, benches, cars, trucks, even tennis nets; onto banners trailing behind planes, hanging above sporting and concert events and now, in smaller form, bordering Web pages; onto the sides of blimps hovering in the sky. Magazine ads now communicate not only though color and text but also through smell and even sound.

The smog thickens from the insidious blurring of editorial content and commercial messages in "advertorials" and product placements, to the point where it often becomes impossible to determine whether someone is trying to tell you something or merely sell you something. Increasingly, our public spaces are up for rent. "Is it crass?" asks the official marketer for the city of Atlanta, Joel Babbitt, who has designs to sell high-tech advertising on city sidewalks, streets, parks and garbage trucks. "Yes, but so is the Blockbuster Bowl. So is Michael Jordan wearing a Nike cap on the bench and getting a million dollars for it. . . . If it brings in money that helps our citizens, what's the harm?"[15]

What is the harm of an incessant barrage of stimulus captivating our senses at virtually every waking moment? Providing a thorough answer to that question is one of the most important things we can do in our message-dense society.

NOTES

1. Eli M. Noam, "Visions of the Media Age: Taming the Information Monster." In *Multimedia: A Revolutionary Challenge*. Third Annual Colloquium, June 16–17, 1995. Frankfurt am Main: Schaffer-Poeschel Verlag Stuttgart, 1995, p. 21.

2. Jaako Lehtonen, "The Information Society and the New Competence," *American Behavioral Scientist,* November/December 1988, pp. 104–111.

3. Louise Sweeney, *The Christian Science Monitor,* January 26, 1978, p. 26.

4. Orrin Klapp, *Overload and Boredom*. New York: Greenwood Press, 1986, p. 7.

5. Robert E. Calem, *The New York Times* on the Web, February 14, 1996. "We'll be at one million times faster [than ENIAC] in six years if Moore's Law continues to hold true, which it always has," said Prof. Mitchell Marcus, chairman of the University of Pennsylvania's Computer and Information Science Department.

6. *TV Dimensions 1995* and *Magazine Dimensions 1995*.

7. Noam, "Visions of the Media Age," pp. 18–19.

8. Michael Dertouzos, *Technology Review,* August/September 1994.

9. Noam, "Visions of the Media Age," p. 28.

10. Patrick Ames, *Beyond Paper*. Indianapolis: Hayden Press, 1993.

11. Jeff Davidson, "The Frantic Society," *Business and Society Review 83* (September 22, 1992): 4; Noam, "Visions of the Media Age," p. 22.

12. Noam, "Visions of the Media Age," pp. 20–24.

13. David Lewis, "Dying for Information? An Investigation Into the Effects of Information Overload in the U.K. and Worldwide." *Reuters Business Information,* October 1996.

14. Cristina Rouvalis, "Charm, Persistence, and a Telephone." *Pittsburgh Post-Gazette,* May 25, 1997.

15. Petter Applebome, "How Atlanta's Adman Pushes the City to Sell Itself," *The New York Times,* February 9, 1993, p. A16.

RELATED LINKS

- www.davidshenk.com (http://www.technorealism.org/dshenk/homepage.html)
- Technorealism (http://www.technorealism.org)
- Change and Information Overload: Negative Effects (http://pespmc1.vub.ac.be/CHIN-NEG.html)
- Deep Thinking and Deep Reading in an Age of Info-Glut, Info-Garbage, Info-Glitz, and Info-Glimmer (http://www.fno.org/mar97/deep.html)

■   A Few Thoughts on Cognitive Overload (http://icl-server.ucsd.edu/~kirsh/Articles/
     Overload/published.html)

FOR FURTHER RESEARCH

To find out more about the topics discussed in this reading, use InfoTrac College Edition. Type
in keywords and subject terms such as "information overload," "information discrepancy," and
"information society." You can access InfoTrac from the Wadsworth/Thomson Communication Café homepage: http://communication.wadsworth.com.

Social Impacts of Information and Communications Technologies

Part IV provides an overview of the promises and paradoxes of networked computing and surveys the criticisms of computer culture. The readings in Chapter 7 trace the development of the World Wide Web from its humble origins as a hypertext interface for research scientists in the early 1990s to the complex, multifaceted communication medium it has become today. When computers were introduced on a wide scale in business and in the schools, it was hoped they would automatically solve efficiency problems and overcome educational hurdles. Instead, it took decades of investment and experimentation before economists started noticing real productivity gains from networked computing. Not surprisingly, improved productivity performance mirrors the growth and development of the World Wide Web. Businesses, it would appear, are finally reaping the benefits of distributed information technology. In the schools, however, there still is no good evidence that most uses of computers significantly improve teaching and learning. The readings in Chapter 8 that question information technology highlight problems associated with the computer lifestyle, while providing a sober (rather than hyped) assessment of the Internet's known impact on social interaction and individual psychology. As business, education, and government have become dependent on PowerPoint for presentations, criticism of the software has grown for encouraging triteness and redundancy. Perhaps no phenomenon better illustrates the perils of technological dependence than the Y2K computer scare, which resulted in minimal actual disruption but considerable pre-event anxiety. As these readings illustrate, there are no simple technological solutions to enduring social problems.

7

Networked Computing:
Promises and Paradoxes

Reading 7-1

The World Wide Web Unleashed
John December

EDITOR'S NOTE

Since its introduction in the early 1990s, the World Wide Web has revolutionized the media and personal communications landscape while transforming the way business is done. This reading from the World Wide Web Unleashed *by John December traces the origins of hypermedia, discusses the different forms that communication can take online, and describes the many communication functions that the Web serves. Perhaps most importantly, December asserts, the Web gives people a way to develop new relationships with each other.*

CONSIDER

1. What proposals led to the development of the Web, and who was associated with them?
2. Why does December consider the Web to be fundamentally a *communications* system (as opposed to a vast textual database, online encyclopedia, or tool for commerce)?
3. Given the different levels of communication that occur on the Web and the distinct functions that the Web serves, what is the impact of all this complexity on users?

Few inventions in human history have captured as much attention as the World Wide Web. Emerging from technologies used in transmitting information over computer networks, the Web today is an important communication tool in the industrialized world. The Web is now part of world culture and commerce; companies use it, schools use it, governments use it, as do students, radicals, slackers, conservatives, teachers, poets, prisoners, the Pope, liberals, gardeners, cops, and even some dogs. To some, the Web represents a step toward the *information superhighway,* a phrase that up until 1994 had been full of hype and little substance.

Why has the Web assumed such a prominence in the communications landscape? Because people can use the Web to communicate with each other. It's not pure technology that drives the Web's success. The Web's possibilities as a communications system mean that you can use it to distribute information, communicate with others, and interact with other people or even software. There are those who love the bits and bytes of the technology that makes up the Web, but the Web involves much more. I don't think many people would put up with the expense and aggravation that it takes to participate in the Web—to spend the money on a computer, software, a modem, an Internet connection, and hours and hours of time—all in order to merely manipulate technology.

There's a lot to learn about the Web, but remember that the power of the Web all comes down to one word: communication. In this chapter, I want you to learn how the Web evolved and to appreciate the communication it makes possible.

WHAT IS THE WEB?

The Web is a communications system. Technically, the Web is a system for exchanging data over computer networks using special software. The Web can be used to transmit text and graphics. The Web gives people a chance to create and share information—to publish it, to broadcast it, and to accumulate it collaboratively

with others. The Web thus gives people a way to create new relationships with each other.

The Web has become *the* way to organize the panoply of information, communication, and interaction on the global Internet. In fact, the Web has become so popular that many people forget that the Web is [simply] an application that uses the Internet for data communication.

The software that people use to browse and provide information on the Web has risen to such prominence that major software companies such as Microsoft consider Web software to be a key part of their strategic products and plans. The media content industry has similarly embraced the Web as a key part of its overall strategy for communicating with customers.

How has all this happened? If the Web is a communications system, where did it come from and why has it seemed to capture the imagination of many online technology users? Is there something compelling about the Web that will help it live beyond the hype it has experienced over the past years or will it burn out like the citizen's band radio craze of the 1970s? Or, will it suffer the fate of the Picturephone, relegated to museums by the greater priorities of a new millennium?

WHERE DID THE WEB COME FROM?

Some say the Web started from a dream. Others say that its essential nature is nothing new and that humans have been communicating for centuries in the way the Web enables us to.

The technical origins of the system now known as the Web are in Switzerland. In March 1989, Tim Berners-Lee, a researcher at the Conseil Europeen pour la Recherche Nucleaire (CERN) European Laboratory for Particle Physics in Geneva, Switzerland, proposed a system to enable efficient information sharing for members of the high-energy physics community. Berners-Lee had a background in text processing, real-time software, and communications. He had previously developed a system that he called Enquire in 1980. Berners-Lee's 1989 proposal, called HyperText and CERN, circulated for comment. The important components of the proposal were the following:

- A user interface that would be consistent across all platforms and that would enable users to access information from many different computers.

From *The World Wide Web Unleashed 1997* by John December. © 1997. Adapted by permission of Pearson Education, Inc., Upper Saddle River, NJ.

- A scheme for this interface to access a variety of document types and information protocols.

- A specification for the storage of information in the form of documents with references, called "links," to other documents. By using the user interface, the user could follow these links and follow a variety of paths through the information. A set of documents organized this way is called *hypertext*. Berners-Lee was not the first person to propose hypertext, as you'll see.

By late 1990, an operating prototype of the Web ran on a NeXT computer, and a line-mode user interface (called www) was completed. The essential pieces of the Web were in place, although they were not widely available for network use.

In March 1991, the www interface was used on a network, and by May of that year it was made available on central CERN machines. The CERN team spread the word about their system throughout the rest of 1991, announcing the availability of the files in the Usenet newsgroup alt.hypertext on August 19, 1991, and to the high-energy physics community through its newsletter in December 1991.

Berners-Lee's innovation didn't arise from a vacuum of ideas. Researchers had been working on hypertext systems for decades before 1989. In fact, it was Ted Nelson in 1965 who coined the term *hypertext* to characterize text that is not constrained to be sequential. Nelson's dream was Xanadu, a system to link all world literature with provisions for automatically paying royalties to authors. Key to the Xanadu system was the idea of linking information in nonhierarchical ways. These connections among information enable readers to follow links from one document to another, and document authors could create these links among existing documents.

BEFORE XANADU

Like Berners-Lee's idea of the Web, Nelson's idea of Xanadu was connected to previous ideas. The idea of associatively linking information via mechanical devices goes back to work done by the Director of the Office of Scientific Research who was responsible for the development of the first atomic bomb—Vannevar Bush. Having worked on calculating artillery firing tables, Bush knew the tediousness of routine calculations, and he proposed an analog computer. But Bush's

main contribution to the roots of the Web was his July 1945 article, "As We May Think," in *The Atlantic Monthly* (this article is available on the Web at http://www.isg.sfu.ca/~duchier/misc/bush/).

Bush called his system a *memex* (memory extension) and proposed it as a tool to help the human mind cope with information. Having observed that previous inventions had expanded human abilities to deal with the physical world, Bush wanted his memex to expand human knowledge in a way that took advantage of the associative nature of human thought. Bush's design for the memex involved technologies for recording information on film and mechanical systems for manipulation. Although the memex was never built, Bush's article defined, in detail, many concepts of associative linking within an information system.

However, the idea of presenting information in a fashion that is nonlinear did not start with the twentieth century or with computer scientists. *The Talmud,* an important document in the Jewish faith, includes commentaries and opinions of the first five books of the Bible. The Talmud's organization contains commentary and commentaries on commentaries that extend from central paragraphs in the middle of the page. Also, footnotes as used in traditional paper texts have a relational, nonsequential quality that is similar to the spirit of hypertext. Certainly, fiction writers—everyone from James Joyce (*Finnegan's Wake*), William Faulkner (*The Sound and the Fury*), and Julio Cortazar (*Hopscotch*)—have artistically represented the nonlinear nature of human experience in fiction.

One could argue that the Web reflects something more than just a technical ability to publish information globally or store and retrieve information. The Web might be another way to express the relatedness of ideas and words, something humans have been doing for thousands of years.

In the decades since Bush's 1945 article, ideas about the design of information systems as well as working computer systems emerged. In 1962, Doug Englebart began a project called Augment at the Stanford Research Institute. Augment's goal was to unite and cross-reference written material of many researchers into a shared document. One portion of the oN-Line System (NLS) included several hypertext features.

In 1965, Ted Nelson coined the term *hypertext* to describe text that is not constrained to be sequential. Hypertext, as described by Nelson, links documents to form a web of relationships that draws on the possibilities for extending and augmenting the meaning of a "flat" piece of text with links to other texts. Hypertext is thus more than just footnotes that serve as commentary or further information in a text; instead, hypertext extends the structure of ideas by making "chunks" of ideas available for inclusion in many parts of multiple texts.

Nelson also coined the term *hypermedia,* which is hypertext not constrained to be text. Hypermedia can include multimedia pictures, graphics, sound, and movies. In 1967, he proposed a global hypermedia system, Xanadu, that as mentioned above would link all world literature with provisions for automatically paying royalties to authors. Although Xanadu has never been completed, a Xanadu group did convene in 1979, and the project was bought and developed by Autodesk, Inc. from 1988 until the project was canceled in 1992. Afterward, Nelson reobtained the Xanadu trademark, and as of 1994, was working to develop the project further (see http://www.xanadu.net and Ted Nelson's home page at http://ted.hyperland.com).

In 1967, a working hypertext system called Hypertext Editing System was operational at Brown University. Andries van Dam lead a team that developed the system, which was later used for documentation during the Apollo space missions at the Houston Manned Spacecraft Center. By 1985, another hypertext system called Intermedia came out of Brown University. It included bi-directional links and the possibility for different views of a hypertext, including a single node overview and an entire hypertext structure view called a web view.

In 1985, Xerox Palo Alto Research Center (PARC) (http://www.parc.xerox.com) introduced a system called NoteCards. Each node in NoteCards could contain any amount of information, and there were many types of specialized cards for special data structures.

Hypertext's stature as an important approach to information organization in industry and academia was marked in 1987, when the Association for Computing Machinery (http://www.acm.org) held its first conference on hypertext at the University of North Carolina. This was the same year that Apple Computer Corporation (http://www.apple.com) introduced its HyperCard system. Bundled free with each Macintosh computer sold, HyperCard became popular. Users organized the cards and stacks in HyperCard and took advantage of the possibilities for ordering the cards in various ways in the stack. Using HyperCard, people could quickly and easily create their own hypertext

works. Because all other Macintosh users also had HyperCard, these works could be easily shared. This ease of creation and ease of sharing information later became important reasons why the Web became popular.

THE CONNECTION AT CERN SPARKS AN IDEA IN THE USA

Many ideas from throughout history can converge in an inventor's mind. The ideas of Vannevar Bush, Ted Nelson, and others showed up in Tim Berners-Lee's proposal for the Web at CERN in 1989. This is when the Web was born; CERN was where most of the Web's character was formed—up until 1993.

In early 1993, a young undergraduate student at the University of Illinois at Urbana-Champaign named Marc Andreessen shifted attention to the United States. Working on a project for the National Center for Supercomputing Applications (NCSA), Andreessen led a team that developed an X Windows System browser for the Web called Mosaic. In alpha version, Mosaic was released in February 1993 and was among the first crop of graphical interfaces for the Web.

Mosaic—with its fresh look and graphical interface that presented the Web using a point-and-click design—fueled great interest in the Web. While Mosaic rose in popularity, Berners-Lee continued promoting the Web at CERN, presenting a seminar in February 1993 outlining the Web's components and architecture.

Communication using the Web continued to increase throughout 1993 as Mosaic's popularity increased. Data communication traffic from Web servers grew from 0.1 percent of the U.S. National Science Foundation Network (NSFNet) backbone traffic in March to 1 percent of the backbone traffic in September. Although it was not a complete measure of Web traffic throughout the world, the NSFNet backbone measurements give a sample of Web use. In September 1993, NCSA released the first (version 1.0) operational versions of Mosaic for the X Windows System, Macintosh, and Microsoft Windows platforms. By October, there were 500 known Web servers (versus 50 at the beginning of the year). During Mecklermedia's Internet World in New York city in 1993, John Markoff, writing on the front page of the business section of the

New York Times, hailed Mosaic as the "killer app [application]" of the Internet. The Web ended 1993 with 2.2 percent of the NSFNet backbone traffic for the month December.

In 1994, more commercial players got into the Web game. Companies announced commercial versions of Web browser software, including Spry, Incorporated. Marc Andreessen and colleagues left the NCSA project in March to form, with Jim Clark (former chairman of Silicon Graphics), a company that later became known as Netscape Communications Corporation (http://home.netscape.com). By May 1994, interest in the Web was so intense that the first international conference on the World Wide Web, held in Geneva, overflowed with attendees. By June 1994, there were 1,500 known (public) Web servers.

By mid-1994, it was clear to the original developers at CERN that the stable development of the Web should fall under the guidance of an international organization. In July, the Massachusetts Institute of Technology (MIT) and CERN announced the World Wide Web Organization (which later became known as the World Wide Web Consortium, or W3C). Today, the W3C (http://www.w3.org) guides the technical development and standards for the evolution of the Web. The W3C is a consortium of universities and private industries, run by the Laboratory for Computer Science at MIT collaborating with CERN, the Institut National de Recherche en Informatique et en Automatique, and Keio University, with support from the U.S. Defense Advanced Research Projects Agency and the European Commission. [Berners-Lee now serves as director of the W3C.]

In 1995, the Web's development was marked by rapid commercialization and technical change. Netscape Communication's browser, called Netscape Navigator [and, later, Netscape Communicator] continued to include more Netscape-specific extensions of the HyperText Markup Language (HTML), and issues of security for commercial cash transactions garnered much attention. By May 1995, there were more than 15,000 known public Web servers, a tenfold increase over the number from a year before. Many companies had joined the W3C by 1995, including AT&T, Digital Equipment Corporation, Enterprise Integration Technologies, FTP Software, Hummingbird Communication, IBM, MCI, NCSA, Netscape Communications, Novell, Open Market, O'Reilly & Associates, Spyglass, and Sun Microsystems.

THE SOCIAL EXPANSION OF THE WEB

Technical innovations throughout history have often failed because of their lack of social acceptance and use —for example, the picture phone and other technically "good ideas" that people simply never wanted and never used.

The Web doesn't seem doomed to the scrap heap. The Web appears to have caught on, at least among the technologically rich people and countries of the world, as part of the communications environment. From Wall Street (http://dowjones.com) to Wal-Mart (http://www.wal-mart.com), the Web has become part of communications culture. In the consumer world, the Web is routinely used to promote everything from Coca-Cola (http://www.cocacola.com) to movies (http://www.toystory.com).

Many businesses see the Web now as a key component of their work. As a key part of future business on the Web, the banking industry is gradually taking steps toward serving its customers online. Systems of "virtual cash" are in development that might create not only a widespread promotional market on the Web, but an actual market for trade. With financial payments, the Web is poised to become an even more important part of global communications and trade systems.

THE CULTURAL ROLE OF THE WEB

Neither Vannevar Bush's compulsively detailed description of the mechanics of his memex nor the gory technical details of the hypertext transport protocol reveal what the World Wide Web has brought to our culture. If you've not been living in a cave, you've heard and seen URLs (uniform resource locators), the naming scheme for referring to resources on the Web. If the cryptic syntax of URLs confuse you, you might have laughed along with David Letterman's fans when he satirically announced his own show's URL in an interview with Larry King as "WWW.com.com.com . . . com.com.diggedy.diggedy.dank.dot.com.diggedy .www.com.Dave.com.com.DOT" (actually, the uniform resource locator for David Letterman's Late Show on CBS is http://www.cbs.com/lateshow).

Letterman's satire of URLs and their ubiquity in many media is perhaps apt. The Web's URLs seem to appear everywhere— on t-shirts, hats, newspaper and magazine ads, radio spots, movie posters, television and radio commercials, promotional flyers, business cards, underwear, and tattoos. But the number of people who use the Web is a minority of the world's, and even the United States', population. Analysis by researchers at Vanderbilt University in 1996 put the number of Web users worldwide at around 20 million [today, there are over 140 million users internationally and some estimate there will be upwards of 500 million users by mid-decade]. Similarly, the face of the Web also isn't like the world's. The Georgia Tech surveys (http://www.cc.gatech.edu/gvu/user_surveys) reveal a Web that is mostly used by relatively old (average age 33 years), highly educated, white, American males.

The Web has opened up new cultural expressions, but these compete with all other forms of media for the scarcest resource on earth, the resource that no technology will ever make more of—human attention. The future of the Web will no doubt depend on its own value to people: If it doesn't provide compelling content, people won't use it, no matter what the flash of its technology.

WHAT GOOD IS THE WEB?

On the Web, you can read the current news, look up a book in a library catalog, check the weather, make airplane reservations, look at the current view of the Empire State Building, find college courses, read the *New York Times,* look up a word in a dictionary or thesaurus, locate stops on the Paris Metro, buy a book, incorporate a business, buy a CD, fall in love, dissect a frog, write to the President of the United States, sell advertising, look at cars, find out what's on CNN, look for a long lost friend in phone directories, gamble, publish your own magazine, reserve a hotel room, rent a car, learn about Mediterranean architecture, find a job, or choose a college.

Today, many people find the Web a valuable way to connect to other people. Remember, the bottom line of the Web is *communication.* If you think about it just as a kind of vending machine, you won't see its full potential. The Web isn't just a publishing medium or a place to sell things, but a medium in which many kinds of communication contexts coexist simultaneously.

COMMUNICATION CONTEXTS ON THE WEB

Communication on the Web can take many forms and can take place in many contexts. Different levels for communicating have evolved on the Web. These levels correspond, in many ways, to offline human communication contexts.

- *Interpersonal.* The Web enables users to create a home page, which typically conveys personal or professional information. The practice of creating a home page emerged from the technical necessity of defining the "default" page that a Web browser displays when you are requesting information from a Web server when only the host name or a host and directory name is given. Home pages are thus traditionally the top-level page for a server, organization, or individual. When created by individuals, home pages often reveal detailed personal information about their authors and are often listed in directories of home pages. Also, individuals often follow the tradition of linking to colleagues' or friends' pages, creating "electronic tribes." When used interpersonally, personal home pages offer one-to-one communication, although the technical operation of all pages on the Web is one-to-many.

- *Group.* Cliques of personal pages can define a particular Web "tribe" or group. Similarly, people can form associations on the Web that are independent of geography and focused on interest in a common topic. Subject-tree breakdowns of information on the Web often evolve from collaborative linking and the development of resource lists and original material describing a subject. Similarly, groups of people associate on the Web based on common interests in communication (a professional association, for example, that has a Web server to announce conferences or calls for participation in its publications). Web groups also can form around a focus on interaction based on social or professional discourse or symbolic exchange (perhaps nontextual) intended to define and indicate relationships in "play" systems such as Web interfaces to Multiple User Dialogue/Object Oriented/Simulations (MU★s) or Web-based "chat" or conferencing systems.

- *Organizational.* Many of the initial Web servers appearing on the Web belong to an organization, not an individual, so the home page for a server often identifies the institution or organization that owns the server. In this way, the genre of the Campus Wide Information System (CWIS) evolved on Web servers of educational institutions. Similarly, commercial, governmental, and nongovernmental organizations have followed the pattern established by CWIS to a large degree.

- *Mass.* Just as other media have been used for one-to-many dissemination of information (newspapers, radio, television), so too is the Web used for mass communication. Many commercial and noncommercial magazines and other publications are distributed through the Web. Moreover, as noted previously, all publicly available Web pages are potentially readable to anyone using the Web, and are thus potentially one-to-many communication.

The key concept to understand is that the Web as a communication system can be flexibly used to express many kinds of communication. The classification of the communication (in the categories listed previously) depends on who is taking part in the communication. The exact classification of any expression on the Web can be blurred by the potentially global reach of any Web page. Thus, a personal home page can be used interpersonally, but it can be accessed far more times on the Web than a publication created and intended for mass consumption. In addition to these contexts, the Web serves many communication functions.

- *Information Delivery.* A Web browser gives the user a "viewer" to "look into" data provided over networks. The structure of hypertext enables user selectivity because of the many ways that a user can choose to follow links in hypertext.

- *Communication.* People can use Web hypertext to create forums for sharing information and discussion and helping group members make contact with each other. With special interactive languages such as Java or Limbo, users can interact in real-time discussions.

- *Interaction.* Using special programming, a Web developer can build interactivity into an application, giving the user a way to receive customized information based on queries. Computer programs also can enable a user to change or add to an information structure.

- *Computation.* Using gateway programming or a language such as Java, the Web can be used to provide an interface to other applications and programs for information processing. Based on user selections, a Web application can return a computed or customized result.

SUMMARY

The Web emerged from ideas about the associative, nonlinear organization of information. Its protocols and technical standards were defined at the Conseil Europeen pour la Recherche Nucleaire in the early 1990s. Subsequent development of graphical user interfaces to the Web in the United States has lead to the widespread use of the Web in industry, education, government, and in the general culture. Today, the Web is a hypertext information and communication system popularly used on the Internet. Communication on the Web can assume many forms and take place in many contexts, ranging from individual communication to group and mass communication.

RELATED LINKS

- Tim Berners-Lee Home Page (http://www.w3.org/People/Berners-Lee)
- December Communications (http://www.december.com)
- Internet Literacy Web Site (http://www.udel.edu/interlit/contents.html)
- Internet Society (http://www.isoc.org)
- Network Solutions: Domain Registration (http://www.networksolutions.com)

FOR FURTHER RESEARCH

To find out more about the topics discussed in this reading, use InfoTrac College Edition. Type in keywords and subject terms such as "information superhighway," "Xanadu," and "hypermedia." You can access InfoTrac from the Wadsworth/Thomson Communication Café homepage: http://communication.wadsworth.com.

Reading 7-2

The Productivity Puzzle
Thomas K. Landauer

EDITOR'S NOTE

Since 1960 over $4 trillion has been spent computerizing the American workplace. And yet, until very recently, solid evidence that information technology leads to increased productivity was very hard to find. Economists refer to this conundrum—large investments in computers resulting in small gains for industry—as the productivity paradox. *With the exception of telecommunications, the net impact of computers on productivity was quite disappointing through the mid-1990s. This reading explains why.*

CONSIDER

1. What is the difference between phase one and phase two computing, according to Landauer?

2. Why does Landauer use the term "augmentation" to describe phase two computing?

3. Of all the industries that are computer intensive, why was telecommunications the least affected by the productivity slowdown of the mid-1970s to mid-1990s?

I went into a department store to buy a cheap watch. The man ahead of me said to the sales clerk, "I really like this one."

"I can't find its stock number; I can't enter the sale."

The clerk went off to a back room where I heard her consulting one person, then another. A loudspeaker paged the manager. Eventually the clerk returned, apologizing, "It isn't in the book, and I can't find the manager."

"There's one right here. Can't I just pay for it?"

"I'm terribly sorry, I can't sell it without the number. Do you like this one? I have the number for it."

"I like the first one better."

From *The Trouble with Computers: Usefulness, Usability, and Productivity* by Thomas K. Landauer (Cambridge, MA: MIT Press, 1995). Copyright © 1995 The MIT Press. Reprinted with permission.

"Well, let's wait for the manager. Gosh, I'm sorry."

"I don't have much time. Can't I just give you the money?"

"I'm really sorry. The manager should be along any minute."

After five minutes of fidgeting and apologies, the manager appeared. She said, "Did you look for the number on the box?"

"Yes, but I didn't find it. And I asked the others. They didn't know either."

"I'll go look."

Off she went. Five minutes later the PA system spoke: "I can't find the number either, would the customer like a different watch?"

"No."

What's going on here? Computers are wonderful. Maybe, if you're like me a few years back, the very title of this book [*The Trouble with Computers*] would have puzzled or made you mad. Trouble? Trouble indeed! Computers are far awesome. You love them; I love them. They're selling like hotcakes: maybe a little slower than they used to, but still they're the biggest spot in modern industry. Everyone wants one. Everyone uses them, one way or another. They're here, they're everywhere. Every accountant, author, secretary, scientist, businessperson, engineer has to have one. They're making new millionaires—no, billionaires—all over the place. Trouble? What trouble?

So finally it was my turn. By now I'd had plenty of time to select a watch and a couple of backups, just in case. No problem. My first pick had a number. So I gave the clerk my credit card. She put it in the machine for verification. The machine didn't take my card. She tried again, sliding the card faster. Again, slower. Again really fast. No go. Four more tries. Then she called across to the sales clerk at a nearby register. "What do I do when it won't accept the card?"

"Enter it with the keys."

"I tried." Dutifully, she tried again. Once. Twice. Three times. Then she called across: "Do you put in the first three numbers?"

"Yes."

"Six, three, eight?"

"No, four, seven, two for that machine."

"Oh, thanks."

The rest of the transaction went smoothly.

This sad but true example is not an isolated case. I suspect that everyone in America has run into computerized check-out machines that slow transactions and frustrate operators and customers alike. Many companies have had sorely disappointing experiences with the introduction of information technology, failing to realize the economies that they were expecting, often promised. Indeed, everywhere you look, some computer system is gobbling dollars while doing silly things and making life hard for its masters and servants alike. Millions of "micros" bought for homes end up in closets. Millions of PCs bought for white-collar workers gather dust. And it gets worse—wait and see.

Computers should make life easier and better. Computers are truly marvelous machines and getting more marvelous every year. Every day they get programmed to do astonishing new things. We're told over and over that we are in a computer revolution, that computers are leading us into a wonderful new information age. The computer and information revolution is widely predicted to be as consequential as the industrial revolution of the previous two centuries—throw in the printing press and agriculture as well. The money being invested in computers is probably comparable to the earlier investment in power-driven machines. "Muscle and movement" machines brought enormous increases in labor productivity. Solid evidence that the computer revolution has brought increased productivity, however, is very hard to find.

> The Internal Revenue Service invested over $50 million in PCs for its agents. The systems were supposed to help agents enter and look up data and make calculations more quickly and accurately. But the number of cases processed by each agent in a week went down by 40 percent.

I believe that computers are in deep trouble. Certainly they have had and continue to have amazing triumphs; they've helped put humans on the moon, totally revised warfare, finally made it possible to solve centuries-old mathematics problems, led bursts of new scientific knowledge, taken over our bookkeeping and our telephone switches. Their raw power for calculation and storage continues to double every few years. But the promise that they would contribute to economics, to a vast improvement in standard of living, has not been kept. The nations, industries, and people who have invested in them heavily have not prospered proportionally (except those who sell computers). There is some sign that some corporations, usually very large ones, have had major successes with computers in the last few years, but it is not clear yet whether these successes were due to the computers themselves or to dramatic business revamping bred of recession pressures. We expected computers to bring across-the-board productivity help, work efficiency improvements for small and large alike. This they have not delivered.

> A major insurance underwriter spent $30 million on a computer system to streamline the operation of its dental insurance claims department. Within a year, the number of claims processed each day by its sixty-five employees increased by over 30 percent. And the total cost of each claims transaction went up from $3.50 to $5.00.[1]

Don't get me wrong. I'm a devoted software designer and a user and fan of computer systems. I'm an electronic mail devotee. It saves me hours of telephone tag, lets me keep work communications short and to the point and personal interactions tactful, and allows me and my correspondents to do our communicating when it's most convenient, not just when we're both available. But I'm a very critical fan. Like others, I have a love-hate relationship with the computer. I get twenty to fifty electronic messages each day—not instead of paper mail and telephone calls but *in addition,* and not all useful or entertaining.

My personal experience more or less captures the overall situation with computers: they do a lot of great things that could make us more efficient and they do a lot of stupid or unintended things that get in our way, and they're not cheap. The bottom line is pretty smudgy. Not only are the economic data equivocal on the productivity effects of computing, but more direct evaluations of their effects on work efficiency are pretty disappointing—much, much inferior to the hope and hype attached in the popular press and mind.

WHY? POOR USEFULNESS AND USABILITY DUE TO POOR EVALUATION, THAT'S WHY

So what's going on here? How did computer systems get this way? How come they aren't better than they are? Here's my overview of what has happened.

Since first leaving the research laboratories in the 1950s, computers as practical devices have been through two partly overlapping phases of evolution corresponding to two major realms of application. In the first phase, computers have been used for automation, to replace humans in the performance of tasks, either doing tasks that humans could do with no help or doing tasks no human would be capable of. All of these tasks involve the manipulation of numbers. The amazing feats that computers perform in mathematics and science all depend on doing well-known mathematical calculations that in principle could be done by humans with a pencil and paper. The difference, of course, is that computers do calculations millions of times as fast as people and with many fewer errors.

Computers can do anything that can be reduced to numerical or logical operations, and that includes a vast array of chores. Almost any process that science, engineering, and statistics have captured in their theories can be carried out by a properly instructed (programmed) computer. This has also meant that we could invent things like radar-directed gunfire, where data arrive in such volume and have to be acted upon so quickly that humans couldn't do the necessary additions and multiplication. It has made it possible to in-

vent CAT scan X-ray and MRI machines that allow doctors to see our insides in glorious three-dimensional detail. Each picture takes billions of calculations. They have allowed us to build much bigger, faster, cheaper electronic means for connecting telephones to each other, replacing the switchboards and electromechanical devices of the not-so-distant past. Without these new computer-based switches, we'd need 2 million more telephone operators than we had in 1950 and would get much worse service at much higher prices. Computers have allowed us to build robots and electronically controlled lathes and milling machines and automatic process controllers for chemical plants and production lines. On the commercial front, their most important contribution has been the relief of bookkeepers. The endless, tedious copying, adding and subtracting, entering and retrieving of numbers on which banks and other businesses depend has almost all been handed over to computers.

Phase one is now running out of steam. Most jobs that could be simply taken over by numerical processors have already been taken over. It's getting hard to think of useful new jobs to do by arithmetic. Certainly the excitement is not over; many more marvelous computer-based inventions will come our way. But the pace of gain from automation will be much slower. The easily reached fruits have been picked.

Phase two of computer application is augmentation, encompassing that wide range of things that people do that cannot be taken over completely by a numerical machine. Most of the things people do—talk, understand speech and language, write, read, create art and science, persuade, negotiate, decide, organize, administer, entertain, socialize—fall into this category. None of these things has yet been, or is likely soon to be, captured in a quantitative theory that can be executed as well by a computer as by a person. Although researchers are working busily, we're not nearly ready to replace humans with machines—even if we wanted to. Instead, computer systems have been designed and built to act as assistants, aids, and "power tools." It is here, in the design of these kinds of computer systems, that we have failed. Impressed with the successes of the automation machines, we have been eager to employ their offspring, the augmentation machines. And we have been paying good money for their services. But so far, they're just not working out. The evidence is that phase two helpers are not helpful enough to be worth their wages. Thus, the trouble with computers is that in their most recent applications—

the jobs for which we now want them—they are not doing enough. Partly the problem is that they are still too hard to operate. Partly the problem is that they get misused, applied badly, and to the wrong jobs. Mostly the problem is that they don't yet do a sufficient number of sufficiently useful things.

THE EVIDENCE

For over five years a debate has been in progress about how much—or even whether—computers contribute to improved productivity. Economists, work sociologists, computer scientists, and other relevant experts have offered a variety of facts, analyses, and opinions. Many have concluded that computers have had very little positive effect on productivity. The bottom line, it has been variously asserted, is that while there are exceptions, most business investments in computers have yielded significantly lower returns than investments in bonds at market interest rates. Two analysts dissent from this view. Stanford University economist Timothy Bresnehan thinks there must be huge gains somewhere because there has been tremendous increase in the ratio of performance to price of computers themselves. Eric Brynjolfsson of MIT weighs in with a minority analysis purporting to show excellent results for heavy hardware investors among the Fortune 500 in recent years.[2] Others have examined the possibility of errors in the measurement of productivity or proposed alternative explanations for the facts.

What seems most striking about this debate is that it has occurred at all. Given the marvelous powers of modern computing, its reputation in the public mind, and the vast amounts of money spent on its application, its economic benefits should be manifest. The fact that many serious and competent scholars can conclude that there has been little net productivity gain attributable to this technology seems enough proof that something is wrong.

HISTORY

In the United States, computers first entered commercial use in a big way in the early 1960s. In 1950 the decennial census counted fewer than 900 computer operators in the entire United States. In 1960 there were still only 2,000. However, by 1970 there were 125,000 and by 1985 close to half a million (or, for comparison, about twice the number of telephone operators).[3] By 1985 computer and related information technology equipment purchases accounted for about 16 percent of total capital stock in the service sector, some $424 billion, up from 6 percent fifteen years earlier.[4] By 1991, the annual equipment outlay was running over $100 billion.[5] And initial equipment costs are only the tip of the iceberg; the serious spending, which starts after the boxes arrive, at least triples the total. Operating and maintaining hardware costs as much as buying it. Software purchase or development adds another approximately equal share; most of the major applications of computers have required new software customized for the business or firm. Finally, computer use eats a comparable large slice. Expensive specialized labor is needed to debug, repair, or modify software. Because systems are so complicated and hard to use, end users (those whom the computer is intended to serve, as opposed to those who serve the computer) not only need extensive training but usually cannot use the computer fully by themselves; they need the assistance of systems analysts, consultants, trainers, or other intermediaries. Moreover, all of this needs supervision, organization, and management—whole electronic data processing and management information systems departments, not to mention the floor space and air-conditioning that they and their machines consume. Most of this outlay should be considered capital expense. It is all intended to make available a tool that is supposed to make other functions of production more efficient. Almost none of it is directly productive; almost none can be considered an input to production in the sense that raw material, energy, or most labor is.

Adding it all up, since 1960, something over $4 trillion (much more than an average year's GNP, or Gross National Product, during that period) has been spent on computing, and total current expenditures for the United States amount to around 10 percent of GNP. Although there was significant computerization, primarily of the phase one variety—complete automation in which the machine replaces a human—in the sixties, the overwhelming amount of phase two computer investment—in which computers are used as aids in the mentally demanding jobs of information workers—occurred from the early seventies onward, at a time when the United States experienced much slower growth in productivity than in any previous period for which comparable data are available.[6]

Quantitative estimates of productivity are usually calculated as the amount of value added for each person-hour employed—so-called labor productivity —or as the number of dollars worth of output for each dollar spent on labor and capital combined—so-called multifactor productivity. Between 1948 and 1965, overall growth in productivity ranged between 2 percent and 7 percent for industrialized nations. From the end of World War II through the sixties, GNP, productivity, and the standard of living of industrial nations grew steadily.[7] Annual labor productivity gains were in the range of 2 percent (for the United States) to 7 percent (for Japan). From about 1970–1975 onward productivity gains have been much smaller, ranging from 0 to 1 percent for the United States, up to 2⅔ percent for Japan. Gains in productivity since 1948 have always been largest in farming and manufacturing, but before 1970, they were nearly as good in other industries as well. Since the early seventies, productivity in the non-farm, non-manufacturing sphere has been essentially flat, even declining in some years. During this same period, of course, manufacturing and farming have become smaller portions of the overall economy, so the slow growth of productivity in other areas has affected the overall picture even more strongly.

Phase one computer application had considerable impact on manufacturing. There were major early phase one computer applications in some non-manufacturing, non-farming segments as well, notably in banking, finance, and insurance, where computers were first used to automate record keeping, accounting, report generation, and billing. Some analysts have found healthy productivity growth for some periods in some segments of these businesses and for particular functions within them. For example, the insurance industry maintained normal labor productivity growth while its extensive bookkeeping, contract preparation, and arithmetic for figuring premiums were automated.[8] As a group, however, these closely related industries have registered declines in productivity growth since widespread adoption of electronic information processing beginning in the late fifties, despite a six-to-one increase in real (inflation-adjusted) investment per employee—largely in computers and other information technology. The number of bookkeepers and billing clerks even continued to grow briskly in U.S. industry as a whole as computers ostensibly took over all the record copying and arithmetic. The number of file clerks multiplied by two and a half between 1960 and 1970 as computers were reputedly replacing them. And although their increase was very modest in later years,

file clerk jobs were still not on the endangered species list.[9]

With the important exception of telecommunications, the remaining non-farm, non-manufacturing industries, such as transportation, public utilities, trade, and services, have shown near flat productivity over the last two decades. These industries should be, and have been, the primary candidates for phase two computer applications. It is for them that word processors, PCs, laptops, spreadsheets, office automation machinery in general, electronic cash registers, inventory management, and management information systems have been designed.

While it would be rash to conclude solely from the recent stagnation of productivity that computers have no positive net effects on work efficiency, the historical trends in productivity certainly give no evidence of large improvements during the period when phase two computer use has been rapidly expanding.

The only major subclassification within non-farm, non-manufacturing that had nontrivial productivity gains between 1973 and 1987 was communications. Communications is composed primarily of television, radio, and telecommunications; the telephone companies are the biggest component, with total revenues over $100 billion a year. From more detailed data, it appears that the telephone business accounts for the superior productivity record of this category.

From 1973 to 1983, telephone company productivity increased over 6 percent annually. During the same period, there were productivity increases of just 1.5 percent in air transport, under 1 percent in retail food stores, and absolute declines in restaurants.[10] All of these, like the telephone business, are non-goods producing but have easily countable output. They are also industries that were using computers and in which one might have imagined computerization to be effective. However, telephone companies were the leading and largest users of both phase one and phase two computing, and they did well.

Most other service industries have also invested heavily in computers but have not done well at all. Probably the second largest investors in phase two computing, as well of phase one application for record keeping, have been the brokerage, banking, and insurance businesses. Although there was apparently significant variation among subsectors, these businesses as a whole have shown a strong net decline in both labor and multifactor productivity since 1973.

NOTES

1. Shoshana Zuboff, *In the Age of the Smart Machine*. New York: Basic Books, 1988.

2. Timothy F. Bresnehan, "Measuring the Spillovers from Technological Advance: Mainframe Computers in Financial Services," *American Economic Review, 76* (September 1986): 742–755; Erik Brynjolfsson and Lorin Hitt, *Is Information Systems Spending Productive? New Evidence and New Results*. Working paper. Cambridge, MA: Sloan School of Management, Center for Information Systems Research, MIT, 1993.

3. H. Allan Hunt and Timothy L. Hunt, *Clerical Employment and Technological Change*. Kalamazoo, MI: W. E. Upjohn Institute for Employment Research, 1986.

4. Stephen S. Roach, "America's Technology Dilemma: A Profile of the Information Economy," Memorandum. New York: Morgan Stanley, 1987.

5. Stephen S. Roach, *Inside the U.S. Economy*. New York: Morgan Stanley, 1992.

6. McKinsey Global Institute, *Service Sector Productivity*. New York: McKinsey and Co., 1992.

7. Martin Neil Baily and Alok K. Chakrabarti, *Innovation and the Productivity Crisis*. Washington, DC: Brookings Institution, 1988; Edward Fulton Denison, *Estimates of Productivity Change by Industry*. Washington, DC: Brookings Institution, 1989.

8. Heidi I. Hartmann, Robert E. Kraut, and Louise A. Tilly (Eds.), *Computer Chips and Paper Clips: Technology and Women's Employment*. Washington, DC: National Academy Press, 1986.

9. Roslyn L. Feldberg and Evelyn Nakano Glenn, "Technology and the Transformation of Clerical Work." In Robert E. Kraut (Ed.), *Technology and the Transformation of White Collar Work*. Hillsdale, NJ: Erlbaum Associates, 1987, pp. 77–97.

10. U.S. Department of Labor, *Productivity Measures for Selected Industries, 1954– 82*. Washington, DC: Government Printing Office, 1983.

RELATED LINKS

- Explaining the Productivity Paradox (http://www.neweconomyindex.org/productivity.html)

- The Productivity Paradox: A Reading List (http://averia.unm.edu/ITProductivity.html)

- Probing the Productivity Paradox (http://www.misq.org/archivist/vol/no18/issue2/edstat.html)

- The Productivity Paradox of Information Technology: Review and Assessment (http://ccs.mit.edu/papers/CCSWP130/ccswp130.html)

FOR FURTHER RESEARCH

To find out more about the topics discussed in this reading, use InfoTrac College Edition. Type in keywords and subject terms such as "productivity paradox," "computerization of industry," and "labor productivity." You can access InfoTrac from the Wadsworth / Thomson Communication Café homepage: http://communication.wadsworth.com.

Reading 7-3

Computer Age Gains Respect of Economists
Steve Lohr

EDITOR'S NOTE

After a two-decade lull, workplace productivity started to pick up in the mid- to late-1990s, prompting even the most hardened skeptics to reconsider technology's contribution to the economy. As this reading points out, economists are attributing this increase in productivity to the gains in speed and efficiency that the Internet and other information technologies make possible.

Interestingly, improved productivity performance mirrors the growth and development of the World Wide Web. Businesses, it would appear, are finally reaping the benefits of information technology.

CONSIDER

1. In terms of increased workplace productivity, is the nation's massive investment in computers and communication technology finally paying off?

2. In your opinion, which single information or communication technology has had the greatest impact on improved productivity, and why?

3. In an information-age economy, do we need a broader definition of productivity and output that goes beyond the industrial-era concept of widgets coming off an assembly line? Is fundamental change afoot in the nature of economic output?

In a nation of technophiles, where Internet millionaires are minted daily, it seems heresy to question the economic payoff from information technology—the billions upon billions spent each year by companies and households on everything from computers to software to cell phones.

But for more than a decade, most of the nation's leading economists have been heretics. They have not been much impressed by the high-tech dogma—embraced by corporate executives, business school professors, and Wall Street alike—that regards the transformation of the economy through the magic of information technology as a self-evident truth.

"You can see the Computer Age everywhere," Robert Solow, a Nobel prizewinner at the Massachusetts Institute of Technology wrote, "but in the productivity statistics."

For years, even as the computer revolutionized the workplace, productivity—the output of goods and services per worker—stagnated, barely advancing 1 percent a year. So it is easy to see how Solow's pithy comment became the favorite punchline of the economic naysayers.

Yet today, even renowned skeptics on the subject of technology's contribution to the economy, like Solow, are having second thoughts. Productivity growth has picked up, starting in 1996, capped by a surge in

the second half of 1998, after eight years of economic expansion. That has drawn attention because past upward swings in productivity typically occurred early in a recovery as economic activity rebounded. Once companies increased hiring, it slowed again.

But something seems fundamentally different this time, something apparently having a lot to do with the increased speed and efficiency that the Internet and other pervasive information-technology advances are bringing to the mundane day-to-day tasks of millions of businesses.

The question, posed by economists, is whether the higher productivity growth, averaging about 2 percent in the last three years, roughly double the pace from 1973 to 1995, is the long-awaited confirmation that the nation's steadily rising investment in computers and communications is finally paying off. The evidence is starting to point in that direction.

"My beliefs are shifting on this subject," said Solow. "I am still far from certain. But the story always was that it took a long time for people to use information technology and truly become more efficient. That story sounds a lot more convincing today than it did a year or two ago."

Another pillar in the pessimist camp was Daniel Sichel, an economist at the Federal Reserve. His work, along with another Fed economist, Stephen Oliner, in 1994, and on his own in 1997, found that computers contributed little to productivity growth. But recently, Sichel ran similar calculations for the last few years and came to a different conclusion.

In a paper recently published in the quarterly *Business Economics,* Sichel wrote that his new work points

From "Computer Age Gains Respect of Economists" by Steve Lohr, *The New York Times,* April 14, 1999, p. A1. Copyright © 1999 The New York Times Company. Reprinted with permission.

to "a striking step up in the contribution of computers to output growth." And the nation's improved productivity performance, he noted, is "raising the possibility that businesses are finally reaping the benefits of information technology."

The impact of information technology on the economy is more than an academic debate. If, as some experts assert, the technology dividend is a key reason for the nation's extraordinary run of high growth, rising wages and low inflation, there are significant policy implications. If the recent gains are not just a temporary blip, it suggests that the Federal Reserve can be less fearful of inflation and keep interest rates stable rather than be forced to raise them to cool off what would otherwise be considered an overheated economy.

Alan Greenspan, the Fed chairman, seems to believe a fundamental change is under way. He told Congress early this year that the economy was enjoying "higher, technology-driven productivity growth."

Erik Brynjolfsson, an associate professor at the MIT Sloan School of Management, asserts that the economic value of speed, quality improvements, customer service and new products are often not captured by government statistics. "These are the competitive advantages of information technology," he said. "We need a broader definition of output in this new economy, which goes beyond the industrial-era concept of widgets coming off the assembly line."

The government, after years of defending its figures, recently conceded that productivity growth may be understated. The core of the problem, government economists say, is the increasingly complex challenge of defining and measuring output in much of the economy's fast-growing service sector, which includes the vast reaches of banking, finance, health care, and education.

According to the official statistics, a bank today is only about 80 percent as productive as a bank in 1977. Yet that seems to take scant account of, say, 24-hour automated teller machines, which clearly benefit customers who no longer have to wait in lines to be served by human tellers during regular "bankers' hours."

Edwin Dean, chief of the productivity division of the Bureau of Labor Statistics, wrote in a research paper that the agency was increasingly concerned that its measurements did not "fully reflect changes in the quality of goods and services" or "capture the full impact of new technology on economic performance."

Still, the government's methods of measurement will not be overhauled any time soon. "These are tough, tough questions and we are not going to get instant solutions," Dean explained in an interview.

American corporations long ago made up their minds, voting for technology with their dollars. Investment in information technology—computing and telecommunications gear—has quadrupled over the last decade, rising as a share of all business spending on equipment, from 29 percent to 53 percent, according to the Commerce Department. And that is only the hardware. There have been similar surges in corporate spending on software, consulting, technical support, and training related to the field.

"The payoff from information technology is unquestionably there with individual companies and we're seeing it over and over again," said Chuck Rieger, a senior consultant at IBM's services division.

Of course, anecdotal evidence from individual companies is no proof of broad-based benefits in an $8.5-trillion economy. But what many experts find encouraging is that the rapid introduction of low-cost Internet technology means most companies can now afford to set up electronic links with customers and suppliers. For example, a recent survey of 2,500 manufacturing companies, conducted by Pricewaterhouse-Coopers, found that the number of factories with Internet links to customers and suppliers doubled in just one year.

At more and more companies, these Internet-based networks are already streamlining the mundane chores of business life like invoicing, purchasing, and inventory control. This is not the glamorous side of Internet commerce, occupied by Amazon.com and others selling consumer products. Yet if a technology dividend in productivity is at hand, the place to look is in the back offices of business. "That is where it will be," Solow, the MIT economist, said, "in the wholesale automation of corporate transactions."

This business-to-business commerce over the Internet is projected to jump from $48 billion in 1998 to $1.5 trillion by 2003, according to Forrester Research. During the same period, the research firm estimates that consumer sales over the Internet will rise from $3.9 billion to $108 billion.

The service sector of the economy is where productivity gains appear to have been especially sluggish and where experts are looking most closely for evidence of an efficiency payoff from technology.

In Chicago, banker Michael Rushmore speaks of how Internet computing has "fundamentally changed the way we do business" over the last three or four years.

Take the way corporate loans are syndicated among many banks, notes Rushmore, a managing director of Nationsbanc Montgomery Securities, the securities arm of BankAmerica Corp.

Until a few years ago, syndicating a large corporate bank loan meant distributing a lengthy offering document, often running more than 200 pages, to 50 or 100 banks. It was, Rushmore recalled, a nightmarish, inefficient process that involved waves of overnight mail, constant faxing and armies of messengers.

Today, much of that process is handled over the Internet on bank Web sites that other banks tap into to read and download the offering document, ask questions and exchange views. Rushmore estimates that the Internet-based system trims 25 percent from the time it takes to close a deal, not just improving the ease of the transaction but also saving an immense number of hours of work.

About a year ago Booz Allen & Hamilton began using the Internet to bill several federal agencies that are its clients. Booz Allen estimates that it has saved $150,000 a year by eliminating the paper handling on its $10 million in monthly billings to the government. The greater speed and efficiency of electronic billing also means that the consulting firm is being paid 30 percent, or six business days per month, faster than before.

"Getting that money into the bank much more quickly is probably the biggest benefit," said Mark Arnsberger, an assistant controller for Booz Allen & Hamilton.

The rapid spread of Internet-based computing, experts say, promises to compress the time it takes for any new technology to enhance economic welfare in general. The classic study of the phenomenon, "The Dynamo and the Computer: An Historical Perspective on the Modern Productivity Paradox," by Paul David, an economic historian at Stanford University, was published in 1990.

The electric motor, David noted, was introduced in the early 1880s but did not generate discernible productivity gains until the 1920s. It took that long, he wrote, not only for the technology to be widely distributed but also for businesses to reorganize work around the industrial production line, the efficiency breakthrough of its day.

"The process takes longer than people think, but I still believe that we will get a revival of productivity growth led by the spread of computing," David said.

His is a misplaced faith, according to the dwindling band of techno-pessimists whose own beliefs remain unshaken. Sure, they concede, there has been surprisingly strong productivity growth as of late. Could this represent a break in the trend? Possibly, they grudgingly admit, but only a tiny shift at best, they insist.

The real problem, they explain, lies in the composition of the nation's vast service economy. More than half of all white-collar workers are what they term "knowledge workers"—managers, executives and professionals like doctors, lawyers, teachers, even economists.

"The work they do does not lend itself to technology-driven improvements in productivity, and any gains are really difficult to eke out and are glacial," said Stephen Roach, chief economist at Morgan Stanley Dean Witter. "Paul David's electrical motor has nothing to do with the knowledge-intensive process of work in a service economy."

Paul Strassmann, former chief information officer at Xerox and the Pentagon, is a real technology cynic. Strassmann, author of *The Squandered Computer* (Information Economics Press, 1997), believes that corporate America's spending spree on information technology amounts to an "economic arms race," fueled by misguided management theories.

The recent improvement in productivity, according to Strassmann, is mainly attributable to the lower cost of capital because of low interest rates. His summary view, though at odds with those of technology optimists like Brynjolfsson of MIT, may also be received warmly by the Fed.

"The explanation for the productivity improvement is interest rates, not information technology," Strassmann said. "The hero here is not Bill Gates. It's Alan Greenspan."

Yet even Strassmann finds the technology undeniably useful, if not a productivity elixir. When asked a detailed question, he replied, "Just look it up on my Web site. It's a lot more efficient that way."

 RELATED LINKS

- Beyond the Productivity Paradox (http://grace.wharton.upenn.edu/~lhitt/bpp.pdf)
- National Productivity Statistics (http://www.rich.frb.org/pubs/eq/pdfs/winter1998/webb.pdf)

- Perspectives on Productivity Growth (http://www.nabe.com/publib/be/990207.pdf)
- Bureau of Labor Statistics, U.S. Department of Labor (http://www.bls.gov)

 FOR FURTHER RESEARCH

To find out more about the topics discussed in this reading, use InfoTrac College Edition. Type in keywords and subject terms such as "new economy," "productivity growth," and "benefits of information technology." You can access InfoTrac from the Wadsworth/Thomson Communication Café homepage: http://communication.wadsworth.com.

Reading 7-4

The Computer Delusion
Todd Oppenheimer

EDITOR'S NOTE

As noted in the original preface to this article in the Atlantic Monthly, *there is no good evidence that most uses of computers significantly improve teaching and learning, yet school districts are cutting such time-honored programs as music, art, and physical education—programs that demonstrably enrich children's lives—to make room for this dubious nostrum. The stated political goal of "computers in every classroom" may not be the panacea that rescues education from its current troubles.*

CONSIDER

1. Do you agree that music, art, and physical education classes ought to be cut when necessary to fund computer classrooms and technology coordinators? Why or why not?

2. In your opinion, why do politicians and school administrators put so much faith in computer technology?

3. According to child-development experts, what difference can hands-on learning make compared to computer learning, especially for young children?

In 1922 Thomas Edison predicted that "the motion picture is destined to revolutionize our educational system and . . . in a few years it will supplant largely, if not entirely, the use of textbooks." Twenty-three years

Copyright © 1997 Todd Oppenheimer, as first published in *The Atlantic Monthly* (July 1997, cover story). Oppenheimer expanded this article, which received the 1998 National Magazine Award for public interest journalism, into a book titled *The Flickering Mind: The False Promise of Technology in the Classroom and How Learning Can Be Saved* (Random House, 2003; www .flickeringmind.net). This excerpt is reprinted by permission of the author.

later, in 1945, William Levenson, the director of the Cleveland public schools' radio station, claimed that "the time may come when a portable radio receiver will be as common in the classroom as is the blackboard." Forty years after that the noted psychologist B. F. Skinner, referring to the first days of his "teaching machines," in the late 1950s and early 1960s, wrote, "I was soon saying that, with the help of teaching machines and programmed instruction, students could learn twice as much in the same time and with the same effort as in a standard classroom." Ten years after Skinner's recollections were published, President Bill Clinton campaigned for "a bridge to the twenty-first century . . . where computers are as much a part of the classroom as blackboards."

If history really is repeating itself, the schools are in serious trouble. In *Teachers and Machines: The Classroom Use of Technology Since 1920* (Teachers College Press, 1986), Larry Cuban, a professor of education at Stanford University and a former school superintendent, observed that as successive rounds of new technology failed their promoters' expectations, a pattern emerged. The cycle began with big promises backed by the technology developers' research. In the classroom, however, teachers never really embraced the new tools, and no significant academic improvement occurred. This provoked consistent responses: the problem was money, spokespeople argued, or teacher resistance, or the paralyzing school bureaucracy. Meanwhile, few people questioned the technology advocates' claims. As results continued to lag, the blame was finally laid on the machines. Soon schools were sold on the next generation of technology, and the lucrative cycle started all over again.

Today's technology evangels argue that we've learned our lesson from past mistakes. As in each previous round, they say that when our new hot technology—the computer—is compared with yesterday's, today's is better. "It can do the same things, plus," Richard Riley, the U.S. Secretary of Education, told me this spring.

How much better is it, really?

The promoters of computers in schools again offer prodigious research showing improved academic achievement after using their technology. The research has again come under occasional attack, but this time quite a number of teachers seem to be backing classroom technology. In a poll taken early last year U.S. teachers ranked computer skills and media technology as more "essential" than the study of European history, biology, chemistry, and physics; than dealing with social problems such as drugs and family breakdown; than learning practical job skills; and than reading modern American writers such as Steinbeck and Hemingway or classic ones such as Plato and Shakespeare.

In keeping with these views New Jersey cut state aid to a number of school districts this past year and then spent $10 million on classroom computers. In Union City, California, a single school district is spending $27 million to buy new gear for a mere eleven schools. The Kittridge Street Elementary School, in Los Angeles, killed its music program last year to hire a technology coordinator; in Mansfield, Massachusetts,

administrators dropped proposed teaching positions in art, music, and physical education, and then spent $333,000 on computers; in one Virginia school the art room was turned into a computer laboratory. Ironically, a half dozen preliminary studies have recently suggested that music and art classes may build the physical size of a child's brain—and its powers for subjects such as language, math, science, and engineering—in one case far more than computer work did. Meanwhile, months after a New Technology High School opened in Napa, California, where computers sit on every student's desk and all academic classes use computers, some students were complaining of headaches, sore eyes, and wrist pain.

Throughout the country, as spending on technology increases, school book purchases are stagnant. Shop classes, with their tradition of teaching children building skills with wood and metal, have been almost entirely replaced by new "technology education programs." In San Francisco only one public school still offers a full shop program—the lone vocational high school. "We get kids who don't know the difference between a screwdriver and a ball-peen hammer," James Dahlman, the school's vocational department chair, told me recently. "How are they going to make a career choice? Administrators are stuck in this mindset that all kids will go to a four-year college and become a doctor or a lawyer, and that's not true. I know some who went to college, graduated, and then had to go back to technical school to get a job." Last year the school superintendent in Great Neck, Long Island, proposed replacing elementary school shop classes with computer classes and training the shop teachers as computer coaches. Rather than being greeted with enthusiasm, the proposal provoked a backlash.

Interestingly, shop classes and field trips are two programs that the National Information Infrastructure Advisory Council, the Clinton Administration's technology task force, suggests reducing in order to shift resources into computers. But are these results what technology promoters really intend? "You need to apply common sense," Esther Dyson, the president of EDventure Holdings and one of the Advisory Council's leading school advocates, told me recently. "Shop with a good teacher probably is worth more than computers with a lousy teacher. But if it's a poor program, this may provide a good excuse for cutting it. There will be a lot of trials and errors with this. And I don't know how to prevent those errors."

The issue, perhaps, is the magnitude of the errors.

Alan Lesgold, a professor of psychology and the associate director of the Learning Research and Development Center at the University of Pittsburgh, calls the computer an "amplifier" because it encourages both enlightened study practices and thoughtless ones. There's a real risk, though, that the thoughtless practices will dominate, slowly dumbing down huge numbers of tomorrow's adults. As Sherry Turkle, a professor of the sociology of science at the Massachusetts Institute of Technology and a longtime observer of children's use of computers, told me, "The possibilities of using this thing poorly so outweigh the chance of using it well, it makes people like us, who are fundamentally optimistic about computers, very reticent."

Perhaps the best way to separate fact from fantasy is to take supporters' claims about computerized learning one by one and compare them with the evidence in the academic literature and in the everyday experiences I have observed or heard about in a variety of classrooms.

Five main arguments underlie the campaign to computerize our nation's schools.

- Computers improve both teaching practices and student achievement.

- Computer literacy should be taught as early as possible; otherwise students will be left behind.

- To make tomorrow's work force competitive in an increasingly high-tech world, learning computer skills must be a priority.

- Technology programs leverage support from the business community—badly needed today because schools are increasingly starved for funds.

- Work with computers—particularly using the Internet—brings students valuable connections with teachers, other schools and students, and a wide network of professionals around the globe. These connections spice the school day with a sense of real-world relevance, and broaden the educational community.

THE FILMSTRIPS OF THE 1990S

The Administration's vision of computerized classrooms arose partly out of the findings of the presidential task force—thirty-six leaders from industry, education, and several interest groups who have guided the Administration's push to get computers into the schools. The report of the task force, *Connecting K–12 Schools to the Information Superhighway* (produced by the consulting firm McKinsey & Co.), begins by citing numerous studies that have apparently proved that computers enhance student achievement significantly.

Unfortunately, many of these studies are more anecdotal than conclusive. Some, including a giant, oft-cited meta-analysis of 254 studies, lack the necessary scientific controls to make solid conclusions possible. The circumstances are artificial and not easily repeated, results aren't statistically reliable, or, most frequently, the studies did not control for other influences, such as differences between teaching methods. This last factor is critical, because computerized learning inevitably forces teachers to adjust their style—only *sometimes* for the better. Some studies were industry-funded, and thus tended to publicize mostly positive findings. "The research is set up in a way to find benefits that aren't really there," Edward Miller, a former editor of the *Harvard Education Letter,* says. "Most knowledgeable people agree that most of the research isn't valid. It's so flawed it shouldn't even be called research. Essentially, it's just worthless." Once the faulty studies are weeded out, Miller says, the ones that remain "are inconclusive"—that is, they show no significant change in either direction.

Why are solid conclusions so elusive? Look at Apple Computer's "Classrooms of Tomorrow," perhaps the most widely studied effort to teach using computer technology. In the early 1980s Apple shrewdly realized that donating computers to schools might help not only students but also company sales, as Apple's ubiquity in classrooms turned legions of families into Apple loyalists. Last year, after the *San Jose Mercury News* (published in Apple's Silicon Valley home) ran a series questioning the effectiveness of computers in schools, the paper printed an opinion-page response from Terry Crane, an Apple vice-president. "Instead of isolating students," Crane wrote, "technology actually encouraged them to collaborate more than in traditional classrooms. Students also learned to explore and represent information dynamically and creatively, communicate effectively about complex processes, become independent learners and self-starters, and become more socially aware and confident."

Crane didn't mention that after a decade of effort and the donation of equipment worth more than $25 million to thirteen schools, there is scant evidence of greater student achievement. To be fair, educators on both sides of the computer debate acknowledge that today's tests of student achievement are shockingly crude. They're especially weak in measuring intangibles such as enthusiasm and self-motivation, which do seem evident in Apple's classrooms and other computer-rich schools. In any event, what is fun and what is educational may frequently be at odds. "Computers in classrooms are the filmstrips of the 1990s," Clifford Stoll, the author of *Silicon Snake Oil: Second Thoughts on the Information Highway* (Anchor Books, 1995), told the *New York Times* last year, recalling his own school days in the 1960s. "We loved them because we didn't have to think for an hour, teachers loved them because they didn't have to teach, and parents loved them because it showed their schools were high-tech. But no learning happened." [See Reading 8-1 for Stoll's perspective on the culture of computing.]

Stoll somewhat overstates the case—obviously, benefits can come from strengthening a student's motivation. Still, Apple's computers may bear less responsibility for that change than Crane suggests. In the beginning, when Apple did little more than dump computers in classrooms and homes, this produced no real results, according to Jane David, a consultant Apple hired to study its classroom initiative. Apple quickly learned that teachers needed to change their classroom approach to what is commonly called "project-oriented learning." This is an increasingly popular teaching method, in which students learn through doing and teachers act as facilitators or partners rather than as didacts. (Teachers sometimes refer to this approach, which arrived in classrooms before computers did, as being "the guide on the side instead of the sage on the stage.") But what the students learned "had less to do with the computer and more to do with the teaching," David concluded. "If you took the computers out, there would still be good teaching there." This story is heard in school after school, including two impoverished schools—Clear View Elementary School in southern California, and the Christopher Columbus middle school in New Jersey—that the Clinton Administration has loudly celebrated for turning themselves around with computers. At Christopher Columbus, in fact, students' test scores rose before computers arrived, not afterward, because of relatively basic changes: longer class periods, new books, after-school programs, and greater emphasis on student projects and collaboration.

The value of hands-on learning, child-development experts believe, is that it deeply imprints knowledge into a young child's brain, by transmitting the lessons of experience through a variety of sensory pathways. "Curiously enough," the educational psychologist Jane Healy wrote in *Endangered Minds: Why Children Don't Think and What We Can Do About It* (Simon & Schuster, 1990), "visual stimulation is probably not the main access route to nonverbal reasoning. Body movements, the ability to touch, feel, manipulate, and build sensory awareness of relationships in the physical world, are its main foundations." The problem, Healy wrote, is that "in schools, traditionally, the senses have had little status after kindergarten."

Some computerized elementary school programs have avoided these pitfalls, but the record subject by subject is mixed at best. Take writing, where by all accounts and by my own observations the computer does encourage practice—changes are easier to make on a keyboard than with an eraser, and the lettering looks better. Diligent students use these conveniences to improve their writing, but the less committed frequently get seduced by electronic opportunities to make a school paper look snazzy. The easy "cut and paste" function in today's word-processing programs, for example, is apparently encouraging many students to cobble together research materials without thinking them through. Reading programs get particularly bad reviews. One small but carefully controlled study went so far as to claim that Reader Rabbit, a reading program now used in more than 100,000 schools, caused students to suffer a 50 percent drop in creativity. (Apparently, after forty-nine students used the program for seven months, they were no longer able to answer open-ended questions and showed a markedly diminished ability to brainstorm with fluency and originality.) What about hard sciences, which seem so well suited to computer study? Logo, the high-profile programming language refined by Seymour Papert and widely used in middle and high schools, fostered huge hopes of expanding children's cognitive skills. As students directed the computer to build things, such as geometric shapes, Papert believed, they would learn "procedural thinking," similar to the way a computer processes information. According to a number of studies, however, Logo has generally failed to deliver on its promises. Judah Schwartz, a professor of education at Harvard and a co-director of the school's Educational Technology Center, told me that a few newer applications, when used properly, can dramatically expand children's math and science thinking by giving them new tools to "make and explore conjectures." Still, Schwartz acknowledges that perhaps "ninety-nine percent" of the educational programs are "terrible, really terrible."

Even in success stories important caveats continually pop up. The best educational software is usually complex—most suited to older students and sophisticated teachers. In other cases the schools have been blessed with abundance—fancy equipment, generous financial support, or extra teachers—that is difficult if not impossible to duplicate in the average school. Even if it could be duplicated, the literature suggests, many teachers would still struggle with technology. Computers suffer frequent breakdowns; when they do work, their seductive images often distract students from the lessons at hand—which many teachers say makes it difficult to build meaningful rapport with their students.

HYPERTEXT MINDS

In schools throughout the country administrators and teachers demonstrate the same excitement, boasting about the wondrous things that children of five or six can do on computers: drawing, typing, playing with elementary science simulations and other programs called "educational games."

The schools' enthusiasm for these activities is not universally shared by specialists in childhood development. The doubters' greatest concern is for the very young—preschool through third grade, when a child is most impressionable. Their apprehension involves two main issues.

First, they consider it important to give children a broad base—emotionally, intellectually, and in the five senses—before introducing something as technical and one-dimensional as a computer. Second, they believe that the human and physical world holds greater learning potential.

The importance of a broad base for a child may be most apparent when it's missing. In *Endangered Minds,* Healy wrote of an English teacher who could readily tell which of her students' essays were conceived on a computer. "They don't link ideas," the teacher says. "They just write one thing, and then they write another one, and they don't seem to see or develop the relationships between them." The problem, Healy argued, is that the pizzazz of computerized schoolwork may hide these analytical gaps, which "won't become apparent until [the student] can't organize herself around a homework assignment or a job that requires initiative. More commonplace activities, such as figur-

ing out how to nail two boards together, organizing a game . . . may actually form a better basis for real-world intelligence."

Others believe they have seen computer games expand children's imaginations. High-tech children "think differently from the rest of us," William D. Winn, the director of the Learning Center at the University of Washington's Human Interface Technology Laboratory, told *Business Week* in a cover story on the benefits of computer games. "They develop hypertext minds. They leap around. It's as though their cognitive strategies were parallel, not sequential." Healy argues the opposite. She and other psychologists think that the computer screen flattens information into narrow, sequential data. This kind of material, they believe, exercises mostly one half of the brain—the left hemisphere, where primarily sequential thinking occurs. The "right brain," meanwhile, gets short shrift—yet this is the hemisphere that works on different kinds of information simultaneously. It shapes our multifaceted impressions, and serves as the engine of creative analysis.

Opinions diverge in part because research on the brain is still so sketchy, and computers are so new, that the effect of computers on the brain remains a great mystery. "I don't think we know anything about it," Harry Chugani, a pediatric neurobiologist at Wayne State University, told me. This very ignorance makes skeptics wary. "Nobody knows how kids' internal wiring works," Stoll wrote in *Silicon Snake Oil,* "but anyone who's directed away from social interactions has a head start on turning out weird. . . . No computer can teach what a walk through a pine forest feels like. Sensation has no substitute."

This points to the conservative developmentalists' second concern: the danger that even if hours in front of the screen are limited, unabashed enthusiasm for the computer sends the wrong message—that the mediated world is more significant than the real one. "It's like TV commercials," Barbara Scales, the head teacher at the Child Study Center at the University of California at Berkeley, told me. "Kids get so hyped up, it can change their expectations about stimulation, versus what they generate themselves."

Faced with such sharply contrasting viewpoints, which are based on such uncertain ground, how is a responsible policymaker to proceed? "A prudent society controls its own infatuation with 'progress' when planning for its young," Healy argued in *Endangered Minds.*

Unproven technologies . . . may offer lively visions, but they can also be detrimental to the development of the young plastic brain. The cerebral cortex is a wondrously well-buffered mechanism that can withstand a good bit of well-intentioned bungling. Yet there is a point at which fundamental neural substrates for reasoning may be jeopardized for children who lack proper physical, intellectual, or emotional nurturance. Childhood—and the brain—have their own imperatives. In development, missed opportunities may be difficult to recapture.

The problem is that technology leaders rarely include these or other warnings in their recommendations. When I asked Dyson why the Clinton task force proceeded with such fervor, despite the classroom computer's shortcomings, she said, "It's so clear the world is changing."

REAL JOB TRAINING

Although projections are far from reliable, it's a safe bet that computer skills will be needed for a growing proportion of tomorrow's work force. But what priority should these skills be given among other studies?

Listen to Tom Henning, a physics teacher at Thurgood Marshall, the San Francisco technology high school. Henning has a graduate degree in engineering, and helped to found a Silicon Valley company that manufactures electronic navigation equipment. "My bias is the physical reality," Henning told me, as we sat outside a shop where he was helping students to rebuild an old motorcycle. "I'm no technophobe. I can program computers." What worries Henning is that computers at best engage only two senses, hearing and sight—and only two-dimensional sight at that. "Even if they're doing three-dimensional computer modeling, that's still a two-D replica of a three-D world. If you took a kid who grew up on Nintendo, he's not going to have the necessary skills. He needs to have done it first with Tinkertoys or clay, or carved it out of balsa wood." As David Elkind, a professor of child development at Tufts University, puts it, "A dean of the University of Iowa's School of Engineering used to say the best engineers were the farm boys," because they knew how machinery really worked.

Surely many employers will disagree and welcome the commercially applicable computer skills that today's high-tech training can bring them. What's striking is how easy it is to find other employers who share Henning's and Elkind's concerns.

Kris Meisling, a senior geological-research adviser for Mobil Oil, told me that "people who use computers a lot slowly grow rusty in their ability to think." Meisling's group creates charts and maps—some computerized, some not—to plot where to drill for oil. In large one-dimensional analyses, such as sorting volumes of seismic data, the computer saves vast amounts of time, sometimes making previously impossible tasks easy. This lures people in his field, Meisling believes, into using computers as much as possible. But when geologists turn to computers for 'interpretive' projects, he finds, they often miss information, and their oversights are further obscured by the computer's captivating automatic design functions. This is why Meisling still works regularly with pencil and paper—tools that, ironically, he considers more interactive than the computer, because they force him to think implications through.

"You can't simultaneously get an overview and detail with a computer," he says. "It's linear. It gives you tunnel vision. What computers can do well is what can be calculated over and over. What they can't do is innovation. If you think of some new way to do or look at things and the software can't do it, you're stuck. So a lot of people think, 'Well, I guess it's a dumb idea, or it's unnecessary.'"

I have heard similar warnings from people in other businesses, including high-tech enterprises. A spokeswoman for Hewlett-Packard, the giant California computer-products company, told me the company rarely hires people who are predominantly computer experts, favoring instead those who have a talent for teamwork and are flexible and innovative. Much the same perspective came from several recruiters in film and computer-game animation. In work by artists who have spent a lot of time on computers "you'll see a stiffness or a flatness, a lack of richness and depth," Karen Chelini, the director of human resources for LucasArts Entertainment, George Lucas's interactive-games maker, told me recently. "With traditional art training, you train the eye to pay attention to body movement. You learn attitude, feeling, expression. The ones who are good are those who as kids couldn't be without their sketchbook."

Some educators worry that as children concentrate on how to manipulate software instead of on the subject at hand, learning can diminish rather than grow. Simulations, for example, are built on hidden assumptions, many of which are oversimplified if not highly questionable. All too often, Turkle wrote in *The American Prospect,* "experiences with simulations do not open up questions but close them down." Turkle's concern is that software of this sort fosters passivity, ultimately dulling people's sense of what they can change in the world. There's a tendency, Turkle told me, "to take things at 'interface' value." Indeed, after mastering SimCity, a popular game about urban planning, a tenth-grade girl boasted to Turkle that she'd learned the following rule: "Raising taxes always leads to riots."

JUST A GLAMOROUS TOOL

It would be easy to characterize the battle over computers as merely another chapter in the world's oldest story: humanity's natural resistance to change. But that does an injustice to the forces at work in this transformation. This is not just the future versus the past, uncertainty versus nostalgia; it is about encouraging a fundamental shift in personal priorities—a minimizing of the real, physical world in favor of an unreal "virtual" world. It is about teaching youngsters that exploring what's on a two-dimensional screen is more important than playing with real objects, or sitting down to an attentive conversation with a friend, parent, or teacher. By extension, it means downplaying the importance of conversation, of careful listening, and of expressing oneself in person with acuity and individuality. In the process, it may also limit the development of children's imaginations.

Perhaps this is why Steven Jobs, one of the founders of Apple Computer and a man who claims to have "spearheaded giving away more computer equipment to schools than anybody else on the planet," has come to a grim conclusion: "What's wrong with education cannot be fixed with technology," he told *Wired* magazine in an interview last year. "No amount of technology will make a dent. . . . You're not going to solve the problems by putting all knowledge onto CD-ROMs. We can put a Web site in every school—none of this is bad. It's bad only if it lulls us into thinking we're doing something to solve the problem with education."

The solution is not to ban computers from classrooms altogether. But it may be to ban federal spending on what is fast becoming an overheated campaign. After all, the private sector, with its constant supply of used computers and the computer industry's vigorous competition for new customers, seems well equipped to handle the situation. In fact, if schools can impose some limits rather than indulging in a consumer frenzy, most will probably find themselves with more electronic gear than they need. That could free the billions [the Administration] wants to devote to technology and make it available for impoverished fundamentals: teaching solid skills in reading, thinking, listening, and talking; organizing inventive field trips and other rich hands-on experiences; and, of course, building up the nation's core of knowledgeable, inspiring teachers. These notions are considerably less glamorous than computers are, but their worth is firmly proved through a long history.

RELATED LINKS

- Connecting K–12 Schools to the Information Superhighway (http://www.uark.edu/mckinsey)

- Child Study Center, University of California at Berkeley (http://ihd.berkeley.edu/child.htm)

- Learning Research and Development Center (http://www.lrdc.pitt.edu)

- edtechnot.com's Jane Healy Links (http://www.edtechnot.com/nothealy.html)

- edtechnot.com's Todd Oppenheimer Links (http://www.edtechnot.com/notoppenheimer.html)

FOR FURTHER RESEARCH

To find out more about the topics discussed in this reading, use InfoTrac College Edition. Type in keywords and subject terms such as "technology education programs," "computerized classrooms," and "computer literacy." You can access InfoTrac from the Wadsworth/Thomson Communication Café homepage: http://communication.wadsworth.com.

8

Questioning Information Technology

Reading 8-1

Further Explorations into the Culture of Computing
Clifford Stoll

EDITOR'S NOTE

Silicon Snake Oil, first published in 1995, stands as one of the most influential critiques of the Internet lifestyle to appear in print. In this excerpt, author Clifford Stoll, an astrophysicist and avid computer user himself, discusses the limitations of network dependence and asserts that there are no simple technological solutions to enduring social problems. Rather than bringing us together, computer networks may instead isolate us from one another. What's missing from the ersatz neighborhood of online community, Stoll argues, is the very essence of a real neighborhood: a feeling of permanence and belonging, a sense of location, and the warmth that can be derived only from an understanding and appreciation of local history.

CONSIDER

1. Why does Stoll take issue with the technocratic belief that computers and networks will make a better society?
2. Are computers merely tools for thinking, or do they alter our thinking processes to conform to their own idiosyncratic demands?
3. Stoll maintains that computer networks isolate us from one another, rather than bringing us together. Do you agree? Why or why not?

I just saw a video from Pacific Bell—I mean the Pacific Telesis Group—showing an imaginary couple buying a coat from Mongolia. We listen to them chat with a yak dealer; a computer interprets on the fly. In the background, children happily play with a three-dimensional game that teaches math.

The phone company wants me to believe that they'll invent automatic translation and worldwide video-phones. And that virtual reality will be primarily used for teaching.

They might equally well show us a less benign future: boring corporate conferences held via satellite and big-screen music videos. Junk mail brought to us at the speed of light. Children avoiding their homework by playing shoot-'em-down, slash-'em-up games. Pornography downloaded into home computers. Credit companies sending dunning letters to a young couple via e-mail.

Now, I've also seen plenty of encouraging things over the networks: seventh-grade students exchanging poetry with friends. A shy woman who met her husband-to-be through the Usenet. International collaborations in sciences and humanities. Specialized mailings for nonprofit groups. Friendly support for a man whose child has leukemia. A family that used the Internet to get the latest research results on a disease. A retarded 25-year-old woman who used a children's math program to practice addition.

Those aren't eye-popping uses like computerized translators or three-dimensional virtual realities, but they're the blossoms in today's garden—much more real than the dreamland painted by network futurists.

In 1986, while managing a cluster of Unix workstations, I viewed networks mechanistically, as a collection of cables, connectors, and computers. After all, my job was to keep the system running, and the main ingredients are hardware. It hadn't occurred to me that the Internet, then so young, formed a community.

Experience dealing with people—not computers—changed my point of view. Other system operators and government agents went out of their way to help me out of a bind. Cooperating together—not only to link our computers, but to track down a renegade [chronicled in Stoll's 1989 book, *The Cuckoo's Egg,*

From *Silicon Snake Oil: Second Thoughts on the Information Superhighway* by Clifford Stoll (New York: Anchor Books, 1995). Copyright © 1995 by Clifford Stoll. Used by permission of Doubleday, a division of Random House, Inc.

published by Doubleday]—showed me that a computer network is, indeed, a community.

But what an impoverished community! One without a church, cafe, art gallery, theater, or tavern. Plenty of human contact, but no humanity. Cybersex, cybersluts, and cybersleaze, but no genuine, lusty, roll-in-the-hay sex.

And no birds sing.

Even ignoring everything palpable—children's laughter, plum jam, my sister Rosalie's green sports car—what's missing from this ersatz neighborhood? A feeling of permanence and belonging, a sense of location, a warmth from the local history. Gone is the very essence of a neighborhood: friendly relations and a sense of being in it together.

Oh—I hear you: It's only a metaphorical community. Much of what happens over the networks is a metaphor—we chat without speaking, smile without grinning, and hug without touching.

On my screen, I see several icons—a mailbox, a theater, a newspaper. These represent incoming messages, an entertainment video, and a news wire. But they're not the real thing. The mailbox doesn't clunk, the movie theater doesn't serve popcorn, and the newspaper doesn't come with a cup of coffee at the corner cafe.

How sad—to dwell in a metaphor without living the experience. The only sensations are a glowing screen, the touch of a keyboard, and the sound of an occasional bleep. All synthetic.

The common claim is that networks, like computers, are tools—utensils to get work done. I've heard this so often that I'm beginning to doubt it.

"A tool for what?" I ask my friends. Their replies are telling: It's a tool for thinking.

Ouch. We need a tool to spare us the effort of thinking? Is reasoning so painful that we require a labor-saving device? What is it we're trying to avoid?

Maybe we're obsessed with computers as tools because, as Thomas Carlyle wrote, man is a tool-using animal . . . without tools he is nothing, with tools he is all.

And so everything within our scope becomes a tool. Advertisements promote pens, dictionaries, and word processors as writing tools. I search in vain for something that isn't a tool: My shoes are personal-transportation tools; chewing gum is a relaxation tool; and the moon is a tool for telling time and illuminating the evening.

But I've never heard of a typewriter user's group, or schools spending thousands of dollars to put a radial-arm saw on every student's desk. Nor do I know of any screwdriver that inspires the same slavish infatuation as the Internet. The computer is a remarkably different kind of tool—one which can turn kids into reactive zombies, adults into frustrated bumblers.

Calling a computer a tool gives us a warm feeling that we're craftsmen, burgeoning with physical skills and manual dexterity. It imparts none of these.

Rather, the computer requires almost no physical interaction or dexterity, beyond the ability to type. And unlike a chisel, drill, or shovel, the computer demands rote memorization of nonobvious rules. You subjugate your own thinking patterns to those of the computer.

Using this tool alters our thinking processes. When Gutenberg invented the printing press, the prevailing style of writing changed, and again when the typewriter became common. Telegraphs, too, influenced literature. Stop. Think of the terseness of Hemingway. In turn, word processors change not just how but *what* we write. The handwritten bread-and-butter note gives way to an e-mail greeting.

Databases aren't just computer programs—there are other ways to organize information, like Rolodexes, address books, and manila folders in filing cabinets. These mechanical filing systems are intuitive, easy to use, and simple to set up. Yet the person deeply committed to a relational database system won't recognize opportunities where these physical devices might work better.

Nor is the computer the only tool for doing mathematics—analytic equations, calculus, approximations, and trigonometry have worked for centuries, if not millennia.

Simply by turning to a computer when confronted with a problem, you limit your ability to recognize other solutions. When the only tool you know is a hammer, everything looks like a nail.

Which is the tool: the computer or the user?

This leads to some important questions that I'm not smart enough to frame. When your thinking is strictly logical—when you're constrained to a digital mode of work—you lose the ability to leapfrog over conceptual walls.

The stiff-walled logic of computers rewards those who can rigorously follow strict-thought rules. These incentives include prestige and employment . . . our software and networks nourish drones.

At the same time, computers punish the imaginative and inventive by constraining them to prescribed channels of thought and action.

For example, we think that painting and drawing programs open up new vistas to graphic artists. But they strongly limit the artist's choices of colors, sizes, shapes, and textures. Moreover, the artist must strictly follow the program's rules. The artist working at a computer never lays a hand on media like origami, textiles, or alabaster.

When we find dance and music on computers, it seems so refreshingly delightful simply because the nature of computing is antithetical to flights of fancy.

And what of the person who can't follow instructions? Often he's the one who comes up with original solutions to problems. Yet this is the guy who cannot boot up without a snag. He has constant troubles with computers, simply because his thoughts are out of sync with the conventions of software designers. In a Darwinian manner, creative people are ill-adapted for survival around computers.

In short, the medium in which we communicate changes how we organize our thoughts. We program computers, but the computers also program us.

Marshall McLuhan divided media into hot and cool—movies and radio were hot, television and the telephone were cool. Hot media are low in participation; cool ones high in it. I'm not sure what he means, but on that scale the Internet, especially the Usenet, is certainly cool.

Think of these media as social interactions. Movies can be participatory, even if you don't get to choose who's on-screen. Get a group of friends together to watch Casablanca at a campus cinema some weekend. There's gossip while waiting in line, along with the smell of popcorn, and the anticipation of seeing a classic film. You nudge each other during the good scenes, or perhaps put an arm around your sweetie. Or head over to the Rocky Horror Picture Show, and don't forget the toast.

Compare this to an intense night surfing the Internet—you have nobody to compare notes with, nobody to harmonize as you hum "As Time Goes By," nobody to spill popcorn on your favorite blanket. Your community disappears when your modem disconnects.

What's the nature of this networked community? It runs in all directions. Professorial, technocratic, punk. Sparks of intellect scattered across electronic fields, without coherent direction.

Listening to traffic crossing the Usenet, I hear a distinct libertarian political leaning: Stay off my back and let me do whatever I please.

It attracts extreme political positions and long-standing international feuds. They spill out of newsgroups frequented by Turks and Armenians, by Israelis and Palestinians, and by Serbs and Croats.

Thousands of Internet users will tell you that I'm giving but one side of a complex story. They'll point to hundreds of self-help groups that work as effectively as any neighborhood counseling organization. They'll show you the comp.risks forum, where anyone can read about the social implications of computing. They'll talk about the World Wide Web, where a click of a mouse will bring the latest news from London, Tokyo, or Berlin.

They're right. The Usenet is a community where hundreds of thousands engage in friendly banter. From across the net and across the ocean, I hear the latest jokes on rec.humor.funny, reports on travel adventures on rec.travel, and listings of jobs on misc.jobs.offered. Before checking out an old Dracula film, I check into rec.arts.movies.

If I were being fair to the Usenet, I'd have to mention the experts who thanklessly help newcomers on such forums as comp.unix.questions, news.answers, and news.newusers.questions. I'd probably have to include some of the lesser-known watering holes, like rec.arts.books, where book-folk congregate, and alt.best-of-usenet, where every day I read gaffes by newcomers as well as exceptionally creative flames.

Don't get me wrong: There's lots of good things happening online. I've seen bulletin boards for cancer survivors, bagpipers, and cave explorers. A carpenter's union in New York State gets the news out over a bulletin board.

Another way to spread the word is through electronic mailing lists. These lists let exclusive groups thrive over the networks, whether medieval English scholars, feminist authors, or Japanese animation addicts.

Mailing lists are universally available over e-mail. To get on the mailing list for postcard collectors, just send mail to postcardrequest@bit.listserv.postcard, with the subject line of *subscribe*. They're simple, too: A user sends mail to one site, and everyone down the line gets a copy.

The neatness of these mailing lists extends beyond their simplicity and wide availability. It's a great way to make a closed discussion, say for sensitive topics like gender issues or recovery groups. There's a place for folk dancers to compare steps and accordion players to exchange notes. Around San Francisco, book fanatics send mail to ead@netcom.com to get the latest scoop on bookstore happenings.

But mailing lists almost guarantee mailbox over-

flow. When the comet crashed into Jupiter, I picked up 50 messages from the Net; another 100 fell into the bitbucket. And mailing-list traffic, like Usenet newsgroups, often has little content.

Virtually everything is debated on the Usenet: whether computers are best left on at night, if cats can be fed a vegetarian diet, if abortion should be legal.

Predictable replies—maybe, maybe, and maybe, but each with more stridency. Plenty of opinions, but not much informed dialogue, and even less consensus.

Of course, since there are no easy answers, arguments over the Usenet are seldom resolved. They'll degenerate into name-calling; eventually one of the participants figuratively walks away, and a new debate begins.

Now, recurrent debates aren't bad—they're just circular and tedious. Next time I have to spend a week in traction, I'll check into the Usenet. One of the joys of computers is how they're great at wasting time that might otherwise be difficult to waste.

A UNIVERSAL PANACEA, OR SILICON SNAKE OIL?

Imagine driving from Yankee Stadium in the Bronx to Jones Beach on Long Island. You'd likely take the Cross Bronx Expressway, the Throgs Neck Bridge, the Cross Island Parkway, the Long Island Expressway, and the Meadowbrook State Parkway. Say thanks to Robert Moses—he created these public works.

From 1930 to 1970, Robert Moses built roads, bridges, parks, and housing projects. Nothing stopped him—not politicians, community leaders, urban planners, neighborhoods. Quite the contrary: He bribed politicians, intimidated community leaders, hired the urban planners, and plowed under the neighborhoods. Anyways, in 1955 only a reactionary Luddite would possibly oppose highway construction. The automobile was clearly the key to the future.

Your imaginary trip across the Cross Bronx Expressway won't show you the thousands of people evicted from their homes, the old brownstone apartments paved over, the diverse neighborhoods cleaved by noisy traffic arteries. Robert Moses did more to destroy New York City than any one individual.

Moses disdained anyone who couldn't afford a car, so he built parkways with low overpasses that blocked buses. No walkways or bike paths, either. In a similar way, computer mavens shun the technophobes, so they write manuals that can't be understood by novices.

Internet merchants want government subsidies to build ever faster links, but they won't offer lower connect rates for the poor.

Today's Internet hustlers invade our communities with computers, not concrete. By pushing the Internet as a universal panacea, they offer a tempting escape from this all-too-mundane world. They tell us that we need not get along with our neighbors, heck, we needn't even interact with them. Won't need to travel to a library either; those books will come right to my desk. Interactive multimedia will solve classroom problems. Fat pay checks and lifelong employment await those who master computers.

They're well-meaning, of course. They truly believe in virtual communities and electronic classrooms. They'll tell you how the computer is a tool to be used, not abused. Because clearly, the computer is the key to the future.

The key ingredient of their silicon snake oil is a technocratic belief that computers and networks will make a better society. Access to information, better communications, and electronic programs can cure social problems.

I don't believe them. There are no simple technological solutions to social problems. There's plenty of distrust and animosity between people who communicate perfectly well. Access to a universe of information cannot solve our problems: We will forever struggle to understand one another. The most important interactions in life happen between people, not between computers.

Computer networks isolate us from one another, rather than bring us together. We need only deal with one side of an individual over the net. And if we don't like what we see, we just pull the plug. Or flame them. There's no need to tolerate the imperfections of real people. It's the same intolerance found on the highway, where motorists direct intense anger at one another.

By logging on to the networks, we lose the ability to enter into spontaneous interactions with real people. Evening time is now spent watching a television or a computer terminal—safe havens in which to hide. Sitting around a porch and talking is becoming extinct, as is reading aloud to children.

The Internet puts me in touch with thousands of people across the country. But it's more important to spend time with my friends and neighbors. Karen Anderson, the penguin keeper at San Francisco's Steinhart Aquarium, puts it this way: "The people who are right close to me are the most important ones in my life. Why should I get excited about personal relationships on some computer network?"

Karen told me of the work of Dr. Luis Baptista, the curator of ornithology at the California Academy of Sciences. This guy knows his birds—he can whistle the songs of doves and sparrows. Jeez, he did his dissertation on the dialects of these birds.

Well, to see how birds learn songs, he raised white-crowned sparrows. When they left the nest, Dr. Baptista placed single fledglings in a special cage where they could see and hear an Asian strawberry finch. The young birds could also hear several dialects of their own sparrow songs in the same room, but they couldn't see those sparrows.

The fledgling sparrows didn't learn their own songs. Instead, they matured, singing the songs of the Asian finches with whom they socially interacted. And later, as parents, these sparrows taught their young to sing Chinese songs, too. Sparrows learn from living teachers, not from machines.

In the same way, the isolation of computers and online networks causes us to sing others' songs. Children, raised with less social interaction, adopt the ways of the first people they come in close contact with. It encourages a divorce from parental values and the dominance of peer culture. Kids that interact with computers rather than their parents miss out on the most important part of growing: being close to their families.

Think I'm exaggerating? One teenager in Berkeley began using a computer when he was three years old; today, he's utterly fluent in getting around the Internet, but can't converse with an adult. I know several computer wizards who can tell you details of their computer's disk cache, but don't know when their family immigrated to America. And I've met dozens of high school students who can proficiently use a word processor, but have never written a thank-you letter.

 RELATED LINKS

- Clifford Stoll (http://www.ocf.berkeley.edu/~stoll)
- Cyberspace, Hypertext, and Critical Theory (http://www.cyberartsweb.org/cpace/)

- edtechnot.com's Clifford Stoll Links (http://www.edtechnot.com/notstoll.html)
- edtechnot.com's Neil Postman Links (http://www.edtechnot.com/notpostman.html)

FOR FURTHER RESEARCH

To find out more about the topics discussed in this reading, use InfoTrac College Edition. Type in keywords and subject terms such as "information superhighway," "technological utopia," and "technorealism." You can access InfoTrac from the Wadsworth/Thomson Communication Café homepage: http://communication.wadsworth.com.

Reading 8-2

Plan 9 from Cyberspace: The Implications of the Internet for Personality and Social Psychology

Katelyn Y. A. McKenna and John A. Bargh

EDITOR'S NOTE

Whenever a new communication medium is introduced into society, three things tend to happen: (1) the technology is feared for its potential to harm or compromise the morals of users, particularly young users; (2) the technology tends to have unintended consequences not foreseen by designers and programmers; and (3) the technology takes longer to mature, or assume a stable form, than originally anticipated. This reading from Personality & Social Psychology Review *by researchers Katelyn McKenna and John Bargh provides an accurate assessment of the Internet's known impact on social life and individual psychology. Counter to the initial, and widely publicized, claim that Internet use causes depression, loneliness, and social isolation, the authors find that the evidence is mainly to the contrary—going online tends to enhance social life, not diminish it. In and of itself, McKenna and Bargh argue, the Internet is not a main effect cause of anything but should be understood as one of several social domains in which individuals now act out important aspects of their lives and attempt to fulfill needs and achieve goals.*

CONSIDER

1. Why was it initially assumed by psychologists and public alike that Internet use leads to depression and social isolation?

2. What are the effects of your own Internet/World Wide Web use on various aspects of your personal and social life?

3. How do online communication and interaction differ from that in real life? According to the authors, there are four major differences that serve as important moderators.

Just as with most other communication breakthroughs before it, the initial media and popular reaction to the Internet has been largely negative, if not apocalyptic. For example, it has been described as "awash in pornography," and more recently as making people "sad and lonely." Yet, counter to the initial and widely publicized claim that Internet use causes depression and social isolation, the body of evidence (even in the initial study on which the claim was based) is mainly to the contrary. More than this, however, it is argued that like the telephone and television before it, the Internet by itself is not a main effect cause of anything, and that psychology must move beyond this notion to an informed analysis of how social identity, social interaction, and relationship formation may be different on the Internet than in real life.

The growth of the Internet has been truly exponential over the past decade. Until recently there were relatively few nodes in that network to carry digitized information from one part of the world to another and relatively few people (mainly academics and government workers) accessing that network. Personal computers for the home were expensive and the interface used to view, send, and receive data over the Internet was not user friendly. However, in recent years personal computers have dropped drastically in price. Sophisticated Internet browser software, such as Internet Explorer and Netscape, is now readily available. Although the Internet is not yet a vital utility such as the telephone, it will not be long before having a connection to the Internet will be equally as important. Indeed, in a recent poll of 1,000 Internet users, 64% said that "using an online or Internet service is a necessity to me" (D'Amico, 1998, p. 1).

These developments have made it possible for the average person to become an active user of the Internet.

More important, for personality and social psychology, the Internet is a place where people are engaging in social interaction. Indeed, the number one use of the Internet at home is for interpersonal communication (Kraut, Mukopadhyay, Szczypula, Kiesler, & Scherlis, 1998). People are increasingly turning to the Internet as a quick and easy way to maintain con-

From "Plan 9 from Cyberspace: The Implications of the Internet for Personality and Social Psychology" by Katelyn Y. A. McKenna and John A. Bargh, *Personality & Social Psychology Review,* 4(1), 2000, pp. 57–76. Copyright © 2000 Personality & Social Psychology Review. Reprinted with permission.

tact with family and friends who live far away. In the survey mentioned earlier, fully 94% reported that the Internet made it easier for them to communicate with friends and family, and 87% regularly use it for that purpose (D'Amico, 1998).

There are a wide variety of electronic venues available on the Internet for interpersonal communication. There are thousands of Internet chat rooms, message boards, listservs, and news groups each dedicated to a specific topic or area of interest for those interested in taking part in group interactions. People can also communicate privately through the creation of private chat rooms, personal messaging, and of course electronic mail. Text-based online adventure games called Multi-User Dungeons (MUDs) and their more socially oriented relatives, the Mud Object Orienteds and Multi-User Shared Hallucinations, are attractive venues for many, particularly younger, Internet users.

FEAR AND LOATHING ON THE INTERNET

The public, however, is somewhat apprehensive about the changes the Internet may or will bring. This fear of the unknown is to be expected to some extent, and it has been a feature of the introduction of most previous technological breakthroughs that greatly affect nearly everyone's lives. Many people were reluctant to have telephones installed when they first became available because it was rumored that outsiders could listen in on the household through the mouthpiece, even when the phone was on the hook. It was also not uncommon for people to resist the installation of electricity because it might leak out of the outlets. Soon after television was invented and publicly demonstrated around 1930, Bela Lugosi made a horror movie called *Murder by Television* that capitalized on public fears of this emerging technology. More recently, there was an initial negative reaction to the introduction of microwave ovens, because of the possibility of escaping radiation, but today microwave cooking is a mundane feature of modern kitchens.

The Internet has fared no differently. For most of the 1990s most people only heard about the Internet in terms of being a dangerous conveyor of pornography to the unwitting eyes of children, or as causing "Internet addiction" (Young, 1998). Politicians responded to public fears of the uncontrolled dissemination of information on the Internet: The U.S. Congress has repeatedly passed legislation such as the Computer Decency

Act (CDA) that seeks to censor or regulate the content of Internet Web sites, only to have such legislation ruled unconstitutional as a violation of the First Amendment by the courts. In fact, the CDA came about largely because of the furor in the media and in Congress caused by the publication, in 1995, of a study by a student at Carnegie Mellon University (Rimm, 1995) that purportedly showed that the Internet was awash in pornography, although this conclusion was "based on false premises and quickly discredited" (Caruso, 1998, p. C5; e.g., the study was never subjected to peer review; see also Hoffman & Novak, 1995; Rossney, 1995).

More recently, another Carnegie Mellon study received U.S. national media coverage when it concluded that using the Internet leads to significant increases in loneliness and depression (Kraut, Patterson, et al., 1998). The participants in this study were people from the Pittsburgh area who had never been on the Internet before; in fact, most had never before used a computer at home. They were not randomly selected but recruited for the "HomeNet" study because their families included high school students, or an adult who was on a community board of directors. These participants had unusually large social circles at the beginning of the study, an average of 49 friends and associates each. Kraut, Patterson, et al. followed these families for 2 years, measuring among other variables the number of hours each individual was on the Internet per day, their levels of depression and loneliness both at the beginning and at the end of the 2-year period, and the number of people in their social circle at the end of the study.

Kraut, Patterson, et al. (1998) found a small but statistically reliable partial correlation of .15 between amount of Internet use and self-reported loneliness, accounting for less than 1% of the change in loneliness over the 2-year period. They also reported that using the Internet for as little as 2 hours per week over the 2-year period resulted in a reduction in the size of the average participant's social network—defined as the number of people in Pittsburgh with whom the participant socialized at least once a month—from 24 to 23 people. The authors also obtained a small but statistically reliable increase in level of self-reported depression (actually, self-reported dysphoric mood) with increased amount of Internet use, again accounting for less than 1% of the change in depression level over the 2-year period. The authors concluded that using the Internet causes increases in loneliness and depression,

and this was the "sound bite" conclusion reported widely by the media.

It is one of the standard principles of journalism (and horror films as well) that "scare headlines sell newspapers": A threat, no matter how statistically rare and unlikely, to which nearly everyone is vulnerable, whether it be poisoned Tylenol tablets or mad-cow disease, is sure to capture the public's attention (e.g., Fuller, 1996; Gans, 1979). So the media play given the "Internet causes loneliness" conclusion is understandable; it is doubtful much coverage would have been given a study showing a slight but statistically significant decrease in loneliness and depression level with Internet use.

However, this becomes more than merely a hypothetical question, because such a decrease is, in fact, what the study did find.

For the entire group of participants, the average reported level of depression for participants after 2 years of being on the Internet was less than it had been before being on the Internet, and the average reported level of loneliness for this group was also lower at the end of the study than when the study began. Furthermore, whereas the average number of people in the local social network declined one person over the 2-year period, the size of the average participant's distant social network—defined as the number of people outside of Pittsburgh with whom the participant talked or visited at least once per year—substantially increased after 2 years of using the Internet, from 25 to 32. Thus, the total number of people in the average participant's social network in the Kraut, Patterson, et al. (1998) study actually increased over the 2 years, from 49 to 55. Of course, there could have been many other factors over the course of the 2 years in participants' lives besides Internet use that could have produced these decreases in depression and loneliness, and increases in number of friends and acquaintances, but because the Kraut, Patterson, et al. study did not include a control group of comparable people who were not given and did not use home computers over the same 2-year period,[1] the only known potential causal factor was participants' use of the Internet. The study's design provided no basis for concluding anything other than that the reason for these changes was the introduction of home computers and Internet access into participants' lives.

Unfortunately, the take-home sound bite message reported by the media was the opposite one. For instance, the headline on the front page of the *New York*

Times read "Sad, lonely world discovered in cyber-space" (Harmon, 1998), and that on the front page of the American Psychological Association's (APA) *Monitor* for that month was similar ("Isolation increases with Internet use"; Sleek, 1998). Due to the great deal of publicity the study received, both within APA and in the national and international media, it is widely accepted by psychologists and public alike that Internet use leads to depression and social isolation.

In the previous case of the Internet pornography study (Rimm, 1995), the (entirely false) conclusion that 83.5% of pictorial content on the Internet was pornographic (and that much of this was child pornography) received immediate media fanfare (most notably the cover of *Time* magazine, before the actual article had appeared), and was a major reason for the passage of CDA in 1996. Although that study was quickly debunked for its gross distortions and its extremely inadequate methodology (e.g., Hoffman & Novak, 1995; Rossney, 1995), these problems were not reported in the media (if at all) to anything approaching the extent of the initial (false) report.

It may well be that the "sad, lonely Internet" conclusion will similarly influence public policy decisions about Internet access and regulation. This would be despite the facts that, according to several large-scale national and international surveys of Internet users, the great majority of respondents consider Internet use to have improved their lives (D'Amico, 1998; Katz & Aspden, 1997; McKenna & Bargh, 1999a), that a substantial proportion (over 50%) of over 600 Internet users surveyed had brought an Internet relationship into their real life (i.e., met in person), and that over 20% of those respondents had formed a romantic relationship and were now living with or engaged to someone they met on the Internet (McKenna, 1998).

Our goal is to set the record straight among personality and social psychologists about the actual social and interpersonal consequences of the Internet—both as to what the existing body of research has found, and as to what further research is likely to find.

The first important point is that there is no simple main effect of the Internet on the average person (e.g., as to make the individual lonelier or more depressed). Like everything else learned in the past 25 years of personality and social psychology research, situational variables such as modes of Internet communication interact with individual differences or "person" variables to produce psychological and behavioral outcomes (e.g., Mischel, 1973). One of the central messages is an old one in communications research (known widely as the uses and gratifications model; Blumler, 1979; Blumler & Katz, 1974; Katz, 1959): How a person is affected by a given communications medium depends on that person's reasons and goals for using that medium (Bargh, 1988). People use the Internet for a variety of reasons and motivations (see McKenna & Bargh, 1999b), and will thus use it differently and it will have different effects on them accordingly. There is, in short, no simple sound bite for how using the Internet will affect an individual.

The related second point is that the Internet per se is neither entirely good or entirely bad as to the kinds of interactive social effects it can have on individuals. Although in this article the positive aspects and outcomes are emphasized (but at the same time point to the potential downsides to Internet communication), this is motivated by the need for a corrective to the overly negative portrayals that have received so much emphasis to date. Television can link a world together and help bring down the Berlin wall (Friedman, 1999), but it is also fertile ground for the cultivation of couch potatoes. The Internet can bring people of like interests and minds together in ways heretofore unseen, but those similarities can range from a past history of sexual abuse among people in great need of anonymous social support, to virulent hatred of other racial groups.

HOW IS THE INTERNET DIFFERENT?

The Internet is a virtual world that is the same in some ways but different in others from the one traditionally studied. How well will existing theory apply to the world of the Internet?

We begin by considering how communication and interaction on the Internet may be different from that in real life. There are four major differences that are likely to be important moderators. First, it is quite possible to be anonymous while on the Internet. For many of us, our names appear in our e-mail addresses, and even if they do not, our identity (and much other information about us) can be ascertained through "fingering" programs and other means. However, it is quite possible, such as on AOL and other Internet service providers, to have an anonymous e-mail name. Moreover, even when using one's real name, one is relatively anonymous when interacting with people from other cities and countries.

That physical distance, or propinquity, does not matter on the Internet means that one can interact with, and meet, people from all over the world, at least those who speak the same languages. Physical distance is the major determinant of who one will meet and form relationships with in the real world, but the Internet vastly expands the range and variety of interaction partners.

Also, unlike in real life, physical appearance and visual cues more generally are not present and not an influential factor on the Internet. As these are powerful determinants of initial attraction and the potential for relationship formation, as well as strong cues for stereotype and other social categorization processes, their absence on the Internet should alter the course of interactions and relationship formation.

Finally, time becomes relatively immaterial on the Internet. Not only can an individual engage in a social exchange without the other person being online at the same time but also he or she has far greater control over his or her side of the interaction than is possible in a conversation by telephone or in person, because there is no need for an instantaneous response. An individual can take all the time he or she needs to formulate a response, perhaps polishing and editing the phrasing until it seems perfect in his or her eyes, rather than having to respond off the cuff.

To summarize, people via the Internet are engaging in largely anonymous but repeated interactions with others who are equally anonymous. They are forming close relationships with others sight unseen. They are also able to construct and reconstruct their identity in numerous ways on the Internet—something not possible for the average individual in non-Internet life. People can and are thus engaging in very different behaviors on the Internet than they do in the real world.

THE EFFECTS OF ANONYMITY IN CYBERSPACE

Deindividuation

When an individual's self-awareness is blocked or seriously reduced by environmental conditions (e.g., such as darkness, presence of large numbers of other people), deindividuation can occur (Diener, 1980; Zimbardo, 1970). Anonymity, feelings of close group unity, a high level of physiological arousal, and a focus on external events or goals are conditions that have been shown to encourage, and often produce, deindividuation. Some of the outcomes produced by deindividuation include a weakened ability for an individual to regulate his or her own behavior, reduced ability to engage in rational, long-term planning, and a tendency to react to

immediate cues or based largely on his or her current emotional state. Furthermore, an individual will be less likely to care what others think of his or her behavior and may even have a reduced awareness of what others have said or done. These effects can culminate in impulsive and disinhibited behaviors (Zimbardo, 1970).

The negative, deindividuating effects of anonymous communication via the Internet have been among the most discussed aspects of computer-mediated communication to date. Researchers have found that people tend to behave more bluntly when communicating by e-mail or participating in other electronic venues such as news groups, than they would in a face-to-face situation. Moreover, misunderstandings, greater hostility and aggressive responses, and nonconforming behavior are more likely to occur in computer-mediated interactions than in interactions that take place face to face (Culnan & Markus, 1987; Dubrovsky, Kiesler, & Sethna, 1991; Kiesler, Siegal, & McGuire, 1984; Siegal, Dubrovsky, Kiesler, & McGuire, 1986). Researchers have also found that under some conditions computer-mediated communication can foster an inability to form group consensus, increased verbal hostility and impersonalization, and an inability to become task focused (Siegal et al., 1986).

More alarmingly, racists and members of hate groups have used the cloak of anonymity afforded by the Internet to harass minority group members through sending hateful or threatening e-mail (Mendels, 1999). For example, the perpetrators of the recent shootings at Columbine High School in Colorado had disseminated racist views anonymously on personal Web pages (Clausing, 1999). The publicity and notoriety of such cases of abuse have led to federal and state legislative efforts to outlaw anonymous Internet (e-mail, newsgroup) communications.

At the same time, the anonymity of the Internet played a major role in getting accurate information about the conflict in Kosovo out to the rest of the world despite heavy Serbian government censorship, and many give the Internet credit for the grassroots communication that facilitated the independence movement in Indonesia (Frankel & Teich, 1999).

Positive Effects of Anonymity

In the social and personality psychology literature, less research has been done on the positive effects that may result from anonymous communication on the Internet and anonymous communication in general. In part, this lack of research stems from the fact that, prior to the advent of the Internet, anonymous interpersonal communication between individuals (as opposed to individuals interacting as a part of a larger group) tended to occur mainly in fleeting, relatively impersonal exchanges (e.g., conversations with one's unknown seatmate on an airplane or a train, polite—or not so polite—exchanges with the latest telemarketer). Such interactions are generally limited to a one-time occurrence and are of short duration. By contrast, on the Internet, people are commonly communicating with others over time behind the shroud of anonymity.

Deindividuation, as through anonymity, does not by itself produce negative behavior. Rather, it decreases the influence of internal (i.e., self) standards of or guides to behavior, and increases the power of external, situational cues (Johnson & Downing, 1979). If those external cues are associated with negative and antisocial behavior, such as Ku Klux Klan hoods, behavior will be negative (Zimbardo, 1970), but if those same hoods are portrayed as those worn by recovery room nurses, the resultant behavior of the person hidden under it is more positive than normal (Johnson & Downing, 1979). A classic example of the positive effects of anonymity is a study by Gergen, Gergen, and Barton (1973), in which individuals who met and conversed in a situation where they could not see one another, sitting in the dark, disclosed much more intimate details of their lives and of the self than did those who met and conversed in a lighted room. Indeed, those who were in the darkened condition left the encounter feeling more positively about the other person, compared to a control condition in which people interacted with the lights on.

Communicating with another via the Internet is much like being in a darkened room in that one cannot see the other person, nor can one be seen. The relative anonymity of Internet communication may allow individuals to take greater risks in making disclosures to their Internet friends than they would with someone they met in a more traditional, anonymous setting. Under the protective cloak of anonymity users can express the way they truly feel and think (Spears & Lea, 1994). If individuals do share more intimate confidences and do so earlier in a potential Internet relationship than in a potential real-life one, Internet relationships should develop intimacy and closeness more quickly than do offline relationships.

The assurance of anonymity gives one far greater play in identity construction than is conceivable in face-to-face encounters. One can, for instance, change one's gender, one's way of relating to others, and literally everything about oneself. Even those who do not log in from an anonymous account experience almost as much freedom in identity construction. On the Internet, where one can be anonymous, where one does not deal in face-to-face interactions, where one is simply responding to other anonymous people, the roles and characters one maintains for family, friends, and associates can be cast aside. One very important and interesting direction for future research, then, concerns the implications of this greater freedom in identity construction for the individual. As Turkle (1995) argued, the Internet provides a kind of experimental laboratory in which one can try out various possible selves (Markus & Nurius, 1986) and different roles in a safe and risk-free manner.

This ability to carve out different identities or roles may be particularly important for those who are role poor (i.e., they have few self-defining roles and identities) and for those who feel that important aspects of their identity are constrained in the relationships they maintain in the non-Internet world. People have a need to present their true or inner self to the outside world and to have others know them as they know themselves (e.g., Gollwitzer, 1986; McKenna & Bargh, 1998; Swann, 1983). When an individual is unable to do this in his or her current relationships, there is likely to be a strong motivation to establish relationships in which those needs and preferences can be expressed and accepted. The Internet makes it much easier for an individual to establish such new relationships and express these important aspects of identity without the risk of upsetting the balance of their offline relationships. We therefore expect to observe a great deal of the taking on of inner personae in Internet social interactions.

Numerous case studies demonstrate that individuals do indeed engage in a great deal of role playing and the expression of multiple identities on the Internet (e.g., Rheingold, 1993; Turkle, 1995). In a survey and in in-depth interviews, hundreds of Internet participants described how they try on different personalities and aspects of personality on the Internet that they feel are closed to them in their non-Internet relationships and situations (McKenna, 1998). What is not yet known are what possible consequences may result from such expression of multiple roles and identities online. For example, do individuals who express multiple roles and self-aspects on the Internet experience the same benefits of better health, greater life satisfaction, and the ability to better deal with stressful life changes as do those who can do the same in the non-Internet realm?

Under what conditions are individuals motivated or willing to incorporate their online identities into their offline world?

TURNING THE TABLES ON ATTRACTION

Considerable research has shown that physical appearance plays a major role in determining whether a relationship will even start between two people. If initial attraction is not there, that is often the end of the story (Hatfield, Aronson, Abrahams, & Rottman, 1966)—not only for potential intimate relationships but also for possible friendships as well (Hatfield & Sprecher, 1986).

On the Internet, however, physical attractiveness cannot be assessed, at least initially. Due to the fact that one cannot see the interaction partner, physical appearance does not stop potential relationships from getting off the ground. Liking, attraction, and friendship on the Internet, therefore, must be based on different grounds, such as similarity, values, and interests, or an engaging conversational style. As these are also powerful determinants of friendship and attraction (Byrne, 1971; Byrne, Clore, & Smeaton, 1986), the Internet may foster the formation of relationships that never would have begun in real life. In fact, relationships formed at these deeper levels may be more durable and important to the individual than those that form based on more superficial physical features.

Liking and Attraction

In first-time encounters, an individual will be liked better if the encounter takes place in an Internet chat room than if the two strangers were to meet face to face (McKenna & Bargh, 1999a, Study 3). Furthermore, this greater liking continued to hold (and indeed significantly increased for those who had first met on the Internet) after the interaction partners met a second time, this time in person. That is, those who first met on the Internet and then talked face to face liked one another more than did those who met face to face in both encounters. Even when participants thought that they had met two different people, one on the Internet and one face to face, they significantly liked the person they talked with on the Internet better: In actuality, these participants had talked with the same person both times.

What causes this increased liking and attraction when people meet on the Internet rather than face to face? Is it simply because physical appearance and non-verbal cues are absent and thus more attention and importance is placed on what the other person says than the way the other person looks? Research has long shown, of course, that first impressions are critical to subsequent interactions and that people are reluctant to change their initial assessment even when presented with new information (Asch, 1946; Belmore, 1987; Higgins & Bargh, 1987). Thus, one may speculate, if physical appearance does not interfere with initial liking and so a positive impression is formed, then once Internet interaction partners meet in person and physical appearance does come into play, it may carry far less weight. However, other factors may contribute or cause this increased liking—for example, the greater intimacy and consequent liking established through self-disclosure (Collins & Miller, 1994) due to the relative anonymity of the Internet relative to the face-to-face initial meeting. Teasing apart the causes for liking and attraction on the Internet will tell us not only about how and why Internet relationships form but also a great deal about the role played by physical attraction for relationships in general.

The Shared Virtual Space of the Internet (The Negation of Physical Proximity)

A considerable body of research has demonstrated that people are much more likely to begin relationships with others who are regularly in close physical proximity, and far less likely to do so with those who are even a short additional distance away (Festinger, 1950; Hays, 1984, 1985; Segal, 1974; Whitbeck & Hoyt, 1994). Similarly, Brockner and Swap (1976) found that the more a person had seen, but not interacted with, another person, the more likely he or she was to initiate an interaction. Berscheid and Reis (1998) noted that familiarity is the most basic determinant of attraction.

When taking part in social gathering places on the Internet (e.g., newsgroups, chat rooms, and MUDs) a person cannot physically see the other people present, but he or she nonetheless becomes familiar with these people through their nicknames, e-mail addresses, or character names. If one regularly joins a particular chat room or news group, one will begin to notice others who frequently post messages or pop in to chat and in turn will be noticed by others. The mere exposure effect (Zajonc, 1968) would predict that repeatedly being exposed to these Internet personae, perhaps even by just seeing their names again and again in the list of posters, will lead to positive feelings about the person behind the name. Despite the fact that these people may live on the far corners of the earth, when they are all gathered in this shared virtual space they may well be perceived and experienced as being in much closer proximity. After all, people often talk about how they get together to chat in a chat room, and use phrases such as "when I am in the MUD with my friends" as if they were all in one physical locality.

Research has shown that we tend to be more attracted to those who are similar to us and who share our opinions (Byrne, 1971; Newcomb, 1961). Indeed, even within married couples the more similar two people are the more compatible they are (Houts, Robins, & Huston, 1996) and the more likely they are to remain married (Byrne, 1997). When individuals begin to get to know one another in the traditional way, however (i.e., not via the Internet), it generally takes some time for them to establish if they have anything in common and to what extent. Hill, Rubin, and Peplau (1976) followed more than 200 dating couples who stated that they were "in love" for a period of 2 years. By the end of the 2 years, nearly 50% of the couples had broken up and the main reason given for the breakup was that they discovered that they had, in fact, different interests and attitudes.

On the Internet, however, the unique structure of newsgroups and Internet relay chat allows individuals to easily find others who share highly specialized interests. There may be, for example, 50,000 people in the world who share one's special passion, but these people are scattered across all five continents and dispersed among over 5 billion human beings. The Internet enables all of them (who have connections to the Internet) to come together in the same virtual space, transcending the problems of physical distance and wide dispersion, and of finding each other. Especially in more rural areas, if it were not for the Internet many people would never have the opportunity to share these important interests and passions with another person.

Thus, when a person enters a chat channel devoted to discussions about exotic butterfly collecting, he or she is already aware of sharing a base of knowledge and interest with the others who are on the channel. This allows them to cut to the chase (so to speak). They do not have to spend time discovering if they have any interests in common with the other participants, but rather can move quickly forward to find out what other key interests they may share. As one person who took part in a series of in-depth interviews put it:

It seems to be easier to recognize who is similar to you and who you'll like on the net. Maybe this is because chat rooms and newsgroups are more personalized (i.e. the "golf room" or "ferret lovers") and so you come into the room knowing you have something in common. (McKenna, 1998, p. 57)

A TIME AND PACE
UNLIKE FACE TO FACE

The timing and the pacing of social exchanges on the Internet differ from face-to-face and telephone interactions in several ways. First of all, it is not necessary for the other person to be online at the same time for a conversation to take place. Rather than having to engage in a groggy telephone conversation in the middle of the night to reach a friend who lives overseas, for instance, one can simply send an e-mail before going to bed and a reply is likely to be waiting in the morning. It is not unusual when engaging in an exchange via e-mail to wait minutes, hours, or days to receive the next piece in the conversation.

Unlike conversations that take place in person or on the telephone that require immediate and spontaneous responses, an individual can take as much time as he or she needs to respond to another person on the Internet. In an e-mail message or newsgroup post, individuals are able to carefully select what they want to say and how they want to say it. They can change and edit their messages before sending them. In contrast, in verbal exchanges, as soon as someone opens his or her mouth the cat is out of the bag and cannot, at least not easily, be put back in.

Finally, in electronic exchanges, a person can "hold the floor" to an extent quite unusual in verbal conversations. Relatively short explanations are the norm in spoken conversations and people often interrupt one another in midsentence. In e-mail or a newsgroup post, however, an individual can say as much or as little about a subject as he or she pleases, without fear of interruption before being able to fully make his or her point (McKenna, 1998).

These differences in timing and pacing provide an individual with a great deal more control over his or her side of a conversation. This higher degree of control, coupled with anonymity, seems to contribute to individuals taking greater risks and chances with making self-disclosures to those with whom they talk on the Internet compared to real life (McKenna, 1998).

INDIVIDUAL DIFFERENCES: WHO IS MORE LIKELY TO GO TO THE NET?

The Internet does not affect everyone in the same way. People vary as to what goals they have, or needs to be met, while using the Internet. In this focus on social interaction and relationship formation, the question becomes: Who will be more likely than others to seek out interactions and to form relationships with others on the Internet?

Social Anxiety

Forging social connections is quite difficult for those individuals who experience high levels of anxiety when in social situations (see Leary, 1983; Leary & Kowalski, 1995). Those who become anxious when meeting new people, talking to individuals they find attractive, or engaging in social group activities (e.g., parties or work-related social affairs), may be barred from the benefits of close personal relationships and group membership. Their basic needs for belonging and intimacy (Baumeister & Leary, 1995; Brewer, 1991) may therefore go unmet. On the Internet, however, many of the situational factors that foster feelings of social anxiety (e.g., talking to someone face to face, having to respond on the spot with verbal exchanges) are absent. Socially anxious individuals may thus be motivated to turn to the Internet as a means through which they can make social connections and meet these needs.

Indeed, recent research (McKenna & Bargh, 1999a, Study 1) has found that social anxiety is a strong predictor of who will be likely to form Internet relationships. Those who scored highly on the Interaction Anxiousness Scale (Leary, 1983) were found to be significantly more likely than their more socially comfortable counterparts to form relationships with others via the Internet. Moreover, socially anxious individuals were more likely to have formed very close Internet friendships and romantic relationships as opposed to weaker relationships (e.g., acquaintanceships).

What is not yet known, however, is whether the formation of such close relationships in the "virtual" realm will have the downstream results of lessening feelings of social anxiety in the offline realm. It may be that the successful formation of relationships in an online setting will lead to increases in the individual's feelings of self-confidence and self-efficacy. He or she may then become more confident of his or her social abilities when placed in face-to-face settings. As one participant who took part in a series of in-depth interviews (McKenna, 1998) stated:

> I used to be a complete disaster when it came to talking with women. In fact, I was so nervous about it that I would go to great lengths to avoid having to meet or talk with them, especially if I found them pretty or intelligent. On the Internet I discovered that talking with women was much easier and not only that, many of them seemed to really like me, found me humorous, and sought me out to talk to. I have become so much more confident with women and not just on-line. (p. 85)

Concluding that the Internet is a positive source of interactions for those who are socially anxious as a means for overcoming anxiety in meeting people assumes that the individual is still trying (and perhaps often failing) to interact with people in real life, outside of the Internet. As the McKenna and Bargh (1998) and McKenna (1998) research showed, in general people are motivated to bring their newly gained Internet identities and relationships into their real-life world. However, it may prove too seductive for some, perhaps the most socially anxious individuals, to escape the trauma of real-life interactions almost entirely, and live their entire social life on the Internet (see Green & Brock, 1998).

Loneliness

Although socially anxious individuals are often also lonely, it is also the case that there are many individuals who are lonely but not socially anxious. In some cases, loneliness may be a temporary condition, occasioned perhaps by changing jobs or moving to a new city. In others, it may be more chronic (e.g., for the homebound, for single working mothers with small children and little or no time left over for socializing). Loneliness is another individual difference that predicts who will form online relationships (McKenna & Bargh, 1999a, Study 1). The Internet would seem to be double edged when it comes to loneliness; lonely people may meet others over the Internet and so decrease their degree of loneliness, but protracted time on the Internet necessarily takes time away from one's existing, non-Internet relationships and could thus impact those, thus increasing loneliness eventually for some individuals (Kraut, Patterson, et al., 1998). Another critical question concerns the quality of relationships that currently lonely people form on the Internet, and their duration and quality.

RELATIONSHIP FORMATION ON THE INTERNET

The culmination of these various forces can be found in data on the formation of acquaintanceships, friendships, and even intimate relationships on the Internet. Due to the greater anonymity, differences in self-presentation, lack of physical gating features that prevent people from getting to know each other better, the fact that physical distance is no longer a barrier to meeting someone, and that the virtual shared space of the Internet brings together far-flung individuals with core shared interests and passions, one may expect the Internet to be a fertile ground for the formation and establishment of relationships. It is indeed that (McKenna, 1998; Parks & Floyd, 1995; Parks & Roberts, 1998). Parks and Roberts (1998), for example, found that 94% of surveyed participants in online text-based games had formed close friendships or romantic relationships with other players. A separate survey conducted with 600 randomly selected news group participants also showed that the formation of strong relationships is quite common on the Internet, with 51% reporting that they had formed close friendships and 35% that they had forged romantic relationships with others on the Internet (McKenna, 1998). It is important to note that, fully 79% of the survey respondents considered their Internet relationships to be as close, as real, and as important as their non-Internet relationships.

Two conclusions should be drawn from the aforementioned. First, far from being solely a cause of loneliness and isolation, people can and do use the Internet to meet others with similar interests and values, and get to know them in a safe environment at their own preferred pace. Second, these relationships are not of lesser quality than real-life relationships; instead, they become real-life relationships. People tend to bring their Internet friends and romantic interests into their real life by talking on the telephone, exchanging pictures and letters, eventually meeting many of them in person, and in many cases moving in with them. It is too early in the Internet game to tell, but it is possible that relationships formed on the Internet are deeper,

more stable and lasting than those formed in the real-world environment in which physical attractiveness and proximity are such powerful constraining and determining forces.

CONCLUSIONS

Plan 9 from Outer Space was Bela Lugosi's final movie (actually, he died while making it). Its rather simple plot was that aliens were trying to conquer the earth by turning freshly deceased humans into zombies that they could control by remote control (thanks to their advanced technology). What does this have to do with this article? Simply that the Internet does not, contrary to current popular opinion, have by itself the power or ability to control people, to turn them into addicted zombies, or make them dispositionally sad or lonely (or, for that matter, happy or popular), and neither does the telephone, or television, or movies. Rather, the Internet is one of several social domains in which an individual can live his or her life, and attempt to fulfill his or her needs and goals, whatever they happen to be (see McKenna & Bargh, 1999b).

We sought in the first part of this article to identify and highlight the key situational variables that make the Internet a unique and special social domain: anonymity, the mitigation of physical proximity, and physical attractiveness as gating features to relationship formation, and the enhanced personal control over the time and pacing of interpersonal interactions and communications. These are important situational variables but they do not operate in isolation, as main effects on all Internet users; rather, they have their effect in interaction with the individual's needs and purposes. Like the communications advances before it, the Internet will always and only be what individuals make of it.

NOTE

1. This is a design problem that, in addition to the nonrepresentative and nonrandomly selected sample of civic leaders and their teenage children (with very few people between the ages of 22–40 years old) who as of 1995 had no computer in the home (Kraut, Kiesler, Mukopadhyay, Scherlis, & Patterson, 1998), makes it quite difficult to draw any conclusions about the social consequences of Internet use for the general population (see also Caruso, 1998).

REFERENCES

Asch, S. E. (1946). Forming impressions of personality. *Journal of Abnormal and Social Psychology, 41,* 258–290.

Bargh, J. A. (1988). Automatic information processing: Implications for communication and affect. In L. Donohew, H. E. Sypher, & E. T. Higgins (Eds.), *Communication, social cognition, and affect* (pp. 9–32). Hillsdale, NJ: Lawrence Erlbaum Associates, Inc.

Baumeister, R. F., & Leary, M. R. (1995). The need to belong: Desire for interpersonal attachments as a fundamental human motivation. *Psychological Bulletin, 117,* 497–529.

Belmore, S. M. (1987). Determinants of attention during impression formation. *Journal of Experimental Psychology: Learning, Memory, and Cognition, 13,* 480–489.

Berscheid, E., & Reis, H. T. (1998). Attraction and close relationships. In D. T. Gilbert, S. T. Fiske, & G. Lindzey (Eds.), *Handbook of social psychology* (4th ed., pp. 193–281). New York: McGraw-Hill.

Blumler, J. (1979). The role of theory in uses and gratifications studies. *Communication Research, 6,* 9–33.

Blumler, J., & Katz, E. (1974). *The uses of mass communications.* Thousand Oaks, CA: Sage.

Brewer, M. B. (1991). The social self: On being the same and different at the same time. *Personality and Social Psychology Bulletin, 17,* 475–482.

Brockner, J., & Swap, W. C. (1976). Effects of repeated exposure and attitudinal similarity on self disclosure and interpersonal attraction. *Journal of Personality and Social Psychology, 33,* 531–540.

Byrne, D. (1971). *The attraction paradigm.* New York: Academic.

Byrne, D. (1997). An overview (and underview) of research and theory within the attraction paradigm. *Journal of Social and Personal Relationships, 14,* 417–431.

Byrne, D., Clore, G. L., & Smeaton, G. (1986). The attraction hypothesis: Do similar attitudes affect anything? *Journal of Personality and Social Psychology, 51,* 1167–1170.

Caruso, D. (1998, September 14). Critics pick apart study on Internet and depression. *New York Times,* p. C5.

Clausing, J. (1999, May 20). Congressional Internet debate turns to issues of violence. *New York Times* [Internet edition], p. 1.

Collins, N. L., & Miller, L. C. (1994). Self-disclosure and liking: A meta-analytic review. *Psychological Bulletin, 116,* 457–475.

Culan, M. J., & Markus, M. L. (1987). Information technologies. In F. Jablin, L. L. Putnam, K. Roberts, & L. Porter (Eds.), *Handbook of organizational communication* (pp. 420–443). Newbury Park, CA: Sage.

D'Amico, M. L. (1998, December 7). Internet has become a necessity, U.S. poll shows. *CNNinteractive* [Internet magazine], p. 1. Retrieved June 20, 1999 from the World Wide Web: http://cnn.com/tech/computing/9812/07/neednet.idg/index.htm

Diener, E. (1980). De-individuation: The absence of self-awareness and self-regulation in group members. In P. Paulus (Ed.), *The psychology of group influence* (pp. 1160–1171). Hillsdale, NJ: Lawrence Erlbaum Associates, Inc.

Dubrovsky, V. J., Kiesler, S. B., & Sethna, B. N. (1991). The equalization phenomenon: Status effects in computer-mediated and face-to-face decision-making groups. *Human-Computer Interaction, 6,* 119–146.

Festinger, L. (1950). Informal social communication. *Psychological Review, 57,* 271–282.

Frankel, M. S., & Teich, A. (Eds.). (1999). Anonymous communication on the Internet [Special issue]. *The Information Society, 15*(2).

Friedman, T. L. (1999). *The Lexus and the olive tree.* New York: Farrar, Straus & Giroux.

Fuller, J. (1996). *News values.* Chicago: University of Chicago Press.

Gans, H. J. (1979). *Deciding what's news: A study of CBS Evening News, NBC Nightly News, Newsweek, and Time.* New York: Random House.

Gergen, K. J., Gergen, M. M., & Barton, W. H. (1973). Deviance in the dark. *Psychology Today, 7,* 129–130.

Gollwitzer, P. M. (1986). Striving for specific identities: The social reality of self-symbolizing. In R. Baumeister (Ed.), *Public self and private self* (pp. 143–159). New York: Springer.

Green, M., & Brock, T. (1998). Trust, mood, and outcomes of friendship determine preferences for real versus ersatz social capital. *Political Psychology, 19,* 527–544.

Harmon, A. (1998, August 30). Sad, lonely world discovered in cyberspace. *New York Times,* p. A1.

Hatfield, E., Aronson, E., Abrahams, D., & Rottman, L. (1966). The importance of physical attractiveness in dating behavior. *Journal of Personality and Social Psychology, 4,* 508–516.

Hatfield, E., & Sprecher, S. (1986). *Mirror, mirror: The importance of looks in everyday life.* Albany: State University of New York Press.

Hays, R. B. (1984). The development and maintenance of friendship. *Journal of Social and Personal Relationships, 1,* 75–98.

Hays, R. B. (1985). A longitudinal study of friendship and development. *Journal of Personality and Social Psychology, 48,* 909–924.

Higgins, E. T., & Bargh, J. A. (1987). Social cognition and social perception. *Annual Review of Psychology, 38,* 369–425.

Hill, C. T., Rubin, Z., & Peplau, L. A. (1976). Breakups before marriage: The end of 103 affairs. *Journal of Social Issues, 32,* 147–168.

Hoffman, D. L., & Novak, T. P. (1995, July 2). *A detailed analysis of the conceptual, logical, and methodological flaws in the article: "Marketing pornography on the information superhighway."* Available: http://ecommerce.vanderbilt.edu/cyberporn.debate.html

Houts, R. M., Robins, E., & Huston, T. L. (1996). Compatibility and the development of premarital relationships. *Journal of Marriage and the Family, 58,* 7–20.

Johnson, R. D., & Downing, L. L. (1979). Deindividuation and valence of cues: Effects on prosocial and antisocial behavior. *Journal of Personality and Social Psychology, 37,* 1532–1538.

Katz, E. (1959). Mass communication research and the study of culture. *Studies in Public Communication, 2,* 1–6.

Katz, J. E., & Aspden, P. (1997). A nation of strangers? *Communications of the ACM, 40,* 81–86.

Kiesler, S., Siegal, J., & McGuire, T. (1984). Social psychological aspects of computer-mediated communication. *American Psychologist, 39,* 1123–1134.

Kraut, R., Kiesler, S., Mukopadhyay, T., Scherlis, W., & Patterson, M. (1998). Social impact of the Internet: What does it mean? *Communications of the ACM, 41,* 21–22.

Kraut, R., Mukopadhyay, T., Szczypula, J., Kiesler, S., & Scherlis, W. (1998). Communication and information: Alternative uses of the Internet in households. In *Proceedings of the CHI 98* (pp. 368–383). New York: ACM.

Kraut, R., Patterson, M., Lundmark, V., Kiesler, S., Mukopadhyay, T., & Scherlis, W. (1998). Internet paradox: A social technology that reduces social involvement and psychological well-being? *American Psychologist, 53,* 1017–1031.

Leary, M. R. (1983). Social anxiousness: The construct and its measurement. *Journal of Personality Assessment, 47,* 66–75.

Leary, M. R., & Kowalski, R. M. (1995). *Social anxiety.* New York: Guilford.

Markus, H. R., & Nurius, P. (1986). Possible selves. *American Psychologist, 41,* 954–969.

McKenna, K. Y. A. (1998). *The computers that bind: Relationship formation on the Internet.* Unpublished doctoral dissertation, Ohio University.

McKenna, K. Y. A., & Bargh, J. A. (1998). Coming out in the age of the Internet: Identity "de-marginalization" through virtual group participation. *Journal of Personality and Social Psychology, 75,* 681–694.

McKenna, K. Y. A., & Bargh, J. A. (1999a). *Can you see the real me? Relationship formation and development on the Internet.* Manuscript submitted for publication.

McKenna, K. Y. A., & Bargh, J. A. (1999b). Causes and consequences of social interaction on the Internet: A conceptual framework. *Media Psychology, 1,* 249–270.

Mendels, P. (1999, July 21). The two faces of on-line anonymity. *New York Times* [Internet edition]. Available: http://www.nytimes.com/library/tech/99/07/cyber/articles/21anonymity.html

Mischel, W. (1973). Toward a cognitive social learning reconceptualization of personality. *Psychological Review, 80,* 252–283.

Newcomb, T. M. (1961). *The acquaintance process.* New York: Holt, Rinehart & Winston.

Parks, M. R., & Floyd, K. (1995). Making friends in cyberspace. *Journal of Communication, 46,* 80–97.

Parks, M. R., & Roberts, L. D. (1998). "Making MOOsic": The development of personal relationships on line and a comparison to their off-line counterparts. *Journal of Social and Personal Relationships, 15,* 517–537.

Rheingold, H. (1993). *The virtual community: Homesteading on the electronic frontier.* New York: Harper & Row.

Rimm, M. (1995). Marketing pornography on the information superhighway. *Georgetown Law Review, 83,* 1839–1934.

Rossney, R. (1995, July 13). Time's story on cyberporn of questionable validity. *San Francisco Chronicle,* p. C3. Available: http://www.sfgate.com/net/rossney/0713.htm

Segal, M. W. (1974). Alphabet and attraction: An unobtrusive measure of the effect of propinquity in a field setting. *Journal of Personality and Social Psychology, 30,* 654–657.

Siegal, J., Dubrovsky, V., Kiesler, S., & McGuire, T. W. (1986). Group processes in computer-mediated communication. *Organizational Behavior and Human Decision Processes, 37,* 157–187.

Sleek, S. (1998). Isolation increases with Internet use. *American Psychological Association Monitor, 29,* 1.

Spears, R., & Lea, M. (1994). Panacea or panopticon? The hidden power in computer-mediated communication. *Communication Research, 21,* 427–459.

Swann, W. B. (1983). Self-verification: Bringing social reality into harmony with the self. In J. Suls & A. G. Greenwald (Eds.), *Psychological perspectives on the self* (Vol. 2, pp. 33–66). Hillsdale, NJ: Lawrence Erlbaum Associates, Inc.

Turkle, S. (1995). *Life on the screen: Identity in the age of the Internet.* New York: Simon & Schuster.

Whitbeck, L. B., & Hoyt, D. R. (1994). Social prestige and assortitative mating: A comparison of students from 1956 and 1988. *Journal of Social and Personal Relationships, 11,* 137–145.

Young, K. (1998). *Caught in the net: How to recognize the signs of Internet addiction and a winning strategy for recovery.* New York: Wiley.

Zajonc, R. B. (1968). Attitudinal effects of mere exposure. *Journal of Personality and Social Psychology Monograph, 9* (Pt. 2).

Zimbardo, P. (1970). The human choice: Individuation, reason, and order versus deindividuation, impulse, and chaos. In

W. J. Arnold & D. Levine (Eds.), *Nebraska symposium on motivation* (Vol. 17, pp. 237–307). Lincoln: University of Nebraska Press.

RELATED LINKS

- The HomeNet Project (http://homenet.hcii.cs.cmu.edu/progress)
- HomeNetToo Project (http://www.msu.edu/user/jackso67/homenettoo)
- Oxford Internet Institute (http://www.oii.ox.ac.uk)
- Association of Internet Researchers (http://www.aoir.org)

FOR FURTHER RESEARCH

To find out more about the topics discussed in this reading, use InfoTrac College Edition. Type in keywords and subject terms such as "Internet addiction," "HomeNet study," and "online relationships." You can access InfoTrac College Edition from the Wadsworth/Thomson Communication Café homepage: http://communication.wadsworth.com.

Reading 8-3

Absolute PowerPoint: Can a Software Package Edit Our Thoughts?

Ian Parker

EDITOR'S NOTE

With the wholesale adoption of computer technology by business, education, and government has come the rise of presentation software used to communicate messages, ranging from the ridiculous to the sublime, to a waiting audience. By far the most widely used presentation package is PowerPoint, which comes bundled with Microsoft's Office program and can be found on some 400 million PCs globally. According to Microsoft estimates, some 30 million PowerPoint presentations are made each day. But as PowerPoint has grown in popularity, so has criticism about the software for encouraging triteness and redundancy; even worse, critics claim, the software reduces human contact and expression to a series of easily digested but meaningless bullet points. At the heart of criticism about the program is the software's AutoContent Wizard, which provides templates such as Managing Organizational Change or Communicating Bad News that are "so close to finished presentations you barely need to do more than add your company logo." As this reading from The New Yorker *observes, PowerPoint both "lifts the floor" of public speaking for bad presenters and "lowers the ceiling" for good communicators, efficiently delivering content but removing much of the thinking in the process.*

CONSIDER

1. According to the reading, what exactly is lost when PowerPoint is used as a medium of communication?

2. On the other hand, what are the benefits of using PowerPoint for giving shape to and structuring arguments?

3. Do you agree with the author that using PowerPoint teaches us not only how to organize and present infor-
    mation but how to look at the world? Why or why not?

Before there were presentations, there were conversations, which were a little like presentations but used
fewer bullet points, and no one had to dim the lights.
A woman we can call Sarah Wyndham, a defense-
industry consultant living in Alexandria, Virginia, recently began to feel that her two daughters weren't listening when she asked them to clean their bedrooms
and do their chores. So, one morning, she sat down
at her computer, opened Microsoft's PowerPoint program, and typed:

Family Matters
An approach for positive change to the
Wyndham family team

On a new page, she wrote:

- Lack of organization leads to confusion and
  frustration among all family members.

- Disorganization is detrimental to grades and
  to your social life.

- Disorganization leads to inefficiencies that
  impact the entire family.

Instead of pleading for domestic harmony, Sarah
Wyndham was pitching for it. Soon she had eighteen
pages of large type, supplemented by a color photograph of a generic happy family riding bicycles, and,
on the final page, a drawing key—the key to success.
The briefing was given only once, last fall. The experience was so upsetting to her children that the threat
of a second showing was enough to make one of the
Wyndham girls burst into tears.

PowerPoint, which can be found on two hundred
and fifty million computers around the world, is software you impose on other people. It allows you to
arrange text and graphics in a series of pages, which
you can project, slide by slide, from a laptop computer
onto a screen, or print as a booklet (as Sarah Wyndham
did). The usual metaphor for everyday software is the
tool, but that doesn't seem to be right here. Power-

Point is more like a suit of clothes, or a car, or plastic
surgery. You take it out with you. You are judged by
it—you insist on being judged by it. It is by definition a social instrument, turning middle managers into
bullet-point dandies.

But PowerPoint also has a private, interior influence. It edits ideas. It is, almost surreptitiously, a business manual as well as a business suit, with an opinion
—an oddly pedantic, prescriptive opinion—about the
way we should think. It helps you make a case, but
it also makes its own case: about how to organize information, how much information to organize, how
to look at the world. One feature of this is the Auto-
Content Wizard, which supplies templates—"Managing Organizational Change" or "Communicating Bad
News," say—that are so close to finished presentations
you barely need to do more than add your company
logo. The "Motivating a Team" template, for example,
includes a slide headed "Conduct a Creative Thinking
Session":

Ask: In what ways can we . . . ?

- Assess the situation. Get the facts.

- Generate possible solutions with green light,
  nonjudgmental thinking.

- Select the best solution.

The final injunction is "Have an inspirational close."
It's easy to avoid these extreme templates—many
people do—as well as embellishments like clip art, animations, and sound effects. But it's hard to shake off
AutoContent's spirit: even the most easygoing Power-
Point template insists on a heading followed by bullet
points, so that the user is shepherded toward a staccato,
summarizing frame of mind, of the kind parodied, for
example, in a PowerPoint Gettysburg Address posted
on the Internet: "Dedicate portion of field—fitting!"

Because PowerPoint can be an impressive antidote
to fear—converting public-speaking dread into moviemaking pleasure—there seems to be no great impulse
to fight this influence, as you might fight the unre-
lenting animated paperclip in Microsoft Word. Rather,
PowerPoint's restraints seem to be soothing—so much
so that where Microsoft has not written rules, businesses write them for themselves. A leading U.S. com-

From "Absolute PowerPoint: Can a Software Package Edit Our
Thoughts?" by Ian Parker, *The New Yorker,* May 28, 2001, An-
nals of Business Section, pp. 76–87. Copyright © 2001 by Ian
Parker. Reprinted with permission.

puter manufacturer has distributed guidelines to its employees about PowerPoint presentations, insisting on something it calls the "Rules of Seven": "Seven bullets or lines per page, seven words per line."

Today, after Microsoft's decade of dizzying growth, there are great tracts of corporate America where to appear at a meeting without PowerPoint would be unwelcome and vaguely pretentious, like wearing no shoes. In darkened rooms at industrial plants and ad agencies, at sales pitches and conferences, this is how people are communicating: no paragraphs, no pronouns—the world condensed into a few upbeat slides, with seven or so words on a line, seven or so lines on a slide. And now it's happening during sermons and university lectures and family arguments, too. A New Jersey PowerPoint user recently wrote in an online discussion, "Last week I caught myself planning out (in my head) the slides I would need to explain to my wife why we couldn't afford a vacation this year." Somehow, a piece of software designed, fifteen years ago, to meet a simple business need has become a way of organizing thought at kindergarten show-and-tells. "Oh, Lord," one of the early developers said to me. "What have we done?"

Forty years ago, a workplace meeting was a discussion with your immediate colleagues. Engineers would meet with other engineers and talk in the language of engineering. A manager might make an appearance—acting as an interpreter, a bridge to the rest of the company—but no one from the marketing or production or sales department would be there. Somebody might have gone to the trouble of cranking out mimeographs—that would be the person with purple fingers.

But the structure of American industry changed in the nineteen-sixties and seventies. Clifford Nass, who teaches in the Department of Communication at Stanford, says, "Companies weren't discovering things in the laboratory and then trying to convince consumers to buy them. They were discovering—or creating—consumer demand, figuring out what they can convince consumers they need, then going to the laboratory and saying, 'Build this!' People were saying, 'We can create demand. Even if demand doesn't exist, we know how to market this.' SpaghettiOs is the great example. The guy came up with the jingle first: 'The neat round spaghetti you can eat with a spoon.' And he said, 'Hey! Make spaghetti in the shape of small circles!'"

As Jerry Porras, a professor of organizational behavior and change at Stanford Graduate School of Business, says, "When technologies no longer just drove the product out but the customer [began having influence], then you had to know what the customer wanted, and that meant a lot more interaction inside the company." There are new conversations: Can we make this? How do we sell this if we make it? Can we do it in blue?

America began to go to more meetings. By the early nineteen-eighties, when the story of PowerPoint starts, employees had to find ways to talk to colleagues from other departments, colleagues who spoke a different language, brought together by SpaghettiOs and by the simple fact that technology was generating more information. There was more to know and, as the notion of a job for life eroded, more reason to know it.

In this environment, visual aids were bound to thrive. In 1975, fifty thousand overhead projectors were sold in America. By 1985, that figure had increased to more than a hundred and twenty thousand. Overheads, which were developed in the mid-forties for use by the police, and were then widely used in bowling alleys and schools, did not fully enter business life until the mid-seventies, when a transparency film that could survive the heat of a photocopier became available. Now anything on a sheet of paper could be transferred to an overhead slide. Overheads were cheaper than the popular alternative, the 35-mm slide (which needed graphics professionals), and they were easier to use. But they restricted you to your typewriter's font—rather, your secretary's typewriter's font—or your skill with Letraset and a felt-tipped pen. A businessman couldn't generate a handsome, professional-looking font in his own office.

In 1980, though, it was clear that a future of widespread personal computers—and laser printers and screens that showed the very thing you were about to print—was tantalizingly close. In the Mountain View, California, laboratory of Bell-Northern Research, computer research scientists had set up a great mainframe computer, a graphics workstation, a phototypesetter, and the earliest Canon laser printer, which was the size of a bathtub and took six men to carry into the building—together, a cumbersome approximation of what would later fit on a coffee table and cost a thousand dollars. With much trial and error, and jogging from one room to another, you could use this collection of machines as a kind of word processor.

Whitfield Diffie had access to this equipment. A mathematician, a former peacenik, and an enemy of exclusive government control of encryption systems, Diffie had secured a place for himself in computing legend in 1976, when he and a colleague, Martin Hellman, announced the discovery of a new method of protecting secrets electronically—public-key cryptography. At Bell-Northern, Diffie was researching the security of telephone systems. In 1981, preparing to give a presentation with 35-mm slides, he wrote a little program, tinkering with some graphics software designed by a B.N.R. colleague, that allowed you to draw a black frame on a piece of paper. Diffie expanded it so that the page could show a number of frames, and text inside each frame, with space for commentary around them. In other words, he produced a storyboard—a slide show on paper—that could be sent to the designers who made up the slides, and that would also serve as a script for his lecture. (At this stage, he wasn't photocopying what he had produced to make overhead transparencies, although scientists in other facilities were doing that.) With a few days' effort, Diffie had pointed the way to PowerPoint.

Diffie has long gray hair and likes to wear English suits. Today, he works for Sun Microsystems, as an internal consultant on encryption matters. I recently had lunch with him in Palo Alto, and for the first time he publicly acknowledged his presence at the birth of PowerPoint. It was an odd piece of news: as if Lenin had invented the stapler. Yes, he said, PowerPoint was "based on" his work at B.N.R. This is not of great consequence to Diffie, whose reputation in his own field is so high that he is one of the few computer scientists to receive erotically charged fan mail. He said he was "mildly miffed" to have made no money from the PowerPoint connection, but he has no interest in beginning a feud with an old friend. "Bob was the one who had the vision to understand how important it was to the world," he said. "And I didn't."

Bob is Bob Gaskins, the man who has to take final responsibility for the drawn blinds of high-rise offices around the world and the bullet points dashing across computer screens inside. His account of PowerPoint's parentage does not exactly match Diffie's, but he readily accepts his former colleague as "my inspiration." In the late nineteen-seventies and early eighties, Gaskins was B.N.R.'s head of computer science research. A former Berkeley Ph.D. student, he had a family background in industrial photographic supplies and grew up around overhead projectors and inks and gels. In 1982, he returned from a six-month overseas business trip and, with a vivid sense of the future impact of the Apple Macintosh and of Microsoft's Windows (both of which were in development), he wrote a list of fifty commercial possibilities—Arabic typesetting, menus,

signs. And then he looked around his own laboratory and realized what had happened while he was away: following Diffie's lead, his colleagues were trying to make overheads to pitch their projects for funding, despite the difficulties of using the equipment. (What you saw was not at all what you got.) "Our mainframe was buckling under the load," Gaskins says.

He now had his idea: a graphics program that would work with Windows and the Macintosh, and that would put together, and edit, a string of single pages, or "slides." In 1984, he left B.N.R., joined an ailing Silicon Valley software firm, Forethought, in exchange for a sizeable share of the company, and hired a software developer, Dennis Austin. They began work on a program called Presenter. After a trademark problem, and an epiphany Gaskins had in the shower, Presenter became PowerPoint.

Gaskins is a precise, bookish man who lives with his wife in a meticulously restored and furnished nineteenth-century house in the Fillmore district of San Francisco. He has recently discovered an interest in antique concertinas. When I visited him, he was persuaded to play a tune, and he gave me a copy of a forthcoming paper he had co-written: "A Wheatstone Twelve-Sided 'Edeophone' Concertina with Pre-MacCann Chromatic Duet Fingering." Gaskins is skeptical about the product that PowerPoint has become—AutoContent and animated fades between slides—but he is devoted to the simpler thing that it was, and he led me through a well-preserved archive of PowerPoint memorabilia, including the souvenir program for the PowerPoint reunion party, in 1997, which had a quiz filled with in-jokes about font size and programming languages. He also found an old business plan from 1984. One phrase—the only one in italics—read, "Allows the content-originator to control the presentation." For Gaskins, that had always been the point: to get rid of the intermediaries—graphic designers—and never mind the consequences. Whenever colleagues sought to restrict the design possibilities of the program (to make a design disaster less likely), Gaskins would overrule them, quoting Thoreau: "I came into this world, not chiefly to make this a good place to live in, but to live in it, be it good or bad."

PowerPoint 1.0 went on sale in April, 1987—available only for the Macintosh, and only in black-and-white. It generated text-and-graphics pages that a photocopier could turn into overhead transparencies. (This was before laptop computers and portable projectors made PowerPoint a tool for live electronic presentations. Gaskins thinks he may have been the first person to use the program in the modern way, in a Paris hotel in 1992—which is like being the first person ever to tap a microphone and say, "Can you hear me at the back?") The Macintosh market was small and specialized, but within this market PowerPoint—the first product of its kind—was a hit. "I can't describe how wonderful it was," Gaskins says. "When we demonstrated at trade shows, we were mobbed." Shortly after the launch, Forethought accepted an acquisition offer of fourteen million dollars from Microsoft. Microsoft paid cash and allowed Bob Gaskins and his colleagues to remain partly self-governing in Silicon Valley, far from the Microsoft campus, in Redmond, Washington. Microsoft soon regretted the terms of the deal; PowerPoint workers became known for a troublesome independence of spirit (and for rewarding themselves, now and then, with beautifully staged parties—caviar, string quartets, Renaissance-period fancy dress).

PowerPoint had been created, in part, as a response to the new corporate world of interdepartmental communication. Those involved with the program now experienced the phenomenon at first hand. In 1990, the first PowerPoint for Windows was launched, alongside Windows 3.0. And PowerPoint quickly became what Gaskins calls "a cog in the great machine." The PowerPoint programmers were forced to make unwelcome changes, partly because in 1990 Word, Excel, and PowerPoint began to be integrated into Microsoft Office—a strategy that would eventually make PowerPoint invincible—and partly in response to market research. AutoContent was added in the mid-nineties, when Microsoft learned that some would-be presenters were uncomfortable with a blank PowerPoint page —it was hard to get started. "We said, 'What we need is some automatic content!'" a former Microsoft developer recalls, laughing. "'Punch the button and you'll have a presentation.'" The idea, he thought, was "crazy." And the name was meant as a joke. But Microsoft took the idea and kept the name—a rare example of a product named in outright mockery of its target customers.

Gaskins left PowerPoint in 1992, and many of his colleagues followed soon after. Now rich from Microsoft stock, and beginning the concertina-collecting phase of their careers, they watched as their old product made its way into the heart of American business culture. By 1993, PowerPoint had a majority share of the presentation market. In 1995, the average user created four and a half presentations a month. Three years later, the monthly average was nine. PowerPoint began to appear in cartoon strips and everyday conversation.

A few years ago, Bob Gaskins was at a presentations-heavy conference in Britain. The organizer brought the proceedings to a sudden stop, saying, "I've just been told that the inventor of PowerPoint is in the audience—will he please identify himself so we can recognize his contribution to the advancement of science?" Gaskins stood up. The audience laughed and applauded.

Cathleen Belleville, a former graphic designer who worked at PowerPoint as a product planner from 1989 to 1995, was amazed to see a clip-art series she had created become modern business icons. The images were androgynous silhouette stick figures (she called them Screen Beans), modelled on a former college roommate: a little figure clicking its heels; another with an inspirational light bulb above its head. One Screen Bean, the patron saint of PowerPoint—a figure that stands beneath a question mark, scratching its head in puzzlement—is so popular that a lawyer at a New York firm who has seen many PowerPoint presentations claims never to have seen one without the head-scratcher. Belleville herself has seen her Beans all over the world, reprinted on baseball caps, blown up fifteen feet high in a Hamburg bank. "I told my mom, 'You know, my artwork is in danger of being more famous than the "Mona Lisa."'" Above the counter in a laundromat on Third Avenue in New York, a sign explains that no responsibility can be taken for deliveries to doorman buildings. And there, next to the words, is the famous puzzled figure. It is hard to understand the puzzlement. Doorman? Delivery? But perhaps this is simply how a modern poster clears its throat: Belleville has created the international sign for "sign."

According to Microsoft estimates, at least thirty million PowerPoint presentations are made every day. The program has about ninety-five per cent of the presentations-software market. And so perhaps it was inevitable that it would migrate out of business and into other areas of our lives. I recently spoke to Sew Meng Chung, a Malaysian research engineer living in Singapore who got married in 1999. He told me that, as his guests took their seats for a wedding party in the Goodwood Park Hotel, they were treated to a PowerPoint presentation: a hundred and thirty photographs—one fading into the next every four or five seconds, to musical accompaniment. "They were baby photos, and courtship photos, and photos taken with our friends and family," he told me.

I also spoke to Terry Taylor, who runs a Web site called eBibleTeacher.com, which supplies materials for churches that use electronic visual aids. "Jesus was a storyteller, and he gave graphic images," Taylor said. "He would say, 'Consider the lilies of the field, how they grow,' and all indications are that there were lilies in the field when he was talking, you know. He used illustrations." Taylor estimates that fifteen per cent of American churches now have video projectors, and many use PowerPoint regularly for announcements, for song lyrics, and to accompany preaching. (Taylor has seen more than one sermon featuring the head-scratching figure.) Visitors to Taylor's site can download photographs of locations in the Holy Land, as well as complete PowerPoint sermons—for example, "Making Your Marriage Great":

- Find out what you are doing to harm your marriage and heal it.
- Financial irresponsibility
- Temper
- Pornography
- Substance abuse
- You name it!

When PowerPoint is used to flash hymn lyrics, or make a quick pitch to a new client, or produce an eye-catching laundromat poster, it's easy to understand the enthusiasm of, say, Tony Kurz, the vice president for sales and marketing of a New York-based Internet company, who told me, "I love PowerPoint. It's a brilliant application. I can take you through at exactly the pace I want to take you." There are probably worse ways to transmit fifty or a hundred words of text, or information that is mainly visual—ways that involve more droning, more drifting. And PowerPoint demands at least some rudimentary preparation: a PowerPoint presenter is, by definition, not thinking about his or her material for the very first time. Steven Pinker, the author of *The Language Instinct* and a psychology professor at the Massachusetts Institute of Technology, says that PowerPoint can give visual shape to an argument. "Language is a linear medium: one damn word after another," he says. "But ideas are multidimensional . . . When properly employed, PowerPoint makes the logical structure of an argument more transparent. Two channels sending the same information are better than one."

Still, it's hard to be perfectly comfortable with a product whose developers occasionally find themselves trying to suppress its use. Jolene Rocchio, who is a product planner for Microsoft Office (and is upbeat about PowerPoint in general), told me that, at a recent meeting of a nonprofit organization in San Francisco, she argued against a speaker's using PowerPoint at a future conference. "I said, 'I think we just need her to get up and speak.'" On an earlier occasion, Rocchio said, the same speaker had tried to use PowerPoint and the projector didn't work, "and everybody was, like, cheering. They just wanted to hear this woman speak, and they wanted it to be from her heart. And the PowerPoint almost alienated her audience."

This is the most common complaint about PowerPoint. Instead of human contact, we are given human display. "I think that we as a people have become unaccustomed to having real conversations with each other, where we actually give and take to arrive at a new answer. We present to each other, instead of discussing," Cathy Belleville says. Tad Simons, the editor of the magazine *Presentations* (whose second-grade son used PowerPoint for show-and-tell), is familiar with the sin of triple delivery, where precisely the same text is seen on the screen, spoken aloud, and printed on the handout in front of you (the "leave-behind," as it is known in some circles). "The thing that makes my heart sing is when somebody presses the 'B' button and the screen goes black and you can actually talk to the person," Simons told me.

In 1997, Sun Microsystems' chairman and CEO, Scott McNealy, "banned" PowerPoint (a ban widely disregarded by his staff). The move might have been driven, in part, by Sun's public relations needs as a Microsoft rival, but, according to McNealy, there were genuine productivity issues. "Why did we ban it? Let me put it this way: If I want to tell my forty thousand employees to attack, the word 'attack' in ASCII is forty-eight bits. As a Microsoft Word document, it's 90,112 bits. Put that same word in a PowerPoint slide and it becomes 458,048 bits. That's a pig through the python when you try to send it over the Net." McNealy's concern is shared by the American military. Enormously elaborate PowerPoint files (generated by presentation-obsessives—so-called PowerPoint Rangers) were said to be clogging up the military's bandwidth. Last year, to the delight of many under his command, General Henry H. Shelton, the chairman of the Joint Chiefs of Staff, issued an order to U.S. bases around the world insisting on simpler presentations.

PowerPoint was developed to give public speakers control over design decisions. But it's possible that those speakers should be making other, more important decisions. "In the past, I think we had an inefficient system, where executives passed all of their work to secretaries," Cathy Belleville says. "But now we've got highly paid people sitting there formatting slides—spending hours formatting slides—because it's more fun to do that than concentrate on what you're going to say. It would be much more efficient to offload that work onto someone who could do it in a tenth of the time, and be paid less. Millions of executives around the world are sitting there going, 'Arial? Times Roman? Twenty-four point? Eighteen point?'"

In the glow of a PowerPoint show, the world is condensed, simplified, and smoothed over—yet bright and hyperreal—like the cityscape background in a PlayStation motor race. PowerPoint is strangely adept at disguising the fragile foundations of a proposal, the emptiness of a business plan; usually, the audience is respectfully still (only venture capitalists dare to dictate the pace of someone else's slide show), and, with the visual distraction of a dancing pie chart, a speaker can quickly move past the laughable flaw in his argument. If anyone notices, it's too late—the narrative presses on.

Last year, three researchers at Arizona State University, including Robert Cialdini, a professor of psychology and the author of *Influence: Science and Practice,* conducted an experiment in which they presented three groups of volunteers with information about Andrew, a fictional high-school student under consideration for a university football scholarship. One group was given Andrew's football statistics typed on a piece of paper. The second group was shown bar graphs. Those in the third group were given a PowerPoint presentation, in which animated bar graphs grew before their eyes.

Given Andrew's record, what kind of prospect was he? According to Cialdini, when Andrew was Power-Pointed, viewers saw him as a greater potential asset to the football team. The first group rated Andrew four and a half on a scale of one to seven; the second rated him five; and the PowerPoint group rated him six. PowerPoint gave him power. The experiment was repeated, with three groups of sports fans that were accustomed to digesting sports statistics; this time, the first two groups gave Andrew the same rating. But the group that saw the PowerPoint presentation still couldn't resist it. Again, Andrew got a six. PowerPoint seems to be a way for organizations to turn expensive, expert decision-makers into novice decision-makers. "It's frightening," Cialdini says. He always preferred to use slides when he spoke to business groups, but one high-tech company recently hinted that his authority

suffered as a result. "They said, 'You know what, Bob? You've got to get into PowerPoint, otherwise people aren't going to respond.' So I made the transfer."

Clifford Nass has an office overlooking the Oval lawn at Stanford, a university where the use of PowerPoint is so widespread that to refrain from using it is sometimes seen as a mark of seniority and privilege, like egg on one's tie. Nass once worked for Intel, and then got a Ph.D. in sociology, and now he writes about and lectures on the ways people think about computers. But, before embarking on any of that, Professor Nass was a professional magician—Cliff Conjure—so he has some confidence in his abilities as a public performer.

According to Nass, who now gives PowerPoint lectures because his students asked him to, PowerPoint "lifts the floor" of public speaking: a lecture is less likely to be poor if the speaker is using the program. "What PowerPoint does is very efficiently deliver content," Nass told me. "What students gain is a lot more information—not just facts but rules, ways of thinking, examples."

At the same time, PowerPoint "lowers the ceiling," Nass says. "What you miss is the process. The classes I remember most, the professors I remember most, were the ones where you could watch how they thought. You don't remember what they said, the details. It was 'What an elegant way to wrap around a problem!' PowerPoint takes that away. PowerPoint gives you the outcome, but it removes the process."

"What I miss is, when I used to lecture without PowerPoint, every now and then I'd get a cool idea," he went on. "I remember once it just hit me. I'm lecturing, and all of a sudden I go, 'God! "The Wizard of Oz"! The scene at the end of "The Wizard of Oz"!'" Nass, telling this story, was almost shouting. (The lecture, he later explained, was about definitions of "the human" applied to computers.) "I just went for it—twenty-five minutes. And to this day students who were in that class remember it. That couldn't happen now: 'Where the hell is the slide?'"

PowerPoint could lead us to believe that information is *all* there is. According to Nass, PowerPoint empowers the provider of simple content (and that was the task Bob Gaskins originally set for it), but it risks squeezing out the provider of process—that is to say, the rhetorician, the storyteller, the poet, the person whose thoughts cannot be arranged in the shape of an AutoContent slide. "I hate to admit this," Nass said, "but I actually removed a book from my syllabus last year because I couldn't figure out how to PowerPoint it. It's a lovely book called *Interface Culture,* by Steven Johnson, but it's very discursive; the charm of it is the throwaways. When I read this book, I thought, My head's filled with ideas, and now I've got to write out exactly what those ideas are, and—they're not neat."

He couldn't get the book into bullet points; every time he put something down, he realized that it wasn't quite right. Eventually, he abandoned the attempt, and instead of a lecture, he gave his students a recommendation. He told them it was a good book, urged them to read it, and moved on to the next bullet point.

RELATED LINKS

- Microsoft Office Online (http://office.microsoft.com/home)
- Keynote Software (http://www.apple.com/keynote)
- Lotus Freelance Graphics (http://www.lotus.com/products/smrtsuite.nsf/wPages/freelance)
- Win Squared Software (http://www.winxwin.com)
- WordPerfect Office (http://www.corel.com/servlet/Satellite?pagename=Corel/Home)
- The Gettysburg PowerPoint Presentation (http://www.norvig.com/Gettysburg)
- The Cognitive Style of PowerPoint (http://www.edwardtufte.com/tufte/powerpoint)

FOR FURTHER RESEARCH

To find out more about the topics discussed in this reading, use InfoTrac College Edition. Type in keywords and subject terms such as "PowerPoint," "presentation software," and "AutoContent Wizard." You can access InfoTrac College Edition from the Wadsworth/Thomson Communication Café homepage: http://communication.wadsworth.com.

Reading 8-4

The Myth of Order. The Real Lesson of Y2K

Ellen Ullman

EDITOR'S NOTE

After years of media hype, the Year 2000 (Y2K) computer problem, known to many as the "millennium bug," resulted in only minimal disruption of a few systems. Perhaps the worst glitch was experienced by the Pentagon, which quietly endured three days of malfunctioning spy satellites. In the months before the millennial transition, concern over possible power grid and transportation disruptions prompted the banking industry to reassure nervous customers through television ads, publications like the Utne Reader *to issue a 120-page* Y2K Citizen's Action Guide, *and the American Red Cross to recommend that the public have enough food and supplies on hand to last several days to a week. In this reading, writer and computer programmer Ellen Ullman draws on her 20 years of programming experience and concludes that the real lesson of Y2K is that software operates just like any natural system: beyond the control of any individual. Y2K also illustrates the importance of advanced planning and disaster prevention—an estimated $250 billion was spent on Y2K-related repairs worldwide—in an era of growing complexity and technological dependence.*

CONSIDER

1. What was the origin of the Y2K problem, and what could have been done to prevent it from becoming such a pressing issue?

2. How do inevitable design flaws or system defects such as the "millennium bug" cause us to rethink the reliability and trustworthiness of information technology?

3. As a cultural phenomenon, what does society's reaction to the Y2K episode say about our reliance on computer hardware and software?

Bugs are an unintended source of inspiration. Many times I've seen a bug in a game and thought, "That's cool—I wouldn't have thought of that in a million years."
—Will Wright, creator of SimCity and chief game designer at Maxis

I've fixed about 1,000 bugs in my life. How many have I created? Undoubtedly more.
—Patrick Naughton, executive vice president of products, Infoseek

Y2K has uncovered a hidden side of computing. It's always been there, of course, and always will be. It's simply been obscured by the pleasures we get from our electronic tools and toys, and then lost in the zingy glow of techno-boosterism. Y2K is showing everyone what technical people have been dealing with for years: the complex, muddled, bug-bitten systems we all depend on, and their nasty tendency toward the occasional disaster.

It's almost a betrayal. After being told for years that technology is the path to a highly evolved future, it's come as something of a shock to discover that a computer system is not a shining city on a hill—perfect and ever new—but something more akin to an old farmhouse built bit by bit over decades by nonunion carpenters.

The reaction has been anger, outrage even—how could all you programmers be so stupid? Y2K has challenged a belief in digital technology that has been almost religious. But it's not surprising. The public has had little understanding of the context in which Y2K exists. Glitches, patches, crashes—these are as inherent to the process of creating an intelligent electronic system as is the beauty of an elegant algorithm, the satisfaction of a finely tuned program, the gee-whiz pleasure of messages sent around the world at light speed. Until you understand that computers contain both of these aspects—elegance and error—you can't really understand Y2K.

Technically speaking, the "millennium bug" is not a bug at all, but what is called a design flaw. Programmers are very sensitive to the difference, since a bug means the code is at fault (the program isn't doing what it was designed to do), and a design flaw means it's the designer's fault (the code is doing exactly what was specified in the design, but the design was wrong or inadequate). In the case of the millennium bug, of course, the code was designed to use two-digit years. The problem comes if computers misread the two-digit numbers—00, 01, et cetera. Should these be seen as 1900 and 1901, or as 2000 and 2001? Two-digit dates were used originally to save space, since computer memory and disk storage were prohibitively expensive. The designers who chose to specify these two-digit "bugs" were not stupid, and perhaps they were not even wrong. By some estimates, the savings accrued by using two-digit years will have outweighed the entire cost of fixing the code for the year 2000.

But Y2K did not even begin its existence as a design flaw. Up until the mid-1980s—almost 30 years after two-digit years were first put into use—what we now call Y2K would have been called an "engineering trade-off," and a good one. A trade-off: to get something you need, you give up something else you need less urgently; to get more space on disk and in memory, you give up the precision of the century indicators. Perfectly reasonable. The correct decision. The surest sign of its correctness is what happened next: two-digit years went on to have a long, successful life as a "standard." Computer systems could not work without standards—an agreement among programs and systems about how they will exchange information.

From "The Myth of Order. The Real Lesson of Y2K" by Ellen Ullman, *Wired,* April 1999, pp. 126–129, 183–184. Copyright © 1999 by Ellen Ullman. Reprinted with permission.

Dates flowed from program to program, system to system, from tape to memory to paper, and back to disk —it all worked just fine for decades.

Though not for centuries, of course. The near immortality of computer software has come as a shock to programmers. Ask anyone who was there: We never expected this stuff to still be around.

Bug, design flaw, side effect, engineering trade-off —programmers have many names for system defects, the way Eskimos have many words for snow. And for the same reason: They're very familiar with the thing and can detect its fine gradations. To be a programmer is to develop a carefully managed relationship with error. There's no getting around it. You either make your accommodations with failure, or the work will become intolerable. Every program has a bug; every complex system has its blind spots. Occasionally, given just the right set of circumstances, something will fail spectacularly. There is a Silicon Valley company, formerly called Failure Analysis (now Exponent), whose business consists of studying system disasters. The company's sign used to face the freeway like a warning to every technical person heading north out of Silicon Valley: Failure Analysis.

In the popular imagination, the programmer is a kind of traveler into the unknown, venturing near the margin of mind and meatspace. Maybe. For moments. On some extraordinary projects, sometimes—a new operating system, a newly conceived class of software. For most of us, though, programming is not a dramatic confrontation between human and machine; it's a confused conversation with programmers we will never meet, a frustrating wrangle with some other programmer's code.

Most modern programming is done through what are called application programming interfaces, or APIs. Your job is to write some code that will talk to another piece of code in a narrowly defined way using the specific methods offered by the interface, and only those methods. The interface is rarely documented well. The code on the other side of the interface is usually sealed in a proprietary black box. And below that black box is another, and below that another—a receding tower of black boxes, each with its own errors. You can't envision the whole tower, you can't open the boxes, and what information you've been given about any individual box could be wrong. The experience is a little like looking at a madman's electronic bomb and trying to figure out which wire to cut. You try to do it carefully but sometimes things blow up.

At its core, programming remains irrational—a time-consuming, painstaking, error-stalked process, out of which comes a functional but flawed piece of work. And it most likely will remain so as long as we are using computers whose basic design descends from ENIAC, a machine constructed to calculate the trajectory of artillery shells. A programmer is presented with a task that a program must accomplish. But it is a task as a human sees it, full of unexpressed knowledge, implicit associations, allusions to allusions. Its coherence comes from knowledge structures deep in the body, from experience, memory. Somehow all this must be expressed in the constricted language of the API, and all of the accumulated code must resolve into a set of instructions that can be performed by a machine that is, in essence, a giant calculator. It shouldn't be surprising if mistakes are made.

There is irrationality at the core of programming, and there is irrationality surrounding it from without. Factors external to the programmer—the whole enterprise of computing, its history and business practices—create an atmosphere in which flaws and oversights are that much more likely to occur.

The most irrational of all external factors, the one that makes the experience of programming feel most insane, is known as "aggressive scheduling." Whether software companies will acknowledge it or not, release schedules are normally driven by market demand, not the actual time it would take to build a reasonably robust system. The parts of the development process most often foreshortened are two crucial ones: design documentation and testing.

Even if programmers were given rational development schedules, the systems they work on are increasingly complex, patched together—and incoherent. Systems have become something like Russian nesting dolls, with newer software wrapped around older software, which is wrapped around software that is older yet. We've come to see that code doesn't evolve; it accumulates.

The problem of old code is many times worse in a large corporation or a government office, where whole subsystems may have been built 20 or 30 years ago. Most of the original programmers are long gone, taking their knowledge with them—along with the programmers who followed them, and ones after that. The code, a sort of *palimpsest* by now, becomes difficult to understand. Even if the company had the time to replace it, it's no longer sure of everything the code does. So it is kept running behind wrappers of newer code—

so-called middleware, or quickly developed user interfaces like the Web—which keeps the old code running, but as a fragile, precious object. The program runs, but is not understood; it can be used, but not modified. Eventually, a complex computer system becomes a journey backward through time. Look into the center of the most slick-looking Web banking site, built a few months ago, and you're bound to see a creaky database running on an aged mainframe.

Adding yet more complexity are the electronic connections that have been built between systems: customers, suppliers, financial clearinghouses, whole supply chains interlinking their systems. One patched-together wrapped-up system exchanges data with another patched-together wrapped-up system—layer upon layer of software involved in a single transaction, until the possibility of failure increases exponentially.

It's from deep in there—somewhere near the middle-most Russian doll in the innermost layer of software—that the millennium bug originates. One system sends it on to the next, along with the many bugs and problems we already know about, and the untold numbers that remain to be discovered. One day —maybe when we switch to the new version of the Internet Protocol, or when some router somewhere is replaced—one day the undiscovered bugs will come to light and we'll have to worry about each of them in turn. The millennium bug is not unique; it's just the flaw we see now, the most convincing evidence yet of the human fallibility that lives inside every system.

It's hard to overstate just how common bugs are. Every week, the computer trade paper *Info World* prints a little box called The Bug Report, showing problems in commonly used software, some of them very serious. And the box itself is just a sampling from www.bugnet.com, where one day's search for bugs relating to "security" yielded a list of 68 links, many to other lists and to lists of links, reflecting what may be thousands of bugs related to this keyword alone. And that's just the ones that are known about and have been reported.

If you think about all the things that can go wrong, it'll drive you crazy. So technical people, who can't help knowing about the fragility of systems, have had to find some way to live with what they know. What they've done is develop a normal sense of failure, an everyday relationship with potential disaster.

One approach is to ignore all thoughts about the consequences—to stay focused on the code on your desk. This is not that difficult to do, since programmers get high rewards for spending large amounts of time in front of a computer workstation, where they're expected to maintain a very deep and narrow sort of concentration.

If you can't stay focused on your code, another approach is to develop an odd sort of fatalism, a dark, defensive humor in the face of all the things you know can go wrong. Making fun of bugs is almost a sign of sophistication. It shows you know your way around a real system, that you won't shy back when things really start to fall apart. A friend of mine once worked as a software engineer at a Baby Bell. He liked to tell people how everyone in the company was amazed to pick up a handset and actually get a dial tone. It was almost a brag: Ha ha, my system's so screwed up you wouldn't believe it.

Now here comes a problem that's no joke. Technical people can't help hearing about the extreme consequences that will come down on the world if they don't find all the places problems like Y2K are hiding. And they simultaneously know that it is impossible to find all the problems in any system, let alone in ones being used long beyond their useful life spans.

"Y2K is a sort of perverse payback from the universe for all the hasty and incomplete development efforts over the last 10 years," said the Y2K testing lead for a midsize brokerage. Also speaking on condition of anonymity, Lawrence Bell (a pseudonym) said it like an I-told-you-so, a chance for him to get back at every programmer and programming manager who ever sent him junky software.

Bell is a tall, impeccably groomed young man whose entire workday consists of looking for bugs. He's in QA, quality assurance, the place where glitches are brought to light, kept on lists, managed, prioritized, and juggled—a complete department devoted to bugs. He has the tester's crisp manner, the precision of the quality seeker, in whom a certain amount of obsessive fussiness is a very good thing.

The only thing about Y2K that was really bothering Bell was the programmers. There is a classic animosity between programmers and testers—after all, the tester's role in life is to find everything the programmer did wrong. But Y2K and its real-world time pressures seem to have escalated the conflict.

The source of the hostility is documentation: Programmers are supposed to make a record of the code they've written. Documentation is how quality assurance people know what the system is supposed to do, and therefore how to test it. But programmers hate to write documentation, and so they simply avoid doing it. "The turnover is high," said Bell, "or the programmers who have been here a long time get promoted. They don't want to go back to this project they wrote 10 years ago—and get punished for not documenting it."

Programmers have fun and leave us to clean up their messes, is Bell's attitude. They want to go off to new programs, new challenges, and the really annoying thing is, they can. "They say, 'I want to do something new,'" said Bell, truly angry now, "and they get away with it."

"No more programmers working without adult supervision!"

This was declaimed by Ed Yardeni, chief economist for Deutsche Bank Securities, before a crowded hotel ballroom. On the opening day of the Year 2000 Symposium, August 10, 1998 (with cameras from *60 Minutes* rolling), Yardeni explained how the millennium bug would bring about a world recession on the order of the 1973–1974 downturn, and this would occur because the world's systems "were put together over 30 to 40 years without any adult supervision whatsoever." Blame the programmers. The mood at the conference was like that of a spurned lover: All those coddled boys in t-shirts and cool eyewear, formerly fetishized for their adolescent ways, have betrayed us.

It has become popular wisdom to say that Y2K is the result of "shortsightedness." It's a theme that has been taken up as a near moral issue, as if the people who created the faulty systems were somehow derelict as human beings.

In fact, some of the most successful and long-lived technologies suffer from extreme shortsightedness. The design of the original IBM PC, for example, assumed there would never be more than one user, who would never be running more than one program at a time, which would never see more than 256K of memory. The original Internet protocol, IP, limited the number of server addresses it could handle to what seemed like a very large number at the time, never imagining the explosive growth of the Web.

I once worked on a Cobol program that had been running for more than 15 years. It was written before the great inflation of the late 1970s. By the time I saw it, in 1981, the million-dollar figure in all dollar amounts was too large for the program's internal storage format, and so multiple millions of dollars simply disappeared without a trace.

We are surrounded by shortsighted systems. Right at this moment, some other program is surely about to burst the bounds of its format for money or number of shares traded or count of items sold. The Dow Jones Industrial Average will one day break 20,000, the price of gas will top $9.99, the systems we're renovating now may live long enough to need renovation again. Some system designer, reacting to the scarce computer resource of our day—not memory but bandwidth—is specifying a piece of code that we will one day look back on as folly.

At the Year 2000 Symposium where Yardeni spoke, there was a technical workshop about creating a "time machine"—a virtual time environment for testing "fixed" Y2K programs. One of the presenters, Carl Gehr of the Edge Information Group, patiently explained that, when designing the test environment, "you have to specify an upper limit" for the year. While everyone scribbled notes, an awful thought occurred to me. "But what upper limit?" I said out loud. "Should we be worrying about the year 9000? 10,001?"

Gehr stopped talking, heads came up from their notes, and the room went quiet. It was as if this were the first time, in all the rush to fix their systems, the attendees had been able to stop, reflect, think about a faraway future. Finally, from the back of the room came a voice: "Good question."

Things can go very, very wrong and still not be the end of the world. Says Bell: "It's just a big user test."

Gehr glanced over at his colleague, Marilyn Frankel, who was waiting to talk about temporary "fixes" for Y2K-affected code. "Marilyn will address that later, I'm sure," he said.

RELATED LINKS

- Salon.com Directory: Ellen Ullman (http://archive.salon.com/directory/topics/ellen_ullman)
- *Wired's* Y2K Archive (http://www.wired.com/wired/archive/y2k)
- Year 2000 Crisis: Resources (http://bladecomputing.com/y2k/resources.htm)

- The Year 2000 Problem (http://www.nytimes.com/library/tech/reference/millennium index.html)
- Y2K Citizen's Action Guide (http://www.utne.com/web_special/web_specials_archives/ articles/404-1.html)

 FOR FURTHER RESEARCH

To find out more about the topics discussed in this reading, use InfoTrac College Edition. Type in keywords and subject terms such as "Y2K," "millennium bug," and "technological failure." You can access InfoTrac from the Wadsworth/Thomson Communication Café homepage: http://communication.wadsworth.com.

PART V

≈

New Technologies
and the Public Sphere

Part V addresses the relationship between new communication technologies and the public sphere with articles that analyze the role of electronic media in democratic processes as well as the problem of unequal access to information technology, a circumstance referred to as the "digital divide." The readings in Chapter 9 reconsider civic involvement and citizen empowerment in light of networked communications and new media/formats, which create new opportunities for individual and collective action. Veteran cyber explorer Howard Rheingold predicts that the shift to coordinated mobile and wireless communications will be as dramatic as the widespread adoption of the PC in the 1980s and the Internet in the 1990s. The interconnectedness of new technology does not necessarily mean that it promotes more tolerance and diversity, however. Dispersed but like-minded individuals can find each other and form virtual communities, but online communication within narrowly focused bounds may encourage a type of group isolation. Readings in Chapter 10 discuss how access to computer technology remains problematic for many people. Despite recent gains, high-income white households still have greater access to the Internet than minority and rural households at the lowest income levels. One proposal to help overcome the digital divide, presented in a report by the RAND Corporation, involves providing nearly universal access to e-mail to all U.S. residents, along the lines of universal telephone service. The authors of the report maintain that the unique properties of e-mail allow individuals to engage in an active civic dialog, fostering interactive communication and providing significant social and political benefits to citizens in the process.

9

Electronic Democracy

Reading 9-1

Media Participation: A Legitimizing Mechanism of Mass Democracy

Erik P. Bucy and Kimberly S. Gregson

EDITOR'S NOTE

This reading reconsiders civic involvement and citizen empowerment in light of interactive media and elaborates on the concept of media participation. Departing from conventional notions of political activity that downplay the participatory opportunities inherent in communication media, the authors argue that since 1992 new media/formats have made accessible to citizens a political system that had become highly orchestrated, professionalized, and exclusionary. Unlike voting and campaign activity, which are sporadic and short lived, new media satisfy the need for popular involvement in public life by delivering a continuous stream of opportunities for civic engagement without overextending the political system's ability to respond. Even if it is only symbolically empowering in the realm of political action, civic engagement through new media provides the individual with an array of civic rewards and ultimately serves as an important legitimizing mechanism of mass democracy.

CONSIDER

1. Which new media/formats do the authors consider rich in civic potential, and why?
2. Why are participatory mechanisms vital to the effective functioning of a strong democracy?

3. The 1988 presidential election was a pivotal moment in national politics. In terms of responsiveness, what changed by the time of the 1992 campaign?

After his career in public life was over, Thomas Jefferson lamented in a series of letters that the American Constitution he was instrumental in shaping "had given all power to the citizens without giving them the opportunity of *being* republicans and of *acting* as citizens" (Arendt, 1963: 256). Modern democracy suffers a similar fate. In the wake of the 1988 presidential election a Markle Commission study found that voters were increasingly resigned to occupying a spectator position and perceived campaigns to be more the property of candidates, insiders, and establishment media than citizens for whom the election drama was staged (Buchanan, 1991). Since the 1990s, however, the infusion of new media/formats into politics has altered the participatory landscape in important ways; with the possible exception of voting, most forms of active political involvement can now take place through new media (Bucy, D'Angelo, and Newhagen, 1999).

New media/formats rich in civic potential include the obvious, and much discussed, participatory venues —the Internet/World Wide Web, talk radio, call-in television, and electronic townhall forums—as well as entertainment programs that feature spontaneous, informal discussions about politics with both political and nonpolitical guests.[1] Yet the civic richness and growing accessibility of these new media/formats (sometimes called the *new news;* see Rosen and Taylor, 1992) does not mean that a vibrant, electronic republic will necessarily replace the existing world of traditional politics. Indeed, given the tendency of the traditional party system to normalize political activity, hopes for a radical transformation of politics, even in cyberspace, are likely to go unrealized (Margolis and Resnick, 2000). Instead, the new media's main contribution to political life may be to make accessible a system that had become highly orchestrated, professionalized, and exclusionary (see Dionne, 1991; Hume, 1991) and to produce positive citizen evaluations of the public sphere.

A previous investigation found that political audiences regarded certain new media/formats, especially call-in shows and the Internet, as useful and valuable to civic life (Bucy, D'Angelo, and Newhagen, 1999). This paper builds on the "new media use as political participation" argument by specifying that this emergent form of electronic democracy, a type of political participation *through* media, involves not just Net activism, as recent works have addressed (e.g. Hill and Hughes, 1998; Schwartz, 1996), but the broader range of citizen actions that can take place online, over the airwaves, and through exposure to political messages that invite involvement. Such actions include but are not limited to direct leader/legislator contact, public opinion formation, participating in civic discussions and agenda building, mediated interactions with candidates and other political actors, donating to political causes, and joining mobilizing efforts—each of which may contribute to the psychological feeling of being engaged with the political system.[2] Collectively, we refer to this class of activity as *media participation*. The article concludes by making the case that civic engagement through media, even if only symbolically empowering for the citizen, contributes substantially to legitimizing the political systems of mass democracies.

Before addressing the specific nature of media participation, traditional conceptions of political participation are examined to provide a context for the changing nature of civic involvement.

POLITICAL PARTICIPATION AND DEMOCRATIC THEORY

Political participation is typically defined as direct citizen involvement in, or influence over, governmental processes. Thus, Verba and Nie (1987: 2) describe participation as "activities by private citizens that are more or less directly aimed at influencing the selection of governmental personnel and/or the actions they take." Conway (2000: 3) more specifically defines participation as "activities of citizens that attempt to influence the structure of government, the selection of government officials, or the policies of government." She notes that these activities may either be supportive of the

From "Media Participation: A Legitimizing Mechanism of Mass Democracy" by Erik P. Bucy and Kimberly S. Gregson, *New Media and Society: An International Journal, 3*(3), 2001, pp. 359–382. Copyright © 2001 by Sage Publications Ltd. Reprinted with permission.

existing politics, authorities, or structure, or they may seek to change current arrangements. Conway distinguishes between active and passive forms of involvement, as well as conventional and unconventional participation. Active participation, which is goal-oriented and motivated by the desire for a specific, personally rewarding outcome, includes such activities as voting, seeking office, writing letters to public officials, or working for a candidate, party or interest group. Passive forms of involvement, which are more ritualized and suggest a certain amount of detachment, include attending ceremonies or other meetings supportive of the government, being aware of government actions and decisions, or merely paying attention to the political environment, for instance, following campaigns and elections through the mass media (Conway, 2000).

Regardless of their exact form, participatory mechanisms are considered vital to the effective functioning of a strong democracy, in part because they are viewed as maintaining open access to the political system (Barber, 1984; Conway, 2000). Rather than burdening elites, classical theories of democracy place the onus of civic vitality on the citizenry, requiring popular interest and self-initiated participation in public affairs. The electorate, in the classical view, should not only be informed and judge political realities rationally but also engage in thoughtful deliberation, possess a democratic disposition, and consider community interests over individual concerns (Berelson, 1952). Systematic research has consistently revealed that these high standards and historically perceived requisites for democracy were not met or even approached by any western democratic nation, however (Cobb and Elder, 1983: 2). Instead of political omnicompetence, most people tend to have little interest in public affairs and few participate actively. Neuman (1986) and more recently Schudson (1998) describe the typical citizen as someone who is only semi-attentive to politics and politically unsophisticated but who, at the prompting of alert others or extreme media attention, can be mobilized into action.

Empirically, then, active citizen participation in politics, at least as traditionally conceptualized, is sporadic despite ample normative encouragement. In an analysis of political participation in the United States between 1967 and 1987, Verba, Schlozman, and Brady (1995) found the proportion of Americans who regularly voted in presidential and local elections was decreasing (down to 58% and 35%, respectively), while persuading others *how* to vote and contributing money to a party or candidate—indirect forms of participa-

tion—was increasing (to 32% and 23%, respectively). In addition, they found that only 34% of the American public reported *ever* initiating contact with a government official; less than that, 29%, had attended a meeting of a political organization (although 48% were affiliated with an organization that took a stand in politics). Aside from voting, they conclude that there is no form of participation in which a majority of the public engages (Verba, Schlozman, and Brady, 1995: 52),[3] perhaps because voting, as Neuman (1986: 176) observes, "is culturally defined as an important, symbolic, civic duty; active participation in campaigns and contact with political authorities are not." In the 1996 U.S. presidential election, an admittedly lackluster and noncompetitive contest, less than half (49%) of all eligible voters turned out on election day, the lowest turnout since 1924; although the 2000 presidential race between Al Gore and George W. Bush was hotly contested, voter turnout only increased slightly, to 51% (Center for Voting and Democracy, 2001).

Evidence of scant political interest, knowledge, and participation among citizens has presented political science with the problem of reconciling democratic theory with reality (Cobb and Elder, 1983). Under theories of elite or stratified pluralism (Neuman, 1986), the dominant response to this theory-reality disconnect, low levels of interest and participation are accepted as normal and interpreted as a sign of general system satisfaction. Voting is still considered important because it helps insure responsiveness of elected officials. But much participation beyond this is regarded as detrimental because it may result in too many demands being placed on the system, interfere with the government's ability to act swiftly when events demand a quick response, and over-politicize social relationships. As Pateman (1970: 6) noted, "limited participation and apathy have a positive function for the whole system by cushioning the shock of disagreement, adjustment, and change" when groups that may not share the same values and norms as the majority press for recognition and accommodation. Low pubic interest also provides political elites with the maneuvering room necessary for policy shifts that may contradict previously stated positions. Popular participation, in this view, should thus be limited to elections; voters can control their leaders by voting them in or out of office but direct citizen influence on policy making between elections should be minimal.

Elite pluralism stems from the political writings of Walter Lippmann (1922, 1927), who felt that ordinary citizens were not competent to deal effectively with the complexities of political affairs. Lippmann would rather see society governed by a technocratic elite of experts who relied on scientific methods to rationally administer government than depend on the sentiments of a disengaged, "phantom" public. Instead of prescribing that individuals actively participate in politics, elite pluralism thus places the onus of civic vitality on diverse and competing elites who should remain circulating and accessible to the masses. In theory, the ability of political "spectators" in a pluralist system to enter the civic arena and become "gladiators" in competition for resources or political influence provides a check on power holders and compels them to act responsively (Milbrath, 1965). Politicians and other elites may anticipate and proactively respond to potential demands not because citizens on balance make many demands but because political action helps to keep spectators from becoming active in the arena (Almond and Verba, 1963: 487).

Despite systemic constraints against mass involvement and genuine public disinterest in politics, the myth that widespread popular participation is desirable is nevertheless perpetuated because it is functional for the system. Milbrath has noted:

> It is important to continue moral admonishment for citizens to become active in politics, not because we want or expect great masses of them to become active, but rather because the admonishment helps keep the system open and sustains the belief in the right of all to participate, which is an important norm governing the behavior of political elites (1965: 152).

Responsiveness is also maintained through open channels of communication between citizens and elites, facilitated through such intermediaries as interest groups and the media, which "keep citizens informed of what public officials are doing and public officials informed of what citizens want" (Milbrath, 1965: 144). Thus, mass media, and in particular new media/formats with their two-way flows and open mike function (Crittenden, 1971), play a vital role in maintaining the perception, and reality, of system openness.

Should the system as a whole fail to remain accessible and responsive, the propensity for tyranny and abuse by elites not only increases but citizen faith, trust, and confidence in institutions may erode, precipitating a crisis of legitimacy. Before rise of the new media in politics, the political system in the view of many

observers (e.g. Blumler, 1983; Dionne, 1991; Kellner, 1990) was experiencing just such a crisis. Among other reasons, American democracy had reached a critical stage because the necessary conditions for civic participation, namely adequate information, an accurate picture of public life, and a sense of citizen connectedness to governmental institutions, had been endangered by politicians and distorted by the press (see Bucy and D'Angelo, 1999).[4] Moreover, the rise of corporate lobbying, the growth of the political consulting industry, and the organization of civic life around media imperatives had served to marginalize the role of citizens in contemporary democracies (Blumler and Gurevitch, 1995). By some accounts, the apex of this crisis occurred during the 1988 presidential election.

ORIGINS AND IMPLICATIONS OF THE NEW MEDIA IN POLITICS

Following the 1988 presidential election, political journalists entered into an extended period of self-criticism and evaluation beyond the regular campaign postmortems and debriefings (Hume, 1991), committing themselves to reconnect citizens to the political process. David Broder (1990: A15) of the *Washington Post* declared that the time had come "for those of us in the world's freest press to become activists, not on behalf of a particular party or politician, but on behalf of the process of self government." The press' civic response was perhaps motivated as much by self preservation as democratic duty; as perceptions that political institutions and processes were inaccessible grew, much of this criticism was directed toward the media. Campaign journalism, once mindful of the average voter, had become increasingly evaluative and elitist, critics charged, and political actors, once hesitant to use advertising, came to *rely* on political spots and staged media events for message control (Hallin, 1992; Jamieson, 1992). These forms of one-way communication maximized campaign influence over the message *du jour* but limited audience interactivity, effectively silencing citizens in the process.

Whether due to frustration with the attack politics and event staging that characterized campaigns of the 1980s, the suggestions of influential, reform-minded writers like Broder, or the unique confluence of events and personalities that shaped the subsequent election, political actors and journalists alike took several steps to empower citizens and make public life more participa-

Table 9-1. Distinguishing Features of New Media/Formats

| | NEW MEDIA/FORMAT | | | | |
Modality	Web	Townhalls	Call-in TV	Talk Radio	TV
Multimedia	■				
Audience Participation	■	■			
Caller Feedback	■	■	■	■	
Visuals	■	■	■		■
Audio	■	■	■	■	■

Note: Audience participation incorporates caller feedback, which both the Web and electronic townhall forums may accommodate to varying degrees depending on the particular program.

tory in 1992. Surveillance measures such as ad watches were adopted to counterbalance misleading or suggestive ads. Public journalism projects were launched at small- and medium-sized newspapers, on National Public Radio, and public television stations, reintroducing the idea of citizen influence over the campaign agenda (Rosen, 1996). And, perhaps most theoretically interesting, new media/formats came to the fore, allowing candidates to address the electorate unencumbered by journalistic commentary and enabling citizens to speak directly to candidates.

INTERACTIVITY AND THE NEW MEDIA

New media/formats that came to national prominence during the 1992 election, and which have been a staple of campaigns since, popularized the concept of interactivity in politics. A principal component of the new media is the notion of political interactivity, or mediated real-time feedback between political actors and citizens (Hacker, 1996). A primary feature setting interactive media apart from traditional campaign news coverage or political advertising is the potential for spontaneous interaction between political figures, journalists, and citizens (Newhagen, 1994). Rather than being proscribed a passive role in the political process, the electorate is symbolically or materially empowered (as discussed below) through the two-way communication architecture to interact directly with candidates. Although constrained by such structural factors as available air time, social conventions that inhibit extended conversations between people of high and low social status, and the sheer number of audience members (both in studio and at home) relative to political guests, interactive formats provide the appearance at least of

an unscripted, unrehearsed civic discussion. If nothing else, new media/formats may cultivate the perception of system responsiveness, offering citizens the opportunity to engage in corrective communication with power holders. This form of mediated talk has the capacity to adjust elite impressions of mass opinion to better reflect actual public sentiment.

Given the time and role constraints on audiences, not to mention status and political knowledge differentials, full interactivity between public figures and private citizens is clearly not achievable even through new media/formats. However, a semblance or subjective sense of it might be. Some election research has found, for instance, that political television audiences may perceive new media/formats to allow for feedback, even if true interactivity is only partially realized, via the mechanism of *perceived interactivity* (Bucy and Newhagen, 1999; Newhagen, 1994). From this perspective, whether a communication event is regarded as interactive by an outside observer may be irrelevant if the experience of participation leads to a heightened sense of self-efficacy and system responsiveness in the individual.

Table 9-1 illustrates the distinguishing features of new media/formats and arrays them according to the number of communication modalities they possess, from most (the Internet/World Wide Web) to least (entertainment television).[5] Entertainment television shows are shown with the fewest modalities because they generally lack direct audience participation mechanisms and a real-time feedback loop that facilitates viewer interaction. Call-in television formats are considered more featureful than talk radio on account of visuals. Electronic townhall forums are distinguished from televised call-in shows by the presence of both a studio and remote viewing audience, either of which may interact with the elite guest depending on the format. Finally, the Internet/World Wide Web features the most choices and options, including all of the previous features as well as multimedia, or communication channel choice, which allows the user to select the message delivery method. The civic relevance of each new media/format is briefly discussed below.

CIVIC RELEVANCE OF NEW MEDIA/FORMATS

- *Political entertainment television:* Set in the casual atmosphere of an informal conversation or comedy skit, political entertainment television relies on interpersonal humor, insider gossip, and banter with celebrities and other high-status guests —frequently politicians—to foster a sense of parasocial involvement or illusion of intimacy with media *personae* (Horton and Wohl, 1956). Through the host's interaction with the show's guests and staff, or through the cast's acting in a bit, members of the audience are invited to feel that this sense of fellowship and social intimacy extends to them, fostering the perception of a face-to-face exchange about a political topic. Shows that feature political entertainment, such as Politically Incorrect, Saturday Night Live, and The Late Show with David Letterman, benefit from their parasocial character and accessibility, but their interactivity is limited by the lack of a real-time feedback mechanism (other than applause from the studio audience). Recent surveys by the Pew Research Center (2000) have documented the information value of political entertainment shows, especially for young viewers, and during the 2000 campaign CBS broadcasted a weekly round-up of political humor from the late-night television talk shows. Since the 1988 presidential election the Center for Media and Public Affairs in Washington, DC has also tracked political jokes told on late-night television (the vast majority of which have been leveled at presidents or presidential contenders).
- *Political talk radio:* Perhaps more than any of the other new media/formats, political talk radio gives voice to the average citizen through its "open mike" character (Crittenden, 1971). Talk radio provides verbal proximity to media and political elites, as well as access to a mass audience of fel-

low listeners, via the direct feedback of listener calls. By extending the voice, radio facilitates a sort of amplified conversation that may shape public sentiments and crystallize opinion on certain issues. Moreover, talk radio programs often deliberately attempt to mobilize the public to participate in civic affairs or contact officials (Hollander, 1995/96), serving as a vehicle for political socialization. For reception to be meaningful, talk radio listening requires dedicated attention with the intent of comprehending the discussion (Tankel, 1998). Listening, in turn, may teach the important civic skill of heeding and tolerating opposing arguments. Indeed, Tankel (1998) asserts that a major attraction of talk radio is the multiplicity of voices heard on the air. Research on the talk radio audience has shown listeners to be significantly more civic-minded and participatory than nonlisteners (Hollander, 1995/96). Callers, in particular, are more likely to participate in other political activities. Talk radio can be best understood, Tankel (1998: 45) suggests, "as a behavior in which the listener is an active participant rather than as a process that constructs a passive recipient."

- *Political call-in television:* Combining the strengths of talk radio with the power of visuals, political call-in television places the viewer in the front row, if not of the political *action,* at least of the political *discussion.* Because of television's visual nature, this format invites close scrutiny of the political guest's physical appearance and nonverbal demeanor, perhaps at the expense of what's said. Importantly, call-in television endows the audience member with more sensory modalities— sight as well as sound—than the guest, who can only hear the audio of the caller. The disembodied voice of the caller is awkward for the elite guest and host but in some way empowers the caller because the transparency, though at a distance, is unidirectional. The guest is visually impaired, the caller visually enabled. Call-in formats thus provide visual *and* verbal proximity to elites, as well as open-mike access to a wide audience (although small by television standards). Public affairs cable channels such as C-SPAN and CNN, which feature daily call-in segments, "may well stimulate increased levels of political involvement or create new vehicles for political participation" (Frantzich and Sullivan, 1996: 246). Such participation has the potential for changing the climate of opinion and influencing the behavior of decision makers, while enhancing the political efficacy of citizens.

- *Electronic townhall forums:* Electronic townhall forums that feature a participatory studio audience, and sometimes an interactive viewing audience, offer a form of vicarious participation unrivaled by other media. For the home audience, the surrogate experience of viewing a townhall forum is intensified by the ability to witness the active involvement of fellow citizens, whose presence reminds viewers of their own democratic role and civic identity. In response to a citizen question during the second presidential debate of 1996 (which was conducted as a townhall forum) about opening the political process to more grassroots involvement, President Clinton referred to surrogate participation and commented on the need to make elections more accessible through campaign finance reform and by opening the airwaves to citizen control: "You see, it's not just you that are participating here. For every one of you who stood up here and asked a question tonight, I promise you, there's 100,000 Americans that said, 'I wish I could have asked that question'" (Federal News Service, 1996). Through the airing of issues and questions that represent citizen interests rather than journalistic fixations—the two diverge considerably—the public debate is recast so voters come to know their own minds, as it were, before facing a critical choice and thereby have the opportunity to build "a more conscious democracy" (Elgin, 1993: 9). The visibility of citizen stand-ins who vocalize collective sentiment and concerns creates a sense of civic relevance that consultant-controlled campaigning all but obliterates.

- *Internet/World Wide Web:* Through convergence and remediation—the repurposing or refashioning of old media with new media, not just in terms of content but by incorporating old media forms into new media venues (Bolter and Grusin, 1999)—the Internet/World Wide Web introduces myriad ways to engage voters and facilitate participation in politics. As a civic medium, the Internet fulfills at least four political functions (Davis and Owen, 1998). First, it provides access to news and political information, frequently faster and more in-depth than traditional media. Second, the Internet links candidates and office

holders with citizens through political Web sites. Third, the Internet provides a space for political discussion, especially through Usenet groups organized around various topics. And, fourth, the Internet can serve as a barometer of public opinion with the capacity of offering reaction to events and decisions in real-time (although, as Wu and Weaver [1997] caution, the validity of online polling is dubious). Quite possibly, the Internet/World Wide Web presents more political information and opportunities for civic engagement than has ever existed. The Web is a complex symbolic environment, however, and users spend a considerable amount of time just orienting to the medium. Before it becomes a true medium of the masses, questions of *social access*—the mix of technical knowledge, psychological skills, and economic resources required for effectual use of information and communication technologies—will have to be addressed (Bucy, 2000).

A question inevitably arises as to whether new media/formats allow citizens to influence the actual substance and outcome of politics. According to net activists (Schwartz, 1996) and some early confirmatory research (Bucy, D'Angelo, and Newhagen, 1999; Newhagen, 1994), interactive political experiences that occur in cyberspace, via cable channels, and over the airwaves, are deemed every bit as "real," useful, and important as their nonmediated corollaries—such traditional measures of political activity as attending meetings and rallies, volunteering, writing legislators, and contacting community leaders. And, citizen action through new media/formats already has had direct political influence in certain instances, as the talk radio furor over congressional pay raises and Zoe Baird's 1993 ill-fated nomination to U.S. attorney general demonstrated (Hollander, 1995/96; Page and Tannenbaum, 1996). Yet an over-emphasis on the traditional, political value of media participation risks losing sight of the more important *individual* consequence of daily citizen involvement with new media—the psychological rewards and personal empowerment derived from civic media use.

DISCUSSION

Elite theories of democracy stress that optimal civic conditions depend on a certain amount of citizen involvement but not too much as to cause instability. In direct contradiction to this limited view of public life is the democratic ethos, well entrenched in American society, that all citizens have the *option* to participate, regardless of whether their participation is healthy for the system. Fortunately for government, not everyone chooses to exercise their political rights. To the contrary, conventional public participation in civic life has been on a downward spiral for the past three or four decades (Putnam, 2000). During the same period, media use (notably television and more recently the Internet) has been on the rise, prompting some political thinkers to sound the alarm bell of social and political erosion (e.g. Robinson, 1977; Putnam, 1995). Conceptualizing new media use as a form of political participation that provides symbolic empowerment resolves the dilemma of civic decline; suddenly, there is a form of participation in which a growing segment of the public regularly engages. Importantly, media participation entails *active* civic involvement, not just passive surveillance of the political environment. Recognizing the value of mediated citizenship reconciles the desire of realists to keep public involvement in (actual) political affairs minimal with the admonitions of classical democracy's proponents for full citizen participation.

In contrast to passive spectatorship under a one-way communication system, media participation in an interactive environment presents the citizen with a civic role and ready avenue of involvement across a variety of communication modalities. Indeed, rather than being slighted by a form of "pseudo participation," as traditionalists (e.g. Kerbel, 1999) might characterize new media use, the citizen benefits from the awareness that media participation provides proximity to political elites, makes politics continuously available and entertaining (i.e. accessible), offers open-mike access to a wide audience, socializes citizens to participate in public affairs, and allows voters to cultivate a civic identity and know their own minds. For the electorate, regular involvement with media, particularly new media/formats, may well be taking the place of direct, sporadic participation in politics. Even if only symbolically empowering for the individual, the experience of media participation is pivotal to maintaining the perception of system responsiveness and thereby serves as an important legitimizing mechanism for mass democracy. Through the generalized occurrence of media participation throughout society, the political world has achieved a previously unknown openness. This should be viewed as a positive development: No other system of civic involvement and public communication seems to shoulder the needs of participatory democracy so effectively.

Except under unusual circumstances when the mass public becomes highly attentive to and mobilized over an issue, as with a controversial high-level nomination, new media/formats probably have little or no direct impact on political decisions. There is no guarantee, for example, that policy makers will pay attention to, let alone heed the advice from, an online discussion or instant survey. Often skewed and typically produced from unscientific samples, these "public opinion" indicators can be highly inaccurate (although the results of a growing number of legitimate surveys are now posted online). The vast majority of media participation, then, may have no direct political impact except to encourage others to register their opinion. Nevertheless, new media/formats provide a public space for citizens to debate politics and express their support for, or discontent with, policies or a particular office holder without requiring any material response from the political system. This arrangement is advantageous for both the individual and the system. For the individual, the psychological rewards and peer activation that new media/formats provide may spur previously inactive spectators to initiate some limited form of civic engagement and motivate already active citizens to further their involvement, despite the wishes of those already active in the arena. For the system, media participation may enhance the perception of governmental accessibility and openness by, first and foremost, giving citizens the opportunity to act *as* citizens. Democracy thus benefits from opportunities for civic activity through media, even though citizen involvement by traditional standards is indirect.

Critics of media participation who view it as a watered-down or thin form of democracy should bear in mind that even conventional political participation seldom brings immediate results from government. Continuous involvement in civic affairs through media, however, may produce immediate and ongoing psychological benefits for the citizen. Although it has been presented as a theoretical proposition here, media participation has already been empirically associated with increased feelings of efficacy and conventional participation in studies of the new media audience (Hollander, 1995/96; Newhagen, 1994). From the skeptic's vantage point, new media/formats sacrifice certain forms of interpersonal deliberation for mediated versions and increase the potential for manipulation by political professionals. But the capabilities of the new technology can also be used to "tie individuals and institutions into networks that will make real participatory discussion and debate possible across great distances" (Barber, 1984: 274). Even if elections were conducted purely by way of new media, they would still be participatory in nature. At the very least, new media/formats expose elites to views and opinions they might not otherwise have heard and, in the case of electronic townhall forums, provide citizens with the sense of front-row participation that political correspondents routinely enjoy at press conferences (Barber, 1984). Rather than relying on journalistic stand-ins, citizens can question authority without media interference.

To the extent that media participation contributes to the agenda-building process of public issue formation, it may be *more* important to long-term stability than voting and other sporadic forms of conventional political activity (see Cobb and Elder, 1983). Campaigns and elections may fortify the short-term stability of a system, especially if they generate high voter turnout, but their infrequent occurrence does not provide the ongoing, interstitial involvement that participatory democracy demands. Indeed, when the republic was young Jefferson expressed concern over the danger inherent in allowing the people "a share in public power without providing them at the same time with more public space than the ballot box and with more opportunity to make their voices heard in public than election day" (Arendt, 1963: 256). New media/formats satisfy this need for popular involvement by delivering a continuous stream of opportunities for civic engagement without overextending the government's ability to respond. The new media thereby increase the number of access points in the political pressure system, improving though not guaranteeing the likelihood that citizen concerns will be heard. By making allowances for continuing mass involvement, new media/formats serve the socially valuable purpose of bringing closer to reality the classical goal of full participation without over-extending already burdened political institutions.

NOTES

1. Examples of political entertainment television shows include ABC's Politically Incorrect with Bill Maher [now Real Time with Bill Maher on HBO], MTV's Choose or Lose campaign specials, and Comedy Central's mock news program, The Daily Show, on which former Senator Bob Dole and other prominent politicians regularly appeared as guest com-

mentators during the 2000 presidential election. These programs are categorized as new media/formats because they routinely provide the appearance of spontaneous interaction, they address political topics with nonpolitical guests in an unconventional manner, and they invite the audience to take an active role in the discussion, even if only in a reactive capacity. Moreover, these programs each have their own interactive Web sites that viewers can visit to continue their involvement with the show online.

2. The activities enumerated here roughly correspond to the four key transactions of democracy identified by Tambini (1999): information provision/access to information; preference measurement (referenda, polls, and representation); deliberation; and will formation/organization.

3. Neuman (1986: 175) estimates that less than 1 in 20 citizens participate in politics beyond voting.

4. The "credibility gap" that arose during the Johnson administration's attempts to explain American involvement in Vietnam and the distrust bred by the Watergate scandal of the Nixon era are often cited as critical turning points in the spread of public cynicism (see, for example, Robinson, 1977).

5. Although they are arrayed by modality, new media/formats don't necessarily vary by level of interactivity because the perception of interactive communication is unique to the individual. Technology can set the upper bounds of message reciprocality, but the *experience* of interactivity ultimately resides in the user (Laurel, 1991).

REFERENCES

Almond, G. and Verba, S. (1963) *The Civic Culture*. Princeton, NJ: Princeton University Press.

Arendt, H. (1963) *On Revolution*. New York: The Viking Press.

Barber, B. R. (1984) *Strong Democracy: Participatory Politics for a New Age*. Berkeley: University of California Press.

Berelson, B. (1952) "Democratic Theory and Public Opinion," *Public Opinion Quarterly* 16(3): 313–30.

Blumler, J. G. (1983) "Communication and Democracy: The Crisis Beyond and the Ferment Within," *Journal of Communication* 33(3): 166–73.

Blumler, J. G. and Gurevitch, M. (1995) *The Crisis of Public Communication*. London: Routledge.

Bolter, J. D. and Grusin, R. (1999) *Remediation: Understanding New Media*. Cambridge, MA: The MIT Press.

Broder, D. S. (1990, January 3) "Democracy and the Press," *Washington Post* A15.

Buchanan, B. (1991) *Electing a President: The Markle Commission Research on Campaign '88*. Austin: University of Texas Press.

Bucy, E. P. (2000) "Social Access to the Internet," *Press/Politics* 5(1): 50–61.

Bucy, E. P. and D'Angelo, P. (1999) "The Crisis of Political Communication: Normative Critiques of News and Democratic Processes," *Communication Yearbook* 22: 301–39.

Bucy, E. P., D'Angelo, P., and Newhagen, J. E. (1999) "Engaging the Electorate: New Media Use as Political Participation," in L. L. Kaid and D. Bystrom (eds.) *The Electronic Election: Perspectives on the 1996 Campaign Communication*, pp. 335–47. Mahwah, NJ: Lawrence Erlbaum.

Bucy, E. P. and Newhagen, J. E. (1999) "The Micro- and Macrodrama of Politics on Television: Effects of Media Format on Candidate Evaluations," *Journal of Broadcasting & Electronic Media* 43(2): 193–210.

Center for Voting and Democracy (2001, February) "Voter Turnout," URL (consulted February 2001): http://www.fairvote.org/turnout/index.html

Cobb, R. W. and Elder, C. D. (1983) *Participation in American Politics: The Dynamics of Agenda-Building* (2nd edn). Baltimore: The Johns Hopkins University Press.

Conway, M. M. (2000) *Political Participation in the United States* (3rd edn). Washington, DC: CQ Press.

Crittenden, J. (1971) "Democratic Functions of the Open Mike Radio Forum," *Public Opinion Quarterly* 35(1): 200–10.

Davis, R. and Owen, D. (1998) *New Media and American Politics*. New York: Oxford University Press.

Dionne, E. J., Jr. (1991) *Why Americans Hate Politics*. New York: Simon & Schuster.

Elgin, D. (1993) "Revitalizing Democracy Through Electronic Town Meetings," *Spectrum* 66(2): 6–13.

Federal News Service (1996, October 16) "Presidential Debate Between President Bill Clinton and GOP Presidential Candidate Robert Dole" [On-line transcript]. Available: Lexis-Nexis Academic Universe.

Frantzich, S. and Sullivan, J. (1996) *The C-SPAN Revolution*. Norman: University of Oklahoma Press.

Hacker, K. L. (1996) "Missing Links in the Evolution of Electronic Democratization," *Media, Culture & Society* 18(2): 213–32.

Hallin, D. C. (1992) "Sound Bite News: Television Coverage of Elections, 1968–1988," *Journal of Communication* 42(2): 5–24.

Hill, K. A. and Hughes, J. E. (1998) *Cyberpolitics: Citizen Activism in the Age of the Internet*. Lanham, MD: Rowman & Littlefield.

Hollander, B. A. (1995/96) "The Influence of Talk Radio on Political Efficacy and Participation," *Journal of Radio Studies* 3: 23–31.

Horton, D. and Wohl, R. R. (1956) "Mass Communication and Para-Social Interaction: Observations on Intimacy at a Distance," *Psychiatry* 19(3): 215–29.

Hume, E. (1991) *Restoring the Bond: Connecting Campaign Coverage to Voters: A Report of the Campaign Lessons for '92 Project*.

Cambridge, MA: The Joan Shorenstein Barone Center on the Press, Politics and Public Policy, Harvard University.

Jamieson, K. H. (1992) *Dirty Politics: Deception, Distraction, and Democracy*. New York: Oxford University Press.

Kellner, D. (1990) *Television and the Crisis of Democracy*. Boulder, CO: Westview.

Kerbel, M. R. (1999) *Remote & Controlled: Media Politics in a Cynical Age* (2nd edn). Boulder, CO: Westview Press.

Laurel, B. (1991) *Computers as Theatre*. Reading, MA: Addison-Wesley.

Lippmann, W. (1922) *Public Opinion*. New York: The Free Press.

Lippmann, W. (1927) *The Phantom Public*. New York: Macmillan.

Margolis, M. and Resnick, D. (2000) *Politics as Usual: The Cyberspace Revolution*. Thousand Oaks, CA: Sage.

Milbrath, L. W. (1965) *Political Participation: How and Why Do People Get Involved in Politics?* Chicago: Rand McNally.

Neuman, W. R. (1986) *The Paradox of Mass Politics: Knowledge and Opinion in the American Electorate*. Cambridge, MA: Harvard University Press.

Newhagen, J. E. (1994) "Self Efficacy and Call-in Political Television Show Use," *Communication Research* 21(3): 366–79.

Page, B. I. and Tannenbaum, J. (1996) "Populistic Deliberation and Talk Radio," *Journal of Communication* 46(2): 33–54.

Pateman, C. (1970) *Participation and Democratic Theory*. Cambridge: Cambridge University Press.

Pew Research Center for the People & the Press (2000, January) "The Tough Job of Communicating with Voters: Audiences Fragmented and Skeptical," URL (consulted July 2000): http://www.people-press.org/jan00rpt2.htm

Putnam, R. D. (1995) "Tuning In, Tuning Out: The Strange Disappearance of Social Capital in America," *PS: Political Science & Politics* 28(4): 664–83.

Putnam, R. D. (2000) *Bowling Alone: The Collapse and Revival of American Community*. New York: Simon & Schuster.

Robinson, M. J. (1977) "Television and American Politics: 1956–1976," *Public Interest* 48: 3–39.

Rosen, J. (1996) *Getting the Connections Right: Public Journalism and the Troubles in the Press*. New York: Twentieth Century Fund Press.

Rosen, J. and Taylor, P. (1992) *The New News v. the Old News: The Press and Politics in the 1990s*. New York: The Twentieth Century Fund Press.

Schudson, M. (1998) *The Good Citizen: A History of American Civic Life*. New York: The Free Press.

Schwartz, E. (1996) *NetActivism: How Citizens Use the Internet*. Sebastopol, CA: Songline Studios.

Tambini, D. (1999) "New Media and Democracy: The Civic Networking Movement," *New Media & Society* 1(3): 305–29.

Tankel, J. D. (1998) "Reconceptualizing Call-in Talk Radio as Listening," *Journal of Radio Studies* 5(1): 36–47.

Verba, S. and Nie, N. H. (1987) *Participation in America: Political Democracy and Social Equality.* Chicago: University of Chicago Press.

Verba, S., Schlozman, K. L., and Brady, H. E. (1995) *Voice and Equality: Civic Volunteerism in American Politics.* Cambridge, MA: Harvard University Press.

Wu, W. and Weaver, D. (1997) "On-line Democracy or On-line Demagoguery? Public Opinion 'Polls' on the Internet," *Press/Politics* 2(4): 71–87.

RELATED LINKS

- Pew Center for Civic Journalism (http://www.pewcenter.org)

- Minnesota e-Democracy Project (http://www.e-democracy.org)

- e-Democracy Home Page (http://www.edemocracy.gov.uk)

- The Daily Show with Jon Stewart (http://www.comedycentral.com/tv_shows/ds)

- MTV: Choose or Lose (http://www.chooseorlose.com)

- Rock the Vote (http://www.rockthevote.org)

- Real Time with Bill Maher (http://www.hbo.com/billmaher)

FOR FURTHER RESEARCH

To find out more about the topics discussed in this reading, use InfoTrac College Edition. Type in keywords and subject terms such as "new media formats," "civic involvement," and "political participation." You can access InfoTrac College Edition from the Wadsworth/Thomson Communication Café homepage: http://communication.wadsworth.com.

Reading 9-2

Smart Mobs: The Power of the Mobile Many
Howard Rheingold

EDITOR'S NOTE

The convergence of mobile communications and computing is driving the next social revolution, veteran cyber explorer Howard Rheingold asserts in this reading from Smart Mobs, *transforming the ways in which wired citizens meet, work, govern, and create. Most pressing, perhaps, are the new ways in which people are engaging in collective action using mobile communications. In the Philippines, political activists mobilized to overthrow a repressive regime by forwarding text messages via cell phones, while in Seattle protestors formed mobile networks that could quickly swarm and disperse to disrupt authorities attempting to maintain order during the World Trade Organization talks. Rheingold predicts that this techno-cultural shift— to coordinated mobile and wireless communications—will be as dramatic as the widespread adoption of the PC in the 1980s and the Internet in the 1990s.*

CONSIDER

1. As more technology becomes wearable and more users rely on mobile communications, people will start using these new media to invent new forms of sex, commerce, entertainment, communion, and conflict. Do you agree? Why or why not?

2. Short Message Service (SMS) was introduced in 1995 as a promotional gimmick. Do you think the technology's designers ever foresaw its use as a tool of political protest?

3. What are the social and political implications of the growing instances of "swarm intelligence" that Rheingold describes?

NETWAR—DARK AND LIGHT

On January 20, 2001, President Joseph Estrada of the Philippines became the first head of state in history to lose power to a smart mob. More than 1 million Manila residents, mobilized and coordinated by waves of text messages, assembled at the site of the 1986 "People Power" peaceful demonstrations that had toppled the Marcos regime.[1] Tens of thousands of Filipinos converged on Epifanio de los Santas Avenue, known as "Edsa," within an hour of the first text message volleys: "Go 2EDSA, Wear blck."[2] Over four days, more than a million citizens showed up, mostly dressed in black. Estrada fell. The legend of "Generation Txt" was born.

Bringing down a government without firing a shot was a momentous early eruption of smart mob behavior. It wasn't, however, the only one.

- On November 30, 1999, autonomous but internetworked squads of demonstrators protesting the meeting of the World Trade Organization used "swarming" tactics, mobile phones, Web sites, laptops, and handheld computers to win the "Battle of Seattle."[3]

- In September 2000, thousands of citizens in Britain, outraged by a sudden rise in gasoline prices, used mobile phones, SMS, email from laptop PCs, and CB radios in taxicabs to coordinate dispersed groups that blocked fuel delivery at selected service stations in a wildcat political protest.[4]

- A violent political demonstration in Toronto in the spring of 2000 was chronicled by a group of roving journalist-researchers who webcast digital video of everything they saw.[5]

- Since 1992, thousands of bicycle activists have assembled monthly for "Critical Mass" moving

demonstrations, weaving through San Francisco streets en masse. Critical Mass operates through loosely linked networks, alerted by mobile phone and email trees, and breaks up into smaller, tele-coordinated groups when appropriate.[6]

Filipinos were veteran texters long before they toppled Estrada. Short Message Service (SMS) messaging was introduced in 1995 as a promotional gimmick.[7] SMS messaging, free at first, remained inexpensive. Wireline telephone service is more costly than mobile service, and in a country where 40 percent of the population lives on one dollar a day, the fact that text messages are one-tenth the price of a voice call is significant.[8] A personal computer costs twenty times as much as a mobile telephone; only 1 percent of the Philippines' population own PCs, although many more use them in Internet cafes.[9] By 2001, however, 5 million Filipinos owned cell phones out of a total population of 70 million.[10]

Filipinos took to SMS messaging with a uniquely intense fervor. By 2001, more than 70 million text messages were being transmitted among Filipinos every day.[11] The word "mania" was used in the Manila press. The *New York Times* reported in 2001:

> Malls are infested with shoppers who appear to be navigating by cellular compass. Groups of diners sit ignoring one another, staring down at their phones as if fumbling with rosaries. Commuters, jaywalkers, even mourners—everyone in the Philippines seems to be texting over the phone. . . . Faye Slytangco, a 23-year-old airline sales representative, was not surprised when at the wake for a friend's father she saw people bowing their heads and gazing toward folded hands. But when their hands started beeping and their thumbs began to move, she realized to her astonishment that they were not in fact praying. "People were actually sitting there and texting," Slytangco said. "Filipinos don't see it as rude any more."[12]

Like the thumb tribes of Tokyo and youth cultures in Scandinavia, Filipino texters took advantage of one

---

From *Smart Mobs: The Next Social Revolution* by Howard Rheingold (Cambridge, MA: Perseus Publishing, 2002), pp. 157–182. Copyright © 2002 by Howard Rheingold. Reprinted with permission.

of the unique features of texting technology: the ease of forwarding jokes, rumors, and chain letters. Although it requires effort to compose messages on mobile telephone keypads, only a few thumb strokes are required to forward a message to four friends or everybody in your telephones address book. Filipino texting culture led to a national panic when a false rumor claimed that Pope John Paul II had died.[13]

Many Filipino text message jokes and rumors were political. Vicente Rafael, professor at the University of California, San Diego, sees Filipino texting culture as inherently subversive:

> Like many third world countries recently opened to more liberal trade policies, the Philippines shares in the paradox of being awash in the latest technologies of communication such as the cell phone while mired in deteriorating infrastructures such as roads, postal services, railroads, power generators and land lines. With the cell phone, one appears to be able to pass beyond these obstacles. And inasmuch as such infrastructures are state run so that their breakdown and inefficiencies are a direct function of governmental ineptitude, passing beyond them also feels like overcoming the state, which to begin with is already overcome by corruption. It is small wonder then that cell phones could prove literally handy in spreading rumors, jokes, and information that steadily eroded whatever legitimacy President Estrada still had.[14]

The "People Power II" demonstrations of 2001 broke out when the impeachment trial of President Estrada was suddenly ended by senators linked to Estrada. Opposition leaders broadcast text messages, and within seventy-five minutes of the abrupt halt of the impeachment proceedings, 20,000 people converged on Edsa.[15] Over four days, more than a million people showed up. The military withdrew support from the regime; the Estrada government fell, as the Marcos regime had fallen a decade previously, largely as a result of massive nonviolent demonstrations.[16] The rapid assembly of the anti-Estrada crowd was a hallmark of early smart mob technology, and the millions of text messages exchanged by the demonstrators in 2001 was, by all accounts, a key to the crowd's esprit de corps.

Professor Rafael sees the SMS-linked crowd that assembled in Manila as the manifestation of a phenomenon that was enabled by a technical infrastructure but that is best understood as a social instrument:

> The power of the crowd thus comes across in its capacity to overwhelm the physical constraints of urban planning in the same way that it tends to blur social distinctions by provoking a sense of estrangement. Its authority rests on its ability to promote restlessness and movement, thereby undermining the pressure from state technocrats, church authorities and corporate interests to regulate and contain such movements. In this sense, the crowd is a sort of medium if by that word one means the means for gathering and transforming elements, objects, people and things. As a medium, the crowd is also the site for the generation of expectations and the circulation of messages. It is in this sense that we might also think of the crowd not merely as an effect of technological devices, but as a kind of technology itself. . . . Centralized urban planning and technologies of policing seek to routinize the sense of contingency generated in crowding. But at moments and in areas where such planning chronically fails, routine can at times give way to the epochal. At such moments, the crowd . . . takes on a kind of telecommunicative power, serving up channels for sending messages at a distance and bringing distances up close. Enmeshed in a crowd, one feels the potential for reaching out across social space and temporal divides.[17]

The Battle of Seattle saw a more deliberate and tactically focused use of wireless communications and mobile social networks in urban political conflict, more than a year before texting mobs assembled in Manila. A broad coalition of demonstrators who represented different interests but were united in opposition to the views of the World Trade Organization planned to disrupt the WTO's 1999 meeting in Seattle. The demonstrators included a wide range of different "affinity groups" who loosely coordinated their actions around their shared objective. The Direct Action Network enabled autonomous groups to choose which levels of action to participate in, from nonviolent support to civil disobedience to joining mass arrests—a kind of dynamic ad hoc alliance that wouldn't have been possible without a mobile, many-to-many, real-time communication network. According to a report dramatically titled, "Black Flag Over Seattle," by Paul de Armond:

> The cohesion of the Direct Action Network was partly due to their improvised communications network assembled out of cell phones, radios,

police scanners and portable computers. Protesters in the street with wireless Palm Pilots were able to link into continuously updated web pages giving reports from the streets. Police scanners monitored transmissions and provided some warning of changing police tactics. Cell phones were widely used.

Kelly Quirke, Executive Director of the Rainforest Action Network reports that early Tuesday, "the authorities had successfully squashed DAN's communications system." The solution to the infrastructure attack was quickly resolved by purchasing new Nextel cell phones. According to Han Shan, the Ruckus Society's WTO action coordinator, his organization and other protest groups that formed the Direct Action Network used the Nextel system to create a cellular grid over the city. They broke into talk groups of eight people each. One of the eight overlapped with another talk group, helping to quickly communicate through the ranks.

In addition to the organizers' all-points network protest communications were leavened with individual protesters using cell phones, direct transmissions from roving independent media feeding directly onto the Internet, personal computers with wireless modems broadcasting live video, and a variety of other networked communications. Floating above the tear gas was a pulsing infosphere of enormous bandwidth, reaching around the planet via the Internet.[18]

From Seattle to Manila, the first "netwars" have already broken out. The term "netwar" was coined by John Arquilla and David Ronfeldt, two analysts for the RAND corporation (birthplace of game theory and experimental economics), who noticed that the same combination of social networks, sophisticated communication technologies, and decentralized organizational structure was surfacing as an effective force in very different kinds of political conflict:

Netwar is an emerging mode of conflict in which the protagonists—ranging from terrorist and criminal organizations on the dark side, to militant social activists on the bright side—use network forms of organization, doctrine, strategy, and technology attuned to the information age. The practice of netwar is well ahead of theory, as both civil and uncivil society actors are increasingly engaging in this new way of fighting.

From the Battle of Seattle to the "attack on America," these networks are proving very hard to deal with; some are winning. What all have in common is that they operate in small, dispersed units that can deploy nimbly—anywhere, anytime. All feature network forms of organization, doctrine, strategy, and technology attuned to the information age. They know how to swarm and disperse, penetrate and disrupt, as well as elude and evade. The tactics they use range from battles of ideas to acts of sabotage—and many tactics involve the Internet.[19]

The "swarming" strategies noted by Arquilla and Ronfeldt rely on many small units like the affinity groups in the Battle of Seattle. Individual members of each group remained dispersed until mobile communications drew them to converge on a specific location from all directions simultaneously, in coordination with other groups. Manila, Seattle, San Francisco, Senegal, and Britain were sites of nonviolent political swarming. Arquilla and Ronfeldt cited the nongovernmental organizations associated with the Zapatista movement in Mexico, which mobilized world opinion in support of Indian peasants, and the Nobel Prize–winning effort to enact an anti-landmine treaty as examples of nonviolent netwar actions. Armed and violent swarms are another matter.

The Chechen rebels in Russia, soccer hooligans in Britain, and the FARC guerrillas in Colombia also have used netwar strategy and swarming tactics.[20] The U.S. military is in the forefront of smart mob technology development. The Joint Expeditionary Digital Information (JEDI) program links troops on the ground directly to satellite communications. JEDI handheld devices combine laser range-finding, GPS location awareness, direct satellite telephone, and encrypted text messaging.[21] Remember the DARPA-funded startup MeshNetworks . . . the company whose technology enables military swarms to parachute onto a battlefield and self-organize an ad hoc peer-to-peer wireless network? Small teams of special forces, wirelessly networked and capable of calling in aircraft or missile strikes with increasing accuracy, were introduced by the United States and its allies in Afghanistan: netwar.

Netwars do share similar technical infrastructure with other smart mobs. More importantly, however, they are both animated by a new form of social organization, the network. Networks include nodes and links, use many possible paths to distribute information from any link to any other, and are self-regulated through flat governance hierarchies and distributed power. Arquilla and Ronfeldt are among many who believe networks constitute the newest major social organizational form. Although network-structured communications hold real potential for enabling democratic forms of decision-making and beneficial instances of collective action, that doesn't mean that the transition to networked forms of social organization will be a pleasant one with uniformly benevolent outcomes. Arquilla and Ronfeldt note the potential for cooperation in examples like the nongovernmental organizations that use netwar tactics for public benefit, but they also articulated a strong caution, worth keeping in mind when contemplating the future of smart mobs:

> Most people might hope for the emergence of a new form of organization to be led by "good guys" who do "the right thing" and grow stronger because of it. But history does not support this contention. The cutting edge in the early rise of a new form may be found equally among malcontents, ne'er-do-wells, and clever opportunists eager to take advantage of new ways to maneuver, exploit, and dominate. Many centuries ago, for example, the rise of hierarchical forms of organization, which displaced traditional, consultative, tribal forms, was initially attended, in parts of the world, by the appearance of ferocious chieftains bent on military conquest and of violent secret societies run according to rank—long before the hierarchical form matured through the institutionalization of states, empires, and professional administrative and bureaucratic systems. In like manner, the early spread of the market form, only a few centuries ago, was accompanied by a spawn of usurers, pirates, smugglers, and monopolists, all seeking to elude state controls over their earnings and enterprises.[22]

In light of the military applications of netwar tactics, it would be foolish to presume that only benign outcomes should be expected from smart mobs. But any observer who focuses exclusively on the potential for violence would miss evidence of perhaps an even more profoundly disruptive potential—for beneficial as well as malign purposes—of smart mob technologies and techniques. Could cooperation epidemics break out if smart mob media spread beyond warriors—to citizens, journalists, scientists, people looking for fun, friends, mates, customers, or trading patterns?

Consider a few experiments on the fringes of mobile communications that might point toward a wide variety of nonviolent smart mobs in the future:

- "Interpersonal awareness devices" have been evolving for several years.[23] Since 1998, hundreds of thousands of Japanese have used Lovegety keychain devices, which signal when another Lovegety owner of the opposite sex and a compatible profile is within fifteen feet.[24] In 2000, a similar technology for same-sex seekers, the "Gaydar" device, was marketed in North America.[25] Hong Kong's "Mobile Cupid Service" (www.sunday.com) sends a text description of potential matches who are nearby at the moment.[26]

- ImaHima ("are you free now?") enables hundreds of thousands of Tokyo i-mode users to alert buddies who are in their vicinity at the moment.[27]

- Upoc ("universal point of contact") in Manhattan sponsors mobile communities of interest; any member of "manhattan celebrity watch," "nyc terrorism alert," "prayer of the day," or "The Resistance," for example, can broadcast text messages to and receive messages from all the other members.[28]

- Phones that make it easy to send digital video directly to the Web make it possible for "peer-to-peer journalism" networks to emerge;[29] Steve Mann's students in Toronto have chronicled newsworthy events by webcasting everything their wearable cameras and microphones capture.[30]

- Researchers in Oregon have constructed "social middleware," which enables wearable computer users to form ad-hoc communities, using distributed reputation systems, privacy and knowledge sharing agents, and wireless networks.[31]

In 2000, WearComp researcher, innovator, and evangelist Steve Mann launched "ENGwear, an experiment in wearable news-gathering systems conducted by students and researchers at the Humanistic Intelligence Lab at the University of Toronto."[32] In the spring of 2000, Mann and a group of his students, all wearing computers equipped with "EyeTaps," which broadcast everything they saw and heard to the Web, showed up at a demonstration in Toronto called by the Ontario Coalition Against Poverty (OCAP). Violence broke out. Mann reported, "We, along with the journalists and various television crews, ran for cover. However, unlike the reporters, my students and I were

still broadcasting, capturing almost by accident the entire event. Whatever we saw before us was captured and sent instantly in real time to the World Wide Web, without our conscious thought or effort."[33]

Mann claims that the WearComp journalist-researchers who made their first appearance at the OCAP demonstration could be a model for a wider movement, which could influence as well as chronicle events:

> WearComp represents a solution to this legacy of suppressed creativity and confining imagination in an age where ever-fewer sources of information seem to reach us, even as the conduits of information grow exponentially. What my students and I undertook in deciding to "cover" the OCAP protest was an experiment in media diversification. This is the process by which we merge our cyborg narratives with the demands of a growing cyberspace that we should, and one day will, be able to interact with control. Facilitating the individual's creation and broadcast of their own narratives and perspectives is an important part of wearable computing technology. What my students and I did—and continue to do— is something far more important than just providing "home movies" and "alternative" images for viewing on the Internet. We are also engaging in a process of cultural reclamation, where the individual is put back into the loop of information production and dispensation.[34]

SWARM INTELLIGENCE AND THE SOCIAL MIND

Massive outbreaks of cooperation precipitated the collapse of communism. In city after city, huge crowds assembled in nonviolent street demonstrations, despite decades of well-founded fear of political assembly. Although common sense leads to the conclusion that unanimity of opinion among the demonstrators explained the change of behavior, Natalie Glance and Bernardo Huberman, Xerox PARC researchers who have studied the dynamics of social systems, noted that a *diversity* of cooperation thresholds among the individuals can tip a crowd into a sudden epidemic of cooperation. Glance and Huberman pointed out that a minority of extremists can choose to act first, and if the conditions are right, their actions can trigger actions by others who needed to see somebody make the first move before acting themselves—at which point the bandwagon-jumpers follow the early adopters who followed the first actors:

> Those transitions can trigger a cascade of further cooperation until the whole group is cooperating.
>
> The events that led to the mass protests in Leipzig and Berlin and to the subsequent downfall of the East German government in November 1989 vividly illustrate the impact of such diversity on the resolution of social dilemmas. . . . The citizens of Leipzig who desired a change of government faced a dilemma. They could stay home in safety or demonstrate against the government and risk arrest—knowing that as the number of demonstrators rose, the risk declined and the potential for overthrowing the regime increased.
>
> A conservative person would demonstrate against the government only if thousands were already committed; a revolutionary might join at the slightest sign of unrest. That variation in threshold is one form of diversity. People also differed in their estimates of the duration of a demonstration as well as in the amount of risk they were willing to take. Bernhardt Prosch and Martin Abram, two sociologists from Erlangen University who studied the Leipzig demonstrations, claim that the diversity in thresholds was important in triggering the mass demonstrations.[35]

Sudden epidemics of cooperation aren't necessarily pleasant experiences. Lynch mobs and entire nations cooperate to perpetrate atrocities. Decades before the fall of communism, sociologist Mark Granovetter examined radical collective behavior of both positive and negative kinds and proposed a "threshold model of collective behavior." I recognize Granovetter's model as a crucial conceptual bridge that connects intelligent (smart mob) cooperation with "emergent" behaviors of unintelligent actors, such as hives, flocks, and swarms.

What happens when the individuals in a tightly coordinated group are more highly intelligent creatures rather than simpler organisms like insects or birds? How do humans exhibit emergent behavior? As soon as this question occurred to me, I immediately recalled the story Kevin Kelly told at the beginning of *Out of Control,* his 1994 book about the emergent behaviors in biology, machinery, and human affairs.[36] He described an event at an annual film show for computer graphics professionals. A small paddle was attached to each seat in the auditorium, with reflective material of contrasting colors on each side of the paddle. The screen in the auditorium displayed a high-contrast, real-time video view of the audience. The person leading the exercise, computer graphics wizard Loren Carpenter, asked those on one side of the auditorium aisle to hold the paddles with one color showing and asked the other half of the audience to hold up the opposite color. Then, following Carpenter's suggestions, the audience self-organized a dot that moved around the screen, added a couple of paddles on the screen, and began to play a giant game of self-organized video Pong, finally creating a graphical representation of an airplane and flying it around the screen. Like flocks, there was no central control of the exercise after Carpenter made a suggestion. Members of the audience paid attention to what their neighbors were doing and what was happening on the screen. Kelly used this as an example of a self-conscious version of flocking behavior.[37]

Musician and cognitive scientist William Benzon believes that the graphical coordination exercise led by Carpenter and described by Kelly is similar to what happens when musicians "jam" and that it involves a yet unexplored synchronization of brain processes among the people involved:[38]

> The group in Carpenter's story is controlling what appears on the screen. Everyone can see it all, but each can directly affect only the part of the display they control with his or her paddle. In jamming, everyone hears everything but can affect only that part of the collective sound that they create (or withhold).
>
> Now consider a different example. One of the standard scenes in prison movies goes like this: We're in a cell block or in the mess hall. One prisoner starts banging his cup on the table (or on one of the bars to his cell). Another joins in, then another, and another, until everyone's banging away and shouting some slogan in unison. This is a simple example of emergent behavior.
>
> But it's one that you won't find in chimpanzees. Yes, you will find them involved in group displays where they're all hooting and hollering and stomping. But the synchrony isn't as precise as it is in the human case.
>
> And that precision is critical to my argument. That precision allows me to treat the human group as a collection of coupled oscillators. Oscil-

lation is one of the standard and simplest emergent phenomena. Once a group has become coupled in oscillation, we can treat the group as a single entity. To be sure, there's more to music than simple oscillation. But oscillation is the foundation, the starting point, and all the elaboration and complexities take place within this framework.

> In effect, in musical performance (and in dance), communication between individuals is pretty much the same as communication between components of a single nervous system. It's continuous and two-way, and it does not involve symbolic mediation. Think of Goffman's interaction order, but drop verbal communication from it. It is a public space that is physically external to the brains of participating individuals, but it is functionally internal to those brains.[39]

Kevin Kelly traced back the new theories regarding emergent properties to William Morton Wheeler, an expert in the behavior of ants.[40] Wheeler called insect colonies "superorganisms" and defined the ability of the hive to accomplish tasks that no individual ant or bee is intelligent enough to do on its own as "emergent properties" of the superorganism. Kelly drew parallels between the ways both biological and artificial "vivisystems" exhibit the same four characteristics of what he called "swarm systems":

- the absence of imposed centralized control
- the autonomous nature of subunits
- the high connectivity between the subunits
- the webby nonlinear causality of peers influencing peers[41]

Steven Johnson's 2001 book *Emergence,* shows how the principles that Kelly extrapolated from biological to technological networks also apply to cities and Amazon.com's recommendation system: "In these systems, agents residing on one scale start producing behavior that lies on one scale above them: ants create colonies; urbanites create neighborhoods; simple pattern-recognition software learns how to recommend new books. The movement from low-level rules to higher level sophistication is what we call emergence."[42] In the case of cities, although the emergent intelligence resembles the ant-mind, the individual units, humans, possess extraordinary onboard intelligence—or at least the capacity for it.

At this point, connections between the behavior of smart mobs and the behavior of swarm systems must be tentative, yet several of the earliest investigations have shown that the right kinds of online social networks know more than the sum of their parts: Connected and communicating in the right ways, populations of humans can exhibit a kind of "collective intelligence."

Decades ago, computer scientists thought that someday there would be forms of "artificial intelligence," but with the exception of a few visionaries, they never thought in terms of computer-equipped humans as a kind of social intelligence. Although everyone who understands the use of statistical techniques to make predictions hastens to add the disclaimer that surprises are inevitable, and one of the fundamental characteristics of complex adaptive systems is their unpredictability, the initial findings that internetworked groups of humans can exhibit emergent prediction capabilities are potentially profound.

The Internet is what happened when a lot of computers started communicating. The computer and the Internet were designed, but the ways people used them were not designed into either technology, nor were the most world-shifting uses of these tools anticipated by their designers or vendors. Word processing and virtual communities, eBay and e-commerce, Google and weblogs and reputation systems *emerged*. Smart mobs are an unpredictable but at least partially describable emergent property that I see surfacing as more people use mobile telephones, more chips communicate with each other, more computers know where they are located, more technology becomes wearable, more people start using these new media to invent new forms of sex, commerce, entertainment, communion, and, as always, conflict.

NOTES

1. Michael Bociurkiw, "Revolution by Cell Phone," *Forbes,* 10 September 2001, <http://www.forbes.com/asap/2001/0910/028.html> (1 March 2002).

2. Ibid.

3. Paul de Armond, "Black Flag Over Seattle," *Albion Monitor* 72, March 2000, <http://www.monitor.net~monitor/seattlewto/index.html> (1 March 2002).

4. Alexander MacLeod, "Call to Picket Finds New Ring in Britain's Fuel Crisis," *Christian Science Monitor,* 19 September 2000. See also: Chris Marsden, "Britain's Labour Government and Trade Union Leaders Unite to Crush Fuel Tax Protest," *World Socialist Web Site,* 15 September 2000, http://www.wsws.org/articles/2000/sep2000/fuel-sl5.shtml (1 March 2002).

5. Steve Mann and Hal Niedzviecki, *Cyborg: Digital Destiny and Human Possibility in the Age of the Wearable Computer* (Mississauga: Doubleday Canada, 2001), 177–178.

6. Critical Mass, <http://www.critical-mass.org/> (6 March 2002).

7. Anne Torres, "4 SME, Txtng is Lyf," *TheFeature.com,* 18 April 2001, <http:/www.thefeature.com> (1 March 2002).

8. Bociurkiw, "Revolution by Cell Phone."

9. Vincente Rafael, "The Cell Phone and the Crowd: Messianic Politics in Recent Philippine History," 13 June 2001. http://communication.ucsd.edu/people/f_rafael.cellphone.html.

10. Ibid.

11. Arturo Bariuad, "Text Messaging Becomes a Menace in the Philippines," *Straits Times,* 3 March 2001.

12. Wayne Arnold, "Manila's Talk of the Town Is Text Messaging," *New York Times,* 5 July 2000, C1.

13. Bariuad, "Text Messaging Becomes a Menace."

14. Rafael, "The Cell Phone and the Crowd."

15. Ibid.

16. Richard Lloyd Parry, "The TXT MSG Revolution," *Independent Digital,* 23 January 2001, <http://www.independent.co.uk/storyjsp?story=51748> (1 March 2002).

17. Rafael, "The Cell Phone and the Crowd."

18. de Armond, "Black Flag Over Seattle."

19. David Ronfeldt and John Arquilla, "Networks, Netwars, and the Fight for the Future," *First Monday* 6, 10 (October 2001), <http://firstmonday.org/issues/issue6_10/ronfeldt/index.html> (1 March 2002).

20. John Arquilla and David Ronfeldt, eds., *Networks and Netwars: The Future of Terror, Crime, and Militancy* (Santa Monica, Calif.: RAND, 2001).

21. Ian Sample, "Military Palmtop to Cut Collateral Damage," *New Scientist,* 9 March 2002 <http://www.newscientist.com/news/news.jsp?id=nw99992005> (29 March 2002).

22. Arquilla and Ronfeldt, eds., *Networks and Netwars,* 310–313.

23. Nick Montfort, "My Pager, My Matchmaker," *Ziff Davis Smart Business,* 7 July 2000, <http://www.techupdate.zdnet.com/techupdate/stories/main/0,14179,2577889,0.html> (1 March 2002).

24. "Bleep at First Sight," *Reuters,* 15 May 1998, <http://www.wired.com/news/news/culture/story/12342.html> (1 March 2002).

25. Craig Wilson, "Gaydar Device Clears Up Mixed Signals," *USA Today,* 25 February 2000,

<http://www.usatoday.com/life/cyber/tech/review/crg942.htm> (1 March 2002).

26. Montfort, "My Pager, My Matchmaker."

27. ImaHima, <http://www.imahima.com/index.jsp> (1 March 2002).

28. Diego Ibarguen, "Tracking Celebrities Via Cell Phones, Web Sites," *San Francisco Chronicle,* 21 January 2001.

29. Justin Hall, "Mobile Reporting: Peer-to-Peer News," *TheFeature.com,* 20 February 2002, <http://www.thefeature.com/printable.jsp?pageid=14274> (1 March 2002).

30. Mann and Niedzviecki, *Cyborg.*

31. Gerd Kortuem et al., "Close Encounters: Supporting Mobile Collaboration through Interchange of User Profiles," in *Proceedings of the First International Symposium on Handheld and Ubiquitous Computing* (HUC99), 1999 Karlsruhe, Germany, <http://www.cs.uoregon.edu/research/wearables/Papers/HUC99-kortuem.pdf> (6 March 2002).

32. ENGwear: Wearable Wireless Systems for Electronic News Gathering, <http://www.eyetap.org/hi/ENGwear> (1 March 2002).

33. Mann and Niedzviecki, *Cyborg,* 175–176.

34. Ibid., 177–178.

35. Natalie S. Glanae and Bernardo A. Huberman, "The Dynamics of Social Dilemmas," *Scientific American,* March 1994, 76–81.

36. Kevin Kelly, *Out of Control* (Reading, Mass.: Addison-Wesley, 1994), <http://www.kk.org/outofcontrol/index.html> (6 March 2002).

37. Ibid.

38. William Benzon, *Beethoven's Anvil: Music in Mind and Culture* (New York: Basic Books, 2001).

39. William Benzon, e-mail interview by author.

40. William Morton Wheeler, *Emergent Evolution and the Development of Societies* (New York: W. W. Norton, 1928).

41. Ibid.

42. Steven Johnson, *Emergence: The Connected Lives of Ants, Brains, Cities, and Software* (New York: Scribner, 2001).

RELATED LINKS

- Smart Mobs website and weblog (http://www.smartmobs.com/index.htm)

- Edge: Smart Mobs (http://www.edge.org/3rd_culture/rheingold/rheingold_print.html)

- Rheingold's Brainstorms (http://www.rheingold.com/index.html)

- The Emergence of the Mobile Tech Smart Flash Mob (http://www.webtalkguys.com/article-smartflashmobs.shtml)

FOR FURTHER RESEARCH

To find out more about the topics discussed in this reading, use InfoTrac College Edition. Type in keywords and subject terms such as "smart mobs," "swarm intelligence," and "netwar." You can access InfoTrac College Edition from the Wadsworth/Thomson Communication Café homepage: http://communication.wadsworth.com.

Reading 9-3

Universal Access to E-mail
Robert H. Anderson, Tora K. Bikson, Sally Ann Law, and Bridger M. Mitchell

EDITOR'S NOTE

This 1995 report from the respected RAND think tank, a bestseller among policy proposals, outlines the rationale for guaranteeing nearly universal access to e-mail in the United States, along the lines of universal telephone service. The authors main-

tain that the unique properties of e-mail allow individuals to engage in an active civic dialog, fostering interactive communication among citizens and delivering significant social and political benefits in the process.

CONSIDER

1. Despite the arguments in favor of universal access, do you think providing e-mail accounts to nearly all U.S. citizens is a desirable and feasible idea?

2. In your view, will increased access to e-mail help reduce the feelings of alienation that many citizens feel and revitalize the involvement of ordinary citizens in the political process?

3. What are some of the disadvantages of making e-mail universally accessible, and why?

Over the last 15 years, the burgeoning use of personal computers has popularized a number of new information services, including in particular electronic mail or "e-mail." E-mail is a form of information interchange in which messages are sent from one personal computer (or computer terminal) to another via modems and a telecommunications system. The use of e-mail began on the ARPAnet (the precursor of the Internet) in the 1960s and 1970s in the United States, gradually spread along with the use of mainframe- and minicomputer-based local nets in the 1970s, and "exploded" along with the rapid growth of personal computers (PCs) and the Internet in the 1980s. E-mail began as a means of information interchange for small, select groups; its use has spread to encompass millions of people in the United States and all over the world. E-mail has given rise to the formation of many "virtual communities"—groups of individuals, often widely separated geographically, who share common interests. The interpersonal linkages and loyalties associated with these virtual communities can be real and powerful.

E-mail has unique properties that distinguish it from other forms of communication; for example, it supports true interactive communication among many participants. For the first time in human history, we would assert, the means of "broadcasting" or "narrowcasting" are not confined to the few with printing presses, TV stations, money to buy access to those scarce resources, and the like. E-mail is also, unlike telephone calls (with the exception of voice mail and

answering machines), asynchronous, so that communication does not depend on the simultaneous availability and attention of sender and recipient. Generalizing greatly, e-mail increases the power of individuals, permitting them to be active participants in a dialog extended in both time and space, rather than passive recipients of "canned" programming and prepackaged information. These characteristics give rise to the question: Can e-mail's novel properties address society's most compelling problems? If so, by what means?

PROBLEM STATEMENT

It is now possible to imagine the arrangement or construction of systems in which nearly universal access to e-mail within the United States could become feasible within a decade—indeed, that is one aspiration of the U.S. National Information Infrastructure (NII) initiative. Since e-mail use is growing rapidly (e.g., within individual corporations, CompuServe, America Online, Internet, and Bitnet systems and on numerous dial-in electronic bulletin boards), the question may be asked: "Why bother? It's happening anyway." Three important answers to this question are: (1) In spite of the growth of these e-mail systems, the majority of U.S. residents probably will continue to lack access to e-mail well into the next century without societal intervention; (2) there is today a significant lack of active participation by many citizens in the dialog that forms the basis for the U.S. democratic process[1]; and (3) some citizens, such as inner-city minorities and the rural poor, are relatively disenfranchised and constitute groups that will be the last to be reached by commercial e-mail systems that evolve in private markets. Because the properties of e-mail allow individuals to en-

From "Universal Access to E-mail," in *Universal Access to E-mail: Feasibility and Societal Implications* by Robert H. Anderson, Tora K. Bikson, Sally Ann Law, and Bridger M. Mitchell (Santa Monica, CA: RAND Corporation, 1995), pp. 1–11. Copyright © 1995 RAND Corporation. Reprinted with permission.

gage in an active civic dialog, with informative and affiliative dimensions, universal e-mail might provide significant benefits in creating interactive communication among U.S. citizens and residents.

The problem, then, is achieving active, responsive citizen participation in our national dialog for all citizens—participation not only in national politics but in local affairs, job markets, educational systems, health and welfare systems, international discourse, and all other aspects of our society.

There are hints that the distinctive properties of electronic mail systems (including access to, and the ability to post and retrieve messages from, various electronic bulletin boards) may well be relevant to this re-enfranchisement of all citizens. Civic networks exemplify these opportunities.

It is also clear that widespread citizen access to an e-mail system could have profound economic implications that might provide new sources of business and revenue to entrepreneurs providing new services; for example, installation of the French Programme Télétel system resulted in a flourishing of electronic services available to virtually all French citizens (and, for that matter, many visitors—through terminals available in hotel rooms and public sites).

It is important to note, however, that the Minitel terminal used by Télétel was not originally conceived of as access to an e-mail system but rather as an "electronic telephone directory." As is often the case, when some facility for communication becomes possible within a system (e.g., ARPAnet, Télétel, and to a growing extent the Dialog system within the United States), its convenience and empowerment of individuals quickly cause e-mail to become an important form of usage. Lack of true e-mail capabilities may be a major contributor to the failure of other electronic service ventures such as teletext experiments, although too many factors may be involved to confirm this assessment.

UNIVERSAL E-MAIL

The initial forays into widespread availability of electronic mail, such as the ARPAnet (and now Internet) experience, Télétel, and growing Prodigy, Compu-Serve, and America Online usage, lead to an intriguing question: What about "universal e-mail?" What about providing all residents of the United States with access to e-mail service, just as they now all (or almost all) have

access to telephone service and postal service? What would be involved in such an undertaking? What are the pros and cons? What are the advantages and disadvantages? Could this have beneficial effects for U.S. society? Greater cohesion? Reduced alienation? Increased participation in the political process? Influence national security? What about beneficial effects for the U.S. economy? Or other productive side effects? And who would pay for the infrastructure and its usage?

More specific questions arise immediately regarding the services and functions to be provided by a universal e-mail system: the required degree of access to such a "universal" service; the provision of privacy; alternative system architectures and implementation schemes; the cost of such a system/service and the method of payment; the likely social and international effect of universal e-mail; and finally, public versus private roles in creating and operating such a service. This report describes our initial study of these and related issues over a two-year period and presents the results of our analyses.

SOME DEFINITIONS

Electronic Mail

For the purposes of this report, we have adopted a definition of electronic mail provided in an earlier RAND report (Anderson et al., 1989):

An electronic mail system:

1. Permits the asynchronous electronic interchange of information between persons, groups of persons, and functional units of an organization; and

2. Provides mechanisms supporting the creation, distribution, consumption, processing, and storage of this information.

The words in this definition all have significance. Key among them are the following:

- *Asynchronous:* One defining attribute of e-mail is the ability to send a message when the recipient is not at that moment logged in; the message is placed in an "inbox" for later inspection by the recipient at his or her convenience.

- *Electronic:* The message travels over telecommunication systems at the speed of electricity in copper, of light in a fiber optic cable, or of microwave or a satellite link (plus additional switching delays). Although some system "gateways" buffer messages for periodic transmission, the result still has a dynamic fundamentally different from postal mail, newspapers, and other traditional media.

- *Interchange of information:* Anyone within the system can send as well as receive messages.

- *Between persons, groups of persons, and functional units of an organization:* Messages may be sent to "mailboxes" representing individuals or groups; "aliases" may be established representing a number of individual addresses, so that a message may be sent to a group of individuals in one action; mailboxes such as "purchasing@abc.com" or "president@whitehouse.gov" may be established that represent a function, to be used by whomever is presently handling that function.

- *Mechanisms supporting the creation, distribution, consumption, processing, and storage:* It must be possible to create messages, send and receive them, store them for future inspection and re-use, and "process" them (e.g., copy portions and paste them into later messages, forward them to others, modify their contents, and reuse them in other applications).

By the above definition, multipart messages containing embedded formatted word-processing documents, video clips, bitmapped pictures, sound clips, and the like are certainly e-mail. Faxes sent from one dedicated fax machine to another, appearing only on output paper are not (because they are not processable in a useful manner), but a "fax" sent from one PC to another meets the definition (because it may be stored for later retransmission, and its contents may be "processed"—e.g., by character recognition or graphics enhancement programs; in fact, some recipients may never get it in paper form. Similarly, using a personal computer to interact with "chat" groups and MUDs[2] usually qualifies as a form of e-mail, because most communication programs through which this interaction is carried out allow the transcript of the interaction to be saved, processed, reused, and so on.

We have tried to use a rather narrow definition of e-mail to focus this report on electronic mail, although it will be clear that most e-mail users will also have facilities at hand to browse the World Wide Web, participate in multi-user simulations and games, and so forth.

UNIVERSAL ACCESS

The other key concept in this report is "universal access." By this, we simply mean e-mail facilities and services that are:

- Available at modest individual effort and expense to (almost) everyone in the United States in a form that does not require highly specialized skills; or,

- Accessible in a manner analogous to the level, cost, and ease of use of telephone service or the U.S. Postal Service.

We do not, therefore, envision that every single person will have access, but that e-mail can achieve the same ubiquity that telephones (including the availability of payphones) and TVs have. . . .

Note that [related technologies] are not distributed uniformly across various sectors of our society. For example, a recent report (Mueller & Schement, 1995) describes telephone access in Camden, New Jersey, by family income, ethnicity, age, and other demographic factors. The report indicates that, overall, only 80.6 percent of households in Camden have telephones; notable disparities include families on food stamps, who lag 20.4 percentage points behind households not on food stamps. For many households, "universal access" means traveling to the nearest working payphone (where receiving incoming messages is sometimes precluded either socially or by the technology). Similarly, universal access to e-mail for many may require using public terminals in shared spaces such as libraries and schools (but where barriers to message reception can readily be eliminated).

ADVANTAGES OF UNIVERSAL E-MAIL

E-mail services can be used both for "telephone-type" messages and for other, usually longer, messages or documents that might otherwise be sent using facsimile or hard-copy postal services, both public and private. Compared with the telephone system, one primary advantage of an e-mail service is that it eliminates "telephone tag." It also provides a content record of the interactions that can be retrieved, printed, studied, selectively forwarded, and in general reused. Other advantages are that it permits (but certainly does not require) more deliberative and reflective, but still interactive, conversational dialogs, as well as one-to-many and many-to-many conversations. These features have led to many new social, commercial, and political groupings of people: the "virtual communities" mentioned above, using e-mail as the linkage. It provides a common context among a set of participants.

Compared with postal services, an e-mail service offers much faster mail delivery—usually minutes between any two locations in the United States (although currently, delays up to a day occur with some Internet access providers), compared with one to several days for postal systems. E-mail systems also afford much more flexibility (both locational and temporal) in that delivery. In the current postal system, a person's mail is delivered to one or two (or at most a few) fixed addresses (e.g., home or office). In most e-mail systems, a person with the proper (portable) terminal equipment can log in to his or her "mailbox" from any location that has electronic access to the system. Today, this means that people can pick up their e-mail from their office, their home, their hotel rooms, another office (perhaps in another city) they are visiting, or any site with a phone jack.[3] In the future, as terminal equipment gets smaller and cellular telephones become more ubiquitous, one will be able to pick up or send e-mail while traveling in a car and flying in an airplane. This results in more geographic independence (*where* one gets mail) and temporal flexibility (*when* one gets mail).

These advantages are available in any e-mail system. The additional advantage of a universal e-mail system is that since everyone belongs to the system, a user can send e-mail to anyone, not just a limited group, and receive e-mail from anyone. This makes the special advantages of e-mail available for all of one's correspondence, not just a subset. If the costs of such a service permit attractive pricing, it could take over a significant portion of the business of current postal services[4]—especially when next-generation e-mail systems allow the transmission and viewing of multimedia messages containing high resolution color pictures, "movie clips" of image sequences, and sound, which could, among other things, support a variety of "electronic commerce."

DISADVANTAGES OF UNIVERSAL E-MAIL

The concept of universal e-mail raises serious concerns as well. For example, individual users could get "flooded" with messages, unless some means of "filtering" incoming message traffic is provided. Also, some

virtual communities enabled by e-mail could be bad for U.S. society, rather than good; they could conceivably lead to a less cohesive society, rather than a more cohesive one. It is also clear that within any e-mail system, some users will be "more equal" than others; they will be able to purchase more powerful equipment, giving them more power over their electronic communication. Some will become more knowledgeable in the features and facilities of the system—permitting them, for example, to assemble tailored mailing lists for broadcast of their messages—allowing them to take advantage of those features for their own personal benefit or gain. Special-interest groups may in particular be motivated to become further empowered by use of these communication tools. Some (but not all) would also consider it a disadvantage that national borders become more transparent to international commerce and influences (Ronfeldt et al., 1993).

MOTIVATIONS FOR UNIVERSAL E-MAIL

The apparent advantages of universal e-mail, despite the possible side effects and disadvantages, lead to a number of possible motivations for establishing such a service in the United States, ranging across the spectrum from the utilitarian to the idealistic. At the utilitarian end is efficiency. Electronic mail uses modern information and telecommunications technology to provide a much faster and more efficient means of conveying information from one point to another than current postal systems, which rely on "technologies"—letters written on paper, put in sealed envelopes, and physically transported from sender to receiver—over two millennia old. The increased speed and efficiency of information delivery by e-mail could have many commercial and economic benefits, contributing to increased U.S. economic competitiveness.

At the idealistic end of the spectrum of motivations, the hypothesis is made that electronic mail makes possible much more egalitarian, deliberative, and reflective dialogs among individuals and groups (see Sproull & Kiesler, 1991, for supporting evidence). It might therefore lead to new social and political linkages within U.S. society, reduce the feelings of alienation that many individuals in the United States feel and give them a new sense of "community," revitalize the involvement of the common citizen in the political process, etc., and in general strengthen the cohesion of U.S. society.

Different motivations across this spectrum will appeal to different elements of U.S. society. To achieve widespread appeal—and political/economic support—a U.S. universal e-mail service should satisfy a broad spectrum of these motivations, whether the system is "designed" to meet these objectives (e.g., with heavy U.S. government involvement) or evolves through private initiative and entrepreneurship subject to constraints, incentives, or standards that encourage universal access.

—with Christopher Kedzie, Brent Keltner, Constantijn Panis, Joel Pliskin, Padmanabhan Srinagesh

NOTES

1. Documentation about the decline in U.S. "social capital" and its effect on the performance of representative government may be found in Putnam (1993) and Putnam (1995). Among the data cited in his 1995 article: U.S. voter turnout has declined by nearly a quarter from the early 1960s to 1990; Americans who report they have "attended a public meeting on town or school affairs in the past year" declined from 22 percent in 1973 to 13 percent in 1993; participation in parent-teacher organizations dropped from more than 12 million in 1964 to approximately 7 million today; since 1970, volunteering is off for Boy Scouts by 26 percent and for the Red Cross by 61 percent.

2. A MUD is variously defined as Multiple User Domain, Multiple User Dimension, Multiple User Dungeon, or Multiple User Dialogue. It is a computer program allowing users to explore and help create an on-line environment. Each user takes control of a computerized persona/avatar/incarnation/character. The user can walk around, chat with other characters, explore dangerous monster-infested areas, solve puzzles, and even create his or her very own rooms, descriptions, and items.

3. E-mail can also be forwarded automatically to an alternative mailbox (e.g., closer to a vacation spot or sabbatic location).

4. In this regard, it should be noted that the current U.S. postal services deliver two things: information (e.g., letters) and bulk material (e.g., packages). A universal e-mail system should, in principle, be able to take over much of the information delivery functions; it obviously cannot handle the bulk material delivery functions. However, some bulk material consists of catalogs and advertising that may, in fact, increasingly become accessible electronically.

REFERENCES

Anderson, R. H., Shapiro, N. Z., Bikson, T. K., & Kantar, P. H. (1989). *The Design of the MH Mail System.* Santa Monica, CA: RAND, N-3017-IRIS.

Klein, H. K. (1995). "Grassroots Democracy and the Internet: The Telecommunications Policy Roundtable—Northeast USA (TPR-NE)." Internet Society: INE '95 Proceedings. Available at http://inet.nttam.com/HMP/PAPER/164/txt/paper.txt.

Lynch, D., & Rose, M. (1993). *The Internet System Handbook.* Reading, MA: Addison-Wesley.

Mueller, M., & Schement, J. R. (1995). *Universal Service from the Bottom Up: A Profile of Telecommunications Access in Camden, New Jersey.* Rutgers University Project on Information Policy, Rutgers University School of Communication.

Putnam, R. D. (1995). "Bowling Alone: America's Declining Social Capital." *Journal of Democracy, 6*(1).

Putnam, R. D. (1993). *Making Democracy Work: Civic Traditions in Modern Italy.* Princeton, NJ: Princeton University Press.

Ronfeldt, D., Thorup, C., Aguayo, S., & Frederick, H. (1993). *Restructuring Civil Society Across North America in the Information Age: New Networks for Immigration Advocacy Organizations.* Santa Monica, CA: RAND, DRU-599-FF.

Sproull, L., & Kiesler, S. (1991). *Connections: New Ways of Working in the Networked Organization.* Cambridge, MA: MIT Press.

RELATED LINKS

- December.com: Tools (http://www.december.com/net/tools)
- E-mail Guide (http://www.emailaddresses.com/email_guide.htm)
- Internet Literacy: Electronic Mail (http://www.udel.edu/interlit/chapter6.html)
- Universal Access to E-Mail Web Site (http://www.rand.org/publications/MR/MR650)

FOR FURTHER RESEARCH

To find out more about the topics discussed in this reading, use InfoTrac College Edition. Type in keywords and subject terms such as "universal service," "universal e-mail," and "civic participation." You can access InfoTrac from the Wadsworth/Thomson Communication Café homepage: http://communication.wadsworth.com.

Reading 9-4

Fragmentation and Cybercascades
Cass R. Sunstein

EDITOR'S NOTE

Since emerging as a mass medium, the Internet has enabled unprecedented democratic discourse among users with divergent views on any number of issues of common concern. One of the signal benefits of distributed communication in cyberspace is the ability to locate people with similar interests and views so that dispersed but like-minded individuals can find each other and form online communities regardless of distance. At the same time, however, online communication within narrowly focused interest groups may encourage a type of group isolation in which Internet users mostly hear "more and louder echoes of their own voices," as this reading explains. From his original investigation of political Web sites, Cass Sunstein finds that people who create a site with one point of view are unlikely to promote or even acknowledge their adversaries and are also unlikely to link to sites with opposing views. Combined with the questionable credibility of much online information, such isolationism may have negative repercussions for a healthy public sphere.

CONSIDER

1. What does the author mean by the term *cybercascades* and why is the Internet an obvious breeding ground for them?

2. With the capacity to customize and make individualized selections, how does the emerging world of interactive media represent a significant change from the commonly shared experience of mass media?

3. According to the author, what are the social and political repercussions of such highly specialized content choices and opinion clustering?

There is a discussion group in cyberspace. The group was started two years ago by about a dozen political activists, who were concerned about the increasing public pressure for gun control and the perceived "emasculation" of the Second Amendment (in the group's view, a clear ban on government restrictions on the sale of guns). But the group was also troubled by the growing authority of government, especially the national government, over the lives of ordinary people, and worried as well about the threat to our "European heritage" and to "traditional moral values" that is posed by the increasing social power of African-Americans and "radical feminist women." The group's members were

From *republic.com* by Cass R. Sunstein. © 2001 by Princeton University Press. Reprinted by permission of Princeton University Press.

fearful that the Republican and Democratic parties had become weak-willed "twins," unable and unwilling to take on the "special interests" who were threatening to "take away our constitutional liberties." The group called itself the Boston Tea Party.

The members of the Boston Tea Party now number well over four hundred people, who regularly exchange facts and points of view, and who share relevant literature with one another. For a majority of the participants, the discussion group provides most of the information on which they base their judgments about political issues. Over the last two years the Boston Tea Party's concerns have been greatly heightened. Nearly 70 percent of the members carry firearms, some as a result of the group's discussions. Small but vigorous protests have been planned, organized, and carried out in three state capitols. A march on Washington, DC, is now in the works. Recent discussion has occasionally turned to the need for "self-protection" against the state, through civil disobedience and possibly through selective "strikes" on certain targets in the public and private sectors. The motivation for this discussion is the widely disseminated view that the "FBI and possibly the CIA" are starting to take steps to "dismember" the group. One member has sent bomb-making instructions to all members of the Boston Tea Party. No violence has occurred as yet. But things are unquestionably heading in that direction.

So far as I know, there is no Boston Tea Party. This story is not true. But it is not exactly false. It is a composite based on the many discussion groups and Websites, less and often more extreme, that can be found on the Internet. Discussion groups and Websites of this kind have been around for a number of years. On March 23, 1996, for example, the *Terrorist's Handbook* was posted on the Internet, including instructions on how to make a bomb (the same bomb, as it happens, as was used in the Oklahoma City bombing, where dozens of federal employees were killed). On the National Rifle Association's "Bullet 'N' Board," a place for discussion of matters of mutual interest, someone calling himself "Warmaster" explained how to make bombs out of ordinary household materials. Warmaster explained, "These simple, powerful bombs are not very well known even though all the materials can be easily obtained by anyone (including minors)." After the Oklahoma City bombing, an anonymous notice was posted not to one but to dozens of Usenet news groups, listing all the materials in the Oklahoma City bomb and exploring ways to improve future bombs. Hun-

dreds of hate groups are now reported to be communicating on the Internet, often about conspiracies and (this will come as no surprise) formulas for making bombs. Members of such groups tend to communicate largely or mostly with one another, feeding their various predilections. The two students who launched the attack in Littleton, Colorado, actually had an Internet site containing details about how to make a bomb. Often such sites receive and spread rumors, many of them false and even paranoid.

Of course these are extreme cases. But they reveal something about the consequences of a fragmented speech market. In a system with robust public forums and general interest intermediaries, self-insulation is more difficult, and people will frequently come across views and materials that they would not have chosen in advance. For diverse citizens, this provides something like a common framework for social experience. "Real-world interactions often force us to deal with diversity, whereas the virtual world may be more homogeneous, not in demographic terms, but in terms of interest and outlook. Place-based communities may be supplanted by interest-based communities."[1] Let us suppose that the communications market continues to become far more fragmented, in exactly the sense prophesied by those who celebrate the "Daily Me" [individualized newspaper] and in a way that invites the continuing emergence of highly specialized Websites and discussion groups of innumerable sorts.

What problems would be created as a result?

FLAVORS AND FILTERS

It is obvious that if there is only one flavor of ice cream or only one kind of toaster, a wide range of people will make the same choice. (Some people will refuse ice cream and some will rely on something other than toasters, but that is another matter.) It is also obvious that as choice is increased, different individuals, and different groups, will make increasingly different choices. This has been the growing pattern with the proliferation of communications options. Consider the celebratory words David Bohnett, founder of geocities .com: "The Internet gives you the opportunity to meet other people who are interested in the same things you are, no matter how specialized, no matter how weird, no matter how big or how small."[2]

The specialization of Websites is obviously important here; so too for the existence of specialized discussion groups of countless kinds. But other technologies are important as well. Consider the World Wide Web Consortium's Platform for Internet Content Selection (PICS), which serves to rate and filter content on the Internet. The authors of PICS hope to put in place a system in which users can filter out materials of any kind, through choosing ratings systems from their preferred sources. Those who seek the ratings of the Conservative Coalition could use its ratings system, whereas those who prefer the ratings system of the American Civil Liberties Union could use its ratings system. This is merely an illustration of the multiple ways in which new technologies reduce the "friction" of ordinary life and permit people, with increasing ease, to devise a communications universe of their choosing. But this is not only an occasion for celebration.

To see this point, it is necessary to think a bit about why people are likely to engage in filtering. The simplest reason is that people often know, or think they know, what they like and dislike. A friend of mine is interested in Russia; he subscribes to a service that provides him with about two dozen stories about Russia each day. If you are bored by news stories involving Russia, or the Middle East, or if you have no interest in Wall Street, you might turn your mind off when these are discussed; and if you can filter your newspaper or video programming accordingly, it's all the better. And many people like hearing discussions that come from a perspective that they find sympathetic. If you are a Republican, you might prefer a newspaper with a Republican slant, or at least without a Democratic slant. Perhaps you will be most willing to trust "appropriately slanted" stories about the events of the day. Your particular choices are designed to ensure that you can trust what you read. Or maybe you want to insulate yourself from opinions that you find implausible, indefensible, or invidious. Everyone considers some points of view beyond the pale, and we filter those out if this is at all possible. Consider the fact that after people make automobile purchases, they often love to read advertisements for the very car that they have just obtained. The reason is that those advertisements tend to be comforting, because they confirm the wisdom of the decision.

We can make some distinctions here. Members of some groups want to wall themselves off from most or all others simply in order to maintain a degree of comfort and possibly a way of life. Some religious groups self-segregate for this reason. Such groups are tolerant of pluralism and interested largely in self-protection; they do not have ambitions on others. Other groups have a self-conscious "combat mission," seeking to convert others, and their desire to self-segregate is intended to strengthen their members' convictions in order to promote long-term recruitment plans. Political parties sometimes think in these terms, and they often ignore the views of others, except when they hold those views up to ridicule. My own empirical study of political Websites (discussed below) suggests that when links are provided to other Websites, it is often to show how dangerous, or how contemptible, competing views really are.

OVERLOAD, GROUPISM, AND *E PLURIBUS PLURES*

In the face of dramatic recent increases in communications options, there is an omnipresent risk of information overload—too many options, too many topics, too many opinions, a cacophony of voices. Indeed the risk of overload and the need for filtering go hand-in-hand. Bruce Springsteen's music may be timeless, but his 1992 hit, "57 Channels (and Nothin' On)," is hopelessly out of date in light of the number of current programming options, at least if contemporary television is put together with the Internet. (Contradicting Springsteen, TiVo exclaims, "There's always something on TV that you'll like!") Filtering, often in the form of narrowing, is inevitable to avoid overload, to impose some order on an overwhelming number of sources of information.

By itself this is not a problem. But when options are so plentiful, many people will take the opportunity to listen to those points of view that they find most agreeable. For many of us, of course, what matters is that we enjoy what we see or read, or learn from it, and it is not necessary that we are comforted by it. But there is a natural human tendency to make choices, with respect to entertainment and news, that do not disturb our preexisting view of the world. I am not suggesting that cyberspace is a lonely or antisocial domain. In contrast to television, many of the emerging technologies are extraordinarily social, increasing people's capacity to form bonds with individuals and groups that would otherwise have been entirely inaccessible. E-mail and Internet discussion groups provide increasingly remarkable opportunities, not for isolation, but for the creation of new groups and connections. This is the foundation for the concern about the risk of fragmentation.

Table 9-2. Links to Allies and Adversaries

Political Orientation	Links to Opposition	No Links to Opposition	Links to Like-Minded Sites	No Links to Like-Minded Sites	Total Number of Sites
Republican	3	7	7	3	10
Democrats	1	11	7	5	12
Conservative	1	20	12	9	21
Liberal	4	13	9	8	17
Total	9	51	35	25	60

Consider some relevant facts about the current communications market. If you take the ten most highly rated television programs for whites, and then take the ten most highly rated programs for African-Americans, you will find little overlap between them. Indeed, seven of the ten most highly rated programs for African-Americans rank as the very *least* popular programs for whites. Similar divisions can be found on the Internet. Some sites are specifically designed for African-Americans and (it is fair to speculate) are not often consulted by others. American Visions, for example, describes itself as "the magazine of Afro-American culture" and as the biggest, if not the first, "Internet site aimed at African-Americans." Afritech was established primarily "as a forum for black professionals and academics to discuss technical issues." Tony Brown Online is said to be, among other things, "a place where blacks can meet one another." Melanet describes itself as offering "the Uncut Black Experience" focused on "peoples throughout the African Diaspora" and provides a number of services, many of them involving African themes. Of course thousands of Websites, probably millions, are written primarily by and for whites (even if their designers were not self-conscious about this). There are sharp divides along lines of gender as well. Only one site (hotmail.com) can be found on both the list of top sites among women over fifty and the list of top sites among men over fifty. Among girls aged twelve to seventeen, the top entertainment sites in 1998 were Eonline.com, Pathfinder.com, and Titanicmovie.com, whereas the top entertainment sites among boys in the same age group were ESPN.com, Playboy.com, and Song Online.

All this is just the tip of the iceberg. Not surprisingly, people of certain interests and political convictions tend to choose sites and discussion groups that support their convictions. "Because the Internet makes it easier to find like-minded individuals, it can facilitate and strengthen fringe communities that have a common ideology but are dispersed geographically. Thus, particle physicists, Star Trek fans, and members of militia groups have used the Internet to find each other, swap information and stoke each other's passions. In many cases, their heated dialogues might never have reached critical mass as long as geographical separation diluted them to a few parts per million."[3] Many of those with committed views on one or another topic —gun control, abortion, affirmative action—speak mostly with each other. In the mid-1990s, a study found "a bleak vision of democratic discourse on the Web," with only 15 percent of partisan sites offering links to opposing viewpoints.[4] The author concludes that "far from fostering deliberative political discourse, most of the surveyed Websites sought to consolidate speech power and served to balkanize the public forum."[5]

My own study, conducted with Lesley Wexler for this book in June 2000, found the same basic picture. Of a random study of sixty political sites, only nine (15%) provide links to sites of those with opposing views, whereas thirty-five (almost 60%) provide links to like-minded sites (see Table 9-2).

One of the most striking facts here is that when links to opposing sites are provided, it is often to show how dangerous, or dumb, or contemptible the views of the adversary really are. Talkleft.com, for example, provides links to several Websites with opposing viewpoints, calling them "Political Sites: The Danger Zone." (There are impressive exceptions. To its credit, the National Organization for Women provides links to Promise Keepers, which it considers an antifeminist organization; the American Conservative Union provides a neutral-sounding set of links to sites of presidential candidates.) Even more striking is the extent to which sites are providing links to like-minded sites. Table 9-2 shows the number of sites that have one or more such links; but in a way it greatly understates what is happening. Several organizations, for example, offer links to dozens or even hundreds of like-minded sites.

All this is perfectly natural, even reasonable. Those who visit certain sites are probably more likely to want to visit similar sites, and people who create a site with one point of view are unlikely to want to promote their adversaries. Nor is definitive information yet available about the extent to which people who consult sites with one point of view are restricting themselves to like-minded sources of information. But what we now know, about both links and individual behavior, supports the general view that many people are mostly hearing more and louder echoes of their own voices. This may well be damaging from the democratic standpoint.

I do not mean to deny the obvious fact that any system that allows for freedom of choice will create some balkanization of opinion. Long before the advent of the Internet, and in an era of a handful of television stations, people made choices among newspapers and radio stations. Magazines and newspapers, for example, often cater to people with definite interests in certain points of view. Since the early nineteenth century, African-American newspapers have been widely read by African-Americans, and these newspapers offer distinctive coverage of common issues and also make distinctive choices about what issues are important.[6] Whites rarely read such newspapers.

But what is emerging nonetheless counts as a significant change. With a dramatic increase in options, and a greater power to customize, comes a corresponding increase in the range of actual choices, and those choices are likely, in many cases, to match demographic characteristics, preexisting political convictions, or both. Of course this has many advantages; among other things, it will greatly increase the aggregate amount of information, the entertainment value of choices, and the sheer variety of options. But there are problems as well. If diverse groups are seeing and hearing quite different points of view, or focusing on quite different topics, mutual understanding might be difficult, and it might be increasingly hard for people to solve problems that society faces together.

Take some extreme examples. Many Americans now believe that AIDS is a minor problem, one that is diminishing in degree and faced largely by people who have recklessly chosen to take risks. Many other Americans think that AIDS is an extremely serious problem, growing in degree, and fueled by government indiffer-

ence and perhaps even by deliberate efforts by white doctors to spread the disease within African-American communities. Many Americans fear that certain environmental problems—abandoned hazardous waste sites, genetic engineering of food—are extremely serious and require immediate government action. But others believe that the same problems are imaginative fictions generated by zealots and self-serving politicians. Many Americans think that most welfare recipients are indolent and content to live off of the work of others. On this view, "welfare reform," to be worthy of the name, consists of reduced handouts, a step necessary to encourage people to fend for themselves. But many other Americans believe that welfare recipients generally face severe disadvantages and would be entirely willing to work if decent jobs were available. On this view, "welfare reform," understood as reductions in benefits, is an act of official cruelty.

To say the least, it will be difficult for people, armed with such opposing perspectives, to reach anything like common ground or to make progress on the underlying questions. Consider how these difficulties will increase if people do not know the competing view, consistently avoid speaking with one another, and are unaware how to address competing concerns of fellow citizens.

A BRIEF NOTE ON HATE GROUPS

As noted, there are hundreds of Websites created and run by hate groups and extremist organizations. They appear to be obtaining a large measure of success, at least if we measure this by reference to "hits." My own informal survey shows that several hate groups have had well over one hundred thousand visitors, and in at least one case well over one million. What is also striking is that many extremist organizations and hate groups provide links to one another, and expressly attempt to encourage both recruitment and discussion among like-minded people.

Consider one extremist group, the so-called Unorganized Militia, the armed wing of the Patriot movement, "which believes that the federal government is becoming increasingly dictatorial with its regulatory power over taxes, guns and land use."[7] A crucial factor behind the growth of the Unorganized Militia "has been the use of computer networks," allowing members "to make contact quickly and easily with like-minded individuals to trade information, discuss cur-

Table 9-3. Links Among "Hate Sites"

Site	Links to Like-Minded Sites	Links to Opposition
Adelaide Institute (holocaust revisionism)	16	6
Aggressive Christianity	0	0
All Men Must Die	5	0
Altar of Unholy Blasphemy	11	0
Aryan Nations	28	0
Crosstar (nationalistic)	29	0
David Duke Online	11	0
God Hates Fags	7	3
Islam Monitor	0	12
KKK.com	72	0
Martin Luther King, Jr. (revisionist view of King)	0	0
Misogyny Unlimited	92	1
National Association for the Advancement of White People	0	0
Skinheads of the Racial Holy War	100	0
Stormfront (white nationalism)	60	5
Voice of Freedom (anti-Semitic)	27	5
Vote for USA (anti-Semitic)	17	0
White Aryan Resistance	0	0
World Church of the Creator	11	0
Total (19)	14 with; 5 without	6 with; 13 without

rent conspiracy theories, and organize events."[8] The Unorganized Militia has a large number of Websites, and those sites frequently offer links to related sites. It is clear that Websites are being used to recruit new members, to allow like-minded people to speak with one another, and to reinforce or strengthen existing convictions. It is also clear that the Internet is playing a crucial role in permitting people who would otherwise feel isolated, or who might move on to something else, to band together and to spread rumors, many of them paranoid and hateful.

There are numerous other examples along similar lines. A group naming itself the "White Racial Loyal-ists" calls on all "White Racial Loyalists to go to chat rooms and debate and recruit with NEW people, post our URL everywhere, as soon as possible." Another site announces that "Our multi-ethnic United States is run by Jews, a 2% minority, who were run out of every country in Europe. . . . Jews control the U.S. media, they hold top positions in the Clinton administration . . . and now these Jews are in control—they used lies spread by the media they run and committed genocide in our name." Table 9-3 gives a brief sense of what is now happening.

Here in particular, the provision of opposition links is designed to produce not discussion but instead fear and contempt. Holocaust denial organizations, for example, describe their adversaries as "extermination-ists" or "Holocaust enforcers" and provide links with the evident goal of discrediting them. With respect to like-minded sites, several hate groups have formal linking agreements: "You link to us and we'll link to you." One such site lists nearly one hundred such groups, each with a link, under the title "White Pride World Wide." The listed sites include European Knights of the Ku Klux Klan, German Skin Heads, Aryan Nations, Knights of the Ku Klux Klan, Siegheil88, Skinhead Pride, Intimidation One, SS Enterprises, and White Future.

We can sharpen our understanding here if we attend to the phenomenon of group polarization. This phenomenon raises serious questions about any system in which individuals and groups make diverse choices, and many people end up in echo chambers of their own design.

GROUP POLARIZATION

The term *group polarization* refers to something very simple: *After deliberation, people are likely to move toward a more extreme point in the direction to which the group's members were originally inclined.* With respect to the Internet and new communications technologies, the implication is that groups of like-minded people, engaged in discussion with one another, will end up thinking the same thing that they thought before—but in more extreme form.

The point has important implications about the effects of exposure to ideas and claims on television, radio, and the Internet even in the absence of a chance for interaction. Because group polarization occurs merely on the basis of exposure to the views of others, it is likely to be a common phenomenon in a balkanized speech market. Suppose, for example, that conservatives are visiting conservative Websites; that liberals are visiting liberal Websites; that environmentalists are visiting sites dedicated to establishing the risks of genetic engineering and global warming; that critics of environmentalists are visiting sites dedicated to exposing frauds allegedly perpetrated by environmentalists; that people inclined to racial hatred are visiting sites that express racial hatred. To the extent that these exposures are not complemented by exposure to competing views, group polarization will be the inevitable consequence.

THE ENORMOUS IMPORTANCE OF GROUP IDENTITY

For purposes of understanding modern technologies, a particularly important point has to do with perceptions of identity and group membership. Group polarization will significantly increase if people think of themselves, antecedently or otherwise, as part of a group having a shared identity and a degree of solidarity. If they think of themselves in this way, group polarization is both more likely and more extreme.[9] If, for example, a number of people in an Internet discussion group think of themselves as opponents of high taxes, or advocates of animal rights, or critics of the Supreme Court, their discussions are likely to move them in quite extreme directions, simply because they understand each other as part of a common cause. Similar movements should be expected for those who listen to a radio show known to be conservative, or who watch a television program dedicated to traditional religious values or to exposing white racism. Considerable evidence so suggests.[10]

Group identity is important in another way. If you are participating in an Internet discussion group, but you think that other group members are significantly different from you, you are less likely to be moved by what they say. If, for example, other group members are styled "Republicans" and you consider yourself a Democrat, you might not shift at all—even if you would indeed shift, as a result of the same arguments, if you were all styled "voters" or "jurors" or "citizens." Thus a perception of shared group identity will heighten the effect of others' views, whereas a perception of unshared identity, and of relevant differences, will reduce that effect, and possibly even eliminate it.

GROUP POLARIZATION AND THE INTERNET

Group polarization is unquestionably occurring on the Internet. From the discussion thus far, it seems plain that the Internet is serving, for many, as a breeding ground for extremism, precisely because like-minded people are deliberating with greater ease and frequency with one another, and often without hearing contrary views. Repeated exposure to an extreme position, with the suggestion that many people hold that position, will predictably move those exposed, and likely predisposed, to believe in it. One consequence can be a high degree of fragmentation, as diverse people, not originally fixed in their views and perhaps not so far apart, end up in extremely different places, simply because of what they are reading and viewing. Another consequence can be a high degree of error confusion.

FRAGMENTATION, POLARIZATION, RADIO, AND TELEVISION

An understanding of group polarization casts light on the potential effects not only of the Internet but also of radio and television, at least if stations are numerous and many take a well-defined point of view. Mere exposure to the positions of others creates group polarization. It follows that this effect will be at work for nondeliberating groups, in the form of collections of individuals whose communications choices go in the same direction, and who do not expose themselves to alternative positions. Indeed the same process is likely to occur for newspaper choices. General interest intermediaries have a distinctive role here, by virtue of their effort to present a wide range of topics and views. Polarization is far less likely to occur when such intermediaries dominate the scene. A similar point can be made about the public forum doctrine. When diverse speakers have access to a heterogeneous public, individuals and groups are less likely to be able to insulate themselves from competing positions and concerns. Fragmentation is correspondingly less likely.

Group polarization also raises more general issues about communications policy. Consider the "fairness doctrine," now largely abandoned but once requiring radio and television broadcasters to devote time to public issues and to allow an opportunity for those with opposing views to speak. The latter prong of the doctrine was designed to ensure that listeners would not be exposed to any single view—if one view was covered, the opposing position would have to be allowed a right of access. When the Federal Communications Commission abandoned the fairness doctrine, it did so on the ground that this second prong led broadcasters, much of the time, to avoid controversial issues entirely, and to present views in a way that suggested a bland uniformity. Subsequent research has suggested that the elimination of the fairness doctrine has indeed produced a flowering of controversial substantive programming, frequently expressing extreme views of one kind or another; consider talk radio.[11]

Typically this is regarded as a story of wonderfully successful deregulation. The effects of eliminating the fairness doctrine were precisely what was sought and intended. But from the standpoint of group polarization, the evaluation is far more complicated. On the good side, the existence of diverse pockets of opinion would seem to enrich society's total argument pool, potentially to the benefit of all of us. At the same time, the growth of a wide variety of issues-oriented programming—expressing strong, often extreme views, and appealing to dramatically different groups of listeners and viewers is likely to create group polarization. All too many people are now exposed largely to louder echoes of their own voices, resulting, on occasion, in misunderstanding and enmity. Perhaps it is better for people to hear fewer controversial views than for them to hear a single such view, stated over and over again.

ENCLAVES AND THE PUBLIC SPHERE

Whenever group discussion tends to lead people to more strongly held versions of the same view with which they began, there is legitimate reason for concern. This does not mean that the discussions can or should be regulated. But it does raise questions about the idea that "more speech" is necessarily an adequate remedy for bad speech—especially if many people are inclined and increasingly able to wall themselves off from competing views. In democratic societies, the best response is suggested by the public forum doctrine, whose most fundamental goal is to increase the likelihood that at certain points, there is an exchange of views between enclave members and those who disagree with them. It is total or near-total self-insulation, rather than group deliberation as such, that carries with it the most serious dangers, often in the highly unfor-

tunate (and sometimes literally deadly) combination of extremism with marginality.

CYBERCASCADES: INFORMATION AS WILDFIRE, AND TIPPING POINTS

The phenomenon of group polarization is closely related to the widespread phenomenon of social cascades. No discussion of social fragmentation and emerging communications technologies would be complete without an understanding of cascades—above all because they become more likely when information, including false information, can be spread to hundreds, thousands, or even millions by the simple press of a button.

It is obvious that many social groups, both large and small, move rapidly and dramatically in the direction of one or another set of beliefs or actions.[12] These sorts of cascades typically involve the spread of information; in fact they are usually driven by information. Most of us lack direct or entirely reliable information about many matters of importance—whether global warming is a serious problem, whether there is a risk of war in India, whether a lot of sugar is really bad for you, whether Mars really exists and what it is like. If you lack a great deal of private information, you might well rely on information provided by the statements or actions of others. A stylized example: If Joan is unaware whether abandoned toxic waste dumps are in fact hazardous, she may be moved in the direction of fear if Mary thinks that fear is justified. If Joan and Mary both believe that fear is justified, Carl may end up thinking so too, at least if he lacks reliable independent information to the contrary. If Joan, Mary, and Carl believe that abandoned hazardous waste dumps are hazardous, Don will have to have a good deal of confidence to reject their shared conclusion. And if Joan, Mary, Carl, and Don present a united front on the issue, others may well go along.

The example shows how information travels and can become quite widespread and entrenched, even if it is entirely wrong. An illustration is, in fact, the widespread popular belief that abandoned hazardous waste dumps rank among the most serious environmental problems; science does not support that belief, which seems to have spread via cascade.[13] Some cascades are widespread but local; consider the view, with real currency in some African-American communities, that white doctors are responsible for the spread of AIDS among African-Americans. One group may end up believing something and another group the exact opposite, and the reason is the rapid transmission of information within one group but not the other.

It should be obvious that the Internet, with Websites containing information designed for particular groups, greatly increases the likelihood of diverse but inconsistent cascades. "Cybercascades" occur every day. Many of us have been deluged with e-mail involving the need to contact our representatives about some bill or other—only to learn that the bill did not exist and the whole problem was a joke or a fraud. Even more of us have been earnestly warned about the need to take precautions against viruses that do not exist. And many thousands of hours of Internet time have been spent on elaborating paranoid claims about alleged nefarious activities, including murder, on the part of President Clinton. A number of sites and discussion groups spread rumors and conspiracy theories of various sorts. "Electrified by the Internet, suspicions about the crash of TWA Flight 800 were almost instantly transmuted into convictions that it was the result of friendly fire. . . . It was all linked to Whitewater. . . . Ideas become E-mail to be duplicated and duplicated again."[14] In 2000, an e-mail rumor specifically aimed at African-Americans alleged that "No Fear" bumper stickers bearing the logo of the sportswear company of the same name really promote a racist organization headed by former Ku Klux Klan Grand Wizard David Duke. (If you're interested in more examples, you might consult http://urbanlegends.about.com, a Website dedicated to widely disseminated falsehoods, many of them spread via the Internet.)

As an especially troublesome example, consider widespread doubts in South Africa, where about 20 percent of the adult population is infected by the AIDS virus, about the connection between HIV and AIDS. South African President Mbeki is a well-known Internet surfer, and he learned the views of the "denialists" after stumbling across one of their Websites. The views of the "denialists" are not scientifically respectable—but to a nonspecialist, many of the claims on their (many) sites seem quite plausible. At least for a period, President Mbeki both fell victim to a cybercascade and, through his public statements, helped to accelerate one, to the point where many South Africans at serious risk are not convinced about an association between HIV and AIDS. It remains to be seen to what extent this cascade effect will turn out to be literally deadly.

With respect to information in general, there is even a "tipping point" phenomenon, creating a potential for dramatic shifts in opinion. After being presented with new information, people typically have different thresholds for choosing to believe or do something new or different. As the more likely believers, that is people with low thresholds, come to a certain belief or action, people with somewhat higher thresholds then join them, soon producing a significant group in favor of the view in question. At that point, those with still higher thresholds may join, possibly to a point where a critical mass is reached, making large groups, societies, or even nations "tip."[15] The result of this process can be to produce snowball or cascade effects, as large groups of people end up believing something—whether or not that something is true—simply because other people, in the relevant community, seem to believe that it is true.

There is a great deal of experimental evidence of informational cascades, which are easy to induce in the laboratory;[16] real world phenomena also have a great deal to do with cascade effects. Consider, for example, going to college, smoking, participating in protests, voting for third-party candidates, striking, recycling, filing lawsuits, using birth control, rioting, even leaving bad dinner parties.[17] In each of these cases, people are greatly influenced by what others do. Often a tipping point will be reached. The Internet is an obvious breeding ground for cascades, and as a result thousands or even millions of people, consulting sources of a particular kind, will believe something that is quite false.

The good news is that the Internet can operate to debunk false rumors as well as to start them. But at the same time, the opportunity to spread apparently credible information to so many people can induce fear, error, and confusion, in a way that threatens many social goals, including democratic ones. As we have seen, this danger takes on a particular form in a balkanized speech market, as local cascades lead people in dramatically different directions. When this happens, correctives, even via the Internet, may not work, simply because people are not listening to one another.

OF DANGERS AND SOLUTIONS

I hope that I have shown enough to demonstrate that for citizens of a heterogeneous democracy, a fragmented communications market creates considerable dangers. There are dangers for each of us as individuals;

constant exposure to one set of views is likely to lead to errors and confusions, sometimes as a result of cyber-cascades. And to the extent that the process entrenches existing views, spreads falsehood, promotes extremism, and makes people less able to work cooperatively on shared problems, there are dangers for society as a whole.

To emphasize these dangers, it is unnecessary to claim that people do or will receive all of their information from the Internet. There are many sources of information, and some of them will undoubtedly counteract the risks I have discussed. Nor is it necessary to predict that most people will speak only with those who are like-minded. Of course many people will seek out competing views. But when technology makes it easy for people to wall themselves off from others, there are serious risks, for the people involved and for society generally.

NOTES

1. Robert Putnam, *Bowling Alone* (2000), p. 178.

2. See Alfred C. Sikes, *Fast Forward* (2000), pp. 13–14.

3. Marshall Van Alstyne and Erik Brynjolfsson, *Electronic Communities: Global Village of Cyberbalkans?* Available at: http://mit.edu/marshall/www/Abstracts.html.

4. Andrew Chin, Making the World Wide Web Safe for Democracy, *Hastings Communications and Entertainment Law Journal, 309* (1997).

5. Ibid., p. 328.

6. For a fascinating discussion, see Ronald Jacobs, *Race, Media, and the Crisis of Civil Society* (2000).

7. See Matthew Zook, *The Unorganized Militia Network: Conspiracies, Computers, and Community I* (1996), available at http://socrates.berkeley.edu/~zoon/pubs/Militia_paper.html.

8. Ibid.

9. See Russell Spears, Martin Lee, and Stephen Lee, Deindividuation and Group Polarization in Computer-Mediated Communication, *British Journal of Social Psychology, 121* (1990); Abrams et al., *Knowing What to Think*, p. 112; Patricia Wallace, *The Psychology of the Internet* (1999), pp. 73–76.

10. See John Turner et al., *Rediscovering the Social Group* (1987).

11. Thomas W. Hazlett and David W. Sosa, Was the Fairness Doctrine a "Chilling Effect"? Evidence from the Post-deregulation Radio Market. *Journal of Legal Studies, 279* (1997).

12. See, e.g. Sushil Bikhchandani et al., Learning from the Behavior of Others, *Journal of Economic Perspectives, 151* (Summer 1998); Andrew Daughety and Jennifer Reinganum, Stampede to Judgment, *American Law and Economics Review, 158* (1999).

13. See Timur Kuran and Cass R. Sunstein, Availability Cascades and Risk Regulation, *Stanford Law Review, 683* (1998).

14. George Johnson, "Pierre, Is that a Masonic Flag on the Moon?" *New York Times,* Nov. 24, 1996, section 2, p. 4.

15. See Mark Granovetter, Threshold Models of Collective Behavior, *American Journal of Sociology* (1978); for a vivid popular treatment, see Malcolm Gladwell, *The Tipping Point* (2000).

16. See Lisa Anderson and Charles Holt, Information Cascades in the Laboratory, *American Economic Review, 847* (1997).

17. Several of these examples are discussed in Anderson and Holt and in Granovetter, *Threshold Models*, 1422–24.

RELATED LINKS

- Republic.com (http://pup.princeton.edu/titles/7014.html)

- Cass R. Sunstein (http://www.law.uchicago.edu/faculty/sunstein)

- TalkLeft (http://www.talkleft.com)

- Urban Legends and Folklore (http://urbanlegends.about.com)

FOR FURTHER RESEARCH

To find out more about the topics discussed in this reading, use InfoTrac College Edition. Type in keywords and subject terms such as "group polarization," "social fragmentation," and "hate speech." You can access InfoTrac College Edition from the Wadsworth/Thomson Communication Café homepage: http://communication.wadsworth.com.

10

The Digital Divide

Rethinking the Digital Divide
Jennifer S. Light

EDITOR'S NOTE

The term digital divide *entered the American vocabulary in the mid-1990s to refer to unequal access to information technology. However, public debate has addressed the digital divide as a technical issue rather than as a reflection of broader social problems. In this reading, Jennifer Light critically analyzes how access to technology is constructed as a social problem and examines the particular assumptions about technology and inequality that frame the debate. The author examines the striking asymmetries between current debates (about the Internet) and earlier debates (about cable television) concerning the relationship between technology and society. She invites us to consider the different ways in which the problem of access to technology has been constructed and suggests that these differences may generate ways to enrich the current debate and spark a conversation leading to more robust solutions.*

CONSIDER

1. Beyond simply providing access to computer hardware and software, how should educators and policy makers concerned with closing the digital divide proceed?

2. In what ways are debates over access to the Internet similar to earlier debates over access to cable television —and in what ways are they different?

3. What does the author mean when she says that "successfully closing a digital divide will have few important consequences for educational or social inequalities if the technology's uses and content evolve in the direction of its predecessors" (radio, telephone, television, and cable)?

The "digital divide" is a reality acknowledged by individuals and organizations that do not always see eye to eye on education matters. CEOs of 45 U.S. corporations, including Microsoft, Cisco Systems, and General Electric, recently issued a report characterizing the divide as a threat to American prosperity. During the 2000 U.S. presidential campaign, candidates George W. Bush and Albert Gore Jr. spoke frequently about their ideas for narrowing the divide. From the National Council of Black Churches to America Online, a remarkable coalition across public, private, and nonprofit sectors has thrown its support behind efforts to eliminate the digital divide.

Americans are engaged in a vigorous public debate about the digital divide—its scope and possible solutions. Yet in our focus on access to computers and computer skills, we have allowed the debate to proceed along remarkably narrow lines, with little attention paid to the strengths and weaknesses of the concept of a digital divide and the assumptions behind it as a focus for intervention. Policies and programs encouraging the use of technology subtly redefine complex problems of inequality in simpler technological terms. Expanding and enriching the debates about technology and inequality are the goals of this article.

This is not the first time Americans have launched an examination of the relationship between technology and inequality into the public spotlight. The debate about cable television regulation and cable's anticipated social impact during the 1960s and 1970s is a close cousin of the digital divide debate. Discussions during the cable era engaged a diverse group of participants— academics, activists, policymakers, and leaders in the private sector. While participants in the cable debates viewed technology policy as inseparable from broader social policy, public leaders addressing the digital divide today largely separate the two. Cable's ultimate incarnation as an entertainment medium should not overshadow the intelligence and sophistication with which the debate proceeded. Educators, policymak-

From Jennifer S. Light, "Rethinking the Digital Divide," *Harvard Educational Review,* 71(4), 2001, pp. 709–733. Copyright © 2001 by the President and Fellows of Harvard College. All rights reserved. Excerpted with permission.

ers, and public leaders in the information age, as well as the people they seek to assist, can benefit from this more nuanced appreciation of the social dimensions of technology.

Making computers and computer instruction widely available remains a useful effort. Yet simultaneously, going beyond an understanding of educational and social inequality that hinges on a "technological fix," it quickly becomes apparent that public leaders seeking to end current—and future—divides must embrace a different understanding of technology. Technology is not a neutral tool with universal effects, but rather a medium with consequences that are significantly shaped by the historical, social, and cultural context of its use.

CONSTRUCTING THE DIGITAL DIVIDE: DEFINING THE PROBLEM

Periodical indices show 1996 as the first year the digital divide leapt into the spotlight as a focus of public attention and action.

Thus, the Clinton administration's National Telecommunications and Information Administration (NTIA) issued a report in 1995 calling attention to information "haves" and "have nots," without mention of a digital divide (NTIA, 1995). A second NTIA report in 1998 and its accompanying publicity helped to popularize the term. Three commonly reported shorthand definitions equate the digital divide with a "disparity between various groups in the areas of computer and Internet use" (Henderson, 2000, p. 60), differences between information haves and have nots ("'Digital Divide' Goes beyond Internet Access," 1999), and disparities in computer ownership and computer usage (Crews, 2000).

From electricity to the telephone and the automobile, most technologies did not enter U.S. society equitably. Disparities in access generally persisted for a time and then lessened as innovations were transformed from luxury to mass-market goods. Only in the case of a few technologies have early or continuing disparities in access become constructed as public problems. The telephone is among them, with "universal service" having been part of the impetus for creating a Federal Communications Commission (FCC) in 1934. Access to telephone service had to be constructed as a "necessity" so that its diffusion could become a legitimate focus for government intervention.

Expounding the wonders of information and communication technology, supporters of alleviating the digital divide have successfully created the public perception that access to computers and computing skills is a new necessity for the Information Age. They have done so by analogizing computer literacy to basic literacy, computer access to owning an automobile, and information infrastructure to the telephone network so vital to the economy of the American past and present (see Cha, 1999; Lawrence, 2000; Poole, 1996).

MEASURING INEQUALITY

Government officials, corporate executives, academic researchers, and nonprofit advocacy organizations now agree that there is a digital divide. However, they are engaged in vigorous debates about the problem's magnitude and how measures should be linked to action. Research findings differ based on what is being measured. For instance, some researchers approach the digital divide as a purely racial issue, while others combine race and socioeconomic status in their analysis. Evaluating the effects of access to computers at home or in public places is another popular approach. It is fascinating to see the explosive growth in data generated from research in the five years since the term *digital divide* was coined. These data have been used as the basis for recommending specific policies and programmatic interventions.

Government research during the Clinton administration suggested that digital inequalities had worsened over time. For example, the NTIA's *Falling Through the Net II* (1998) and *Falling Through the Net III* (1999) noted that the gap in computer ownership between White and Hispanic households increased more than 42 percent from 1994 to 1998. Gaps in Internet access between White and Hispanic households and between White and African American households grew by five percentage points between 1997 and 1999. Gaps in Internet access from home between households at the highest and lowest income levels widened by 29 percent from 1997 to 1999. The NTIA's 2000 figures show White and Asian American households with 46 percent and 57 percent access, respectively, more than double the access of African American and Hispanic house-

holds, with 23.5 percent and 23.6 percent, respectively. These numbers have been used to argue for government intervention and public-private partnerships.

A different approach focuses on the information technology market, in particular the costs of computers and Internet access. Observers note that race-related gaps in ownership and use have diminished as computer prices fall, and that African Americans are buying computers faster than Whites ("What Digital Divide?" 2000). Some politically conservative commentators have argued that government policy proposals base their initiatives' urgency on outmoded data in order to manufacture a crisis that requires government intervention (Powell, 1999). Several fiscally conservative commentators cite falling computer prices as evidence that competition in the technology market will eventually solve the problem on its own (Glassman, 2000; Theirer 2000).

Other analysts point to additional factors exacerbating the digital divide. For example, a business school professor's focus on consumer markets explains that the divide persists in part due to a lack of relevant online content, arguing for a better match between the interests of minority groups and online information (Hoffman, Novak, & Schlosser, 2000).

Studies describing and measuring the divide, and the policy reports that use those studies, tend to share two basic assumptions: that introducing computers mitigates inequality, and that life in the new geography of cyberspace frees individuals from other social constraints. In other words, access to the economic potential of an Information Society holds the potential to alleviate critical problems faced by America's disadvantaged, yet America's disadvantaged lack access to that potential (Goslee, 1998; Lacey, 2000; Poole, 1996).

HOW TECHNOLOGIES REDEFINE THE PROBLEMS THEY ARE ADOPTED TO SOLVE

In the United States, public discourse about information technology is filled with visions of the future. However, a careful reading of our history suggests that we should pause before assuming that educational, economic, and social inequalities will be eliminated, or even significantly mitigated, by simply increasing the availability and use of computers. The interactions between technology and society are complex, and examples from U.S. history suggest that past efforts to make earlier technologies available to the have nots did not inevitably transform social relations.

Consider the long-term effects of the hand calculator. Educators of the 1970s and 1980s wrote widely that bringing calculators to underachieving students would help to close a performance gap in mathematics (Walton, 1983). Now, a generation later, results from the National Assessment of Educational Progress (NAEP) and the Third International Math and Science Study (TIMSS) reveal an unexpected result. The access gap has closed, but the performance gap has not. According to the NAEP, among fourth graders, 50 percent of African Americans, 44 percent of Hispanics, and 27 percent of Whites report using calculators for math class. Students who now use calculators at the highest rates—racial minorities—tend to have the lowest mathematics performance in school and on standardized tests (Loveless, 2000). Inequalities in outcomes for students, what really matters, did not substantially change, despite access to calculators.

This is a paradigmatic example of a technological solution redefining a problem. Social inequality was redefined as a problem of access to technology. These initiatives relied on the shaky causal inference that closing one gap would close another. If we fast-forward a generation and substitute "computers and Internet access" for "calculators" and "social inequality" for "disparities in math achievement," is it obvious that the outcomes will be different? Can we reasonably expect the inequalities that correlate with a lack of access to technology to disappear?

Technologies are not independent of the society in which they are created or of the context in which they are used (Bijker, Hughes, & Pinch, 1987; Cuban, 1986; MacKenzie & Wajcman, 1985). Their array of interactions with different people, organizations, institutions, and cultures—such as individual teachers, schools, or academic subjects—makes it difficult for any particular technology to have uniform or even entirely predictable effects (Fischer, 1992; Wajcman, 1991). Findings from empirical research on computers and social interaction bear this out, revealing that the same technologies have multiple and sometimes contradictory consequences.

Thus, in some studies, computers and the Internet have been found to diminish hierarchies in communication by erasing social cues that signal status (Hiltz & Turoff, 1978; Sproull & Kiesler, 1991). In others they have been found to reinforce existing social cues, for example, gendered speech patterns (Herring, 1993). Some studies show that computers and the Internet

create new forms of community (Hampton & Wellman, 2001; Rheingold, 1993), while other studies conclude that they lead to diminished human interactions (Kraut et al., 1998; Nie, 2000). Research on computers as educational media comes to similar contradictory conclusions.

These studies' varied results suggest that the context of a technology's use matters as much as the technology itself. By extension, this body of research calls into question the basic assumption of most policy proposals to alleviate the digital divide—that increased access to computers at school and at home will inevitably improve educational performance and reduce economic and social inequality. Empirical research suggests that isolating the effects of changing technology is difficult if not impossible.

In light of evidence calling into question basic assumptions of proposals to alleviate a digital divide, how then should educators, policymakers, and the many constituencies who care about closing the digital divide proceed? One course of action is to simply ignore these potential problems and push ahead with existing programs that focus on closing the gap in access. A second possibility is to step back from the research findings to critically reflect on how current public debates define "the problem" and to consider whether public discourse might constructively change.

As a physical artifact, technology offers a convenient platform onto which we can project complex concerns in a simplistic way. It is comforting to imagine that the diffusion and use of a particular technology will remedy complex social problems. Hopes for a more equal future society are one of the most popular fantasies fastened onto new technologies.

Yet fastening such hopes onto computers and the Internet evades the complex causes of inequality and instead focuses on treating one of its symptoms, unequal access to technology, with the assumption that closing one gap will close the others. The digital divide offers a narrow way to talk about inequality that is noncontroversial because, while claims makers might disagree about the causes of social and economic inequality, they agree that increasing the use of computers is a "good thing."

While the digital divide debate appears to concern social inequality, it equally concerns consumer markets. Notably, the NTIA, the agency spearheading federal efforts to address the digital divide, is part of the Department of Commerce.

Certainly, for the myriad of claims makers, the simplicity of the concept and the restricted scope of existing debates are virtues. These simplifications help to generate broad support that more comprehensive constructions of inequality could not. Bipartisan public-private support for bringing computers into schools and homes is far less threatening to the status quo than government-sponsored desegregation or other policies designed to attack inequality, and computer education simultaneously builds a more skilled labor force and future consumers. The concept of a "digital divide" as now debated appeals to liberals who favor substantial increases in spending on public education, conservatives who want a more skilled labor force with minimal government intrusion, and leaders of both the private and public sectors, who want to look like they are doing something about a social problem.

Yet if history is any guide, the consequences of conceptualizing a digital divide that focuses almost exclusively on computer equipment and skills may be a short-term technological fix. Given the speed with which electronics become outmoded, it is not hard to imagine a new technological divide not so far down the road, as access to information infrastructure depends not on dial-up, but on satellite or hand-held personal communication devices. For example, in the five years since the term *digital divide* was coined, we have already seen the introduction of cable modems, palm pilots with wireless email, and other forms of access to information networks. As with the case of the calculator, the broader inequalities that may correlate with a lack of access to technology will not go away. Technology will not solve the problems of students who lack basic skills or school supplies or who have poorly trained teachers.

The calculator is not the only technology from the American past whose failure to achieve educational goals and close gaps can enrich contemporary debates about the digital divide (Cuban, 1986). Discussions about cable regulation during the urban crises of the 1960s included much attention to closing an information gap, another goodhearted public intervention that did not succeed as planned. Yet this failure was not for lack of sophisticated debate.

THE CABLE DEBATES: REFRAMING TECHNOLOGY AND INEQUALITY

The rhetoric that links civil rights concerns to information and communications technology is not unique to the Internet era. In the late 1960s, a time when civil rights and racial justice were a prominent part of the national conversation, the "revolutionary" technology debated as a potentially constructive agent of social change was cable television. Contemporary visions of "wired cities" and a "wired nation" have roots in urban policy and communications policy debates of the 1960s. This was an era when academics, public leaders, and average citizens began to characterize many of the problems faced by America's minorities as information and communications issues. Cable technology was said to provide a possible antidote to the isolation of "ghetto residents" (Dordick, Chesler, Firstman, & Bretz, 1969). Talk of wired cities and a wired nation, then as now, served as a hopeful metaphor for a more integrated society.

Observers' hopes for cable, both their specific visions for the future and their enthusiastic embrace of technology, offer a useful parallel that might temper excitement about technologies today. Scholars have noted rhetorical similarities between today's excitement about an information revolution and similar speculation about a revolution during the formative days of cable (Streeter, 1997; Surman, 1996). Their focus is the disjuncture between optimistic rhetoric filled with possibilities for a better society, and how, in the face of clashing interests, the new medium ended up falling far short of its early promise.

A brief discussion of the debates during the FCC freeze on cable licensing (1966–1972) and the eventual failure of cable to reduce social inequality offers much to enrich contemporary conversations. A key point is that in the minds of many participants in debates about cable, technology policy was an important component of a broader, multifaceted urban social policy. The opportunities offered by cable were important, but they were only part of a set of interventions designed to reduce educational, social, and economic inequalities.

Despite this elevated level of public discourse, political factors intervened to remake cable from an interactive, two-way educational medium into a wing of broadcast television's empire, diminishing its potential to extend learning beyond the classroom. By the 1980s, discussions about cable no longer referred to the "public information utility," or to cable as a medium for job training and placement. Instead it described movies on demand and music television. This shift deserves highlighting today. The digital divide discourse banks on the assumption that computers, the Internet, and other emerging information technology will persist in a form and with content relevant to educators' broad goals. Historical studies of technological change indicate that this is not a safe assumption.

COMPARING THE CABLE DEBATES
AND THE DIGITAL DIVIDE DEBATES

The cable era had no catchy term to describe its technological divide, yet similar assumptions about the broad social benefits that would follow from closing gaps in access to information and communications technology pervaded academic research and policy analysis. For example, the Kerner Commission Report, which characterized a nation divided, focused attention on how existing media made little room for minority voices (U.S. Kerner Commission, 1968). In its recommendations for action, the commission called for better uses of television to connect Black and White Americans, including the creation of an Institute for Urban Communications to move racial minorities and minority issues into the media industry. Similarly, the Eisenhower Commission identified news media as a critical component in the disconnect between Black and White America. Its report focused on violence on television, and urged broadcasters to take a more critical stance toward violence in programming. Both commissions' reports suggested that technological changes in the media business, coordinated with changes in programming content, must become partners in a co-ordinated effort for social change. This would be an important step on the complicated path toward a more unified society.

Recognizing that change to the broadcast establishment would come slowly, a broad coalition of academics, activists, and policymakers suggested that the emerging cable medium might quickly become a potent force for personal development and group empowerment—if an effort were made to get minority voices in at the ground level. It was no secret that racial minorities were less likely to subscribe to cable than Whites, and that few minorities owned or developed cable programming (Powledge, 1972). In an early observation of electronic redlining, former President of CBS News Fred Friendly noted that "cable entrepreneurs consistently seek to build their systems in areas populated by well-to-do citizens, bypassing whenever possible those who need access the most" (cited in Powledge, 1972, p. 16). While the lack of distance between residential units made it cheaper for cable operators to wire densely populated poor urban areas, these areas were never the first to obtain services.

Proponents of cable as a tool for social reform share three key ideas with their contemporary digital divide counterparts. First, reports from think tanks and the alternative print media of the 1960s and 1970s followed the Kerner Commission in stressing that access to information and communication was a civil right, and thus media should not be separate but equal. The Kerner Commission report singled out the lack of racial minorities both in the television industry and on the television screen as a serious problem. Bringing minority voices into the information and communications industries would simultaneously encourage group solidarity and facilitate communications across social groups (Pool, 1973; Price & Wicklein, 1972; Smith, 1970). Contemporary calls to close a digital divide evoke the Kerner Commission report and the civil rights movement as they suggest that "the network society is creating two parallel information and communications systems—one for whites and one for blacks"—and call for a national commitment to close this gap ("News and Views," 1999, p. 57).

Second, many observers focused on the absence of both an established cable industry and a fixed regulatory framework to suggest that there was a window of opportunity to create a new power dynamic. Making technology seem relevant and urging racial minorities to become producers of programming, as well as consumers, took on new importance (Pool, 1973; Tate, 1971). Contemporary observations from FCC Commissioner Michael Powell and others who argue for minorities to close a digital divide by producing, not merely consuming, information products sound strikingly like comments from Charles Tate of the Urban Institute's National Cable Information Service in 1971 (Powell, cited in "Digital Divide Goes Beyond Internet Access," 1999; Tate, 1971). Tate posed the choice in stark terms: minorities could continue to be passive recipients of still more entertainment channels from White America, or they could seize an opportunity to shape a medium with potential reach beyond the modest audiences of the minority press.

Third, the belief that information is power and the recognition of an information gap motivated initiatives to increase access to the cable medium for minority citizens (Dordick et al., 1969; Pool, 1973; Yin, 1972). Much like the Neighborhood Network Centers promoted by the NTIA, HUD, the Department of Education, and the National Urban League today, neighborhood telecommunications centers of the 1960s and 1970s that focused on cable began to serve both as centers for adult education and job training and as places to centralize the production of community programming (Dordick et al., 1969; Yin, 1972). Bringing local cable programming to community centers in minority residential areas responded to concerns that most early cable subscribers were likely to be affluent, and it capitalized on the historical fact that in low-income areas the multiservice center as neighborhood institution dated back many decades.

Like contemporary discourse about closing the digital divide, public discourse about cable expressed the belief that the medium could help to restructure society.

HOW THE DIGITAL DIVIDE DEBATES ARE DIFFERENT

The cable debate's lack of a determinist outlook is a subtle yet key difference that sets it apart from contemporary discussions about the digital divide. The digital divide debate is based on a technologically determinist assumption that closing gaps in access to computers will mitigate broader inequalities—an assumption requiring enormous faith in the capacity of a technology to bring about major social change. While reports on the digital divide often mention race or income, they do so in the service of an argument that focuses on access to computers and not on other causes of inequality.

A second contrast with the cable era is that in those earlier debates the problem of inequality and its possible solution were defined much more broadly. While one can find technological determinists in the cable era, the idea that a technological revolution would not bring about social change on its own served as a bedrock principle for public debate in the early 1970s. Analysts treated the communications divide as one manifestation of a physical, economic, and social phenomenon—race-based inequality. In this context, cable alone could not solve America's problems, but it could be part of a solution. Even technological optimists recognized that the potential of communications technologies to reduce inequality would only be realized if cable were introduced alongside other social policies and programs. This sense of coordination is absent from the digital divide literature, with rare exceptions (see Goslee, 1998).

Today, the focus of most policy discussions is more narrowly attentive to access to technology. Policies that encourage the adoption of technologies subtly shift the problem of social inequalities and segregation, redefining them in technological terms.

How might our national conversation change if we brought some of the assumptions of the cable era to the digital divide debates? First, the cable episode, which puts the relationship between communications systems and urban systems at its center, suggests that geography would be a constructive addition to contemporary discussions. The promise of computers and Internet skills is to raise status, increase social mobility, and decrease stratification—all spatial metaphors. Yet despite the popular conception of cyberspace as an extension of physical space, public debates and policy interventions for the digital divide make minimal reference back to the physical world.

This omission is striking, given widespread agreement about continuing forms of segregation and inequality in the urban environment. For the nation's less advantaged citizens in particular, place matters (Massey & Denton, 1993; Wilson, 1987).

Digital divide initiatives can help low-income Americans who are segregated in poor neighborhoods gain new job skills. Yet, simultaneously, transportation constraints may not allow them practical access to existing employment opportunities. We have seen early versions of this dilemma already, in difficulties with good-spirited initiatives aimed at encouraging Silicon Valley companies to hire and train more African Americans from Oakland, California. The success of these programs presumes the ownership of a car, an improved public transportation system, or housing prices low enough so people can afford to live relatively close to work. Telecommuting and remote work may mitigate some of these constraints, yet they simultaneously present new forms of segregation.

CONCLUSION

Ours is not the first generation to imagine technology as an instrument to reduce social inequality. Some champions of computing make the "computer exceptionalism" argument, claiming that the current information technology revolution fundamentally differs from the effects of other technologies, including computers in their early form as programming instruments (Starr, 1996). Yet historians of technology are generally skeptical of such claims. Instead, to regain the hope that we can in fact reduce disparities requires close analysis of why—despite well-intentioned past efforts—it has not already happened.

A central assumption in discussions of the digital divide is that computers, the Internet, and other emerging technologies will persist in a recognizable form with continuing value as educational tools both inside and outside the classroom. Yet initial assumptions about the future form and uses of media, even from experts, are often mistaken. Radio, telephone, television, and cable were each in turn predicted to be the next great educational technology, both for the classroom (Cuban, 1986) and for at-home instruction (Day, 1995; Frank, 1935; Rao, 1977). Yet all evolved into media whose primary function is entertainment. As cable, computers, and the Internet converge, who is to say that the form and function of this new new medium will not shift? Perhaps as the technology develops its entertainment potential, it might become a medium focused on video games and chat room play, not on continuing education and community programming. Successfully closing a digital divide will have few important consequences for educational or social inequalities if the technology's uses and content evolve in the direction of its predecessors [e.g. radio, telephone, television, and cable].

Historically, powerful political and commercial interests have shaped the ultimate form and uses of technology. This profit orientation helps to explain why cable and other media have not realized their potential as broadly educational tools, particularly for self-improvement beyond the classroom. The early phases of the digital divide debate are a classic case of a determinist public discourse that assumes technologies evolve along Darwinian lines and that the "best" technologies survive. Yet evidence suggests that the Internet is moving in a direction similar to its predecessors. Without more prominent contributions from the education community, there is little reason to believe that the trend will be reversed.

A historian's challenge is to answer, with the benefit of historical distance, the question "How could they possibly have thought that?" The examples of calculators and cable illustrate how technologies can disappoint. A goal for educators should be to reduce the chance that future scholars will look at current efforts to close the digital divide and ask, with the benefit of their historical distance, "how could they possibly have thought that?" For this to happen, we must put in place a set of educational policies and practices attentive to the complex and even contradictory consequences of technological innovations.

REFERENCES

Bijker, W., Hughes, T., & Pinch, T. (Eds.) (1987). *The social construction of technological systems*. Cambridge, MA: The MIT Press.

Cha, A. E. (1999, December 10). Initiatives outlined for digital divide. *Washington Post,* E3.

Crews, C. (2000, February 28). Technology program works to close "digital divide." *Philadelphia Tribune,* 6G.

Cuban, L. (1986). *Teachers and machines: The classroom use of technology since 1920.* New York: Teachers College Press.

Day, J. (1995). *The vanishing vision.* Berkeley: University of California Press.

Digital divide goes beyond Internet access (1999, August 29). *Jacksonville Free Press,* 2.

Dordick, H., Chesler, L., Firstman, S., & Bretz, R. (1969). *Telecommunications in urban development* (Staff Paper for the Task Force on Communications Policy). Santa Monica, CA: RAND.

Fischer, C. (1992). *American calling: A social history of the telephone.* Berkeley: University of California Press.

Frank, G. (1935). Radio as an educational force. *Annals of the American Academy of Political and Social Science, 177,* 119–122.

Glassman, J. (2000, April 24). Digital divide: The search for victims continues. *Reason Online.* Available: http://reason.com/tcs/042400.html.

Goslee, S. (1998). *Losing ground bit by bit. Low-income communities in the information age.* Washington, DC: Benton Foundation.

Hampton, K., & Wellman, B. (2001). Examining community in the digital neighborhood: Early results from Canada's wired suburb. In T. Ishida & K. Isbister (Eds.), *Digital cities: Lecture notes in computer science 165* (pp. 194–208). Heidelberg: Springer-Verlag.

Henderson, G. (2000, January 31). The digital divide. *Emerge,* p. 60.

Herring, S. (1993). Gender and democracy in computer-mediated communication. *Electronic Journal of Communication, 3*(2) [Online]. Available: http://www.cios.org/www/ejc/v3n293.htm.

Hiltz, S. R., & Turoff, M. (1978). *The network nation: Human communication via computer.* Reading, MA: Addison-Wesley.

Hoffman, D., Novak, T., & Schlosser, A. (2000). The evolution of the digital divide: How gaps in Internet access may impact electronic commerce. *Journal of Computer-Mediated Communication, 5*(3) [Online]. Available: http://www.ascusc.org/jcmc/vol5/issue3.

Kraut, R., Lundmark, V., Patterson, M., Kiesler, S., Mukopadhyay, T., & Scherlis, W. (1998). Internet paradox: A social technology that reduces social involvement and psychological well-being? *American Psychologist, 53,* 1017–1031.

Lacey, M. (2000, February 3). Clinton enlists top-grade help for plan to increase computer use. *The New York Times,* A25.

Lawrence, J. (2000, April 27). Internet equality in town and country. *USA Today,* 7A.

Loveless, T. (2000). *How well are American students learning? Focus on math achievement.* Washington, DC: Brookings Institution, Brown Center on Education Policy.

MacKenzie, D., & Wajcman, J. (Eds.) (1985). *The social shaping of technology: How the refrigerator got its hum.* Milton Keynes, UK: Open University Press.

Massey, D., & Denton, N. (1993). *American apartheid: Segregation and the making of the underclass.* Cambridge, MA: Harvard University Press.

National Telecommunications and Information Administration (1995). *Falling through the Net: A survey of the "have nots" in rural and urban America.* Washington, DC: U.S. Department of Commerce. [Online] Available: http://www.ntia.doc.gov/ntiahome/fallingthru.html.

National Telecommunications and Information Administration (1998, July 28). *Falling through the Net II: New data on the digital divide. Washington, DC: U.S. Department of Commerce.* [Online] Available: http://www.ntia.doc.gov/ntiahome/net2/falling.html.

National Telecommunications and Information Administration (1999, July 8). *Falling through the Net: Defining the digital divide.* Washington, DC: U.S. Department of Commerce. [Online] Available: http://www.ntia.doc.gov/ntiahome/fttn99/contents.html.

News and views: The large and growing digital divide for Black and White college students (1999, October 31). *Journal of Blacks in Higher Education,* 25, 57.

Nie, N. (2000). Study of the social consequences of Internet use [Online]. Available: http://www.stanford.edu/group/siqss/Press_Release/internetStudy.html.

Pool, I. de S. (Ed.) (1973). *Talking back: Citizen feedback and cable technology.* Cambridge, MA: The MIT Press.

Poole, G. (1996, January 29). A new gulf in American education, the digital divide. *The New York Times,* D3.

Powledge, F. (1972). *An ACLU guide to cable television.* New York: ACLU.

Powell, A. C. (1999, November). Falling for the gap: Whatever happened to the digital divide? *Reason,* pp. 43–44.

Price, M., & Wicklein, J. (1972). *Cable television: A guide for citizen action.* Philadelphia: Pilgrim Press.

Rao, P. (1977). Telephone and instructional communications. In I. de S. Pool (Ed.), *The social impact of the telephone* (pp. 473–486). Cambridge, MA: The MIT Press.

Rheingold, H. (1993). *The virtual community: Homesteading on the electronic frontier.* Reading, MA: Addison-Wesley.

Smith, R. L. (1970, May 18). The wired nation. *The Nation,* pp. 582–606.

Sproull, L., & Kiesler, S. (1991). *Connections: New ways of working in the networked organization.* Cambridge: The MIT Press.

Starr, P. (1996, July/August). Computing our way to educational reform. *American Prospect,* pp. 50–60.

Streeter, T. (1997). Blue skies and strange bedfellows: The discourse of cable television. In L. Spigel & M. Curtin (Eds.), *The revolution wasn't televised: Sixties television and social conflict* (pp. 221–242). New York: Routledge.

Surman, M. (1996). *Wired words: Utopia, revolution, and the history of electronic highways.* Paper presented at the Internet Society Conference, Montreal, Canada. Available: http://www.isoc.org/inet96/proceedings/e2/e2_1.htm.

Tate, C. (Ed.) (1971). *Cable television in the cities: Community control, public access, and minority ownership.* Washington, DC: Urban Institute.

Theirer, A. (2000, July). Is the "digital divide" a virtual reality? *Consumers Research,* pp. 16–20.

Wajcman, J. (1991). *Feminism confronts technology.* Cambridge: Polity Press.

Walton, S. (1983, July 27). Add understanding, subtract drill. *Education Week* [Online archives]. Available: http://www.edweek.org.

What digital divide? (2000, April 24). *Reason Online.* Available: http://www.reason.com/bi/d-divide.html.

Wilson, W. J. (1987). *The truly disadvantaged: The inner city, the underclass, and public policy.* Chicago: University of Chicago Press.

U.S. Kerner Commission (1968). *Report of the National Advisory Commission on Civil Disorders.* New York: Dutton.

Yin, R. (1972). *Cable television: Applications for municipal services.* Santa Monica, CA: RAND.

RELATED LINKS

- Digital Divide Network (http://digitaldividenetwork.org)
- Closing the Digital Divide (http://www.digitaldivide.gov)
- The Digital Divide: A Resource List (http://www.gseis.ucla.edu/faculty/chu/digdiv)
- Digital Divide Links (http://www.pbs.org/digitaldivide/links.html)

FOR FURTHER RESEARCH

To find out more about the topics discussed in this reading, use InfoTrac College Edition. Type in keywords and subject terms such as "digital divide," "information inequality," and "technological fix." You can access InfoTrac College Edition from the Wadsworth/Thomson Communication Café homepage: http://communication.wadsworth.com.

Reading 10-2

Routes to Media Access
John E. Newhagen and Erik P. Bucy

EDITOR'S NOTE

Although much research attention and policy discussion relating to the digital divide remains focused on physical access to information and communication technology—what percentage of the public has access to an Internet-ready computer—this reading argues that the way information technology is used is a larger concern than simple access to computer hardware. Importantly, the authors argue, a distinction should be made between having access to the Internet as a technology and being able to access the content that resides on it. Profitable use of new media hinges more on the motivations, characteristics, and abilities of individual users—issues beyond pricing and availability. Perhaps more interesting than the economic issues associated with the Web's development and use is the cognitive cost of access to the user. Without the requisite training, a significant portion of the population may get left behind—socially, economically, and perhaps politically—not because they lack interest in the Internet, but because they do not have the appropriate skills, information processing ability, or self confidence necessary to hold their own in cyberspace.

CONSIDER

1. What do the authors mean by "media access"—access to what?

2. How do the authors explain the differences between system and physical access on one hand and social and cognitive access on the other?

3. If social, culture, or cognitive barriers to Internet use do exist, then will certain groups be excluded from online opportunities entirely, regardless of access to hardware and software (and infrastructure)? Why or why not?

Politicians, civic leaders, and a host of other good-minded citizens agree that Internet access is good.

From "Routes to Media Access" by John E. Newhagen and Erik P. Bucy, in *Media Access: Social and Psychological Dimensions of New Technology Use,* edited by Erik P. Bucy and John E. Newhagen (Mahwah, NJ: Lawrence Erlbaum Associates, 2004), pp. 3–23. Copyright © 2004 by Lawrence Erlbaum Associates. Reprinted with permission.

Some go so far as to see access to the Internet as a key to the reinvigoration of democratic society (e.g. Rheingold, 2000).[1] While the topic receives a great deal of public attention, discussions frequently omit the critical question, "access to what?" One approach would reduce the issue of access to a simple discussion of power (Marx, 1867/1967). From that perspective power resides in the hands of those controlling the means of production: land in an agrarian society, machines in an industrial society, and information in a postmodern society. If the Internet represents the enabling technology for the Information Age, then it follows that access to the Internet is a necessary condition for access to power. But is it sufficient? If the concept is limited to mean physical access to computer apparatus, the answer is "no." Access must be conceptualized in much broader human and technological terms.

The idea that physical access to a computer is sufficient to enable Internet use, however, seems to dominate the thinking of many policy makers looking for simple or immediate solutions. The idea of access as a social imperative usually manifests itself in television news spots featuring a local politician dedicating a new computer lab at a school or public library. But, as the readings in this section demonstrate, these events may be no more than mere token gestures if the users of these machines do not possess the requisite skills, cognitive ability, and social motivation needed to enable full access to the content conveyed by the technology.

In any case there seems to be a clear distinction between having access to the Internet as a technology and being able to access the content that resides on it. The first kind of access, technological, has two dimensions —physical access to a computer and access to the network itself, which we term system access. Once technological access is accomplished the task shifts to content. Content access also has two dimensions, social and cognitive access.

Categorizing access in this manner is epistemologically parsimonious because it accommodates both aggregate and individual-level considerations. Table 10-1 shows the technological and content dimensions of access and their corresponding levels of analysis. On the technological side, physical access treats computers as individual nodes, while system access looks at the Internet in aggregation. On the content side, cognitive access addresses the individual user, while social access considers aggregations of users. The category labeled "social" describing content aggregation points to an important difference between the Internet and previous mass media systems. In a mass media system, the inhabitants of this quadrant would be referred to as audience members. However, the idea of an audience as a passive grouping of content consumers (or "receivers" of broadcast messages) just does not describe the diversity of users who are online at a given point in time. Moreover, Internet users typically do not experience simultaneous exposure to the same message in the way that mass media audiences do.

Table 10-1. Dimensions of Access Across Levels of Analysis

Level of Analysis	DIMENSIONS OF ACCESS	
	Content	Technological
Individual	Cognitive	Physical
Aggregate	Social	System

DIMENSIONS OF ACCESS

In Internet parlance, the answer to the question "access to what?" is content. The online industry's distinction between service providers and content providers implies two levels of access. A service provider is someone who connects the user's computer to the Internet. A content provider is someone who posts information on the Internet. The development of America Online's marketing philosophy is a good example of how this distinction emerged. As a service provider, AOL connects millions of users to the Internet by charging a monthly connect charge, but its management has always had a vision of controlling what their clients see and do once they get there. In the early days of the Web, AOL fashioned itself as a stand-alone network, hoping to work outside the publicly accessible Internet. As the Internet grew it became clear that working outside the global network was no longer a viable strategy and the service gradually granted its users wider Internet access. But it did so begrudgingly; even today some complain the service's browser is not up to snuff.

In recent years the company has articulated a role beyond that of mere service provider and has embraced the notion that the real money is in content. AOL's merger with Time Warner symbolizes this change of philosophy. But the dilemma posed by being both a service provider and content provider persists for the Internet's largest online service. In its advertising and promotion, AOL avidly promotes its ease of use, especially for novice users ("so easy to use, no wonder it's number one"), but this usability advantage applies mostly to e-mail and other chat features and avoids the thorny issue of content access. Perhaps AOL's top management did not hear the rallying cry of radical Internet politics: *information wants to be free.* While Microsoft and AOL still aspire to be both service and content providers, a substantial portion of the market, made up of regional and local service providers, has no aspirations to provide content. The same is true for nonprofit providers, especially universities.

The distinction between providing access to media technology and making content accessible was not as pronounced in the high era of mass media. Because of their low literacy barrier, radio and television are (mostly) understood by all. Marshall McLuhan's (1964/1994) dictum, that "the medium is the message," resonated for the precise reason that the content of television seemed to follow its form, giving rise in McLuhan's view to new structures of feeling and thought. If television is an intuitive, emotionally involving, close-up medium, then it follows that the content will bear those characteristics, regardless of genre or program. Trying to make the distinction between medium and message doesn't make much sense with newspapers either. Is a newspaper like *The Washington Post* a content provider or a service provider? True, it provides the service of running huge printing presses and managing an equally large distribution system to ensure subscribers receive their daily newspaper. But it also maintains a large information-processing organization to generate the content that fills its pages.

The division of labor between service and content providers began to emerge as cable television matured, when it started making sense to think about the difference between delivering a signal to subscribers' homes as one function, and providing the content through that cable as another. Cable companies have tried their best to project themselves as content providers, an argument made easier to sustain by the fact most of them until recently enjoyed regional monopolies. But direct broadcast television, with its inexpensive satellite dishes and growing number of high quality digital signals, has broken that monopoly and made many subscribers aware that they have content options independent of the technological delivery system. Some media economists fear that big media will come to dominate the Internet just as they have mass media, enclosing the online world with a costly commercial fence (McChesney, 1997). However, this may prove difficult if the Internet actually marks the divorce between service provision and content generation.

Technological Access

Technological access addresses hardware and infrastructure considerations and has two dimensions, physical access to computers and access to the Internet as a system.

Physical Access   Physical access entails actually being able to sit down in front of an Internet-ready computer. Arguments centering on the issue of physical access frequently point to the high cost of owning a multimedia computer as a barrier for economically disadvantaged groups (see Schon, Sanyal, & Mitchell, 1999). One solution to this problem is to promote installation of public terminals in schools and libraries. However, that position is difficult to sustain given the decreasing cost of computers. For most of the past two decades the cost of a good computer did not drop much below $2,000. It seemed as if the cost of a computer was pegged at that price. While the per-unit cost of components such as memory chips or disk space fell, each succeeding generation of machine required more resources to be fully functional and the price remained relatively constant. The cost of computers finally plummeted in the late 1990s, when computer stores began to offer powerful machines to customers at no charge in exchange for signing a three-year contract with an Internet service provider at the cost of about $400. Usually those contracts offered full Internet access for much less than the cost of cable television.

This drop in price brings the opportunity for access to home computing to a much broader segment of the population than previous economic realities allowed and lessens the need for public terminals. Those who forecasted that computers would never be affordable enough for the economic underclass are reminiscent of the skeptics in the 1960s who similarly predicted color television would remain so expensive it would always be a privilege of the wealthy. Large scale surveys show that Internet use is becoming increasingly more pervasive, with Internet access above 50% nationwide (NTIA, 2002). A case can even be made that the cost of a computer is not an overwhelming obstacle in many (though not all) parts of the Third World. A large portion of computer components are actually manufactured in Asia, and the technology is readily available, albeit primarily to the middle class, in Latin America as well.

System Access   System access doesn't get mentioned as much as it should. Brenda Laurel (1991) uses the dramatic stage as a metaphor for the computer interface and makes the point that the computer user, like the theater goer, is not aware of what is going on behind the scenes. Yet that is an important area where the Internet differs from other communication technologies, especially television.[2]

The distributed nature of Internet architecture technologically enables its interactivity, the single most important feature that distinguishes the new medium from earlier media systems. The architecture of the

Internet in many ways reflects the neural networks that make up the brain. Cognitive psychologists David Rumelhart and James McClelland (1986) describe human thought in terms of a network of interconnected nodes, where mental processes are distributed across the system and function in parallel. When one node is activated in the network, other nodes become active as well according to the strength of their connection with the original node. An active group of nodes becomes a schema, which might be a memory or attitude. One of the revolutionary aspects of the neural net approach is the claim that meaning does not reside in individual nodes, but in the *connection strengths* between nodes. For instance, for most people the connection between the node for the color green would be very strong with the node for grass. At a system level, the connections between computers on the Internet looks like a neural network, where the strength of the nodes makes the difference in meaning. This again has to do with bandwidth, or the capacity and speed of a connection.

From the user's point of view the issue of connection quality boils down to download times, which can range from annoyingly long to completely disabling. A bandwidth problem, download times really have to do with how close you are to the Internet backbone. Large research universities are the most likely to be a part of the backbone itself, but the increasing availability of high capacity fiber optic cable ties commercial enterprises to it as well. From a hardware standpoint fiber optic cable has the most bandwidth, followed by coaxial cable and twisted pair copper wire. Software engineering also enters into the picture, designing data compression techniques which have been responsible for increasing bandwidth to levels not imagined just a few years ago. The bandwidth of Internet connections is usually described in terms of line capacity, where T1 and T3 connections are the fastest and highest volume but usually only employed by institutions. Telecommunications firms offer commercial and residential customers premium connections such as ISDN or cable modems. While an improvement over modem access, these commercially offered services are still peripheral to the system's backbone. In any event, the days of individual users logging on to the Internet via standard twisted-pair telephone line with a 56kb modem are not likely to last long. Already cable companies are upgrading their lines to fiber optic cable and are providing two-way connections with high speeds compared to what was available just a few years ago.

In the long run, system access may be a more chronic problem than physical access to computers, especially in areas where basic telecommunications infrastructure has lagged.

Content Access

Content access concerns the motivation to use information technology and the ability to process meaning once the user is connected to a communication system and also has two dimensions, social and cognitive access.

Social Access   Since the mid-1990s, researchers and policy makers have called attention to a digital divide, where some social or demographic groups are systematically excluded from the information revolution [see Reading 10-1]. Early research showed typical Internet users to be predominantly young, white, middle class males (NTIA, 1998). However, as new communication technology diffuses into society, the demographic base of users appears to broaden. For instance, the percentage of women on the Internet has dramatically increased over the past decade and age appears to be playing less of a role. More recent research shows the strongest factor determining access is education (Nie & Erbring, 2000; NTIA, 2000, 2002).

Simply focusing on central demographic tendencies among disadvantaged social groups may not, however, allow us to fully understand the barriers to access at the societal level. It is important to remember that the theoretical level of analysis employed here is the group, and the description of a "typical" group member is a statistical aggregation; even while African-Americans may lag behind in Internet use as a group, many are indeed wired. During the initial phase of research in this area one important exercise might be to take a hard look at what statisticians call the outliers—those who do not fit the group pattern. Do African-Americans and Hispanics who are wired fit the mainstream demographic pattern for Internet use? Demographic variables, such as race, are frequently confounded by other factors, such as education and income. The problem is how to unpack this set of important societal determinants. One way to address this area of concern is to ask the question: Would increasing education solve the access problem, or is it more deeply rooted?

One construct that offers some promise in the early going of media access research is efficacy. Efficacy has been researched in several contexts, notably by psychologists and political scientists. Two types of efficacy have been established—self and system—which correspond to individual and social outlooks. Self efficacy is the sense of being able to cope with the social world (Bandura, 1997). Self efficacy combines with system efficacy, a sense of how well the social system works, to generate individual motivation. The reason both self and system efficacy are important at the social level is that they can be group attributes. For instance, African-Americans have lower system efficacy assessments for the American political system than Caucasians (Shingles, 1981).

If *self* efficacy, an internally regulated state determined almost entirely by education, is an important constraint to Internet access, then society should be able to educate its way out of any disparity in Internet access between groups. On the other hand, *system* efficacy may be the driving force impeding access for some social groups. There is evidence, for instance, that Hispanic culture promotes the notion among young men that computers as a system are too complex for them to manage. Notice the subtle but important difference between system and self efficacy. Here the culture is telling the individual that the Internet may be too complex, rather than the individual making a self assessment. While social class usually correlates with self efficacy, there can be exceptions. For instance, during the Black Power movement of the late 1960s and early 1970s, blue collar African-Americans showed unusually high political self efficacy, emphasizing poor system performance for their inability to advance economically and socially (Shingles, 1981). Bandura (1997) attributes this to the fact that low system efficacy can challenge the individual and actually increase self efficacy toward goal attainment. If this is the case for Internet access, then one strategy might be to present the acquisition of computer skills as a challenge rather than a *fait accompli*.

In any case, cultural norms tend to be quite conservative and slow in changing. Thus, while a group might hope to educate itself out of a problem in a generation or so, that may not be an option if the problem resides within deeper-rooted cultural norms.

Cognitive Access   Cognitive access describes the psychological resources the user brings to the computer interface and addresses how individuals orient to the medium, process information, and engage in problem-solving when using information and communication technologies.

Cognitive access differs from the study of human-computer interaction and usability studies in that it deals not only with efficient interface design and successful navigation in hypermedia environments but also the reception of meaning from content, whether from new or old media. The Internet, as mentioned, displays both text and images in high resolution. Some Web developers, enamored with the bells and whistles of full motion video and high fidelity digital sound, see on-line text as transitional—an artifact of the Web's early development. However, a closer examination of Internet use leads to the conclusion that text will continue to be an important, if not dominant, component of Internet content. Because of its high level of abstraction as a representational system, text stands out as the best way to use a computer to communicate messages that are dense in information (Stephenson, 1999). While the navigational component of Web pages may become more graphically oriented and user friendly, basic content will likely continue to be dominated by text.

The prospect of a medium which renders images and text with equal fidelity invites an examination of how the two modalities interact in the online environment in ways that they do not in mass media and adds another layer of complexity to the issue of cognitive access. Studying the simultaneous interaction of text and image suggests that a broader range of psychological processes will have to be considered than has been the case for traditional mass media.

Image processing is "natural" or automatic in the sense that mediated images correspond to an analogical system of communication, whereas words are almost wholly arbitrary and require a language system to have meaning. As Messaris and Abraham (2001) note, "the relationship between most words and their meanings is purely a matter of social convention, whereas the relationship between images and their meanings is based on similarity or analogy" (p. 216). Visual recognition of objects does not seem to require prior familiarity with different representational styles or media, either. Because images "appear more natural, more closely linked to reality than words" (Messaris & Abraham, 2001, p. 217), cognitive access to mediated images is egalitarian; regardless of socioeconomic status, viewers all generally call the same psychological processes into play while viewing. Thus, on the morning of September 11, 2001, the images of the ill-fated jetliners plunging into the World Trade Center towers were processed in much the same way by all viewers who saw them, at least for the first few seconds of exposure. After initial exposure, individual differences in knowledge or literacy determined by such factors as education level and viewer sophistication may come into play.

The extraction of meaning from textual information, on the other hand, requires the recognition and decoding of abstract symbols. Unlike the processing of images, text processing is not natural or automatic. It is a learned skill and varies widely between individuals. This fact makes the issue of access to textual content much more salient than it does for the processing of images. The low literacy barrier enjoyed by television (due to the medium's visual orientation) is not shared by the Web. This is true even for Web sites that are purely image-based on account of the technological literacy required to access the online environment.

Given these constraints, the relationship between textual and visual content has important implications for the issue of content access. Cognitive access to the Internet is more than an interface design issue. Granted, interface design driven by attention to human cognition can greatly enhance navigation (Shneiderman, 1998). However, the more complex, or information-dense the content, the more that learned skills will become a factor—and the greater the chance for a "cognitive divide." Further, it does not matter whether cognitive obstacles to access are real or imagined, either way they will still impede access.

THE TEMPORAL SEQUENCE OF ACCESS

The four dimensions of access discussed here—physical, system, social, and cognitive—exist, more or less, for all media technologies. The critical factor distinguishing Internet from mass media experiences concerns the way these dimensions are interrelated, both in terms of temporal sequence and linearity. Newhagen and Levy (1998) argue that the Internet stands apart from mass media due to its nonlinear architecture. Information flow in a mass media system is linear, passing through an hourglass-shaped system of filters, gatekeepers, and value enhancers. The neck of the hourglass represents the place where data are converted into media content. This task is usually carried out by information professionals, such as journalists or entertainment producers. On the other hand, the Internet is made up of interconnected nodes that allow content formation to take place simultaneously and at locations distributed across the network. The idea of juxtaposing the linearity of mass media with the nonlinearity of the Internet has important implications for access.

Access as a Linear Process

The one-way flow of information in a mass media system encourages modeling access as a linear process. This model generally sees technological access as the first step, where users must acquire the system connections and physical hardware before progressing into the content access domain. For example, with mass media such as newspapers, readers must have a hard copy to know what the journalists at *The Washington Post* are talking about; television viewers must have a receiver to watch this evening's lineup on NBC.[3] With the Internet, users similarly need a computer. As communication media converge, however, what "having a computer" means should be defined broadly so that discussions about access may embrace a range of different scenarios. Similarly, the scope of what is meant by "the Internet" should be defined as broadly as possible so that discussions about access may embrace as many scenarios as possible. Some prefer to use the term "matrix" in place of Internet because matrix is more inclusive (see December, 1996). In any case, it can generally be said that technological access is linear in the sense that the physical interface generator, usually a personal computer, must be present in order to access the content residing in the information system to which it is connected.

Once technological access is achieved, attention turns to the issue of content access. Here, the linear model generally places social access ahead of cognitive access, where individual characteristics such as education, gender, race, socioeconomic status, and cultural circumstances are viewed as determinants of cognitive access. Full media access can be achieved only after each level has been penetrated in turn. Thus, the policy maker concerned about African-Americans being on the wrong side of the digital divide might sponsor a program to place computers in predominantly black schools and offer Internet connections. This approach implies that the physical presence of the technology in the right place will enable access for the target group. This approach baits the issue of cognitive access but leaves for school officials the task of figuring out how to put the technology to gainful use after the public relations event celebrating the installation of the computers is over, the politicians have left, and the television camera lights have gone dim. Each successive level of access brings potential users closer to full media access, but proximity to content no more assures its sophisticated use and enjoyment than does being handed a book without the ability to read.

Limitations of the Linear Model

The inability of the linear model to deal with the issue of cognitive access calls the assumption of linearity into question. In the parlance of social science methodology, the model commits the ecological fallacy by using aggregate level data to tell individual level stories. Here, we have technological access ostensibly enabling content access. But let's not forget to do a follow-up visit to the fortunate high technology high school after a few months to see how their computers are being used. If the machines are piled in the corner gathering dust, the linear model must be insufficient.

Another limitation of the linear model has to do with the assumption that content is pre-produced and free standing. Content providers who use the linear model, which assumes pre-produced content is the motor for income generation, may be in real trouble here. Implied by this linear process is the idea that content creation takes place somewhere behind the user interface and that exposure and enjoyment occur after development. If, however, the user is an active participant in content generation, as is the case with a growing number of interactive media, the content-as-income-generator model breaks down. Why would users pay for something they have a hand in creating? Remember the mantra of Internet radicals: *information wants to be free*. Here, free means readily available at no monetary cost.

Landow (1992) suggests the nonlinearity of hypertext on the Internet provides an interesting test bed for the postmodern problem of meaning and content. His proposition can be extended to the issue of access.

Media Access as a Nonlinear Process

The nonlinear model conceptualizes access as a process of content creation as well as acquisition. Here, some subtle but important distinctions need to be stated. Humans are surrounded by a vast and complex data ecology; data objects are the stuff of the physical world. The warming rays of the sun and the cold blast of the winter wind are data. Information is data given structure by humans through the use of an abstract symbol system such as language; access to that information is contingent on an understanding of that language. Content is information given meaning, or narrative structure. Information construction, then, is something that happens on the production side of communication technologies. In a mass media system it is something professionals such as journalists do. On the Internet, information resides on the server side of the client-server dyad. Content, on the other hand, can be generated by the client side of the interface; it is something that emerges when the user creates meaning from information. Thus, the fundamental difference between a linear mass media system and the interactive Internet

is that the locus of content creation can shift partly if not wholly from the sender (or server) side of the communication dyad to the receiver (or client) side.

While assumptions about technological access may not change much in a nonlinear system, maintaining a clear distinction between social and cognitive access is not as straightforward. To begin with, the linear model never really addresses the process of cognitive access; conceptually, it seems like an artifact of social access. Survey data describing who surfs the Internet tell us that education, income, geographic location, and martial status are all statistically associated with physical access to computer technology (Bucy, 2000; NTIA, 1998, 2000, 2002; van Dijk, 2000). But sociodemographic markers, which serve as external indicators, do not specify the psychological processes involved in accessing, apprehending, and making gainful use of on-line content.

Social or cultural factors may play more of a role in basic psychological responses to media than currently believed. The facial expression of emotion, for instance, has been found to be remarkably constant across cultures (Ekman, 1982). Little work has been done, however, investigating the role emotion might play in the reception of media content by different social or cultural groups. There may be subtle differences in over-learned skills between cultural groups, for example, that only become apparent when the processing task becomes more complex. The Internet, still far from a universally usable system, challenges users who have limited textual and technological literacy and who lack the social motivation to engage with the system in the first place. Chances are that the specific skills needed for cognitive access are learned in a specific cultural context. Interestingly, race persists as a determinant of Internet use and awareness, especially for African-Americans, even after controlling for the effects of income and education (Katz, Rice, & Aspden, 2001).

Moreover, the Internet's ability to present information-dense material, both textual and graphical, with comparable fidelity will require consideration of psychological processes employed by computer users that may differ from users of other electronic media. This again calls for closer examination of the social or cultural backdrop, where some groups may employ much different processing strategies than others. In summary, two things have to be considered as caveats to the assumption that cognitive access is invariant across users. First, cultural and social circumstances may affect basic psychological processes in ways not yet fully considered. Second, a wider range of psychological processes must be brought to bear in processing Internet content than is the case for other electronic media. Again, if cognitive access was consistent across individuals, then it would precede and determine social access.

If social or cultural barriers to new technology use do exist, then certain groups may be excluded from online opportunities entirely, regardless of access to or computer hardware or telecommunications infrastructure. This is perhaps the clearest of all issues at a policy level. Liberal democracy works under the assumption that individual characteristics such as gender, race, and class should not impede access to economic opportunity and political power. If the Internet represents the enabling technology in a society where information is power, then the implications of access in all its various manifestations are indeed serious.

NOTES

1. Nevertheless, there are those who would constrain, control, or ban access to certain kinds of content, such as pornography, on the Internet. Some argue that access per se can be psychologically harmful, especially for the young. There is a sporadic but steady stream of articles in the popular press (e.g. Rosenstiel & Kovach, 1999) and in academic journals (e.g. Kraut, Patterson, Lundmark, Kiesler, Mukopadhyay, & Scherlis, 1998) critical of unrestricted access, sometimes going so far as to see intensive use as an addiction.

2. See Newhagen and Levy (1998) for a discussion of the possible impact of the Internet's distributed architecture on the mass communication process.

3. This example obviously oversimplifies the process. Mass media are now available online and information from the newsroom of *The Washington Post* might reach consumers through other routes, such as opinion leaders who previously read the newspaper. But the principle of the model still stands behind such variations.

REFERENCES

Bandura, A. (1997). *Self-efficacy: The exercise of control.* New York: W. H. Freeman and Company.

Bucy, E. P. (2000). Social access to the Internet. *Harvard International Journal of Press/Politics, 5*(1), 50–61.

December, J. (1996). Units of analysis for Internet communication. *Journal of Communication, 46*(1), 14–38.

Ekman, P. (1982). *Emotions in the human face.* Cambridge: Cambridge University Press.

Katz, J. E., Rice, R. E., & Aspden, P. (2001). The Internet, 1995–2000: Access, civic involvement, and social interaction. *American Behavioral Scientist, 45*(3), 405–419.

Kraut, R., Patterson, M., Lundmark, V., Kiesler, S., Mukopadhyay, T., & Scherlis, W. (1998). Internet paradox: A social technology that reduces social involvement and psychological well-being? *American Psychologist, 53*(9), 1017–1031.

Landow, G. P. (1992). *Hypertext: The convergence of contemporary critical theory and technology.* Baltimore, MD: The Johns Hopkins Press.

Laurel, B. (1991). *Computers as theatre.* New York: Addison-Wesley.

Marx, K. (1867/1967). *Capital: A critical analysis of capitalist production.* New York: International Publishers.

McChesney, R. W. (1997). *Corporate media and the threat to democracy.* New York: Seven Stories Press.

McLuhan, M. (1964/1994). *Understanding media: The extensions of man.* Cambridge, MA: The MIT Press.

Messaris, P., & Abraham, L. (2001). The role of images in framing news stories. In S. D. Reese, O. H. Gandy, Jr., & A. E. Grant (Eds.), *Framing Public Life: Perspectives on Media and Our Understanding of the Social World* (pp. 215–226). Mahwah, NJ: Lawrence Erlbaum Associates.

Newhagen, J. E., & Levy, M. R. (1998). The future of journalism in a distributed communication architecture. D. L. Borden & Harvey Kerric (Eds.), *The Electronic Grapevine: Rumor, Reputation, and Reporting in the New On-line Environment* (pp. 9–21). Mahwah, NJ: Lawrence Erlbaum Associates.

Nie, N. H., & Erbring, L. (2000). *Internet and society: A preliminary report.* Retrieved September 30, 2000, from http://www.stanford.edu/group/siqss/Press_Release/Priliminary_Report-4-21.pdf

NTIA (1998, July). *Falling through the Net: Defining the digital divide.* National Telecommunications and Information Administration, U.S. Department of Commerce. Retrieved July 23, 2002, from http://www.ntia.doc.gov/ntiahome/fttn99/contents.html

NTIA (2000, October). *Falling through the Net: Toward digital inclusion.* National Telecommunications and Information Administration, U.S. Department of Commerce. Retrieved July 23, 2002, from http://www.ntia.doc.gov/ntiahome/fttn00/contents00.html

NTIA (2002, February). *A nation online: How Americans are expanding their use of the Internet.* National Telecommunications and Information Administration, U.S. Department of Commerce. Retrieved July 23, 2002, from http://www.ntia.doc.gov/ntiahome/dn/index.html

Rheingold, H. (2000). *The virtual community: Homesteading on the electronic frontier* (rev ed.). Cambridge, MA: MIT Press.

Rosenstiel, T., & Kovach, B. (1999, February 28). And now . . . the unfiltered, unedited news. *The Washington Post,* B1.

Rumelhart, D., & McClelland, P. (1986). *Parallel distributed processing: Explorations in the microstructure of cognition.* Cambridge, MA: The MIT Press.

Schon, D. A., Sanyal, B., & Mitchell, W. J. (Eds.) (1999). *High technology and low-income communities.* Cambridge, MA: The MIT Press.

Shingles, R. (1981). Black consciousness and political participation: The missing link. *American Political Science Review, 75,* 76–91.

Shneiderman, B. (1998). *Designing the user interface: Strategies for effective human-computer interaction* (3rd ed.). Reading, MA: Addison-Wesley.

Stephenson, N. (1999). *In the beginning . . . was the command line.* New York: Avon Books.

van Dijk, J. (2000). Widening information gaps and policies of prevention. In K. L. Hacker & J. van Dijk (Eds.), *Digital Democracy: Issues of Theory & Practice* (pp. 166–183). London: Sage.

RELATED LINKS

- National Telecommunications and Information Administration (http://www.ntia.doc.gov)
- The Digital Divide Network (http://www.digitaldividenetwork.org/content/sections/index.cfm)
- Digital Divide Series Home (http://www.pbs.org/digitaldivide)
- Second-Level Digital Divide (http://www.firstmonday.dk/issues/issue7_4/hargittai)

FOR FURTHER RESEARCH

To find out more about the topics discussed in this reading, use InfoTrac College Edition. Type in keywords and subject terms such as "Internet access," "digital divide," and "Internet self-efficacy." You can access InfoTrac College Edition from the Wadsworth/Thomson Communication Café homepage: http://communication.wadsworth.com.

Reading 10-3

The Rise of the Overclass: How the New Elite Scrambled Up the Merit Ladder— and Wants to Stay There Any Way It Can

Jerry Adler

EDITOR'S NOTE

In 1984, Newsweek *marked the arrival of a new species of successful American—the Yuppie, or upwardly mobile professional. A decade later, the magazine took stock of another breed of upwardly mobile achievers and declared that "we are witnessing an epochal moment in American sociology"—the birth of a new elite of highly paid, high-tech strivers somewhat ominously dubbed "the overclass." They might not send their kids to private schools and they might not even think of themselves as members of an overclass, but, as writer Jerry Adler notes, they are technologically savvy and they are pulling away from the rest of America in some ways too important to ignore.*

CONSIDER

1. How does membership in the overclass differ from inheriting wealth or an aristocratic title?

2. What distinguishes and defines members of the overclass? What are their common cultural and professional interests?

3. Unlike the word "yuppie," which was widely used to describe overachievers in the 1980s, the term "overclass" never quite caught on. Why do you suppose this is?

You've probably never heard of the overclass, which is just how its members like it; they have a lot to answer for. They are the people who put Jim Carrey on magazine covers, who renamed blue-green "teal," and keep loaning money to Donald Trump—not out of any sinister conspiracy to ruin the country but because, well, it's their job. As "professionals" and "managers" they lay claim to an increasing share of the national income, but they wind up spending most of it at mirror-walled restaurants where they have to eat $10 arugula salads. They're famous for having opinions, but it's hard to know what these are, since they never call talk-radio shows. If they didn't exist we'd have to invent them, because otherwise we'd have no answer to the question, *whatever happened to all those Yuppies we used to see running around, anyway?*

We are witnessing an epochal moment in American sociology, the birth of a new class. There is, obviously, nothing new in the fact that some people in America have more money, influence and prestige than others. But designating them "the overclass" is not just another way for journalists to package the squeal of the skewered bourgeoisie. When "the poor" became "the underclass" it meant no longer thinking of them as just "a lot of people without money," but as the inheritors of a "culture of poverty." Similarly, the overclass refers to a group with a common culture and interests, with the obvious difference from the underclass that nobody is trying to get *out* of the overclass.

Important discoveries like this always galvanize the national dialogue. Michael Lind, who gives a neo-Marxian analysis of the overclass in his book *The Next American Nation* (The Free Press, 1995), was being attacked last week from both the left and the right, even

as *The Atlantic Monthly* was arriving in mailboxes with a cover story by Nicholas Lemann on "The Structure of Success in America." Lind puts more emphasis on race and parentage, while Lemann dwells more on the role of SAT tests in determining who gets the goodies in American society. But they're talking about the same people, who are also part of the IQ elite described in last year's [controversial and disputed] best seller *The Bell Curve* (The Free Press, 1994).

And this same insight resonates throughout society. Marketing consultants are already whacking the overclass into demographic slices so thin that they can peel off the Lexus segment from that for Infinitis. Political consultants study how to covertly appeal to the newly identified bloc, while simultaneously attacking their opponents for pandering to it. Bashing an elite is always great political sport. But somehow the people derided by the Left as "corporate America" and by the Right as the "liberal establishment" seldom find their real interests seriously threatened.

Who *is* the overclass? It is hard to talk about class in America, a country in which 90 percent of adults in defiance of statistics and common sense identify themselves to pollsters as "middle class." What distinguishes the overclass, in fact, is precisely its effort to distance itself *from* the middle class, rather than lay claim to it. If the overclass is hard to define, it's because it is a state of mind *and* a slice on the income curve. But it is not a ruling class: Bill Clinton seems to belong, but Newt Gingrich clearly doesn't; Bill Gates does, but probably not the chairman of Dow Chemical. The overclass obviously is affluent, but how much is that in dollars? Lind refers to families in the top "quintile," or 20 percent, of household income, because most government statistics are kept that way. But that implies a cutoff of only about $67,000 a year. Any figure is necessarily arbitrary, but it seems more logical to speak of a class consisting of the top 5 percent in household income, roughly 12.5 million people with incomes starting at $113,182.

From "The Rise of the Overclass: How the New Elite Scrambled Up the Merit Ladder—and Wants to Stay There Any Way It Can" by Jerry Adler, *Newsweek,* July 31, 1995, pp. 32–46. Copyright © 1995 Newsweek, Inc. All rights reserved. Reprinted by permission.

That figure—more than three times the median household income—probably seems extravagant to most Americans, but *Fortune* magazine recently proclaimed on its cover the alarming news that the new standard for executive pay is "four times your age"— in other words, $120,000 at the age of 30. The fact is that no matter how many Danielle Steel novels we read most of us have only the vaguest idea of the lives of people much richer (or poorer) than we are. Mark Mellman, a Democratic pollster, once asked voters to imagine what it would be like to have dinner with their member of Congress. Overwhelmingly they described a meal out of an Edith Wharton novel, with liveried servants and string quartets. Congress members make $133,600 a year.

But money is not the only entry requirement. Inherited wealth doesn't count for much, unless you're actively investing it yourself, preferably in something creative like a yogurt plant in Kazakhstan, nor does income from a local business like a fast-food franchise. (Owning a Cajun or Tuscan restaurant is okay, though, even if it loses money.) The overclass is national, or even transnational, in outlook, although its members mostly cluster on both coasts. It judges people, itself included, mainly on "merit," a quality that can be demonstrated only by a continual and strenuous accumulation of academic and professional credentials. Even more than money, it values competitive achievement: books published, screenplays produced, products launched, elections won. Of course, those things generally translate into money in the end anyway.

You might think that anyone would be proud to be associated with such a productive and successful class, but somehow that's not the case. The overclass, in fact, is one of the most anguished and self-doubting oligarchies in history, a habit of mind that began in the first act that defined it as a generation, its resistance to being drafted for Vietnam. "We've kept our compact with *ourselves,*" says Chicago novelist and lawyer Scott Turow. "We know the unexamined life is not worth living, we're good parents, we recycle. But what have we done for anybody else? That's the question people of this class will ask when their kids are grown." Who wants to be in that position? *Not I,* says Eric Redman, a partner in a big Seattle law office, with a corner office on the 61st floor of Seattle's tallest building. Also a Rhodes scholar, a Harvard Law graduate and a member of the Harvard class of 1970—of whom nearly 30 percent, responding to an anonymous survey for their 25th reunion, reported a net worth of more than

$1 million. But Redman describes himself as just a "glorified hourly wage slave . . . My broker told me the really big money isn't being made in salaries, but real estate and stock options." So count him out. What about Faith Popcorn, the endlessly quotable president of a marketing firm called BrainReserve, who lives and works in her own townhouse in the most expensive part of Manhattan? Not her either. "I'm not psychologically like those rich people," she says. "I lived in a studio apartment for 25 years before I bought my brownstone, and my cottage in Wainscott [a fashionable section in the Hamptons] is only 750 square feet."

Perhaps they just don't realize that the overclass is not the old-fashioned, discredited, morally bankrupt aristocracy. "They're the first wave of people who went to Ivy League schools on their merits, did well and are still hustling to do well," says Nelson W. Aldrich, Jr. —himself a scion of an old aristocratic family and the author of *Old Money*. The overclass was made possible by the transformation in the 1950s and 1960s of the Ivy League from a closed network dedicated to serving the least disreputable offspring of the WASP elite into a great machine for identifying future national leaders. A degree from an Ivy League or equivalent school is an almost indispensable credential of overclass membership—and not only because it presumes that you learned something while getting it. "At the highest levels," Lind says, "everyone was a roommate in college." Turow, who has degrees from Amherst, Stanford, *and* Harvard, says friends sometimes ask him whether their children really need $100,000 worth of higher education to get ahead in life. "If you're asking me whether an Ivy League graduate will have access in ways that don't exist to graduates of otherwise outstanding schools like the University of Illinois," he tells them, "the answer is yes."

The overclass leads a distinctive lifestyle, which basically reflects Yuppie tastes updated to take into account its increased affluence, sophistication, and of course weight—often a simple matter of substituting a Mercedes SL320 for a 10-speed bicycle. It is a lifestyle founded on privilege—on the premise, according to Stan Schultz, a cultural historian at the University of Wisconsin, that "we are terribly busy souls doing important things that no one else can do . . ." so of course we have to fly business class, we need a full-time nanny instead of day care, we eat out four nights a week instead of trying to make our own risotto with squid ink. The widespread belief that Yuppies as a class would perish from Brie-cheese poisoning turned out to be over-optimistic. They're still at it, according to the consumer-research wizards of Claritas, Inc., who have identified a specific segment of the overclass, comprising mostly urban singles and couples without children, whose members eat Brie cheese at *more than five times the national average.*

Politically, the overclass exists in a state of perpetual tension between its economic interests, which lie with the Republicans, and its psychological affinity for the Democrats. "One trait that comes through the data is the economic conservatism of this group," says Tom W. Smith of the National Opinion Research Center at the University of Chicago. "They don't like to give money away." But their values are libertarian and cosmopolitan—typically pro-choice on abortion, pro-NAFTA on trade, environmentally aware. And at odds, therefore, with the Republican social agenda, which is driven by groups like the Christian Coalition (founded by Yale Law School alumnus Pat Robertson) and The Family Research Council, which actively loathe everything about the overclass, except its money. "If you're making six figures, Republicans aren't hurting you," said Diana Sperraza, a TV news producer vacationing on Nantucket Island this summer. "You don't want to think about it," she says. "You have a foot in each camp, really."

It's likely those tendencies described by Sperraza actually cancel each other out. As far as political power goes, individual members of the overclass naturally serve in high positions—such as the presidency—in both parties. But except for those whose careers are actually in politics or journalism, they don't seem to wield extraordinary influence. "These people want access and power," says Maria Cantwell, a former Democratic congresswoman who represented Seattle's East Side, home to many Microsoft millionaires. "But they're too busy to use it. They're used to the fast track to make things happen. That's not government."

One of Lind's most controversial points is that the overclass has used its money and access to manipulate public policy, enriching itself at the expense of everyone else. But the money and access that count in Congress are wielded by institutions, not "classes" composed of disparate individuals. Much has been made of the reduction in marginal tax rates since 1980. But over the same period many loopholes were closed, so that while tax burdens were shifted around some among individuals, as a group the top 5 percent paid 31 percent of all federal income taxes last year—up from 27.8 percent in 1977. It is true that the gap in after-tax income

between the richest Americans and all the others has been growing. But economists now agree that the government's consumer price index, which is used to adjust income statistics, overstates the effect of inflation on people's wages. By other measures, middle-class income is growing—slowly—the poor are stagnating, and the rich are getting richer, very rapidly.

If it lacks a distinctive political interest, the overclass nevertheless has an ideology, the ideology of "merit." Its success validates its intelligence and effort. Other oligarchies in the past have made similar assertions, of course, but the overclass is the first that is able to demonstrate superiority mathematically, with the help of SAT scores. "They believe they create their job, their opportunity and their wealth," says Edward Blakely, dean of urban planning at the University of Southern California. The attitude he describes may account for the peculiar reaction the overclass has to failure, such as the loss of a job. Its members decline to acknowledge it. "Their view," says Peter Meder, who runs an executive-search firm in the Chicago suburb of Deerfield, "is still one of total entitlement . . . The opening line is, 'I'm networking right now. I'm taking some time off to evaluate my options.' Can you imagine a factory worker or a retail-store manager getting fired and saying, 'I'm taking time off to evaluate my options'?"

In the abstract, "merit" is a wonderful ideal, and a far more efficient way to allocate rewards in a modern society than, say, primogeniture [ancestry]. Of course, in the real world luck plays a role in everyone's life; some people go to high school in Beverly Hills and some in East St. Louis. But people who believe that all rewards flow from merit tend not to have much sympathy for life's failures. "As you do well, you convince yourself that anyone can do well," says Stephen Klineberg, a sociologist at Rice University. "They don't feel particularly connected to the plight of the working class," says Blakely. When a factory worker loses his job, the overclass isn't hostile, just uncomprehending, he says: "It's a case of 'What's wrong with them? Why can't they go back to school?'"

Failure just is not an option for the overclass. Elise Gunter, a successful Hollywood lawyer, recently had dinner with an investment banker friend, who explained his theory that America is becoming a two-tier society. One class will have the autonomy to live where and how it wants; the other will be increasingly constrained and shut out. Pedigree and power, money and education will make the difference, and so he had set out to become as rich and successful as possible. "You couldn't imagine anyone saying that 10 or 15 years ago," she said with a shudder. "But he said it matter-of-factly, as if to say, 'Of course that's the way it is.' On the one hand it was disturbing, but part of me agrees with that."

Gunter's friend had an extreme case, verging on paranoia, of a more general overclass anxiety. "You could call them scared to death, leading lives of quiet desperation," says Aldrich. "Or not-so-quiet desperation. They talk about their desperation while eating out." This belief in the coming triumph of the smart and rich helps explain why the overclass is so driven to reject so vehemently middle-class values and tastes. Is health the only reason so few of them smoke? Or is it also a way of choosing sides with the winners? "We are the talented few," says Schultz. "We wouldn't think of going to Las Vegas, except once to be able to comment on how tacky America is." Can anyone doubt that arugula would quickly be seen for the bitter, stringy vegetable it actually is if Burger King began offering it on sandwiches?

Of course, salad vegetables don't have much significance, even symbolically. But other personal choices, such as where to live and send children to school, very much do. Increasingly the overclass is choosing to live in ways that minimize its mixing with the middle class (which is doing the same, of course, with respect to the poor). Sometimes it just moves farther out into the suburbs, or higher up the highrise. But increasingly often it chooses to live in a walled and gated community guarded by private security forces. "It becomes a matter of status not to have contact [with strangers]," observes Mike Davis, a perceptive critic of Los Angeles society. "Physical isolation is a luxury." In Laguna Niguel, a wealthy Orange County beach town, a group of homeowners won permission to put gates at their entry roads—guarding not just the 250 homes, but a public park right in the middle of their subdivision. The plan is being challenged in court by another resident of the town.

No issue is more fraught with desperation for the overclass than schools. Their conviction that they rose to their eminence in one generation on "merit" leads inescapably to the conclusion that their own kids might not make it, or deserve to. But few are willing to put that proposition to the test; instead, they maneuver frantically to get their offspring into the best possible private schools, starting (in highly competitive environments such as Manhattan) with preschool before the age of 3. "Those who believe in public education as a democratic ideal," says Pearl Kane, an authority on independent schools at Columbia University Teachers College, "move to Greenwich, Connecticut, and pay a million dollars for their homes." Those who don't are like one well-to-do Los Angeles mother, a former public-school teacher herself, who says bluntly that the problem with the public schools is having children of different social classes, where "they don't have the same values in their home . . . if I'm working hard to push my child I want to make sure the other parents are, too." One residential development soon to be built in California has hit on the perfect overclass solution: a gated community with a private school inside.

And let's wish the future residents long and happy lives, in contented ignorance of people like Michael Brennan, a union electrician from Arlington Heights, Illinois. He had a few years of college, intending to be a teacher, but lost interest. When a friend from college derided people with "dead-end jobs," Brennan thought to himself, "Hey, some people just want to feed their kids and meet their responsibilities." He's working now on a job at a big Chicago law firm, and when he shows up at 2 a.m. to shut off the power, he finds lawyers still at their desks from 18 hours before, even on weekends. Some of them probably feel sorry for or even contemptuous toward him. They probably think, if they think about it at all, that he envies them. They're very wrong. "Some of these people I feel sorry for," he says. "You wonder if they've sold their souls. Life's pretty short." Even for the overclass.

—with John McCormick in Chicago, Andrew Murr in Los Angeles, Rich Thomas and Thomas Rosenstiel in Washington, Nina Biddle in New York, Daniel Glick in Seattle, Debra Rosenberg in Nantucket, and Ginny Carroll in Houston.

RELATED LINKS

- A Kinder, Gentler Overclass (http://www.theatlantic.com/unbound/interviews/ba2000-06-15.htm)

- *Time* Digital Archive: Cyber Elite (http://www.time.com/time/digital/cyberelite/list.html)

- To have and to have not (http://www.hartford-hwp.com/archives/45/006.html)
- Who Are the Digerati? (http://www.edge.org/digerati)

FOR FURTHER RESEARCH

To find out more about the topics discussed in this reading, use InfoTrac College Edition. Type in keywords and subject terms such as "overclass," "upwardly mobile professionals," and "meritocracy." You can access InfoTrac from the Wadsworth/Thomson Communication Café homepage: http://communication.wadsworth.com.

Reading 10-4

Tech Savvy: Educating Girls in the New Computer Age
Sherry Turkle, Patricia Diaz Dennis, et al.

EDITOR'S NOTE

One of the lesser-discussed aspects of the digital divide is the disparity between women and men in attitudes toward, and mastery of, new technologies. In high school, girls represent just 17 percent of computer science AP (Advanced Placement) test takers. In college, women receive less than a third of the computer science degrees awarded. And in the workforce, women represent just 1 in 5 information technology professionals. This report sponsored by the American Association of University Women Educational Foundation concludes that the way information technology is used, applied, and taught in the nation's classrooms must change to resolve the digital gender divide.

CONSIDER

1. How does the report define information technology fluency—what three kinds of knowledge does technological fluency consist of?

2. Do you agree with the report's key recommendations? Which recommendation should be implemented first, and why? Can you think of any other steps that should be taken?

3. Sherry Turkle, one of the report's authors, argues that girls are not so much computer phobic as they are critical of computer culture. How could computer culture become more inviting for girls?

In contemporary culture, the computer is no longer an isolated machine: It is a centerpiece of science, the arts, media, industry, commerce, and civic life. Information technology is transforming every field, and few citizens are unaffected by it. The commission has chosen to use the terms "computers" and "computer technology" to refer to this larger "e-culture" of information and simulation, and has focused its inquiries, discussion, and recommendations on computers and education.

The question is no longer whether computers will be in the classroom, but how computers can be used to enhance teaching and learning—ideally, in ways that

From *Tech-Savvy: Educating Girls in the New Computer Age* by Sherry Turkle, Patricia Diaz Dennis, and associates (Washington, DC: American Association of University Women Educational Foundation, 2000). Copyright © 2000 AAUW Educational Foundation. Reprinted with permission.

promote the full involvement by girls and other groups currently underrepresented in many computer-related endeavors. The commission's themes and recommendations, while focused on girls in schools, would, if addressed, improve the quality of the computer culture for all students.

KEY THEMES

1. Girls have reservations about the computer culture—and with good reason. In its inquiries into gender issues in computers and education, the commission found that girls are concerned about the passivity of their interactions with the computer as a "tool"; they reject the violence, redundancy, and tedium of computer games; and they dislike narrowly and technically focused programming classes. Too often, these concerns are dismissed as symptoms of anxiety or incompetence that will diminish once girls "catch up" with the technology.

   The commission sees it differently: In some important ways, the computer culture would do well to catch up with the girls. In other words, girls are pointing to important deficits in the technology and the culture in which it is embedded that need to be integrated into our general thinking about computers and education. Indeed, girls' critiques resonate with the concerns of a much larger population of reticent users. The commission believes that girls' legitimate concerns should focus our attention on changing the software, the way computer science is taught, and the goals we have for using computer technology.

2. Teachers in grades K–12 have concerns—and with good reason. Teachers, three-fourths of whom are women, critique the quality of educational software; the "disconnect" between the worlds of the curriculum, classroom needs, and school district expectations; and the dearth of adequate professional development and timely technical assistance. Even those teachers technologically savvy enough to respond to the commission's online survey had incisive criticisms of the ways that computer technology has come into the classroom, and of the ways that they are instructed and encouraged to use it.

   Often, teachers' concerns are met with teacher bashing: "Teachers are not measuring up" to the new technology, is our frequent response. Again, the commission sees it differently. Rather than presume teachers' inadequacies, the commission believes that teachers need opportunities to design instruction that takes advantage of technology across all disciplines. Computing ought to be infused into the curriculum and subject areas that teachers care about in ways that promote critical thinking and lifelong learning.

3. Statistics on girls' participation in the culture of computing are of increasing concern, from the point of view of education, economics, and culture. Girls are not well-represented in computer laboratories and clubs, and have taken dramatically fewer programming and computer science courses at the high school and postsecondary level. Therefore, girls and women have been labeled as computer-phobic.

   The commission sees it differently: It interprets such behavior not as phobia but as a choice that invites a critique of the computing culture. We need a more inclusive computer culture that embraces multiple interests and backgrounds and that reflects the current ubiquity of technology in all aspects of life. As this report describes, girls assert a "we can, but I don't want to" attitude toward computer technology: They insist on their abilities and skills in this area even as they vividly describe their disenchantment with the field, its careers, and social contexts. Although some of this attitude may be defensive, it is important to take a hard look at what these girls are feeling defensive about.

4. Girls' current ways of participating in the computer culture are a cause for concern. A common alternative to computer science courses—and a common point of entry for girls into the computer world—has been courses on computer "tools," such as databases, page layout programs, graphics, online publishing, and other "productivity software."

   The commission believes that while mastery of these tools may be useful, it is not the same thing as true technological literacy. To be "technologically literate" requires a set of critical skills, concepts, and problem-solving abilities that permit full citizenship in contemporary e-culture. Girls' grasp of specific computer tools—use of the Internet and e-mail, and competency with productivity software such as PowerPoint or page layout programs—may have satisfied an older standard of computer literacy and equity; the new definition of computer literacy and equity described in this report is a broader one (see below).

The new standard of "fluency" assumes an ability to use abstract reasoning; to apply information technology in sophisticated, innovative ways to solve problems across disciplines and subject areas; to interpret vast amounts of information with analytic skill; to understand basic principles of programming and other computer science fundamentals; and to continually adapt and learn new technologies as they emerge in the future. It is our job as a society to ensure that girls are just as competent as their male peers in meeting these standards.

When they began their deliberations, commissioners explored various ways of defining what it would mean to achieve "gender equity" in the computer culture. Some commissioners emphasized concrete suggestions to get more girls into the "pipeline" to computer-related careers and to participate in these disciplines as they are presently constituted. Other commissioners emphasized ways that the computer culture itself could be positively transformed through the integration of girls' and women's insights, concentrating on the "web" of cultural associations that women's greater participation might create.

The commission does not view the two perspectives as dichotomous or competing. They are mutually reinforcing. One of the values in getting more girls and women in the computer pipeline is that their greater presence may transform the computer culture overall; by the same token, changes in the e-culture itself—the ways technology is discussed, valued, and applied—would invite more girls and women to participate fully in that culture.

WHAT IS FLUENCY WITH INFORMATION TECHNOLOGY?

What "everyone should know" about technology cannot be a static list of prescriptions to use word processing programs or e-mail. Instead, fluency goals must allow for change, enable adaptability, connect to personal goals, and promote lifelong learning. Like language fluency, information technology fluency should be tailored to individual careers and activities.

As described by a National Research Council report, fluency with information technology* requires the acquisition of three kinds of interdependent knowledge that must be taught in concert: skills, concepts, and capabilities. Skills are necessary for job preparedness, productivity, and other aspects of fluency. They include such things as using the Internet to find information, or setting up a personal computer. Skills change as technology advances: Using the Internet became essential in the past five years, and designing a home page will be essential soon. Concepts explain how and why information technology works. Capabilities, essential for problem solving, include managing complex systems as well as testing solutions.

Fluency is best acquired when students do coherent, ongoing projects to achieve specific goals in subjects that are relevant and interesting to them.

A project for biology students might be: Design an information system to track HIV testing and notification; communicate the design to potential participants; and convince users that privacy will be maintained. In this example, students would need content knowledge about HIV testing and about notification practices. They would use fluency skills such as organizing a database and communicating with others, and fluency concepts such as algorithmic thinking and an understanding of personal privacy concerns. To complete the project, students would use fluency capabilities such as sustained reasoning, testing solutions, and communicating about information technology.

A project for German language learners might be: Critique a program that translates directions for using a cellular phone by researching alternative cellular phone interfaces; devise tests of the program; evaluate the translation with potential users; and design a presentation to communicate recommendations to program designers. Students would need content knowledge of contemporary German language, such as referring to a cellular phone as a "handy," as well as appreciation of the diverse cellular phone interfaces. Students would need fluency skills, such as using the Internet to find information and using a graphic or artwork package to create illustrations. They would use fluency concepts, such as algorithmic thinking and awareness of the so-

---

*The term *fluency* and its description are adapted from the National Research Council, Computer Science and Telecommunications Board, *Being Fluent with Information Technology* (Washington, DC: National Academy Press, 1999).

cial impact of information technology. To complete the project, they would use fluency capabilities, such as testing solutions, managing complex systems, and thinking about information technology abstractly.

The commission has reviewed existing research, considered research that the AAUW Educational Foundation commissioned on the topic, talked with researchers, and listened to girls' and teachers' observations about computing. The commissioners urge immediate action on the following recommendations to ensure social equity as well as a more thoughtful integration of technology in education and our lives.

KEY RECOMMENDATIONS

- *Compute across the curriculum.* Computers can no longer be treated as a "set aside," lab-based activity. Computation should be integrated across the curriculum, into such subject areas and disciplines as art, music, and literature, as well as engineering and science. This integration supports better learning for all, while it invites more girls into technology through a range of subjects that already interest them.

- *Redefine computer literacy.* Computer literacy needs to be redefined to include the lifelong application of relevant concepts, skills, and problem-solving abilities. What does this mean? Students must be trained to be literate citizens in a culture increasingly dependent on computers. Students—especially females, who predominate in clerical and service occupations—must be educated to move beyond word processing and presentation software to solve real-life problems with technology. While a tally of girls in computer science classes is a convenient benchmark, empowering girls and other nontraditional users to mine computer technology for sophisticated, innovative uses requires a mastery of these literacies and abilities, not quickly outdated programming skills alone.

- *Respect multiple points of entry.* Different children will encounter different entry points into computing—some through art, for example, some through design, some through mathematics. These multiple entry points need to be respected and encouraged, while we remain sensitive to activities and perspectives that are appealing to girls and young women.

- *Change the public face of computing.* Make the public face of women in computing correspond to the reality rather than the stereotype. Girls tend to imagine that computer professionals live in a solitary, antisocial, and sedentary world. This is an alienating—and incorrect—perception of careers that will rely heavily on computer technology and expertise in this century.

- *Prepare tech-savvy teachers.* Schools of education have a special responsibility: They need to develop teachers who are able to design curricula that incorporate technology in a way that is inclusive of all students. Schools of education also must be able to assess "success" for students and teachers in a tech-rich classroom. The focus for professional development needs to shift from mastery of the hardware to the design of classroom materials, curricula, and teaching styles that complement computer technology.

- *Begin a discussion on equity for educational stakeholders.* A more equitable and inclusive computer culture depends on consciousness-raising within schools about issues of gender, race, and class. School districts should put in place institutional mechanisms that will facilitate such conversations in partnership with parents, community leaders, and representatives from the computer and software industry.

- *Educate students about technology and the future of work.* Schools have a message to communicate about the future of work: All jobs, including those in the arts, medicine, law, design, literature, and the helping professions, will involve more and more computing. Conversely, technological careers will increasingly draw on the humanities, social science, and "people skills." It is especially important that girls not bound immediately for college understand career options in computer and network support, and the impact of new technologies on more traditional fields.

- *Rethink educational software and computer games.* Educational software and games have too often shown significant gender bias. Girls need to recognize themselves in the culture of computing. Software should speak to their interests and girls should be treated as early as possible as designers, rather than mere end users, of software and games.

- *Support efforts that give girls and women a boost into the pipeline.* Create and support computing clubs and summer school classes for girls, mentoring programs, science fairs, and programs that encourage girls to see themselves as capable of careers in technology.

RELATED LINKS

- American Association of University Women (http://www.aauw.org)
- Being Fluent with Information Technology (http://stills.nap.edu/html/beingfluent)
- *Multimedia Literacy* Web Site (http://www.mhhe.com/cit/hofstetter/multilit3e/student/contents.html)

FOR FURTHER RESEARCH

To find out more about the topics discussed in this reading, use InfoTrac College Edition. Type in keywords and subject terms such as "information technology fluency," "computer culture," and "educational software." You can access InfoTrac from the Wadsworth/Thomson Communication Café homepage: http://communication.wadsworth.com.

Policing the Electronic World: Issues and Ethics

Part VI takes up the thorny issues involved in policing the electronic world, including file-sharing and copyright protection, privacy and surveillance, and questions arising from disk sanitization practices. The readings in Chapter 11 examine the implications of copyright protections, which are designed to discourage unauthorized copying and distribution of intellectual property. In the case of the MP3 music format, however, many argue that charging a fee—in essence, penalizing the consumer—is the wrong answer to the question of file-sharing over the Web. Pay sites have emerged, but free ventures like Kazaa continue to flourish and the entertainment industry's lawyers are having a difficult time stopping peer-to-peer networks that require no central entity to run. Another area of electronic concern pertains to privacy and the new technology. Due to the growing use of computerized tracking software, biometrics, and miniaturized recording devices, individual privacy has come increasingly under siege. As the readings in Chapter 12 point out, the proliferation of surveillance technologies may help vanquish crime but at the expense of unprecedented monitoring of public spaces and private places. Another potential source of personal information exposure is discarded hard drives, which, even if reformatted or thought to contain worthless data, continue to harbor information that is both confidential and recoverable. The availability of information from old hard drives is little publicized, but awareness of such potentially risky consumer exposure will surely spread once identity thieves and law enforcement agencies start looking to repurposed drives for confidential material. Too few computer users, it appears, are fully aware that neither the delete key nor the format command really do their job.

11

Copyright and Regulation

Reading 11-1

Who Will Own Your Next Good Idea?

Charles C. Mann

EDITOR'S NOTE

Intellectual property, the legal term for any idea, piece of knowledge, or expression in tangible form that has an owner, is the primary product of the Information Age. Copyright laws are designed to discourage illegal copies of someone else's intellectual property from being made. But, as this article from the Atlantic Monthly *notes, when electronic media are exported internationally, the laws that govern copyright in the United States don't always apply. Widespread pirating of software, music, and videos, made simple by the introduction of digital technology, costs U.S. firms as much as $20 billion a year.*

CONSIDER

1. Do you agree with John Perry Barlow of the Electronic Frontier Foundation that digitized expression makes traditional notions of copyright outmoded and irrelevant? Why or why not?

2. In your view, is the threat of piracy and counterfeiting of digital media as real and damaging as industry representatives claim? Why or why not?

3. How do digital technologies lower the reproduction and distribution costs of pirated media content?

About twelve years ago I walked past a magazine kiosk in Europe and noticed the words *temple des rats* on the cover of a French magazine. Rat temple! I was amazed. A few months before, a friend of mine had traveled to northwestern India to write about the world's only shrine to humankind's least favorite rodent. The temple was in a village in the Marusthali Desert. That two Western journalists should have visited within a few months of each other stunned me. Naturally, I bought the magazine.

The article began with a Gallic tirade against the genus *Rattus. Le spectre du rat, le cauchemar d'humanité! Quel horreur!*—that sort of thing. Then came the meat: an interview, in Q&A form, with a "noted American journalist" who had just gone to the rat temple. The journalist, who was named, was my friend. No such interview had occurred: the article was a straight translation, with fake interruptions by the "interviewer" such as *Vraiment?* and *Mon Dieu!*

I was outraged. To my way of thinking, these French people had ripped off my friend. I telephoned him immediately; he had the same reaction. Expletives crackled wildly across the Atlantic. Reprinting his copyrighted article without permission or payment was the same, we decided, as kicking down his door and stealing his CD player.

We were wrong. Although the magazine had done my friend wrong, what was stolen was not at all like a CD player. CD players are physical property. Magazine articles are *intellectual* property, a different matter entirely. When thieves steal CD players, the owners no longer have them, and are obviously worse off. But when my friend's writing was appropriated, he still had the original manuscript. What, then, was stolen? Because the article had been translated, not one sentence in the French version appeared in the original. How could it be considered a copy? Anomalies like this are why intellectual property has its own set of laws.

Intellectual property is knowledge or expression that is owned by someone. It has three customary domains: copyright, patent, and trademark (a fourth form, trade secrets, is sometimes included). Copyrighted songs, patented drugs, and trademarked soft drinks have long been familiar denizens of the American landscape, but the growth of digital technology has pushed intellectual property into new territory. Nowadays one might best define intellectual property as anything that can be sold in the form of zeroes and ones. It is the primary product of the Information Age.

All three forms of intellectual property are growing in importance, but copyright holds pride of place. In legal terms, copyright governs the right to make copies of a given work. It awards limited monopolies to creators on their creations: for a given number of years no one but Walt Disney can sell Mickey Mouse cartoons without permission. Such monopolies, always valuable, are increasingly lucrative. For the past twenty years the copyright industry has grown almost three times as fast as the economy as a whole, according to the International Intellectual Property Alliance, a trade group representing film studios, book publishers, and the like. Last year, the alliance says, copyrighted material contributed more than $400 billion to the national economy and was the country's single most important export.

These figures may actually understate the value of copyright. Today it is widely believed that personal computers, cable television, the Internet, and the telephone system are converging into a giant hose that will spray huge amounts of data—intellectual property—into American living rooms. As this occurs, according to the conventional scenario, the economic winners will be those who own the zeroes and ones, not those who make the equipment that copies, transmits, and displays them. Because copyright is the mechanism for establishing ownership, it is increasingly seen as the key to wealth in the Information Age.

At the same time, the transformation of intellectual property into electronic form creates new problems. If the cost of manufacturing and distributing a product falls, economic forces will drive down its price, too. The Net embodies this principle to an extreme degree. Manufacturing and distribution costs collapse almost to nothing online: zeroes and ones can be shot around the world with a few clicks of a mouse. Hence producers of digital texts, music, and films will have trouble charging anything at all for copies of their works—competitors can always offer substitutes for less, pushing the price toward the vanishing point.

In addition, creators must deal with piracy, which is vastly easier and more effective in the digital environment. People have long been able to photocopy texts, tape-record music, and videotape television shows. Such leakage, as copyright lawyers call it, has existed since the first day a reader lent a (copyrighted) book to

From "Who Will Own Your Next Good Idea?" by Charles C. Mann, *The Atlantic Monthly,* September 1998, pp. 57–82. Copyright © 1998 by The Atlantic Monthly Company. All rights reserved. Reprinted with permission.

a friend. With the rise of digital media, the leakage threatens to turn into a gush. To make and distribute a dozen copies of a videotaped film requires at least two videocassette recorders, a dozen tapes, padded envelopes and postage, and considerable patience. And because the copies are tapes of tapes, the quality suffers. But if the film has been digitized into a computer file, it can be e-mailed to millions of people in minutes; because strings of zeroes and ones can be reproduced with absolute fidelity, the copies are perfect. And on-line pirates have no development costs—they don't even have to pay for paper or blank cassettes—so they don't really have a bottom line. In other words, even as digital technology drives the potential value of copyright to ever greater heights, that same technology threatens to make it next to worthless.

How real is the threat of piracy? Very real, according to Jack Valenti, of the Motion Picture Association of America. The world, in his view, is a "heartbreaking," "devastating," "pirate bazaar" in which counterfeiters with "no sense of morality" steal billions from America's moviemakers. In December the MPAA estimated that piracy, chiefly in the form of illegal videocassettes, costs the U.S. motion-picture industry more than $2.5 billion a year.

Movies are not the only losers. Publishers complain that pirates knock off expensively produced textbooks in fields ranging from business management and computer science to medicine and English. Music companies hire a firm called GrayZone to hunt down bootleg-CD makers and Web-site pirates around the globe. In some countries—Russia and China, for example—more than 90 percent of all new business software is pirated, according to the Business Software Alliance and the Software Publishers Association, the two major trade associations in the field. The International Intellectual Property Alliance claims that foreign copyright infringement alone costs U.S. firms as much as $20 billion a year.

Critics charge that these huge figures are absurd, and not only because of the obvious difficulty of measuring illicit activity. While researching this article I obtained a CD-ROM called "CAD Xpress" for about $30 ("CAD" is the acronym for "computer-assisted design"). It contained a copy of the current version of AutoCAD, the leading brand of architectural-drafting software, which has a list price of $3,750. According to the Software Publishers Association, my copy of CAD Xpress represents a $3,750 loss to Autodesk, the manufacturer of AutoCAD. This assumes, of course, that I,

and every other buyer of CAD Xpress, would otherwise pony up thousands of dollars for AutoCAD.

More important, in the view of Stanley Besen, an economist at Charles River Associates, a consulting firm in Washington, DC, the huge estimates of piracy losses don't take into account the copyright owners' responses to copying. "Suppose I know that people are going to copy Lotus 1-2-3," he said to me. "So I sell it for $500, knowing that four people will make copies of each program, whereas I might sell it for only $100 if all five users purchased programs for themselves." The price takes copying into account, and no loss occurs.

JAMES BROWN HAS A PROBLEM

If there is a totemic example of the vexations of copyright infringement, it's James Brown, the Godfather of Soul. Now sixty-five, Brown was born horribly poor and raised by his aunt in a Georgia brothel. As a child, he shilled for the brothel by singing and dancing in the streets. He was caught stealing clothes from cars and was sent away for several years when still in his teens. But rather than slide into full-fledged delinquency, Brown emerged to begin a fifty-year music career that shaped the course of gospel, rhythm and blues, rock-and-roll, disco, and funk (which he more or less invented). Spinning, falling on his knees, dropping into splits, he climaxed shows with an exuberant fake heart attack, after which he was carried offstage on a cape and "resurrected" by screaming fans. Brown was one of the first African-American pop singers to wrest control of his career—including the copyright to his songs—from the white music establishment.

In the 1980s Brown's commercial star dimmed. But his music was heard more than ever before, because rappers by the dozen built their songs around recorded snippets—"samples," in the jargon, which are "looped," or played over and over—of such Brown hits as "Cold Sweat" and "Get on the Good Foot." Thirty years after the release of "Say It Loud (I'm Black and I'm Proud)," Brown's black-power anthem from 1968, bits and pieces of the song are still all over the airwaves. "It is impossible to listen to more than 15 minutes of rap radio on any given night in Boston without hearing a back beat, a guitar hook, or a snatch of vocals from 'Say It Loud,'" Mark Costello and David Foster Wallace wrote in *Signifying Rappers,* a critical study of the genre.

What does Brown think of his place on the cutting

edge of intellectual-property regulation? I called him to find out. A receptionist patched me through to a cell phone. Brown was in a car and somewhat distracted; he had discerned clues to a fellow driver's mental condition and unwholesome fondness for his mother from his behavior at the wheel. I knew that the unlicensed copying of Brown's music had been curtailed in the aftermath of a 1991 court decision, which prevented the rapper Biz Markie from distributing a record that sampled the singer Gilbert O'Sullivan without permission. I wanted to know what Mr. Please, Please, Please thought of the new software that allows people to put entire albums on the World Wide Web. The previous night, for instance, I had downloaded part of his landmark 1963 album, "The James Brown Show Live" at the Apollo, from a computer in Finland. "This technology," he said, "I hate it. Hate it!" Then he hung up.

In the age of the Internet, Xerox PARC researcher Mark Stefik argues, the only way to foil piracy—indeed, the only way to charge for intellectual property—will be to equip all televisions, telephones, computers, music players, and electronic books with chips that regulate the flow of copyrighted material. "Kind of like having V-chips for copyright," he says. When I download *The Sound and the Fury* into my electronic book, the ©-chip will register the transaction, speeding my payment to the copyright owner and invisibly encoding the record in my copy of the text. If I lend the novel to my sister by e-mailing her a copy, my e-book will erase the original copy, so that only one is in circulation. The software won't permit my sister to dump the text into any e-book without a ©-chip, so the copy will always remain within a closed circle. Similar rules will apply to videos, music, journalism, databases, photographs, and broadcast performances—any configuration of zeroes and ones that can be sold and delivered by wire. Current, if primitive, examples of what Stefik calls "copyright boxes" include Nintendo machines, whose proprietary hardware is meant to ensure that only Nintendo-approved games work on them, and digital audio tape (DAT) recorders, which contain a chip that prevents the copying of previously copied tapes.

Copyright boxes could let copyright owners subdivide usage rights, creating new markets for information. If I want to download music by James Brown, for example, I could negotiate the terms at the Web site of his company, James Brown Enterprises. By paying a little extra, I could obtain the right to send a copy of "Say It Loud" to my sister without deleting it from my computer. By paying a little less, I could rent the music for a party next week, with the ©-chip expunging the music the morning after. I might buy a site license, so that everyone in the family could listen to "Say It Loud." I might acquire only the right to listen myself, typing in a password to prove my identity every time I wanted to hear the Hardest Working Man in Show Business. Copyright boxes, Stefik says, "open up a lot of possibilities."

These possibilities, he concedes, will not be easy to achieve: "I don't see this as a debate about next week." People may find ways to circumvent ©-chips; others may regard the chips as unworkably inconvenient. But perhaps the greatest obstacle, Stefik thinks, is attitude. A small but significant group of technophiles scoffs at the whole idea of copyright boxes, believing that the Internet changes the role of intellectual property so much that the chips will be useless. Some Web denizens believe that the change is profound enough that efforts to safeguard copyright in the digital world actually work against the interests of a democratic society.

FREE SOFTWARE

Perhaps the most widely known copyright skeptic is John Perry Barlow, who co-founded the Electronic Frontier Foundation, a civil-liberties group for cyberspace. Intellectual-property law "cannot be patched, retrofitted, or expanded to contain digitized expression," Barlow declared in a widely read manifesto from 1994. "These towers of outmoded boilerplate will be a smoking heap sometime in the next decade." Barlow's idea derives from his experiences writing for the Grateful Dead. Unlike most bands, the Dead allowed fans to record concerts and trade the tapes, which ended up increasing their audience. "Not that we really planned it, but it was the smartest thing we could have done," Barlow told me recently. "We raised the sales of our records considerably because of it."

Experiences like his, he said, show that copyright is not so much wrong as outmoded: "Copyright's not about creation, which will happen anyway—it's about distribution." In Barlow's view, copyright made sense when companies had to set up elaborate industrial processes for "hauling forests into Waldenbooks or encapsulating music on CDs and distributing them to Tower Records." To make such investments feasible, unauthorized copying had to be stopped—that's why the Dead let fans trade homemade tapes of concerts but sent "nasty lawyers" after counterfeiters who duplicated and sold official recordings. In the future, Barlow told me, people will be able to download music and writing so easily that they will be reluctant to take the trouble to seek out hard copies, let alone want to pay for them. Musicians or writers who want to be heard or read will have to thumbtack their creations onto the Web for fans to download—free, Barlow insisted. Because distributing material on the Internet costs next to nothing, there will be no investment in equipment and shipping to protect. Record companies and publishers will be obviated, and the economic justification for copyright will vanish.

Some people may still try to control their works with copyright boxes, concedes Esther Dyson, a cyberpundit who puts out *Release 1.0,* an insiders' newsletter about technology. But they will have a tough time. Even if creators can use ©-chips to forestall piracy, they will still have to compete for an audience with everyone else posting material on the Net—that is, with the entire world. Like television stations on cable systems with hundreds of channels, writers and musicians on the Internet will be so desperate for audiences that, Dyson says, they will be glad to be copied, because their increased notoriety will translate into lucrative personal-appearance fees. "It's a new world," Dyson says. "People will have to adjust."

CLICKWRAP WORLD

David Nimmer has a story. Imagine the year 2010, he says. The last Barnes & Noble-Walden-Borders-Broadway store in the United States has just closed. Now no offline book, music, or video stores remain, except for a replica bookstore in Disneyland. Anyone who wants to obtain poems, essays, or novels must download them from the Internet into an electronic book. Anyone who wants to watch a movie, listen to recorded music, or look at a reproduction of a painting must download it into the appropriate copyright box. But before getting books, music, and films, people must first click on the "OK" button to accept the terms of the ubiquitous standard download contract—the "Gates from Hell Agreement," Nimmer and two co-authors call it in an article in the *California Law Review.*

The agreement prohibits the contractee from letting anyone else view the copyrighted material. If problems surface, the agreement authorizes private police officers to descend on users' houses to check for il-

licit printouts and copies. Should search victims whine about unwarranted search and seizure, the courts reply that they freely signed away those Fourth Amendment rights by clicking the "OK" button.

"Crazy, isn't it?" Nimmer says of this scenario. "But that's what they're talking about." A former federal prosecutor, Nimmer is now at the Los Angeles firm of Irell and Manella, and is an author, with his late father, of *Nimmer on Copyright,* a widely cited treatise. A lawyer who represents entertainment, publishing, and technology companies, Nimmer is an advocate for the rights of copyright holders. Yet he is greatly distressed by some of the proposed legislation. "You're talking not about copyright but about an attack on copyright," he says. "I'm extremely bothered by where we might be heading."

Because the copyright industry has energetically campaigned for protection against illicit copying, Congress is knee-deep in copyright bills. One of the most important would bring this country into conformity with a treaty adopted in 1996 by the World Intellectual Property Organization. WIPO administers the Berne Convention, an international-copyright agreement enacted in 1887. The WIPO treaty, which is universally lauded, asks signatory nations to "provide adequate legal protection . . . against the circumvention of effective technological measures" against piracy. To implement this request, the Clinton Administration and many prominent Republicans have backed legislation that bans making or using any device that can evade any method of copy protection. In making the vague language of the treaty harshly specific, the Administration set off an explosion of protest.

When these proposals appeared, last year, they aroused violent opposition from what Barlow proudly calls "a ragtag assembly of librarians, law professors, and actual artists." He adds, "This will sound hyperbolic, but I really feel that the copyright industry, its congressional supporters, and the Clinton Administration were trying to propose that if you read a book, you were making a copy in your memory and should therefore pay a proper license." The underlying legislative problem is that "the movement is all in one direction," says James Boyle, a copyright specialist at the Washington College of Law at American University. "There's no movement [in the other direction] to contract copyright terms or increase fair use."

Microsoft Agent is a program that makes cute little animated figures. The license not only tells customers they can't "rent, lease or lend" the program but also informs them that they have no right to make the figures "disparage" Microsoft. McAfee VirusScan, the leading anti-virus software, has a license term that is every writer's dream: nobody may publish a review of the program "without prior consent" from the company. But even that is surpassed by Digital Directory Assistance, maker of PhoneDisc, a CD-ROM containing millions of phone numbers and addresses. According to the license, the software can't be "used . . . in any way or form without prior written consent of Digital Directory Assistance, Inc."

If agreements like these govern electronic books in the future, the ©-chip inside will not permit the text to be transmitted unless the customer first accepts the clickwrap license. Because current licenses typically forbid copying or lending intellectual property, Nimmer fears that copyright owners will end up with all the protections of copyright while the public is forced to surrender its benefits—especially the right to lend privately or copy within the limits of fair use the expressions of others. Any reader who wants to challenge the licenses for overreaching copyright will be forced into litigation—a situation that inevitably redounds to the benefit of large companies that can afford to pay legal fees. "It's an end run around copyright," Nimmer says. "It provides a mechanism to put a stranglehold on information, and that in itself is a bad idea."

I submit that it is even worse than he thinks. Copyright, according to Martha Woodmansee, an English professor at Case Western Reserve University, is implicitly based on the "romantic notion of the author." During the Renaissance, she explains in *The Author, Art, and the Market,* writers generally considered themselves vehicles for divine inspiration, and thus not entitled to benefit personally from their work. "Freely have I received," Martin Luther said of his writing, "freely given, and want nothing in return." In the eighteenth century the book trade grew; some writers changed their minds about making a living from the pen. Justifying the switch, the German philosophers Johann Fichte and Immanuel Kant evolved the image of the artist as a sovereign being who creates beauty out of nothing but inspiration.

This picture, though lovely, is incomplete. Artists often combine the materials around them into new forms—inconveniently for copyright, which assumes solitary originality. As the critic Northrop Frye put it, "Poetry can only be made out of other poems; novels out of other novels." Shakespeare derived some of the language in *Julius Caesar* from an English translation of a French translation of Plutarch; he followed a printed

history so closely for *Henry V* that scholars believe he had the book open on his desk as he wrote. In this century Eugene O'Neill gleaned *Mourning Becomes Electra* from Aeschylus. Charles Ives was an inveterate borrower; in his Fourth Symphony the second movement alone quotes at least two dozen tunes by other composers. Andy Warhol filled galleries with reproductions of Brillo boxes, Campbell's soup cans, and photographs of Marilyn Monroe. And so on.

Warhol's place in art history is uncertain, but in one respect he was right on target. In a time increasingly dominated by corporate products and commercial media, the raw materials out of which art is constructed seem certain to include those products and media. In the 1940s little girls bonded emotionally with anonymous dolls and had elaborate self-transformative fantasies about Cinderella, whose story they might have heard from their parents. Today girls bond with Barbie™ and dream of the broadcast exploits of Sabrina the Teenage Witch™. Fans fill the Internet with homemade stories about Captain Kirk, Spiderman, and Special Agent Fox Mulder—skewed, present-day versions of the folktales our forebears concocted about Wotan, Paul Bunyan, and Coyote the Trickster. Five hundred channels watched six hours a day—how can art that truly reflects the times ignore it?

Copyright should not impede artistic efforts to explain our times. Nor should we let it interfere with the relation between producers and consumers of art. Any work of art is a gift, at least in part—something done not purely from motives of calculation. Knowing this, people approach works of art in a more receptive state than they do, say, advertisements. The same people who would unhesitatingly copy Microsoft Word at their jobs, the novelist Neal Stephenson said to me recently, "would no more bootleg a good novel than they would jump the turnstile at an art museum." Stephenson, the author of *The Diamond Age,* a witty, imaginative science-fiction novel about pirating an electronic book, believes that in the long run this relationship of respect and trust is the only safeguard that works of art have. It is also the reason they are worth safeguarding. What will the act of reading be like if every time I open a book I must negotiate the terms under which I read it? The combined changes in copyright law could lead us closer to what Michael Heller, a law professor at the University of Michigan, calls "the tragedy of the anticommons," in which creators and writers cannot easily connect, because they are divided by too many gates and too many toll-keepers.

It seems unlikely that in the foreseeable future all

ties will be severed. But opposing pressures from the Internauts who want to open copyright up and the software companies and publishers who want to clamp it shut presage major change in the way our culture is created and experienced. Unfortunately, as Hal Varian points out, we will be changing laws today to fit a tomorrow we can as yet only guess at. The likelihood of guessing correctly now, he says, is "close to minimal." Yet it's easy to feel the pressure to make—and force—decisions right away. As I write this, knowing that I am close to finished, I realize what will be one of the first questions my editors ask: whether they can put this article on the Web.

RELATED LINKS

- *The Atlantic Monthly* Digital Edition (http://www.theatlantic.com)
- Copyright and Related Issues for Multimedia and Online Entrepreneurs (http://www.medialawyer.com/lec-copy.htm#III)
- International Intellectual Property Alliance (http://www.IIPA.com)
- U.S. Copyright Office (http://www.copyright.gov)

FOR FURTHER RESEARCH

To find out more about the topics discussed in this reading, use InfoTrac College Edition. Type in keywords and subject terms such as "intellectual property," "copyright infringement," and "software pirating." You can access InfoTrac from the Wadsworth/Thomson Communication Café homepage: http://communication.wadsworth.com.

Reading 11-2

The Next Economy of Ideas
John Perry Barlow

EDITOR'S NOTE

File-sharing software, perhaps the third "killer application" of the Internet (the first and second being e-mail and the graphical Web browser), has taken the music-sharing community by storm. But popular file-sharing programs have enraged the recording industry and supporters of existing copyright law. In the view of John Perry Barlow, a former songwriter for the Grateful Dead and opinionated cofounder of the Electronic Frontier Foundation, the noncommercial distribution of information through file-sharing programs such as Napster actually increases *the sale of commercial work. File-sharing, Barlow asserts, allows artists to enter into a more interactive relationship with audiences. In return, audiences may reward artists by becoming loyal fans—and consumers. In this reading, a follow-up to his influential 1994* Wired *essay "The Economy of Ideas," Barlow boldly asserts that copyright won't survive the Napster, Kazaa, and Morpheus bomb—but creativity will.*

CONSIDER

1. Why does Barlow think that the free proliferation of expression does not decrease its commercial value? Do you agree?

2. If great artists throughout history produced and authored works without royalties and copyright protections, why do we consider them so essential today?

3. Why is the Recording Industry Association of America convinced that the easy accessibility of freely downloadable commercial songs will bring about an economic apocalypse?

An invasion of armies can be resisted, but not an idea whose time has come.
    —Victor Hugo

The great cultural war has broken out at last.

Long awaited by some and a nasty surprise to others, the conflict between the industrial age and the virtual age is now being fought in earnest, thanks to that modestly conceived but paradigm-shattering thing called Napster.

What's happening with global, peer-to-peer networking is not altogether different from what happened when the American colonists realized they were poorly served by the British Crown: The colonists were obliged to cast off that power and develop an economy better suited to their new environment. For settlers of cyberspace, the fuse was lit last July [2000], when Judge Marilyn Hall Patel tried to shut down Napster and silence the cacophonous free market of expression, which was already teeming with more than 20 million directly wired music lovers.

Despite an appeals-court stay immediately granted [to] the Napsterians, her decree transformed an evolving economy into a cause, and turned millions of politically apathetic youngsters into electronic Hezbollah. Neither the best efforts of Judge Patel—nor those of the Porsche-driving executives of the Recording Industry Association of America [RIAA], nor the sleek legal defenders of existing copyright law—will alter this simple fact: No law can be successfully imposed on a huge population that does not morally support it and possesses easy means for its invisible evasion.

To put it mildly, the geriatrics of the entertainment industry didn't see this coming. They figured the Internet was about as much of a threat to their infotainment empire as ham radio was to NBC. Even after that assumption was creamed, they remained as serene as sunning crocodiles. After all, they still "owned" all that stuff they call "content." That it might soon become possible for anyone with a PC to effortlessly reproduce

their "property" and distribute it to all of humanity didn't trouble them at all.

But then along came Napster. Or, more to the point, along came the *real* Internet, an instantaneous network that endows any acne-faced kid with a distributive power equal to Time Warner's. Moreover, these were kids who don't give a flying byte about the existing legal battlements, and a lot of them possess decryption skills sufficient to easily crack whatever lame code the entertainment industry might wrap around "its" goods.

Practically every traditional pundit who's commented on the Napster case has, at some point, furrowed a telegenic brow and asked, "Is the genie out of the bottle?" A better question would be, "Is there a bottle?" No, there isn't.

Which is not to say the industry won't keep trying to create one. In addition to ludicrously misguided (and probably unconstitutional) edicts like the Digital Millennium Copyright Act, entertainment execs are placing great faith in new cryptographic solutions. But before they waste a lot of time on their latest algorithmic vessels, they might consider the ones they've designed so far. These include such systems as the pay-per-view videodisc format Divx, the Secure Digital Music Initiative (SDMI), and CSS, aka the Content Scrambling System—the DVD encryption program, which has sparked its own legal hostilities on the Eastern front, starting with the New York courtroom of Judge Lewis Kaplan.

Here's the score: Divx was stillborn. SDMI will probably never be born owing to the wrangling of its corporate parents. And DeCSS (the DVD *de*cryptor) is off and running, even though the Motion Picture Association of America (MPAA) has prevailed in its lawsuit aimed at stopping Web sites from posting—or even linking to—the disc-cracking code. While that decision is appealed, DeCSS will keep spreading: As the Electronic Frontier Foundation was defending three e-distributors inside Kaplan's court last summer, nose-

From "The Next Economy of Ideas" by John Perry Barlow, *Wired*, October 2000, pp. 238–242, 251–252. Copyright © 2000 by John Perry Barlow. Reprinted with permission.

ringed kids outside were selling t-shirts with the program silk-screened on the back.

The last time technical copy protection was widely attempted—remember when most software was copy-protected?—it failed in the marketplace, and failed miserably. Earlier attempts to ban media-reproduction technologies have also failed. Even though entertainment execs are exceptionally slow learners, they will eventually realize what they should have understood long ago: The free proliferation of expression does not decrease its commercial value. Free access *increases* it, and should be encouraged rather than stymied.

The war is on, all right, but to my mind it's over. The future will win; there will be no property in cyberspace. Behold DotCommunism. (And dig it, ye talented, since it will enrich you.) It's a pity that entertainment moguls are too wedged in to the past to recognize this, because now they are requiring us to fight a war anyway. So we'll fatten lawyers with a fortune that could be spent fostering and distributing creativity. And we may be forced to watch a few pointless public executions—Shawn Fanning's [Napster's inventor] cross awaits—when we could be employing such condemned genius in the service of a greater good.

Of course, it's one thing to win a revolution, and quite another to govern its consequences. How, in the absence of laws that turn thoughts into things, will we be assured payment for the work we do with our minds? Must the creatively talented start looking for day jobs?

Nope. Most white-collar jobs already consist of mind work. The vast majority of us live by our wits now, producing "verbs"—that is, ideas—rather than "nouns" like automobiles or toasters. Doctors, architects, executives, consultants, receptionists, televangelists, and lawyers all manage to survive economically without "owning" their cognition.

I take further comfort in the fact that the human species managed to produce pretty decent creative work during the 5,000 years that preceded 1710, when the Statute of Anne, the world's first modern copyright law, passed the British parliament. Sophocles, Dante, da Vinci, Botticelli, Michelangelo, Shakespeare, Newton, Cervantes, Bach—all found reasons to get out of bed in the morning without expecting to own the works they created.

Even during the heyday of copyright, we got some pretty useful stuff out of Benoit Mandelbrot, Vint Cerf, Tim Berners-Lee, Marc Andreessen, and Linus Torvalds, none of whom did their world-morphing work with royalties in mind. And then there are all those great musicians of the last 50 years who went on making music even after they discovered that the record companies got to keep all the money.

Nor can I resist trotting out, one last time, the horse I rode back in 1994, when I explored these issues in a *Wired* essay called "The Economy of Ideas." The Grateful Dead, for whom I once wrote songs, learned by accident that if we let fans tape concerts and freely reproduce those tapes—"stealing" our intellectual "property" just like those heinous Napsterians—the tapes would become a marketing virus that would spawn enough Deadheads to fill any stadium in America. Even though Deadheads had free recordings that often were more entertaining than the band's commercial albums, fans still went out and bought records in such quantity that most of them went platinum.

My opponents always dismiss this example as a special case. But it's not. Here are a couple of others closer to Hollywood. Jack Valenti, head of the MPAA and leader of the fight against DeCSS, fought to keep VCRs out of America for half a dozen years, convinced they would kill the film industry. Eventually that wall came down. What followed reversed his expectations (not that he seems to have learned from the experience). Despite the ubiquity of VCRs, more people go to the movies than ever, and videocassette rentals and sales account for more than half of Hollywood's revenues.

The RIAA is unalterably convinced that the easy availability of freely downloadable commercial songs will bring on the apocalypse, and yet, during the two years since MP3 music began flooding the Net, CD sales have *risen* by 20 percent.

Finally, after giving up on copy protection, the software industry expected that widespread piracy would surely occur. And it did. Even so, the software industry is booming. Why? Because the more a program is pirated, the more likely it is to become a standard.

All these examples point to the same conclusion: Noncommercial distribution of information *increases* the sale of commercial information. Abundance breeds abundance.

This is precisely contrary to what happens in a physical economy. When you're selling nouns, there is an undeniable relationship between scarcity and value. But in an economy of verbs, the inverse applies. There is a relationship between familiarity and value. For ideas, fame *is* fortune. And nothing makes you famous faster than an audience willing to distribute your work for free.

All the same, there remains a general and passionate belief that, in the absence of copyright law, artists and other creative people will no longer be compensated. I'm forever accused of being an antimaterialistic hippie who thinks we should all create for the Greater Good of Mankind and lead lives of ascetic service. If only I were so noble. While I do believe that most genuine artists are motivated primarily by the joys of creation, I also believe we will be more productive if we don't have to work a second job to support our art habit. Think of how many more poems Wallace Stevens could have written if he hadn't been obliged to run an insurance company to support his "hobby."

Following the death of copyright, I believe our interests will be assured by the following practical values: relationship, convenience, interactivity, service, and ethics.

Before I explain further, let me state a creed: Art is a service, not a product. Created beauty is a relationship, and a relationship with the Holy at that. Reducing such work to "content" is like praying in swear words. End of sermon. Back to business.

The economic model that supported most of the ancient masters was patronage, whether endowed by a wealthy individual, a religious institution, a university, a corporation, or—through the instrument of governmental support—by society as a whole.

Patronage is both a relationship and a service. It is a relationship that supported genius during the Renaissance and supports it today. Da Vinci, Michelangelo, and Botticelli all shared the support of both the Medicis and, through Pope Leo X, the Catholic Church. Bach had a series of patrons, most notably the Duke of Weimar. I could go on, but I can already hear you saying, "Surely this fool doesn't expect the return of patronage."

In fact, patronage never went away. It just changed its appearance. Marc Andreessen was a beneficiary of the "patronage" of the National Center for Supercomputer Applications when he created Mosaic [the first graphical Web browser]; CERN was a patron to Tim Berners-Lee when he created the World Wide Web. DARPA was Vint Cerf's benefactor; IBM was Benoit Mandelbrot's.

"Aha!" you say, "but IBM is a corporation. *It* profited from the intellectual property Mandelbrot created." Maybe, but so did the rest of us. While IBM would patent air and water if it could, I don't believe it ever attempted to patent fractal geometry.

Relationship, along with *service,* is at the heart of what supports all sorts of other modern, though more anonymous, "knowledge workers." Doctors are economically protected by a relationship with their patients, architects with their clients, executives with their stockholders. In general, if you substitute "relationship" for "property," you begin to understand why a digitized information economy can work fine in the absence of enforceable property law. Cyberspace is *un*real estate. Relationships are its geology.

Convenience is another important factor in the future compensation of creation. The reason video didn't kill the movie star is that it's simply more convenient to rent a video than to copy one. Software is easy to copy, of course, but software piracy hasn't impoverished Bill Gates. Why? Because in the long run it's more convenient to enter into a relationship with Microsoft if you hope to use its products in an ongoing way. It's certainly easier to get technical support if you have a real serial number when you call. And that serial number is not a thing. It's a contract. It is the symbol of a relationship.

Think of how the emerging digital conveniences will empower musicians, photographers, filmmakers, and writers when you can click on an icon, upload a cyber-dime into their accounts, and download their latest songs, images, films, or chapters—all without the barbaric *inconvenience* currently imposed by the entertainment industry.

Interactivity is also central to the future of creation. Performance is a form of interaction. The reason Deadheads went to concerts instead of just listening to free tapes was that they wanted to interact with the band in meatspace. The more people knew what the concerts sounded like, the more they wanted to be there.

I enjoy a similar benefit in my current incarnation. I'm paid reasonably well to write, despite the fact that I put most of my work on the Net before it can be published. But I'm paid a lot more to speak, and still more to consult, since my real value lies in something that can't be stolen from me—my point of view. A unique and passionate viewpoint is more valuable in a conversation than the one-way broadcast of words. And the more my words self-replicate on the Net, the more I can charge for symmetrical interaction [i.e. interactivity].

Finally, there is the role of *ethics.* (I can hear you snickering already.) But hey, people actually *do* feel inclined to reward creative value if it's not too inconvenient to do so. As Courtney Love said recently, in a brilliant blast at the music industry: "I'm a waiter. I live on tips." She's right. People want to pay her because they like her work. Indeed, actual waitpeople get by even though the people they serve are under no legal obligation to tip them. Customers tip because it's the right thing to do.

I believe that, in the practical absence of law, ethics are going to make a major comeback on the Net. In an environment of dense connection, where much of what we do and say is recorded, preserved, and easily discovered, ethical behavior becomes less a matter of self-imposed virtue and more a matter of horizontal social pressure.

Besides, the more connected we become, the more obvious it is that we're all in this together. If I don't pay for the light of your creation, it goes out and the place gets dimmer. If no one pays, we're all in the dark. On the Net, what goes around comes around. What has been an ideal becomes a sensible business practice.

Think of the Net as an ecosystem. It is a great rain forest of life-forms called ideas, which, like organisms —those patterns of self-reproducing, evolving, adaptive information that express themselves in skeins of carbon—require other organisms to exist. Imagine the challenge of trying to write a song if you'd never heard one.

As in biology, what has lived before becomes the compost for what will live next. Moreover, when you buy—or, for that matter, "steal"—an idea that first took form in my head, it remains where it grew and you in no way lessen its value by sharing it. On the contrary, my idea becomes *more* valuable, since in the informational space between your interpretation of it and mine, new species can grow. The more such spaces exist, the more fertile is the larger ecology of mind.

I can also imagine the great electronic nervous system producing entirely new models of creative worth where value resides not in the artifact, which is static and dead, but in the real art—the living process that brought it to life. I would have given a lot to be present as, say, the Beatles grew their songs. I'd have given even more to have participated. Part of the reason Deadheads were so obsessed with live concerts was that the audience *did* participate in some weird, mysterious way. They were allowed the intimacy of seeing the larval beginnings of a song flop out onstage, wet and ugly, and they could help nurture its growth.

In the future, instead of bottles of dead "content,"

I imagine electronically defined venues, where minds residing in bodies scattered all over the planet are admitted, either by subscription or a ticket at a time, into the real-time presence of the creative act.

I imagine actual storytelling making a comeback. Storytelling, unlike the one-way, asymmetrical thing that goes by that name in Hollywood, is highly participatory. Instead of "the viewer" sitting there, mouth slack with one hand on a Bud while the TV blows poisonous electronics at him, I imagine people actually engaged in the process, and quite willing to pay for it.

This doesn't require much imagination, since it's what a good public speaker encourages now. The best of them don't talk at the audience, but *with* them, creating a sanctuary of permission where something is actually *happening*. Right now this has to happen in meatspace, but the immense popularity of chat rooms among the young natives of cyberspace presages richer electronic zones where all the senses are engaged. People will pay to be in those places—and people who are good at making them exciting will be paid a lot for their conversational skills.

I imagine new forms of cinema growing in these places, where people throw new stuff into the video stew. The ones who are good enough will be paid by the rest of us to shoot, produce, organize, and edit.

People will also pay to get a first crack at the fresh stuff, as Stephen King is proving by serializing novels on the Web. Charles Dickens proved the same thing long ago with his economic harnessing of serialization. Though Dickens was irritated that the Americans ignored his British copyright, he adapted and devised a way to get paid anyway, by doing public readings of his works in the U.S. The artists and writers of the future will adapt to practical possibility. Many have already done so. They are, after all, creative people.

It's captivating to think about how much more freedom there will be for the truly creative when the truly cynical have been dealt out of the game. Once we have all given up regarding our ideas as a form of property, the entertainment industry will no longer have anything to steal from us. Meet the new boss: no boss.

We can enter into a convenient and interactive relationship with audiences, who, being human, will be far more ethically inclined to pay us than the moguls ever were. What could be a stronger incentive to create than that?

We've won the revolution. It's all over but the litigation. While that drags on, it's time to start building the new economic models that will replace what came before. We don't know exactly what they'll look like, but we do know that we have a profound responsibility to be better ancestors: What we do now will likely determine the productivity and freedom of 20 genera-tions of artists yet unborn. So it's time to stop speculating about when the new economy of ideas will arrive. It's here. Now comes the hard part, which also happens to be the fun part: making it work.

RELATED LINKS

- The Berkman Center for Internet and Society, Harvard Law School (http://cyber.law.harvard.edu)
- The Economy of Ideas (http://www.wired.com/wired/archive/2.03/economy.ideas.html)
- Electronic Frontier Foundation (http://www.eff.org)
- Fair Use Online (http://cyber.law.harvard.edu/fairuse)
- Selling Wine Without Bottles: The Economy of Mind on the Global Net (http://www.eff.org/IP/idea_economy.article)

FOR FURTHER RESEARCH

To find out more about the topics discussed in this reading, use InfoTrac College Edition. Type in keywords and subject terms such as "Kazaa," "file-sharing programs," and "peer-to-peer networking." You can access InfoTrac from the Wadsworth / Thomson Communication Café homepage: http://communication.wadsworth.com.

Reading 11-3

Free
Lawrence Lessig

EDITOR'S NOTE

With the publication of his second book about innovation, networked media, and the law, Lawrence Lessig has become perhaps the leading authority on creativity and free expression in cyberspace. In this excerpt from The Future of Ideas: The Fate of the Commons in a Connected World, *the Stanford law professor argues that freeing cultural and intellectual resources (rather than controlling them through overly restrictive laws and regulations) is absolutely vital to the creation and sharing of new art forms, whether manifested as remixed movies and music, digital art and poetry, nonlinear storytelling, or forms of po-litical activism. Digital technology, he asserts, "could enable an extraordinary range of ordinary people to become part of a cre-ative process . . . where one can individually and collectively participate in making something new"—but only if we recognize and abide by the noncommercial values that make for a truly "free society."*

CONSIDER

1. From the standpoint of maximizing innovation, why is Lessig reluctant to distinguish innovation from cre-ativity or creativity from commerce?

2. In what sense are free resources crucial to the processes of innovation and invention? In other words, how do overly restrictive controls cripple creativity?

3. Lessig claims that digital tools "dramatically change the horizon of opportunity for those who could create something new." Do you agree? Why or why not?

A time is marked not so much by ideas that are argued about as by ideas that are taken for granted. The character of an era hangs upon what needs no defense. Power runs with ideas that only the crazy would draw into doubt. The "taken for granted" is the test of sanity; "what everyone knows" is the line between us and them.

This means that sometimes a society gets stuck. Sometimes these unquestioned ideas interfere, as the cost of questioning becomes too great. In these times, the hardest task for social or political activists is to find a way to get people to wonder again about what we all believe is true. The challenge is to sow doubt.

And so it is with us. All around us are the consequences of the most significant technological, and hence cultural, revolution in generations. This revolution has produced the most powerful and diverse spur to innovation of any in modern times. Yet a set of ideas about a central aspect of this prosperity—"property"—confuses us. This confusion is leading us to change the environment in ways that will change the prosperity. Believing we know what makes prosperity work, ignoring the nature of the actual prosperity all around, we change the rules within which the Internet revolution lives. These changes will end the revolution.

That's a large claim, so to convince you to carry on, I should qualify it a bit. I don't mean "the Internet" will end. "The Internet" is with us forever, even if the character of "the Internet" will change. And I don't pretend that I can prove the demise that I warn of here. There is too much that is contingent, and not yet done, and too little good data to make any convincing predictions.

But I do mean to convince you of a blind spot in our culture, and of the harm that this blind spot creates. In the understanding of this revolution and of the creativity it has induced, we systematically miss the role of a crucially important part. We therefore don't even notice as this part disappears or, more important, is removed. Blind to its effect, we don't watch for its demise.

This blindness will harm the environment of innovation. Not just the innovation of Internet entrepreneurs (though that is an extremely important part of what I mean), but also the innovation of authors or artists more generally. This blindness will lead to changes in the Internet that will undermine its potential for building something new—a potential realized in the original Internet, but increasingly compromised as that original Net is changed.

The struggle against these changes is not the traditional struggle between Left and Right or between conservative and liberal. To question assumptions about the scope of "property" is not to question property. I am fanatically pro-market, in the market's proper sphere. I don't doubt the important and valuable role played by property in most, maybe just about all, contexts. This is not an argument about commerce *versus* something else. The innovation that I defend is commercial and noncommercial alike; the arguments I draw upon to defend it are as strongly tied to the Right as to the Left.

Instead, the real struggle at stake now is between *old* and *new*. The story on the following pages is about how an environment designed to enable the new is being transformed to protect the old—transformed by courts, by legislators, and by the very coders who built the original Net.

Old versus *new*. That battle is nothing new. As Machiavelli wrote in *The Prince*:

> Innovation makes enemies of all those who prospered under the old regime, and only lukewarm support is forthcoming from those who would prosper under the new. Their support is indifferent partly from fear and partly because they are generally incredulous, never really trusting new things unless they have tested them by experience.[1]

And so it is today with us: those who prospered under the old regime are threatened by the Internet;

From *The Future of Ideas: The Fate of the Commons in a Connected World* by Lawrence Lessig (New York: Vintage Books, 2002), pp. 5–15. Copyright © 2001, 2002 by Lawrence Lessig. Reprinted with permission.

this is the story of how they react. Those who would prosper under the new regime have not risen to defend it against the old; whether they will is the question this [reading] asks. The answer so far is clear: They will not.

There are two futures in front of us, the one we are taking and the one we could have. The one we are taking is easy to describe. Take the Net, mix it with the fanciest TV, add a simple way to buy things, and that's pretty much it. It is a future much like the present. Though I don't (yet) believe this view of America Online (AOL), it is the most cynical image of Time Warner's marriage to AOL: the forging of an estate of large-scale networks with power over users to an estate dedicated to almost perfect control over content. That content will not be "broadcast," to millions at the same time; it will be fed to users as users demand it, packaged in advertising precisely tailored to the user. But the service will still be essentially one-way, and the freedom to feed back, to feed creativity to others, will be just about as constrained as it is today. These constraints are not the constraints of economics as it exists today— not the high costs of production or the extraordinarily high costs of distribution. These constraints instead will be burdens created by law—by intellectual property as well as other government-granted exclusive rights. The promise of many-to-many communication that defined the early Internet will be replaced by a reality of many, many ways to buy things and many, many ways to select among what is offered. What gets offered will be just what fits within the current model of the concentrated systems of distribution: cable television on speed, addicting a much more manageable, malleable, and sellable public.

The future that we could have is much harder to describe. It is harder because the very premise of the Internet is that no one can predict how it will develop. The architects who crafted the first protocols of the Net had no sense of a world where grandparents would use computers to keep in touch with their grandkids. They had no idea of a technology where every song imaginable is available within thirty seconds' reach. The World Wide Web (WWW) was the fantasy of a few MIT computer scientists. The perpetual tracking of preferences that allows a computer in Washington State to suggest an artist I might like because of a book I just purchased was an idea that no one had made famous before the Internet made it real.

Yet there are elements of this future that we can fairly imagine. They are the consequences of falling costs, and hence falling barriers to creativity. The most dramatic are the changes in the costs of distribution; but just as important are the changes in the costs of production. Both are the consequences of going digital: digital technologies create and replicate reality much more efficiently than nondigital technology does. This will mean a world of change.

These changes could have an effect in every sphere of social life. Begin with the creative sphere, and let's start with creativity off-line, long before the law tried to regulate it through "copyright."

There was a time (it was the time of the framing of our Constitution) when creativity was essentially unregulated. The law of copyright effectively regulated publishers only. Its scope was just "maps, charts, and books." That meant every other aspect of creative life was free. Music could be performed in public without a license from a lawyer; a novel could be turned into a play even if the novel was copyrighted. A story could be adapted into a different story; many were, as the very act of creativity was understood to be the act of taking something and re-forming it into something (ever so slightly) new. The public domain was vast and rich—the works of Shakespeare had just fallen from the control of publishers in England; they would not have been protected in the United States even if they had not.[2]

It's not clear who got to participate in this creativity. No doubt social norms meant that the right did not reach blindly across the sexes or races. But the spirit of the times was storytelling, as a society defined itself by the stories it told, and the law had no role in deciding who got to tell what stories. An old man fortunate enough to read might learn of the struggles with pirates in the Gulf of Tripoli. He would retell this story to others in the town square. A local troupe of actors might stage the struggle for patrons of a local pub. If compelling, the troupe might move to the town next over and retell the story.

It makes no sense to say that that world was "more creative" than ours. My point is not about quantity, or even quality, and my argument does not imagine a "golden age." The point instead is about the nature of the constraints on this practice of creativity: no doubt there were technical constraints on it; no doubt these were important and real. But except for important subject matter constraints imposed by the law, the law had essentially no role in saying how one person could take and remake the work of someone else. This act of creativity was free, or at least free of the law.

Skip ahead to just a few years and think about the

potential for creativity then. Digital technology has radically reduced the cost of digital creations. As we will see more clearly below, the cost of filmmaking is a fraction of what it was just a decade ago. The same is true for the production of music or any digital art. Using what we might call a "music processor," students in a high school music class can compose symphonies that are played back to the composer. Imagine the cost of that just ten years ago (both to educate the composer about how to write music and to hire the equipment to play it back). Digital tools dramatically change the horizon of opportunity for those who could create something new.[3]

And not just for those who would create something "totally new," if such an idea is even possible. Think about the ads from Apple Computer urging that "consumers" do more than simply consume:

Rip, mix, burn,

Apple instructs.

After all, it's your music.

Apple, of course, wants to sell computers. Yet its ad touches an ideal that runs very deep in our history. For the technology that they (and of course others) sell could enable this generation to do with our culture what generations have done from the very beginning of human society: to take what is our culture; to "rip" it—meaning to copy it; to "mix" it—meaning to reform it however the user wants; and finally, and most important, to "burn" it—to publish it in a way that others can see and hear.[4] Digital technology could enable an extraordinary range of ordinary people to become part of a *creative* process. To move from the life of a "consumer" (just think about what that word means—passive, couch potato, *fed*) of music—and not just music, but film, and art, and commerce—to a life where one can individually and collectively participate in making something new.

Now obviously, in some form, this ability predates digital technology. Rap music is a genre that is built upon "ripping" (and, relatedly, "sampling") the music of others, mixing that music with lyrics or other music, and then burning that remixing onto records or tapes that get sold to others.[5] Jazz was no different a generation before. Music in particular, but not just music, has always been about using what went before in a way that empowers creators to do something new.[6]

But now we have the potential to expand the reach of this creativity to an extraordinary range of culture and commerce. Technology could enable a whole generation to *create*—remixed films, new forms of music, digital art, a new kind of storytelling, writing, a new technology for poetry, criticism, political activism—and then, through the infrastructure of the Internet, *share* that creativity with others.

This is the art through which free culture is built. And not just through art. The future that I am describing is as important to commerce as to any other field of creativity. Though most distinguish innovation from creativity, or creativity from commerce, I do not. The network that I am describing enables both forms of creativity. It would leave the network open to the widest range of commercial innovation; it would keep the barriers to this creativity as low as possible.

Already we can see something of this potential. The open and neutral platform of the Internet has spurred hundreds of companies to develop new ways for individuals to interact. E-mail was the start; but most of the messages that now build contact are the flashes of chat in groups or between individuals—as spouses (and others) live at separate places of work with a single window open to each other through an instant messenger. Groups form easily to discuss any issue imaginable; public debate is enabled by removing perhaps the most significant cost of human interaction—synchronicity. I can add to your conversation tonight; you can follow it up tomorrow; someone else, the day after.

And this is just the beginning, as the technology will only get better. Thousands could experiment on this common platform for a better way; millions of dot.com dollars will flow down the tube; but then a handful of truly extraordinary innovations comes from these experiments. A wristwatch for kids that squeezes knowingly as a mother touches hers, thirty miles away. A Walkman where lovers can whisper to each other between songs, though separated by an ocean. A technology to signal two people that both are available to talk on the phone—*now*. A technology to enable a community to decide local issues through deliberation in virtual juries. The potential can only be glimpsed. And contrary to the technology doomsayers, this is a potential for making human life more, not less, human.

But just at the cusp of this future, at the same time that we are being pushed to the world where anyone can "rip, mix, [and] burn," a countermovement is raging all around. To ordinary people, this slogan from Apple seems benign enough; to lawyers in the content industry, it is high treason. To the lawyers who prosecute the laws of copyright, the very idea that the music on "your" CD is "your music" is absurd. "Read the license," they're likely to demand. "Read the law," they'll say, piling on. This culture that you sing to yourself, or that swims all around you, this music that you pay for many times over—when you hear it on commercial radio, when you buy a CD, when you pay a surplus at a large restaurant so that it can play the same music on its speakers, when you purchase a movie ticket where the song is the theme—this music is *not yours*. You have no "right" to rip it, or to mix it, or especially to burn it. You may have, the lawyers will insist *permission* to do these things. But don't confuse Hollywood's grace with your rights. These parts of our culture, these lawyers will tell you, are the property of the few. The law of copyright makes them so, even though . . . the law of copyright was never meant to create any such power.

Indeed, the best evidence of this conflict is again Apple itself. For the very same machines that Apple sells to "rip, mix, [and] burn" music are programmed to make it impossible for ordinary users to "rip, mix, [and] burn" Hollywood's movies. Try to "rip, mix, [and] burn" Disney's *101 Dalmatians* and it's your computer that will get ripped, not the content. Software, or *code*, protects this content, and Apple's machine protects this code. It may be your music, but it's not your film. Film you can rip, mix, and burn only as Hollywood allows. *It* controls that creativity—it, and the law that backs it up.

This struggle is just a token of a much broader battle, for the model that governs film is slowly being pushed to every kind of content. The changes we see affect every front of human creativity. They affect commercial as well as noncommercial activities, the arts as well as the sciences. They are as much about growth and jobs as they are about music and film. And how we decide these questions will determine much about the kind of society we will become. It will determine what the "free" means in our self-congratulatory claim that we are now, and will always be, a "free society."

This is a struggle about an ideal—about what rules should govern the freedom to innovate. I would call it a "moral question," but that sounds too personal, or private. One might call it a political question, but most of us work hard to ignore the absurdities of ordinary politics. It is instead best described as a *constitutional* question: it is about the fundamental values that define this society and whether we will allow those values to change. Are we, in the digital age, to be a free society? And what precisely would that idea mean?

To answer these questions, we must put them into context. Step back from the conflict about music or innovation, and think about *resources* in a society more generally. How are resources, in this vague, general sense, ordered? Who decides who gets access to what?

Every society has resources that are *free* and resources that are *controlled*. Free resources are those available for the taking. Controlled resources are those for which the permission of someone is needed before the resource can be used. Einstein's theory of relativity is a free resource. You can take it and use it without the permission of anyone. Einstein's last residence in Princeton, New Jersey, is a controlled resource. To sleep at 112 Mercer Street requires the permission of the Institute for Advanced Study.

Over the past hundred years, much of the heat in political argument has been about which system for controlling resources—the state or the market—works best. The Cold War was a battle of just this sort. The socialist East placed its faith in the government to allocate and regulate resources; the free-market West placed its faith in the market for allocating or regulating resources. The struggle was between the *state* and the *market*. The question was which system works best.

That war is over. For most resources, most of the time, the market trumps the state. There are exceptions, of course, and dissenters still. But if the twentieth century taught us one lesson, it is the dominance of private over state ordering. Markets work better than Tammany Hall in deciding who should get what, when. Or as Nobel Prize-winning economist Ronald Coase put it, whatever problems there are with the market, the problems with government are far more profound.

This, however, is a new century; our questions will be different. The issue for us will not be which system of exclusive control—the government or the market—should govern a given resource. The question for us comes before: not whether the market or the state but, for any given resource, whether that resource should be *controlled* or *free*.

"Free."

So deep is the rhetoric of control within our culture that whenever one says a resource is "free," most believe that a price is being quoted—free, that is, as in zero cost. But "free" has a much more fundamental meaning—in French, *libre* rather than *gratis*, or for us non-French speakers, and as the philosopher of our age and founder of the Free Software Foundation Richard Stallman puts it, "free, not in the sense of free beer, but free in the sense of free speech."[7] A resource is "free" if (1) one can use it without the permission of anyone else; or (2) the permission one needs is granted neutrally. So understood, the question for our generation will be not whether the market or the state should control a resource, but whether that resource should remain free.[8]

This is not a new question, though we've been well trained to ignore it. Free resources have always been central to innovation, creativity, and democracy. The roads are free in the sense I mean; they give value to the businesses around them. Central Park is free in the sense I mean; it gives value to the city that it centers. A jazz musician draws freely upon the chord sequence of a popular song to create a new improvisation, which, if popular, will itself be used by others. Scientists plotting an orbit of a spacecraft draw freely upon the equations developed by Kepler and Newton and modified by Einstein. Inventor Mitch Kapor drew freely upon the idea of a spreadsheet—VisiCalc—to build the first killer application for the IBM PC—Lotus 1-2-3. In all of these cases, the availability of a resource that remains outside the exclusive control of someone else—whether a government or a private individual—has been central to progress in science and the arts. It will also remain central to progress in the future.

Yet lurking in the background of our collective thought is a hunch that free resources are somehow inferior. That nothing is valuable that isn't restricted. That we shouldn't want, as Groucho Marx might put it, any resource that would willingly have us. As Yale professor Carol Rose writes, our view is that "the whole world is best managed when divided among private owners,"[9] so we proceed as quickly as we can to divide all resources among private owners so as to better manage the world.

This is the taken-for-granted idea that I spoke of at the start: that control is good, and hence more control is better; that progress always comes from dividing resources among private owners; that the more dividing we do, the better off we will be; that the free is an exception, or an imperfection, which depends upon altruism, or carelessness, or a commitment to communism.

Free resources, however, have nothing to do with communism. (The Soviet Union was not a place with either free speech or free beer.) Neither are the resources that I am talking about the product of altruism. I am not arguing that there is such a thing as a "free lunch." There is no manna from heaven. Resources cost money to produce. They must be paid for if they are to be produced.

But how a resource is *produced* says nothing about how access to that resource is granted. Production is different from consumption. And while the ordinary and sensible rule for most goods is the "pay me this for that" model of the local convenience store, a second's reflection reveals that there is a wide range of resources that we make available in a completely different way.

Think of music on the radio, which you consume without paying anything. Or the roads that you drive upon, which are paid for independently of their use. Or the history that we hear about without ever paying the researcher. These too are resources. They too cost money to produce. But we organize access to these resources differently from the way we organize access to chewing gum. To get access to these, you don't have to pay up front. Sometimes you don't have to pay at all. And when you do have to pay, the price is set neutrally or without regard to the user, inside or outside the company. And for good reason, too. Access to chewing gum may rightly be controlled all the way down; but access to roads, and history, and control of our government must always, and sensibly, remain "free."

My argument is that always and everywhere, free resources have been crucial to innovation and creativity; that without them, creativity is crippled. Thus, and especially in the digital age, the central question becomes not whether government or the market should control a resource, but whether a resource should be controlled at all. Just because control is possible, it doesn't follow that it is justified. Instead, in a free society, the burden of justification should fall on him who would defend systems of control.

No simple answer will satisfy this demand. The choice is not between all or none. Obviously many resources must be controlled if they are to be produced or sustained. I should have the right to control access to my house and my car. You shouldn't be allowed to rifle through my desk. Microsoft should have the right to control access to its source code. Hollywood should have the right to charge admission to its movies. If one couldn't control access to these resources, or resources called "mine," one would have little incentive to work to produce these resources, including those called mine.

But likewise, and obviously, many resources should be free. The right to criticize a government official is a resource that is not, and should not be, controlled. I shouldn't need the permission of the Einstein estate before I test his theory against newly discovered data. These resources and others gain value by being kept free rather than controlled. A mature society realizes that value by protecting such resources from both private and public control.

We need to learn this lesson again. The opportunity for this learning is the Internet. No modern phenomenon better demonstrates the importance of free resources to innovation and creativity than the Internet. To those who argue that control is necessary if innovation is to occur, and that more control will yield more innovation, the Internet is the simplest and most direct reply. For . . . the defining feature of the Internet is that it leaves resources free. The Internet has provided for much of the world the greatest demonstration of the power of freedom—and its lesson is one we must learn if its benefits are to be preserved.

Yet at just the time that the Internet is reminding us about the extraordinary value of freedom, the Internet is being changed to take that freedom away. Just as we are beginning to see the power that free resources produce, changes in the architecture of the Internet—both legal and technical—are sapping the Internet of this power. Fueled by a bias in favor of control, pushed by those whose financial interests favor control, our social and political institutions are ratifying changes in the Internet that will reestablish control and, in turn, reduce innovation on the Internet and in society generally.

I am dead against the changes we are seeing, but it is too much to believe I could convince you that the full range is wrong. My aim is much more limited. My hope is to show you the other side of what has become a taken-for-granted idea—the view that control of some sort is always better. I want you to leave simply with a question about whether control is best. I don't have the data to prove anything more than this limited hope. But we do have a history to show that there is something important here to understand.

NOTES

1. Niccolo Machiavelli, *The Prince,* 2nd ed. (London and New York: W. W. Norton, 1992), 17.

2. In 1710, the English Parliament passed the Statute of Anne, which, to the horror of its original supporters, was amended to limit the term of copyright to twenty-eight years. In 1774, the House of Lords finally upheld the limit, permitting the works of Shakespeare to fall into the public domain for the first time. *Donaldson v. Becket, English Reports* 98 (House of Lords, 1774), 251, overturning *Millar v. Taylor, Burroughs* 4 (1769): 2303, 2308. See Mark Rose, *Authors and Owners* (Cambridge, Mass.: Harvard University Press, 1993), 97. Had the work of Shakespeare not fallen into the public do-

main, it would not have been protected in the United States, because foreign copyrights were not protected in the United States until 1891. T. Bender and D. Sampliner, "Poets, Pirates, and the Creation of American Literature," *New York University Journal of International Law & Politics* 29 (1997): 255. Americans were free to copy English works without the permission of English authors and were free to translate foreign works without the permission of foreign copyright holders.

3. For an introduction, see "The Future of Digital Entertainment" (Special Report), *Scientific American* 283 (2000): 47.

4. Apple, of course, means something a bit narrower by the term mix. See http://www.apple.com/imac/digitalmusic .html: "Because iTunes is really about freedom. The freedom, first and foremost, to play songs in the order you want, not the order they were first recorded on CD. The freedom to mix and match artists and musical categories as it suits you. The freedom to create your own music CDs. And the freedom to put more than a hundred MP3 songs on a single CD."

5. The relationship to low-cost production is no accident with some modern music. As John Leland describes it, "The digital sampling device has changed not only the sound of pop music, but also the mythology. It has done what punk rock threatened to do: made everybody into a potential musician, bridged the gap between performer and audience." Siva Vaidhyanathan, *Copyrights and Copywrongs: The Rise of Intellectual Property and How It Threatens Creativity* (New York: New York University Press, 2001), 138. By keeping the cost low, and hence the distance between creator and consumer short, the genre aspires to keep the range of creators as broad as possible. That aspiration for music could, I argue, become an aspiration for creativity more generally.

6. This is the character of Caribbean music as well. "Every new version will slightly modify the original tune," but then, obviously, draw upon and copy it. Ibid., 136.

7. Richard Stallman has been likened to the Moses of what I will call the "open code" movement. The likeness is indeed striking. Stallman began the movement to build a free operating system. But as with Moses, it was another leader, Linus Torvalds, who finally carried the movement into the promised land by facilitating the development of the final part of the OS puzzle. Like Moses, too, Stallman is both respected and reviled by allies within the movement. He is an unforgiving, and hence for many inspiring, leader of a critically important aspect of modern culture. I have deep respect for the principle and commitment of this extraordinary individual, though I also have great respect for those who are courageous enough to question his thinking and then sustain his wrath.

Stallman insists that those who would advance the values of the free software movement must adopt the language "free" rather than "open." This seems to me an unproductive debate. To the extent Stallman believes that people dilute the insights of the free software movement by minimizing its connection to fundamental values, he is correct. The importance of free and open source software is much more than business, or efficient code. But the remedy to narrowness is not magic words—especially when the magic words tend to confuse rather than clarify. I am partial to the term *open*—as in open society; I believe it is properly a reference to values as well as the licenses under which code is distributed; and by "open code" I mean to refer to the values across both technical and legal contexts that promote a world where governing structures—code—are fundamentally free.

For an exceptional study of free and open source software, and the incentives that are behind it, see Working Group on Libre Software, "Free Software/Open Source: Information Society Opportunities for Europe?," Version 1.2 (April 2000), http://eu.conecta.it/paper.pdf.

8. In the terms of legal theory, there are two distinct ways in which a resource could be "free" in the sense I mean. Either no one would have any entitlement to the resource, or if someone did have an entitlement, the resource would be protected by a liability rather than a property rule. See Guido Calabresi and Douglas Melamed, "Property Rules, Liability Rules, and Inalienability: One View of the Cathedral," *Harvard Law Review* 85 (1972): 1089. See also Robert P. Merges, "Institutions for Intellectual Property Transactions: The Case of Patent Pools," in *Expanding the Boundaries of Intellectual Property,* Rochelle Cooper Dreyfuss and Diane Leenheer Zimmerman, eds. (Oxford: Oxford University Press, 2001), 123, 131. ("The essence of this Framework is this: Calabresi and Melamed assign all legal entitlements to one of two rules, 'property rules' and 'liability rules.' The former are best described as 'absolute permission rules': one cannot take these entitlements without prior permission of the owner. The rightholder, acting individually, thus sets the price. Most real estate fits this description. By contrast, liability rules are best described as 'take now, pay later.' They allow for nonowners to take the entitlement without permission of the owner, so long as they adequately compensate the owner later. In the Calabresi–Melamed Framework, ex post adequate compensation is deemed 'collective valuation'").

9. Carol Rose, "The Comedy of the Commons: Custom, Commerce, and Inherently Public Property," *University of Chicago Law Review* 53 (1986): 711, 712.

 RELATED LINKS

- Lawrence Lessig's blog (http://www.lessig.org/blog)
- Stanford Center for Internet and Society (http://cyberlaw.stanford.edu)
- Creative Commons Project (http://creativecommons.org)
- *The Future of Ideas* (http://the-future-of-ideas.com)
- *Code and Other Laws of Cyberspace* (http://cyberlaw.stanford.edu/code)

 FOR FURTHER RESEARCH

To find out more about the topics discussed in this reading, use InfoTrac College Edition. Type in keywords and subject terms such as "copyright law," "technological innovation," and "public goods." You can access InfoTrac College Edition from the Wadsworth/Thomson Communication Café homepage: http://communication.wadsworth.com.

Reading 11-4

The Race to Kill Kazaa
Todd Woody

EDITOR'S NOTE

Even though history shows that new technologies help expand their markets, the entertainment industry has a history of pursuing legal action against inventors and other media entrepreneurs who facilitate the unauthorized distribution of media content. Recent lawsuits brought against file-sharing services, including Napster and now Kazaa, demonstrate the industry's resolve and aversion to ceding control. However, unlike Napster, Kazaa has no central server indexing songs and other content that would allow the industry to take the company to court for copyright infringement. In the case of Kazaa, the servers are in Denmark, the software is in Estonia, the domain is registered Down Under, and the corporation's legal address is on a tiny island in the South Pacific. The users—60 million of them—are everywhere around the world. As this article from Wired *magazine points out, the entertainment industry's lawyers are having a difficult time stopping a peer-to-peer network that requires no central entity to run.*

CONSIDER

1. What makes Kazaa fundamentally different from earlier file-sharing services, such as Napster, and why is it more insulated from legal prosecution?

2. What is the solution to the file-sharing issue, which purportedly causes the entertainment industry to lose millions of dollars in lost revenue each year?

3. Do you agree that the power to kill Kazaa ultimately rests solely in the hands of the service's users? Why or why not?

On October 2, 2001, the weight of the global entertainment industry came crashing down on Niklas Zennström, cofounder of Kazaa, the wildly popular file-sharing service. That was the day every major American music label and movie studio filed suit against his company. Their goal was to shutter the service and shut down the tens of millions of people sharing billions of copyrighted music, video, and software files. Only problem: Stopping Napster, which indexed songs on its servers, was easy—the recording industry took the company to court for copyright infringement, and a judge pulled the plug. With Kazaa, users trade files through thousands of anonymous "supernodes." There is no plug to pull.

Nor, as attorneys would soon discover, was there even a single outfit to shut down. That's because on a January morning three months after the suit was filed, Amsterdam-based Kazaa.com went dark and Zennström vanished. Days later, the company was reborn with a structure as decentralized as Kazaa's peer-to-peer service itself. Zennström, a Swedish citizen, transferred control of the software's code to Blastoise, a strangely crafted company with operations off the coast of Britain—on a remote island renowned as a tax haven—and in Estonia, a notorious safe harbor for intellectual property pirates. And that was just the start.

Ownership of the Kazaa interface went to Sharman Networks, a business formed days earlier in the South Pacific island nation of Vanuatu, another tax haven. Sharman, which runs its servers in Denmark, obtained a license for Zennström's technology, FastTrack. The Kazaa.com domain, on the other hand, was registered to an Australian firm called LEF Interactive—for the French revolutionary slogan, *liberté, égalité, fraternité.*

Confused? So were the copyright cops. "It's hard to know which one to sue," complains Michael Speck, an investigator with the Australian Record Industry Association. Hollywood lawyers figured the best way to bring Kazaa to justice was to squeeze Sharman. Trouble was, Sharman, which operates out of Sydney, had no employees. All its workers, including CEO Nikki Hemming, are contracted through LEF. The names of Sharman's investors and board members are locked away in Vanuatu, a republic that bills itself as an asylum whose "strict code of secrecy" is "useful in any number of circumstances where the confidentiality of ownership, or control, want to be preserved."

Why all the subterfuge? It's an international business model for the post-Napster era. A close look at Kazaa reveals a corporate nesting doll that frustrated Hollywood attorneys for more than a year. From Estonia to Australia, they pleaded with courts to force Kazaa's operators out from the shadows. Meanwhile, every week that Sharman was able to hold the law at bay, countless copies of Kazaa software were being downloaded. In the last six months alone, PC users have downloaded more than 90 million copies. Kazaa

From "The Race to Kill Kazaa" by Todd Woody, *Wired,* February 2003, pp. 104–107, 138. Copyright © 2003 by Todd Woody. Reprinted with permission.

has 60 million users around the world and 22 million in the U.S.—an irresistible audience to marketers. Last year, Sharman raked in millions from U.S. advertisers like Netflix and DirecTV, without spending a penny on content. The chase could have gone on forever.

And then, suddenly, a few days before Thanksgiving, it ended.

Hollywood's disdain for file-sharing can be measured in the 10-foot stack of papers that make up *Metro Goldwyn Mayer Studios v. Grokster et al.*, which sits on file in the Los Angeles federal courthouse. In the suit, a roster of entertainment conglomerates accuse Fast-Track-enabled services Kazaa, Morpheus, and Grokster of profiting from a "21st-century piratical bazaar." Record labels and movie studios want the services closed and fined $150,000 for each illegally traded song or movie. Given the billions of files changing hands every week, the damages could be astronomical.

With U.S. operations, Grokster and Morpheus were easy to pin down. But before attorneys could make their case against Kazaa, they had to find Sharman, which hadn't left so much as a paper trail to the U.S. Many of its contracts with U.S. companies are negotiated through LEF, whose sole director is, not coincidentally, Nikki Hemming. So the lawyers asked their Australian counterparts to track her down. "They're doing everything they can to avoid being located," grumbles Richard Mallett, an executive with the Australasian Performing Right Association. One Australian attorney invoked the Hague Convention to obtain a court order compelling Hemming to turn over documents. Even then, the lawyer claims it took the subpoena server a week of cat-and-mouse games to corner her.

Finally, the company decided to stop running. Hemming chose to be deposed in Vancouver; she feared that simply stepping foot in the U.S. could complicate matters. Likewise, she didn't show up at the late-November jurisdiction hearing in Los Angeles. Sharman's lawyers were there, however. The question before U.S. District Court judge Stephen Wilson was simple: Does Sharman do enough business in the U.S. to be lawfully included as part of the Morpheus-Grokster lawsuit? But the proceeding quickly became a referendum on the company's alleged sins. "Sharman has done everything it can to exploit and enhance the copyright-infringing activity of its members," said the industry's lead attorney David Kendall. "There is no intention to promote wrongful uses," countered Sharman lawyer Rod Dorman. "Is my client aware that people do that? Yes."

"I realize that some of these issues are uncharted," the judge told the attorneys. "I'm inclined to find there is jurisdiction against Sharman."

It was bad news for Sharman but, with the hearing on the industry's home turf, not surprising. Sharman has been preparing for litigation. For months, the company has been bundling Kazaa with Altnet, a P2P network that delivers encrypted songs, movies, and videogames. But while Kazaa downloads are free, Altnet works on a micropayment model—and has attracted legitimate technology and entertainment clients. As a result, Sharman is ready to argue that Kazaa can be put to legal uses and so, under the law, does not violate copyright statutes. With Altnet, Sharman has begun the transformation to an upstanding business.

Can a company built on the trafficking of other people's property shed the secrecy surrounding its operations and go legit? Hollywood's pinstriped suits think they know the answer to that question—it's a ruse. For every legal file on Altnet, there are millions of illegal ones on Kazaa. Altnet may be a good idea by itself, but on the back of Kazaa, it's one more tactic to delay prosecution while Sharman sells more advertising.

But of course that's what they'd say. The question is better posed to the company's mysterious and elusive CEO, Nikki Hemming—if I can find her.

As it turns out, getting a table with Hemming is easier without a subpoena in your hand. "You're the first journalist to see our office," says the 36-year-old CEO, dressed in a white blouse, tan slacks, and sandals. It's a Sunday afternoon in a quiet Sydney neighborhood overrun with Mercedes SUVs and yellow-crested cockatoos. A marketing manager sits with us in the lime-green office, painted in the color of the Kazaa site, and records me recording his boss's first interview in months.

Hemming left her native England for Sydney in 1995 to establish a Virgin Interactive outpost. There, she befriended Kevin Bermeister, a tech entrepreneur. In 1996, Bermeister started a company called Brilliant Digital Entertainment and moved it to L.A.—where he and Zennström eventually signed an agreement to bundle an early version of Altnet with Kazaa. Early last year, Zennström, under legal siege in America, decided he wanted out. Bermeister introduced Zennström to Hemming, who corralled some investors, formed Sharman, and acquired Kazaa. Hemming also established LEF, which she calls "an independent organization with a long-term contract to provide services to Sharman."

I ask Hemming about Sharman's unconventional

structure. "It's not uncommon to register an offshore organization and provide management services from where you live," she says, trying not to sound defensive. "LEF does business as a normal Australian company. Sharman abides by the regulations of Vanuatu. I'm quite happy to declare that there are tax efficiencies in doing that. It really is as simple as that."

But there are more than just tax advantages in Vanuatu. Matt Oppenheim, head of legal affairs for the Recording Industry Association of America in Washington, maintains that Sharman calls Vanuatu home because it provides camouflage for revenue. Also, Vanuatu's vaunted "code of secrecy" means the nation would be unlikely to honor a summons to reveal assets, investors, or a board of directors. "The fact that Sharman is registered in Vanuatu," he says, "is a sham."

Oppenheim's colleagues go even further. They call Sharman's Sydney operation a take on *The Sting*, in which Paul Newman and Robert Redford set up a phony bookie joint in a Chicago storefront—except that in this version, Bermeister is running the whole thing from L.A. "Mate, when you go to their office, you'll see that only a few people work there," one insider tells me.

Very conspiratorial. But not true. When I return to Sharman's office the next day, a dozen people are tapping away in front of monitors. The London-based biz dev guy is here en route to a board meeting in Vanuatu. Whiteboards are full of the jargon-laden scribbles of marketers and programmers. Phil Morle, Sharman's director of technology, knows the rap about the headquarters being an empty shell, and he jokes about it: "I hired actors to come in here."

For all Sharman's obsessive secrecy, there's a desire among the employees to be seen as respectable renegades. At one point, a marketing manager shows off a homemade *Wired* cover playing off Kazaa's lime colors, featuring two colleagues striking tough-guy poses under the headline "IT'S HARD BEING GREEN." Hemming plays the role, too. Given the chance, she lashes out at Hollywood for its attitude toward Altnet: "What does it take for an industry to wake up to an amazing opportunity? They have this misconceived idea that we're the threat, but we're the solution."

So why aren't they getting on board? Hemming shrugs. "People dig their heels in because they want to maintain an existing business model when a new one appears to be a threat."

Altnet is the anti-Kazaa. Both networks use Fast-Track and coexist as part of the Kazaa Media Desktop, a Web page-like application. But while Kazaa is a feast for users, Altnet—49 percent of which is owned by Zennström's firm—returns control to the content creators. Unsigned bands can distribute free music via an Altnet server. Publishers can use the digital rights management system to allow time-limited downloads or to sell copyrighted files through the micropayment service, introduced in November. You might pay 49 cents for one of 300 songs on Altnet or $10 to $20 for a videogame, with charges appearing on your credit card statement or phone bill. Publishers pay fees and commissions to Altnet, which are shared with Sharman.

The bundle gives Altnet access to 60 million Kazaa users. But because search results come back together, Altnet's 600 pay-as-you-download files seem laughably unappealing next to hundreds of millions of free copyrighted files. Sure, Altnet's results appear atop the page, but that only gives users an indication of how far to scroll to get what they're really after.

Bermeister insists that, with Hollywood's cooperation, Altnet can change the way the masses think of file-sharing. "The only way to influence users is to increase the volume of non-infringing files," he tells me at Altnet's L.A. office. He's betting that quick downloads, high-quality songs, and a frequent-flier program that rewards legal downloads will turn the tide. Not to mention the warm feeling you get from doing the right thing.

According to a declaration he gave in the copyright case, it's already working. The creators of the animated Wallace and Gromit series distribute encrypted video through Altnet. Same for movie studio Lions Gate Entertainment, which cooperated on a campaign to promote Microsoft's new multimedia software. In October, various Infogrames videogames generated 90,000 paid downloads—even while free versions were available on Kazaa. *RollerCoaster Tycoon* sold 250 copies in one weekend.

And yet despite early signs that Altnet could succeed, Sharman continues to tweak Kazaa in ways that encourage illegal file-sharing. In September, it added a feature that makes it easier to download entire albums, according to the RIAA, and another that rewards active uploaders by letting them "jump the queue" for downloads. Bermeister admits that such options add to Hollywood's skepticism. "We were ridiculed when we had discussions at a very high level within the entertainment industry," he says.

Why does Sharman do it? Because the more users, the better. A bigger consumer base allows Sharman to sell more ads and to devise new revenue opportunities—like the complex scheme Kazaa (and other file-sharing services) tried to deploy last year. It involved hijacking commissions from ecommerce sites like Amazon that were earmarked for referring organizations (everything from blogs to nonprofit sites), and diverting them to a third party, which in turn paid Sharman. Having more users helps Altnet, too. Bermeister plans to introduce an opt-in distributed computing scheme this year to resell idle processing power and hard drive storage of Kazaa-member computers. The more Kazaa users, the more who will sign up.

Of course, any business plan that depends on a large user base clearly benefits from the lure of illegal file-sharing, which in turn undermines Sharman's argument for legitimacy.

Back in Los Angeles a few days after Thanksgiving, a battalion of high-priced attorneys fill out an art deco federal courtroom. Both sides—the Hollywood insiders and the file-sharing scofflaws—are asking the judge for a quick, trial-free ruling in their favor. Two men in black are seated amid a sea of suits: plaintiffs Lamont Dozier, who penned such Motown hits as "Stop! In the Name of Love," and Jerry Leiber, who with partner Mike Stoller gave Elvis "Jailhouse Rock." "If we don't stop it in its tracks, it will become a monster," the 69-year-old Leiber says of Kazaa. Then there are the guys sitting behind Sharman's attorneys, from Tech-9 —an industrial rock band that distributes its music online. They're wearing T-shirts emblazoned with the letters FTI. Fuck the industry.

The day ends without a decision from Wilson. That could take months. If he does find in favor of Hollywood, then what? The law may take out Hemming and Zennström, but it can't stop a peer-to-peer network that requires no central entity to run. Ultimately, the power to snuff Kazaa rests solely in the hands of Kazaa users. Getting them to do so means first giving them a better place to go.

RELATED LINKS

- Kazaa (http://www.kazaa.com)
- Altnet (http://www.altnet.com)
- Grokster (http://www.grokster.com)
- Morpheus (http://www.morpheus.com)
- Recording Industry Association of America (http://www.riaa.org)

FOR FURTHER RESEARCH

To find out more about the topics discussed in this reading, use InfoTrac College Edition. Type in keywords and subject terms such as "peer-to-peer network," "file-sharing," and "FastTrack software." You can access InfoTrac College Edition from the Wadsworth/Thomson Communication Café homepage: http://communication.wadsworth.com.

12

Privacy and Surveillance

Reading 12-1

Remembrance of Data Passed:
A Study of Disk Sanitization Practices

Simson L. Garfinkel and Abhi Shelat

EDITOR'S NOTE

Many discarded hard drives, although thought to be reformatted or simply lacking worthwhile data, contain information that is both confidential and recoverable. As this fascinating study in data recovery by Simson L. Garfinkel and Abhi Shelat shows, discarded drives contain a bounty of revealing information—from personal letters and pornography to bank account and credit card numbers—readily retrievable by data sleuths and computer hackers. In the study, just 9% of the 129 usable drives they purchased from eBay and analyzed had been properly cleaned (or "sanitized") by having their sectors completely overwritten with zero-filled blocks. The availability of information from old hard drives is little publicized, but awareness of such potentially risky consumer exposure will surely spread once identity thieves and law enforcement agencies start looking to repurposed drives for confidential material. As this reading and the article by James Rosenbaum (Reading 12-2) illustrate, neither the delete key nor the format command really do their job.

CONSIDER

1. What is the difference between a sanitized file and a deleted file? Similarly, what is the difference between sanitizing and (re)formatting a hard drive?

2. Despite the ready availability of sanitization tools, most computer users seem to make little effort to erase the information on their discarded hard drives. What explanations do the authors advance for this state of affairs?

3. Compare three data destruction techniques: reformatting, overwriting, and physical destruction. If you had a hard drive with sensitive information that needed to be discarded, which method would you be most comfortable with?

A fundamental goal of information security is to design computer systems that prevent the unauthorized disclosure of confidential information. There are many ways to assure this information privacy. One of the oldest and most common techniques is physical isolation: keeping confidential data on computers that only authorized individuals can access. Most single-user personal computers, for example, contain information that is confidential to that user.

Computer systems used by people with varying authorization levels typically employ authentication, access control lists, and a privileged operating system to maintain information privacy. Much of information security research over the past 30 years has centered on improving authentication techniques and developing methods to assure that computer systems properly implement these access control rules.

Absent a cryptographic file system, confidential information is readily accessible when owners improperly retire their disk drives. In August 2002, for example, the United States Veterans Administration Medical Center in Indianapolis retired 139 computers. Some of these systems were donated to schools, while others were sold on the open market, and at least three ended up in a thrift shop where a journalist purchased them. Unfortunately, the VA neglected to *sanitize* the computer's hard drives—that is, it failed to remove the drives' confidential information. Many of the computers were later found to contain sensitive medical information, including the names of veterans with AIDS and mental health problems. The new owners also found 44 credit card numbers that the Indianapolis facility used.[1]

The VA fiasco is just one of many celebrated cases in which an organization entrusted with confidential information neglected to properly sanitize hard disks before disposing of computers. Other cases include:

- In the spring of 2002, the Pennsylvania Department of Labor and Industry sold a collection of computers to local resellers. The computers contained "thousands of files of information about state employees" that the department had failed to remove.[2]

- In August 2001, Dovebid auctioned off more than 100 computers from the San Francisco office of the Viant consulting firm. The hard drives contained confidential client information that Viant had failed to remove.[3]

- A Purdue University student purchased a used Macintosh computer at the school's surplus equipment exchange facility, only to discover that the computer's hard drive contained a FileMaker database containing the names and demographic information for more than 100 applicants to the school's Entomology Department.

- In August 1998, one of the authors purchased 10 used computer systems from a local computer store. The computers, most of which were three to five years old, contained all of their former owners' data. One computer had been a law firm's file server and contained privileged client-attorney information. Another computer had a database used by a community organization that provided mental health services. Other disks contained numerous personal files.

- In April 1997, a woman in Pahrump, Nevada, purchased a used IBM computer for $159 and discovered that it contained the prescription records of 2,000 patients who filled their prescriptions at Smitty's Supermarket pharmacy in Tempe, Arizona. Included were the patient's names, addresses and Social Security numbers and a list of all the medicines they'd purchased. The records included people with AIDS, alcoholism, and depression.[4]

These anecdotal reports are interesting because of their similarity and their relative scarcity. Clearly, confidential information has been disclosed through com-

Reprinted with permission from "Remembrance of Data Passed: A Study of Disk Sanitization Practices" by Simson L. Garfinkel and Abhi Shelat, *IEEE Security & Privacy, 1*(1) (January/February 2003), pp. 17–27. Copyright © 2003 IEEE.

puters sold on the secondary market more than a few times. Why, then, have there been so few reports of unintended disclosure? We propose three hypotheses:

1. Disclosures of this type are exceedingly rare.
2. Confidential information is disclosed so often on retired systems that such events are simply not newsworthy.
3. Used equipment is awash with confidential information, but nobody is looking for it—or else there are people looking, but they are not publicizing that fact.

To further investigate the problem, we purchased more than 150 hard drives on the secondary market. Our goal was to determine what information they contained and what means, if any, the former owners had used to clean the drives before they discarded them. Here, we present our findings, along with our taxonomy for describing information recovered or recoverable from salvaged drives.

THE HARD DRIVE MARKET

Everyone knows that there has been a dramatic increase in disk-drive capacity and a corresponding decrease in mass-storage costs in recent years. Still, few people realize how truly staggering the numbers actually are. According to the market research firm Dataquest, nearly 150 million disk drives [were] retired in 2002—up from 130 million in 2001. Although many such drives are destroyed, a significant number are repurposed to the secondary market. (This market is rapidly growing as a supply source for even mainstream businesses, as evidenced by the cover story in *CIO Magazine,* "Good Stuff Cheap: How to Use the Secondary Market to Your Enterprise's Advantage."[5])

According to the market research firm IDC, the worldwide disk-drive industry [shipped] between 210 and 215 million disk drives in 2002; the total storage of those disk drives [was] 8.5 million terabytes (8,500 petabytes, or 8.5 x 1018 bytes). While Moore's Law dictates a doubling of integrated circuit transistors every 18 months, hard-disk storage capacity and the total number of bytes shipped are doubling at an even faster rate.

It's impossible to know how long any disk drive will remain in service; IDC estimates the typical drive's life-span at five years. Dataquest estimates that people will retire seven disk drives for every 10 that ship in the year 2002; this is up from a retirement rate of three for 10 in 1997. As the VA Hospital's experience demonstrates, many disk drives that are "retired" by one organization can appear elsewhere. Unless retired drives are physically destroyed, poor information security practices can jeopardize information privacy.

THE UBIQUITY OF HARD DISKS

Compared with other mass-storage media, hard disks pose special and significant problems in assuring long-term data confidentiality. One reason is that physical and electronic standards for other mass-storage devices have evolved rapidly and incompatibly over the years, while the Integrated Drive Electronics/Advanced Technology Attachment (IDE/ATA) and Small Computer System Interface (SCSI) interfaces have maintained both forward and backward compatibility. People use hard drives that are 10 years old with modern consumer computers by simply plugging them in: the physical, electrical, and logical standards have been remarkably stable.

This unprecedented level of compatibility has sustained both formal and informal secondary markets for used hard drives. This is not true of magnetic tapes, optical disks, flash memory, and other forms of mass storage, where there is considerably more diversity. With current devices, people typically cannot use older media due to format changes (a digital audio tape IV drive, for example, cannot read a DAT I tape, nor can a 3.5-inch disk drive read an 8-inch floppy.)

A second factor contributing to the problem of maintaining data confidentiality is the long-term consistency of file systems. Today's Windows, Macintosh, and Unix operating systems can transparently use the FAT16 and FAT32 file systems popularized by Microsoft in the 1980s and 1990s. FAT stands for File Allocation Table and is a linked list of disk clusters that DOS uses to manage space on a random-access device; 16 or 32 refers to the sector numbers' bit length. Thus, not only are 10-year-old hard drives mechanically and electrically compatible with today's computers, but the data they contain is readily accessible without special-purpose tools. This is not true with old tapes, which are typically written using proprietary backup systems, which might use proprietary compression and/or encryption algorithms as well.

A common way to sanitize a cartridge tape is to use a bulk tape eraser, which costs less than US$40 and can erase an entire tape in just a few seconds. Bulk erasers can erase practically any tape on the market. Once erased, a tape can be reused as if it were new. However, bulk erasers rarely work with hard disks, creating a third factor that complicates data confidentiality. In some cases, commercially available bulk erasers simply do not produce a sufficiently strong magnetic field to affect the disk surface. When they do, they almost always render the disk unusable: in addition to erasing user data, bulk erasers remove low-level track and formatting information. Although it might be possible to restore these formatting codes using vendor-specific commands, such commands are not generally available to users.

THE SANITIZATION PROBLEM

Most techniques that people use to assure information privacy fail when data storage equipment is sold on the secondary market. For example, any protection that the computer's operating system offers is lost when someone removes the hard drive from the computer and installs it in a second system that can read the on-disk formats, but doesn't honor the access control lists. This vulnerability of confidential information left on information systems has been recognized since the 1960s.[6]

Legal protections that assure data confidentiality are similarly void. In *California v. Greenwood,* the U.S. Supreme Court ruled that there is no right to privacy in discarded materials.[7] Likewise, it is unlikely that an individual or corporation could claim that either has a privacy or trade-secret interest in systems that they themselves have sold. Experience has shown that people routinely scavenge electronic components from the waste stream and reuse them without the original owner's knowledge.

Thus, to protect their privacy, individuals and organizations must remove confidential information from disk drives before they repurpose, retire, or dispose of them as intact units—that is, they must sanitize their drives.

The most common techniques for properly sanitizing hard drives include

- Physically destroying the drive, rendering it unusable
- Degaussing the drive to randomize the magnetic domains—most likely rendering the drive unusable in the process
- Overwriting the drive's data so that it cannot be recovered

Sanitizing is complicated by social norms. Clearly, the best way to assure that a drive's information is protected is to physically destroy the drive. But many people feel moral indignation when IT equipment is discarded and destroyed rather than redirected toward schools, community organizations, religious groups, or lesser-developed nations where others might benefit from using the equipment—even if the equipment is a few years obsolete.

SANITIZING THROUGH ERASING

Many people believe that they're actually destroying information when they erase computer files. In most cases, however, delete or erase commands do not actually remove the file's information from the hard disk [see Reading 12-2]. Although the precise notion of "erase" depends on the file system used, in most cases, deleting a file most often merely rewrites the metadata that pointed to the file, but leaves the disk blocks containing the file's contents intact.

When the operating system erases a FAT file, two things occur. First, the system modifies the filename's first character in the file's directory entry to signal that the file has been deleted and that the directory entry can be recycled. Second, the system moves all of the file's FAT clusters to the hard drive's list of free clusters. The actual file data is never touched. Indeed, there are many programs available that can recover erased files, as we discuss later.

Although our semantic notion of "erasing" implies data removal, the FAT file system (and many other modern file systems) doesn't meet our expectations.

SANITIZING THROUGH OVERWRITING

Because physical destruction is relatively complicated and unsatisfying, and because using the operating system to erase files does not effectively sanitize them, many individuals prefer to sanitize hard-drive information by intentionally overwriting that data with other data so that the original data cannot be recovered. Although overwriting is relatively easy to understand and to verify, it can be somewhat complicated in practice.

One way to overwrite a hard disk is to fill every addressable block with ASCII NUL bytes (zeroes). If the disk drive is functioning properly, then each of these blocks reports a block filled with NULs on read-back.

We've observed this behavior in practice: for most home and business applications, simply filling an entire disk with ASCII NUL bytes provides sufficient sanitization.

One organization that has addressed the problem of sanitizing storage media is the U.S. Department of Defense, which has created a "Cleaning and Sanitizing Matrix"[8] that gives DoD contractors three government-approved techniques for sanitizing rigid disk drives:

- Degauss with a Type I or Type II Degausser
- Destroy by disintegrating, incinerating, pulverizing, shredding, or melting
- Overwrite all addressable locations with a random character, overwrite against with the character's complement, and then verify. (However, as the guidelines state—in all capital letters no less—this method is not approved for sanitizing media that contains top-secret information.)

The DoD's overwriting strategy is curious, both because it does not recommend writing a changing pattern, and because the method is specifically not approved for top-secret information. This omission and restriction is almost certainly intentional. Peter Gutmann, a computer security researcher at the University of Auckland who has studied this issue, notes: "The . . . problem with official data destruction standards is that the information in them may be partially inaccurate in an attempt to fool opposing intelligence agencies (which is probably why a great many guidelines on sanitizing media are classified)."[9]

Indeed, some researchers have repeatedly asserted that simple overwriting is insufficient to protect data from a determined attacker. In a highly influential 1996 article, Gutmann argues that it is theoretically possible to retrieve information written to any magnetic recording device because the disk platter's low-level magnetic field patterns are a function of both the written and overwritten data. As Gutmann explains, when a computer attempts to write a one or a zero to disk, the media records it as such, but the actual effect is closer to obtaining 1.05 when one overwrites with a one and 0.95 when a one overwrites a zero. Although normal disk circuitry will read both values as ones, "using specialized circuitry it is possible to work out what previous 'layers' contained."[10] Gutmann claims that "a high-quality digital sampling oscilloscope" or Magnetic Force Microscopy (MFM) can be used to retrieve the overwritten data. We refer to such techniques as exotic because they do not rely on the standard hard-disk interface.

Gutmann presents some 22 different patterns that you can write in sequence to a disk drive to minimize data recovery. In the eight years since the article was published, some sanitation tool developers (such as those on the WIPE project, for example[11]) have taken these "Gutmann patterns" as gospel, and have programmed their tools to painstakingly use each pattern on every disk that is sanitized. Moreover, other organizations warn that failure to use these patterns or take other precautions, such as physically destroying a disk drive, means that "someone with technical knowledge and access to specialized equipment may be able to recover data from files deleted."[12]

But in fact, given the current generation of high-density disk drives, it's possible that none of these overwrite patterns are necessary—a point that Gutmann himself concedes. Older disk drives left some space between tracks; data written to a track could occasionally be recovered from this inter-track region using special instruments. Today's disk drives have a write head that is significantly larger than the read head: tracks are thus overlapping, and there is no longer any recoverable data "between" the tracks. Moreover, today's drives rely heavily on signal processing for their normal operation. Simply overwriting user data with one or two passes of random data is probably sufficient to render the overwritten information irrecoverable—a point that Gutmann makes in the updated version of the article, which appears on his Web site (www.cryptoapps.com/~peter/usenix01.pdf).

Indeed, there is some consensus among researchers that, for many applications, overwriting a disk with a few random passes will sufficiently sanitize it. An engineer at Maxtor, one of the world's largest disk-drive vendors, recently told us that recovering overwritten data was something akin "to UFO experiences. I believe that it is probably possible . . . but it is not going to be something that is readily available to anyone outside the National Security Agency."

A SANITIZATION TAXONOMY

Modern computer hard drives contain an assortment of data, including an operating system, application programs, and user data stored in files. Drives also contain backing store for virtual memory, and operating system meta-information, such as directories, file attributes, and allocation tables. A block-by-block disk-drive ex-

Table 12-1. A Sanitization Taxonomy

Level	Where Found	Description
Level 0	Regular files	Information contained in the file system. Includes file names, file attributes, and file contents. By definition, no attempts are made to sanitize Level 0 files' information. Level 0 also includes information that is written to the disk as part of any sanitization attempt. For example, if a copy of Windows 95 had been installed on a hard drive in an attempt to sanitize the drive, then the files installed into the C:\WINDOWS directory would be considered Level 0 files. No special tools are required to retrieve Level 0 data.
Level 1	Temporary files	Temporary files, including print spooler files, browser cache files, files for "helper" applications, and recycle bin files. Most users either expect the system to automatically delete this data or are not even aware that it exists. Note: Level 0 files are a subset of Level 1 files. Experience has shown that it is useful to distinguish this subset, because many naive users will overlook Level 1 files when they are browsing a computer's hard drive to see if it contains sensitive information. No special tools are required to retrieve Level 1 data, although special training is required to teach the operator where to look.
Level 2	Deleted files	When a file is deleted from a file system, most operating systems do not overwrite the blocks on the hard disk that the file is written on. Instead, they simply remove the file's reference from the containing directory. The file's blocks are then placed on the free list. These files can be recovered using traditional "undelete" tools, such as Norton Utilities.
Level 3	Retained data blocks	Data that can be recovered from a disk, but which does not obviously belong to a named file. Level 3 data includes information in slack space, backing store for virtual memory, and Level 2 data that has been partially overwritten so that an entire file cannot be recovered. A common source of Level 3 data is disks that have been formatted with Windows Format command or the Unix newfs command. Even though the output of these commands might imply that they overwrite the entire hard drive, in fact they do not, and the vast majority of the formatted disk's information is recoverable with the proper tools. Level 3 data can be recovered using advanced data recovery tools that can "unformat" a disk drive or special-purpose forensics tools.
Level 4	Vendor-hidden data	This level consists of data blocks that can only be accessed using vendor-specific commands. This level includes the drive's controlling program and blocks used for bad-block management.
Level 5	Overwritten data	Many individuals maintain that information can be recovered from a hard drive even after it is overwritten. We reserve Level 5 for such information.

amination also reveals remnants of previous files that were deleted but not completely overwritten. These remnants are sometimes called *free space,* and include bytes at the end of partially filled directory blocks (sometimes called *slack space*), startup software that is not strictly part of the operating system (such as boot blocks), and virgin blocks that were initialized at the factory but never written. Finally, drives also contain blocks that are not accessible through the standard IDE/ATA or SCSI interface, including internal drive blocks used for bad-block management and for holding the drive's own embedded software.

To describe data found on recovered disk drives and facilitate discussion of sanitization practices and forensic analysis, we created a *sanitization taxonomy* (see Table 12-1).

Sanitization Tools

Many existing programs claim to properly sanitize a hard drive, including $1,695 commercial offerings that boast government certifications, more than 50 tools licensed for a single computer system, and free software/open-source products that seem to offer largely the same features. Broadly speaking, two kinds of sanitization programs are available: disk sanitizers and declassifiers, and slack-space sanitizers.

Disk sanitizers and declassifiers aim to erase all user data from a disk before it's disposed of or repurposed in an organization. Because overwriting an operating system's boot disk information typically causes the computer to crash, disk sanitizers rarely operate on the boot disk of a modern operating system. Instead, they're usually run under an unprotected operating system, such as DOS, or as standalone applications run directly from bootable media (floppy disks or CD-ROMs). (It's relatively easy to sanitize a hard disk that is not the boot disk. With Unix, for example, you can sanitize a hard disk with the device /dev/hda using the command dd if=/dev/zero of=/dev/hda.) Using our taxonomy, disk sanitizers seek to erase all of the drive's Level 1,

2, 3, and 5 information. Sanitizers equipped with knowledge of vendor-specific disk-drive commands can erase Level 4 information as well.

Slack space sanitizers sanitize disk blocks (and portions of disk blocks) that are not part of any file and do not contain valid file system meta-information. For example, if a 512-byte block holds a file's last 100 bytes and nothing else, a slack-space sanitizer reads the block, leaves bytes 1–100 untouched, and zeros bytes 101–512. Slack-space sanitizers also compact directories (removing ignored entries), and overwrite blocks on the free list. Many of these programs also remove temporary files, history files, browser cookies, deleted email, and so on. Using our taxonomy, slack-space sanitizers seek to erase all Level 1 through Level 4 drive information, while leaving Level 0 information intact.

Forensic Tools

The flip side of sanitization tools are forensic analysis tools, which are used for recovering hard-disk information. Forensic tools are harder to write than sanitization tools and, not surprisingly, fewer of these tools are available. Many of the packages that do exist are tailored to law enforcement agencies.

Almost all forensic tools let users analyze hard disks or hard-disk images from a variety of different operating systems and provide an Explorer-style interface so you can read the files. Tools are of course limited by the original computer's operating system, as different systems overwrite different amounts of data or metadata when they delete a file or format a disk. Nevertheless, many of these forensic tools can find "undeleted" files (Level 2 data) and display hard-drive information that is no longer associated with a specific file (Level 3 data). Most tools also offer varying search capabilities. Hence, an operator can search an entire disk image for keywords or patterns, and then display the files (deleted or otherwise) containing the search pattern.

Programs tailored to law enforcement also offer to log every keystroke an operator makes during the hard-drive inspection process. This feature supposedly prevents evidence tampering.

O Sanitization, Where Art Thou?

Despite the ready availability of sanitization tools and the obvious threat posed by tools that provide forensic analysis, there are persistent reports that some systems containing confidential information are being sold on the secondary market.

We propose several possible explanations for this state of affairs:

- *Lack of knowledge.* The individual (or organization) disposing of the device simply fails to consider the problem (they might, for example, lack training or time).

- *Lack of concern for the problem.* The individual considers the problem, but does not think the device actually contains confidential information.

- *Lack of concern for the data.* The individual is aware of the problem—that the drive might contain confidential information—but doesn't care if the data is revealed.

- *Failure to properly estimate the risk.* The individual is aware of the problem, but doesn't believe that the device's future owner will reveal the information (that is, the individual assumes that the device's new owner will use the drive to store information, and won't rummage around looking for what the previous owner left behind).

- *Despair.* The individual is aware of the problem, but doesn't think it can be solved.

- *Lack of tools.* The individual is aware of the problem, but doesn't have the tools to properly sanitize the device.

- *Lack of training or incompetence.* The individual attempts to sanitize the device, but the attempts are ineffectual.

- *Tool error.* The individual uses a tool, but it doesn't behave as advertised. (Early versions of the Linux wipe command, for example, have had numerous bugs which resulted in data not being actually overwritten. Version 0.13, for instance, did not erase half the data in the file due to a bug; see http://packages.debian.org/unstable/utils/wipe .html.)

- *Hardware failure.* The computer housing the hard drive might be broken, making it impossible to sanitize the hard drive without removing it and installing it in another computer—a time-consuming process. Alternatively, a computer failure might make it seem that the hard drive has also failed, when in fact it has not.

Among nonexpert users—especially those using the DOS or Windows operating systems—lack of training might be the primary factor in poor sanitization practices.

Among expert users, we posit a different explanation: they are aware that the Windows format command does not actually overwrite a disk's contents.

Paradoxically, the media's fascination with exotic methods for data recovery might have decreased sanitization among these users by making it seem too onerous. In repeated interviews, users frequently say things like: "The FBI or the NSA can always get the data back if they want, so why bother cleaning the disk in the first place?" Some individuals fail to employ even rudimentary sanitization practices because of these unsubstantiated fears. This reasoning is flawed, of course, because most users should be concerned with protecting their data from more pedestrian attackers, rather than from U.S. law enforcement and intelligence agencies. Even if these organizations do represent a threat to some users, today's readily available sanitization tools can nevertheless protect their data from other credible threats.

However interesting they might be, informal interviews and occasional media reports are insufficient to gauge current sanitization practices. To do that, we had to acquire numerous disk drives and actually see what data their former owners left behind.

OUR EXPERIMENT

We acquired 158 hard drives on the secondary market between November 2000 and August 2002. We purchased drives from several sources: computer stores specializing in used merchandise, small businesses selling lots of two to five drives, and consolidators selling lots of 10 to 20 drives. We purchased most of the bulk hard drives by winning auctions at the eBay online auction service.

As is frequently the case with secondary-market equipment, the drives varied in manufacturer, size, date of manufacture, and condition. A significant fraction of the drives were physically damaged, contained unreadable sectors, or were completely inoperable.

Because we were interested in each drive's data, rather than its physical deterioration, our goal was to minimize drive handling as much as possible. Upon receipt, we recorded each drive's physical characteristics and source in a database. We then attached the drives to a workstation running the FreeBSD 4.4 operating system, and then copied the drive's contents block-by-block—using the Unix dd command from the raw ATA device—into a disk file we called the "image file." Once we completed this imaging operation, we attempted to mount each drive using several file systems: FreeBSD, MS-DOS, Windows NT File System, Unix File System, and Novell file systems. If we successfully mounted the drive, we used the Unix tar command to

transverse the entire file system hierarchy and copy the files into compressed tar files. These files are exactly equal to our taxonomy's Level 0 and Level 1 files.

We then analyzed the data using a variety of tools that we wrote specifically for this project. In particular, we stored the complete path name, length, and an MD5 cryptographic checksum of every Level 0 and Level 1 file in a database. (MD5 is a one-way function that reduces a block of data to a 128-bit electronic "fingerprint" that can be used for verifying file integrity.)

Initial Findings
We acquired a total of 75 Gbytes of data, consisting of 71 Gbytes of uncompressed disk images and 3.7 Gbytes of compressed tar files.

From the beginning, one of the most intriguing aspects of this project was the variation in the disk drives. When we briefed people on our initial project plans, some people were "positive" that all the recovered drives would contain active file systems, while others were sure that all of the drives would be reformatted. Some were certain we'd find data, but that it would be too old to be meaningful, and others were sure that nearly all of the drives would be properly sanitized, "because nobody could be so stupid as to discard a drive containing active data."

File System Analysis
The results of even this limited, initial analysis indicate that there are no standard practices in the industry. Of the 129 drives that we successfully imaged, only 12 (9 percent) had been properly sanitized by having their sectors completely overwritten with zero-filled blocks; 83 drives (64 percent) contained mountable FAT16 or FAT32 file systems. Another 46 drives did not have mountable file systems.

Of the 83 drives with mountable file systems, 51 appeared to have been freshly formatted—that is, they either had no files or else the files were created by the DOS format c:/s command; another six drives were formatted and had a copy of DOS or Windows 3.1 installed. Of these 51 drives, 19 had recoverable Level 3 data—indicating that the drives had been formatted after they had been used in another application.

Document File Analysis
We performed limited analysis of the mountable file systems to determine the type of documents left on the drives. Table 12-2 summarizes these results.

Overall, the 28 drives with active file systems con-

Table 12-2. Recoverable Level 0 and 1 Files by Type

File Type	Number Found	On Drives	Max Files per Drive
Microsoft Word (.doc)	675	23	183
Outlook (.pst)	20	6	12
Microsoft PowerPoint (.ppt)	566	14	196
Microsoft Write (.wri)	99	21	19
Microsoft Works (.wks)	68	1	68
Microsoft Excel (.xls)	274	18	67

tained comparatively few document files—far fewer than we'd expect to find on actively used personal computers. We believe that this is because the drives' previous owners intentionally deleted these files in an attempt to at least partially sanitize the drives before disposing of them.

To test this theory, we wrote a program that lets us scan for deleted files and directories. Using this program, we can scan the disks for data that was presumably deleted by the drive's original owner prior to disposing of the drive. The results are illuminating: with the exception of the cleared disks (all blocks zeroed), practically every disk had significant numbers of deleted directories and files that are recoverable. Even the 28 disks with many undeleted files contained significant numbers of deleted-but-recoverable directories and files as well. A close examination of the deleted files indicates that, in general, users deleted data files, but left application files intact.

Recovered Data

Some of the information we found in these files included:

- Corporate memoranda pertaining to personnel issues

- A letter to the doctor of a 7-year-old child from the child's father, complaining that the treatment for the child's cancer was unsatisfactory

- Fax templates for a California children's hospital (we expect that additional analysis of this drive will yield medically sensitive information)

- Love letters

- Pornography

Using slightly more sophisticated techniques, we wrote a program that scans for credit card numbers. The program searches for strings of numerals (with possible space and dash delimiters) that pass the mod-10 check–digit test required of all credit card numbers, and that also fall within a credit card number's feasible numerical range. For example, no major credit card number begins with an eight.

In our study, 42 drives had numbers that passed these tests. Determining whether a number is actually a valid credit card number requires an attempted transaction on the credit card network. Rather than do this, we inspected the number's context. Two drives contained consistent financial-style log files. One of these drives contained 2,868 numbers in a log format. Upon further inspection, it appeared that this hard drive was most likely used in an ATM machine in Illinois, and that no effort was made to remove any of the drive's financial information. The log contained account numbers, dates of access, and account balances. In addition, the hard drive had all of the ATM machine software.

Another drive contained 3,722 credit card numbers (some of them repeated) in a different type of log format. The files on this drive appeared to have been erased, and the drive was formatted. Yet another drive contained 39 credit card numbers in a database file that included the correct type of credit card, and still another had a credit card number in a cached Web page URL. The URL is a 'GET'-type HTTP form that was submitted to an e-commerce site; it contained all of the address and expiration information necessary to execute an e-commerce transaction. Finally, another drive had 21 credit card numbers in a file.

We also wrote a program that searches for RFC mail headers. Of the 129 drives analyzed, 66 drives had more than five email messages. We use this threshold because some programs, such as Netscape Navigator, include a few welcome emails upon installation. One drive in our batch contained almost 9,500 email messages, dated from 1999 through 2001. In all, 17 drives had more than 100 email messages and roughly 20 drives had between 20 and 100 email messages. During this analysis, we only investigated the messages' subject headers; contents seemed to vary from typical spam to grievances about retroactive pay.

UNDERSTANDING DOS FORMAT

It's not clear if the 52 formatted drives were formatted to sanitize the data or if they were formatted to determine their condition and value for sale on the secondary market.

In many interviews, users said that they believed DOS and Windows format commands would properly remove all hard drive data. This belief seems reasonable, as the DOS and Windows format commands specifically warn users that "ALL DATA ON NON-REMOVABLE DISK DRIVE C: WILL BE LOST" when a computer is booted from floppy and the user attempts a format C: command. This warning might rightly be seen as a *promise* that using the format command will in fact remove all of the disk drive's data.

Many users were surprised when we told them that the format command does not erase all of the disk's information. As our taxonomy indicates, most operating system format commands only write a minimal disk file system; they do not rewrite the entire disk. To illustrate this assertion, we took a 10-Gbyte hard disk and filled every block with a known pattern. We then initialized a disk partition using the Windows 98 FDISK command and formatted the disk with the format command. After each step, we examined the disk to determine the number of blocks that had been written.

Despite warnings from the operating system to the contrary, the format command overwrites barely more than 0.1 percent of the disk's data. Nevertheless, the command takes more than eight minutes to do its job on the 10-Gbyte disk—giving the impression that the computer is actually overwriting the data. In fact, the computer is attempting to *read* all of the drive's data so it can build a bad-block table. The only blocks that are actually written during the format process are those that correspond to the boot blocks, the root directory, the file allocation table, and a few test sectors scattered throughout the drive's surface.

Although 158 disk drives might seem like a lot, it's a tiny number compared to the number of disk drives that are sold, repurposed, and discarded each year. As a result, our findings and statistics are necessarily qualitative, not quantitative. Nevertheless, we can draw a few conclusions.

First, people can remove confidential information from disk drives before they discard, repurpose, or sell them on the secondary market. Moreover, freely available tools make disk sanitization easy.

Second, the current definition of "medical records" might not be broad enough to cover the range of medically sensitive information in the home and work environment. For example, we found personal letters containing medically sensitive information on a computer that previously belonged to a software company.

Many routine email messages also contain medically sensitive information that should not be disclosed. If an employee sends a message to his boss saying that he'll miss a meeting because he has a specific problem requiring a doctor visit, for example, he has created a record of his medical condition in the corporate email system.

Third, our study indicates that the secondary hard-disk market is almost certainly awash in information that is both sensitive and confidential.

Based on our findings, we make the following recommendations:

- Users must be educated about the proper techniques for sanitizing disk drives.

- Organizations must adopt policies for properly sanitizing drives on computer systems and storage media that are sold, destroyed, or repurposed.

- Operating system vendors should include system tools that securely delete files, and clear slack space and entire disk drives.

- Future operating systems should be capable of automatically sanitizing deleted files. They should also be equipped with background processes that automatically sanitize disk sectors that the operating system is not currently using.

- Vendors should encourage the use of encrypting file systems to minimize the data sanitization problem.

- Disk-drive vendors should equip their drives with tools for rapidly or even instantaneously removing all disk-drive information. For example, they could equip a disk drive with a cryptographic subsystem that automatically encrypts every disk block when the block is written, and decrypts the block when it is read back. Users could then render the drive's contents unintelligible by securely erasing the key.[13]

With several months of work and relatively little financial expenditure, we were able to retrieve thousands of credit card numbers and extraordinarily personal information on many individuals. We believe that the lack of media reports about this problem is simply because, at this point, few people are looking to repurposed hard drives for confidential material. If sanitization practices are not significantly improved, it's only a matter of time before the confidential information on repurposed hard drives is exploited by individuals and organizations that would do us harm.

NOTES

1. J. Hasson, "V.A. Toughens Security after PC Disposal Blunders," *Federal Computer Week,* 26 Aug. 2002; www.fcw.com/fcw/articles/2002/0826/news-va-08-26-02.asp.

2. M. Villano, "Hard-Drive Magic: Making Data Disappear Forever," *New York Times,* 2 May 2002.

3. J. Lyman, "Troubled Dot-Coms May Expose Confidential Client Data," *NewsFactor Network,* 8 Aug. 2001; www.newsfactor.com/perl/story/12612.html.

4. J. Markoff, "Patient Files Turn Up in Used Computer," *New York Times,* 4 Apr. 1997.

5. S. Berinato, "Good Stuff Cheap," *CIO,* 15 Oct. 2002, pp. 53–59.

6. National Computer Security Center, "A Guide to Understanding Data Remanence in Automated Information Systems," Library No. 5-236,082, 1991, NCSC-TG-025; www.radium.ncsc.mil/tpep/library/rainbow/NCSC-TG-028.ps.

7. *California v. Greenwood,* 486 U.S. 35, 16 May 1988.

8. U.S. Department of Defense, "Cleaning and Sanitization Matrix," DOS 5220.22-M, Washington, D.C., 1995; www.dss.mil/isec/nispom_0195.htm.

9. P. Gutmann, "Secure Deletion of Data from Magnetic and Solid-State Memory," *Proc. Sixth Usenix Security Symp.,* Usenix Assoc., 1996; www.cs.auckland.ac.nz/~pgut001/pubs/secure_del.html.

10. Ibid.

11. T. Vier, "Wipe 2.1.0," 14 Aug. 2002; http://sourceforge.net/projects/wipe.

12. D. Millar, "Clean Out Old Computers Before Selling/Donating," June 1997; www.upenn.edu/computing/security/advisories/oldcomputers.html.

13. G. Di Crescenzo et al., "How to Forget a Secret," *Symposium Theoretical Aspects in Computer Science* (STACS 99), Lecture Notes in Computer Science, Springer-Verlag, Berlin, 1999, pp. 500–509.

RELATED LINKS

- AutoClave (http://staff.washington.edu/jdlarios/autoclave)
- CyberScrub (http://www.cyberscrub.com)
- Wipe (http://wipe.sourceforge.net)
- Disk and File Shredders: A Comparison (http://www.fortunecity.com/skyscraper/true/882/Comparison_Shredders.htm)
- Simson Garfinkel's blog (http://www.simson.net/blog)

FOR FURTHER RESEARCH

To find out more about the topics discussed in this reading, use InfoTrac College Edition. Type in keywords and subject terms such as "disk sanitization," "drive reformatting and overwriting," and "data confidentiality." You can access InfoTrac College Edition from the Wadsworth/Thomson Communication Café homepage: http://communication.wadsworth.com.

Reading 12-2

In Defense of the Delete Key

James M. Rosenbaum

EDITOR'S NOTE

The computer delete key doesn't really do its job. Allegedly erased files are merely removed from sight, not from your hard drive. As a result, a growing number of individuals and corporations, from Monica Lewinsky to Microsoft, are finding themselves liable for acts never committed, only expressed. Once expressed electronically, however, ideas and desires seem to take on a life of their own—often times well beyond the author's actual intent. In this short but eloquent plea, James M. Rosenbaum, a federal district court judge for the District of Minnesota, argues that because we are not free to make mistakes online or retract messages once sent, we are gradually enforcing "a dangerous self-censorship over our ideas and expressions."

CONSIDER

1. Do you agree with Judge Rosenbaum that the computer delete key represents an "elaborate deception"? Should anything be done to change its operation?

2. How would individuals and companies be protected if the courts recognized cyber trash, "the stuff which, in less electronic times, would have been wadded up and thrown into a wastebasket"?

3. What is lost, in a digital age, when an increasing number of passing comments uttered electronically are forever archived?

It is becoming widely known that a computer's DELETE key represents an elaborate deception. The deception is pure, and inheres in the key's name: When the DELETE key is used, nothing is deleted.[1] It is now clear that relatively simple devices can recover almost everything that has been "deleted." This durability of computerized material compounds itself, because once a computer file is generated—let alone disseminated—internal and external copies proliferate. And each is impervious to deletion.

In practice, this once-arcane fact has spawned a new legal industry: the mining of e-mails, computer files, and especially copies of hard drives to obtain deleted material.

Knowing these facts leads me to two thoughts: one, we have now placed an electronic recording device over every office door; and two, we should not stand for it. Finally, I suggest a possible remedy.

THE ELECTRONIC RECORDER

There was a time when people spoke casually "off the record" amongst themselves. That time has passed. At this earlier time, two people could easily say something—even, perhaps, something politically incorrect—simply between themselves. They might even have exchanged nasty notes between themselves. And when

---

From "In Defense of the Delete Key" by James M. Rosenbaum, *The Green Bag, An Entertaining Journal of Law,* Summer 2000, pp. 393–396. Copyright © 2000 by James M. Rosenbaum.

they had moved past this tacky, but probably innocent, moment, it was truly gone.

Their words either vanished into the air, or the note was wadded up and thrown into a wastebasket. From there, the note was removed to a "delete" device called an incinerator. Once there, it was destroyed forever. The computer, and its evil spawn the e-mail, have ended this earlier time forever. For many of us, e-mail and the computer now substitute for those doorway conversations and those idle notes. But unlike those notes, they are not easily thrown away.

In the computer, the conversation lingers, and the note persists. In my view, this is wrong.

A PRECEPT SOME THOUGHTS ON THE LAW

None of us is perfect. But the preservation and persistence of evidence of our imperfections does not prove we are wrong, vile, venal, or even duplicitous. It just proves we are human—perhaps even farther beneath the angels than we might have wished—but lower nonetheless.

Today, legal discovery deep-sea fishes for snippets of deleted e-mails and deleted files in search of proof of imperfections. And the fish which are caught are thrown, as proof, into courtrooms throughout the land. In my view, they are just fish, and as valueless as the same fish might be if allowed to rot as long as the finally recovered file has been deleted.

Sometimes people just have bad ideas, or might just pass an idle—if imperfect—thought. This does not mean the person is vile. Mere evidence that a person who has done "A," but once expressed "B," does not prove that the person is lying or deceitful. The fallacy in the "truth" of the recovered e-mail or computer file is that it might just have been a bad idea, properly rejected, and consigned to an imperfectly labeled wastebasket. The problem is that on the computer's hard drive, it looks like more.

The second part of the fallacy is the almost universal—and I argue almost universally wrong—idea that finding this deleted material is the electronic equivalent of finding the inculpatory "second set of books." The evil of the second set of books lies not in the fact of their conception, but that they were used. The fact that one conceives of something—even something improper—does not necessarily mean it was acted upon.

The preservation and discovery of computer-deleted material has forced companies and prudent individuals to severely curtail the practice of using e-mails for all but the most innocuous materials. Any other course of action subjects the computer user to long term liability for idle thoughts.

THE LARGER RISK

In some ways, the greater risk in the preservation and discovery of computerized material lies in the knowledge that things will not be expressed, and ideas will not be exchanged, out of a pernicious—but valid—fear that their mere expression will be judged tantamount to the act. This is dangerous indeed.

One of the United States Constitution's many geniuses lies in its lofty protection of free speech. Legally, it protects the speaker only from state rather than private regulation. But the Constitution's words express a higher ideal: The First Amendment's premise is that a society is freer and in less danger when the wrong, the venal, the potentially evil is expressed and subjected to the light of day and to the "marketplace of ideas." Conversely, but importantly, is the negative concept: the marketplace of ideas and expression is impoverished and demeaned when it is deprived of ideas which may be discussed and tested, and ultimately, perhaps, rejected. Knowledge of the computer's awesome power to always remember, and never forget, a bad idea once expressed erodes and endangers this powerful concept.

People who recognize that whatever you say on a computer "can and will be used against you," prudently avoid saying anything "dangerous" via computer. But does anyone believe that people are "thinking" more perfect thoughts simply because they are increasingly reluctant to express them? I seriously doubt it.

We are, instead, enforcing a dangerous self-censorship over our ideas and expressions. And we do not restrict this censorship to ourselves. Businesses and organizations regularly adopt restrictions on the words and ideas which can be input into the company's or organization's computers. Why? Because of the intersection of legal developments and technology.

Once upon a time, liability was based on objective acts done or omitted. Did the person threaten violence (assault); did he or she strike a victim (battery); did he or she fail to act reasonably under the circumstances (negligence)? If so, the actor was liable for the consequent act. Unless the actor's intentions were objectively manifest, however, no liability accrued. In the 1950s, the song "Standing on the Corner" was correct: "Brother, you can't go to jail for what you're thinking, or for the 'oooh' look in your eye. You're only standing on the corner, watching all the girls go by."

This is, unquestionably, a new century. And since the end of the last, the song's proposition has been somewhat modified. At least in some cases, there has been a shift to subjective proof. In these areas, courts and the law consider the recipient's perception of the actor's behavior. But even here, purely subjective views do not alone suffice—there must be some outward manifestation of the impure thoughts.

Into this classic legal environment comes the computer. It never forgets, and never forgives. An idle thought "jotted" onto a calendar, a tasteless joke passed to a once-trusted friend, a suggestive invitation directed at an uninterested recipient, if done electronically, will last forever. Years later, it can subject its author to liability.

A PROPOSAL

While recognizing the difficulties inherent in such a suggestion, I recommend a cyber statute of limitations. This limitation recognizes that even the best humans may have a somewhat less than heavenly aspect. It acknowledges that anyone is entitled to make a mistake and to think a less than perfect thought. I suggest that, barring a pattern of egregious behavior, or an objective record of systematic conduct—absent, if you will, a real "second set of books"—that the courts recognize the existence of cyber trash. This is the stuff, which, in less electronic times, would have been wadded up and thrown into a wastebasket. This is what the DELETE button was meant for, and why pencils still have erasers.

The length of this cyber statute of limitations can be set as arbitrarily as any other. In light of the free expression risks I perceive, I suggest the length should be short—perhaps 6 months for an isolated message. If an idea was merely a lousy one, or was an isolated cyber utterance, and the actor/author did not objectively manifest some untoward behavior, he or she would be considered presumptively human, and—at least for the law's purposes—DELETE would mean delete. If, to the contrary, there was an objective continuation of the challenged conduct, or a continuing pattern of wrongful acts, the cyber statute of limitations would be tolled as any other.

This suggestion is feasible. Computers internally record the date on which a "document" was created. Once the limitations period has passed, documents should be legally consigned to the cyber wastebasket.

My solution is imperfect. But so are humans. If perfect recall defines perfection, computers have achieved it. But their operators have not achieved it with them, and humans are unlikely to do so. A legal system which demands human perfection, and which penalizes a momentary failing, cannot operate in the real world.

THE ULTIMATE FLAW

This suggestion recognizes that the computer is, itself, flawed. Its permanent memory is a flaw which undermines its value and endangers its users. Its inability to forget weakens and undermines the very ideas it permanently holds. The real flaw is that the computer lies: it lies when it says DELETE. This mechanical lie ought not to debase and degrade the humans who are, and ought to be, its master.

NOTE

1. For those with little knowledge, and less interest, a computer's delete key acts somewhat like a thief who steals a card from the old library's card file. When the card was in place, the librarian could decode the library's filing system and find the book. If the card was gone, or unreadable, the book was still in the library, but it could no longer be found amidst the library's stacked shelves. In a computer, the "lost" book can be found with very little effort.

RELATED LINKS

■ Daemon Seed: Old E-mail Never Dies (http://www.wired.com/wired/archive/7.05/email.html)

■ *The Green Bag: An Entertaining Journal of Law* (http://www.greenbag.org)

■ PC-Webopedia: Delete Key (http://webopedia.internet.com/TERM/D/Delete_key.html)

■ Send Those Computer Files to the Shredder (http://www.law.com/jsp/statearchive.jsp?type=Article&oldid=ZZZY9DVV6MC)

FOR FURTHER RESEARCH

To find out more about the topics discussed in this reading, use InfoTrac College Edition. Type in keywords and subject terms such as "delete key," "e-mail lawsuits," and "digital evidence." You can access InfoTrac from the Wadsworth/Thomson Communication Café homepage: http://communication.wadsworth.com.

Reading 12-3

Privacy and the New Technology: What They Do Know Can Hurt You

Simson Garfinkel

EDITOR'S NOTE

Privacy is under siege from all sides. Over the next 50 years, we will see new types of privacy invasions that find their roots in advanced technology and unbridled information exchange, including the selling of medical records and biological information. That's the assessment of Simson Garfinkel in this excerpt from Database Nation: The Death of Privacy in the 21st Century. *Threats to privacy can be tamed, he argues, by being careful and informed consumers, involving government in the privacy fight, and stepping up our personal privacy protection efforts.*

CONSIDER

1. Why does Garfinkel think that the term "privacy" falls short of conveying the myriad ways in which technology undermines individual autonomy and self-integrity?

2. Many people today say that in order to enjoy the benefits of modern society, we must give up some degree of personal privacy. Do you agree? Why or why not?

3. Should government get involved in the privacy fight and, if so, how? Or would it be better to leave issues of individual freedom to individual citizens?

You wake to the sound of a ringing telephone—but how could that happen? Several months ago, you re-programmed your home telephone system so it would never ring before the civilized hour of 8 am. But it's barely 6:45. Who was able to bypass your phone's programming?

You pick up the receiver, then slam it down a moment later. It's one of those marketing machines playing a recorded message. What's troubling you now is how this call got past the filters you set up. Later on you'll discover how: The company that sold you the phone created an undocumented "back door"; last week, the phone codes were sold in an online auction.

Now that you're awake, you decide to go through yesterday's mail. There's a letter from the neighborhood

Reprinted with permission from *Database Nation: The Death of Privacy in the 21st Century* by Simson Garfinkel (Sebastopol, CA: O'Reilly & Associates, 2000). Copyright © 2000, O'Reilly & Associates, Inc. All rights reserved. Orders and Information: (800) 998-9938, www.oreilly.com. As edited and published by *The Nation*, February 28, 2000.

hospital you visited last month. "We're pleased that our emergency room could serve you in your time of need," the letter begins. "As you know, our fees (based on our agreement with your HMO) do not cover the cost of treatment. To make up the difference, a number of hospitals have started selling patient records to medical researchers and consumer-marketing firms. Rather than mimic this distasteful behavior, we have decided to ask you to help us make up the difference. We are recommending a tax-deductible contribution of $275 to help defray the cost of your visit."

The veiled threat isn't empty, but you decide you don't really care who finds out about your sprained wrist. You fold the letter in half and drop it into your shredder. Also into the shredder goes a trio of low-interest credit-card offers. Why a shredder? A few years ago you would never have thought of shredding your junk mail—until a friend in your apartment complex had his identity "stolen" by the building's superintend-ent. As best as anybody can figure out, the super picked one of those preapproved credit-card applications out of the trash, called the toll-free number and picked up the card when it was delivered. He's in Mexico now, with a lot of expensive clothing and electronics, all at your friend's expense.

On that cheery note, you grab your bag and head out the door, which automatically locks behind you.

This is the future—not a far-off future but one that's just around the corner. It's a future in which what little privacy we now have will be gone. Some people call this loss of privacy "Orwellian," harking back to *1984,* George Orwell's classic work on privacy and autonomy. In that book, Orwell imagined a future in which a totalitarian state used spies, video surveillance, historical revisionism and control over the media to maintain its power. But the age of monolithic state control is over. The future we're rushing toward isn't one in which our every move is watched and recorded by some all-knowing Big Brother. It is instead a future of a hundred kid brothers who constantly watch and interrupt our daily lives. Orwell thought the Communist system represented the ultimate threat to individual liberty. Over the next fifty years, we will see new kinds of threats to privacy that find their roots not in Communism but in capitalism, the free market, advanced technology and the unbridled exchange of electronic information.

WHAT DO WE MEAN BY PRIVACY?

The problem with this word "privacy" is that it falls short of conveying the really big picture. Privacy isn't just about hiding things. It's about self-possession, autonomy and integrity. As we move into the computerized world of the twenty-first century, privacy will be one of our most important civil rights. But this right of privacy isn't the right of people to close their doors and pull down their window shades—perhaps because they want to engage in some sort of illicit or illegal activity. It's the right of people to control what details about their lives stay inside their own houses and what leaks to the outside.

Most of us recognize that our privacy is at risk. According to a 1996 nationwide poll conducted by Louis Harris & Associates, 24 percent of Americans have "personally experienced a privacy invasion." In 1995 the same survey found that 80 percent felt that "consumers have lost all control over how personal information about them is circulated and used by companies." Ironically, both the 1995 and 1996 surveys were paid for by Equifax, a company that earns nearly $2 bil-

lion each year from collecting and distributing personal information.

Today the Internet is compounding our privacy conundrum—largely because the voluntary approach to privacy protection advocated by the Clinton Administration doesn't work in the rough and tumble world of real business. For example, a study just released by the California HealthCare Foundation found that nineteen of the top twenty-one health Web sites have privacy policies, but most sites fail to follow them. Not surprisingly, 17 percent of Americans questioned in a poll said they do not go online for health information because of privacy concerns.

But privacy threats are not limited to the Internet: Data from all walks of life are now being captured, compiled, indexed and stored. For example, New York City has now deployed the Metrocard system, which allows subway and bus riders to pay their fares by simply swiping a magnetic-strip card. But the system also records the serial number of each card and the time and location of every swipe. New York police have used this vast database to crack crimes and disprove alibis. Although law enforcement is a reasonable use of this database, it is also a use that was adopted without any significant public debate. Furthermore, additional controls may be necessary: It is not clear who has access to the database, under what circumstances that access is given and what provisions are being taken to prevent the introduction of false data into it. It would be terrible if the subway's database were used by an employee to stalk an ex-lover or frame an innocent person for a heinous crime.

"New technology has brought extraordinary benefits to society, but it also has placed all of us in an electronic fishbowl in which our habits, tastes and activities are watched and recorded," New York State Attorney General Eliot Spitzer said in late January, in announcing that Chase Manhattan had agreed to stop selling depositor information without clear permission from customers. "Personal information thought to be confidential is routinely shared with others without our consent."

THE ROLE OF TECHNOLOGY

Today's war on privacy is intimately related to the recent dramatic advances in technology. Many people today say that in order to enjoy the benefits of modern society, we must necessarily relinquish some degree of privacy. If we want the convenience of paying for a meal by credit card or paying for a toll with an electronic tag mounted on our rearview mirror, then we must accept the routine collection of our purchases and driving habits in a large database over which we have no control. It's a simple bargain, albeit a Faustian one.

This trade-off is both unnecessary and wrong. It reminds me of another crisis our society faced back in the fifties and sixties—the environmental crisis. Then, advocates of big business said that poisoned rivers and lakes were the necessary costs of economic development, jobs and an improved standard of living. Poison was progress: Anybody who argued otherwise simply didn't understand the facts.

Today we know better. Today we know that sustainable economic development *depends* on preserving the environment. Indeed, preserving the environment is a prerequisite to the survival of the human race. Without clean air to breathe and clean water to drink, we will all die. Similarly, in order to reap the benefits of technology, it is more important than ever for us to use technology to protect personal freedom.

Blaming technology for the death of privacy isn't new. In 1890 two Boston lawyers, Samuel Warren and Louis Brandeis, argued in the *Harvard Law Review* that privacy was under attack by "recent inventions and business methods." They contended that the pressures of modern society required the creation of a "right of privacy," which would help protect what they called "the right to be let alone." Warren and Brandeis refused to believe that privacy had to die for technology to flourish. Today, the Warren/Brandeis article is regarded as one of the most influential law review articles ever published.

Privacy-invasive technology does not exist in a vacuum, of course. That's because technology itself exists at a junction between science, the market and society. People create technology to fill specific needs and desires. And technology is regulated, or not, as people and society see fit. Few engineers set out to build systems designed to crush privacy and autonomy, and few businesses or consumers would willingly use or purchase these systems if they understood the consequences.

FIGHTING BACK

How can we keep technology and the free market from killing our privacy? One way is by being careful and informed consumers. Some people have begun taking simple measures to protect their privacy, measures like making purchases with cash and refusing to provide their Social Security numbers—or providing fake ones. And a small but growing number of people are speaking out for technology *with* privacy. In 1990 Lotus and Equifax teamed up to create a CD-ROM product called Lotus Marketplace: Households, which would have included names, addresses and demographic information on every household in the United States, so small businesses could do the same kind of target marketing that big businesses have been doing since the sixties. The project was canceled when more than 30,000 people wrote to Lotus demanding that their names be taken out of the database.

Similarly, in 1997 the press informed taxpayers that the Social Security Administration was making detailed tax-history information about them available over the Internet. The SSA argued that its security provisions—requiring that taxpayers enter their name, date of birth, state of birth and mother's maiden name—were sufficient to prevent fraud. But tens of thousands of Americans disagreed, several U.S. senators investigated the agency and the service was promptly shut down. When the service was reactivated some months later, the detailed financial information in the SSA's computers could not be downloaded over the Internet.

THE ROLE OF GOVERNMENT

But individual actions are not enough. We need to involve government itself in the privacy fight. The biggest privacy failure of the U.S. government has been its failure to carry through with the impressive privacy groundwork that was laid in the Nixon, Ford and Carter administrations. It's worth taking a look back at that groundwork and considering how it may serve us today.

The 1970s were a good decade for privacy protection and consumer rights. In 1970 Congress passed the Fair Credit Reporting Act, which gave Americans the previously denied right to see their own credit reports and demand the removal of erroneous information. Elliot Richardson, who at the time was President Nixon's Secretary of Health, Education and Welfare, created a commission in 1972 to study the impact of computers on privacy. After years of testimony in Congress, the commission found all the more reason for alarm and issued a landmark report in 1973.

The most important contribution of the Richardson report was a bill of rights for the computer age, which it called the Code of Fair Information Practices. The Code is based on five principles:

- There must be no personal-data record-keeping system whose very existence is secret.

- There must be a way for a person to find out what information about the person is in a record and how it is used.

- There must be a way for a person to prevent information about the person that was obtained for one purpose from being used or made available for other purposes without the person's consent.

- There must be a way for a person to correct or amend a record of identifiable information about the person.

- Any organization creating, maintaining, using or disseminating records of identifiable personal data must assure the reliability of the data for their intended use and must take precautions to prevent misuse of the data.

The biggest impact of the Richardson report wasn't in the United States but in Europe. In the years after the report was published, practically every European country passed laws based on these principles. Many created data-protection commissions and commissioners to enforce the laws. Some believe that one reason for Europe's interest in electronic privacy was its experience with Nazi Germany in the 1930s and 1940s. Hitler's secret police used the records of governments and private organizations in the countries he invaded to round up people who posed the greatest threat to German occupation; postwar Europe realized the danger of allowing potentially threatening private information to be collected, even by democratic governments that might be responsive to public opinion.

But here in the United States, the idea of institutionalized data protection faltered. President Jimmy Carter showed interest in improving medical privacy, but he was quickly overtaken by economic and political events. Carter lost the election of 1980 to Ronald Reagan, whose aides saw privacy protection as yet another failed Carter initiative. Although several privacy-protection laws were signed during the Reagan/Bush era, the leadership for these bills came from Congress, not the White House. The lack of leadership stifled any chance of passing a nationwide data-protection act. Such an act would give people the right to know if their name and personal information is stored in a data-

base, to see the information and to demand that incorrect information be removed.

In fact, while most people in the federal government were ignoring the cause of privacy, some were actually pursuing an anti-privacy agenda. In the early 1980s, the government initiated numerous "computer matching" programs designed to catch fraud and abuse. Unfortunately, because of erroneous data these programs often penalized innocent people. In 1994 Congress passed the Communications Assistance to Law Enforcement Act, which gave the government dramatic new powers for wiretapping digital communications. In 1996 Congress passed two laws, one requiring states to display Social Security numbers on driver's licenses and another requiring that all medical patients in the United States be issued unique numerical identifiers, even if they pay their own bills. Fortunately, the implementation of those 1996 laws has been delayed, thanks largely to a citizen backlash and the resulting inaction by Congress and the executive branch.

Continuing the assault, both the Bush and Clinton administrations waged an all-out war against the rights of computer users to engage in private and secure communications. Starting in 1991, both administrations floated proposals for use of "Clipper" encryption systems that would have given the government access to encrypted personal communications. Only recently did the Clinton Administration finally relent in its seven-year war against computer privacy. President Clinton also backed the Communications Decency Act (CDA), which made it a crime to transmit sexually explicit information to minors—and, as a result, might have required Internet providers to deploy far-reaching monitoring and censorship systems. When a court in Philadelphia found the CDA unconstitutional, the Clinton Administration appealed the decision all the way to the Supreme Court—and lost.

PROTECTING PRIVACY

One important step toward reversing the current direction of government would be to create a permanent federal oversight agency charged with protecting privacy. Such an agency would:

- Watch over the government's tendency to sacrifice people's privacy for other goals and perform government-wide reviews of new federal programs for privacy violations before they're launched.

- Enforce the government's few existing privacy laws.

- Be a guardian for individual privacy and liberty in the business world, showing businesses how they can protect privacy and profits at the same time.

- Be an ombudsman for the American public and rein in the worst excesses that our society has created.

Some privacy activists scoff at the idea of using government to assure our privacy. Governments, they say, are responsible for some of the greatest privacy violations of all time. This is true, but the U.S. government was also one of the greatest polluters of all time. Today the government is the nation's environmental police force, equally scrutinizing the actions of private business and the government itself.

At the very least, governments can alter the development of technology that affects privacy. They have done so in Europe. Consider this: A growing number of businesses in Europe are offering free telephone calls —provided that the caller first listens to a brief advertisement. The service saves consumers money, even if it does expose them to a subtle form of brainwashing. But not all these services are equal. In Sweden both the caller and the person being called are forced to listen to the advertisement, and the new advertisements are played during the phone call itself. But Italy's privacy ombudsman ruled that the person being called could not be forced to listen to the ads.

The Fair Credit Reporting Act was a good law in its day, but it should be upgraded into a Data Protection Act. Unfortunately, the Federal Trade Commission and the courts have narrowly interpreted the FCRA. The first thing that is needed is legislation that expands it into new areas. Specifically, consumer-reporting firms should be barred from reporting arrests unless those arrests result in convictions. Likewise, consumer-reporting firms should not be allowed to report evictions unless they result in court judgments in favor of the landlord or a settlement in which both the landlord and tenant agree that the eviction can be reported. Companies should be barred from exchanging medical information about individuals or furnishing medical information as part of a patient's report without the patient's explicit consent.

We also need new legislation that expands the fundamental rights offered to consumers under the FCRA. When negative information is reported to a credit bureau, the business making that report should be required to notify the subject of the report—the consumer—in writing. Laws should be clarified so that if a consumer-reporting company does not correct erroneous data in its reports, consumers can sue for real damages, punitive damages and legal fees.

Further, we need laws that require improved computer security. In the eighties the United States aggressively deployed cellular-telephone and alphanumeric-pager networks, even though both systems were fundamentally unsecure. Instead of deploying secure systems, manufacturers lobbied for laws that would make it illegal to listen to the broadcasts. The results were predictable: dozens of cases in which radio transmissions were eavesdropped. We are now making similar mistakes in the prosecution of many Internet crimes, going after the perpetrator while refusing to acknowledge the liabilities of businesses that do not even take the most basic security precautions.

We should also bring back the Office of Technology Assessment, set up under a bill passed in 1972. The OTA didn't have the power to make laws or issue regulations, but it could publish reports on topics Congress asked it to study. Among other things, the OTA considered at length the trade-offs between law enforcement and civil liberties, and it also looked closely at issues of worker monitoring. In total, the OTA published 741 reports, 175 of which dealt directly with privacy issues, before it was killed in 1995 by the newly elected Republican-majority Congress.

Nearly forty years ago, Rachel Carson's book *Silent Spring* helped seed the U.S. environmental movement. And to our credit, the silent spring that Carson foretold never came to be. *Silent Spring* was successful because it helped people to understand the insidious damage that pesticides were wreaking on the environment, and it helped our society and our planet to plot a course to a better future.

Today, technology is killing one of our most cherished freedoms. Whether you call this freedom the right to digital self-determination, the right to informational autonomy, or simply the right to privacy, the shape of our future will be determined in large part by how we understand, and ultimately how we control or regulate, the threats to this freedom that we face today.

RELATED LINKS

- Center for Democracy and Technology (www.cdt.org)
- Echelon Watch (www.aclu.org/echelonwatch/index.html)
- Electronic Frontier Foundation (www.eff.org)
- Global Internet Liberty Campaign (www.gilc.org)

FOR FURTHER RESEARCH

To find out more about the topics discussed in this reading, use InfoTrac College Edition. Type in keywords and subject terms such as "privacy invasion," "electronic databases," and "privacy protection." You can access InfoTrac from the Wadsworth/Thomson Communication Café homepage: http://communication.wadsworth.com.

Reading 12-4

The Challenge of an Open Society
David Brin

EDITOR'S NOTE

Fifteen minutes into the future, society faces a dilemma. The proliferation of surveillance cameras and recording equipment— so-called "snoop technology"—has vanquished crime but at the expense of unprecedented monitoring of public spaces and private places. David Brin argues in this excerpt from The Transparent Society *that early in the 21st century, we will confront a troubling choice: live free but under constant scrutiny on the one hand, or retain our supposed privacy while relying on the authorities to responsibly monitor society on the other.*

CONSIDER

1. Given the choice between Brin's two mythical cities, which would be a more desirable place to live, and why?
2. What central issue will the citizens of countless 21st century communities have to confront, according to Brin?
3. Why does Brin consider accountability to be the keystone of Western civilization's success?

You're wondering why I've called you here. The reason is simple. To answer all your questions. I mean—all. This is the greatest news of our time. As of today, whatever you want to know, provided it's in the data-net, you can know. In other words, there are no more secrets.
—John Brunner, *The Shockwave Rider,* 1974

This is a tale of two cities. Cities of the near future, say ten or twenty years from now.

Barring something unforeseen, you are apt to be living in one of these two places. Your only choice may be which one.

At first sight, these two municipalities look pretty much alike. Both contain dazzling technological marvels, especially in the realm of electronic media. Both suffer familiar urban quandaries of frustration and decay. If some progress is being made in solving human problems, it is happening gradually. Perhaps some kids seem better educated. The air may be marginally cleaner. People still worry about overpopulation, the environment, and the next international crisis.

None of these features is of interest to us right now, for we have noticed something about both of these twenty-first century cities that is radically different. A trait that marks them as distinct from any metropolis of the late 1990s.

Street crime has nearly vanished from both towns. But that is only a symptom, a result.

The real change peers down from every lamppost, every rooftop and street sign.

Tiny cameras, panning left and right, survey traffic and pedestrians, observing everything in open view.

Have we entered an Orwellian nightmare? Have the burghers of both towns banished muggings at the cost of creating a Stalinist dystopia?

Consider city number one. In this place, all the myriad cameras report their urban scenes straight to Police Central, where security officers use sophisticated image processors to scan for infractions against public order—or perhaps against an established way of thought. Citizens walk the streets aware that any word or deed may be noted by agents of some mysterious bureau.

Now let's skip across space and time.

At first sight, things seem quite similar in city number two. Again, ubiquitous cameras perch on every vantage point. Only here we soon find a crucial difference. These devices do not report to the secret police. Rather, each and every citizen of this metropolis can use his or her wristwatch television to call up images from any camera in town.

Here a late-evening stroller checks to make sure no one lurks beyond the corner she is about to turn.

Over there a tardy young man dials to see if his dinner date still waits for him by a city fountain.

A block away, an anxious parent scans the area to find which way her child wandered off.

Over by the mall, a teenage shoplifter is taken into custody gingerly, with minute attention to ritual and rights, because the arresting officer knows that the entire process is being scrutinized by untold numbers who watch intently, lest her neutral professionalism lapse.

In city number two, such microcameras are banned from some indoor places . . . but not from police headquarters! There any citizen may tune in on bookings, arraignments, and especially the camera control room itself, making sure that the agents on duty look out for violent crime, and only crime.

Despite their initial similarity, these are very different cities, representing disparate ways of life, completely opposite relationships between citizens and their civic guardians. The reader may find both situations somewhat chilling. Both futures may seem undesirable. But can there be any doubt which city we'd rather live in, if these two make up our only choice?

TECHNOLOGY'S VERDICT

Alas, they do appear to be our only options. For the cameras are on their way, along with data networks that will send a myriad images flashing back and forth, faster than thought.

In fact, the future has already arrived. The trend began in Britain a decade ago, in the town of King's Lynn, where sixty remote-controlled video cameras were installed to scan known "trouble spots," reporting directly to police headquarters. The resulting reduction in street crime exceeded all predictions; in or near zones covered by surveillance, crime dropped to one-seventieth of the former rate. The savings in patrol costs alone paid for the equipment in a few months. Dozens of cities and towns soon followed the example of King's Lynn. Glasgow, Scotland, reported a 68 percent drop in crime citywide, while police in Newcastle fingered over 1,500 perpetrators with taped evidence. (All but seven pleaded guilty, and those seven

From "The Challenge of an Open Society," in *The Transparent Society: Freedom vs. Privacy in a City of Glass Houses* by David Brin. Copyright © 1998 by G. David Brin. Reprinted by permission of Perseus Books Publishers, a member of Perseus Books, LLC.

were later convicted.) In May 1997, Newcastle soccer fans rampaged through downtown streets. Detectives studying video tapes picked out 152 faces and published 80 photographs in local newspapers. In days, all were identified.

Today, over 300,000 cameras are in place throughout the United Kingdom, transmitting round-the-clock images to a hundred constabularies [police stations], all of them reporting decreases in public misconduct. Polls report that the cameras are extremely popular with citizens, though British civil libertarian John Wadham and others have bemoaned this proliferation of snoop technology, claiming, "It could be used for any other purpose, and of course it could be abused."

Visitors to Japan, Thailand, and Singapore will see that other countries are rapidly following the British example, using closed circuit television (CCTV) to supervise innumerable public areas.

This trend was slower coming to North America, but it appears to be taking off. After initial experiments garnered widespread public approval, the City of Baltimore put police cameras to work scanning all 106 downtown intersections. In 1997, New York City began its own program to set up twenty-four-hour remote surveillance in Central Park, subway stations, and other public places.

No one denies the obvious and dramatic short-term benefits derived from this early proliferation of surveillance technology. That is not the real issue. In the long run, the sovereign folk of Baltimore and countless other communities will have to make the same choice as the inhabitants of our two mythical cities. Who will ultimately control the cameras?

Consider a few more examples.

How many parents have wanted to be a fly on the wall while their child was at day care? This is now possible with a new video monitoring system known as Kindercam, linked to high-speed telephone lines and a central Internet server. Parents can log on, type www.kindercam.com, enter their password, and access a live view of their child in day care at any time, from anywhere in the world. Kindercam will be installed in two thousand day care facilities nationwide by the end of 1998. Mothers on business trips, fathers who live out of state, even distant grandparents can all "drop in" on their child daily. Drawbacks? Overprotective parents may check compulsively. And now other parents can observe your child misbehaving!

Some of the same parents are less happy about the lensed pickups that are sprouting in their own workplaces, enabling supervisors to tune in on them in the same way they use Kindercam to check up on their kids.

That is, if they notice the cameras at all. At present, engineers can squeeze the electronics for a video unit into a package smaller than a sugar cube. Complete sets half the size of a pack of cigarettes were recently offered for sale by the Spy Shop, a little store in New York City located two blocks from the United Nations [see http://www.w2.com/docs2/z/spyshop .html]. Meanwhile, units with radio transmitters are being disguised in clock radios, telephones, and toasters, as part of the burgeoning "nannycam" trend. So high is demand for these pickups, largely by parents eager to check on their babysitters, that just one firm in Orange County, California, has recently been selling from five hundred to one thousand disguised cameras a month. By the end of 1997, prices had dropped from $2,500 to $399.

Cameras aren't the only surveillance devices proliferating in our cities. Starting with Redwood City, near San Francisco, several police departments have begun lacing neighborhoods with sound pickups that transmit directly back to headquarters. Using triangulation techniques, officials can now pinpoint bursts of gunfire and send patrol units swiftly to the scene, without having to wait for vague telephone reports from neighbors. In 1995 the Defense Department awarded a $1.7 million contract to Alliant Techsystems for its prototype system secures, which tests more advanced sound pickup networks in Washington and other cities. The hope is to distinguish not only types of gunfire but also human voices crying for help.

So far, so good. But from there, engineers say it would be simple to upgrade the equipment, enabling bored monitors to eavesdrop through open bedroom windows on cries of passion, or family arguments. "Of course we would never go that far," one official said, reassuringly.

Consider another piece of James Bond apparatus now available to anyone with ready cash. Today, almost any electronics store will sell you night vision goggles using state-of-the-art infrared optics equal to those issued by the military, for less than the price of a video camera. Agema Systems, of Syracuse, New York, has sold several police departments imaging devices that can peer into houses from the street, discriminate the heat given off by indoor marijuana cultivators, and sometimes tell if a person inside moves from one room to the next. Military and civilian enhanced vision technologies now move in lockstep, as they have in the computer field for years.

In other words, even darkness no longer guarantees privacy.

Nor does your garden wall. In 1995, Admiral William A. Owens, then vice chairman of the Joint Chiefs of Staff, described a sensor system that he expected to be operational within a few years: a pilotless drone, equipped to provide airborne surveillance for soldiers in the field. While camera robots in the $1 million range have been flying in the military for some time, the new system will be extraordinarily cheap and simple. Instead of requiring a large support crew, it will be controlled by one semiskilled soldier and will fit in the palm of a hand. Minuscule and quiet, such remote-piloted vehicles, or RPVs, may flit among trees to survey threats near a rifle platoon. When mass-produced in huge quantities, unit prices will fall.

Can civilian models be far behind? No law or regulation will keep them from our cities for very long. The rich, the powerful, and figures of authority will have them, whether legally or surreptitiously. And the contraptions will become smaller, cheaper, and smarter with each passing year.

So much for the supposed privacy enjoyed by sunbathers in their own backyards.

Moreover, surveillance cameras are the tip of the metaphorical iceberg. Other entrancing and invasive innovations of the vaunted *Information Age* abound. Will a paper envelope protect the correspondence you send by old-fashioned surface mail when new-style scanners can trace the patterns of ink inside without ever breaking the seal?

Let's say you correspond with others by e-mail and use a computerized encryption program to ensure that your messages are read only by the intended recipient. What good will all the ciphers and codes do, if some adversary has bought a "back door" password to your encoding program? Or if a wasp-sized camera drone flits into your room, sticks to the ceiling above your desk, inflates a bubble lens, and watches every keystroke that you type?

In late 1997 it was revealed that Swiss police had secretly tracked the whereabouts of mobile phone users via a telephone company computer that records billions of movements per year. Swisscom was able to

locate its mobile subscribers within a few hundred meters. This aided several police investigations. But civil libertarians expressed heated concern, especially since identical technology is used worldwide.

The same issues arise when we contemplate the proliferation of vast databases containing information about our lives, habits, tastes, and personal histories. The cash register scanners in a million supermarkets, video stores, and pharmacies already pour forth a flood of statistical data about customers and their purchases, ready to be correlated. (Are you stocking up on hemorrhoid cream? Renting a daytime motel room? The database knows.) Corporations claim this information helps them serve us more efficiently. Critics respond that it gives big companies an unfair advantage, enabling them to know vastly more about us than we do about them. Soon, computers will hold all your financial and educational records, legal documents, and medical analyses that parse you all the way down to your genes. Any of this might be examined by strangers without your knowledge, or even against your stated will.

As with those streetlamp cameras, the choices we make regarding future information networks—how they will be controlled and who can access the data—will affect our own lives and those of our children and their descendants.

A MODERN CONCERN

The issue of threatened privacy has spawned a flood of books, articles, and media exposes—from Janna Malamud Smith's thoughtful *Private Matters,* and Ellen Alderman and Caroline Kennedy's erudite *Right to Privacy* all the way to shrill, paranoid rants by conspiracy fetishists who see Big Brother lurking around every corner. Spanning this spectrum, however, there appears to be one common theme. Often the author has responded with a call to arms, proclaiming that we must become more vigilant to protect traditional privacy against intrusions by faceless (take your pick) government bureaucrats, corporations, criminals, or just plain busybodies.

That is the usual conclusion—but not the one taken here.

For in fact, it is already far too late to prevent the invasion of cameras and databases. The *djinn* cannot be crammed back into its bottle. No matter how many laws are passed, it will prove quite impossible to legislate away the new surveillance tools and databases. They are here to stay.

Light *is* going to shine into nearly every corner of our lives.

The real issue facing citizens of a new century will be how mature adults choose to live—how they can compete, cooperate, and thrive—in such a world. A transparent society.

Our civilization is already a noisy one precisely because we have chosen freedom and mass sovereignty, so that the citizenry itself must constantly argue out the details, instead of leaving them to some committee of sages.

What distinguishes society today is not only the pace of events but the nature of our tool kit for facing the future. Above all, what has marked our civilization as different is its knack for applying two extremely hard-won lessons from the past.

> In all of history, we have found just one cure for error—a partial antidote against making and repeating grand, foolish mistakes, a remedy against self deception. That antidote is criticism.

Scientists have known this for a long time. It is the keystone of their success. A scientific theory gains respect only by surviving repeated attempts to demolish it. Only after platoons of clever critics have striven to come up with refuting evidence, forcing changes, do a few hypotheses eventually graduate from mere theories to accepted models of the world.

If neo-Western civilization has one great trick in its repertoire, a technique more responsible than any other for its success, that trick is accountability. Especially the knack—which no other culture ever mastered—of making accountability apply to the mighty. True, we still don't manage it perfectly. Gaffes, bungles, and inanities still get covered up. And yet, one can look at any newspaper or television news program and see an eager press corps at work, supplemented by hordes of righteously indignant individuals (and their lawyers), all baying for waste or corruption to be exposed, secrets to be unveiled, and nefarious schemes to be nipped in the bud. Disclosure is a watchword of the age, and politicians have grudgingly responded by passing the Freedom of Information Act (FOIA), truth-in-lending laws, open meeting rules, and codes to enforce candor in real estate, in the nutritional content of foodstuffs, in the expense accounts of lobbyists, and so on.

Although this process of stripping off veils has been uneven, and continues to be a source of contention, the underlying moral force can clearly be seen pervading our popular culture, in which nearly every modern film or novel seems to preach the same message—suspicion of authority. The phenomenon is not new to our generation. Schoolbooks teach that freedom is guarded by constitutional "checks and balances," but those same legal provisions were copied, early in the nineteenth century, by nearly every new nation of Latin America, and not one of them remained consistently free. In North America, constitutional balances worked only because they were supplemented by a powerful mythic tradition, expounded in story, song, and now virtually every Hollywood film, that any undue accumulation of power should be looked on with concern.

Above all, we are encouraged to distrust government.

The late Karl Popper pointed out the importance of this mythology in the dark days during and after World War II, in *The Open Society and Its Enemies*. Only by insisting on accountability, he concluded, can we constantly remind public servants that they *are* servants. It is also how we maintain some confidence that merchants aren't cheating us, or that factories aren't poisoning the water. As inefficient and irascibly noisy as it seems at times, this habit of questioning authority ensures freedom far more effectively than any of the older social systems that were based on reverence or trust.

And yet, another paradox rears up every time one interest group tries to hold another accountable in today's society.

> Whenever a conflict arises between privacy and accountability, people demand the former for themselves and the latter for everybody else.

The rule seems to hold in almost every realm of modern life, from special prosecutors investigating the finances of political figures to worried parents demanding that lists of sex offenders be made public. From merchants anxious to see their customers' credit reports to clients who resent such snooping. From people who "need" caller ID to screen their calls to those worried that their lives might be threatened if they lose telephone anonymity. From activists demanding greater access to computerized government records in order to hunt patterns of corruption or incompetence in office to other citizens who worry about the release of personal information contained in those very same records.

In opposing this modern passion for personal and corporate secrecy, I should first emphasize that I *like* privacy! Outspoken eccentrics need it, probably as much or more than those who are reserved. I would find it hard to get used to living in either of the cities described in the example at the beginning of this chapter. But a few voices out there have begun pointing out the obvious. Those cameras on every street corner are coming, as surely as the new millennium.

Oh, we may agitate and legislate. But can "privacy laws" really prevent hidden eyes from getting tinier, more mobile, and clever? In software form they will cruise the data highways. "Antibug" technologies will arise, but the resulting surveillance arms race can hardly favor the "little guy." The rich, the powerful, police agencies, and a technologically skilled elite will always have an advantage.

In the long run, as author Robert Heinlein prophesied years ago, will the chief effect of privacy laws simply be to "make the bugs smaller"?

The subtitle of this book—*Will Technology Force Us to Choose Between Privacy and Freedom?*—is intentionally provocative. I think such a stark choice can be avoided. It may be possible to have both liberty and some shelter from prying eyes.

But suppose the future *does* present us with an absolute either-or decision, to select just one, at the cost of the other. In that case, there can be no hesitation.

Privacy is a highly desirable *product* of liberty. If we remain free and sovereign, we may have a little privacy in our bedrooms and sanctuaries. As citizens, we'll be able to demand some.

But accountability is no side benefit. It is the one fundamental ingredient on which liberty thrives. Without the accountability that derives from openness—enforceable upon even the mightiest individuals and institutions—how can freedom survive?

In the information age to come, cameras and databases will sprout like poppies—or weeds—whether we like it or not. Over the long haul, we as a people must decide the following questions:

Can we stand living exposed to scrutiny, our secrets laid open, if in return we get flashlights of our own that we can shine on anyone who might do us harm—even the arrogant and strong?

Or is an illusion of privacy worth any price, even the cost of surrendering our own right to pierce the schemes of the powerful?

There are no easy answers, but asking questions can be a good first step.

RELATED LINKS

- David Brin's Web Page (http://www.kithrup.com/brin)
- EarthCam: Webcam Network (http://www.earthcam.com)
- HotSeat: The Transparent Society
  (http://hotwired.lycos.com/packet/hotseat/97/22/transcript4a.html)
- Surveillance Camera News (http://www.mediaeater.com/cameras/news.html)
- Video Surveillance (http://www.privacyinternational.org/issues/cctv)

FOR FURTHER RESEARCH

To find out more about the topics discussed in this reading, use InfoTrac College Edition. Type in keywords and subject terms such as "surveillance," "snoop technology," and "transparent society." You can access InfoTrac from the Wadsworth/Thomson Communication Café homepage: http://communication.wadsworth.com.

Index

Access to technology, 255–272
Adaptive systems, 41
Adler, Jerry, 272–277
Advanced Research Projects Agency (ARPA), 6
Advertising
  e-commerce, 27
  history of, 17
  as storytelling, 23
  on television, 81–84, 148–149
  ubiquity of, 160
Agnew, Sean, 106–113
Amazon.com, 28, 31
America Online (AOL)
  merger with Time Warner, 72, 76, 298
  screen names on, 44
Analog versus digital, 71
Anderson, Robert H., 239–245
Ando, Kunitake, 74, 75
Andreessen, Marc, 6, 168, 169, 293, 294
Animation, 88–89
Anonymity, 197–199
Apple Computer, Inc.
  Apple II, 6
  and copyrights, 299–300
  HyperCard, 168
  iPod, 74
  school computers, 183–187
Armstrong, Howard, 37–38
AT&T, 102–105
AT&T/Liberty Media, 93
Attention economy, 27
Audiences
  demand for media, 69
  interactive, 25, 62
  national, 17
  needs and gratifications, 61–62
Aufderheide, Pat, 102–106
Augmentation, 174

Balance of power, 70
Bargh, John A., 193–205
Barlow, John Perry, 288, 291–296

Bell, Alexander Graham, 17
Beniger, James R., 11–21
Berliner, Hans, 17
Berne Convention, 289
Berners-Lee, Tim, 166, 168, 293, 294
Bertelsmann, 93, 97, 98
Bikson, Tora K., 239–245
Blogger.com, 29
Blogs, 29, 46–47, 129–133
Blood, Rebecca, 129–133
Bolter, Jay David, 50–59
Brin, David, 327–332
Brin, Sergey, 119
Broadband services, 102–105
Brown, James, 287–288
Browsers, 6, 168–169
Bucy, Erik P., 221–231, 264–272
Bugs, software, 212–217
Bureaucracy, 14–15
Bush, Vannevar, 167

Cable companies, 102–105
Cairncross, Frances, 3–10
Calculators, 258
Campbell, Michael Ian, 44
Card, Orson Scott, 125–126
Carlyle, Thomas, 15
Cell phones, 232–234
Censorship, 113. *See also* Government regulation
Cerf, Vint, 293
Chaos theory, 40–41
Children
  development of, 185–186
  exposure to media, 142
Clark, Jim, 169
Claude Henri Comte de Saint-Simon, 15
Clear Channel Communications, 106–113
Clinton, Bill, 181–182
CoCoon, 78
Coevolution, 39
Collective action, 231–238
Columbine High School, 44

Comcast, 81
Commercial Revolution (15th century), 13, 19
Communication
    collective action using, 231–238
    complexity, 40–41
    digital language in, 39
    history of, 3–7
    language, 39
    multimedia forms of, 40
    predictions, 7–10
    revolution in, 3–32
Compaine, Benjamin, 97–101
Complexity, 40–41
Compunications, 18
Computer Decency Act (CDA), 194–195, 196
Computers
    access to, 256–263, 266
    augmentation, 174
    business use of, 172–173
    as communication devices, 62
    and creativity, 190–191
    culture of, 188–193
    and education, 181–187
    for job training, 186–187
    history of, 5–7, 174–177
    productivity and, 172–181
    social impact of, 163–187
    as tools, 189–190
Conseil Europeen pour la Recherche Nucleaire (CERN),
        166, 294
Constant television households, 142
Constitution, 71, 222
Content, 68
Content Scrambling System (CSS), 292
Control Revolution, 12–14
Control technologies, 16
Convergence. *See also* Sony Corporation
    and communication content, 68–69
    and communications organizations, 70–71
    consequences of, 67–73
    construct of, 39–40
    definition of, 72
    and digitization, 18
    and media/audience relationships, 69
Cookies, 72
©-chips, 289
Copyright boxes, 288
Copyrights, 73–79, 285–307
Corporations, 92–105. *See also* Time Warner
CUSeeMe, 26
Cybercascades, 252–253
Cyberculture, 23, 25
Cybernetics, 13
Cyberpunk culture, 25, 26

"Daily Me, The," 70
DARPA, 294

Dating, computer, 133–138, 199–200
Death of distance, 3, 7
December, John, 165–172
DeCSS (DVD decryptor), 292, 293
Deindividuation, 197
Deleted files, 319–321
Democracy, electronic, 219–254
Dennis, Patricia Diaz, 277–281
Department of Defense, 6
Depression (economic), 38
Depression (psychological), 194–196
Design flaws, 213
Diffusion theory, 36
Digital broadcasting, 81
Digital divide, 255–272
Digital Millennium Copyright Act, 292
Digital technology
    and cinema, 86–91
    and content distribution, 68–69
    and convergence, 18–19
    and television, 81–85
    versus analog, 71
Digital video recorders (DVRs), 81, 84–85
Dilworth, Bryan, 109–110
Discussion groups, 245–254
Disk drives, sanitation of, 309–318
Disney, 93, 98
Divx, 292
Do-it-yourself (DIY) Internet culture, 25
Dot.com pyramid schemes, 28
DRM software, 79
Dyson, Esther, 289

eBay, 28
Ecology, 1, 21
E-commerce, 6, 27–29
Edison, Thomas, 17, 181
Education
    computers in, 181–187
    fine arts, 182
    of girls in the computer age, 277–281
    job training, 186–187
Ehrlich, Fred, 77
Electronic Frontier Foundation, 288, 291, 292
Ellis Island database, 30
E-mail, 196
    history of, 240–241
    inappropriate, 46
    spam, 151–157
    universal access to, 240–244
Emergent behaviors, 31, 236–238
Ender's Game (Card), 125–126
Englebart, Douglas, 53
Estrada, Joseph, 232
Eyeball hours, 27

Fairness doctrine, 251–252
Federal Communications Commission (FCC), 38, 103, 257

Feedback, 13, 17–18
Fiber-optic cables, 4
Fidler, Roger, 33–42
l5th Annual Communications Industry Forecast, 69
File-sharing, 70, 291, 304–307
Filters, 246–247
Fine arts education, 182
First Amendment to the Constitution, 71
Ford, Henry, 16
Fragmentation, 251–252
Frauenfelder, Mark, 125–128
Fundamentalism, 23–24, 32
Future of Music Coalition, 110

Garfinkel, Simson L., 308–318, 322–327
Gaydar, 235
Gender divisions, 248
General Electric, 93
Generation Txt, 232
Girls, education of, 277–281
Gitlin, Todd, 139–146
Gleick, James, 146–150
Globalization, 93–101
Goldberg, Dave, 78
Google.com, 118–125
Gore, Al, 25
Government regulation, 38, 71, 101, 194–195
Grateful Dead, 288, 293
Gregson, Kimberly S., 221–231
Group identity, 251
Group polarization, 250–252
Grusin, Richard, 50–59
Gutenberg, Johannes, 17, 71

Hackers, 30–31
Hate groups, 249–250
Hiltzik, Michael A., 86–91
Hogan, John, 108–109
Hollerith, Herman, 16
Hoover Dam, 48
Houghton-Mifflin, 98
HyperCards, 168
Hyperlinks, 68, 72
Hypermedia, 56, 168
Hypermediacy, 53–55
HyperText, 166–167
HyperText Markup Language (HTML), 169

Idei, Nobuyuki, 75, 76
ImaHima i-mode service, 235
Immediacy, 51–53, 70
Industrial Revolution, 11
Information overload, 158–161, 247
Information society, 11–20
Information, nonlinear, 167
Initial price offering (IPO), 27
Intellectual property, 286

Interactivity
  joysticks, 25
  mouse and keyboard, 25
  television, 24–25
Interface design, 52–53
Interfaces, 27
International Business Machines (IBM), 16, 294
Internet. *See also* World Wide Web
  access to, 256–263, 264–271
  anonymity on, 197–199
  broadband service, 102–105
  and collective actions, 232–238
  commerce on, 27–29
  as a community, 189, 190–191, 192
  content, 27
  effect on society, 44–49
  emergent behaviors on, 31, 236–238
  fundamentalism affected by, 24
  gender divisions in, 248
  government regulation of, 71, 101, 194–195
  and groups, 245–254
  history of, 6–7, 25–26
  "Internet intoxication," 44
  networked computers, 5–7
  and personality, 193–202
  and political processes, 190–191, 222–229
  publishing model within, 43
  racial divisions in, 248
  radio on, 100
  real-time audio streams, 100
  relationship formation on, 202
  shared virtual space of, 199
  and social psychology, 193–202
  TCP/IP, 6
  telephone line capacity and, 4
  user identities, 44
Internet Archive, 123
Internet Explorer, 26
Internet Project Kosovo (IPKO), 30
Interpersonal awareness devices, 235
iPods, 74

Japan Communications, 75
Jefferson, Thomas, 222
Job training, 186–187
Joblove, George, 86–89
Jobs, Steven, 6, 187

Kazaa, 304–307
Kimura, Keiji, 74, 77

Labor force, U.S., 19
Lagardere/Hachette, 98
Landauer, Thomas K., 172–177
Lanier, Jaron, 26
Larsen, Lee, 111–112
Launch Media, 75

Law of suppression of radical potential, 37–38
Law, Sally Ann, 239–245
Laws, libel and obscenity, 71
Lessig, Lawrence, 296–303
Levenson, William, 181
Light, Jennifer S., 255–264
Listservs, 29
Living systems, 41
Lohr, Steve, 177–181
Loneliness, 195–196, 201–202
Long-distance communication, 4
Lovegety keychain devices, 235

Machlup, Fritz, 18
Mailing lists, 191
Mandelbrot, Benoit, 293, 294
Mann, Charles C., 285–291
Marconi, Guglielmo, 17
Mass communication, 17
Mass feedback technologies, 17–18
Matchmaking services, 134–138
Mathematical communication theory, 13
Mathematics, 52–53
McChesney, Robert W., 92–96
McHugh, Josh, 84–85
McIntosh, Shawn, 67–73
McKenna, Katelyn Y. A., 193–205
McLuhan, Marshall, 55, 143, 190
Media
  acceleration of, 146–150
  children's exposure to, 142
  collective action using, 231–238
  concentration of, 92–114
  convergence of, 67–73
  ecology of, 21–32
  globalization of, 92–96, 97–101
  mass media, uses of, 59–63
  mediamorphosis, 1, 33–42
  ownership, 72
  parasocial interaction in, 1
  participation, 222–229
  saturation, 139–146
  theory, 33–64
Mediamorphosis, 1, 33–42
MediaOne, 103
Mergers, corporate, 72, 76, 102–105
Metro Goldwyn Mayer Studios v. Grokster et al., 305
Microsoft, 74, 79
Mill, John Stuart, 15
Millennium bug, 212–217
Mitchell, Bridger M., 239–245
Mobile Cupid Service, 235
Moore, Gordon, 6
Moore's Law, 6
Morita, Akio, 80
Morreale, Jesse, 111

Morse, Samuel F. B., 16
Mosaic, 26, 168, 294
Moses, Robert, 191
Motion Picture Association of America (MPAA), 287, 293
Mottola, Tommy, 77
Movies, digitization of, 86–91
MTV, 149–150
Mulrine, Anna, 133–138
Music, 54. *See also* Sony Corporation
  artificial production of, 54
  car audio systems, 77
  creating, 299
  file-sharing, 304–307
  online services, 77–79
  portable players, 74
  production and distribution, 69–70, 293
  on radio, 106–114
  ripping, 299
  sampling, 287, 299
  on television, 149–150

Napster, 75, 291–292, 304
National Public Radio (NPR), 37
National Telecommunications and Information Administration (NTIA), 256
Negroponte, Nicholas, 39
Nelson, Ted, 26, 167
NetMD Walkman, 77
Netscape, 26, 169
Netwars, 232–236
Networks
  computer, 5–7
  peer-to-peer, 292–296
  protocols, 6
  World Wide Web, 165–171
Newhagen, John E., 264–272
News Corporation, 93
News, individualized, 70, 246
Nintendo, 6, 288
Nozoe, Yuki, 76

Oligopolies, 72, 73, 93
Open access, 102–103
OpenMG, 77, 78
Open source, 23
Oppenheimer, Todd, 181–187
Overclass, 273–277

Page, Larry, 119
Palo Alto Research Center (PARC), 35, 53, 168
Parasocial interaction, 1
Parker, Ian, 205–212
Patel, Marilyn Hall, 292
Pavlik, John, 67–73
Peer-to-peer (P2P) model, 73
Peer-to-peer file-sharing programs, 70, 77, 304–307

Peer-to-peer networking, 292–296
Personality, 193–202
Piracy, 286–287
Platform for Internet Content Selection (PICS), 247
Playlists, 113
Political processes
    advertising, 149
    and democratic theory, 222–224
    election campaigns, 60–61
    political Websites, 248–250
    and technology, 222–229
Pornography, 194–195, 196
Postal system, 16
PowerPoint presentation software, 205–212
Preprocessing, 15
Privacy
    deleted files, 318–321
    discarded drives, 308–318
    google.com, 118–124
    surveillance, 327–332
    and technology, 322–327
Productivity, 172–181
Psychology
    anonymity, 197–199
    attraction, 199–200
    computers and children, 185–186
    depression and loneliness, 194–196
    intelligent cooperation, 236–238
    and the Internet, 43–49, 193–202
    personality, 193–202
    and PowerPoint presentations, 205–212
    relationships, 199–202
Public Broadcasting Act (1967), 37

Racial divisions, 248
Radio
    canned broadcasts, 107–108
    Clear Channel stations, 107–108
    FM vs. AM, 36–39
    formats, 110
    and groups, 251–252
    independent stations, 30
    online, 78, 100
    playlists, 113
    political talk shows, 226
    Voice of America, 72
Radio Corporation of America (RCA), 37
Rationalization, 15
Reality television shows, 31
Recording Industry Association of America (RIAA), 75, 292, 293
Reed-Elsevier, 98
Religion, 25, 32
Remediation, 1, 50–59
Remote control, 146–150
Renaissance, definition of, 22

Restoration, digital, 89–90
Revolution, connotations of the term, 12, 21
Rheingold, Howard, 231–239
Riley, Richard, 182
RoomLink, 78
Rose, Frank, 73–84
Rosenbaum, James M., 318–321
Rushkoff, Douglas, 21–32

Sanda, Frank, 75
Sanitation of disk drives, 308–318
Sarnoff, David, 37–38
Satellites, 4–5
Saturation, media, 139–146
Schwartz, Evan I., 151–157
Seagram, 93
Search engines, 118–124
Secure Digital Music Initiative (SDMI), 292
Severin, Werner J., 59–64
Sharlet, Jeff, 106–114
Shelat, Abhi, 308–318
Shenk, David, 157–161
Short Message Service (SMS) messaging, 232
Simulations, military, 125–128
Skinner, B. F., 181
Smart mobs, 232–238
Smog, data, 157–161
Social anxiety, 201
Social middleware, 235
Social science research, 135
Software, 205–212, 288
Sony Corporation, 73–79, 80, 86, 93, 98
Spam, 151–157
Special effects, 86–91
Spending, online, 135
Spontaneous self-organization, 41
Springsteen, Bruce, 247
Standards
    computer network protocols, 6
    hackers and, 30–31
Statute of Anne, 293
Stefik, Mark, 288
Stickiness, 27
Stoll, Clifford, 184, 188–193
Suhler, Veronis, 69
Sunstein, Cass R., 245–254
Supervening social necessities, 37
Surveillance, 327–332
Swarm intelligence, 236–238
Swidey, Neil, 117–125

Tankard, James W., Jr., 59–64
Taylor, Frederick Winslow, 16
TCP/IP, 6
Technology
    access to, 255–272

Technology (*continued*)
  changes in, 34–35
  coevolution, 39
  and collective actions, 231–238
  communications revolution, 3–32
  connotations of the term, 13
  control, 16–18
  convergence, 39
  dependence on, 212–217
  in education, 181–187
  fear of, 194
  mass feedback, 17–18
  and political processes, 222–229
  predictions, 7–10, 181–182, 189, 299
  questioning, 188–217
  social forces, 37
  social impact of, 163–187
  stages of development, 35
  Y2K bug, 212–217
Technomyopia, 36
Telematics, 18
Telephones
  access to, 256–257
  cell, 232–234
  history of, 4
  in the Philippines, 232
Television
  average hours watched, 141
  cable, 62, 259–261
  future of, 80–85
  and groups, 251–252
  history of, 5
  interactivity, 24–25, 62
  political call-in, 226–227
  political entertainment, 226
  racial divisions in, 248
  reality shows, 31
Terrorist attacks of 9/11, 128
Tethered downloads, 77–78
Text messaging, 232–236
30-Year Rule, 34–35
Time shifting, 80
Time Warner
  as media giant, 93, 98, 103
  merger with AOL, 72, 76, 298
Time zones, standardized, 15
TiVo, 81, 84–85, 247
Torvalds, Linus, 293
Townhall forums, 227
Transatlantic cable, 4
Turing, Alan, 52
Turkle, Sherry, 277–281

Ubiquitous value network, 75
Ullman, Ellen, 212–217

Uniform resource locators (URLs), 169
United States Gramaphone Company, 17
Unlimited media, 143
Upoc ("universal point of contact") text messages, 235
USENET, 29, 190–191
Uses and gratifications approach, 1, 60–64

Valenti, Jack, 76, 287, 293
VCRs, 80, 293
Viacom, 93, 97, 98
Video games, 25, 36, 56, 125–128
Video software, 86
Viral marketing, 70, 73
Virtual reality, 26, 51–53
Vivendi, 72, 98
Voice of America radio, 72
Von Neumann, John, 52

Waldrop, Mitchell, 41
War games, 125–128
Watson, Thomas, 5
Watt, James, 16
WearComp webcasting, 235–236
Webcasting, 235
Weber, Max, 14
Weblogs, 29, 46–47, 129–133
Websites, political, 248–250
Wega TV, 78
Weinberger, David, 42–49
Windows, 53–55
Windows Media platform, 79
Winston, Brian, 36–37
Wire services, 98
Wojcicki, Susan, 119
Woody, Todd, 303–307
World Intellectual Property Organization (WIPO), 289
World Trade Organization protest, 233–234
World Wide Web, 6, 27, 165–171. *See also* Internet
  communication contexts on, 170–171
  cultural role of, 169–170
  description of, 166
  history of, 166–169
  as a new world, 43–49
  social expansion of, 169
  uses for, 170–171
World Wide Web Consortium (W3C), 169
Wozniak, Stephen, 6

Xanadu, 167
Xerox, 35, 46, 53, 168

Y2K, 212–217
Yahoo!, 28, 29, 75, 78

Zennström, Niklas, 304–305